THE MAKING OF
MODERN DRAMA
SERIES

THE CART
AND THE TRUMPET

The Plays of George Bernard Shaw

MAURICE VALENCY

SCHOCKEN BOOKS · NEW YORK

First published by Schocken Books 1983
10 9 8 7 6 5 4 3 2 1   83 84 85 86
Copyright © 1973, 1983 by Maurice Valency

Library of Congress Cataloging in Publication Data
Valency, Maurice Jacques, 1903–
The cart and the trumpet.
(The Making of modern drama)
Reprint. Originally published: New York:
Oxford University Press, 1973. With new pref.
Includes bibliographical references and index.
1. Shaw, Bernard, 1856–1950—Criticism and
interpretation. I. Title. II. Series.
PR5367.V3   1983   822'.912   82–16954

Manufactured in the United States of America
ISBN 0–8052–0740–6

CONTENTS

PREFACE TO THE SCHOCKEN EDITION

In the decade that has passed since this book was first published, the generation to which Shaw chiefly addressed himself has dwindled to a point where few can readily call to mind the piercing eye, the lifting brow, and the sardonic smile that signalized the master's presence on this planet. But though the man has all but faded from our sight, his words have lost neither their savor nor their alcohol. Everything indicates that Shaw will have something for us as long as we have ears to hear.

The generation which now meets Shaw for the first time has in store an interesting experience; yet in all likelihood the shock of the encounter will not be comparable to that with which *Man and Superman* assaulted our sensibilities in the first years of the century which is passing. On the youth of that time Shaw made an unforgettable impression. He celebrated a century of revolutionary thought with a display of verbal fireworks the like of which, it seemed, had never before been seen, and the magnificence of which could not possibly be equaled. Since then, it is true, we have been treated to *feux d'artifice* of even more dazzling brilliance, a flaming rhetoric that is more conducive to reflection than anything that can possibly be put into words. And to this, in some sense, his words are a fitting prelude.

Like the image of the Father depicted on the Sistine ceiling, Shaw manifested himself from a vast height, stretching toward a languid Adam a shapely finger charged with lightning. He inhabited his heaven for a very long time. Inevitably, there were those who grew weary of his gesture, for he was, it must be admitted, an extremely ubiquitous presence. H. G. Wells, his friend and admirer, complained that it was impossible to go anywhere in Europe without being confronted with his effigy. Nevertheless, unlike the portraits with which the rulers of his day plastered the walls of their cities, Shaw's face terrified no one. On the contrary, his was a face that made one smile. Perhaps this was his difficulty, for, though he was preeminent as a leader, he was sadly lacking in followers.

Shaw played the clown. It was, of course, no ordinary clown he played—he played the Clown of God. As the apostle of the Life Force he approached divinity as closely as a nineteenth-century Irishman might dare to come. That was close enough; but it left a certain distance between the ostensible Shaw and the God within, and he hastened to fill the gap with grotesqueries of protean ingenuity.

In public, by preference, he wore motley. He undertook to save mankind through laughter. Possibly this is not the way to go about it. Possibly it is only through pain that the human soul can bear salvation. But a man so deeply conscious of the misery of the human condition was not quite capable of inflicting pain, though he was certainly capable of feeling it. Thus the pathos that underlies his joyous comedies is never far from the comic sparkle that enlivens the darker plays and, like Molière, he found it difficult to purge his characters of melancholy. It seems a far cry from John Tanner to Captain Shotover, yet Shaw created them both in his image, and it would be a bold man who could say with confidence which of these best resembled him.

Many have joined the hue and cry in pursuit of Shaw, and some have shown much skill in the chase. But in the main the peelers have lost their time. Shaw proves to be beyond our grasp. It is when he seems to be just within reach that he slips through our fingers. A consummate actor, he played characters of consequence. He played them well. Among other roles, he created the part of the Fabian socialist, an earnest man of the highest dedication, assiduous, indefatigable, unsparing: by no means a frivolous character. The cap and bells with which periodically he embellished this impressive figure had little to add to the performance; and even his closest associates found it hard to say at what point he began to jingle. He advertised himself shamelessly and, very likely, needlessly. He used all the tricks of the midway to hustle the sucker into his booth; yet it was never his purpose to deceive. He had only the most reputable stuff to sell. The snake oil he purveyed was of unexceptionable quality. It was only the medicine show that made it seem dubious.

Obviously Shaw had considerable need to show himself to advantage, and apparently he was never quite sure of the effect. At home he surrounded himself with portraits of himself. In staging his plays actors were encouraged to make themselves up to resemble him whenever possible. It became traditional to play John Tanner as young Bernard Shaw, and Captain Shotover was usually made up with whiskers to recall the Shaw of later years. Ultimately these mummeries served no great purpose. They helped to keep him in the public eye; but the image thus displayed to the world was a more or less conscious fabrication in which the author took little satisfaction, for he could not wholly identify with these displays in which, as he said, he dramatized himself. "I have never pretended that G.B.S. was real," he wrote. "I have over and over again taken him to pieces before the audience to shew the trick of him."

It is, however, in vain that we look to his plays for these instances of self-revelation. Almost all his plots center on a climactic unmasking of the characters, but nowhere does the author unmask himself. He teases the beholder into an exhilarating game of hide-and-go-seek, but he rarely plays fair, and it is with a mounting sense of frustration that we realize that while we watch for him on the stage, our author is off somewhere holding a meeting in the preface.

"Others abide our question. Thou art free." One can aptly apostrophize Shakespeare in this vein, for Shakespeare very wisely forbore to lecture his posterity. But when Shaw mounts the platform he not merely abides our question, he engulfs us in answers, so many and so various that the questioner may well yearn for the silence of Shakespeare's victorious brow. The result, nevertheless, is in some respects the same. Ultimately both artists preserve their mystery. Shakespeare's reticence is the source of an endless stream of interpretation. Shaw's volubility invites interminable debate. The literary consequences in each case eloquently attest the vitality of their source and, after so much effort, it would be strange if nothing resulted to lessen the confusion. We cannot pretend to understand these masters, but at least we can venture to find our way around the more troublesome questions that are posed in their works.

However it may be with Shakespeare, with Shaw this much at least is clear. At the height of his tenure as comedian-in-chief of the age, Shaw laid aside the more obvious *lazzi* of his profession and, with a degree of elegance that recalls Isaiah, he donned the sober mantle of that prophet. It is true that in this solemn guise he was not altogether convincing, but this is understandable: it is not in the nature of prophets to be altogether convincing. As their names seem to indicate, neither Undershaft nor Shotover quite hits the mark, though between them they straddle it well enough to give us pause; but beyond them there is the gospel of the brothers Barnaby to clarify the author's prediction, insofar, at least, as it can be clarified.

Life, we are told, offers us a choice, and we are at this moment under some constraint to come to a decision. We may choose, in the fullness of our wisdom, to blow ourselves up once and for all, in which case the Will to Live will doubtless undertake some further physiological adventures along lines other than human. Or we may decide to engender that superior humanity of which the poet dreamed, and develop a race of men more durable than ours. Such is the tenor of the message that Shaw left for us to ponder. It seems singularly opposite to our time.

It is a sad comment on the temper of the age that what is least characteristic of Shaw should come first to mind when we attempt a summary sketch of his character. Needless to say, there is more to Shaw than this. His art is compendious. There is God's plenty in it. For the rest, gentle reader, look not on his picture, but his book.

1983   M.J.V.

FOREWORD

I began this study some years ago with the intention of writing a short work that might serve as an introduction to modern drama. But it soon became apparent that the subject was too complex to reward any such summary treatment, and that the best way to deal with it was to attack it piecemeal, beginning with the major figures and ending God knows where. Two volumes of this work have already appeared. The first deals primarily with the works of Ibsen and Strindberg; the second, with the plays of Chekhov. The present volume has to do mainly with Shaw and the English theater.

Those who venture to write about Shaw face unusual difficulties, the chief of which is that the best things about him have been said by himself and are not improved by paraphrase. He is nevertheless the subject of a literature so vast that anyone who undertakes to read it in detail will have time for little else. Yet in spite of all that has been done to document him and to explicate him, the man remains mysterious. His genius was framed on a scale so ample that he inspired even himself with wonder, and he ended by thinking of himself as a force commensurate with God. He was not equally sure of himself as an individual. He knew himself to be an actor, a man of many moods and guises. Out of these he devised an image that might represent him with some consistency to the world; but behind this official profile, there is, as all his biographers have noted, another and more elusive semblance which in spite of much attempt at portraiture, quite defies definition.

In putting these chapters together it has been my purpose not so much to attempt an interpretation of the man as to offer some analysis of his works. Nevertheless the one is so intimately bound up with the other that in trying to interpret his art I have doubtless gone further than I in-

xi

tended in portraying the artist. The result is necessarily a very personal sketch. I think perhaps it will serve; but I cannot warrant the likeness, and I offer it quite without prejudice to the impressive gallery of portraits which attest to the fascination which this extraordinary man exerts on those who read him.

It was my aim in this study to exhibit Shaw's drama with relation to the thought and art of his time, and more particularly in the light of the conditions of the theater in the nineteenth century. Needless to say, it is hardly possible to give anything like an exhaustive account of the Victorian stage in a single chapter of a book devoted to an exceptional phase of its development. I have therefore contented myself with indicating the main currents of the drama in this period and have carefully refrained from touching upon those aspects of its history which are not directly relevant to the matter in hand, considering that the reader who desires to make a more thorough survey of this field will find the region very thoroughly laid out and charted.

In this, as in the previous volumes of this work, I have tried to limit myself, so far as is possible, to a discussion of primary materials, that is to say, to the plays themselves and their immediate context. But no matter how narrow the path one tries to follow in a book of this sort, it is virtually impossible to avoid some occasional excursion into precincts where, it may be considered, a student of the drama has no special business. My only excuse for such trespasses is that they seemed necessary or, at least, inviting; and I take this opportunity to acknowledge my indebtedness to the many brilliant scholars whose work in nineteenth-century studies has made it possible for transients to venture into their bailiwick with some feeling of confidence. Some of my more direct obligations I have acknowledged in the text and the notes; for the rest I can only express generally my gratitude to those on whose work I have levied, perhaps unwittingly, for facts and insights without which this book would have been poor indeed.

Shaw's revisions are occasionally of interest to the specialist; they are rarely relevant to a study of general nature. With few exceptions, I have avoided troubling the reader with textual matters. For the purpose of quotation I have made regular use of the superb Ayot St. Lawrence edition of 1930–32. This was supervised by the author at the height of his powers, and I believe it offers the best available text of the works with which the present study is concerned. The Standard Edition of 1930–50 is more readily available and includes works written subsequent to *The Apple Cart*, the last of the plays I have considered. Since the notes to this volume are easily referred from the one to the other edition, I cannot think that my choice of text will cause the reader any considerable inconvenience; but if there should be any, I solicit his forgiveness.

I cannot bring this preface to a close without a word of thanks to my friends and colleagues who have read the manuscript critically prior to its publication. I am especially indebted in this respect to Dr. Toby Lelyveld and Dr. Carl R. Woodring, who have offered expert advice and made valuable suggestions. I am deeply grateful also to Mr. Sheldon Meyer, Mrs. Ann Lindsay, and the production staff of Oxford University Press, whose aid and encouragement have added immeasurably to the pleasure I have had in preparing this book for the printer. Finally I must express my thanks to the staffs of the various libraries I have haunted, both here and abroad, and particularly to the staff of the library of Columbia University.

New York   M.J.V.
January 1973

ACKNOWLEDGMENTS

W̲e express appreciation for permission to reprint to the following: The Society of Authors, for: *Bernard Shaw and Mrs. Patrick Campbell: Their Correspondence*, edited by Alan Dent, London, 1952 (permission also granted by the estate of Mrs. Patrick Campbell; *Collected Letters of Bernard Shaw*, edited by Dan H. Laurence, Dodd, Mead & Company, New York, 1965—on behalf of the Bernard Shaw Estate; *Collected Works of George Bernard Shaw*, Ayot St. Lawrence edition, New York, 1930–1932—on behalf of the Bernard Shaw Estate; *Bernard Shaw and Ellen Terry: Their Correspondence*, edited by Christopher St. John, New York, 1931. I also am grateful for permission to reprint: *Bernard Shaw's Letters to Granville Barker*, edited by C. B. Purdom, Theatre Art Books, New York, 1957; Manuscript Letters to Siegfried Trebitsch, Henry W. and Albert A. Berg Collection, New York Public Library, Astor, Lenox and Tilden Foundations; and Beatrice Webb: *Diaries, 1912–24*, edited by Margaret Cole, London and New York, 1952, copyright "The London School of Economics and Political Science."

The Cart and the Trumpet

THE GREEN YEARS

In the spring of 1876 George Bernard Shaw came to London to seek his fortune.

He was at this time a tall, reedy youth of twenty, pale and red-haired, with sharp gray eyes deep set under prominent brows, protruding ears, and a very large nose.

The sparse red beard came five years later. It was apparently intended at first to conceal the marks of an attack of smallpox he suffered when he was twenty-five. It suited him, and he let it stay. His various eccentricities came later still, together with the carefully constructed reputation which served him the better part of his life. He was at this time not beautiful. Evidently he found his appearance a matter of concern. Before he left his native Dublin he had himself photographed five times.

At twenty Shaw had reason to bewail his destiny. He had been born into a middle-class family of impoverished Protestants, but he clung firmly all his life to a dream of inherited nobility, based on a distant relationship to an Irish baronet. This tinge of Irish snobbery, characteristic of class-conscious Dublin, evidently colored all his future thinking. He was poor until middle age. But it was essential for him to be considered a member of the upper classes, and he was firmly resolved not to work if he could help it.

His father, George Carr Shaw, was a pleasant, easygoing man who drank in secret. Having run rapidly through his capital in the wholesale grain business, he settled himself comfortably into a life of chronic alcoholism, sustained by a small income. Shaw's mother, Lucinda Elizabeth Gurley, was a thoroughly frustrated woman of a type at one time characteristic of the genteel poor, a woman, according to her son, "incapable of unkindness," and without any warmth beyond what is necessary to sustain life.

Mrs. Shaw apparently understood that it was her lot to cope diligently with the manifold difficulties of existence. Among these was the management of a seedy household, and the keeping up of appearances. She was, however, not much given to domestic cares. She was mainly interested in music, cultivated her voice, and for a time cherished an ambition to shine on the concert stage. She had married the elder Shaw under some misapprehension as to the state of his finances. Her subsequent disappointment was intense, and it was further aggravated by the discovery that her genial consort was a drunkard. In these circumstances, she bore her husband's occasional advances, and the resulting children, without pleasure or complaint. The man's cheerful ineptitude, and his lack of responsibility, however, forced her to earn a living by giving music lessons while she waited hopefully for the turn of fortune which was to deliver her from poverty.

During those years the Shaw ménage—mother, father, son, and two daughters—was largely sustained by a singular individual whose house they shared. This was a romantic personage, a lame gypsy who called himself Vandeleur Lee and who developed extravagant pretensions as a music master. Mrs. Shaw studied with him and also assisted him with his teaching. When Lee's highly touted method of voice production was eventually published, he took leave of Dublin, and went to London to exploit his success. The house on Hatch Street was sold. "Bessie" Shaw promptly consigned her husband and her son to their fate and, taking her surviving daughter Lucy with her, set off for London in the wake of her teacher. In London she took a large ramshackle house at 13 Victoria Grove and set up as a singing teacher with Lee's vocal system as her basis.

At this time young Shaw was sixteen, a lanky romantic boy, with hair parted in the middle, whom nobody loved. He had little schooling, but his temper was artistic, his imagination fervent. He had opinions and, since he believed himself to be pathologically timid, asserted them belligerently. He was subject to migraines, which periodically laid him low. From his boyhood he was inclined to be finicky in his diet and overly dainty in his personal habits. In a house which all day echoed the piano, nobody had troubled to teach him the rudiments of music. He taught himself, painfully, to master the keyboard, and dreamed of becoming a great composer like Verdi. He prowled the drafty halls of the National Gallery in Dublin and thought of one day rivaling Titian and Michelangelo. He read Dickens avidly and recognized in himself the talents of a great novelist. In the end he took a course in bookkeeping, after which his uncle Frederick managed to get him a job as a clerk in a real estate office.

His life henceforth was a matter of collecting rents in slum tenements and posting the amounts in ledgers. He detested this work, rose to the position of cashier, and then was suddenly demoted. After four years of employment, he cut himself adrift, put his savings in his pocket, and went off to London to join his mother. In the four years since he had seen her she had not written him so much as a word. But he knew her address.

Mrs. Shaw received him without pleasure and lodged him in a vacant room. He was plainly a burden to her, but she was a woman accustomed to burdens, and she harbored him until he married, twenty-two years later, in 1898. It was not a cozy arrangement. George was an overtidy youth and, at the same time, extremely indolent. His mother and his sister Lucy were negligent housekeepers, profoundly absorbed in their professional interests, and seldom at home. From Shaw's account of the situation, which doubtless reflects a Dickensian sense of social injustice, one gathers that his dear ones found his presence barely endurable. For his part, he found it impossible to leave his bed before noon, and, day after day, after a late breakfast, he wandered off to the British Museum reading room to justify his existence by improving his mind and, presumably, his prospects.

After some months in London, he wrote his friend McNulty in Dublin:

> My prospects in Dublin were stupendous. The employer's daughter would have been mine for the asking and partnership in the firm assured. The only obstacle to the fortune was that I cared neither for the post nor for the daughter, not insuperable, I admit. I was full of politics and religion and these were, as you know, forbidden. Here am I, in London, without the credentials of a peasant immigrant, and I shall bear the traces of the Shaw snobbery which considers manual work contemptible, and on no account will I enter an office again.[1]

His loneliness during this period was, apparently, immense. "My mother and I lived together," he wrote toward the end of his life, "but there was hardly a word between us."[2]

He had charm, and made friends easily, but he was an unhappy youth. After some months of inactivity in London, when his savings were exhausted, his sister Lucy threatened to turn him out unless he found work. This posed a problem. He had come to London in a period of hard times. There were no jobs to be had, and he was unable to enter the civil service. In this emergency, Vandeleur Lee came to his rescue. He had contracted to do a column on music for a satirical periodical called *The Hornet*. Since he had no aptitude for writing, he employed Shaw for some months as his ghost writer. When *The Hornet* died, Shaw took a cram course in French, then one in Italian, presumably in order to write operas. He began to study harmony. He had no prospect of regular employment. He was now twenty-one.

His life in the following years was uneventful. The economic depression into which England was plunged grew progressively more grim until it culminated in the strikes and riots of the mid-eighties. For a young Irishman without connections, without regular education or any special skill, it was all but impossible to get a foothold anywhere in the capital. Shaw found it useless even to try, and he soon fell to contemplating the bastions of the economic citadel with rancor, dreaming of the time when the walls would somehow topple at his approach. In the meantime he cultivated his acquaintances and made efforts to acquire the polished manner and the speech of an English gentleman.

For a young man in Shaw's position there were certain advantages in the economic situation. He was now completely dependent on a mother who evidently regarded him as a congenital good-for-nothing; but the general absence of economic opportunity gave him an unanswerable excuse for idleness. He whiled away luxurious afternoons in the complacent atmosphere of the British Museum reading room, studying books on etiquette and books on philosophy. He spent pleasant evenings arguing with people in one or another of the discussion groups which flourished all over London. He luxuriated in the English *bohème*, the natural refuge of the jobless intellectual.

Discussion groups were by no means new to the London scene. It is said that by 1840 there were nearly two thousand coffeehouses and tea shops in the capital, all amply supplied with newspapers and periodicals for the use of the patrons who gathered daily to mull over the state of the world. The next decades saw a significant floriation of literary and philosophic societies where discussion was on a plane sufficiently exalted to warrant regular visits to the library for those who desired to shine in the proceedings. These clubs were generally modest in size, and were open to all who wished to attend. They were under the leadership of literary clergymen of the type of Stopford Brooke, P. H. Wicksteed, and F. J. Furnivall, or socialist thinkers like Charles Bradlaugh. It was in this earnest atmosphere that Shaw formed himself as a public speaker.

Shaw's ideas were rooted in the depression of 1879; but there is nothing to indicate that he was specifically interested at this time in social questions. He was interested in music, art, and love, the normal pursuits of a boy of his type. The economic problems of the day, however, were inescapable. They soon absorbed his attention.

By the time Shaw came to England, the great tide of English prosperity had turned. The golden years had lasted from 1851 to 1873. In this period England had become, in the stock phrase, the workshop of the world. The middle class, firmly established in power after the Reform Bill of 1832, had risen to a position of complete supremacy in the English economy, and the lot of the working classes, vastly swelled by the demand for cheap labor in the factories, was miserable. Wages rose rapidly, but never in proportion to the rise in prices. The workmen who thronged to the cities, attracted by what seemed to be a dazzling opportunity to better their lives, were caught in an inflationary spiral from which there was no foreseeable escape. When German competition cut down the demand for English goods, inventories piled up and production lagged. So long as conditions were favorable, the recently organized labor unions remained strong; but organization was of little use to the unemployed, and in the course of the depression the labor movement languished and died.

Long before the dangers of free enterprise became generally apparent, the uncontrolled, and seemingly uncontrollable, growth of the industrial machine was alarming the intellectual classes. During the 1850's and 1860's there was a mounting attack on the middle class which stressed its aggressiveness, its hypocrisy, and the squalor of the system on which its wealth depended. Historically this was an extension of the reaction that had followed the failure of the Great Revolution in France; but in England, in the 1860's, it had special characteristics.

In England the fundamental issue centered on the right of the individual to advance his personal interests free of social control. A consequence of the English reaction against the revolutionary ideas that had precipitated the expropriation of the landed gentry in France was an enhanced sense of the sanctity of individual ownership. The eighteenth-century philosophers, in particular John Locke, had described property as a right anterior to the existence of the state. It was argued, in consequence, that it was the function of the state to protect property rights, not to curtail them. The disciples of Adam Smith considered that individual enterprise operated in accordance with the natural law of supply and demand and must therefore on no account be the subject of governmental interference. The ideas of the classical economists found unexpected support in the Darwinian hypothesis and the idea of the survival of the fittest as a fundamental law of nature. The consequence was the sanctification of unbridled competition, and the concept of laissez faire as a basic element in the constitution of states. It was in some such terms that Herbert Spencer formulated his "social statics" of 1851.

The question of the relation of individual enterprise to the common good was not, however, so easily resolved. Even in utilitarian terms it was debatable whether the greatest good of the greatest number was better served through free competition or social control. The position of Adam Smith, who had based the principle of social utility on self-interest, was directly opposed to the growing socialist temper of the times, supported by the awakening conscience of the evangelical clergy. Eventually J. S. Mill repudiated this tenet of the utilitarian theory and threw in his lot with those who espoused the cause of governmental control of industrial enterprise.

The issue began to take on religious connotations. In 1860 Protestantism and the mercantile system were so firmly allied as to appear indissoluble. The qualities prized by the bourgeois entrepreneur—obedience and devotion to work—were precisely those that recommended themselves to the church. The life of the time was seasoned with useful slogans: "Work is blessed"; "*Laborare est orare*"; "The devil finds work for idle hands." The evangelical clergy saw it as part of its holy mission to extol the felicity of those who were content with their lot and exerted itself in praise of the cheerful acceptance of life's hardships and the nobility of honest poverty. It was easy for the radically minded of every stripe to see in this alliance of piety and wealth an unholy conspiracy to sanctify the inequalities of the existing order. Socialists as far apart ideologically as Karl Marx and Charles Kingsley considered religion the opiate of the poor; many of the poor were of the same opinion.[3]

In this period even the aristocracy joined the attack on middle-class industrial exploitation. Marx had observed, in a passage that was endlessly quoted in socialist writings, that "the *bourgeoisie*, wherever it got the upper hand, put an end to all feudal, patriarchal, idyllic relations . . . and left remaining no other bond between man and man than naked self-interest and callous cash payment."[4] A widening split was perceptible in clerical circles. Within the ranks of the ethical humanists, particularly, there was a growing awareness of the injustice of the industrial system. Such writers as Leslie Stephen and Frederic Harrison brought a "puritan" conscience to the consideration of social problems, and to John Morley, the least emotional of the writers of his day, it seemed that evangelical theology was narrow, unhistoric, and rancorous, "even though it impressed a kind of moral organization on the mass of barbarism which surged chaotically into the factory towns."[5]

In the little debating societies which Shaw frequented, at first his attention was drawn mainly to aesthetic and philosophical problems. But there were groups which concentrated on the ills of society as well as on abstract questions such as the nature of idealism, the revaluation of morals, and the social function of art, and Shaw soon found himself absorbed in social questions. He frequented many such groups, listened to many opinions, and tried to find a secure basis for forming judgments. The lines along which his thinking was oriented in this manner were progressively elaborated and extended, but in their essential direction they determined his thought for the better part of his life. He read a great deal in these years and abstracted from his reading whatever he needed to form a consistent system. It was not long before he had one.

At twenty-four he felt he had read enough and was ready to write. He began sending articles to newspapers and popular periodicals. These were systematically rejected.[6] In the spring of 1879 he began his first novel, entitled *Immaturity*. He worked at it "like a beaver" five months, and sent it off to a publisher that very year. The publisher hastened to return it. The other publishers he tried—there were nine in all—did as much. He was not perturbed in the least: he was already working on his second novel, *The Irrational Knot*. It met the same fate. He started another novel, and then yet another. He wrote five novels in six years without finding a publisher. The seventh year he rested.

It was normal in this period to blame the ills of the individual on the injustice of society. *The Irrational Knot* may be said to illustrate this tendency; but Shaw did not stress it. In this novel he was mainly interested in describing the unfortunate consequences of the union of a young workman and a young lady of the upper classes. The young man, an electrician named Conolly, has a beautiful baritone voice, as well as a sister who sings in a music hall. The sister marries a nobleman, takes to drink, and dies. Conolly's marriage falls apart. It is a sad story, and it shows the influence of the discussion groups which Shaw was attending at this time. Five years after it was finished, Annie Besant thought it sufficiently interesting to warrant its publication, in installments, in her periodical *Our Corner*. It came out in book form in 1905, but no one who reads it will have difficulty in understanding why it took so long to be published.

The Irrational Knot in some measure reflects Shaw's mood in these years. In Catholic Ireland, he had felt he was an alien. He was an alien in England. For a young Irishman without means or connections it was scarcely possible to penetrate English society on any desirable level. It was necessary to transcend it; and for this he required a springboard. The only circle open to him was the world of art, a realm which had no fixed frontiers, and to which his musical background provided a passport. His earliest acquaintances were poets and musicians. He did not play the piano very well, but well enough so that he was in some demand as an accompanist. Like Conolly, his hero, he had a pleasant baritone voice, and was therefore invited to parties at homes he might not have visited otherwise. It was in this manner that he gained some modest introduction to the intellectual life of the capital.

To judge by his third novel, *Love Among the Artists* (1881), Shaw's literary interests at the age of twenty-five were largely autobiographical; like most debutants he had begun by writing his memoirs. In the contrast of his two heroes, Jack and Adrian—the one, a blunt, workmanlike musician of low birth; the other, a poetic and aristocratic painter—it is possible to see the polarity of the writer's own self-consciousness. Both heroes are resolutely pursued by women. Meanwhile Adrian is deeply involved in a struggle with his beautiful mother, the elegant Mrs. Herbert, whose manifest contempt for her son's abilities, and masterful attempts to arrange his life, obviously sublimate Shaw's actual domestic situation.

Shaw had brought with him from Ireland a burning sense of social injustice, but there is no indication at this time that he had any idea of making a career of it. It is certain that when his friend James Lecky took him in the winter of 1879 to a meeting of the Zetetical Society neither of them had any inkling of the extent to which this visit was to influence Shaw's future.

In 1879 the Zetetical was barely a year old. It was, by all accounts, a random assemblage of earnest young people who met weekly in the rooms of The Women's Protective and Provident League in Great Queen Street, Longacre, to exercise their wits in the "unrestricted discussion of social, political and philosophical subjects." Its orientation was liberal and progressive, Millite, Malthusian, and evolutionary, and it admitted women on equal terms with men. As it happened, its membership included a number of surprisingly gifted people, among them Sidney Webb and Sidney Olivier, Webb's fellow clerk in the Colonial Office, both of whom were fated to exert an important influence on Shaw's career.

It was the practice at this club for the members to read prepared papers on solid topics as a basis for discussion. Shaw plunged headlong into these exercises and at once became conscious of his shortcomings as a public speaker. Many years later he wrote:

> I had an air of impudence, but was really an arrant coward, nervous and self-conscious to a heartbreaking degree. Yet I could not hold my tongue. I started up and said something in the debate, and then, feeling that I had made a fool of myself . . . I vowed I would join the society; go every week; speak in every debate; and become a speaker or perish in the attempt. I carried out this resolution.[7]

The account of his heroic efforts to overcome his shyness has doubtless been exaggerated, since their source is Shaw's own recollection, and he was by no means averse to self-dramatization. At any rate, beginning with the Zetetical he appears to have practised his oratory with the single-minded absorption of an opera singer. One after the other, he joined all the clubs he could manage—among others, the Dialectical Society, the Bedford Club, the Browning Club, the Shelley Club, and the New Shakespeare Society. He talked incessantly, and he ceased to tremble.

These early exercises colored his future writing. To the end of his days he considered himself a journalist, but from the first his style was oratorical rather than journalistic. A letter he addressed to Mrs. Pattie Moye, a member of the Zetetical executive committe, explaining his forthcoming paper on capital punishment, is written in the same style as his most mature writing of later years. It is the style of a witty schoolmaster addressing a class.[8] Even in his most intimate letters he was evidently aware of a roomful of critical listeners whom he must at all costs impress.

His shyness, on which he dwelt often in his later years, was obviously based on a feeling of inferiority: for a long time he was uncertain of his reception. Nevertheless, his earliest journalistic efforts were phrased in the language of the omniscient, and by 1882, having drawn a blank in his every attempt at publication, he felt that he had mastered his profession and was now qualified to instruct others. An aspiring lady novelist asked him if he would revise her manuscript professionally. He proposed a fee of three guineas, ten if he had to copy the text over, and in the meantime wrote her a gratuitous letter full of sound advice on the art of writing.[9]

The next step was to write something himself that people might wish to read. In 1882 he wrote *Cashel Byron's Profession.* It is the most successful and the least sensible of Shaw's novels. The book publishers rejected it with their customary celerity, but in 1885 the socialist journal *To-day* agreed to run it in serial form, and its editor issued it as a book the following year. This marked a peak in the young man's career. He was an established author.

This story was the fruit of Shaw's friendship with the amateur boxer Pakenham Beatty, and here the question of social equality was posed in its most obvious form. The plot is sheer melodrama. In this version, the beautiful bad mother is an actress. Her son, a professional pugilist, turns out to be a nobleman in disguise. In the end he triumphs both over his mother and his detractors: nothing more banal can be imagined. Yet for all its manifest shortcomings, *Cashel Byron's Profession* has a certain sparkle and easily supports the reading. Not so much can be said for the last of Shaw's novels. *An Unsocial Socialist* is unbearably dull, though from a biographical viewpoint it is interesting, since it marks a distinct point of departure in the writer's orientation. In his earlier works his socialist tendencies unquestionably stemmed from a sense of personal injury. In this novel, his indignation is on a cosmic scale. By this time he was no longer a poor relation of the upper classes. He was a Socialist.

When Shaw joined the Zetetical in 1879 there was not much talk in England of social revolution. Deeper questions were being debated. The question of social equality, loudly raised during the revolutionary outbursts of 1848 and 1871, was not at this time being pressed. Badly weakened by the depression, the Labor leaders had entered upon an uneasy alliance with the Liberal party, which undertook to represent their interests in Parliament, and socialism as an active influence was now virtually nonexistent. The mounting economic crisis, however, brought the labor question once again into focus. In 1881 the radical journalist Henry Hyndman founded a Marxist organization, which some years later adopted the name of the Social Democratic Federation, and advanced a politically oriented socialist program. The first result of its activities was a split in its ranks and the formation of a rival body of anarchist tendencies called the Socialist League, with William Morris as its head. These two organizations did what they could during the depression years to organize the working class into an effective force.

According to his own account, Shaw first became aware of the economic aspects of history in 1882, when he heard Henry George lecture on land nationalization at the Memorial Hall in Farringdon Street. Up to this time, apparently, he had considered his economic problem a private affliction. Henry George made him understand that he was by no means singular in his misfortune. Poverty was the destiny of the majority of men in a distorted social environment; but it was not irremediable. The world could be changed. This realization, Shaw said later, changed the course of his life. He bought a copy of *Progress and Poverty*, found the contents utterly convincing, and became a single-taxer.

But at Hyndman's Social Democratic Federation, where he tried to spread his newly found creed, he was at once made aware of his naïveté as a social theorist. He had never heard of Karl Marx. They spoke there of nothing else. He hastened to repair his shortcomings in this respect by reading through the first book of *Das Kapital* in the French translation of Deville. When he laid the book down, he had a cause. He was a socialist. "From that hour," he said later, "I became a man with some business in the world."

Capital is by no means the clearest of books, nor the easiest to read, and it is not likely that Shaw entirely understood its drift, even in French. But he was entirely responsive to the passionate fervor that motivated it, and in it he saw a more or less scientific exposition of his own grievances against middle-class society. His interpretation of Marx's book, written nineteen years after he first read it, was entirely characteristic of the standpoint from which he came to view the class struggle. For Shaw, poor and jobless, socialism was a matter of life and death; but for Shaw, rich and successful, it was a matter of *noblesse oblige*. He wrote:

> Marx's *Capital* is not a treatise on Socialism, it is a jeremiad against the *bourgeoisie* supported by such a mass of evidence and such a relentless genius for denunciation as had never been brought to bear before. It was supposed to be written for the working classes; but the working man respects the *bourgeoisie* and wants to be a *bourgeois*; Marx never got hold of him for a moment. It was the revolting sons of the *bourgeoisie* itself—Lasalle, Marx, Liebknecht, Morris, Hyndman, Bax, all, like myself, *bourgeois* crossed with squierarchy—that painted the flag red. Bakunin and Kropotkin, of the military and noble caste (like Napoleon) were our extreme left. The middle and upper classes are the revolutionary element in society. . . .[10]

In 1883 Marx died in London, poor, friendless, and generally disliked by those who knew him. The following year Shaw joined the newly formed Fabian Society. Once again his horizons widened.

The Fabian Society, like the Zetetical, had a modest beginning. About 1880 Thomas Davidson, a Scot who was deeply impressed by Rosmini's Ethical Philosophy, assembled a small coterie in his rooms in Chelsea, to discuss philosophical questions. This group called itself The Fellowship of the New Life. Eventually its members split off into two groups, one of which carried on, more or less seriously, discussions aimed at the improvement of individual character. The other, under the leadership of Frank Podmore, dedicated its energies to the cause of social reform. This group, consisting of some dozen people, met in E. R. Pearse's apartment early in 1884 and organized itself as the Fabian Society, with the avowed purpose of reconstructing society "in accordance with the highest moral possibilities." The members were in no immediate hurry to bring about the necessary changes. Podmore had named his club after that Fabius Maximus who had distinguished himself by biding his time patiently while Hannibal wore himself out marching about Italy. The Fabians felt they too could serve by standing and waiting.

In their inception they were neither rich nor powerful. The first collection of contributions is said to have amounted to 13s. 6d. But the Fabians were resolute. The moment to strike, they felt, would surely come and, since they had no idea of when it might be, they devoted themselves to preparing the moment. Shaw joined the Society in September 1884. Four months later he was elected to the executive committee. He promptly recruited Sidney Webb and Sidney Olivier, and henceforth the Fabian tracts, under Shaw's editorship, were given a solid statistical documentation. Webb served Shaw as a living reference library. Shaw wrote, many years later, with his usual candor:

> The difference between Shaw with Webb's brains and knowledge at his disposal, and Shaw by himself is enormous. Nobody has yet gauged it because as I am an incorrigible mountebank, and Webb is one of the simplest of geniuses, I have always been in the centre of the stage whilst Webb has been prompting me, invisible, from the side. I am an expert picker of other men's brains; and I have been exceptionally fortunate in my friends.[11]

The Fabians soon included a group of brilliant radicals, among them William Clarke, Graham Wallas, Hubert Bland, and, later, Annie Besant. It was never a large group: in 1885 it numbered some twenty young people, predominantly Millite in their orientation, bohemian in appearance, flamboyant in their opinions. They do not seem to have taken themselves with the utmost seriousness. To begin with, in spite of the name they had chosen, their watchwords were "Educate, Agitate, Organize," and their ultimate purpose was, in Shaw's words, "to bring about a tremendous smashup of existing society, to be succeeded by complete socialism." This ambitious plan was soon relinquished. By 1886, as the economic depression reached climactic proportions, the Fabians had already matured sufficiently to give up any insurrectionist ideas they may have harbored. They now adopted a quiet gradualistic approach to socialism and made earnest attempts to infiltrate the Liberal party leadership, in the meantime seeking to influence public opinion by publishing tracts and giving lectures. Their policy by this time was frankly opportunistic and practical. They considered themselves to be sober citizens, the realists of the socialist movement.

Ten years later they had so far mellowed as to declare, in 1896, that the object of socialism was not to destroy private enterprise completely but to spur it forward into new avenues of endeavor by nationalizing the common industries. The line that Shaw consistently developed in his writings and lectures during this decade was the gradual extension of state power; the progressive augmentation of the income tax as a means of equalizing privilege; the extinction of private enterprise through state competition, and distribution in accordance with the value of the individual in the collective effort of production—substantially the program developed by Proudhon. Politically the consequence would be social democracy, with the best minds in control of the government. The immediate concern of the Fabians was to acquire the necessary voting power to bring about this result through legislation. As in great measure the Fabian policy became the policy of the English Labor movement, this program eventually met with considerable success.

Fabian Essays in Socialism was published, under Shaw's editorship, in 1889. It was a series of papers by the seven members of the Fabian Executive—Shaw, Webb, Clarke, Olivier, Wallas, Besant, and Bland—that set forth the Fabian idea with persuasive clarity. The society now numbered more than 150 members and was by this time extremely articulate, though not yet influential. Both its membership and its influence grew rapidly in the course of the next decade. By the turn of the century it had passed its peak of influence; but by that time its membership list numbered 2500 names.[12]

Thus, by the time he was thirty, Shaw found what he most needed—a place in the world, a moral orientation, and a group of friends whose ideas he shared. There remained the question of his own economic situation. The Fabian Society did not support anyone financially; on the contrary, it had to be supported. Shaw had been writing assiduously for nine years. His total earnings in that time amounted, by his own reckoning, to six pounds; but his stars were already assuming a favorable aspect.

In 1885 his friend Henry Salt had introduced him to William Archer, a young man of exactly Shaw's age, who was then reviewing books for the *Pall Mall Gazette*. Archer had excellent connections. He proved to be as valuable to Shaw along literary lines as was Sidney Webb in his political associations. That very year, through Archer's good offices, Shaw began reviewing books for the *Pall Mall Gazette* at two guineas a thousand words.

Archer now moved over to the *World*, where he took over the theatrical column, and soon he was given the art column also. This he shouldered off on Shaw, who thus suddenly found himself established as art critic for a highly reputable periodical without knowing quite how it had happened. For some three and a half years he reviewed, *tant bien que mal*, all the art exhibitions in London.

During these years he continued lecturing for the Fabian Society whenever the occasion offered, traveling about to workingmen's clubs as often as twice a week. He had by this time become an enchanting speaker, "a blend of bland and blond Mephistopheles with meek and mild curate," and his lectures were very well attended. They brought him no money, but they brought him to the attention of a number of susceptible young women with gratifyingly advanced ideas. He was properly responsive, cultivated his appearance carefully, and began thinking of himself as a dashing young man of irresistible attractions, somewhere between Don Juan and Mephistopheles; in any case, a very devil with the ladies. Many years later he reminisced:

> when Nature completed my countenance in 1880 or thereabouts (I had only the tenderest sprouting of hair on my face until I was 24), I found myself equipped with the upgrowing moustaches and eyebrows, and the sarcastic nostrils of the operatic fiend whose airs (by Gounod) I had sung as a child, and whose attitudes I had affected in my boyhood.[13]

In 1888 the *Star*, a radical journal, began publication under the editorship of T. P. O'Connor. H. W. Massingham, a Fabian friend, saw to it that Shaw was engaged to write music criticism for it, as an assistant to Belfort Bax, at a weekly stipend of two pounds ten. In February 1889 Bax left, and Shaw took over the post of music critic.

His articles, signed "Corno di Bassetto," attracted immediate attention. It was the first time in the history of English journalism that anyone had ventured to write readable music reviews. Shaw continued with the *Star* until October 1890. At this time the post of music critic on the *World*, which Engel had filled, suddenly fell vacant, and William Archer was able to arrange for Shaw to take it. This was steady employment, really well paid, and Shaw continued writing the weekly column for the *World* for more than four years. He now signed himself G. B. S.

As a writer, Shaw had, from the beginning, every gift save brevity. At his best, he was a superb stylist; but he had great facility, so that one is sometimes aware that he could have managed as well with half his text. His love of incremental and climactic constructions betrays the platform orator, accustomed to embellishing his phrases operatically for the sheer pleasure of the performance. Doubtless his discursiveness is a sign of the natural ebullience of an energetic nature; on the other hand, he is sometimes unduly insistent and hangs on unconscionably long to one's lapel. He was more talented than any of his contemporaries, but he was incapable of that self-imposed austerity which is the special gift of the supremely gifted: he did not know when to stop. It was possibly the realization of his exclusion from the community of the very great which spurred his creative faculty to its utmost and also accounted for the blatancy of his efforts at self-aggrandizement. It was also, in all likelihood, the shaping principle of his philosophical system, so that the very distant goal of his personal aspiration came to be identified with the end-point of the evolution of humanity, progressively realizing an unimaginable ideal.

It was evidently no easy thing for Shaw to achieve the intellectual level to which he aspired. He was by nature a performing artist, an actor in the field of letters, and therefore constantly in some danger of self-betrayal. Like most successful journalists, he was expert in the manipulation of his material, and quite willing to employ shock tactics for the sake of effect, or even for their own sake. Thus he wrote: "It is always necessary to overstate a case startlingly to make people sit up and listen to it, and to frighten them into acting on it. I myself do this habitually and deliberately."[14]

In the circumstances, it was natural that so consciously aggressive a figure should occasionally be misunderstood. But it soon became clear that he was not in the least dangerous; and, until the Great War, he passed for an eccentric, who barked a good deal, but, as a professed vegetarian, did not bite. Like Whistler, of whom he did not approve, Shaw exuded an air of novelty and passed readily for an original thinker. In fact, as he often admitted with the complete candor of a man who does not expect to be believed, he was a merchant of ideas, not an innovator. He was strongly motivated by an innate need to disobey, but though he made a very radical effect, his notions of morality and proper decorum were rigidly conservative and of the middle class. With all the sincerity and fervor of the dedicated revolutionary, he expressed, in terms of the most advanced thought of his day, the solid values of the eighteenth century, and in the rationalization of these values he found one of his principal incentives as a logician. Nobody exemplified better than he the paradoxical nature of Victorian radicalism in England.

His literary sources were various and seldom unimpeachable. Since he was sure of his direction, he made use of everything that came to hand. Beatrice Webb, who did not like him, complained of his lack of intellectual stability. In fact, he seems to have adhered to his principles with remarkable firmness. The Webbs, from whom he derived much mental sustenance, based themselves on facts and figures and thus found themselves under the necessity, from time to time, of changing their opinions. Shaw was relatively free from such embarrassments. Figures bored him, and beyond a certain point he found facts confusing. Once he had a mark by which to steer, he sought no further aids to navigation. He knew in advance where his course lay and steered it with the air of one in authority. "Like Goethe," he wrote, "I knew all along, and have added more to my power of handling, illustrating, and addressing my material, than to the material itself."[15]

Very likely there was a strain of skepticism at the core of his faith which contributed to the need he felt for making a strong impression: "To be strong in argument," he wrote in 1881, apropos of the Zetetical debates, "one must have faith in it, whereas to my mind, it is less a means of eliciting truth than of exercising ourselves by pretending to believe what we know in our hearts to be nonsense."[16] He wrote to Ellen Terry, sixteen years later, having in the meantime assumed the mantle of the sage: "In this world you must know *all* the points of view, and take One, and stick to it. In taking your side, don't trouble about its being the right side—north is no righter or wronger than south—but be sure that it is really yours, and back it for all you are worth."[17]

Shaw did not distinguish himself as an art critic. His artistic orientation was essentially literary, and, from the viewpoint of craftsmanship, unequivocally realistic and matter-of-fact. He had, without doubt, an excellent ear for music. There is no evidence that he ever developed an eye for painting. When Archer had him appointed art critic for the *World*, not much time was lost in examining his qualifications. "Shaw didn't know much more about painting than I," Archer later reminisced, "but he thought he did and that was the main point."[18]

Shaw's artistic background was somewhat sketchy. He had done a little drawing and painting as a boy, under a drawing master, and was able to make amusing doodles, with which he sometimes enlivened his letters to friends. He had read Vasari and had come to the conclusion that Michelangelo marked the peak of possible perfection in art. In London, he had for some months looked after the art column in Annie Besant's *Our Corner* and had even gone so far as to write an article for it on painting. He had no other experience in this field.

His first review as an art critic was published on 24 March 1886 and concerned an exhibition of paintings by Holman Hunt, a Pre-Raphaelite, for whose work Shaw professed the deepest admiration. By this time the Pre-Raphaelite movement was in its second generation and could be considered neither new nor revolutionary. Thirty-five years had passed since Rossetti and his friends had first declared war on the Academy. In the ensuing period peace had been made and ratified, the Pre-Raphaelites were largely absorbed into the Establishment, and some had even been elected to the Royal Academy.

In England, at this time, Impressionist art was generally associated with the New English Art Club, recently organized by Walter Sickert, and against this group all the traditional painters, including the Pre-Raphaelites, were firmly united. The first Impressionist exhibition in London took place in April 1886, scarcely a month after Shaw's debut on the *World*. His review amply demonstrated his shortcomings as an art critic. Impressionism, he wrote, apropos of a landscape entitled "St. John's Wood," was the misfortune of having indefinite impressions. It could be cured by "attentive observation and a suitable pair of spectacles." In 1887, his estimate of the Impressionists was somewhat more perceptive. He had by this time made a turn around the Paris art galleries and evidently realized that the movement must be taken seriously. He now conceded its honesty and its realism, but still gave no evidence of knowing what the Impressionists had in mind. In a review written two years later, shortly before he ended his career in this field, he renewed his suggestion that the members of the New English Art Club have their eyes tested. One comes with some astonishment, therefore, upon his statement, six years later in *The Sanity of Art* (1895), that he had been a champion of the Impressionists from the beginning:

> When I was engaged chiefly in the criticism of pictures the Impressionist movement was struggling for life in London; and I supported it vigorously because . . . it was evidently destined to improve pictures

greatly by substituting a natural, observant, real style for a conventional, taken-for-granted, ideal one. The result has entirely justified my choice of sides.[19]

Shaw was by this time under strong Ibsenite influence, and evidently Impressionism had become associated in his mind with realism, as opposed to idealism, and was therefore commendable. From his viewpoint, painting was essentially representative and informative, a dramatic and didactic art. It should therefore center on incident in its subject matter, and on exactness of representation in its form. He was deeply impressed by Hunt's moral earnestness and felt that his "Light of the World" was a great modern masterpiece. Ruskin had warned the Pre-Raphaelites against their medieval leanings. Shaw dutifully followed him by expressing disapproval of Morris's medieval associations, as well as of his idea that the faraway and long ago was a necessary element in the magic of art.

Ruskin had complicated the issue for the Pre-Raphaelites by directing their attention to contemporary problems. By the time Shaw became aware of the movement, it was no longer precisely definable. In the mind of William Morris, its outstanding exponent in this period, Pre-Raphaelitism and socialism were synonymous. The result was an unstable compound in which Paolo and Francesca became somehow involved with the dignity of labor, and in which moral sincerity, honest workmanship, and social reform were associated with the wildest romanticism. It was in terms of this amalgam of aestheticism and social revolt, coupled with some sense of the relation of Pre-Raphaelitism to the symbolist movement across the Channel, that Shaw was later to call *Candida* "a modern Pre-Raphaelite play." Thus Marchbanks, in that play, took on the dignity of a Pre-Raphaelite hero, the modern counterpart, presumably, of that Paolo who played havoc with the domestic arrangements of the Malatesta of Rimini.

It is entirely probable that, as Jacob Epstein was later to remark, Shaw knew nothing at all about art.[20] Judging by his reviews, Shaw's approach to painting was simply bookish. In his view of the matter, art was primarily illustrative, and must therefore be honest, workmanlike, functional, and sensible in order to be good. Consequently, his criticism of painting involved quite practical considerations. Of Ingres's "La Source," which was enjoying a great vogue in these years, he wrote: "Take the young lady painted by Ingres as 'La Source,' for example. Imagine having to make conversation with her for a couple of hours. . . ."[21]

In the 1880's symbolism was virtually inescapable, but Shaw was not yet touched by it. His world was still the world of objective realities, an economic system which poetry might sublimate or interpret, but was powerless to transform, save through its ability to influence legislation. What he particularly admired in the Pre-Raphaelite painters was their realism which, through the anachronistic nature of their subject matter, lent itself readily to allegorical interpretation. On the other hand, the Pre-Raphaelites' tendency toward romanticism embarrassed him; and he disparaged their sloppy execution. He disliked Rossetti because Rossetti was sensual, and Millais because Millais was prudish. Morris, he thought, had precisely the right tone both as artist and socialist, and it was Morris particularly who influenced his ideas of art.

These ideas were such as to remove him effectively from the major artistic influences of the time, which tended above all to separate art from literature and even from the representation of that nature which for four centuries artists had been trying in vain to imitate. For Shaw, at this stage of his career, such tendencies were absolutely incomprehensible, and even in his maturity, after he had come under symbolist influence, they made no sense. The artistic revolution in the theater, however, which Ibsen had initiated, represented a less radical departure from traditional norms, and here Shaw found himself on surer ground. Surest of all was his grasp of music.

The music notes he wrote for the *World*, later collected in three volumes under the title *Music in London, 1890–1894*, have been widely and very justly admired. Shaw has been called the greatest of music critics.[22] There is no reason to deny him this praise: if he is not the greatest, he is certainly the most delightful of those who have followed this ungrateful profession. It would be a mistake, however, to suppose that Shaw's writings on music afford us any unusual insight into the musical currents of his time. Occasionally he made a penetrating observation, but on the whole he was concerned, as a journalist, with the program and the technical aspects of the performances he reviewed, rather than with the music itself. His reviews provide us with a priceless record of the musical scene in London in the early 1890's, but they are not, and certainly were not intended to be, a major contribution to the history of music.

In Shaw's day journalistic writers in the fields of music and art affected the grave pedestrian style associated with wedding announcements and obituaries, and in their columns they wisely preserved their anonymity. Shaw wrote an easy, intimate style, reminiscent of Hazlitt and Addison, that brought a vivid personality sharply to the attention of his readers. He was witty. In the concert hall, far from avoiding attention, he particularly invited it. In his knickerbocker suit of yellow tweed and his bright red tie, he was a conspicuous figure, an exclamation point among the black frock-coated gentry who sat in the stalls. It was naturally assumed that his lack of gravity was proof of his incompetence. The contrary was true. He was more highly versed in musical literature than any of his English colleagues of the press, and thoroughly at home in the musical world. But, clearly, he was more deeply interested in himself than in his subject matter, and this gave his writing a frivolous tone.

As a critic his manner was, in general, informative and benevolent; but he could be brutal. In reading his criticism one is often aware of his impatience and scorn of those who did not please him, as well as of that air of superiority which is among the professional infirmities of the trade. It is difficult in his adverse notice of a singer, or even of an orchestra, to avoid the suggestion that Shaw could have done better himself, had he been asked. Shaw's assumption of personal authority became even more conspicuous when he moved to the drama desk: "Let it be remembered," he wrote,

> that I am a superior person and what seemed incoherent and wearisome fooling to me may have seemed an exhilarating pastime to others. My heart knows only its own bitterness, and I do not desire to intermeddle with the joys of those among whom I am a stranger. I assert my intellectual superiority—that is all.

If the assertion of his intellectual superiority was the basis of Shaw's critical method, and such indeed seems to have been the case, it must be granted that he made his activity an entertaining spectacle. Journalism of this sort necessarily includes a polemic element. Shaw engaged in critical controversy with judolike dexterity. His habitual method of defense was to yield ground gracefully when he was attacked, and then to return to his original position. He made no pretense of objectivity. On the contrary, he asserted more personal hostility than in fact he could possibly have experienced:

> It is the capacity for making good or bad art a personal matter that makes a man a critic. The artist who accounts for my disparagement by alleging personal animosity on my part is quite right; when people do less than their best, and do that less at once badly and self-complacently, I hate them, loathe them, detest them, long to tear

them limb from limb and strew them as gobbets about the stage or platform. . . . In the same way, really fine artists inspire me with the warmest personal regard. . . .[23]

In music Shaw took instinctively to what is sensible, sincere, explicit, and readily intelligible. Thus in most cases time has borne out his opinions. He greatly valued good craftsmanship and a finished execution. Mozart, whom he admired most of all, along with Bach, Handel and Beethoven, furnished him with ready standards for comparison. For reasons not so readily discernible, he rated Elgar almost as high as Beethoven, and far higher than any contemporary composer.[24] He was not partial to Brahms, saw nothing to praise in Schubert, but was enchanted by Verdi.

The idioms of Cyril Scott, Schönberg, Stravinsky, and even Sibelius came hardly within the ken of either Corno di Bassetto or the G. B. S. of the *World*. In his later life, Shaw approved of Stravinsky but, he wrote,

> Elgar could turn out Debussy and Stravinsky music by the thousand bars for fun in his spare time. The enormous command of existing resources, which this orchestral skill of his exemplifies, extends over the whole musical field, and explains the fact that, though he has a most active and curious mind, he does not appear in music as an experimenter and explorer, like Scriabin and Schönberg.

Of the work of Debussy, Schönberg, and Cyril Scott he wrote in 1947: "Much of it has proved the soundness of Oscar Wilde's precept, 'Avoid the latest fashion or you will be hopelessly out of date in six months.' "[25] Gustav Mahler, he spoke of only as an "energetic conductor." He did not appraise the work of Berlioz, only its performance; and while he rose to the defense of Richard Strauss in 1910, he gave no evidence of knowing anything about him during his years as a music critic, although two of Strauss's major tone poems were written before 1890. One can hardly say that as a critic Shaw was abreast of the times, but his times, after all, were extensive beyond the ordinary, and his professional interest in music did not survive his critical career.

It is much to his credit that he recognized the greatness of Wagner's music, where Ruskin heard only the noise, but he was not an early champion of Wagner. The impression he gave in his later writings that he had somehow rescued Wagner from oblivion is largely the result of his habit of rewriting history to suit his taste. In 1935 he described himself as "a violent Wagnerite" at a time when Wagner was a "furiously absurd" figure in London.[26] The truth is that by the time Shaw became a Wagnerite, Wagner's pre-eminence was acknowledged every-where. The eighth, and last, concert of the Wagner festival at the Albert Hall, with Wagner as the guest of honor, was the subject of one of Shaw's earliest reviews, and in it Shaw remarked that the composer was received with tempestuous applause.[27]

In time, Shaw came to regard Wagner as "the greatest of modern composers"; but we cannot overlook the possibility that he admired Wagner, as he did Ibsen, partly for the wrong reasons. The French Wagnerites, most of whom had scant opportunity to hear Wagner's music, had been deeply impressed by the text of his operas, which they considered marvels of symbolist poetry. Shaw, judging by *The Perfect Wagnerite*, was deeply impressed by what he considered Wagner's allegory; but undoubtedly he was also moved by the grandeur of his musical conception and, at a time when Rossini, Meyerbeer, and Verdi were thought to have scaled the pinnacle of operatic art, it is a clear proof of Shaw's extraordinary receptivity that he was able to respond sincerely to Wagner's genius as a composer. *The Perfect Wagnerite* indicates, among other things, how ready Shaw was to absorb into his own system and to publicize according to his own lights, whatever was deemed remarkable in his day. It was his special talent to associate him-self with the best—or almost the best—that was thought and said in his world; but the association was not always a happy event. He invaded the ideas of others with the air of an Alexander enlarging his empire, magnifi-cently heedless of the devastation he might leave in his wake. In this respect he invites comparison with Undershaft, the merchant of death in *Major Barbara*, whose motto also was "Unashamed."

In September 1894 Frank Harris bought the *Saturday Review*, dis-charged the staff, and hired a new group of writers. Shaw's work on the *World* had impressed Harris with his originality, but he considered that after four years of reviewing music, Shaw was ripe for a change, and in January 1895 Harris engaged him to write drama criticism for the newly organized periodical at a weekly salary of six pounds.

Shaw held this post for more than three years. At the end of that time he married, and with his marriage his journalistic career came to an end. His drama reviews, later published in three volumes entitled *Dramatic Opinions and Essays*, and later republished as *Our Theatres in the Nine-ties*, represent his best work as a writer of critical feuilletons.[28] These exhibit all the mannerisms which by this time Shaw affected, as well as the other qualities which characterize his prefaces and essays—his vigor, his waspishness, his shameless egotism, and his eminently sound taste and good judgment. They afford us also an unparalleled perspective of the theatrical world in London during a most significant period in the development of the English stage.

This account, while priceless, is not altogether objective. It is not only a record of the current goings-on in the London theater, but also a memoir of his own personal quarrel with its masters. He acknowledged this with characteristic generosity, when the battle was won:

> I must warn the reader that what he is about to study is not a series of judgments aiming at impartiality, but a siege laid to the theatre of the nineteenth century by an author who had to cut his own way into it at the point of the pen and throw some of its defenders into the moat.
>
> Pray do not conclude from this that the things hereinafter written were not true, or not the deepest and best things I know how to say. Only they must be construed in the light of the fact that all through I was accusing my opponents of failure because they were not doing what I wanted, whereas they were often succeeding very brilliantly in doing what they themselves wanted. I postulated as desirable a certain kind of play in which I was determined ten years later to make my mark as a playwright (as I very well foreknew in the depth of my unconsciousness); and I brought everybody—authors, actors, managers—to the one test: were they coming my way or staying in the old grooves?[29]

One must admire Shaw's honesty in admitting the self-serving element in his drama criticism, but it is as well not to be swept away by it. It is true that in these years he was engaged in a battle with the commercial theater, and that he was zealously advancing the cause of Ibsen against the vested interests of the resident managers. But he was also energetic in his efforts to get those managers to produce the plays he had already written. These were not the masterpieces of his later career, to which his *Apology* alludes. They were the intermediate plays—*Candida, The Man of Destiny*, and *Captain Brassbound's Conversion*—the commercial possibilities of which were not yet apparent to the managers in the West End. These were, obviously, little theater plays directed to an exclusive audience, and very likely they would have been financially disastrous on the commercial stage at a time when they were first offered. In time they all proved their worth on the stage: in the 1890's, their time had not yet come.

It is possible that nobody, since the time of Racine, had tried so shamelessly to advance his interests in the theater as Shaw during these years; but it is questionable that his drama criticism did anything to influence decisively either the course of English drama, or the ultimate destiny of his own plays.

After Ibsen, new currents had set in, the effects of which were inescapable even in England, and European drama entered a new phase. Shaw cast in his lot with the new movement, along with Barker, Hankin, Barrie, and Galsworthy, and did what he could to stimulate its development both as critic and as playwright. Along with William Archer and A. B. Walkley, his most gifted contemporaries in the critical field, Shaw brought to the attention of the British public artistic considerations which, without him, might have been overlooked for some years longer. But it was not Shaw's precepts which influenced the English stage so much as his examples. He was vociferous as a critic; but as a playwright he developed a style of comedy which had not existed before his time and which by its existence demonstrated the poverty of what in this period passed for intellectual drama.

Shaw resigned his post on the *Saturday Review* in May 1898 and was succeeded by Max Beerbohm. The year marked a turning point in his life: when his journalistic career came to an end, his career in the theater began to flower. He wrote, with disarming effrontery, a valedictory to his readers on the *Saturday Review*:

> For ten years past, with an unprecedented pertinacity and obstination, I have been dinning into the public head that I am an extraordinarily witty, brilliant and clever man. That is now part of the public opinion of England; and no power in heaven and earth will ever change it. I may dodder and dote; I may pot-boil and platitudinize; I may become the butt and chopping block of all the bright, original spirits of the rising generation; but my reputation shall not suffer; it is built up fast and solid, like Shakespear's, on an impregnable basis of dogmatic reiteration.[30]

As usual he exaggerated. In 1898 his reputation was still confined to a small group of appreciative readers. But it was destined in some years to become world-wide beyond that of any man in England.

SHAW'S THEATER

By the time Shaw gave up his post on the *Saturday Review* he had written seven plays, only one of which had brought him anything substantial in the way of royalties. His plays had hardly been seen by anybody, and even those who most admired his work conceded willingly that it was destined for an exclusive coterie. The only play Shaw had so far written which was judged to have some chance of success on the commercial stage was *You Never Can Tell*. It had been offered to George Alexander, one of the more perceptive actor-managers of the day. He had returned it with the notation: "When I got to the end, I had no more idea of what you meant by it than a tom-cat."

By 1892 there had been much talk of the renewal of English drama, and a good deal of discussion in the press as to the course which the new serious comedy must take; but it was still by no means clear in what way the new comedy should be new, or in what degree it might become serious. In 1884, Henry Arthur Jones had written, in words reminiscent of the *Entretiens* of Diderot, of the current need for plays of serious intention, dealing with themes of "meaning and importance." Two years later, in the preface to *The Renascence of English Drama*, Jones intimated that this goal had already been reached: "If there had been in 1882 a body of cultivated playgoers sufficiently numerous to understand and welcome such plays as have been eminently successful in some of our West End theatres, not a single word of the following papers would have been written or spoken."[1]

Two years after that, he appeared considerably less optimistic. In his introduction to the survey of the English stage recently published by Augustin Filon, he noted that English taste in the drama was still deplorable. In popular estimation Bulwer-Lytton rivaled Shakespeare: *The*

Lady of Lyons was considered the equal of *Hamlet* as a masterpiece of tragedy; and *Money* was generally thought to be as fine a comedy as *The School for Scandal.* He added: "It is benevolent of M. Filon to write criticism about a nation where such notions have prevailed for half a century." In England, Jones concluded, English drama, as such, did not exist: "there is no drama that even pretends to picture modern English life; I might almost say that pretends to picture human life at all. . . ."[2]

Doubtless Jones's despondency was warranted by the facts; but to many it must have seemed excessive. There were those who thought that the English stage had made enormous strides in the last generation. In his Introductory Statement to *The Ticket of Leave Man*, one of the great successes of the 1860's, Tom Taylor had boasted:

> There has been no period, for the last two centuries, in which invention and activity have been more conspicuous in the dramatic field than during the thirty or forty years which include the epoch of such dramatists as Miss Mitford, Sheridan Knowles, Bulwer-Lytton, James White, Jerrold, Browning, G. Darley, Searle, Marston, Horne, Lovell, Troughton, Bell, Mrs. Gore, Sullivan, Peake, Poole, Hook, Planché, Charles and George Dance, the Mortons, Mark Lemon, Buckstone, Selby, Fitzball (who, whatever may be the literary quality of his plays, has given evidence of genuine romantic invention), Bernard, Coyne, Oxenford, Shirley Brooks, Watts, Phillips, and those peculiar products of our time, the burlesque writers, like the Brothers Brough, and Messrs. Byron and Barnaud.

Nevertheless the theater which Shaw inherited was no great thing. The two centuries that divided Sheridan from Jones had produced nothing of the slightest consequence for the history of the stage. Along with the best of the conservative critics of his time, Jones placed his hopes for a revival of the drama on the refinement of the type of domestic melodrama which, after the time of Robertson, was called realistic. In 1894 he had based his enthusiasm on the success of Pinero's *The Second Mrs. Tanqueray* (1893), and on the glowing reception of his own *The Masqueraders* (1894). In 1896 it was the failure of *Michael and His Lost Angel* that prompted his depression. In common with most of his professional colleagues, he had a hearty distaste for Ibsen and the Ibsenist drama, and he was entirely out of touch with the avant-garde ideas that were influencing the French stage in this period. He had known Shaw since 1885, respected him as a critic, and had given him sound advice on business matters in connection with the production of *Arms and the Man*; but there is not the slightest evidence that he had any inkling at this, or any other time, of Shaw's importance for the rebirth of the theater over which Jones and Pinero presumably presided.

The conditions which make for great drama in any period are far from clear, but surely one of them is the activity of great dramatists. In the two centuries between Sheridan and Shaw there was nobody of that sort in England, and the taste for rubbish asserted itself peremptorily. The actors in this sterile time accommodated themselves to the mediocrity of the drama by cultivating an artificial style that was an end in itself. The English theater, once the domain of the dramatic author, became an actor's theater, and the audience came to see, not the plays, but the stars who performed them.

In the eighteenth century the patent houses had housed professional stock companies which offered a cycle of "classical" plays in repertory, varied by an occasional novelty. As the century drew to its close the competition of the minor houses caused the legitimate theaters to lengthen their bills so as to include a varied offering of theatrical fare. In the early 1800's the curtain at Covent Garden went up at six in the afternoon, in time to bring in the workmen after their tea. It went down about midnight. The Haymarket gave an even longer performance. These innovations entailed putting on from seven to ten acts in the course of an evening. In the patent houses it was customary to open with a short curtain-raiser, followed by a five-act tragedy and a melodrama, the whole topped off with a pantomime or farce; while the unlicensed theaters usually offered three complete plays, perhaps two melodramas and a farce. The spectators who sat through these multiple spectacles were not only exceptionally exigent, but remarkably exhibitionistic. An evening in the theater often involved a spirited contest between actors and audience for the spotlight of attention, for there were performers on both sides, and the spectators were quite willing to entertain one another if they thought the show dull.

In these years the English drama sank to such depths as defy the scrutiny of any but the most intrepid scholar. Judging by the quality of successful offerings, from Colman's *John Bull* (1803) to Robertson's *Caste* (1867), the London public rejoiced in the broadest and most obvious theatrical effects, stagy attitudes, heavy bombast, and cloying sentimentality. The great Elizabethan plays, cobbled up to suit the current fashion, continued meanwhile to find favor, performed in styles that ranged from the "classic" manner of Kemble to the "metaphysical" style of Macready. It was in such grand fashion also that the less great plays of the time were performed. Until the 1860's no actor made an attempt at realistic portraiture, and no dramatic writer had occasion to suggest anything of the sort in his plays. During this period the art of the playwright wholly consisted in arranging a sequence of effective scenes and picturesque tableaux in which the principal actors might display themselves to advantage. "Why, what the devil is the plot good for but to bring in fine things?" Mr. Bayes asks in *The Rehearsal*. The Victorian playwrights were entirely of his opinion.

An anthology such as Lamb's *Specimens of English Dramatic Poets* indicates with some accuracy what an experienced playgoer of the year 1808 might consider the flower of English drama in the great tradition. It is a series of poetic passages particularly suited to stage declamation without reference to the dramatic context, the equivalent of an album of "highlights" from the opera. From this standpoint, *Hamlet* might be given as a concert piece by a single actor; indeed, this is what it often came to in the early Victorian theater, the other actors being considered mere vehicles for the facilitation of the principal's performance. Such plays as Holcroft's famous melodrama *A Tale of Mystery* and Bulwer-Lytton's *The Lady of Lyons* were designed as a sequence of impressive tableaux with music and declamation, linked by an anecdote the details of which nobody was expected to comprehend.

The performance of these declamations, however, was important. The audience of that day, though barely literate, was by no means unsophisticated. Those who sat habitually in the pit were as thoroughly versed in the traditions of the tragic stage as the modern aficionado in the complex rituals of the bull ring. These connoisseurs exercised the most exquisite discrimination in the evaluation of an actor's performance. They knew the actor's points better than he, awaited the crucial speeches with impatience, and expressed their opinion of his execution immediately and imperiously. These conditions determined the character of dramatic art for the better part of a century.

As the mise en scène was mainly designed to focus attention on the star actors, there was no special need for stage management. Aside from the arrangement of the tableaux into which the action was periodically frozen so as to make the effect of a painting, the stage director's problem was principally a matter of controlling the traffic across the stage.

Acting, under these conditions, was an art that required exceptional skill. In the major houses, after 1810, the actors were so far removed from the spectators in the topmost galleries that their features could hardly be discerned. To be heard they had to bellow; and in order to be visible they had to exaggerate their postures far beyond the uses of ordinary humanity. In these circumstances, dramatic writing was necessarily hyperbolic in proportion to the extravagance of the performance. It was normal for the dramatic author to suit his composition to the needs and capacities of the actors whose text he was expected to supply, rather than for the actor to think of himself as a servant of the play.

Writing for the stage was, accordingly, a servile profession which afforded neither much compensation nor much esteem. During the first half of the nineteenth century, writers were often hired on an annual basis to provide an acting company with a steady supply of usable material. Other writers were paid by the act. As speed was essential in a trade of this sort, plays were patched out of other plays, and novels were ransacked for adaptable scenes which might readily be reduced to dialogue. Much of this activity was in the hands of dependable hacks who prided themselves on their professionalism rather than on their artistry. Thus it happened that the rift between the literary and the commercial drama, a distinction which in the days of Shakespeare had not existed, became absolute and permanent. For the greater part of the nineteenth century, those who wrote for the theater were not considered literary artists, while those who were esteemed as poets affected to despise the stage. Lord Byron who, in fact, enjoyed some success as a dramatist, wrote in the preface to *Marino Faliero*: "Were I capable of writing a play which should be deemed stageworthy, success would give me little or no pleasure, and failure great pain. It is for this reason that during the time of being one of the committee of one of the theatres, I never made the attempt and never will."

In the period 1850–80, a time which in the other arts saw an extraordinary flowering of creative activity, the English drama was controlled by a small group of unimaginative professionals—managers, actors, and writers—whose principal aim was to please a sophisticated, but relatively uncultivated audience, whose tastes were known but whose possibilities were not explored. This audience was strongly oriented along moral and patriotic lines. It cherished inviolable ideals, the validity of which no playwright would dare question. It desired the theater to demonstrate, in as vivid and convincing a manner as possible, the rightness of an Englishman's fundamental belief in the infallibility of God's Providence, and the absolute superiority of British ways. It was eager to see how, after many thrilling vicissitudes, the wiliest villains got their just deserts, while innocent virtue, seemingly enmeshed in an impenetrable net of evil, infallibly triumphed in the end. Since this audience desired the stage to provide not an authentic representation of experience, but a means of escape from the discomforts of life, the Victorian drama ordinarily took place in a fantastic never-never land in which only an occasional landmark served to recall the world outside the playhouse. The theater thus developed its own special reality, its own conventions, morality, logic, speech, and gesture, in short, its own world.

Consequently, for the better part of the century, what the audience most admired in the theater was not the representation of truth, but that precise shade of the untrue which it found most agreeable to believe. Essentially this remains the case; the dramatic experience is enjoyable provided it is understood that it is not truth, but a fantasy akin to truth. It is this complex attitude which has always precluded any serious attempt to represent "life as it is" in the theater, so that when in Moscow at the end of the century Stanislavsky pushed his idea of naturalism to the point of counterfeiting reality on the stage, the absurdity of the pretense became embarrassingly apparent.

In the London theaters the dictatorship of the pit reached its peak in the early 1800's. Then slowly the tide began to turn. Doubtless the change reflected some improvement in the cultural level of the London audiences, but the motive appears to have been mainly economic. The theaters as they were constituted simply did not pay. No matter how large the playhouse, the scale of prices was always too low and the demands of the audience too high to yield a substantial profit. It was the dream of every theater manager in London from the time of Macready to drive the pittites from the pit, and to substitute a better-paying audience. The pittites seemed immovable. When at last they began to give way, the managers hastened to accelerate their withdrawal with every means at their disposal.

It was no simple matter. In the 1840's Macready and Phelps made earnest efforts to refine their productions so as to attract a more estimable class of playgoers. It was in vain. The respectable citizenry continued to regard the theater as a place of low resort and could not be induced to go there. A decade later, Charles Kean tried once again, this time with more success; and in the course of the next ten years the character of the theater-going public changed so markedly that the more progressive managers began to think seriously of accommodating the physical aspects of the playhouses to the requirements of an upper-class clientele. As early as 1843 the pit benches at the Haymarket were provided with backs. By 1856 orchestra stalls were common in the London theaters. In 1863 the chairs at the Haymarket were covered in velvet. In 1876 Marie

Wilton ripped out the pit benches completely, carpeted the stalls, and provoked a riot by raising their price at the Haymarket to ten shillings. By this time the more expensive areas of the London playhouses had begun to glitter with well-dressed people, and the drama, which had so far provided a worm's eye view of the world of fashion, began to depict a social class which desired to see itself portrayed on the stage with some show of authenticity.

With the passage of the Theatre Act of 1843 the long monopoly of the patent houses came to an end. It now became possible to present plays without music in any of the London theaters. Since this legislation did no more, in fact, than to regularize what was already current practice, there was no immediate consequence. Seven years after the passage of the bill, however, Charles Kean took advantage of the new freedom to put on an elaborate series of classic revivals at the Princess' Theatre. The following season, in the Exhibition year, the Queen took a box at the Princess', and for the next decade, until the death of the Prince Consort in 1861, she continued to defy public opinion by making frequent visits to the theater.

The effect of Victoria's patronage on the fortunes of the London theater is incalculable. Before her accession the royal family had manifested its interest in the English drama chiefly by attending the yearly performance "Commanded by His Majesty." Now that the Queen's favor was so openly bestowed on it, playgoing took on new dignity. It became possible for the first time to call the theater, as Irving did, a temple of art. The art he had in mind, of course, was the art of acting.

After the Great Exhibition, theater-building began in earnest. In the fifty years between 1850 and 1900 the number of playhouses in and around London trebled. At the turn of the century the city supported 61 theaters, of which 38 were in the West End. There were, in addition, 39 music halls, so that London now rivaled Paris as a center of theatrical enterprise. The renascence of the English drama might be said to be an accomplished fact.[3] Yet its birth pangs were by no means over. Great changes had taken place in the physical appearance of the playhouses and the plays they presented, but the substantive elements of English drama, its conventions, logic, depth, and choice of subject matter were little altered since the earlier days of the century. After 1867 there was much talk of realism in the drama. But realism at this time meant primarily an enhancement of the stage illusion through mechanical means. The theater remained theatrical.

The presence of a more thoughtful and more cultivated clientele made

it possible, nevertheless, to develop the subject matter of drama in areas
that had so far been taboo. The new audience could read and was not
altogether averse to a display of new ideas in the theater provided they
were to its taste. In the 1870's the drama began, at first with great
circumspection, to enter the current of contemporary thought. In this
adventure it had, of course, the precedent and the pattern of the French
thesis plays to which Augier and Dumas *fils* had recently given currency. It was along these lines that the English dramatists proceeded to
put on the stage what passed for the burning issues of the day.

These issues had, in fact, little to do with the problems that actually
confronted Victorian society. They were hypothetical questions concerning domestic and social relations, questions of duty and conscience,
adultery, illegitimacy, and social status. The English dramatists ventured
upon these unaccustomed areas with the delicacy of tightrope walkers,
and the fact that such themes in a realistic context could be discussed at
all in the theater gave rise to some apprehension in the press. Nevertheless the way was opened for the kind of play which in England passed
for social drama, and eventually for the plays of Ibsen, Shaw, and Galsworthy.

The history of the drama in the nineteenth century is essentially the
history of realism, the conceptual transition from the idea of drama as an
abstract and exemplary art distinct from ordinary experience to that of
drama as the actual representation of life. In this respect the drama seems
to have manifested its major trends somewhat later than painting, which
began to reject precise representation at about the time when dramatists
were beginning to take it up most seriously. So long as the theater was
dominated by the classical preconceptions of the Renaissance, dramatic
literature was regarded as a branch of poetry and, no matter how
debased its rhetoric, in theory its compositions were rhetorical fictions
subject to the rules of art. In tragedy, and later in melodrama, this
concept resulted in idealization, hyperbole, and symmetrical design. In
comedy, it resulted in caricature. There was no need, in these circumstances, to imitate actual experience on the stage, and it was seldom that
anything of the sort was attempted.

In the conspiracy to perpetuate the illusion of a special reality, exclusively of the theater, all those professionally concerned with the stage
collaborated—the writers, actors, managers, critics, the censor, and most
significantly, the public. In the time of Victoria, public sentiment was
presumed to be so extraordinarily sensitive that it must be preserved
from the slightest shock. Between the ideal world of the theater and the

sordid realities of life the Licenser of Plays manfully interposed his person, insisting on the revision or deletion of anything that might conceivably cause discomfort to anyone. Apart from the traditional villainies which were invariably thwarted or punished in the last act, the world of the theater was preserved in a state of innocence which was incomparably more agreeable than the conditions of the world outside. Nothing more congenial to established ideas of justice and morality was conceivable than the views of life presented in the current drama, and the fact that it was completely fanciful disturbed no one. Thus the successful partnership of church and stage which was evidenced by the institution of the Church and Stage Guild in 1880 was a perfectly logical outcome of the alliance of the antirealistic forces which had so long controlled English sentiment.

When, in his Royal Institution speech of 1 February 1895, Henry Irving formally presented his claim to have the art of the actor officially classified among the fine arts, he was in effect asking the government to take note of the importance of the theater as a stronghold of conservative idealism. His speech invited knighthood and by conferring this dignity upon him Victoria also conferred nobility upon a profession which had not so far been entirely respectable. Irving fittingly commemorated the occasion by unveiling a statue of Mrs. Siddons in Paddington Green, thus extending the mantle of respectability retroactively over the entire theatrical tradition of England. The change was not altogether advantageous. Before he was ennobled by Imperial decree, there had been some possibility that Irving might play Ibsen at the Lyceum. After he accepted knighthood—as Shaw was quick to see—the case for the new realism became for the time hopeless.[4]

The transition from the idealistic conception of drama which Irving exemplified to the idea that the drama should be an honest reflection of life was neither smooth nor certain, nor in fact, rewarding. It took place, but the process involved a series of awkward compromises. It was easy enough for designers to devise, and for carpenters to execute, a convincing likeness of reality on the stage; and it was no great hardship for actors to mimic the speech of real people, but it was infinitely more difficult for writers to break with dramaturgic patterns which had amply proved their worth at the box office. The trend toward realism, however, was inexorable. In the course of a period of growing materialism, everything conspired to attenuate the ideal basis of the earlier drama. The glaring contrasts of melodrama gave way, albeit reluctantly, to a more extensive spectrum of moral values, relativistic ideas encroached upon the absolutes of the former age, and characterization became progressively more complex. It became difficult to distinguish heroes from villains. The time was not far off when, in serious drama, such concepts would be given up.

The rapid development of impressionism in the 1880's—itself a special aspect of the trend toward realism—helped further to disintegrate the eternal verities upon which the old drama was grounded. Technically, the need to represent each situation with the precision due to its singularity led to a type of detailed stage presentation which had never before been consciously employed in the theater. Instead of the generally useful settings which formerly had served indifferently for any play, special sets began to be designed to suit the requirements of the action, and characters began to be thought of as unique personages instead of as representative types of humanity. The next step was the technique of naturalism, and the attempt to give an exact account of reality on the stage. But before realism could develop to this point it was necessary not only to surmount the extraordinary prudery of the time but, more difficult still, to overcome the idealistic tendency of a culture which had only recently emerged from the mists of romanticism. In the theater one of the chief manifestations of this tendency was the astonishing development of melodrama.

The primary plot pattern of melodrama is traceable to Schiller's *Die Räuber*, a romantic tragedy. The idea of tragedy on which Schiller framed his epoch-making play was, in fact, classical; but in the process of giving movement and romantic coloring to the traditional plot of the cruel tyrant and the innocent victim, the youthful Schiller diluted the Senecan formula to the point where it was barely recognizable. *Die Räuber* is, at bottom, a prodigal son play, but it has wider implications than is usual in this genre, and in the contrast between the warm-hearted Karl and the scheming Franz, Schiller was able to develop a theme of the greatest significance for the literary history of the period.

The contrast between the man of heart and the man of mind which is the dramatic basis of *Die Räuber* represented in unmistakable terms the psychic tensions which engendered the cult of sensibility in the eighteenth century, and this in turn prefigured the conflict between the new romanticism and the classical tradition which it superseded. In Schiller's play, Franz is a self-centered Machiavellian who cuts a wretched figure alongside the wild, but lovable Karl. This characterological contrast—which Sheridan had anticipated four years before in *The School for*

Scandal—provided an indispensable pattern for future melodrama. The character whom Hobbes had described with evident distaste a century earlier as archetypal man single-mindedly engaged in the pursuit of his personal interest thus became a stage villain, infallibly doomed to fail in his nefarious schemes of self-assertion at the expense of those more nobly disposed than he.

Drama conceived along classical lines had traditionally emphasized the supremacy of the intellect over the irrational faculties, and particularly over the passions. In reversing this attitude, in accordance with the progressive tendencies of his day, Schiller initiated a new dramatic genre, which channeled into the traditional modes of tragedy the full spirit of the romantic age. Very likely Schiller based his innovation on the ideas of Shaftesbury and Rousseau, and the current of sensibility which had been rising since the time of Shadwell and Steele. He wrote: "For him who has reached the point of cultivating his intellect at the expense of his heart (and I do not envy him this honor), there is no longer any humanity or divinity; these two worlds are nothing in his eyes. . . ." This described tolerably well the villain of melodrama, a character amply supplied with brains, but heartless.

The vogue of melodrama in France began six years after the first production of Schiller's play, which so impressed the French as a revolutionary manifesto demonstrating the right of noble hearts to rise against corrupt authority that in 1792 the author was made an honorary citizen of France. In 1798 Guilbert de Pixerécourt produced a musical play entitled *Victor, ou l'enfant de la forêt*, the plot of which was largely borrowed from *Die Räuber*. *Victor* had originally been composed as an opera with scenes of spoken dialogue, but by the time it reached the stage, only some portions of the score were left. These were used to enhance important exits and entrances and to underscore the mood of certain scenes. Although there was no lack of precedent for the use of music to accompany stage dialogue, *Victor* was hailed as a new dramatic genre, and its success initiated a long series of plays of similar cut, with romantic plots, thrilling scenes, and elaborate settings, the action of which was supported and accentuated by an appropriate musical score.

Pixerécourt billed his play as a melodrama. It was in fact a tragicomedy with comic scenes and a happy ending. In 1809, five years after its first production, *Victor* was adapted for the English stage by William Dimond under the title of *The Foundling of the Forest*. By this time the vogue of melodrama in London had been assured by the remarkable success of Thomas Holcroft's *A Tale of Mystery* (1802), which was also adapted from the French. *A Tale of Mystery* is indeed so mysterious that the intricacies of its plot seriously tax the attention of the modern reader, but it appears not to have confused the nineteenth-century audience in the least. The inference is either that this audience was remarkably perceptive, or else that it concentrated on the scenes represented without bothering very much about the events that brought them about. At any rate, this piece of dramatic rubbish was incessantly revived over an unbelievably long period—its popularity was exceeded only by Douglas Jerrold's *Black Ey'd Susan* (1829), which held the stage at very frequent intervals for a half-century.

Melodrama was fearlessly eclectic in its choice of subjects. The French authors who supplied the English theater with most of these pieces—Pixerécourt, Caignez, and D'Ennery—borrowed plots and characters wherever they might be found, levying heavily on the *Sturm und Drang* playwrights, as well as on Kotzebue, Shakespeare, and Walter Scott. Melodrama thus presented an astonishing hodgepodge of every kind of sensational fiction from Goethe to Dickens, all of it shaped according to the requirements of an essentially moralistic medium which mixed thrills with sentiment, relieved suspense with comedy, and systematically doled out prizes and punishments in the last act. This genre was proved to be eminently stageworthy even when it ceased to be musical. Before 1843 a few bars of music had sufficed to exempt a play from the monopoly of the patent houses. When the monopoly was abolished, the musical element in melodrama could be dispensed with, and often it was, but the genre was too firmly established in popular estimation to admit of any extensive alteration of its dramatic formula, and eventually found its way into the cinema without any impairment of its heroic outlines.

The revolutionary note in *Die Räuber* was implicit in the play's indictment of a social system which outlawed a man of generous impulses while it provided every advantage for the selfish scoundrel who was able to worm his way into the good graces of the gullible. Its theme was thus in some degree critical of current standards and current authority, and it is significant that this rebellious strain crept into popular melodrama on every level, even the lowest. Conceivably this had something to do with the remarkable popularity of these plays, in most of which may be found some trace of dissatisfaction with the current norms. Among the fruits of the French Revolution, melodrama was certainly the least considerable, but it was among the longest-lived. In the course of the century during which it remained popular it sank to unimaginable depths of stupidity and bathos. It became illogical, incoherent, virtually unintelligible; nevertheless its enormous viability in the theater and its subsequent development in the cinema, radio, and television testify to its importance as a dramatic medium. It was doubtless this, as well as its energy and its undercurrent of social criticism, which recommended it to Shaw as a prime vehicle for the transmission of ideas in the theater.

The resounding success of Hugo's *Hernani* in 1830 indicated the possibilities of melodrama in high style. *Hernani* was called a romantic tragedy. It is in fact an opera without music in which the lyric passages fulfill the function of aria and duet. Since the masters of this short-lived form, Hugo and the elder Dumas, based their style, so they said, on Shakespeare, it was predictable that further efforts would be made in England to revive poetic drama in the Elizabethan manner. Indeed, many of the English poets from Shelley to Tennyson and Browning tried their hands at five-act tragedies in verse, and the imitation of Shakespeare continued throughout the major part of the century to absorb the energies of those who aspired to rise above the trivialities of the popular stage. The results ranged from such pretentious nonsense as J. S. Knowles's *Virginius* (1820) to really distinguished works such as Tennyson's *Becket* (1893), which provided Irving with a magnificent role. Relatively few of these blank verse plays actually reached the stage. The bulk of the poetic tragedy that was published in England served mainly to widen the abyss which separated the literate drama of the time from the plays which were the gainpenny of the commercial theater. Probably, as Matthew Arnold suggested, the conditions for tragedy were not present at this stage of English culture. The reasons, however, could not have been those which he adduced—essentially the lack of a common faith upon which to base the tragic experience.

Tragedy is the luxurious aspect of despair. In its power to transform pain into pleasure it demonstrates human artistry in its most useful aspect. So sublime a genre was doubtless well suited to the temper of life in fifth-century Athens, or in Elizabethan England, or perhaps even in France in the time of Louis XIV. It did not at all suit an age which from the height of the Industrial Revolution look forward to endless vistas of social and scientific progress. The optimistic note of melodrama, on the contrary, was entirely appropriate to this era. Its clouds were dark with menace, but invariably lined with silver. Its heroes and heroines were threatened by dangers calculated to make strong men shudder, and the sorrows patiently endured by its aged couples could wring tears from hearts of stone, but the horrors of melodrama were always lightened by the author's implied warranty of a happy outcome. The melodramatic fantasy, unlike the tragic, proceeded on a very superficial level of masochism, and, since it never really fathomed the depths of pathos, it was always amenable to the enlivening effects of comedy.

A just and thoughtfully administered Providence was indispensable to the melodramatic world-view. Its climate was therefore fundamentally cheerful, and the ingenuity of the playwright was demonstrated by the intricacy of a plot that threaded its way confidently through the labyrinths of misfortune in such a way as to come out exceedingly well. In a world compounded of moral absolutes, the play of good and evil was particularly amenable to pleasing arrangements of light and shade, and the necessary contrasts were best set forth in terms of archetypal characters some steps removed from abstraction.

It is arguable that the decline of melodrama at the end of the century was in greater measure related to the dilution of Christian faith in the post-Darwinian era than to the growing sophistication of the audience or the mounting interest in individual psychology. Melodrama involved a direct affirmation of Christian principles. Unlike tragedy, which regularly demonstrated the instability of fortune, and thus joined victim and tyrant in a higher metaphysical entity, melodrama affirmed faith in the values of this world and invariably demonstrated the material advantages of virtue and the drawbacks of vice. It was, consequently, very well suited to the needs of the constantly rising mercantile class; but it could not survive the skepticism of those who had nothing to hope for in heaven and nothing to fear in hell.

The development of realism was fatal to the melodramatic view of life. Realism implied a disquieting sense of experience as widely incompatible with the idealistic basis of melodrama as it was with the aesthetic basis of tragedy. The consequence was that, with the decline of melodrama, the theater had to find new forms and new matter in order to survive. It branched off, in fact, in two directions, the spiritual and the material. In both cases, its procedures were analytical. The one resulted in the development of symbolism and the new psychological drama. The other extended the areas of the problem play into social criticism and reform, and brought about a re-examination of the moral bases of society.

These realistic tendencies first became apparent some twenty years before Shaw came to London. Tom Taylor's *Our American Cousin* (1858) and *The Ticket of Leave Man* (1863) both indicate some attempt at a portrayal of city life in a manner more convincing than that of Dekker or Middleton. The tendency toward a more exact mimesis is even more evident in the plays of Dion Boucicault, the dominant theatrical influence of the mid-century.

Boucicault began his stage career as an actor, and his subsequent success as a writer is clearly ascribable to his sense of what works effectively on the stage. He first made his mark in 1841 with *London Assurance*, a play in which he tried, though in vain, to recapture the spirit of Restoration comedy. His true gift, as it turned out, was for melodrama. His version of *The Corsican Brothers* (1852), a strange play involving the supernatural relations of twin brothers, was adapted from the French of the elder Dumas, and, for all its success, showed no great originality. But in *The Colleen Bawn* (1860) and *Arrah-na-Pogue* (1865) Boucicault showed his talent. The fictitious Ireland he brought to the English theater was obviously far from any known reality, but it served to extend the scope of melodrama to include characters and situations which had at least, a definite provenience and a native cast. *The Octoroon* (1861), similarly, was outrageously fanciful in its plot, but it brought to the theater a problem which had so far not been considered apt for the stage. *The Streets of London* (1864), on the other hand, was hopelessly theatrical. Very likely it marked the limit to which, in Boucicault's opinion, the drama should go in its representation of reality. Three years later Thomas Robertson produced *Caste* and with it initiated a new realism which, in the opinion of many, was the basis of the modern English style of comedy.

Robertson's principal innovation was a type of melodrama which resembled serious comedy. In the series of six plays he wrote before his early death in 1871 he took up a number of themes of the sort that held the stage in contemporary France, but which had not yet been given any sort of attention in the English theater. Like Ibsen, his contemporary, Robertson took his departure from the type of *drame* in which Dumas *fils*, Augier, and Oscar Feuillet were at that time specializing. Ibsen made use of this thematic material in an attempt to transcend the theatrical conventions of his time. Robertson was not so ambitious. He contented himself with working realistically within the conventional framework of the domestic *drame*.

It was Robertson's idea to develop a type of comedy which would represent through the collision of individual wills the clash of the social forces that determine human destinies. Unhappily his plays did not carry out this laudable intention. His characters were stock types. His plots were contrived after the traditional formulas, and his conclusions were commonplace. The titles of his plays—*Society, Caste, Play, School, War, Ours*—indicate the sort of critical survey of English life which he had in mind, but his plays, in spite of their critical pretensions, hardly detached themselves from the matrix in which they were conceived. Obviously what Robertson wished to bring about in the theater was something like a revolution. In fact, he did little that was new; but it seemed, for a time, a great deal.

Up to this time nineteenth-century plays in England essentially portrayed a group of stock characters engaged in an intrigue. The stock company of the period consisted of a troupe of actors, each of whom had his "line"—in France it was called his *emploi*—beyond which he seldom ventured. The system went back to the time of the *commedia dell'arte*, which was similarly organized. Plays written for companies of this sort were definable in terms of the permutation of a handful of stock masks which served to delineate in the theater the entire spectrum of the human race. By means of a leading man, a light comedian, low comedian, character actor, heavy man, old man, juvenile lead, and walking gentleman every conceivable shade of the masculine personality could be represented. The other sex was similarly suggested in terms of the leading lady, heavy woman, old woman, ingénue, and soubrette. These characters, together with some "utilities" and supernumeraries, made up a cast, and, in relation to one another, a play.

It was quite unnecessary in these circumstances for an author to go into lengthy descriptions of his characters. All that was needed was to allocate the roles, write the speeches, and indicate the actions. Each actor knew what his line entailed. He could be relied upon to supply a ready-made characterization in accordance with his role and even to improvise, if necessary, the dialogue and stage business which he considered requisite to its proper development. The writer who unduly labored his style in devising a new play betrayed his ignorance of the profession. Beyond a certain point, experienced actors did not trouble to study their parts. They depended heavily on the prompter and, failing his assistance, said whatever came into their heads. For the rest, they not only reveled in their specialities but exaggerated their individual idiosyncracies at the expense of the play and the other actors.

Plays composed in accordance with these customs had the advantage of a highly skilled cast, but one which was relatively independent of the intentions of the author. The line actor required no direction, few explanations, and little rehearsal. The writers, for their part, were left free to concentrate on their plots without wasting calories on characterization or dialogue, so that a play, once the sequence of scenes was settled, could be put together without undue waste of time. The disadvantage of the system was that, since the available characters were as rigidly defined as chessmen, plays of this type had virtually interchangeable parts and might easily make an impression of sameness. Moreover in this system each principal had his special prerogatives which it was the business of the author to satisfy. All this left little room for any unusual display of originality, since anything by way of innovation was likely to be submerged under the actor's habitual interpretation.

Bulwer-Lytton's *Money* (1840) was one of the first Victorian plays in which some attempt was made to go beyond the current stereotypes. But *Money* was not a great play. Robertson's *David Garrick* (1864) and *Society* (1865) were arranged conventionally. *Caste* (1867) made a distinct departure. To our eyes, the professional good-for-nothing Eccles, and the honest plumber Gerridge, his son-in-law, seem to be rather ordinary examples of Victorian caricature. Yet in the theater these characters created a sensation; and Shaw—after subjecting Eccles to severe critical manhandling—did him the honor of modeling Drinkwater upon him when he wrote *Captain Brassbound's Conversion*, and Mr. Doolittle as well when he wrote *Pygmalion*.

In creating Eccles, Robertson brought into being a new stock type, convincing chiefly because of its novelty. The genial reprobate who absolutely resists reform was not a character indigenous to melodrama. In that ingenuous genre all reprobates are liable, under proper auspices, to instant conversion. Eccles represents an attempt at realism. He is neither a sympathetic character nor precisely a villain. He is rotten to the core, no doubt, but he is amusing and holds the stage well. Moreover, both he and Gerridge speak a colloquial jargon—comparable in its way to the nautical language of Sweet William in *Black Ey'd Susan*—the artificiality of which passed for truth in the 1860's. On both counts Eccles was said to be not merely realistic but absolutely drawn from life.

Thirty years later, Eccles seemed less convincing. But among Robertson's principal contributions to the progress of English drama, as Shaw pointed out in reviewing the revival of *Caste* in 1897, was the fact that, while his characters were clearly drawn from stock, they are less wooden than the stock types of tradition:

> "Nature! Freshness!" you will exclaim. "In Heaven's name . . . where is there a touch of nature in Caste?" I reply: "In the windows, in the doors, in the walls, in the carpet, in the ceiling, in the kettle, in the

fireplace, in the ham, in the tea, in the bread and butter, in the bassinet, in the hats and sticks and clothes, in the familiar phrases, the quiet, unpumped, everyday utterance; in short, the commonplaces that are now spurned because they are commonplaces, and were then inexpressibly welcome because they were the most unexpected of novelties."

And yet I dare not submit even this excuse to a detailed examination. Charles Mathews was in the field long before Robertson and Mr. Bancroft with the art of behaving like an ordinary gentleman in what looked like a real drawing room. The characters are all very old stagers, very thinly "humanized. . . ." Eccles is caricatured in the vein and by the methods Dickens had made obvious, and the implied moral view of his case is the common Pharisaic one of his day. . . . The "Marquizzy" is not an honest study from life, but simply a ladyfication of the conventional haughty mother. . . . Only, let it not be forgotten that in both there really is a humanization . . . that is, a discovery of saving sympathetic qualities in personages hitherto deemed beyond redemption.

. . . And if from these hints you cannot gather the real nature and limits of the tiny theatrical revolution of which Robertson was the hero, I must leave you in your perplexity for want of time and space for further exposition.[5]

Shaw's reluctance to discuss *Caste* in greater detail is entirely understandable. The play is very amusing, and at the same time quite dreadful. In *Caste* the Honorable George D'Alroy marries Miss Esther Eccles, a chorus girl, to whom his mother, the Marquise de St. Maur has strong objections. The Honorable George is promptly called to arms in India. His wife carries on gallantly in his absence, but the abyss that separates the classes is fully demonstrated by the Marquise's rejection of her son's wife and family, as well as by the protests of Gerridge at the intrusion of the aristocracy into their peaceful lower-class home. The gap is bridged, however, in the Eccles's kitchen, thus demonstrating that the class problem, however grave it may seem, can be solved very simply if the parties will only sit down together and share a pot of tea. In the midst of these ceremonies, moreover, D'Alroy, long given up for dead, puts in a providential appearance, and Eccles—a very resolute parasite—accepts a pensioned exile so that he will no longer embarrass his relatives with his presence. Thus the characters fall with convenient dispatch into conventional roles, and what began as a *drame de déclassement* ends happily as melodrama.

It is only when we try to appraise the effect of this nonsense in historical terms that the importance of Robertson's play becomes apparent. Until his day drama was played on a plane so far removed from reality that it could not possibly be mistaken for it. It was because of its greater vividness and heightened expression, its improbable situations, and the general air of the marvelous that characterized it, that the drama justified itself as an art. In the 1860's the public did not go to the theater to experience "life as it is," but in order to live for a little time more amply than it was permitted to live in the outer world. Accordingly, it was traditional in the theater to exaggerate everything. A play was thought of as a series of exciting moments strung on a narrative thread which served to connect them more or less sensibly, and dramatists from the time of Shakespeare exerted themselves to produce effects of intensity so extreme that they approximated madness.

The essence of Robertson's style was understatement; and amid the current noises of the theater, his quiet style made a most emphatic effect. In his modest efforts to bridge the distance that separated the world of the stage from the real world, Robertson was, whether consciously or not, striking at the root of the English dramatic tradition. Partly because of the enormous success of Shakespeare in creating a super-reality on a bare stage, the nineteenth-century drama had so far resisted any encroachment from sources external to the theater. But the English stage was no longer bare. The intrusion of realistic settings and practical properties—box sets, ceilings, real doors with locks and doorknobs—brought the ideal world of the classical drama to the point where it seemed real only in an atmosphere of madness. At the end of the nineteenth century, aside from the Shakespearean actors, only the symbolists were prepared to push the dramatic fantasy to this point.

Nevertheless, in the nature of things, the dramatists of this period did not, and could not, draw characters from the life. In the theater, characters were drawn from the antique. Everything conspired to perpetuate the ancient models. "Lines" were handed down from father to son. The art of the drama was a process in which plays were made out of plays and characters grafted upon characters. The stage under these conditions nourished itself and was thus capable of perpetuating a life of its own which ran parallel to the life of the outer world without touching it at any point. But its vitality was not inexhaustible. Eventually it became necessary to transfuse into these mummeries the visible characterization of living things. It was in this respect that Robertson was original.

Robertson was certainly not the first to feel the need of injecting new life into the theater. Dion Boucicault and Bulwer-Lytton had tried, each in his way, to create new character-types patterned after living models. Both were limited by the conventions within which they worked. But Robertson had the advantage of a fresh acting company under the sagacious direction of two gifted managers. The troupe for which he wrote, at the Prince of Wales's, was relatively free of tradition, and it was fortunate in numbering such people as Squire Bancroft, John Hare, and Marie Wilton. It was a unique combination for a venture into realism. Even so, it encountered resistance.

In Robertson's day realism was rightly considered to be an unwelcome and unnatural intrusion of ordinary life into the ideal world of the drama, an invasion of the ideal by the mundane. It was noticed that what was perhaps natural and proper in real life was strained and unnatural on the stage. Thomas Purnell expressed in 1871 a view that was widely shared both in France and England twenty years later:

> Mr. Robertson gives us the real conversation he has heard at the "Owl's Roost," or in the West End Square where people come out at night to enjoy the evening breeze under a weeping ash in front of their houses. I cannot say we do not want this commonplace artistically represented on the stage, for it finds an appreciative public. I can only express my surprise that people pay to hear other men say behind footlights what they hear in their own houses.[6]

It is difficult to understand in our day, after a full century of naturalistic writing, how anyone could have mistaken the speech of any of Robertson's characters for the speech of real people. But Purnell was evidently thinking in terms of blank verse, or Restoration rhetoric. Judged by Victorian standards the conversation in Mrs. D'Alroy's kitchen must have sounded shockingly natural, too much so, indeed, to qualify as stage dialogue. At any rate, Robertson's cup-and-saucer style had no immediate consequence in the theater. By the time it was again held up to critical scrutiny, writers like Archer, Walkley, and Shaw were inveighing against the falsity of theatrical idealization, and it had become apparent that before any substantial progress could be made in the theater not only the physical aspects of the stage must be altered, but also the conceptual basis of drama.

Melodrama had so far been concerned with social problems only in the most general way. It concentrated, in effect, upon a single issue, the conflict of good and evil. This was usually resolved most expeditiously by means of a discovery and peripeteia which brought down the curtain in an entirely satisfactory manner. In melodrama, the wicked, though remarkably energetic, had a definite threshold of fatigue; but God was inexhaustible. Villains schemed mightily and worked hard. The good had only to wait.

Such agreeable assumptions, unhappily, could be maintained only so long as the theater ignored the facts of life; and eventually the fictional basis of melodrama became too obvious to sustain an illusion. The development of realism from Diderot to Shaw was inexorable, but its progress was majestically slow. Diderot had not proposed any change in the traditional patterns of drama. He had advocated no more than a change in its subject matter from the tribulations of heroes to the events of contemporary life, chiefly a matter of bringing the antique up to date. But once the drama took contemporary life for its model, it was predictable that "life as it is" would in time make its way to the stage.

The idea was not new, only its application. Within their own dramatic frame, the Elizabethans had long ago shown the way to realism and, in the guise of satire, the comedic writers of the Restoration had sketched recognizable vignettes of contemporary characters. The conditions of the stage did not favor anything like an exact representation of reality in those periods, nor was mimesis at that time intended to be a matter of precise detail. By the end of the nineteenth century, however, the stage was ready for a more or less exact representation of life.

By 1880 the English playhouse was virtually in its modern shape. It had an auditorium of moderate size, with a well-behaved audience seated in relative comfort in front of a picture stage framed by the proscenium arch. In the Georgian theater the scenery had served mainly as a background for the actors, and the principal acting area was the apron of the stage. In the new theater, the play drew back into its setting, and the players actively inhabited the set. The imaginary fourth wall, which sprang spontaneously into being with this new arrangement, served to isolate the play effectively from the audience, so that direct communication in the form of asides and aparts became an evident absurdity, while soliloquies took on a new reflective character and were no longer directed obviously to the house. In theory the audience now no longer existed, and when it insisted on its identity as an audience, it was at the expense of the illusion. In these circumstances, such Antoinesque affectations as the imaginary fireplace or window in the fourth wall were soon dropped as unnecessary pretenses.

As early as 1827 James Boaden complained that "the modern stage affects reality infinitely beyond the proper objects of dramatic representation," and he deplored the fact that audiences were now able to forget that they sat in the theater and watched the performance of actors.[7] In the days of Mrs. Siddons audiences were acutely conscious of the actor's art. Mrs. Siddons retired in 1812. At the midpoint of the century the classic style which she and her brother John Philip Kemble had developed was still in vogue. But in the period 1850–70 the style of acting changed rapidly. Kemble had brought into fashion a technique which aimed at refining the representation of nature by means of ideal postures as far removed from ordinary gesture as declamation is from speech. This was in some sense an extension of the idealizing tendencies which characterized the art of the Renaissance, and which were still the shaping principles of academic sculpture and painting. In the new realistic frame that Robertson devised for the Bancrofts, the archetypal postures of the older actors seemed exaggerated. Beginning with Hare and the Kendals, a school of natural acting developed which influenced even actors who had never worked with Robertson. By the end of the century the realistic style of George Alexander had pretty well replaced the grandeur of the older school, nevertheless the Shakespearian tradition was still robust; and the style which Kean had made famous in the early decades of the century, though somewhat tempered by Fechter and Irving, never quite lost its hold on the tragic stage.[8]

In comedy the ribald mannerisms of the early years did not long survive the refinements of Madame Vestris and Charles Mathews, and the vogue of the low comedian dwindled. The relatively low-keyed style of comic acting inaugurated by the Bancrofts was particularly well suited to the genteel drawing-room atmosphere of the Prince of Wales's. But this style, which the Bancrofts further developed at the Haymarket, was not universally popular. There were complaints that, in consequence of Robertson's influence, the theater was losing its strength, and that only a few players of the old school were still able to sustain a full-bodied performance.[9]

The English theater in the 1880's, however, inclined ever more strongly toward the assimilation of art to nature. It was objected that actors no longer troubled to raise their voices, and that they spoke as if they were actually in a drawing room instead of a theater; but there was no way of excluding the actors from the illusion they themselves created. Stage settings became more accurately imitative as the century wore on. The wing and drop sets of the earlier theater were now chiefly used for outdoor effects. By 1875 interior scenes were regularly played in carpeted box-sets with ceiling clothes, practical doors, and suitable furnishings. Scene changes presented a more difficult problem.

Since the use of the stage curtain interfered with the effective exits which actors prized, the fall of the curtain to hide shifts of scenery—regularly practised in the Paris opera since 1825—did not become common in London until the end of the century. Long after the grooves and shutters of the old theater had been discarded, scenery was still shifted in full view of the audience, and properties were drawn on and off the set by means of cords.

In the last years of the century, however, intense professional interest was concentrated on developing the physical elements that contributed to the dramatic illusion. Considerable advances were made in the lighting of plays, as well as in the general mechanics of the stage. In the 1860's illuminating gas was the principal source of lighting in most London theaters, and the gas table was under the control of the prompter who, from his corner, was able to dim or intensify the lighting of various stage areas in accordance with the cues in his script. About this time the electric arc light became available, but most managers preferred gas, which gave a softer and more manageable light. Among them was Henry Irving, a specialist in stage lighting. It was under his direction that the practice was instituted at the Lyceum of darkening the auditorium during the performance, while the stage was brilliantly lit.

In 1881 the new Savoy, built by D'Oyly Carte especially to house the Gilbert and Sullivan operettas, was lit entirely by electricity, controlled by rheostats, more or less in the modern manner, and by the end of the century Adolphe Appia had substantially laid down the theory of modern stage lighting. The lighting of plays, nevertheless, was flat and glaring until the projector lamp came into use in the 1920's and provided the fluid control of illumination which is characteristic of the contemporary stage.

Meanwhile the art of stage management was also undergoing radical changes. In the early nineteenth century, plays had normally been directed by the actor-manager, and it was usual for him to arrange the play around his own performance. In the stock companies plays were rehearsed largely through line readings. Actors were not expected to show in advance what they intended to do in performance, and since each actor was entrusted with the exclusive control of his part, the opening performance was often something of a surprise for everyone. Only new plays were rehearsed with care, and even then, rehearsal was mainly a matter of arranging the traffic across the stage. In comedy, where the more complex interrelations of the narrative ordinarily required more unified control, the coordination of the action was normally

entrusted to the prompter, whose function it was to see that the lines
were spoken more or less as they stood in the text.[10]

Soon after the mid-century it became usual for the actor-manager to
share the conduct of the play with a "producer," ordinarily the author
himself. Boucicault is said to have originated the directorial idea in England. He was certainly among the first to revive the author's right to
assist at rehearsals, and he took pains to adjust the placement of his actors
and their movements, and the physical settings and lighting arrangements
of his plays. But Boucicault was primarily interested in managing spectacular effects in melodrama. Before Robertson, nobody bothered to
direct drawing-room plays. They were expected to direct themselves.

Under the Bancrofts' management Robertson for the first time established the modern technique of stage direction, co-ordinating the various
elements of a production into a unified presentation. In Robertson's
David Garrick (1864) the scene directions in the printed text were
sufficiently detailed so that the stage business might be readily visualized
by the reader. Robertson's pioneer work in this field enabled future
writers such as Augustus Harris and W. S. Gilbert to take complete
control of their productions, and after them Pinero and Shaw did as
much. The ultimate result was to shift much of the responsibility for a
production from the actor to the author.[11]

In England in the 1880's the idea that the elements of a production
might be directed toward a purpose other than the personal display of
the principals was both new and unsettling. It was rendered more plausible by the visits of foreign acting companies which had abandoned the
star system in favor of a co-ordinated ensemble. A Dutch company from
Rotterdam conceived along such lines made a sensation in London in
1880. It was followed by the Meiningen company, which opened at the
Drury Lane in May of the following year and vividly demonstrated the
advantages of a company commanded by a *régisseur*. It took some time
for this idea to gain favor in England. In spite of the author's invasion of
the actor-manager's prerogatives, actors continued to rule the stage for a
long time. In the case of Shaw, we have amusing anecdotes concerning
his relations with his star actors from Cyril Maude in *You Never Can
Tell* to Beerbohm Tree in *Pygmalion*. The development of the professional director who is neither actor nor author was a late phenomenon in
England. In general, Shaw directed his own plays.

Realism in the drama had so far concerned itself mainly with the more
acceptable aspects of life. The urge to depict "life as it is," however, led

inexorably—from Diderot to Balzac, and from Flaubert to Zola—to a literature which concentrated on the more brutal and pitiable sides of human nature. It was some time before this "naturalistic" literature reached the stage. When it did, it was only briefly popular.

The distinction between realism and naturalism was never clear. As a literary movement, realism was first spoken of in Paris about 1826, though it was only after 1850 that it gained currency as a literary term. Naturalism was a term current among painters as early as the 1860's. About 1880 Zola gave it currency as a movement in literature, and by 1884 the naturalists were so firmly established in France that Louis Deprez undertook to write their history in *L'Evolution naturaliste*. Three years later, in 1887, Antoine offered some examples of this style in his newly established Théâtre Libre. In theory—though Antoine was not much interested in theory—the naturalistic dramatists shared the unemotional objectivity of the realistic tradition but were more consciously "scientific" in their view of life. What distinguished their plays from the traditional drama of the time was the unpleasantness associated with their realism.

Unpleasantness was by no means welcome in the English theater. People went to see plays in order to have agreeable experiences which would confirm an optimistic view of life. The sticky blend of prudishness and hypocrisy which passed for idealism on the Victorian stage made itself evident even in forms that were not meant to be taken seriously. French farces were regularly subject to "refinement" in the process of adaptation to English taste. Native comedy was even more strictly policed. W. S. Gilbert wrote in 1870: "It has become a recognized principle in the unwritten law of criticism that no married man (in an original piece) may be in love with anybody but his wife, and in like manner no single lady may see any charm in a married man."[12]

But already English playwrights, following Robertson, were beginning to see some advantage in developing comedy along less restricted lines. Unfortunately, the chief influences in social comedy continued to come from France, and the English playwrights continued to import, along with their French models, their artificiality and their rhetoric. Accordingly, when they began to deal "realistically" with current problems, Pinero, Wilde, Jones, and the others continued to use dramatic methods against which their French contemporaries were even then reacting in the name of realism.

In the early days of Shaw's dramatic career the effect of bringing social problems to the stage was simply to emphasize the distance that divided the theater from life. It became possible, however, in the lighter genres, particularly in farce and extravaganza, to treat the reigning conventions with a degree of irony that was not yet tolerated in serious comedy. As early as the first version of *Trial by Jury* (1868) and *Engaged* (1877), Gilbert effectively satirized the conventional pretenses of polite courtship. In *H. M. S. Pinafore* (1878) he dealt a hearty buffet at the sacrosanct distinctions of class with which Robertson had tinkered timidly fifteen years before in *Caste*; and in *The Importance of Being Earnest* (1895) Wilde thumbed his nose with unusual gusto at the conventions of upper-class society.

By the time of Gilbert the discrepancy between the norms of acceptable behavior on the stage and the actions of people outside the playhouse was sufficiently apparent to warrant a critical appraisal of the contemporary drama. This was essentially what Shaw desired to bring about, and here he showed himself to be a true follower of Ibsen. In his youth Ibsen had dreamed of revolutionizing the human spirit through the medium of literature.[13] He had soon given up this dream and turned his energies in other and more rewarding directions. Shaw, however, really believed he could revolutionize society by writing for the stage. What he did, in fact, was to revolutionize the theater. It was no mean feat; but it came somewhat short of his intention, and the realization of how little he was able to accomplish certainly contributed to the bitterness that runs through so much of his work.

In the 1880's the Licenser of Plays began to relax his vigilance. He continued to bar oaths and bad language from the stage; but in the course of time his tastes became progressively more sophisticated and his sensibilities less easily ruffled. The limits of his growing permissiveness were, however, not easy to fix. Long before Grein's private production of *Ghosts* in 1891, the battle of morals was joined between such conservative critics as Clement Scott and J. F. Nisbet, and young radicals such as Archer, Walkley, Shaw, and Justin McCarthy. The battle was fought bitterly, but in the end the guardians of public morals had the worst of it. Bit by bit, the censorship was forced to relax its efforts until by 1896 Sydney Grundy feared that the stage had gone completely to the dogs.

In spite of such fears, repeatedly expressed in conservative circles, it was to be many years before a play as conventionally moral as *Widowers' Houses* could be given a public showing in London. *Ghosts* was not licensed for production until 1914. *Mrs Warren's Profession* was banned until after the First World War; and when, on the eve of that debacle, Mrs. Patrick Campbell spoke the memorable words, "Not bloody likely" in *Pygmalion*, the event was discussed for weeks in the press, and people thronged to the theater expressly to hear her say it.

To Henry Arthur Jones, writing in 1891, the English theater seemed to have changed with phenomenal rapidity in the interval between 1870 and 1890; and he wrote enthusiastically of the literary richness and material prosperity of the theater of his day. Yet in 1896 Shaw—at the time drama critic of the *Saturday Review*—complained that "half a dozen visits in the year serve all the purposes of those respectably literate citizens who are anxious to see whatever is good in the threatre."[14]

In fact, before 1895 one finds little in the Victorian repertory that has other than antiquarian interest for the modern reader. The greatness of modern English drama began—and possibly it ended—with Shaw. On the Continent, however, the dramatic history of the later nineteenth century is impressive. By the year 1900 most of the plays that define the course of modern drama had been written—*Peer Gynt* in 1867, *Ghosts* in 1881, *The Power of Darkness* in 1886, *Miss Julie* in 1888, *The Master Builder* in 1891, *The Weavers* in 1892, *The Sea Gull* in 1896, and *Uncle Vanya* about 1900. By the time Shaw was effectively established as a dramatist, Maeterlinck had done his chief work, Ibsen had written his last play, and Chekhov was dead.

The London managers took scant notice of these alien developments. In 1890 their dependence on the Paris stage was complete, but they kept their eyes firmly fixed on the theater of the boulevards. When the salon drama became fashionable, they picked nervously over the new plays, but the boulevard theater offered richer fields for exploration. In the widely circulated survey of the English stage which Filon published in 1897, he complained that *Le Retour de Melun*, the trashy melodrama which was the basis of *The Ticket of Leave Man*, was enormously successful in London, while the *hautes comédies* of the serious playwrights languished and died there of indifference.

The type of high comedy which Filon admired appealed very much, however, to Oscar Wilde. In his three problem comedies Wilde carried on the tradition of Scribe in a style somewhere between the thesis play and domestic melodrama. As a writer of high comedy, Wilde obviously left something to be desired. His technique in the domestic *drame* seems remarkably inept; but his plays were the first successful plays in prose since the time of Sheridan which made any pretensions to literary merit. It may be objected that the aphoristic sparkle of *Lady Windermere's Fan* (1892) is so intrusive as to ruin the play. All the same, with this play

Wilde made it clear that there was a place for literate drama in the English theatre, and Pinero and Jones were quick to take the hint. Wilde went further. Though *A Woman of No Importance* (1893) and *An Ideal Husband* (1895), in spite of their enormous success in their day, are now of little consequence in the theater, *The Importance of Being Earnest* (1895) was a great comedic masterpiece, the first in England since the time of Congreve, and its influence on Shaw's later style is too clear to require emphasis. It is perhaps significant that Shaw professed to see as little in it as he saw in the work of Gilbert, whose influence upon him was equally great, or greater.

The type of comedy which Wilde adapted from the French appealed also to Pinero. Pinero was, like Boucicault, a professional showman chiefly interested in making a success on the stage. He was sufficiently attuned to the spirit of the time to understand that success in the theater would entail a more thoughtful approach to the drama than his contemporaries were inclined to make. When the success of Ibsen on the continent made it clear that the new social drama was likely to become commercially interesting in London, Pinero turned at once to "unpleasant" plays. His first attempt at a serious comedy was *The Profligate* (1889). This was followed by *The Second Mrs. Tanqueray* (1893). These plays were the first efforts made in England to elevate the drama to the plane of the contemporary social novel.

It was obviously no part of Pinero's ambition to break with the tradition in which he had been trained, but only to develop and to extend it. He was, like his earlier contemporary Tom Taylor, a cultivated man. Unlike Robertson, he knew the ways of upper-class society at first hand. But while, from his eminence as a public official, Taylor had been content to write down to popular taste, Pinero, a generation later, aspired to higher things.

In the preface to *Un Père prodigue* (1859), Dumas had written:

> A man without any worth as a thinker, as a moralist, as a philosopher, as a writer, may nevertheless be a man of the first order as a dramatic author, that is to say, as a manipulator of the purely external movements of people; and, on the other hand, to be a thinker, a moralist, a philosopher, a writer who is listened to in the theatre, it is indispensable to be provided with those qualities which are particular and natural to this man of little worth. In short, to be a master in this art, one must be clever in the business.[15]

Like Taylor, Pinero aspired to be clever in the business. But while Taylor, who was really clever in the business, harbored no illusions as to the literary value of his plays, Pinero aspired to distinction as a thinker and a writer, and undoubtedly he believed that through him the English drama was scaling heights it had not hitherto reached. In this estimate of his achievements most of his contemporaries concurred. As late as 1938 Barrett Clark recorded the fact that Pinero was "regarded by certain critics as the best equipped and most skillful writer in the English-speaking world."[16] The fact that a generation later Pinero seems inept as a craftsman, and quite vapid as a thinker, is a useful indication of the provisional quality of literary judgments.

The movement to turn the theater into a forum for the discussion of social problems is traceable particularly to the influence of the Second Empire dramatists. After the publication of *L'Affaire Clemenceau* in 1866, Dumas *fils* turned his attention to the preparation of a collected edition of his dramatic works, for each of which he now wrote a considerable preface. It was not customary for French playwrights to write long essays in connection with their plays, but Dumas had a growing sense of his importance as a thinker and a social reformer. The prefaces he wrote for his plays were not brief critical pieces in the manner of the *examens*, *critiques*, and *avertissemens* of his predecessors in the seventeenth century. Dumas's prefaces are long discourses on a variety of subjects associated with, but not limited by the plays to which they are prefixed, written in the style of a learned essayist whose interests extend far beyond the ordinary horizons of the drama.

In these pieces the author enters upon a relation of some intimacy with his reader, characterizing himself and his work with evident satisfaction, describing the genesis and the history of his play, the difficulties attending its production, and the nature of the critical reception. The dramatist then gives way to the savant, discussing the moral and social problems raised in the play in question, touching upon related questions of a political and philosophical nature, arguing, demonstrating, admonishing, posing questions and resolving them with the authority hitherto reserved to academicians and members of the Institute. The preface to *Un Père prodigue* is virtually a manual for playwrights. The preface to *Un Fils naturel* deplores the growing triviality of the current theater and eloquently urges the dedication of the stage to the high service of humanity:

> This great art of the theatre will . . . become the property of acrobats and the vulgar amusement of the rabble if we do not hasten to put it at the service of the great social causes and the high hopes of humanity. . . . We must no longer represent man as an individual, but with

> great strokes we must paint man as the representative of mankind,
> take him back to his sources, show him the paths he must follow,
> reveal to him his ends, in other words, we must become more than
> moralists, we must become law-givers. . . .

It was, he added, the privilege and the duty of French dramatists to
promote by all means possible the "useful" theater as against the empty
aestheticism of the followers of Scribe: "Through comedy, through
tragedy, through the *drame*, through buffoonery, in the form that suits
us best, let us inaugurate the *useful theatre*, at the risk of hearing the
protests of the apostles of *art for art's sake*—four words absolutely devoid of meaning."[17]

In his later prefaces Dumas assumed a tone of impressive majesty.
They include a note of prophecy which foreshadows the disasters of
1870–71 unless the prophet's voice is heeded. With the aid of these
prefaces his plays assumed a degree of importance as social documents
which is justified intrinsically only by *Les Idées de Mme. Aubray*
(1867). Unhappily, in the end, Dumas felt that as a reformer of society
he had failed. He noted with evident despondency in the preface to
L'Etrangère (1876) that what he had wished to do could perhaps not be
done in the theater:

> The dramatic author who is not only a contriver of more or less
> ingenious plots . . . but who would like them to be not only a source
> of pleasure, but a source of instruction for men finds himself trapped
> between his ideal and his helplessness. He understands that it is not to
> the form which he has so far practised that mankind will ever look
> for the solution of the great problems that beset it even though he
> believes that he has found it for himself. . . .[18]

The consequence of his disappointment was an escape from the problems of reality into a fantastic *au-delà*. *La Femme de Claude* (1873) is of
a high degree of abstraction, and from this point on Dumas, who had
begun as a sober realist in the style of Flaubert, inclined more and more
strongly toward mysticism, and ended, like all the major writers of his
time, as a symbolist.[19]

As early as 1870 Georg Brandes had recognized in Dumas the genius
of the new realism in the drama. In the first part of the lectures later
published as *Main Currents of Literature in the Nineteenth Century*
(1872), he strongly urged Scandinavian authors to follow the example of
the French in dramatizing questions of social importance instead of wasting their talents on idle dreams and idealistic abstractions. In Brandes's

opinion the goal of literature was nothing less than the revolutionizing of the human spirit, and the vitality of current writing was in proportion to its capacity to arouse controversy. Accordingly he considered that the literature that debated the problems of the moment was the only living literature of the time. This meant primarily the novels and plays of Dumas *fils* and the plays of Augier, and it was to these works that Brandes chiefly called attention in his lectures.

Brandes's *Main Currents* aroused deep hostility when the first volume was published. The second volume was not even reviewed in the Danish press; nevertheless Brandes's influence on the avant-garde of the northern countries was very great. Even before he read *Main Currents* Ibsen had written the ailing revolutionist:

> How the old ideas will come tumbling about our ears! And it is high time they did. Up till now we have been living on nothing but crumbs from the revolutionary table of the last century, and I think we have been chewing on that stuff long enough. The old terms must be invested with new meaning and given new explanations. Liberty, equality, and fraternity are no longer what they were in the days of the late-lamented guillotine. . . . What is really needed is a revolution of the human spirit. And in this *you* shall be one of those who took the lead. . . .[20]

After the first volume of Brandes's lectures came into his hands, Ibsen wrote: "No more dangerous book could fall into the hands of a pregnant writer. It is one of those works that place a yawning gulf between yesterday and today. . . . In twenty years one will not be able to comprehend how a spiritual existence was possible at home before these lectures. . . ."[21]

But Ibsen had no wish to join Brandes in anything of a partisan nature. Dumas had hoped to bring about social reform not by influencing legislation, but by changing the ideas of society through literature. It was this notion particularly that appealed to Ibsen. In 1869 he had already come to the conclusion that Brandes and he were of one mind as to the function of drama as a social force. It was not quite what Brandes had in mind. Ibsen wrote: "Thinking it over, I see that what really interests you in literature are the tragedies and comedies that take place in the inner life of the individual and that you care little or nothing about actually existing outward conditions—political or otherwise."[22]

In Brandes, Ibsen saw what he desired to see, just as Shaw later saw his own reflection in Ibsen. Pinero, for his part, shared Ibsen's viewpoint more fully than Shaw. But Pinero was not gifted with any special insight into human nature, nor had he any idea of revolutionizing anything. The sort of play which he developed in the last years of the nineteenth century resembles in everything but elegance the well-made plays of Dumas *fils*.

The Second Mrs. Tanqueray, with Mrs. Patrick Campbell in the role of Paula, made a sensation in London. It is a notably clumsy piece of dramatic writing, no longer playable, and of no great value intellectually, but historically it is an extremely important document. For the first time it made the London managers aware of the commercial possibilities of "unpleasant" plays, and its success loosened the grip of melodrama on the English stage. From this time on, the exploitation of a serious theme was possible in the English theater, provided, of course, it was treated with the necessary decorum—that is to say, with a proper regard to the moral outcome and a proper respect for English prudishness. This was not, at bottom, very different from French prudishness.

Of *The Second Mrs. Tanqueray* William Archer wrote admiringly: "Dumas might have been proud to sign his name to it." He was perhaps mistaken. Dumas would scarcely have been proud of the inept exposition. But, judging by *Le Demi-monde* he would very likely have applauded the manner in which conventional morality was upheld in the drama of a woman haunted by an unsavory past. Very likely also, the extraordinary coincidence through which Paula's former lover turns up unexpectedly as her step-daughter's suitor would not have greatly troubled any disciple of Scribe. In the dramatic pattern that Dumas developed, coincidence is the order of the day, and fact is normally stranger than fiction. Like *Le Demi-monde*, which in some measure it reflects, *The Second Mrs. Tanqueray* belongs to the make-believe realism of the 1850's, in which life was arranged on the stage in conventional festoons which owed more to art than to nature. Dumas's play was written in 1855, Pinero's, thirty-eight years later. In the interval a good deal of history had been made in France, and English society also had undergone considerable changes. Yet if one were to judge by these plays alone, one would say that nothing had changed.

Pinero, unlike Dumas *fils*, had no special pretensions to greatness. The extravagance of the critical fanfare that heralded his productions was a measure of the depths from which he helped to rescue the English theater. He rejoiced in his success without losing his modesty, but his talents did not develop beyond a certain point. Paula Tanqueray lived again as Iris Blundell in *Iris* (1901), as Mrs. Jesson in *His House in Order* (1906), and as Zoe Blundell in *Mid-Channel* (1909); but nothing Pinero wrote fulfilled the promise of *The Second Mrs. Tanqueray*. The main line of development of English drama, nevertheless, passes through Pinero, not Shaw. The succession of English playwrights who brought the spirit of Second Empire drama to its culmination in England includes Jones, Wilde, Barker, Barrie, Galsworthy, Maugham, Coward, and Rattigan—all of whom made a careful detour around Shaw. Most of these writers stemmed from the same root as Pinero—all but three bore the stamp of Scribe. It was not until after the Second World War that English drama sheered away from the methods of the well-made play, and then only with difficulty.

While there is undoubtedly something in Pinero that inspires respect, it is difficult to find anything to admire in the work of Henry Arthur Jones, his most eminent contemporary. Jones, like Shaw, was self-taught. His true gift was for melodrama, and his great success was *The Silver King* (1882). It was, however, his ambition to write on higher intellectual levels than melodrama afforded, provided these served acceptably at the box office. Unhappily, he had neither the imagination nor the courage to make a new departure in the drama. Like most of his contemporaries, Jones worked in the complete conviction that the moral standards of his time were ultimate and universal. His social criticism was therefore limited to a demonstration of the distance that separates reality from the ideal, and his manifest aim was to improve society by uncovering its moral shortcomings.

In this regard British writers of this period showed remarkable unanimity. The revolutionary ideas that were to shape the thought of the next generation made slow progress in England. The prevailing tendency in the Victorian novel was melioristic rather than iconoclastic. From Thackeray to Meredith, English novelists seem to have been conventionally idealistic in their views, and much the same may be said of such robust social critics as Carlyle, Ruskin, and Arnold. It is chiefly in the circles that Shaw frequented that we hear the rumble of the approaching storm. In the drama, until Shaw indicated the possibility, no character questioned the standards of British morality save perhaps Lord Goring in Wilde's *An Ideal Husband*, a personage whose seriousness was itself open to question.

The revival of English comedy at the end of the nineteenth century was not a development of the current Victorian tradition. It was a reversion to the witty plays of the Restoration, the point at which English comedy had lost its way, and was thus in some sense a classic revival. As such it depended upon a rejection of romantic sentimentality. The success of such plays as Boucicault's *London Assurance*, with its vague reminiscences of Vanbrugh and Farquhar, indicated the direction of the type of aphoristic comedy which Wilde was to renew, and Shaw to extend into wider fields.

Comedy in high style depended on the replacement of the professional playwrights who served the theater of the 1890's with a body of dramatic authors of stature and integrity. In the previous decades, doubtless in response to the demands of a play-going public that was rapidly becoming literate, the distance that had so far separated Victorian drama from Victorian literature was gradually lessened. But it was only when writing for the theater became lucrative that the English drama really changed.

Until the time of Robertson professional writers for the stage earned their living either by turning out farces and melodramas wholesale like A. J. Byron and the enormously versatile Planché, or by adapting French plays for a manager for a fee or an annual salary. In France, Scribe had long ago initiated a system of royalties predicated on the gross receipts of his plays. In England, according to Boucicault, a new author at this time could expect to be paid no more than £50 per act for an original play, and a writer of repute could get no more than £500 for a full-length script.

Not all reputable authors did so well. For the four acts of *The Ticket of Leave Man* Tom Taylor is said to have been paid no more than £150 out of which he had to pay for the translation of the French original. He received a similar sum for *Our American Cousin*, which brought the manager £20,000. A generation earlier Elliston had made a fortune with *Black Ey'd Susan*, which Douglas Jerrold sold him for £70. But when the long-run production superseded the repertory cycle as the mainstay of the London theater, it was inevitable that authors should insist on being paid a percentage of the gross receipts. In 1860 Boucicault sold *The Colleen Bawn* to Webster on this basis. His royalties amounted to £10,000. He drove, it is true, an exceptionally hard bargain for the time. It was actually not until 1890 that the practice of fixing royalties on a sliding scale became general in England.[23]

The introduction of the royalty system brought a new sort of writer into the field. Throughout the Victorian age a number of popular novelists such as Charles Reade had worked for the stage as well as for the press. Now that the financial rewards of the drama were significantly enhanced, more serious writers were attracted to the theater. Fixed royalties, however, were not in themselves a sufficient attraction. Before the drama could afford the writer a reasonably secure return for his labor it was necessary that some method be devised of insuring the author's proprietary rights on a continuing basis. In 1833, largely through the efforts of Planché, a bill was passed which made it possible to copyright a play, though only after an actual public performance.[24] This requirement was usually met by means of a single public reading in an out-of-town theater, but the copyright acquired in this manner did not run outside of England. It was only when the International Copyright Convention was concluded in 1877, and the United States Copyright Act was passed in 1891, that English authors felt safe in making their plays available in print.

As the realistic tendencies of the age progressively dispelled the theatricalism of the Victorian theater, compensatory movements developed on the comic stage. The lighter forms had been traditionally parodic. Their subject matter was often no more than a caricature of recent successes in the more solid genres. But these forms also included fairy plays and imaginative fantasies of all sorts, and with the rapid development of realistic drama, these lighter entertainments took on new validity and achieved importance as vehicles of irony and social satire.

Burlesque was the one indigenous comic form of the Victorian period. Walpole's Licensing Act of 1737 had virtually excluded all discussion of political matters in the theater, along with the caricature of political figures. In consequence, burlesque was confined for a time to dramatic parody in the manner of Fielding's *Tom Thumb* (1730). When the great vogue of tragedy passed, the writers of burlesque turned to classic mythology as their natural prey. There ensued a long series of clownish mock-classical pieces of the order of Charles Dibdin's *Poor Vulcan*, pleasantly anarchronistic, and more or less funny, but seldom of a high order of wit.

The refinement of burlesque in the nineteenth century was in large measure the work of James Robinson Planché, a man of astonishing talent. Planché specialized in parody. He began by parodying the classics, then tried his hand at a series of "revues" which commented wittily on current happenings in the theater. After that he turned to *Les Contes de Perrault*, out of which he dramatized *Puss in Boots*, *Beauty and the Beast*, *Bluebeard*, *Sleeping Beauty*, and *The White Cat*. These entertainments were billed as extravangazas. Planché distinguished them carefully from burlesques and travesties which, he explained, were parodic forms depending for their interest on the popularity of the works they caricatured, while extravaganzas were "whimsical treatments of poetical subjects."[25] This genre had a very considerable development in the course of the century and was found especially suitable for musical embellishment. In time it became indistinguishable from the Scandinavian *eventyr*, of the type of Öhlenschläger's *Aladdin*, out of which developed such unexpected masterpieces as *Peer Gynt* and *To Damascus*.

The return of political satire to the English theater was actually the work of W. S. Gilbert. His method was a miracle of tact. Gilbert tailored his plays and his libretti very precisely to the tastes of a fundamentally conservative audience which enjoyed having fun poked at the administration of English institutions, provided their sanctity was clearly recognized. His first plays had been written in imitation of Byron's burlesques and Planché's extravaganzas. Later he tried his hand at Robertsonian comedy. *Engaged* (1877) foreshadows the type of ironic farce which was to culminate in Wilde's *The Importance of Being Earnest*. From the critical reaction to *Engaged* and *Trial by Jury*, however, Gilbert gathered that an infusion of sentiment was essential to success in the ironic vein. A consequence was the special flavor of the operettas he wrote with Sullivan. In these extraordinary pieces his characteristic acerbity was sweetened just enough to please a public which enjoyed satire only if it was permitted at the same time to indulge its sentimentality. This blend of honey and vinegar, which Meilhac, Halévy and Offenbach had already successfully exploited in Paris, made Gilbert's fortune in England. Doubtless it also gave Shaw something to think about when he turned to extravaganza as a vehicle for social satire.

When Shaw made his debut as a dramatist in 1892, the Victorian theater was still thirty years behind the times. In the 1890's there was nothing on the English stage to indicate that its writers were aware of Zola, Jean Jullien, Becque, or Curel; there was no sign of Hauptmann or Strindberg, no hint of Turgenev or Tolstoy, and very little that might suggest an awareness of either Maeterlinck or Ibsen. The most that could be said of English playwrights in the 1890's was that they were pretty well abreast of Sardou.

With the possible exception of W. S. Gilbert, no contemporary English dramatist had so far ventured to stress the ambiguities of middle-class life in this period. The degree of social criticism implied in a play like *The Second Mrs. Tanqueray* was carefully adjusted so that it might serve as a basis for discussion. It was not so far heightened as to give anyone a moment's anxiety as to the validity of the social framework of the time. "Human life," Jones wrote,

> is a larger thing than the theatre, and the theatre can be powerful only in so far as it recognizes this, and allows the chief things in a play to be not the cheap, mechanical tricks of the playwright, the effective curtains, the machinery of cleverly devised situations, but the study of life and character, the portraiture of the infinitely subtle workings of the human heart.

Jones's statement, while impressive, was not borne out by Jones's practice. In *The Second Mrs. Tanqueray* Pinero, indeed, had made an effort, feeble perhaps, but well-intentioned, to plumb the depths of the human heart. It was hardly his fault that his public found Ellean's excessive purity agreeable and praiseworthy. But the play suggested a question, and in its very ambiguity, it indicated the manner in which such questions would one day be posed.

It is perfectly evident that the dramatists of the 1890's in England had a sincere desire to rise above the contrivances of the well-made play, and the summary depiction of character. It was no easy transition. The theater they had inherited had the obvious advantage of being theatrical. The Scribean playwright had no need to dissimulate the nature of his merchandise. It had a ready market, and he rejoiced in his wares. His plays were arranged in accordance with classic rules of design. He tried to produce on the stage, not an effect of life, but a balanced work of art, rationally conceived, elegantly executed, and aesthetically pleasing, what divine Providence might be expected to produce if it had the time and the necessary training.

In France the reaction to this idea of drama set in some years before Scribe's death. Scribe died in 1861, three years after the production of *Le Fils naturel* (1858), which definitely established the concept of *le théâtre utile*. In his preface to *Un Père prodigue*, Dumas had accommodated the Scribean idea to his new concept of dramaturgy: "Le réel dans le fond, le possible dans le fait, l'ingénieux dans le moyen." It was this formula which gave Jones, Pinero, and Wilde their orientation as new dramatists, and for a time it served Shaw as well. "I have fought," Jones wrote,

> for a recognition of the distinction between the art of the drama on the one hand, and popular amusement on the other. . . . I have fought for the entire freedom of the modern dramatist, for his right to portray all aspects of human life, all passions, all opinions; for the

freedom of search, the freedom of phrase, the freedom of treatment, that are allowed to the Bible and to Shakespeare, that must necessarily be allowed to every writer and to every artist that sees humanity as a whole. I have fought for sanity and wholesomeness, for largeness and breadth of view. I have fought against the cramping and deadening influences of modern pessimistic realism; its littleness, its ugliness, its narrowness, its parochial aims.[26]

Obviously Jones felt that he had fought the good fight, and in fact the difference between his work and the work of the writers of the previous generation leaps to the eye. But there is nothing even remotely revolutionary in such plays as *Michael and His Lost Angel* (1896) or *Mrs. Dane's Defense* (1900). One judges that in plays of this sort Jones sincerely felt that he was affording his audience a view of "humanity as a whole."[27] The phrase, as usual with Jones, was borrowed from Dumas; its implications were wholly traditional. In the current state of the theater it was probably out of the question for any dramatist to see humanity otherwise than as an assortment of well-classified character types, represented on the stage by specialists whose *emplois* must be kept in mind in arranging a play. Since, technically, these characters had to be employed in an ingenious action from which a moral might be drawn, it was inevitable that the new English dramatists should be caught in the dilemma of Dumas *fils* in his efforts to write meaningful plays with ingenious plots. Such indeed was the predicament of those who wrote English social comedy from the time of *Lady Windermere's Fan* to the time of Maugham's *The Circle*. But there was already in the offing a sterner breed of English playwright. Such dramatists as St. John Hankin, Granville Barker, and John Galsworthy, under naturalist influences, were quite ready to avoid the entanglements of plot and were seriously resolved to come to grips with social matters. There was also Shaw.

In his youth Ibsen had dreamed, not of patching up the social structure with small reforms, but of sounding such a blast as would bring down the ancient walls in ruins. It was the dream of the 1870's, which the 1880's dispelled. Ten years after *Ghosts* was written, Shaw undertook once again a frontal attack on the society of his time. It was obviously a foolhardy venture. But Shaw's special combination of brashness and good sense, his extraordinary insolence, and superabundant wit, made it easy for the thoughtless to discount the seriousness of the affront, and difficult for the thoughtful to overlook its merit. Shaw was not eager to court failure as a dramatist. After the frustration of his hopes for his first three plays, he cannily shifted his ground from irony to romantic comedy, where his chances were better. By the time he came to write *Arms and the Man* he had learned how to be pleasant in the theater without sacrificing his standing as a social critic. After *Mrs Warren's Profession* all his plays were in some measure pleasantries. All had a serious purpose, but none of them needed to be taken with absolute solemnity, and whatever was unpleasant in them was consigned to prefaces which, like discreet escorts, accompanied his plays as far as the stage door, but no farther.

From the first, Shaw desired to demonstrate his originality by telling the truth; but, as he soon discovered, it is no easier to tell the truth in the theater than anywhere else. Before Shaw could become truly articulate as a dramatist it was necessary for him to discover who he was precisely, and what it was that he believed. The effort must have cost him something. Like all really sincere people he found himself early involved in a maze of contradictions from which it was impossible for him to emerge. He was an avowed socialist, but not a humanitarian. He believed in social equality, but he had no faith in democracy. He was an enemy of capitalism, but he was determined to make his fortune, and in fact became a millionaire. He was a religious enthusiast whose creed could not be defined by an existent faith. In these circumstances it was necessary for him not only to create an image which would represent him properly to the world, but also to devise a believable divinity in terms of which he might justify himself in all his diversity and ambiguity. The task which occupied him from *The Philanderer* to *Back to Methuselah* was the composition of a carefully detailed portrait of himself posed against a background of eternity. Like Dante, the one great poet with whom he disdained to claim comparison, he was ambiguous to sum up his age and himself in terms of an enduring conceit. The English theater was obviously not ready for an enterprise of such magnitude. He set to work at once to make it ready.

THE UNPLEASANT PLAYS

ACCORDING to his biographer, Archibald Henderson, when Shaw was asked about the turning point in his life, he replied, "with a twinkle of his gray eyes under the shaggy brows: 'I haven't had any turning point in my life. I've gone straight on.' "[1]

But in fact there had been some turning points in his life. The year 1898, for one, marked a significant change in his fortunes. That year he survived a dangerous illness which came close to crippling him, and in that year he married.

In May 1898 Shaw suffered an injury which led to a necrosis of the bones in his foot. He was quite helpless for some months, and badly in need of a nurse. Miss Charlotte Payne Townshend, by Shaw's account a millionairess, was a trained nurse in need of a worthy person to look after. She was a lonely, placid Irishwoman of socialist views, generous with her money, but reticent, reserved, and averse to any sort of publicity. Beatrice Webb had intended her to marry Graham Wallas and had arranged for them to meet at a Fabian summer resort. Instead she met Shaw there and, after two years of a singular courtship, they reached a point where a union cleared of all "love interest, happiness interest, & all the rest of the vulgarities of marriage" seemed convenient and tolerable. As a condition of their marriage it was stipulated that their relationship should not be tainted by any suspicion of bodily contact, since sexuality inspired Miss Townshend with horror and her husband with uneasiness. In these circumstances they were married on 1 June 1898 at a Registry Office.

Shaw's financial condition at this time was less delicate than his health. He was by now a successful writer and could expect to support himself in decent comfort provided he continued to work. At the time it seemed doubtful that he could continue in his career as a drama critic, but he was already a well-known journalist, and he had attracted some attention as a playwright. He had so far written eight plays. Five had been given some sort of production, and of these two had proved moderately successful. *The Devil's Disciple* had brought in solid royalties. The other plays had not been produced.

An avant-garde playwright's prospects at the turn of the century were precarious at best. Shaw's marriage changed everything for him. He gave up journalism once and for all and decided to devote himself to the theater. He was forty-two, and for the first time in his life he was financially secure.

It was now thirteen years since his first attempt to write for the stage. He had begun his career as a playwright in 1885, at twenty-nine, in an unfruitful collaboration with William Archer, the most helpful and closest of his friends, and also the most critical of his talents. Archer manifested from beginning to end a surprising degree of hostility to Shaw's dramatic efforts, which he considered inept; and to his drama criticism, which he regarded as effective but perniciously wrongheaded. In reviewing the published version of *Widowers' Houses* in 1893, Archer wondered that Shaw should be "tempted to devote further time and energy to a form of production for which he has no special ability and some constitutional disabilities," and he added that *Widowers' Houses* was "a curious example of what can be done in art by sheer brainpower, apart from natural aptitude. For it does not appear that Mr. Shaw has any more specific talent for the drama than he has for painting or sculpture."[2] Ten years later, in 1903, Archer wrote with regard to his friend's influence as a critic:

> Mr. Shaw was engaged, week by week, in producing dramatic criticisms. Writing for a six-penny paper, he had but a limited audience; and therefore, even his wit, energy, and unique literary power (I use the word deliberately) could do little to influence the course of events. But all that he could do he did, to discredit, crush and stamp out the new movement. Had he been a power at all he would have been a power for evil.[3]

It is an interesting commentary on the steadfastness of Archer's position that in 1921, when Shaw was already beatified, Archer was still of substantially the same opinion as to his merits and his influence. He regretted, he wrote, that his friend should have produced "so little practical effect on his generation." And he added: "I am strongly under the impression (I may be wrong) that you have less of a following to-day than you had twenty years ago."[4]

At twenty-nine Archer had been writing drama criticism for some years, had translated Ibsen's *Pillars of Society*, and had personally interviewed Ibsen. He had therefore every reason to consider himself an expert in the drama. His views on playmaking were identical with those expressed by Francisque Sarcey, the dean of the Paris drama critics: he was convinced that the principles of the well-made play are universal and of eternal validity. The book on playmaking which he later published is a painstaking expression of these principles.

The theme of the play on which he proposed to collaborate with Shaw was of French origin: a young man discovers in the nick of time that his fiancée's dowry consists of "tainted" money. As the collaborators conceived the project, according to Shaw's account, Archer was to devise a plot on this theme, and Shaw, who had written much dialogue during his term as a novelist, was to write the actual speeches. The result would be, it was agreed, a realistic comedy in the quiet manner of Robertson.

According to the amusing account of the play's origin which Archer published in his review of *Widowers' Houses* in 1892, the play was to have been called *Rhinegold*, in obvious reference to Wagner's opera. The first scene was to have taken place in a hotel garden on the Rhine. There were to be two heroines, one sentimental, one comic:

> I fancy the hero was to propose to the sentimental heroine, believing
> her to be the poor niece, instead of the rich daughter of the sweater, a
> slum-landlord, or whatever he may have been, and I know he was to
> carry on in the most heroic fashion, and was ultimately to succeed in
> throwing the tainted treasure of his father-in-law, metaphysically
> speaking, into the Rhine. All this I gravely proposed to Mr. Shaw,
> who listened with no less admirable gravity.[5]

The anecdote was obviously of some value to this pair of enterprising journalists, and they made the most of it. To Archer's version of the matter, which Shaw sardonically printed in the first edition of the play, he added a vigorous postscript in which he denied that there was any substantial difference between Archer's plot and the one he used, except that his story was longer:

> I told him that I had finished up the renunciation and wanted some
> more story to go on with, as I was only in the middle of the second
> act. He said that according to his calculation the renunciation ought to

have landed me at the end of the play. I could only reply that his calculation did not work out, and that he must supply further material.[6]

The comic nature of this dialogue does not altogether obscure the seriousness of Shaw's conception in his first play, nor his originality in ending it as he did. From a dramaturgic viewpoint the hero's renunciation of the tainted gold would provide an effective curtain for the last act of a conventionally conceived play in the style of Dumas *fils*. The play would then have demonstrated the triumph of virtue, and the powerlessness of mammon to corrupt a noble soul, a conclusion calculated to uplift the heart and enrich the box office. This was evidently not Shaw's idea. It was his purpose as "a missionary to the theatre" to expose the corruption of society in a capitalist culture.

Archer intended the renunciation to be the triumphant end of the story. If this renunciation came at the middle rather than at the end of the play, the action might be expected to include a reversal in the final sequence, and the result would be an ironic comedy in which the hero would come to terms, cynically, with both his scruples and his bride. In this manner, love, plus money, would conquer all, Jack would have his Jill, and the world would be somewhat the worse for their union. A comedy conceived in these terms would be both unpleasant and realistic, and quite certain to fail. With intentions of this sort in mind, Shaw at twenty-nine was a bit ahead of his time, and very far ahead of Archer.

Archer had already expressed his conviction that unpleasant plays had no chance in the English theater:

A drama which opens the slightest intellectual, moral, or political question is certain to fail. The public will accept open vice, but it will have nothing to do with a moral problem. Especially it will have nothing to do with a piece to whose theme the word "unpleasant" can be applied. This epithet is of undefined and elastic signification, but once attach it to a play and all chance for it is past.[7]

It may seem, in retrospect, that Archer was somewhat shortsighted in his prediction; the fact is, he had a solid basis for his opinion. It would be a long while before English taste was sufficiently accommodated to the flavor of bitter comedy to ensure its success in the theater. In Archer's day English taste ran to sweetness and light. By 1890 Antoine had done something to naturalize unpalatable comedy in Paris, and Becque had already initiated the vogue—if vogue it might be called—of the *comédie rosse*. But in London unpleasant comedy of the type of *Les Corbeaux*

(1882) and *La Parisienne* (1885) was not a commercial possibility. The English had not yet learned to laugh in this manner. It is therefore remarkable that Shaw, at the very beginning of his dramatic career, should have been so ambitious—or so naïve—as to attempt in England a style that was still in the very forefront of progress across the Channel.

English managers at this time were watching the French stage with the eyes of hawks, but they seem to have paid no attention to Antoine's desperate innovations. Unpleasant drama was firmly associated in their minds with Ibsen. By the time Archer entered into relations with Shaw, he had been promoting the cause of Ibsen for some years and was considered one of the most earnest of the English Ibsenists. He was not the first. English literary circles had first become aware of Ibsen in 1871 when Edmund Gosse, at that time a very young journalist, published a long review of *Peer Gynt* (1867) in *The Spectator*. Gosse sent Ibsen a copy of his article, together with a review of *The Pretenders* (1863), which he intended to publish. Ibsen was then at the critical point of his career. He was struggling to finish *Emperor and Galilean* (1876), had only recently tried his hand at social comedy with *The League of Youth* (1869), and was in great need of critical support. He wrote Gosse a warm reply, and solicited his good offices in promoting his plays in London. Gosse at once appointed himself Ibsen's apostle to the English.

In this evangelical task he was soon joined by Archer. Archer had Norwegian relatives. He had acquired a reading knowledge of Danish in Norway and had read most of Ibsen's early plays. *Pillars of Society* (1877) especially appealed to him. Soon after reading it, he made a hasty translation, and, after peddling his version for three years, succeeded in persuading W. H. Vernon to produce it under the title of *Quicksands; or The Pillars of Society*. Vernon gave the play a single matinee performance at the Gaiety in December 1880, with himself in the role of Consul Bernick, then dropped it with a sigh of relief.

By this time Catherine Ray had published a translation of *Emperor and Galilean* which evoked some interest. Ibsen began to be talked about in London. A. B. Walkley and Philip Wicksteed now joined the cause and, with the help of others, rallied a literary coterie around the Ibsenist banner. In this manner Ibsen became the standard-bearer of the new realism in England, a modest movement that soon became extremely articulate and based itself on the need to repudiate the hypocrisy, sentimentality, and prudishness of the middle-class drama and the culture on which this drama rested.

The Ibsenist group displayed such energy that in 1884 Henry Arthur

Jones was induced to produce an adaptation of *A Doll's House*, written by himself in collaboration with Henry Herman. The play, aptly called *Breaking a Butterfly*, was accommodated to English taste by the omission of the ambiguous Dr. Rank, together with all mention of Krogstad's affair with Mrs. Linde, and the addition of a happy ending. The result was most unfortunate. The London audience saw nothing unusual in a domestic drama which, indeed, no longer had anything unusual in it and, after a month, it was withdrawn.[8] The production, however, served to direct attention to the unpleasant aspects of Ibsenist drama, and the question of whether or not Nora "in fact" returned to her husband sometime after the curtain came down became the subject of debate, though it was easily overshadowed in literary circles by the burning question posed in Stockton's *The Lady and The Tiger*, which had been published two years before.

A Doll's House, however, was not to be brushed off lightly. Eleanora Duse was trouping the play all over Europe in a version tailored specifically to her requirements by Luigi Capuana, so that Nora was becoming a household word on the Continent at the very time that Archer was bitterly insisting that Ibsen was impossible on the English stage. The challenge was at last taken up by Janet Achurch. With considerable fanfare, she and Charles Charrington, her husband, put on Archer's version of *A Doll's House* at the Novelty in the summer of 1889. Much to everyone's astonishment, the production was a success.

The ensuing critical controversy brought the play vividly to the public eye. When the critic George Buchanan wrote contemptuously in the *Pall Mall Gazette* that the play was an inept imitation of French drama in the style of Zola, Shaw promptly retorted in the same periodical that, however little Buchanan may have seen in the play, he himself saw a great deal. For him the characters were archetypal Man and Woman, "she resembling the new Will in her before which must yield all institutions hostile to it . . . he dimly beginning to see that in giving this irresistible Will its way, he is not losing her, since he never really possessed her, but standing at last to win her for the first time."[9]

Evidently by 1889 Shaw was already interpreting life in terms of the evolving Will, the central factor in the philosophical system which he was to expound a dozen years later in *Man and Superman*. He was also by this time so strong a partisan of the Ibsenist movement that he was prepared to go some distance beyond Ibsen in his interpretation of *A Doll's House*. Archer, on the other hand, was less enthusiastic about the feminist implications of the play. By 1887 he had studied Ibsen's work carefully, and, after talking to Ibsen once or twice, had reached the sensible conclusion that Ibsen could not be pinned down to a consistent doctrine. Ibsen was, he decided, "essentially a kindred spirit with Shaw —a paradoxist, a sort of Devil's Advocate, who goes about picking holes in every 'well-known fact.' "[10]

For his part, Shaw hastened to naturalize Ibsen as a Fabian socialist. In June 1897, still very much under Ibsen's spell, Shaw wrote that sixty years before, in 1837, nobody in England knew that "Ibsen had begun the drama of struggle and emancipation, and had declared that the really effective progressive forces of the movement were the revolt of the working classes against economic, and of women against idealistic, slavery."[11] He might have added that at that time Ibsen, as yet only nine years old, must also have been a little vague about the nature of the movement he was setting afoot. Nine years later, in 1906, Shaw found it convenient to deny that Ibsen had exerted any significant influence on English drama. In his obituary essay on Ibsen, he attributed Pinero's moral ideas to Thackeray and Trollope, Wilde's to the school of Gautier, and his own to English socialists of the type of Stuart Glennie and Belfort Bax.[12]

What Shaw thought of Ibsen in 1906 is not entirely clear, but in 1890 he seemed to have no doubt of his significance for English literature. In 1888 Philip Wicksteed had succeeded—in spite of the opposition of his ecclesiastical superiors—in delivering a series of lectures on Ibsen, published three years later in a modest volume entitled *Four Lectures on Ibsen*.[13] In the spring of 1890, following his lead, Shaw agreed to contribute a paper on Ibsen to the series "Socialism in Contemporary Literature" which the Fabian Society had organized for its summer meetings that year.[14] This paper, which Shaw read on 18 July 1890 to a little group of Fabians, presented Ibsen as a passionate realist, a fervent Social Democrat, and a dedicated revolutionary. The resemblance to Shaw was striking.

The gist of the Fabian lecture was duly reported to Ibsen. It drew from him an immediate response, published as an interview in *The Daily Chronicle*, in which he firmly disavowed any knowledge of socialism and all connection with the Social Democratic party.[15] But, on second thought, Ibsen cannily amended this statement. A fortnight later, *The Chronicle* published an English translation of a letter to Hans Brackstad in which Ibsen wrote:

> What I really said was . . . that I was surprised that I, who had made
> it my chief life task to depict human characters and human destinies,

should, without conscious or direct intention, have arrived in several matters at the same conclusions the social democratic moral philosophers had arrived at by scientific processes.[16]

Shaw took this mollifying answer as a complete vindication of his position and, the following year, 1891, he published his Fabian lecture with some amplification as *The Quintessence of Ibsenism*, a title doubtless suggested by Schäffle's *The Quintessence of Socialism*. His interpretation of Ibsen was soon challenged by other Ibsenists, among them Archer. "A grave injustice," Archer wrote,

has been done Ibsen of late by those of his English admirers who have set him up as a social prophet and have sometimes omitted to mention that he is a bit of a poet as well. . . . As a matter of fact, Ibsen has no gospel whatever, in the sense of a systematic body of doctrine. . . . It belongs to the irony of fate that the least dogmatic of thinkers—the man who said of himself, "I only ask, my call is not to answer—" should figure in the imagination of so many English critics as a dour dogmatist.[17]

Archer was right, beyond doubt. Ibsen did not in the least accord with Shaw's approach to the drama. Shaw understood art mainly in terms of meaning. His critical function was primarily interpretative. It was his purpose to expound the *significatio* of Ibsen's work, and he saw it therefore as essentially parabolic and allegorical. "It really matters very little," he wrote in his preface to the third edition of *The Quintessence of Ibsenism* (1913) "whether Ibsen was a great man or not: what does matter is his message and the need of it."[18]

But, as Shaw was forced to concede in the additions he made to the first edition of his work, Ibsenism cannot be reduced to a formula: "its quintessence is that there is no formula." Ibsen's viewpoint was, indeed, consistently relativistic. It was his position that, since truth is impermanent, it is dangerous to insist on an absolute of any sort. His views were therefore constantly amended, supplemented, and contradicted, so that it is necessary to interpret his thought as a dialogue rather than as a doctrine. Shaw was an evangelist and therefore committed to the expression of a consistent doctrine. Yet he does not appear to have been always at ease with his gospel. His plays reflect a constant state of psychic ferment, the nature of which is represented by the conflicting views of his characters, vigorously contrasted, but seldom resolved.

In 1890 Shaw was aware most of all of Ibsen's attack on the dogmatic idealism of Pastor Manders in *Ghosts*. From this viewpoint it would be unthinkable to end Archer's plot with a heroic renunciation in the manner of the Second Empire dramatists. His collaboration with Archer had begun five years after Archer's failure with *The Pillars of Society* and the year after Jones's ill-fated flirtation with *A Doll's House*. At this time, also, Henrietta Lord's translation of *Ghosts* was running in installments in the socialist gazette *To-Day*, almost concurrently with Shaw's *Cashel Byron's Profession*. It is in the highest degree improbable, therefore, that Shaw knew nothing of Ibsen at this time, as he later insisted.[19] On the contrary, everything indicates that in taking up Archer's suggestion for *Rhinegold*, he intended from the start to give the plot an Ibsenist turn, and it is probable that it was because of Archer's prominence as an Ibsenist that Shaw offered to collaborate with him so soon after their initial meeting.

Archer, however, was evidently unwilling to waste his time with an unpleasant play, and, after their initial disagreement, he cheerfully abandoned the project. Shaw also laid it aside.

By 1892 the new theater movement had gained considerable momentum. Both Archer and George Moore were propagandizing vigorously for a Free Theatre in London, organized along the lines of Antoine's Théâtre Libre in Paris, which would produce new English plays privately in spite of the censor and the commercial managers. At this point J. T. Grein, a young journalist of Dutch extraction who was publishing a fortnightly review of art in London, also decided the time was ripe for a new departure in the drama. In 1891, he inaugurated the London Independent Theatre, an enterprise funded more or less at his own expense. Its membership at no time exceeded 175 subscribers, but its plans were ambitious. Grein planned to produce privately, free of commercial considerations, a series of original English plays in which, as he wrote, "real human emotion should be roused by the presentment of real human life."

Unhappily, there were no English plays of this description available for production. Grein decided to open with Ibsen. In March 1891 he invited an audience to see a performance of *Ghosts* at the Royalty in Soho. The production was modest, but the storm of protest it aroused was gratifying. Both the author and the management were resoundingly castigated in the press. Archer rushed to the defense. "The critics' hatred of Ibsen and contempt for the Independent Theatre," he wrote, "is perfectly genuine, perfectly sincere. The plain truth is that the theatrical journalism of to-day is narrow-minded, *borné*, and if not illiterate, at any rate, illiberal in its culture."[20]

Greatly encouraged by the amount of publicity his venture had received, Grein proceeded to put on a series of plays calculated to shock bourgeois sensibilities. That fall he produced Zola's *Thérèse Raquin*. The following March he put on three one-act plays, including Banville's *The Kiss*. In July he produced Van Nouhuys's *The Goldfish* and, in October 1892, Poel's version of *The Duchess of Malfi*. In the search for original English plays, however, Grein was able to turn up only Webster's brutal tragedy as an example of "the presentment of real human life" in the naturalist manner. In these circumstances, when Shaw came up with the offer of a comedy which he judged to be appropriately realistic, Grein accepted it sight unseen.[21]

Shaw's play was the comedy he had begun, with Archer's help, seven years previously. Apparently he had taken it up once again in 1890 and finished it in 1892 with the Independent Theatre in mind.[22] He retitled it *Widowers' Houses*, adapting for the purpose the text in Mark 12:38 in which Jesus reproaches those who "devour widow's houses and for pretence make long prayers." The production was by no means elaborate. The cast was not paid. Florence Farr played Blanche; James Welch took the role of Lickcheese. The play was performed twice and closed. Its reception was much less hysterical than that accorded *Ghosts*; nevertheless, the first performance was such as to give Shaw a memorable evening in the theater. There was loud applause from the socialist contingent in the audience, much booing from the opposition, a general atmosphere of disorder and excitement. Shaw was called to the stage and delivered a lecture on socialism. It was his first, and perhaps his headiest triumph. He wrote Charles Charrington exultantly: "I have proved myself a man to be reckoned with. I have got the blue book across the footlights. . . . I have appeared before the curtain amid transcendent hooting & retired amid cheers. And I have spent so much time in rehearsal that I am stark ruined. . . ."[23]

The second performance was less exciting, but it was more thoughtfully received. There was some comment in the press, very little of which was favorable. Shaw had an excellent opinion of his play. In the preface he wrote for the version which Grein published in 1893, he insisted that his comedy was "a work of art as much as any comedy of Molière's is a work of art, and pretends to be a better made play for actual use and long wear on the boards than anything that has been turned out by the patent constructor's machinery." But in the preface he wrote in 1898 for *Plays Pleasant and Unpleasant*, he stressed rather its shock value than its artistry: "I had not achieved a success, but I provoked an uproar."

It was characteristic of the period that the "uproar" over *Widowers'*

Houses had nothing to do with its merits as drama but was largely concerned with its moral implications. The play is, in fact, not an altogether convincing piece of dramatic writing, though, for its time it is surprisingly original.

The play in which Archer had found the suggestion for his plot was *La Ceinture dorée*, a three-act prose comedy by Emile Augier, originally produced at the Gymnase in Paris in 1855. It was at that time received with the polite indulgence accorded a harmless potboiler from the pen of a writer of repute. The tainted money theme was hardly new. At the beginning of the eighteenth century, plays about corrupt men of money were normally framed along the lines of classic comedy and involved such volatile blackguards as Lesage's Crispin (1707) and Turcaret (1709). In such plays the classic rogue is a low fellow, despicable for his motives, but admirable for his cunning, and amusing in the manner of the clever slave of Latin comedy. Characters of this type were customarily enmeshed in their own snares; often they were cheated by some scoundrel worse than themselves.

Augier's play, however, belonged to the postrevolutionary period. At this time bourgeois morality was no longer a laughing matter, and it was normal for the erring parvenu to be taught a lesson in case he needed one. In *La Ceinture dorée* the hero, Roussel, is a rich man of a realistic turn of mind. His daughter Celeste is sought in marriage by the idealistic Trelan, whose father, it appears, was ruined by Roussel. It is now discovered that Roussel's fortune was acquired, twenty years ago, through a shady deal, the details of which were unknown to him. Trelan attempts to persuade his prospective father-in-law to make restitution; when Roussel refuses, Trelan withdraws from the proposed marriage, renouncing the huge dowry that goes with Celeste, and prepares to leave for Persia. Suddenly war breaks out. Roussel is ruined. The various mercenary suitors who have been attracted by his daughter's dowry vanish as if by magic. It is then that Trelan comes forward to claim the hand of Celeste.

In the romantic comedy of the nineteenth century it was regularly assumed that marriage was the natural solution to the class problem, and that love would eventually bridge the gap between the aristocracy and the wealthy bourgeoisie. This theme was as popular in England as it was in France. In such plays as Morton's *All That Glitters is Not Gold* (1851), Robertson's *Society*, and *Caste*, and Bulwer-Lytton's *The Lady of Lyons*, it is demonstrated that class barriers are of no avail against natural nobility and the power of love. But while the assimilation of classes was greatly facilitated in the nineteenth-century drama, it was not long before other pressures were felt. As the moneyed classes arrogated to themselves the prestige that formerly belonged to the nobility, they had to shoulder also its traditional responsibilities. It was not enough for the possessor of money to be ennobled; his money also had to have its lineage certified.

Plays dealing with money were extremely common during the Second Empire. By 1885 the plot of the rich swindler was already threadbare, but the middle class was once again under scrutiny, and plays of ill-gotten money were in vogue. Sardou had recently demonstrated the popularity of the genre in *La Famille Benoîton* (1865), and Ibsen had even more recently revived the theme in *The Pillars of Society*. Very likely it was Archer's experience with this very play that moved him to suggest the theme of *Rhinegold* to Shaw. But while Archer remained loyal all his days to the Scribean idea of play-making, by 1892 Shaw was well on the way to other things. In his mind, socialism and naturalism were synonymous. *Widowers' Houses* was a slice of life.

The naturalist movement is traceable to a group of disillusioned French intellectuals who saw in the failure of the republic of 1848 the end of their hopes for achieving the goals of the Great Revolution. Convinced that all efforts to reform the social structure through legislation were doomed by the proclamation of the Second Empire, they resolved to break completely with the bourgeois culture they had inherited, and turned instead to the lower classes as a source of both artistic inspiration and the power necessary to overthrow the middle-class regime. The situation with these early socialists was obviously not the same as that which resulted in a renewal of revolutionary effort in similar groups a century or so later; but the analogy seems clear enough.

The rebels were in the main writers and artists, not politicians. Their attack on the existing order was mounted along aesthetic lines and centered on questions of realism, truth, and the depiction of "life as it is." Their weapons were literary—essays, stories, novels, and plays—with some supporting journalism to extend their social criticism into the political field. Their immediate object was to break the strangle-hold of the academies on the art and literature of the time. Substantially this was the program first adopted by the Pre-Raphaelites in England, and it was something of this sort that Ibsen proposed to Georg Brandes in the first years of their acquaintance.

The most influential of the leaders of the realist movement were Gustave Courbet and his literary counterpart Pierre Joseph Proudhon. Like Jean Jacques Rousseau before him, and Tolstoy after, Courbet fancied himself a man of the people. He was in fact a disaffected bourgeois, and his rebellion against his native environment motivated a series of paintings which represented with savage irony the grossness of the provincial middle class and the brutalized peasantry of Franche-Comté. In the 1850's painters were expected to choose pleasant idealistic subjects, and to paint them daintily. Courbet went far beyond the Barbizon painters in his depiction of nature "as it is." In consequence the nine paintings he exhibited in the Paris *Salon* of 1850–51 were accorded a reception very much like that of Ibsen's *Ghosts* in London a generation later.

Luckily for Courbet, in the repressive atmosphere of the 1850's the controversy which he provoked was for the time confined to the aesthetic question, the relation of truth and beauty. Nevertheless the reaction was swift and fierce. Louis Geofroy wrote in the *Revue des deux mondes*: ". . . Voici venir les coryphées de l'ère nouvelle, qui nous rejettent brutalement la face contre cette terre fangeuse d'où nous enlevait l'art de la poésie." Courbet's partisans were no less articulate. Champfleury saw in Courbet's brutal realism a new and profound source of poetry. Radical writers like Proudhon, however, strongly emphasized the social aspect of the new art. For Proudhon, the moral that was implicit in Courbet's *La Baigneuse* was completely explicit: "Yes, there she is, right enough, this plump, rich bourgeoise deformed by fat and opulence, in whose softness and mass the ideal is stifled . . . there she is just as our stupidity, her selfishness and her cuisine have formed her."[24]

In the manifesto which Courbet prefixed to the catalogue of paintings he exhibited in 1855, the year of the Paris International Exposition, he declared that his purpose as an artist was the negation of the ideal, and that only in this manner could democracy be achieved. From his standpoint there was no difference between realism and revolution; the one naturally implied the other: to see life "as it is" is to change it. In this idea he was amply seconded by Zola, who declared that the French republic might choose between naturalism and extinction.[25] Thus, while the realists' revolutionary animus seemed to be in the first place motivated by their exasperation with the artificial standards of academic art, its basis was essentially social, and its consequences were far-reaching. To the static complacency of a cultural system imprisoned in a framework of immutable ideals, the realists opposed the idea of change as the indispensable requisite of social vitality. The idea was stupendous. In large measure it accounted for the spectacular development of the drama

from Ibsen to Pirandello, and its repercussions were felt even in Robertson's modest innovations in the English theater. It was to become the
essential element in Shaw's philosophical system.

Ideas that seemed dangerously extreme in the days of Proudhon were
precisely those that seemed most reasonable to the young radicals of the
succeeding generation. Proudhon, for all his radicalism, was reluctant to
cut himself off from the past. "Il faut marcher," he wrote, "mais tout en
conservant." Those, however, who inherited his views in the 1870's felt
that in order to achieve a vital realistic expression it was necessary to
abandon the past altogether, and they did what they could to sever the
bonds of tradition. "Of course the past is dead," Zola wrote in the
preface to *Thérèse Raquin*:

> We must look to the future, and the future will have to do with
> human problems studied in the framework of reality. We must cast
> aside fables of every sort, and delve into the living drama of the
> twofold life of the character and its environment. . . . The drama will
> either die, or become modern and realistic.[26]

Realistic attitudes, already well developed in the novel through the
influence of Balzac, led the new writers, who now called themselves
naturalists, to concentrate on the precise observation of facts, and this
observation in turn encouraged them to record their findings in a manner that, so they said, approximated scientific reports. Naturalistic art
was, in theory at least, austere. The naturalists tried to avoid sentimentality, avoided preaching, and firmly repudiated the easy humanitarianism
of their romantic predecessors. If their work mainly reflected the
squalor and bestiality of the human condition it was not, ostensibly,
because they took pleasure in ugliness, but because they took pleasure in
truth. The truth was not uniformly agreeable, but there was no other
real source of beauty. Moreover, truth was a most useful irritant, the
indispensable spur to action.

Such considerations brought naturalism well abreast of the social question in the 1880's. Proudhon had given direction to those realists who
had a socialist bias in much the same way as in contemporary England,
Ruskin influenced the Pre-Raphaelites. The results were not uniformly
productive. In France some of the realists were politically minded; many
were not. The result was the splitting of the new movement along diver-
gent paths. The adherents of *l'art pour l'art*, writers such as Flaubert,
Leconte de Lisle, and the Goncourts, developed realism as a purely
aesthetic principle. For them naturalism was a reaction against romantic

idealism and sentimentality. Those who felt more keenly the twinges of social conscience developed the utilitarian aspect of naturalism. Writers of the type of Zola taught "the bitter science of life" in the professed hope of bringing about by this means the improvement of society. For them truth was not only beautiful, but useful.

It is clear, nevertheless, that in holding the mirror up to nature in its more repulsive aspects, the naturalists exhibited a certain perversity of taste. The end of art, the Goncourts had written, is a human document set down in all its truth and all its horror. This was essentially Chekhov's position also as a writer, and also Gorky's; but Chekhov's touch some-how transformed horror into poetry, and Gorky succeeded in giving human degradation a look of tragic grandeur. Unpleasantness for its own sake as a principle of art, however, could hardly be justified in the cultural environment of the 1880's. A successful tour of hell was possible only on condition that it involved the idea of an ultimate ascent to Paradise. In the absence of a sufficient poetic, the utilitarian side of naturalism was indispensable to its survival, and those who professed no interest in any form of idealism soon stirred up a hornet's nest. Thus while the proponents of a purely artistic naturalism simmered, like the Goncourts, in their own bitter juices, the major realists, from Taine to Maupassant, expressed with varying degrees of vigor their dissatisfaction with the existing order, and their desire to change it through some sort of political activity.

By 1885 the reaction against naturalism, materialism, positivism, and the cult of ugliness had already taken shape. In France, after Bourget's *Le Disciple* (1889), the symbolist movement was clearly in the as-cendant, and by 1891, when Jules Huret published the results of his *Enquête*, the great majority of his sixty-four authorities assured him that naturalism was dead.

In the theater, the bankruptcy of naturalism, and the spiritual preoc-cupations of the symbolists left the heirs of the Scribean tradition—Augier, Dumas, Sardou, and Brieux—in full possession of the field. With the notable exception of Brieux, the seriousness of these writers as social critics was open to question. But while their importance at home steadily diminished, outside of France they were taken with complete serious-ness. A consequence was the line of drama developed by Ibsen, Björnson, and Strindberg, and through these writers Second Empire realism was transformed into something of which its founders had not dreamed. This, in essence, was the new movement in the theater.

In France the social drama of the Second Empire, like that of the later

Victorian era in England, was concerned principally with the consequences of individual aberrations from the standards of good society.
These plays were serious in tone and expressed righteous indignation at
the evil-doing of those who hid their rascality behind a façade of piety
and respectability. Plays like Augier's *Le Fils de Giboyer* were deeply
sentimental and invariably affirmed the imperishable ideals of the middle
class, the integrity of the virtuous, the sanctity of family life, and the
rights and obligations of parenthood. It is, of course, to this genre of
drame that *The Pillars of Society* belongs.

The difference between Augier and Ibsen, however, became clear in
the treatment of Nora in *A Doll's House* and of Mrs. Alving in *Ghosts*.
The moral tendency of these plays was clearly revolutionary in the
deepest sense and, although Ibsen vigorously disclaimed any connection
with Zola, his naturalist bias at this time was evident to everyone. Ibsen's
radicalism was actually limited by the misgivings to which he gave expression in *An Enemy of the People* and later in *The Wild Duck*. His
essentially conservative nature, fortified by success, ultimately put an
end to the more patently disturbing aspects of his work. Shaw, however,
formed his idea of Ibsen somewhat short of the point where Ibsen
stopped being an Ibsenist. He had, moreover, two important models in
France on whom to fashion his thought—Becque and Brieux.

Although its initial manifestations in France had suffered an eclipse,
naturalism was certainly not dead in the 1880's. By 1890 its manner had
changed, but not its character. Zola's work was by no means free of
sentimentality. Those who followed him, however, had no illusions to
indulge. In Becque's *Les Corbeaux*, produced in 1882, the rascally Tes-
sier suffers no inconvenience by reason of his villainy. On the contrary,
he is rewarded for it, and it is suggested that, in this world, villainy is the
normal path to success and happiness and that innocence is the surest
way to ruin. After Becque, social comedy—for example, Jean Jullien's
La Sérénade (1887) and George Ancey's *La Dupe* (1891)—both presented by Antoine in his Théâtre Libre, became once again hard and
objective. It was evidently with this sort of bitter comedy in mind that
Shaw began his career in the theater.

Widowers' Houses was the first play by an English author that approached the tone of naturalism. It is a *comédie rosse* which has distinct
affinities with the type of unpleasant comedy in which the writers of the
Théâtre Libre specialized. But it is not quite a naturalistic play.

The naturalists had made a point of avoiding contrivance. They professed a system of dramaturgy which imitated nature as closely as possible, and which thus took account of the fact that nature normally does not trouble to organize its material in interesting plot-sequences. In fact, however, few of the naturalist playwrights, and least of all Zola, were able to avoid designing their plays in accordance with a preconceived pattern. Becque, the most successful of the naturalistic outer fringe, was a professed admirer of Scribe. His comedies were carefully plotted so as to bring out the grim jest which lay at their core. It is impossible to say how well acquainted Shaw was at this time with the work of the French naturalists, but, judging by the preface he wrote for his edition of the translations of Brieux, he knew French drama very well indeed, and it seems clear that in *Widowers' Houses* he meant to follow the latest French fashion.

Like *Les Corbeaux, Widowers' Houses* was plotted so as to make a point, but it was by no means expertly contrived. The degree of liberty which Shaw permitted himself in the collocation of events and coincidences would have put to shame the least scrupulous of the followers of Scribe. It is obviously in the highest degree improbable that Sartorius's daughter should meet her father's mortgagee by accident on a Rhine boat; that she should fall in love with him at first sight; that Lickcheese should rise so suddenly in the world after a lifetime of servility; or that Cockayne—to say nothing of Trench—should become so utterly corrupted in the same short space of time. It is not clear why Shaw believed that his hero could not manage without the assistance of a confidant in the classic manner. Nevertheless, the characterizations are vivid, and if the point is made clumsily, it is certainly made clear.

"*Qu'est-ce que la Propriété?*" Proudhon had asked; and on the first page of his celebrated treatise on that subject he had answered: "La Propriété c'est le vol."[27] In a social system founded on the exploitation of the poor, Shaw suggests, it is impossible to escape the guilt of riches, and it is sheer hypocrisy to pretend that one can. The choices are few. One can give up the world, like Alceste in *Le Misanthrope*; or one can come to terms with it, like the sensible Philinte. In following the example of Philinte, Dr. Trench demonstrates his good sense, but not his moral superiority. When the facts are made clear to him, he faces them squarely, without the "tact" of his friend Cockayne, and once he realizes how completely he is committed to the economics of exploitation, he proceeds very sensibly to make the most of his situation. In this manner he shows himself to be a more honest man than the high-minded gentry who prefer not to know the sources of their income. He is not admirable, but he is no hypocrite.

It is conceivable that Trench might have given up his tainted patrimony, joined the deserving poor, and become the victim of the economic system instead of one of its tyrants. But this is not his genre. Although he begins as a romantic idealist, he is soon educated. He becomes a realist and quickly reaches the conclusion that in a brutal world it is better to inflict pain than to suffer it. It is a thesis which Shaw demonstrated fully some years later in *Major Barbara* and, one might add, it was the conclusion at which he arrived in his own private life. Trench accordingly pockets his conscience along with the mortgage money and joins his fellow brigands with the easy cynicism of those who are able to endure "life as it is."

The difficulty with this arrangement is that, while the reasoning is impeccable, the characterization is not. In the first two acts Trench is presented as a fine example of English upper-class breeding, that is to say, as a foolish, stiff-necked, and honorable young man of romantic tendencies and sympathetic character, the sort of young man who goes gladly to die, if need be, for Queen and Country in the far-off wastes of India. This posture he maintains for rather more than half the play; yet in the relatively short interval between acts three and four, his spine somehow develops the flexibility necessary to bring about the desired outcome. The comedy is thus made to hinge on a recognition and peripety in traditional fashion, but the reversal that follows upon Trench's discovery that he is as bad as Sartorius necessitates a wholly unnatural wrenching of his character. In the one dramatic scene of the play, Sartorius demonstrates convincingly that his own position in the social hierarchy is entirely necessary and proper. He then shows Trench the door. One might expect a violent reaction. On the contrary, when next we see him, some months later, Trench is a new man, completely reconciled to his destiny as a slum-landlord and a begetter of future slum-landlords. In this unexpected change he sacrifices not only our sympathy, but also his dramatic effectiveness, for a change of this sort is neither funny nor tragic, but, at the most, depressing. At this point, therefore, Trench more or less vanishes from the scene, leaving only a parable in his place, the character having been completely absorbed by the thesis.

The fault is a lack of realism. In reality people caught in such situations are likely to justify themselves in a manner that convinces at least themselves. Trench's ready acquiescence in his fall from grace is quite as incredible as Lickcheese's sudden access of business acumen. The lack of verisimilitude in these sudden shifts of character is much more serious than the improbability involved in a sudden change of fortune. In the theater one is prepared to accept almost any eventuality in the narrative, but very little that seems arbitrary in the characterization. It would be normal for Trench to keep his income; but it does not seem normal for him to come to terms with Sartorius, and far from normal for him to marry his daughter. What we should expect, realistically, is that in the future he would completely ignore their existence.

At this point of his career Shaw understood realism as the expression of a philosophic, not a psychological truth. His characters therefore do not follow their natural bent but are put through the paces of the author's syllogism like obedient animals in a circus. It was a long time before Shaw learned the difference between logical and psychological motivation, and perhaps he never learned it fully or cared to learn it. In the type of drama which interested him, it was more useful to employ types of humanity rather than persons.

The parabolic intention of *Widowers' Houses* was quite clear to his American editor. In the brief introduction to the first American edition of *Plays Pleasant and Unpleasant*, the play is recommended in terms which recall the journalistic fervors of a former age:

> Sartorius, the ghoul who fattens upon the living graves of the destitute is limned masterfully. . . . Blanche, the flower growing on this dunghill of corruption is the natural product of her environment. Public opinion has only come to realize the problem involved in "tainted money," but this play written sixteen years ago brings home this moot question into the very heart of family relations. . . . Harry and Blanche are the natural products of their environment and consummate their sordid, fleshly union without a vestige of illusion as to the baseness of their motives.[28]

This formulation, however florid, sums up the action with admirable accuracy. In a later preface Shaw himself noted, "In Widowers' Houses I have shown middle class respectability and younger son gentility fattening on the poverty of the slum as flies fatten upon filth. . . ."[29] The point is made amply clear in both these statements, but there is a difference. The American editor saw the fable by gaslight and presented the play as melodrama. Shaw saw it in the light of day and made it into a comedy. The nuance marks the difference between his talent and that of his less gifted colleagues.

Sartorius is far from a ghoul. He is a pleasant and well-mannered man, and, like Balzac's Mercadet, a most indulgent father. Blanche is a pretty girl with an uncontrollable temper, and Trench is portrayed as an uncommonly attractive young gentleman. The external attractiveness of

these characters enhances the grimness of the moral. It is Trench's cynical acquiescence in the practices of slum-landlordism that provides the
play with its principal effect. This effect is of no great intensity at any
time, but the final scene clearly foreshadows Shaw's later manner. The
little band of social reprobates, having arranged its business, goes off to
dinner, arm in arm, with apparently not a care in the world. The effect is
neither revolting, nor shocking. It is, in its way, funny.

This play represents, of course, the earliest stage in Shaw's development and, while it is in some ways surprisingly well done, it has some
archaic stiffness and an abruptness of manner which betrays the author's
inexperience. In one respect, however, its faults afford a significant measure of Shaw's besetting limitations as a playwright. With the exception
of Blanche, who exhibits some embarrassing traces of humanity, its characters give the impression of actors speaking the author's mind, and
doing his bidding, with robotlike docility. Like the actors of the Japa-
nese doll theater, Shaw's personages are exceptionally lifelike puppets,
but the illusion of their humanity is not so perfect as to prevent the
attention from straying occasionally from the doll to the hand that
manipulates it. This is an inherent drawback of the type of drama that is
intended to demonstrate a thesis and is therefore under constant control.
Drama that deals with living beings, as in the plays of Chekhov, is less
amenable to the author's direction and, since it exhibits a fantasy that is
in some degree emancipated from rational control, it depends for its
effects on inexplicable impulses and indefinable motives. In the theater
such plays create an effect of life; they are in the highest degree realistic,
but in general they prove nothing and their meaning is a matter of
conjecture.

For Shaw, however, a play was chiefly valuable in terms of its meaning. The idea of art for art's sake made no sense to one for whom art was
essentially allegorical, and behavior a basis for moral judgment. There is,
of course, nothing wrong with drama devised according to such conceptions. It is perhaps more straightforward in its theatricality than the
drama that aims at an effect of reality. But it is not at all the same thing.
If one accepts Shaw's theater for what it is, one is overwhelmed with
admiration at the effects he achieves in his *guignol*. It is only when one
looks to him for something that belongs to another type of drama that
one becomes aware of his shortcomings as an artist.

All the faults, and many of the virtues, of Shaw's mature style are
already manifest in this first play—the patently contrived plot, the theatricality of situation, the brightness and flatness of the characters, the

wit and sententiousness of the dialogue, and the shaping force of the idea; as well as a certain sense of its being very good indeed but a little short of the mark. In spite of the evident attempt to elevate the emotional content of certain scenes, the tone of the play is singularly phlegmatic. Only Blanche vibrates with any special vitality, and it is evident that this character, among all the others, is rather more than hypothetical.

Blanche is depicted as a formidable woman, fiercely passionate, strong-willed and given to ungovernable rages. In relation to her parlormaid, she reveals herself, somewhat surprisingly, as a sadist, and the maid is portrayed as a masochist who evidently adores her tormentor. In the final scene with Trench, Blanche's sadism is even further developed, so that even Trench recognizes the erotic nature of her aggressiveness and is shrewdly able to take advantage of it. Blanche is apparently the first example of the nineteenth-century *femme féroce* in English drama—Wilde's *Salomé* was written two years later, in 1894. Her provenience is not altogether clear. It is possible that Blanche was the result of direct observation; she is often said to have been suggested by Jane Patterson, the turbulent mistress of Shaw's early years. But while Mrs. Patterson may have helped to fix the character vividly in Shaw's mind, the stereotype which Blanche represents was actually at the height of its vogue in the 1880's, so much so that Sarah Bernhardt found it advantageous to make a specialty of the role.

Seemingly each age has its own erotic coloring. The type of sexual fantasy that came into fashion in the 1850's probably had its roots in Sade's *Justine*, a novel which initiated a series of memorable female portraits celebrating the spookier aspects of heterosexual love. The type of sadistic beauty in which this age reveled long antedated its romantic versions. Mérimée's Carmen was a modern equivalent of the Angelicas and Alcinas of the Renaissance, who were in turn modern versions in their day of the Circes and Calypsos of an earlier age. For the nineteenth century, Carmen, in Bizet's opera, effectively established the cliché of the beautiful and deadly *allumeuse*, but the *femme fatale* had been in vogue for some time before Bizet put her on the stage in 1875. We have ample intimations of her in the various romantic treatments of Cleopatra, and in works such as Coleridge's *Christabel* and Keats's *Lamia* and *La Belle Dame Sans Merci* in the early years of the century. Soon after, the fascination of evil beauty was felt everywhere, and such writers as Théophile Gautier, Barbey d'Aurevilly, Gustave Flaubert, Stéphane Mallarmé, and Pierre Louÿs did what they could to inflame the imagination of their readers with the perilous enchantments of the lovely woman whose beauty feeds on men. The *femme fatale*, as Louis Deprez pointed out in *L'Evolution naturaliste* (1884), specialized in "the annihilation of the artist." This was only natural. It was those who were particularly sensitive to beauty that found these dangerous ladies irresistible. Others of a more practical turn evidently avoided them. These vampires did not often attack the throats of bankers.

The immediate source of the sadistic heroine was probably French, but the evil power of woman's beauty had long been recognized in England, and the romantic revival of interest in woman as *bête féroce* occasioned no great astonishment. After the early romantics, the Pre-Raphaelites, particularly Rossetti and Burne-Jones, displayed great interest in malevolent beauties of the type of Coleridge's Lady Geraldine, and Swinburne published some extraordinary fantasies of distinctly masochistic nature. Pater excited such interest with his celebrated interpretations of the Gioconda smile in *The Renaissance* (1873) that fashionable ladies of the 1880's found it necessary to practice *"le sourire à la Lise"* before their mirrors in order to cut a proper figure in polite society.[30] Thus, while it is likely that the defensive posture toward women which Shaw assumed in his plays was related to his personal sexual situation, we cannot overlook the possibility that his female characters from *Widowers' Houses* to *Man and Superman* followed the current mode in high-style heroines during this period, and that his Candida, for example, owed as much to Pater's Leonardo as to the Titian's Virgin. Thus, in Eugène Sue's *Les Mystères de Paris* (1843), the unfortunate victim's state of mind is described in terms that accord well with Shaw's description of Blanche's relations with Trench in *Widowers' Houses*:

> Women like Cécile exert a sudden power, a magic omnipotence over men of animal sensuality such as Jacques Fernand.
> At the very first glance they divine the nature of these women, they lust after them, they are drawn to them by a fatal attraction . . . and soon mysterious affinities, sympathies doubtless of magnetic nature, chain them invincibly at the feet of their monstrous loves: for only they can quench the impure fires they kindle.[31]

From Shaw's standpoint this sort of sexual fascination served no useful purpose and must be regarded as a biological aberration in some way related to the evil economic system which fostered it. It was to be some years before the utilitarian purposes of the sex drive became sufficiently clear to him so that he could justify, in *Man and Superman*, the "magic omnipotence" of the alluring female. In *Widowers' Houses*, Blanche's feral attraction does not draw Trench upward in the evolutionary scale. On the contrary, Blanche is the sexual manifestation of the corrupting power of greed. It is not a pretty picture they make together but, such is the intimation, this is what romance amounts to in this naughty world.

In the early part of 1893 Shaw tried his hand once again at a play for the Independent Theatre.[32] He turned to a new theme. *The Philanderer* is chiefly about love and marriage, matters into which Shaw's recent amorous experiences had given him, so he thought, an unusual insight. As drama this play is certainly of no great value. Shaw himself was of two minds about it. He pushed it enthusiastically for many years; but in a letter to Ellen Terry, written in August 1896, he speaks of reading it to some friends, after a long interval, with little satisfaction: "It turned out to be a combination of mechanical farce with realistic filth which quite disgusted me." Some months after that, he described it to Justin Mc-Carthy as "the dullest filth." Nevertheless in December of that year he ended a letter to Ellen Terry: "Mind you tell me something serious about *The Philanderer*. How would you like to play Julia?" Miss Terry did not like *The Philanderer* and did not wish to play Julia. But evidently it was important to Shaw to have the play accepted. As late as 1913 he was assiduous in his attempts to get a star to play Julia. Mrs. Patrick Campbell refused indignantly. The play offended her: "I find it ugly—some mischievous personal experience."[33]

Whatever his feelings about *The Philanderer*, Shaw published it along with *Widowers' Houses* and *Mrs Warren's Profession* in the first volume of *Plays Pleasant and Unpleasant* in 1898 and prefixed to it a note in which he explained that it had become apparent that this play required more expert acting than the Independent Theatre could manage, and so was not played there. The part of Charteris, he wrote, could be played only by Charles Wyndham at the Criterion, but the play was not suitable for the Criterion. In fact, he had offered the play in February 1895 to Richard Mansfield, who was opening a season at the Garrick in New York, on condition that he play Charteris: "Charteris must be played by you—by YOU, Richard Mansfield, not Lancelot nor another—else the contract's off."[34]

The contract had never been on. Mansfield decided that the spectacle of Ibsen "turned inside out" was not "a pleasant or agreeable one." "If you don't like the play," Shaw had written him, "wire me at once the single word 'declined.'" Mansfield hastened to do so. The play was not produced in London until 1905 and then ran very briefly. Shaw had little occasion to rejoice in it.[35]

In discussing the unpleasant aspects of the three plays in his first volume, Shaw justified their acerbity on the ground of their therapeutic value. The purpose of *The Philanderer* was, he wrote, to show

> the grotesque relations between men and women which have arisen under marriage laws which represent to some of us a political neces- sity (especially for other people), to some a divine ordinance, to some a romantic ideal, to some a domestic profession for women, and to some that worst of blundering abominations, an institution which society has outgrown but not modified, and which "advanced" individuals are therefore forced to evade.[36]

In a letter to the young journalist Golding Bright, written some two years before this preface was written, the case was put differently. There he noted that his first three plays were

> what people call realistic. They were dramatic pictures of middle class society from the point of view of a Socialist who regards the basis of that society as thoroughly rotten economically and morally. . . . In "The Philanderer" you had the fashionable cult of Ibsenism and "New Womanism" on a real basis of clandestine sensuality.[37]

The play itself, however, does not conform with either of these specifi- cations. It does not deal with the evils of marriage as an institution, nor is it an attack on what Shaw called "the crimes of society." It is, if any- thing, a protest against the unreasonable possessiveness of women in love.[38]

The antimarital attitude, which Charteris was intended to demon- strate, Shaw had formulated quite explicitly three years before in his lecture on Ibsen to the Fabian Society. At that time he had pointed out that the social organism in the process of being civilized had to force marriage and family life on the individual in order to perpetuate itself, since love could not be counted on as a unifying principle, and the sexual relationship was not stable. In these circumstances, men pretend that marriage is everlastingly congenial, that connubial desire is eternal, that women are both coy and passive, and that one naturally loves one's kindred. Those whose experience differs from this ideal of marriage are forced by the majority to pretend otherwise:

> the policy of forcing individuals to act on the assumption that all ideals are real, and to recognize and accept such action as standard moral conduct, absolutely valid under all circumstances . . . may therefore be described as the policy of Idealism. But the man strong enough to face the truth has another viewpoint. He insists that mar- riage in many cases is a failure.

Shaw added: "Let us provide otherwise for the social ends which the family subserves, and then abolish its compulsory character altogether." Such, he thought, was Ibsen's doctrine in *Ghosts*: "What Ibsen insists on is that there is no golden rule; that conduct must justify itself by its effect upon life, and not by its conformity to any rule or ideal. . . ."[39]

It was according to such ideas that Charteris was conceived. He is, presumably, an exceptional man, a genius, strong enough to face the truth and to behave in accordance with it, instead of submitting to society's dictates. For such an individual the sexual appetite is free of the restrictions placed upon it by others, and he will insist on having his desire without incurring the penalty of lifelong servitude to a domestic arrangement for which he has neither the aptitude nor the inclination. A man of this sort has no alternative but to be a philanderer.

A year or so before he wrote *The Philanderer*, Shaw had solemnly apprised Florence Farr, a young actress with whom he was intimate at this time, that he was a genius of the first order, a godlike man.[40] *The Philanderer* was evidently a description of the difficulties encountered by such men in exercising their talents among women of a lesser order of greatness, particularly among those who use their pretended freedom as a bait for marriage. As the scene of these activities Shaw imagined a club organized to secure for its members the advantages of the perfect equality of the sexes. The Ibsen Club has rooms, house rules, dues, and committees. It serves dinner like other clubs, but it symbolizes the intellectual *bohème* in which Shaw was moving in these years, the group of advanced people who styled themselves Ibsenists and prided themselves mightily on being free of convention. Within the precincts of the Ibsen Club, Leonard Charteris moves with suitable abandon; but far from avoiding the matrimonial entanglements to which ordinary people are subject, he appears to have proposed marriage to all the ladies of the club who have so far taken his fancy, and there is nothing to indicate at the end of the play that he has any intention of relenting in his pursuit of the eternal feminine whom he leads on, and presumably upward.

The seemingly antiseptic Ibsen Club is actually a hotbed of sexual activity. In its rarefied atmosphere the action centers on the efforts of the ingenious Charteris, who is both the protagonist and the *raisonneur*, to elude the determined assault of the beautiful, but inordinately possessive Julia Craven by making love to the less beautiful but less violent Grace Tranfield. Julia is resolved to marry Charteris at any cost. He, on the other hand, has already proposed to Grace. The ladies meet and clash violently. When Grace discovers that her rival is disposed to fight tooth

and nail for her former lover, she retires decorously from the battle
leaving Julia in possession of the field. But Charteris is ingenious. He
escapes his doom by promoting a match between Julia and the susceptible Dr. Paramore. This arrangement leaves Charteris free to marry
Grace, but Grace declines on the ground that she is sincerely in love
with Charteris and therefore would be placing herself in his power if she
became his wife.

"The ideal wife," Shaw wrote in *The Quintessence of Ibsenism*,

> is one who does everything that the ideal husband likes, and nothing
> else. Now to treat a person as a means instead of an end is to deny
> that person's right to live. And to be treated as a means to such an
> end as sexual intercourse with those who deny one's right to live is
> insufferable to any human being. Woman, if she dares face the fact
> that she is being so treated, must either loathe herself or else rebel.

In this passage Shaw was obviously thinking of *A Doll's House* and
Ghosts, but it is in *Love's Comedy* that Ibsen discusses the problem of
people like Grace and Charteris. The conclusion in that play is much the
same as in *The Philanderer*. In the case of Charteris, however, the implication is that, after he has Julia safely married, he will continue to
include her in his philanderings, without prejudice to his pursuit of
Grace. He is, in short, doomed to a life of unrestricted Don Juanism.

However depraved this may seem, as an honest man Charteris has no
alternative. Marriage, in his view, is a form of captivity enforced by all
the rigors of the law and all the pressures of the church. If he marries the
lovely Julia, he becomes her property; if he marries Grace, she becomes
his prisoner. A marriage for love is clearly out of the question for those
who prize their freedom. The only happy possibility is marriage predicated not on love, but on a sound economic basis, with mutual respect
and mutual convenience.

Although Shaw's dependence on Ibsen is clear in this play, it is likely
that *The Philanderer* is in some sense an apology for his own compre-
hensive philanderings in the course of his greener years. From what we
know of his relations with Mrs. Patterson during the time that he was
maintaining somewhat similar relations with Florence Farr it would seem
that he patterned Julia Craven on the one lady and Grace Tranfield on
the other. The scene between Julia and Grace in the first act of *The
Philanderer* was in fact suggested by an actual occurrence involving his
two mistresses, the events of which are amply documented in his correspondence.[41] Shaw's habit of discussing at length with each of his ladies

the idiosyncracies of the others seems to find a clear reflection in the behavior of Charteris, with whose loveless sexuality it is tempting to connect Shaw's own behavior in these years. It is sometimes said that, in Charteris, Shaw attempted for the first time a self-portrait. If it is so, it was retouched almost beyond recognition; at the same time it is perfectly clear that he intended in this play, as formerly in his novels, to turn his amorous experiences to some account. In this regard the play provides an amusing commentary on his biography.[42]

The Philanderer is a curiously dry comedy. Like *Widowers' Houses* it has a tragic undercurrent that gives it a touch of bitterness; but it is not so good a piece of work as Shaw's first play. The principal characters—the two ladies, their fathers, and their lovers, Paramore and Charteris—are linked together in a series of relationships which make a neat, but unconvincing pattern, and they are brought into their respective scenes by methods that smack of conscription. The play suffers also from an especially tedious third act and a most unsatisfactory denouement. Nevertheless it rewards study as a first formulation of motifs which were to figure significantly in Shaw's future work. All of Shaw is present in this play. Dr. Paramore was destined to reappear some years later, in another form, in *The Doctor's Dilemma*. In the absence of the Life Force, as yet not dramatically operative, the metaphysical significance of Julia's beauty is not clarified. But her character is very clear. She is presented as an intermediate stage of the *femme bête-féroce*, of which Blanche Sartorius was the prototype. Similarly, in Charteris it is easy to see the first stage in the development of John Tanner, the hero of *Man and Superman*.

In *The Philanderer*, the Don Juan character is incompletely realized, but already he presents a striking embodiment of male ambivalence. Charteris, still in the pride of his youth and vigor, has the dexterity required to elude capture. He courts his women energetically, but in fear and trembling, maneuvering the chase skillfully so that it appears that it is he who is being pursued. In *Man and Superman* Tanner is less skillful and consequently achieves something like tragic stature. Willy-nilly, protesting violently, he is gobbled up by the eternal feminine when he least expects it. It is evidently a fate worse than death.

Charteris illustrates a preliminary phase of this form of erotic cannibalism. Unlike Tanner, he is a slave of his appetites, but he is definitely on the defensive and seeks safety in numbers. He talks incessantly, desperately attempting to justify an impossible position, and thus foreshadows the typically Shavian character, a talkative, witty, and unashamedly self-centered man who is convinced that his personal needs are in the best interests of the human race.

Charteris comes somewhat closer to the Restoration rake—Etherege's Dorimant, or Congreve's Mirabell—than to anyone Shaw knew or could find in the plays of Ibsen. But he is not really a Restoration character. The Restoration wit, even at his best, is neither an artist nor a thinker. He is a sensible, sensual young man without scruples, bent on pleasure and intent on making a rich marriage. His cruelty, when he is cruel, is the result of heedlessness, not of a desire to vivisect the female soul. Since he has learned to live at his ease within the normal framework of good society, he has no fear of being imprisoned by marriage, and no moral obstacles to impede his acquisition of the things men want. In comparison, Charteris, for all his self-assurance, seems comically fearful, a young man more inclined to eloquence than to the more vigorous amatory exercises.

No doubt it is to the Dorimants of fiction that we must trace the elvish character of Shaw's more famous protagonists. Like their seventeenth-century forebears, these are curiously intangible personages, with great style and little soul. Some, like Charteris, seem unbearably arch; others, like Dick Dudgeon, are blunt and forthright; but all share the mystery of the unrealized. The Restoration wit is, for all his lack of humanity, firmly rooted in the world he inhabits, a sparkish figure in a fictional cosmos. Charteris belongs nowhere. He is a realist in search of reality, a completely bookish conception.

The basis of comedy in *The Philanderer* is quite different from that of the Restoration plays. In *The Country Wife* Horner satisfies his seemingly inexhaustible appetites by flaunting his incapacity. Charteris, on the other hand, attracts women by maintaining an air of fatigue. He too presents a challenge, but, unlike Horner, he has evidently no vocation for the business in hand. He is a philanderer without portfolio. Thus, this play, which is ostensibly about love, is singularly arid. The reason is clear. The philanderer is not a lover of women. He is only an observer. Dr. Paramore is a lover.

The rhetorical tone of *The Philanderer* is also quite different from that of Restoration comedy. The Restoration mode tends largely toward similitude and aphorism as the chief vehicle of wit, and Machiavellian ingenuity in the management of the intrigue. Shaw's comedy comes closer to farce. He depends for variety upon unexpected twists and surprises rather than upon intricate plotting. His characters are much inclined to rhetorical displays and often affect an inappropriately sententious utterance with parallel structure and incremental repetition worthy of a Ciceronian oration. His conceits depend most often upon the inversion of commonplaces, seldom upon figures of speech or imagery, so that the effect is, on the whole, more analytic than decorative. There is, finally, at the bottom of Shaw's comedy a strain of broad humor based on common sense, which is not bookish at all, but depends on a shrewd sense of the absurd, a gift for comic exaggeration which may fairly be called Irish. In this characteristic Shaw does not differ widely from the Restoration dramatists, the best of whom were also Irish.

Since the withdrawal of *The Philanderer* left the Independent Theatre without a play to follow *Widowers' Houses*, Shaw took up in the summer of 1893 an even more sensational theme than that of the earlier play. Prostitution was quite definitely taboo in England as a subject for drama. There can be no doubt that Shaw was aware when he undertook *Mrs Warren's Profession* that the Queen's Reader of Plays would forbid its production, but evidently he hoped his play would provoke a controversy which would bring to public attention not only the social aspects of prostitution but also the question of censorship. Both aspects of the matter were fully exploited in the preface to the published play.[43]

There were deeper considerations. Underlying Shaw's professional attitudes was a gnawing sense of the world's injustice, and particularly its injustice to himself. His autobiographical writings make it clear that he felt he had been unjustly treated from the moment of his birth, that, though he was born a gentleman and was brilliantly endowed by nature, he had been unfairly deprived of the financial advantages that his breeding entailed and his brilliance deserved. He had been undesired, unloved, neglected, and, at last, abandoned to his fate.[44] This sense of personal deprivation was speedily generalized into a grievance of cosmic proportions. When he became aware, first through Henry George, and afterwards through Karl Marx, of the moral depravity of the rich, he hastened to throw in his lot with the poor and soon became adept in collecting examples of social injustice. It was normal that, when he first embarked on his career as a dramatist, these should provide him with points of departure.

The Unpleasant Plays were presented, in the preface to the first edition, as instances of the ills of society. *The Philanderer* does not seem, on the surface, to exhibit any glaring example of social injustice, other than women's efforts to enslave the men they fancy, but Shaw blamed the inequities of love on the antiquated institution of matrimony with which it has somehow become associated. The other two plays are straightforward attacks on the economic exploitation of the poor by the rich and, in presenting them in printed form, Shaw expressed his indignation at being prevented from presenting them publicly on the stage. As a dramatist, he wrote, his standpoint was not properly that of a professional entertainer, but of a professional critic. The two professions were not mutually exclusive. Criticism

> may say things which many would like to say but dare not, and indeed for want of skill could not even if they durst. Its iconoclasms, seditions, and blasphemies, if well turned, tickle those whom they shock; so that the critic adds the privilege of the court jester to those of the confessor.[45]

It was, presumably, from this viewpoint that *Mrs Warren's Profession* was composed. The author professed to take an impartial and dispassionate view of the situation under scrutiny, and to evaluate it as an expert. As playwright, he formulated an amusing fantasy in accordance with the rules of the art. As critic he commented learnedly on the situation he had imagined. This was not in accordance with naturalistic practice. Naturalistic works were supposed to speak for themselves, without intrusion on the part of the author. *Mrs Warren's Profession* is, in fact, not an example of naturalism. It is a *pièce à thèse* in the manner of Dumas *fils* and, as in the case of *Widowers' Houses*, its roots are traceable to the drama of the Second Empire. Its technique is Scribean; its plot is contrived so as to make a point.

The subject was topical. In the mid-eighties the question of white slavery was exciting much attention, particularly with respect to the export trade in English girls. W. T. Stead had recently published an article on the subject in the *Pall Mall Gazette* entitled "The Maiden Tribute of Modern Babylon."[46] In a story entitled *Yvette*, Maupassant told the story of a delicately reared girl who discovers that the source of her support is a mother engaged in prostitution. This story was brought to Shaw's attention by Janet Achurch who, with her husband Charles Charrington, had managed the first successful production of Ibsen in London. Shaw apparently did not share her enthusiasm for Maupassant's story, and later he denied that he had even read this "ultra romantic French novel."[47] Indeed, if the plan of the original were followed, the *scène à faire* of the resulting play would presumably represent the confrontation of the pure daughter and the erring mother, a tearful scene similar to the famous recognition scene in Augier's *Le Fils de Giboyer*.

In these circumstances Shaw evidently declined to follow the tried and true methods of the theater. Miss Achurch, a practical person, thereupon adapted *Yvette* for herself in a version called *Mrs. Daintry's Daughter.* For his part, Shaw developed his view of the matter in a play which he first named *Mrs Jarman's Profession*, a title which recalled the profession of Cashel Byron. This title he later changed to *Mrs Warren's Profession.*

The difference between *Mrs Warren's Profession* and such plays as *The Second Mrs. Tanqueray*, *Iris*, *Zaza*, or *Lady Windermere's Fan* is fundamental. The widespread interest in beautiful courtesans which is one of the more engaging aspects of nineteenth-century fiction had a twofold basis. On the one hand, it served to satisfy popular curiosity as to the ways of glamorous and expensive women whose intimacies only the very rich could afford; on the other, it justified the sedate lives of the virtuous by demonstrating the disadvantages of professional immorality. A favorite formula in this genre involved, as in Dumas's *Le Demimonde*, the efforts of elegant courtesans to rehabilitate themselves in good society through a subterfuge, which was invariably discovered. The fortunes of lower-class whores of the type of Zola's *Nana*, however, were almost exclusively in the domain of naturalistic literature. Such figures did not reach the stage for some time; and stories of the type of Lenormand's *Mixture* and Colette's *Gigi* belong to a more sophisticated environment than Shaw's London afforded.

In portraying Mrs. Warren, Shaw evidently meant to treat his material scientifically from the socialist viewpoint, that is to say, according to Marxist principles. It was customary in plays based on this theme to assume on the part of the protagonist some moral weakness which must be in the long run expiated. Shaw placed the blame, not on Mrs. Warren, but on the social system which in her case made a life of vice both necessary and attractive. From this viewpoint, the protagonist is not Mrs. Warren at all, but the social organization which perverted her, and it is society which is called to account in the play, not its victim.

Shaw did not go so far, however, as to exculpate Mrs. Warren completely. It was one thing to blame society for its sins, quite another thing to coddle Mrs. Warren for hers. Shaw did not intend to be sentimental about Mrs. Warren's choice of a career; moreover, her activities ran counter to his growing squeamishness in sexual matters. Mrs. Warren was therefore conceived in such a way as to inspire respect for her resourcefulness and disgust for her way of life. The resulting complex hardly makes for a consistent characterization. Mrs. Warren manages wonderfully well for three acts. In the fourth act she is mysteriously annihilated by the author. Her daughter, Vivie, in these circumstances, becomes completely incomprehensible. The play thus demonstrates impressively the disadvantages of a character conceived a priori in terms, not of life, but of the abstraction it is intended to embody. This difficulty was pervasive in Shaw's plays. He was, at bottom, an allegorist, intent not on realizing a character, but on working out a doctrine.

Mrs Warren's Profession is a well-made play manufactured according to the rigid tenets of what Shaw was later to call "Sardoodledom." Vivie, the highly cultivated daughter of a highly successful whorehouse madam, is enjoying a romance with Frank Gardner, the disrespectful son of the local rector. It turns out that Vivie's young man is in all likelihood her half-brother, the fruit of the rector's wild oats, long ago sowed in the company, so to speak, of Vivie's mother. Upon making this discovery, Vivie disowns both her mother and her lover and embarks on a professional career as a legal actuary.

Obviously this play turns, like *Widowers' Houses*, upon a most improbable set of coincidences. What is interesting in it is, however, not the material but the manner in which it is managed. In this regard Shaw demonstrated remarkable originality. From Ibsen and from Samuel Butler he had learned that the ties which traditionally bind parents to children are social conventions which need not be treated as if they had divine sanction, even though they figure prominently among the Commandments. With these advanced attitudes, his own filial relations certainly predisposed him to concur, and the need to set forth these attitudes, together with his ideas regarding the economic basis of Mrs. Warren's profession, necessarily gave his play a certain doctrinal stiffness. In her scenes with the romantic Mr. Praed, Vivie makes her position as a liberated woman extremely clear. Mrs. Warren is formed in the image of the mothers in Kotzebue's plays. Her daughter is as hard as stone. Their confrontation provides an interesting contrast:

VIVIE: Are you my mother?

MRS WARREN (*appalled*): Am I your mother? Oh Vivie!

VIVIE: Then where are our relatives—my father—our family friends? You claim the rights of a mother: the right to call me fool and child; to speak to me as no woman in authority over me at college dare speak to me; to dictate my way of life; and to force on me the acquaintance of a brute whom anyone can see to be the most vicious sort of London man about town. Before I give myself the trouble to resist such claims, I may as well find out whether they have any real existence.

MRS WARREN (*distressed, throwing herself on her knees*): Oh no, no.
Stop, stop. I a m your mother: I swear it. . . .[48]

Having shown the relationship of mother and daughter in this manner,
Shaw proceeds to demonstrate in the sequel that the two are actually
very much alike, save that the one makes no secret of her hardness, while
the other cloaks it with traditional sentimentality. The revelation of the
mother's profession is a *coup de théâtre* analogous to that in which the
noble son of the cynical journalist Giboyer in Augier's play discovers
how his father prostituted himself for his sake.

Augier's scene is shamelessly sentimental by any standards, but it made
many people weep, and its cathartic effect is beyond question. Shaw's
scene is powerful in another way. When Mrs. Warren steps out of her
conventional role as self-sacrificing mother, she reveals herself as a hardheaded career woman with no nonsense about her, and Vivie for the first
time feels drawn to her. She understands that they are fellow workers,
faced with a similar problem and engaged in a common cause:

VIVIE (*more and more moved*): Mother, suppose we were both as poor
as you were in those wretched old days, are you quite sure that you
wouldnt advise me to try the Waterloo bar, or marry a laborer, or
even go into the factory?

MRS WARREN (*indignantly*): Of course not. What sort of mother do
you take me for? How could you keep your self-respect in such star-
vation and slavery? . . . Where would we be now if we'd minded the
clergyman's foolishness? Scrubbing floors for one and sixpence a day
and nothing to look forward to but the workhouse infirmary. Dont
you be led astray by people who dont know the world, my girl. . . . [49]

The consequence of this discovery is that Vivie feels such a sudden
surge of affection for her mother that young Frank Gardner—for all his
profligacy as much a snob as the Trollopian rector, his father—is moved
to protest. This generous flow of sympathy, however, is short-lived. It is
quickly transformed into disgust when Vivie learns that her mother is
now operating a string of profitable bawdy-houses on the Continent.

The second reversal is confusing. It is certainly conceivable that Vivie
might sympathize with her mother as a woman, and at the same time
detest her profession. The difficulty is that she is presented as a rigorously logical person, and is therefore quite unable to reconcile her sympathy with her disgust. In the case of Augier's *Le Fils de Giboyer* the
situation is simpler. As between father and son, in that play, the emotional current springs spontaneously from the heart, is completely sentimental and irrational, and may be accepted unequivocally on that basis.

Vivie's reaction, however, is puzzling. She agrees in theory that as between a life of misery and a life of sin, the latter is the only sensible choice. But she cannot reconcile the theory with the fact and, faced with the moral consequences of her mother's logic, she is quite swept away by her revulsion. She tells Crofts, her mother's financial backer:

> VIVIE: . . . When I think of the society that tolerates you, and the laws that protect you! when I think of how helpless nine out of ten young girls would be in the hands of you and my mother! the unmentionable woman and her capitalist bully—
>
> CROFTS (*livid*): Damn you!
>
> VIVIE: You need not. I feel among the damned already.[50]

Vivie's disgust would be comprehensible if it were caused, not by her objection to a life of professional sexuality, but by Crofts's demonstration of the manner in which capital exploits this type of labor. Logically, she should be equally nauseated if he revealed that he cleared his 35 per cent out of a venture involving the employment of young girls in a paint factory. But it is not Crofts's exploitation of labor that revolts Vivie. It is the nature of his enterprise. She is by temperament a Puritan, and evidently a prig, and she detests the subversion of womanhood to the point where all sexuality becomes repugnant to her. The result of these colloquies, together with the sudden revelation that in pursuing her romance with Frank she was on the verge of incest, apparently causes her to renounce love forever.[51]

Thus, in the fourth act, two days after meeting her mother, Vivie has become, to everyone's astonishment, a "woman of business, permanently single, and permanently unromantic." She has also become too sqeamish to speak the words that describe her mother's occupation. She can barely bring herself to write them on a piece of paper. Obviously she has suffered a trauma of impressive proportions which would, in a later age, send her for a time to a psychoanalyst. As it is, at twenty, she has become a New Woman.

Mrs Warren's Profession is obviously no masterpiece, but it is a much better play than *Widowers' Houses*. The thesis is the same, and the characters are in much the same relation to one another: Sartorius is to Trench as Mrs. Warren is to Vivie. Both young people derive their income from a tainted source, and in each case the discovery of this fact is the turning point of the play. The difference is that, while Trench accepts, with disturbing cynicism, the evil system that supports him, Vivie Warren rejects it.

In this play Shaw's dramatic method becomes clear enough to define. Essentially this method involves a revaluation of values, the result of their translation into economic terms. The application of rational analysis to relations which are customarily treated as unquestionable; the substitution of Hobbesian postulates for the conventional axioms of Christian morality—so that all actions become explicable on the basis of relatively enlightened self-interest—give an air of novelty to situations which are in fact resolved more or less in accordance with normal patterns. The outcome of a Shavian comedy is seldom shocking; what is surprising is the motivation. It is along such lines that Shaw developed what he called scientific natural history.

In the case of *Mrs Warren's Profession* the scientific method proved too much. Shaw justified Mrs. Warren's choice of profession, but he obviously did not mean to justify the profession. He was at heart as squeamish as Vivie, and the thought of Mrs. Warren's way of life filled him with disgust. But he was revolted even more by the cultural system which makes prostitution a sensible alternative to poverty. He therefore used Mrs. Warren to reproach society for its sins, then had recourse to Vivie to reproach Mrs. Warren for hers. In the end, having said some very shocking things about social morality, he concluded the play on an impeccably moral note.

Shaw prided himself on his moral sense. A work of the first order, he wrote, is one "in which morality is original and ready-made," and he considered that Ibsen wrote plays of this order.[52] In fact, Ibsen had no interest in any moral system. It was the pressure of an inflexible system operating on the individual with the force of law that provided him with the stuff of drama.

Shaw, however, was a moralist. He wished to substitute for the rigid morality of the day a system which responded more elastically to the requirements of the individual situation, but he had no idea of doing away with morality altogether. The tyranny of his conscience is everywhere apparent in his thinking. Ibsen was firm in rejecting all absolutes. Shaw was a relativist only in theory. He rejected the ideals of society not because they were ideals, but because they were conventional. He insisted on the necessity for subjecting current standards to rational analysis, but it was important to him to maintain standards. Accordingly, in his plays the rationalization is often extraordinary, but the conclusion is usually commonplace. It is not the actions of his characters that are surprising. It is the reasons they give for what they do.

In *Mrs Warren's Profession*, Mrs. Warren's motives are readily comprehensible, and she is extremely articulate in explaining them. Vivie, however, is hardly realized. Her character remains mysterious throughout the play. In all likelihood Shaw had met girls like Vivie in the circles he frequented; but at this time this type of young woman had not been studied carefully, and it is clear that Shaw did not know quite what to make of her. As he saw her at this point of her development, the New Woman was a manly transvestite, with a handshake that made strong men wince, and a desire to relax after a hard day's work with a glass of whisky, a good cigar, and a detective story. It is unlikely that this is what Ibsen's Nora would have become after a year or two at Newnham College.

The desexualization of Vivie is perhaps the most significant point in her characterization. It anticipates the desexualization of Don Juan in the inferno scene of *Man and Superman*, and his decision to forsake the romantic pleasures of his colleagues in hell for the cool intellectualism of the saints in Paradise. The manner in which Vivie reaches this state foreshadows also a prime motive in Shaw's future dramatic method. For Vivie the need to be herself is paramount, but in order to satisfy this need it is necessary for her to discover what that self is. The play is shaped, therefore, in such a way as to bring about the climactic situation in which this moment of self-revelation can take place, and the crisis of identity also initiates a reversal of the action. This anagnorisis became central in Shaw's later plays from *Arms and the Man* to *Heartbreak House*, and the combination of discovery and reversal as central elements in these plays gives them a curiously classical effect.

It would be a mistake, however, to push the Aristotelian analogy too far. Shaw's use of the classical agnition is essentially modern. The ancients made much use of mistaken identities and disguises for comedic purposes, but recognition in ancient drama—even in tragedy—is seldom a matter of the revelation of character. Oedipus discovers at some cost who he is, not what he is. The dramatic unmasking of character does not appear to antedate Shakespeare: psychology is a relatively recent preoccupation in the theater. The concentration on the soul, and its infirmities, which characterizes the major dramatists of our time is perhaps the most significant of the distinctions between ancient and modern drama. In this regard, Shaw was certainly not a pioneer. He was not primarily a psychologist in the theater. But he was an important influence on those who were.

In his letter to Golding Bright, Shaw noted that his first three plays were criticisms of a special phase, the capitalist phase, of modern social organization, and their purpose was to make people thoroughly uncomfortable whilst entertaining them artistically. But my four subsequent plays . . . are not "realistic" plays. They deal with life at large, with human nature as it presents itself through all economic and social phases. "Arms & the Man" is the comedy of youthful romance and disillusion; "Candida" is the poetry of the Wife & Mother—the Virgin Mother in the true sense. . . .[53]

The inference is that in the *Pleasant Plays* Shaw meant to represent psychological processes of a universal nature, while in the earlier plays he meant to portray the reactions of individuals to the evils peculiar to a capitalist society. The distinction, then, is largely one of emphasis, but it will not bear scrutiny. There is no reason to suppose that human nature in its universal aspect is different from human nature under capitalist auspices. Behavior may show the effects of one or another set of economic pressures, but it would be hasty to conclude that the individual nature is the result of its economic environment. The spirit of compromise which Trench exemplifies in *Widowers' Houses* may seem at work both in *Arms and the Man* and in *Candida*; and there is nothing of a psychological nature in *The Philanderer* that would not work as well, or better, under feudalism. But the *Pleasant Plays* are not thesis plays. The characters are therefore relatively free of doctrinal control. Raina is immediately acceptable. Candida is, at least, believable—these characters may be called realistic. Vivie, on the other hand, is a puppet. As a character she demonstrates vividly the disadvantages of the didactic method in the drama.

During these years Shaw insisted that the chief value of his plays lay in their utility.[54] Twenty-five years later, he was no longer so eager to advance the utilitarian aspect of his comedies as their principal justification. He had long thought of Ibsen as primarily a utilitarian writer. In 1895 he wrote: "the highest genius . . . is always intensely utilitarian."[55] However, in 1898, Ibsen in one of his rare speeches had made his literary position clear: "I have been more the poet and less the social philosopher than people generally seem inclined to believe. . . . My task has been the description of humanity. . . ."[56] It took some time for Shaw to arrive at this position; but in one of the autobiographical pieces he wrote after the First World War, he defined himself in much the same terms. He was, he declared, an artist first, and only secondarily a social philosopher:

There is an economic link between Cashel Byron, Sartorius, Mrs Warren and Undershaft, all of them prospering in questionable activi-

ties. But would anyone but a buffle headed idiot of a university
professor, half-crazy with correcting examination papers, infer that
all my plays were written as economic essays, and not as plays of life,
character, and human destiny like those of Shakespeare or Euripides . . . ?[57]

For Shaw realism was not a technique that involved the laboratory
methods of the school of Médan. The realistic imagination was "the
power to imagine things as they are without actually sensing them."[58]
Shaw was consciously engaged on the side of that down-to-earth view of
life which realistic writers long before the time of Boccaccio had advanced against the idealistic attitudes of feudal Christianity. All succeeding ages in some measure inherited this issue. The result is a polarity of
truly impressive proportions, the workings of which are demonstrable at
every stage of Western culture, and particularly clear in the latter half
of the nineteenth century, when realism became a political influence.

Neither Trench in *Widowers' Houses*, nor Vivie in *Mrs Warren's
Profession*, can be considered, from this point of view, realistic characters. It would be realistic for Trench to maintain his aristocratic aloof-
ness and, while persisting in his contempt for Sartorius, to go on living
comfortably on the income he provided. Normally, Vivie would despise
her mother without giving up her monthly tribute. Both Trench and
Vivie are romantic characters, idealists, each in his way. Trench would
rather be a scoundrel than a hypocrite. He accepts his fate. Vivie does
not. She withdraws from the world into the somber fastnesses of
Chancery Lane where young women, presumably, are safe from the
intrusions of passion. If we consider these to be plays of *déclassement*,
like *Caste*, the novelty is that instead of demonstrating the native nobility of the lower classes, as is usual in plays of this type, Shaw's plays
demonstrate their less savory side. Their realism is, however, a relative
matter. In *Mrs Warren's Profession* the tainted money is unacceptable
even to the supposedly unprincipled young man, a practical person who
is resolved above all not to waste his life in useful labor:

FRANK . . . : I cant marry her now.
PRAED (*sternly*): Frank! Let me tell you, Gardner, that if you desert her
now, you will behave very despicably.
FRANK: Good old Praddy! Ever chivalrous! But you mistake: it's not the
moral aspect of the case: it's the money aspect. I really cant bring
myself to touch the old woman's money now.
PRAED: And was that what you were going to marry on?
FRANK: What else? . . .[59]

The inconsistency of viewpoint in these two plays, separated as they were by the interval of a year, is easily explicable. Shaw had a point to make in the theater, and he took his responsibilities in this respect with all the seriousness of which his nature was capable. But in order to make a point in the theater it is necessary to have an audience. Shaw's experience with his first play amply proved Archer's contention that unpleasant plays had no place on the Victorian stage. In consequence, having proved his metal, he began to veer sharply in the direction of producible drama. *Mrs Warren's Profession* was a play on an unpleasant subject, but it was not really an unpleasant play. Its protagonist was a modest girl who—whatever she said—acted according to the strictest standards of morality. Vivie's story was certainly not sentimental, but it was not unromantic.

The attempt did not succeed. Shaw read the play to the Independent Theatre, which, in view of the difficulty of the theme, declined to produce it. In his preface to the published edition Shaw blamed its rejection on the censor. "The play was ready; the Independent Theatre was ready; two actresses, Mrs Theodore Wright and Miss Janet Achurch . . . were ready; but the mere existence of the Censorship, without action or knowledge of the play on its part, was sufficient to paralyze all these forces."[60] His account of the matter was not entirely candid. The Independent Theatre, a private society, was immune from censorship. It was Grein who had vetoed the production.

In 1898 Shaw applied to the censor for a license. It was refused. Shaw then made drastic revisions, including the omission of the second act, deleted all references to Mrs. Warren's profession, and again asked for a license. This version was provisionally approved on 19 March 1898. Three years later, the London Stage Society, which Grein inaugurated in July 1899, decided, over his objections, to produce the play in its original form. After innumerable difficulties in securing a theater, *Mrs Warren's Profession* in the unlicensed version, was given two private performances on January 5 and 6, 1902. It was thoroughly denounced in the press. Even Archer reproached Shaw for handling such a subject since "he could not touch pitch without wallowing in it." He later explained his metaphor with an even stranger comment: "What is fundamentally intolerable in the play is its almost all-pervading flippancy of tone."[61]

Twenty-three years later, after the play had been performed many times abroad, the ban was lifted in England. *Mrs Warren's Profession* was first produced publicly on 27 July 1925 in Birmingham and, some

months later, in London. By that time it was no long
cent, and it enjoyed a profitable run of sixty-eight
ultimately, *Mrs Warren's Profession* achieved acce
be remarkable.

By this time Shaw had long experienced the bittersweet sa .
cess. All his life he affected to despise public taste, but he wasted no .
in adapting himself to it. His standards were high, but he was an eminently practical literary workman who intended to be paid well for his
work. Unlike artists like Ghelderode, of whom hardly anyone in England
had heard until after he was dead, Shaw was determined to gain a public
hearing while he was among those present. He was by nature a critic,
and his art was medicinal; but he did not insist, like Zola, on making a
virtue of its unpleasantness. If his critical pills required sugar-coating to
make them palatable, he was entirely willing to provide the means. He
had already written:

> . . . It is poets and artists who spend their lives in trying to make the
> unreal real; whereas the ordinary man's life-struggle is to escape from
> reality, to avoid all avoidable facts and deceive himself as to the real
> nature of those he cannot avoid. . . . Hence, the more unnatural,
> impossible, unreasonable, and morally fraudulent a theatrical enter-
> tainment is, the better he likes it. He abhors the play with a purpose,
> because it says to him, "Here, sir, is a fact which you ought to attend
> to." This, however, produces the happy result that the great dramatic
> poets, who are all incorrigible moralists and preachers, are forced to
> produce plays of extraordinary interest in order to induce our audi-
> ences of shirkers and dreamers to swallow the pill.[62]

The practical result of these ideas was the *Pleasant Plays.*

THE PLEASANT PLAYS

A*rms and the Man* was written in the early months of 1894, toward the end of Shaw's stint as a music critic. About the beginning of the year, Florence Farr secured the backing of Mrs. Annie Horniman for a season of "advanced" plays to be performed at the Avenue Theatre in the West End. Mrs. Horniman did not wish to publicize her theatrical ventures. She remained anonymous. Florence Farr arranged for a first bill which included Yeats's *The Land of Heart's Desire* and John Todhunter's *A Comedy of Sighs*. Dr. Todhunter's play had a bad reception and had to be withdrawn, leaving Miss Farr at a loss for a replacement. In this emergency she asked Shaw for permission to revive *Widowers' Houses*, in which she had played Blanche. Shaw promised instead to provide her with a new play. In a few weeks he put together *Arms and the Man*.

Under Shaw's direction, with George R. Ross as stage manager, the play went immediately into rehearsal, and opened on 21 April 1894, with an excellent cast of young people. Miss Farr played Louka; Alma Murray was Raina; Yorke Stephens played Bluntschli. The opening performance was roundly applauded, and Shaw was called to the stage to take a bow. It was on this occasion that, on hearing a solitary hiss from the audience, Shaw turned to his detractor with the celebrated quip—"I quite agree with you, sir, but what can two do against so many?"[1]

The notices were favorable. Walkley wrote that the play was a unique piece of work. Archer declared it was quite as funny as *Charley's Aunt* or Lumley's *The New Boy*, "a psychological extravaganza, in which drama, farce and Gilbertian irony keep flashing past the bewildered eye. . . ."[2] But *Arms and the Man* was not a success. With Yeats's play as a curtain-raiser it was kept on the stage for eleven weeks at a loss. It earned a total gross of £1777, recouping half the investment. It is said that His Royal Highness the prince of Wales, later Edward VII, went to see it and pronounced the author mad.

Richard Mansfield, however, saw a performance and was attracted by the idea of presenting it in his forthcoming American tour. The play had certain drawbacks, among them the fact that Bluntschli hardly appears in the second act, a grave fault in the traditional *numérotage* of scenes. In spite of this defect, Mansfield's wife, Beatrice Cameron, persuaded him to buy the play, and Mansfield presented it in New York in September 1894 at the Herald Square Theatre. There was some difficulty about the casting. Shaw had insisted that Mansfield play Sergius, which he considered the better and more difficult part. Mansfield, however, fancied himself as Bluntschli. He was applauded, but the play did no better in New York than in London.

It was, Mansfield complained, the weakest play in his repertory. Nevertheless he considered that it added to his prestige, and he kept it before his public throughout the tour.[3] From Shaw's viewpoint, at least, it was a profitable venture. *Arms and the Man* brought him something over £100 in royalties. It was the largest sum he had ever earned through his writings, and for the first time he felt himself to be a successful playwright.

In an essay called "A Dramatic Realist to his Critics," published in the *New Review*, September 1894, Shaw wrote an exhaustive account of the circumstances attending the composition of the play. From this it appears that his material was the fruit of considerable research, including a careful analysis of the account of the Serbo-Bulgarian war in the *Annual Register* for 1885. This assertion is borne out by the notes he made on the flyleaf of his first draft of the play.[4] But in an interview printed in the *Pall Mall Gazette* some months before the *New Review* article, he had pretended airily that the whole enterprise was in the nature of a lark:

> A month or so ago I thought that Miss Farr might be wanting a play for her Enterprise at the Avenue. It struck me that some interest might be got from the clash of romantic ideal with cold, logical democracy. The play was nearly finished before I settled on its locality. I wanted a war as a background. Now, I am absolutely ignorant of history and geography; so I went about among my friends and asked if they knew of any wars. They told me of several from the Trojan to the Franco-German. At last Sidney Webb told me of the Servo-Bulgarian war, which was the very thing. Put a Republican—

say a Swiss—into the tyrant-ridden East and there you are. So I
looked up Bulgaria and Servia in an Atlas, made all the names of the
characters end in "off" and the play was complete.[5]

The flippancy of this account is characteristic of Shaw, but it is certainly true that he knew little about war in general, and still less about
the war in the Balkans. It is likely that he had read an article on war that
General Wolesley had published some years before in the *Fortnightly
Review*, and an article called "The Philosophy of Courage" published
by General Horace Porter in the *Century*. He seems to have been familiar also with General Marbot's account of the battle of Wagram, Alexander Kinglake's *Invasion of the Crimea* (1887), and some solid works of
realistic war-fiction such as *War and Peace* and Zola's *La Débâcle*
(1892). These gave him some idea of conditions at the front.[6] As for the
Bulgarian situation, he was dependent on the *Annual Register* and what
casual information was available. Sergius Stepniak, a Russian nihilist then
living in London, was his principal informant, and apparently he introduced Shaw to a Russian named Esper Alexandrovitch Serebryakov,
who had commanded the Bulgarian naval forces in the Danube and was
able to tell him something about the terrain. Beyond this it is difficult to
see where Shaw found time to do research, or why further research was
necessary. *Arms and the Man* did not need careful documentation. Its
detail and its coloring were purely theatrical. As Shaw intimated in the
Pall Mall Gazette, the play could have been set in any country of Eastern Europe in the course of almost any war.[7]

Technically *Arms and the Man* is a textbook example of the well-made
play. The exposition is at the same time thrilling and informative. It
includes everything that is necessary for the development of the action.
The complication is gratifyingly symmetrical. It involves the unmasking
of Sergius by Louka, and the unmasking of Raina by Bluntschli. The
confrontation of Sergius and Bluntschli culminates in the climactic scene
which precipitates the denouement. This is brought about, in accordance
with the best Scribean practice, through the convergence of the main
plot and the subplot, the superposition of the Bluntschli-Raina-Sergius
triangle—the triangle of the principals—upon the triangle involving
Sergius, Louka, and Nicola, the triangle of the servants. As the two plots
are interrelated through Sergius, the detonation of the one brings about
the resolution of the other. Nothing neater—or more artificial—can be
imagined. It is clear that by 1894 Shaw had mastered the essentials of the
art of playmaking.

Although *Arms and the Man* made, and still makes, an effect of brilliant originality, it is only the obliquity of the approach that is novel. The story itself belongs to the ages; it is the story of Angelica and Medoro in the *Orlando furioso*, one of the most famous stories in the world. It was customary in late versions of this story for the enemy soldier to return after the war in order to claim the lady who helped him in his desperate hour. This normally involved a duel with a local rival, whom he regularly vanquished. In this form the story of the lady and the soldier retained its popularity for centuries and continues to do so. The results in our day vary from Ouida's *Under Two Flags* to Giraudoux's *Siegfried*.

While this formula was a normal attribute of military melodrama, the representation of war as a muddy business, boring, barbarous, and dependent for its outcome upon chance, was relatively new to the theater. It was a viewpoint which had been found shocking when Tolstoy advanced it in *War and Peace* (1865–72), and it still seemed shocking in the 1890's. In England Robertson had made a vague gesture at this sort of realism in *Ours* (1866) and in *War* (1871); but love and heroism were the warp and filler of military melodrama. In the theater it was a matter of faith that only the brave deserve the fair and that native nobility was best demonstrated on the field of battle. Shaw did not venture to disturb so venerable a tradition. In his depiction of war he did not break new ground; he simply rushed in boisterously where angels feared to tread.

The scene of the fugitive soldier entering the lady's bedroom through the open window was by 1894 more or less commonplace. In England it had been used twenty years before in Tom Taylor's *Lady Clancarty; or, Wedded and Wooed* (1874), and quite recently it had seen service in Sardou's *Madame Sans-Gêne* (Paris, 1893). In levying on Shaw's play for *The Chocolate Soldier*, Oscar Straus's librettists did no more than to reclaim for the popular stage what Shaw had originally borrowed from it. In one respect Shaw's treatment was novel. Where normally the narrative was expected to justify itself purely as entertainment, Shaw made use of it for the propagation of an idea.

The idea was neither original nor complex, but it was amply sufficient to transform a run-of-the-mill comedy into something worth talking about. *Arms and the Man* has to do with the contrast between illusion and reality. It has the importance of a play that deals with large issues. In this regard Straus cannily forbore to follow Shaw's example. The result was that *The Chocolate Soldier* was a resounding success, while *Arms and the Man*, by professional standards, was generally accounted a failure.

For Shaw, however, the production of his play was an affair of moment. It indicated, for the first time, the direction in which his talent lay. It also revealed a fund of dramatic material much more suited to his purpose than the areas covered by Dumas, Augier, and the other writers of the thesis play. At this point in his career, Shaw understood that success in the theater depended upon the use of theatrical methods rather than the methods of the debating platform or the pulpit. It was a precept he could not long keep in mind, but it had an important influence on the *Pleasant Plays*. Moreover, in *Arms and the Man* he developed a technique through which the revelation of character is made to coincide with the ideological development of the action. This technique served him well throughout his life as a dramatist.

Some years later, in *Androcles and the Lion*, Lavinia was to tell Ferrovius: "You will find your true faith in your hour of trial." Henceforth it became Shaw's principal business as a playwright to devise hours of trial in which his characters might discover their identity. It is in this respect that the plays of Shaw's middle period differ from their Scribean models. While the Scribean plays normally unfold a narrative involving the fortunes of the hero, in Shaw's comedies the denouement is not concerned with the protagonist's success or failure, but with his attainment of a higher level of self-awareness. Such is the situation in *Arms and the Man.*

The Bulgarian Arcadia which Bluntschli unwittingly invades in his flight from the battlefield is a world of make-believe in which the principal characters are masquerading in ideal disguises which have little to do with their reality. In this world Sergius and Raina are cast as romantic lovers in the tradition of Viennese operetta. For a time they find their roles enjoyable and take pains to act in conformity with them. But their parts require unusual exertions, and their maintenance proves to be an embarrassing nuisance. The scene in which they drop their poses is the climax of the play. In accordance with received rules of playmaking it is properly deferred until the end of the action; but it is elaborately prepared for from the very first scene and can therefore occasion no shock when it happens. The pleasure of the final sequence is thus the astonishing occurrence of what is entirely foreseeable from the beginning. Such is the normal result of the well-made play, but this effect, being thoroughly anticipated, requires, as always, some accentuation of the denouement by way of an unexpected disclosure. In *Arms and the Man*, the final twist, the catachresis consequent on the revelation of Bluntschli's true character, serves this purpose admirably.

In the plan of the action, Sergius and Bluntschli are presented as contraries. Raina passes from the one to the other, and in the process is redefined into something more closely approximating her true self. The action thus describes an educational experience which foreshadows the education of Cleopatra, Eliza Doolittle, and Barbara Undershaft, each of whom is given a similar lesson in realism. Bluntschli and Sergius are both brave men, but only Bluntschli is adult. The action therefore represents also the growing-up of Sergius, in a manner which parallels the education of Raina.

For his models, Shaw is said to have looked to his friends. Bluntschli is supposedly drawn after Sidney Webb, who was in fact the son of an innkeeper. Sergius was presumably suggested by Robert Cunninghame Graham. The former was a serious, factually minded civil servant, the other a flashy adventurer who claimed descent from a Scottish king.[8]

The idea that it is indispensable in studying the works of a writer to find among his acquaintances real people with whom to identify the characters of his fancy is the source of much pleasant detective work. It is based on the assumption that art is primarily mimetic and that, in consequence, the dramatic artist spends his time in transferring his experience to the stage much as a photographer records his impressions on film. But art implies a more serious involvement with life than the representation of the outer world. It has psychic connotations which are of the utmost significance to the artist, and which normally account for his artistic creativity. For a writer the desire to represent the figures of external experience is usually based on his need to use reality as a means of recreating his inner life, very much as in reverie one weaves together the figments of experience into a more meaningful texture. It is evident that the characters of a play, however derived, live exclusively with the life of the artist.

Drama is undoubtedly in some sense mimetic; but it must be obvious that what the playwright represents in the theater is not the outer world —no matter how close the semblance may seem—but an inner landscape peopled with figures which are all, more or less recognizably, aspects of himself. Like the figures of dreams, these personages wear a variety of disguises, and some are made to resemble real people so closely as to approximate identity, until one reflects upon the nature of the things the dreamer makes them do. Thus a play, whatever its manifest action, is likely to reveal upon careful scrutiny the impress of its shaping principles, that is to say, the movements of the artist's inner life, his soul.

Sergius and Bluntschli haunt the plays of Shaw very much as Brand

and Peer Gynt recur in the works of Ibsen. It is reasonable to assume, therefore, that whatever relation they may have had to real people, essentially these characters represent significant elements of the author's personality which he found it necessary to reconcile in a work of art. In Ibsen's case, it requires no very sharp eye to discern in characters so far abstracted as Brand and Peer Gynt the fundamental dialectic of his personality. Shaw was infinitely more reticent. While Ibsen emerged occasionally in public and attempted to prod his readers into recognizing him in his plays, Shaw remained hidden all his life behind the preposterous self-portrait he foisted on the world. "All autobiographies," he wrote in his autobiography, "are lies; I do not mean unconscious, unintentional lies; I mean deliberate lies."[9]

Nevertheless Shaw's need to become visible was as great as Ibsen's, or greater. In one of his most sincere declarations he directed attention, very much as Ibsen had, to the place where he might actually be found:

> I have had no heroic adventures. Things have not happened to me, on the contrary, it is I who have happened to them; and all my happenings have taken the form of books and plays. Read them, or spectate them, and you have my whole story. . . . The best autobiographies are confessions; but if a man is a deep writer all his works are confessions.[10]

Shaw was a deep writer. There is no doubt that his plays are, in one way or another, confessions, and it is interesting that he himself was aware of it. But confessions of this sort are normally defensive operations framed to conceal less agreeable truths. It is certainly possible to catch a glimpse of Shaw in *Widowers' Houses*, somewhere between Trench and Lickcheese. He publicly identified himself with Charteris in *The Philanderer*. But in that play one is tempted rather to identify Shaw with Grace Tranfield than with her suitor, and there is a strong hint of Shaw in Vivie Warren. But no single character is adequate to represent the psychic debate which it was Shaw's aim to exhibit on the stage. This was evidently a three-sided business. To represent it properly it was necessary to imagine dialectically opposed characters whose opposition might be resolved, but whose viewpoints were irreconcilable. Ibsen had attempted to synthesize Brand and Peer Gynt in the person of the Emperor Julian, but *Emperor and Galilean* ends in the triumph of the Brand-figure, the Galilean aspect of Ibsen's nature, and the Third Kingdom toward which his later plays are oriented is unreachable, an ideal realized only in death. With Shaw, also, the synthesis is never more than provisional. He attempted to achieve it in fantasy in play after play, until at last, after *Back to Methuselah*, he gave up the attempt. But while the psychic conflict was never resolved, the dramatic method was eminently fruitful. It was in this manner that he was really able to extract the quintessence of Ibsenism.

Arms and the Man is a comic play, contrived according to rule, and the last place to which one would look for the artist's candid self-portrait. But its plot was singularly well suited to Shaw's purpose. Accordingly, the play wrote itself quickly and easily and was adorned with such wit and warmth as none of his earlier plays possessed. It is still one of his most useful and most enjoyable comedies, with that air of meaning more than is said which is everywhere the mark of successful drama. In its essential patterns *Arms and the Man* is arranged very simply in terms of the rivalry of Sergius and Bluntschli, with Raina as the center of tension, but there is no real tug of war. The action is largely a description of Raina's development as a woman. She is, to begin with, completely identified with Sergius. When Bluntschli appears, she is moved to reject Sergius and to identify herself with Bluntschli—but only on condition that he assume in her mind something of the romantic character of Sergius. Bluntschli is quite willing to accept this condition. The result is that he and Sergius somehow exchange characters; the idealist is seen to be a realist, and the realist reveals himself as an idealist.

From a psychological viewpoint it would seem that it is in Raina that Shaw prefigured his innermost self, his ego, poised somewhat precariously between the conflicting elements of his nature. If it seems preposterous that so boisterous a nature as Shaw's should choose to portray itself as a young girl, we may recall what we know of his early life—his timidity, his passivity, his long dependence on his mother, his extensive virginity, his pointless and well-publicized philanderings, his excessive daintiness, and the disgust with which, as he says, sexual contacts inspired him. All this indicates a temperament which accords ill with our normal ideas of virility.

In the light of these biographical details, all furnished by himself, it is certainly possible to assume that in his childhood Shaw suffered a trauma that left him so deeply unmanned as to require an immensely long lifetime of unceasing activity to compensate for the injury. If this is true, it must be admitted that in the course of the years he offered himself astonishing proofs of vigor. Nevertheless in his plays he seems to have been deeply identified more often with his women than with his men.

There is no evidence that he had any unusual insight into the female mentality. His women fall into rather obvious molds. Masterful women of the type of Lady Cicely or Candida impressed him most. He had a vivid impression of the sort of sexless spinster represented by Vivie Warren. But women of normally passionate nature seem to have inspired him mainly with fear and therefore showed clear traces of the vampire. The most manageable women in his canon were those who are amenable to the tutelage of a masterful male. These generally resulted in delightful characterizations. The suggestion is therefore tempting that the education of Raina, as well as that of Cleopatra, Eliza, Barbara, and Ellie Dunn represents in some sense the education of Shaw.

Of the male characters in *Arms and the Man* it was doubtless Sergius, not Bluntschli, who was intended to be the protagonist of the action. Sergius binds together the two narrative lines and is the chief source of the comic effect. It is usual to play him as something of a clown, extravagantly costumed, and excessively mannered. This was certainly not Shaw's intention. Everything indicates that, while Shaw meant to ridicule his extravagance as a character, he took the problem of Sergius quite seriously and intended his comic anguish to border on the tragic. Sergius was meant to elicit a pang.

Shaw's idea of comedy was by this time pretty well crystallized. His sense of the absurd was as keen as Ibsen's; his humor, broader. He was gayer than Molière, but at bottom his mood, like that of all great masters of comedy, was melancholy. It was part of his personal tragedy that, even when he had achieved great success as a comedic dramatist, his audience was disposed to share with him the fun, but not the pathos of the jest. Like Molière, whom he much admired, he knew well that the comic writer's vocation is *faire rire les honnêtes gens*. But he had an abiding distrust of laughter. He preferred to evoke the pleasure of tears. He wrote:

> Sometimes the stage custom is not only obsolete, but fundamentally wrong: for instance, in the simple case of laughter and tears, in which it deals too liberally, it is certainly not based on the fact, easily discoverable in real life, that tears in adult life are the natural expression of happiness, as laughter is at all ages the natural recognition of destruction, confusion and ruin. When a comedy of mine is performed, it is nothing to me that the spectators laugh—any fool can make an audience laugh. I want to see how many of them, laughing or grave, have tears in their eyes. And this result cannot be achieved, even by actors who thoroughly understand my purpose, except through an artistic beauty of execution unattainable without long and arduous practice, and an effort which my plays probably do not seem serious enough to call forth.[11]

It would be a mistake to see in this passage only the paradox. People do not cry, ordinarily, when they are happy, but they often cry when they are touched. If Shaw really believed that tears are the sign of happiness, then it must be that for him, as for many others, happiness was sad. Shaw's sense of absurdity is proverbial, but his view of life was at no time comic in the joyful sense. Chekhov also saw life under the aspect of absurdity. He insisted that *The Three Sisters* was a comedy, and *The Cherry Orchard* a farce, but it is difficult to avoid feeling the pathos of these plays. At any rate, his comedies make people cry. Shaw, however, saw modern society as a shocking exhibition of stupidity and waste. In such circumstances, laughter would be a sign either of imbecility or of the hysterical conversion of pain. Shaw never forgot that his father, on learning that he was ruined financially, had burst into a fit of uncontrollable laughter. "My father," he noted in an autobiographical sketch, "found something in a funeral which tickled his sense of humor, and this characteristic I have inherited."[12]

Laughter, in Shaw's view, was aggressive. To laugh was to belittle, or even to destroy, the object. Tears, on the other hand, were a sign of identification, a display of affirmative character. Where laughter was divisive, tears were a token of human kinship. The result of such thinking, obviously, was to assimilate comedy to tragedy, and this perhaps was what Shaw, at bottom, had in mind. He did not share the world's opinion of the ridiculous, any more than he shared its idea of the sublime.

In the stage directions of *Arms and the Man*, Sergius is said to be:

> a tall, romantically handsome man, with the physical hardihood, the high spirit, and the susceptible imagination of an untamed mountain chieftain. But his remarkable personal distinction is of a characteristically civilized type. The ridges of his eyebrows, curving with a ram's horn twist around the marked projections at the outer corners, his jealously observant eye, his nose, thin, keen, and apprehensive in spite of the pugnacious high bridge and large nostril, his assertive chin, would not be out of place in a Paris salon. In short, the clever, imaginative barbarian has an acute critical faculty which has been thrown into intense activity by the arrival of Western civilization in the Balkans; and the result is precisely what the advent of nineteenth century thought first produced in England: to wit, Byronism. By his brooding over the perpetual failure, not only of others, but of himself, to live up to his imaginative ideals, his consequent cynical scorn for humanity, the jejune credulity as to the absolute validity of his ideals and the unworthiness of the world in disregarding them, his wincings and mockeries under the sting of petty disillusions which

every hour spent among men brings to his infallibly quick observation, he has acquired the half tragic, half ironic air, the mysterious moodiness, the suggestion of a strange and terrible history that has left him nothing but undying remorse, by which Childe Harold fascinated the grandmothers of his English contemporaries.[13]

It is evident that this luxurious description was intended to evoke in the reader's mind the Satanic *homme fatal* of romantic fiction, an awe-inspiring figure which held the stage from the time of Byron's Manfred to that of Chekhov's Captain Solyony.[14] Sergius represents the Byronic hero very thoroughly, both in his sadistic and his masochistic aspects, and the uses to which the character is put are in comic contrast to the expectation aroused in his presentation. The description suggests, in more than one particular, the author's personal identification with this glamorous figure. Doubtless the portrait idealized Shaw's appearance at this time; but, judging by the compendious series of photographs which he has left us, Shaw did what he could to remedy the disparity. He carefully trained his eyebrows into the ram's horn twist, thrust out his chin aggressively with the help of his beard, and cultivated the half-tragic, half-ironic air of a latter-day Hamlet. Sergius is no simple man. There are, Shaw suggests, a half-dozen people in residence in this handsome figure:

SERGIUS (*speaking to himself*): Which of the six is the real man? thats the question that torments me. One of them is a hero, another a buffoon, another a humbug, another perhaps a bit of a blackguard. (*He pauses and looks furtively at Louka as he adds, with deep bitter ness*): And one, at least, is a coward: jealous, like all cowards. . . .[16]

Shaw's characters are not generally given to soul-searching. They are normally too busy with the external problems of the plot to wonder very much about their inner situation. Sergius is an exception. He has an inward-looking eye and is perhaps of all Shaw's characters the most introspective. He is a romantic who finds it exhausting to sustain his pose, but impossible to relinquish it. Hector Hushabye in *Heartbreak House* is obviously cut from the same cloth, but if he is less a caricature than Sergius it is only because he preserves his incognito better. In the case of Sergius the loss of his Byronic soul's trappings would, conceivably, involve major surgery. In fact, he never gives them up. He changes his orientation, but he cannot divest himself of his heroic posture. On, the contrary, in marrying a girl of the lower classes, and thus declaring his independence of convention, he proudly affirms his romantic nature. He is, like Shaw, a rebel against the tyranny of the social order and, even more heroically, against the tyranny of his compulsions. Thus, the more attentively one considers the characterization of Sergius, the more clearly one comes to understand the predicament of the character out of whose fantasy he had sprung.

The early realization that life is not beautiful, and that the world is not constructed along operatic lines, could not wholly eradicate the romantic strain in Shaw. All Shaw's memorable characters—Dick Dudgeon, Julius Caesar, Brassbound, Shotover, Saint Joan—have a latent Byronic image, firmly and often comically suppressed, which is eventually developed into visibility. But Shaw was determined to be at all costs a realist. Sergius's romanticism turns out to be a complex affair. Bluntschli's realism is even more complex.

Bluntschli is not, seemingly, in the least neurotic. He makes the impression of a completely integrated individual, as steady as a rock, an eminently practical and efficient manager. One would imagine such a character would be spared analysis. But in the case of Bluntschli, Shaw reserves a surprise. In the final scene of the play it is revealed quite unexpectedly that Bluntschli is aware that he is of an incurably romantic disposition:

> BLUNTSCHLI: . . . I ran away from home twice when I was a boy. I went into the army instead of into my father's business. I climbed the balcony of this house when a man of sense would have dived into the nearest cellar. I came sneaking back here to have another look at the young lady when any other man of my age would have sent the coat back—
>
> PETKOFF: My coat!
>
> BLUNTSCHLI: —yes: thats the coat I mean—would have sent it back and gone quietly home. Do you suppose I am the sort of fellow a young girl falls in love with? . . .[16]

He is, of course, precisely that sort of fellow. The final bit of legerdemain is very skillfully managed. At the end of the play one suddenly realizes that as a figure of romance Bluntschli is much more the genuine article than his comic-opera rival.

The discovery is only momentarily surprising, for the cards have been carefully stacked. The romantic image is established from the moment he first appears, muddy, bloodstained, and exhausted, a dashing and impressive figure, pistol in hand, and saber clanking. The fact that he would rather have chocolates in his cartridge pouch is interesting; but it does not really make him out a practical man since—Shaw to the contrary—cartridges are normally more useful in combat than candy. His preference, however, indicates that he is a brave man, more concerned with his comfort than his safety, an infallible sign of a naturally optimistic disposition. He is, moreover, a fatalist who knows that battles are won by chance and not by skill, and who nevertheless is skillful as a matter of principle. Raina's choice is therefore not in doubt and in making it she affirms her good sense.

Practically, she finds Bluntschli both helpless and masterful—an irresistible combination—and also eminently comfortable. It is an ideal formula for a husband. She demands too much of Sergius. He cannot live up to her expectations and is therefore full of heroic self-torture. Bluntschli, however, makes no pretensions. He has brought the ideal down to manageable proportions and is able to handle himself without strain. Raina has to choose, therefore, not between the romantic hero and the practical man of business, but between the false romantic and the true. In choosing Bluntschli, she manifests her realistic appraisal of what truly constitutes a romantic figure.

In his essays and prefaces, Shaw reveals himself as an enthusiast intent on preaching a revolutionary gospel at whatever cost to himself. The man who emerges from his personal correspondence is, however, a shrewd man of business, unashamedly efficient in advancing his personal interests. There is no way to bridge the gap between these two figures; they are poles apart. Taken together, they compose a personality that must have been incomprehensible even to itself. Shaw resolved this problem, at least partially, by keeping both aspects of his nature constantly before his eyes. In Sergius we may glimpse the romantic idealist yearning for a more solid reality, and in Bluntschli, the solid realist longing for romance. These figures in a measure foreshadow the archetypes in terms of which so much of Shaw's future work was to be cast—the poet and the man of action dancing an interminable pas de deux.

Arms and the Man demonstrated the possibility of being brilliantly original, and even significant, within the framework of conventional melodrama. If the detail is meager, the machinery a little creaky, and the comedy not of uniformly high order, it is necessary to make some allowances for the circumstances of composition. It was the first time anything of the sort had been attempted in England; and the play was written at top speed. The humor is not above reproach. For the English of this period, Bulgarians were ridiculous simply because they were

Bulgarians. In general, foreigners were funny. Such was the theatrical tradition, and Shaw got as much fun out of it as he could. The daring attempt to deflate military glory, something which so far had been sacrosanct in the theater, chiefly aroused discussion; but in fact the novelty of the play lay elsewhere. What was unusual in Shaw's play was that the characters, though drawn from stock, are remarkably conscious of their motives and entirely articulate in exposing them to view. In the main, Sergius and Bluntschli interpret themselves honestly and sensibly, quite unlike real people. This is the source of the vivid impression these characters make and also the cause of their patent artificiality. Moreover, when their motives are held up to scrutiny, their actions, though in themselves entirely conventional, take on unexpected meaning. There was not much precedent for this technique in melodrama. It was new.

The new Ibsenist drama was interesting precisely because of its search for meaning. This realization did much to shape Shaw's future career in the theater. He himself invented little in the way of plot or dramatic design, but he was determined that his plays have significance. In the case of *Arms and the Man* he had not "found" a plot; the plot had, so to speak, found him. It is when a dramatist comes upon the dramatic pattern that properly represents the psychic configuration he needs to exhibit that his career as an artist begins. Perhaps the real significance of *Arms and the Man* was not clear to Shaw at this, or any other time. In the nature of things its truth had to be rationalized in terms of an acceptable allegory. This took the form of the opposition of realism and idealism which Ibsen had made fashionably current in intellectual circles. It was, accordingly, in such terms that *Arms and the Man* was conceived and presented, and in this light it is still usually understood. Perhaps that is best.

Shaw's originality is manifest in the early recognition of the fact that important drama in the coming age would be essentially involved not with plot or poetry but with the reinterpretation of motives. Ibsen had indicated the direction that must be taken to bring the drama into a more direct relation with modern currents of thought. The way was open for a rational interpretation of dramatic values.

To bring this about, in Shaw's judgment, all that was necessary was to present realistically what was currently played fairy-tale fashion. Realism entailed a revaluation of experience in accordance with intellectual rather than emotional standards. The result would be a reaction against

Victorian sentimentality and Victorian prudery, and the substitution of a new classicism for the romantic attributes of the previous age.

In the course of two centuries of growing sensibility, tragedy and comedy had been fused virtually into a single genre, which had completely lost the therapeutic function claimed for the drama by the Renaissance apologists. Shaw proposed to restore the social utility of the theater by returning to the comedic conceptions of Jonson and Molière. He began to speak of his work in Jonsonian terms. Apparently relating his *Unpleasant Plays* to tragedy, he wrote of his *Pleasant Plays* as "plays dealing less with the crimes of society and more with its romantic follies."[17]

Thus far the popular drama had been directed to that level of the mind which eludes the control of the intellect. It was possible to enjoy a play without making head or tail of it. Shaw wished to write comprehensible drama. In his theater the judgment would be suspended only insofar as the fictions of the plot were concerned, but the characters were to be subjected to the full play of the critical faculty. The consequence would be the translation of the dramatic fantasy from the infantile to the adult reaches of the mind. Practically this would be meaningful drama, addressed to the intellect, and calculated to provoke thought. This was the task which Shaw set himself in the next phase of his career.

Immediately after the American opening of *Arms and the Man*, Shaw began work on a new play, his fifth. It took two months to write it. He called it *Candida*.[18]

When it was finished, Shaw read the play to Charles Wyndham at the Criterion and was told that it would be twenty-five years before the London stage was ready for such a play. Early the next year Cyril Maude asked to see it, but Shaw thought it inappropriate for the Haymarket audience and suggested that Maude produce his new play, *You Never Can Tell*, instead. Meanwhile he had offered *Candida* to Mansfield for production in America, suggesting that Mansfield play the eighteen-year-old Marchbanks, and that he engage Janet Achurch, for whom it had been written, to play the title role.[19]

Mansfield was at this time thirty-eight. He had not yet read the play. Shaw described it to him as "the most fascinating work in the world . . . in three acts, one cheap scene, and with six characters." Mansfield was enchanted by the prospect of playing a juvenile lead and, incredible as it seems, he actually engaged Janet Achurch at a salary of £250 a week and paid her travel expenses to New York. Shaw was jubilant. He finished copying out the parts and wrote Mansfield that he was sending him "the full score of Candida, and the band parts (all except the first violin which Janet took to study on the way, and which she will no doubt lose) . . . a labor which leaves its marks on my constitution until the last trumpet."[20]

In preparation for Mansfield's forthcoming production, Shaw now secured the copyright with a reading in South Shields on 30 March 1895. But when Mansfield at last came to read the play, he had grave misgivings. He wrote Shaw:

> The stage is not for sermons. . . . Here are three long acts of talk—talk—talk—no matter how clever that talk is—it is talk—talk—talk. . . . Shaw, if you will write for me a strong, hearty—earnest—noble—genuine play—I'll play it. Plays used to be written for *actors* —actors who could stir and thrill—and that is what I want now—because I can do that—the world is tired of theories and arguments and philosophy and morbid sentiment. . . .

And, warming to his subject, he proceeded to voice his real objection to *Candida*. He liked neither Marchbanks as a role nor Janet Achurch as a woman:

> To be frank and to go further—I am not in sympathy with a young, delicate, morbid and altogether exceptional young man who falls in love with a massive middle-aged lady who peels onions. I couldn't make love to your Candida (Miss Janet Achurch) if I had taken ether—I never fall in love with fuzzy haired persons who purr and are business-like and take a drop when they feel disposed and have weak feminine voices—my ideal is something quite different. I detest an aroma of stale tobacco and gin. I detest intrigue and slyness and sham ambitions. I don't like women who sit on the floor—or kneel by your side and have designs on your shirt bosom—I don't like women who comb their tawny locks with their fingers, and claw their necks and scratch the air with their chins.
>
> You'll have to write a play that a *man* can play and about a woman that heroes have fought for and a bit of ribbon that a knight tied to his lance.
>
> The stage is for romance and truth and honor. . . .
>
> *Candida is* beautiful—don't mistake me—we both understand it and we both appreciate it—there are fine things here—but—we are paid—alas—Shaw—we are paid to *act*.[21]

This unexpected blast from America gave Shaw something to think about. Mansfield, meanwhile, abandoned the play, but kept Miss Achurch in rehearsal in the hope of annoying her into releasing him from his contract. She was not, however, annoyable to that extent and continued to draw her salary to the end of the season. It was not until two years later that *Candida* was produced. The Independent Theatre company gave it a single performance in Aberdeen on 30 June 1897 and then toured the provinces with it and *A Doll's House*, with Miss Achurch starring in both plays. The following spring she played it in Manchester; and on 1 July 1900, a Sunday, it was performed once in London at the Strand under the auspices of the London Stage Society, with Charrington as Morell, and Granville-Barker as Marchbanks. Four years later, after infinite difficulties, Arnold Daly—at that time an uncertain young actor—produced it on the proverbial shoestring at the Princess Theater in New York.

The first New York performance was given on 8 December 1903. "If you think a bustling—striving—hustling—pushing—stirring American audience will sit out calmly two hours of deliberate talk you are mistaken—and I'm not to be sacrificed to their just vengeance." Such had been Mansfield's considered judgment in 1895. But, like most experienced theater managers, he was quite unable to follow the currents of public taste. Daly's production was enormously successful. As an afterpiece, he added *The Man of Destiny*, newly written, and later still, *How He Lied to Her Husband*. In 1904, after a run of 150 performances in New York, Daly took these plays on an extended tour of the United States. That same spring Reinhardt produced *Candida* in German at the Neues Theater in Berlin. In the fall of 1904 Granville-Barker and J. E. Vedrenne organized a series of matinees at the Royal Court Theatre in London. They offered a repertory of plays by "advanced" authors— Euripides, Maeterlinck, Schnitzler, Hauptmann, Barker, and Yeats, along with five of Shaw's comedies. Among these *Candida* was given a prominent place.

The Royal Court productions, culminating in a Shaw season of evening performances beginning 1 May 1905, effectively established Shaw as a dramatist. *Candida* began to be discussed seriously as an important English play, provoking as much earnest talk in radical circles as *A Doll's House*. It was taken up vigorously by the feminists as a revolutionary statement on the relations of man and wife, and in the course of time, it inspired a number of interesting domestic comedies dealing with analogous situations, such as Barrie's *What Every Woman Knows* and *The Ten Pound Look*, and, after some years, Robert Sherwood's *Reunion in Vienna* and Robert Anderson's *Tea and Sympathy*.

In his later years Shaw tired of the play, and spoke disparagingly of its situation, its principal character, and its adherents, the Candidomaniacs. It is not unlikely that, as time went by, his attitude changed considerably with respect to the mother-image he had created in *Candida*. In fact the role of Candida is striking, but not entirely playable, and, although it has tempted every great actress of our time, it is doubtful if anyone has actually succeeded in realizing it.

The reason is, evidently, that in devising *Candida* according to the canons of the *pièce à thèse*, Shaw set up a plot-situation so preposterous that it can hardly be taken seriously. To make the striking effect he needed, it was necessary for him to pose the contrast between the poet and the preacher in the most unmistakable fashion. The consequence is an unequal contest between an effeminate youth and a burly parson of forty, over a woman who seems temperamentally suited to neither. Candida's choice, in these circumstances, is a foregone conclusion. It would be in the highest degree irrational for a grown woman of thirty-five, the mother of several children, to run off with a brilliant but neurotic boy who, at eighteen, has barely survived his adolescence. Nor is it easily conceivable that under normal conditions a well-developed man would say to an arrogant youth who was making earnest efforts to seduce his wife, "She must choose between us now." Morell, clergyman though he is, would seem more likely to administer something more in the nature of physical reproof. Morell is too reasonable a man for that, and the fact that he does nothing of the sort demonstrates his weakness as well as his delicacy, but his weakness seems as exceptional as the boy's brilliance. The action boils down, therefore, to a contest between a strong boy and a weak man, and the contrast between the poet and the man of action, which is ostensibly the point, is obscured by the special characteristics of the contestants.

In her opening scenes with Morell, Candida characterizes herself quite summarily. She is annoyed because Morell takes her for granted and piqued because he is the object of universal feminine adulation. She is quick to point out, however, that her resentment proceeds not from jealousy but from a sense of social injustice. It is manifestly unjust for everyone to love Morell and nobody to love Marchbanks, and she hints that she would willingly retrieve the balance in this regard if she thought it would be helpful. One might conclude at this point that she plans to use Marchbanks in order to teach Morell a lesson in domestic relations. But it would be wrong to jump to such a conclusion. In these scenes Shaw evidently meant to indicate that, unlike Morell, Candida is above ordinary morality, and that the conventional ideas of marital fidelity mean nothing to her in comparison with the demands of that higher morality which is the source of her compassion for the unfortunate young man.

The inference is that, in spite of her motherhood, Candida has preserved and will continue to preserve, her spiritual virginity. She is a mother by vocation, sexually uncommitted to any man, and bound by no law other than her will in which is resident a higher will, which is divine. It is possible, accordingly, to consider *Candida* a precursor of *Man and Superman*. At its core is the evolutionary theory, as yet inchoate, which was to become fundamental in all of Shaw's later work, and it is, very likely, to this idea that must be attributed Shaw's allusions to Candida as the Virgin Mother.

On the stage, however, Candida does not in the least evoke the image of the Bride of God. On the contrary she makes the impression of a vigorous feminist who is determined to be valued at her proper worth and who seizes the first opportunity to make her worth clear to her husband. Thus the play appears to depict, like *A Doll's House*, the emancipation of an intelligent woman from the traditional bonds of matrimony, and the auction scene at the end of the play involves a declaration of independence quite as definite as the slamming of the door in the last act of Ibsen's play. The implication is that the reasons Candida assigns for her decision in this scene are less than candid. The real question is not which of the two men needs her most, but which of them she most needs in order best to fulfill herself as a woman. It is her destiny to be a mother and to raise children. From this viewpoint Marchbanks seems useless. The man for her is Morell, and this entails some sacrifice on her part.

It may well be that in the light of *Man and Superman* Shaw revaluated *Candida* in terms of his later theory; but even on its own terms, the question of the relative weakness of the two men does not seem vital. Each man has his weakness and his special strength. Since Morell is capable of playing the father as well as the son, he is ideally suited for marriage. Marchbanks is capable of neither role. He can be only the lover, a decorative, but disturbing influence in any well-ordered domestic arrangement. His function in the domestic triangle is primarily disruptive. He has no real desire to become Candida's husband. He wishes only to deprive Morell of his wife.

Morell, however, is not easily despoiled. It is by no means obvious that he is the weaker man. On the contrary, his physical preponderance is so evident that it ordinarily requires unusual exertions on the part of the actor to convey the impression that he is spiritually dwarfed by his adversary. The unholy alliance of Marchbanks and Candida is thus based on very questionable assumptions from every standpoint save one, namely, that Marchbanks does not need a woman and that Morell does. Once Marchbanks realizes this, he takes off into the night with the velocity, one imagines, of a bidder at an auction who has barely escaped acquiring at a ruinous price an object for which he has no use.

The greatness of *Candida* as a play depends neither on the ingenuity of the plot nor on its psychological realism. It depends upon the masterful depiction of a young man of genius, an uneasy embodiment of the divine principle in its most uncomfortable form. Marchbanks, not Candida, is the life of the play. In performance, the action heightens immediately upon Marchbanks's entrance, and it drops at once when he leaves the stage.

Like other manifestations of the superman in Shaw's comedies, Marchbanks is remarkably awkward in a social setting. He is, of course, broadly caricatured, but the hyperbole does not obscure the characterization. Marchbanks is a child of terrifying precocity, desperately advancing his own individuality at the expense of the only man who has ever befriended him. One might imagine that it is in this manner that a young homosexual would attempt to disrupt the connubial arrangements of those more comfortably situated than he. But Shaw does not present Marchbanks in this light. His effeminacy, like his waspishness, is merely the sign of his superior sensitivity. Presumably his sexual inclinations are thoroughly masculine. He cuts, nonetheless, a strange figure, at the same time childish and dangerously adult. Possibly this figure out of *Adonais* was meant to suggest young Shelley; but in Eugene, the well-born, it is tempting to see rather the gifted, aggressive, and pathologically shy youth who first came to London nineteen years before *Candida* was written, bringing his tensions with him.

The portrait of Morell leaves less to the imagination than that of Marchbanks. Morell is a Christian Socialist, committed to the idea that political action is futile unless it is accompanied by a strengthening of the moral fiber. His mission, accordingly, is ethically rather than politically oriented, and his influence emanates primarily from the pulpit. It is Morell's oratorical proficiency which principally arouses Candida's scorn. She does not doubt his sincerity. What revolts her is not the man, but the mountebank.

In the 1850's F. D. Maurice, and his disciples Julius Hare, Charles Kingsley, and J. M. Ludlow, felt it was their mission to Christianize socialism by giving a proper religious direction to the cause of social justice. Their efforts were, on the whole, ineffective; but they did much to expose the miserable working conditions in the English factories, and the hypocrisy of what passed in their time for philanthropy. As early as 1854 Maurice organized the first experiment in adult education among the working classes, the Workingman's College, and brought people like Ruskin, Rossetti, Huxley, and Frederic Harrison to lecture there. It was with this movement that Shaw associated Morell.[22]

Kingsley was a more glamorous character than Maurice, and his particularly pungent brand of muscular Christianity was not only vigorously romantic but also immensely effective. In *The Water Babies* (1863), published while he was Professor of Modern History at Cambridge, he turned to advantage the myth of the two titans, Prometheus, the cunning thinker, and Epimetheus, his brother, who rashly accepted the beautiful Pandora and her box of volatile afflictions, along with its compensatory gift of hope. For Kingsley the cautious Prometheus was an impractical prophet, the father of all the "noisy, windy people," while Epimetheus was a maker and a doer, the prototype of those who are willing to cope with their humanity and its attendant ills. Like the earth-bound titan, Kingsley himself was willing to till the soil in the sweat of his brow, and he chose to fight the materialism of his age by inoculating its agents with his own moral fervor and sense of spiritual purpose.[23]

It is more than likely that, in devising Morell, Shaw had in mind someone like Kingsley, and it is arguable that *Candida* is an exemplum founded on the myth that Kingsley popularized in *The Water Babies.* James Mavor Morell is a plausible version of Kingsley's titan, a giant not especially gifted with foresight, but a brave warrior with the courage to accept the gifts of a mischievous god and make the best of the consequences. Among these gifts must be reckoned Candida with her trousseau of domestic chores, her children, her paraffin lamps, her onions, and the rest of it. These connubial burdens Morell cheerfully bears, but the very thought of them sickens Marchbanks, the visionary fire-bringer. Obviously the contrast is not lost on Candida.

In the crusading preacher Shaw exhibited a more adult stage of human development than we see in the feverish Marchbanks, but there is some loss of glamor, for it is not always beautiful to grow up. Morell is Shaw's age at the time *Candida* was written. His library includes the works Shaw held most in esteem at this time—Browning's poems, *Progress and Poverty, Fabian Essays, A Dream of John Ball,* Marx's *Capital.* Moreover, Morell is a practiced orator, robust, genial, kindly, full of energy,

withal, a great baby, pardonably vain of his powers and unconsciously pleased with himself. He has a healthy complexion; good
forehead, with the brows somewhat blunt, and the eyes bright and
eager, mouth resolute, but not particularly well cut, and a substantial
nose, with the mobile spreading nostrils of the dramatic orator, void,
like all his features, of subtlety.

He has, as Marchbanks is at pains to inform him, "the gift of the gab,
nothing more and nothing less." This portrait might well serve as a cruel
caricature of the author at the age of forty.

Shaw was certainly aware of this uncomfortable aspect of himself. In a
letter written almost twenty years later to Mrs. Patrick Campbell, upon
whom he was resolved to make an unforgettable impression, he described himself in terms that would serve very well to characterize
Morell:

> On Tuesday Winifred Holiday called on me on business of the last
> importance, which turned out to be that I should make a great
> religious peroration that night. Which I did, shamelessly, and not
> only brought down the house, but quite touched the bishop in the
> chair. . . . Last night at Blackburn I gassed—its the only fitting
> expression—for an hour and a half, and did another religious
> peroration. After that I scintillated in the Mayor's parlor, being
> screwed up rhetorically to such a pressure that I sparked at every
> touch and terrified and disconcerted the chambermaids and waiters at
> the Old Bull by my intensity.[24]

The description of Eugene is particularly interesting by comparison:

> He is a strange, shy youth of eighteen, slight, effeminate, with a
> delicate childish voice, and a hunted, tormented expression and
> shrinking manner that shew the painful sensitiveness of very swift
> and acute apprehensiveness in youth, before the character has grown
> to full strength. . . . He is so uncommon as to be almost unearthly;
> and to prosaic people there is something noxious in this unearthli-
> ness, just as to poetic people there is something angelic in it.[25]

As an experiment in self-analysis *Candida* goes some steps beyond
Arms and the Man, but the psychic configuration and the technique
through which it is manifested are much the same. As portraiture,
Candida is a triptych. At its center is the Mother, a fantasy figure mysteriously associated with Titian's "Virgin of the Assumption," elusive,
immaculate, and transcendent. To one side stands the Father, impressive,
but not invulnerable. On the other side of her is the aspiring Son, beautiful, fragile, and full of sorrow and pride. In these terms, it becomes

evident that it is the Son who must be sacrificed, but the Father cannot pass unscathed. The picture is classic.

The Shaw who wrote prefaces and lectured in Workmen's Halls was unquestionably much more Morell than Marchbanks, but Marchbanks was the source of Shaw's aesthetic insights. Without the intrusion of the impudent and perceptive child, Shaw's plays would, in all likelihood, have been as dreary as Pinero's. Candida, however, is impervious to either of the entities who struggle for her approval. Between the two, she maintains the singular neutrality which only figures of fantasy possess. Like Lady Cicely in *Captain Brassbound's Conversion*, Candida mothers everyone and loves no one. She is completely self-sufficient. Thus, for all the superior spirituality with which she is theoretically invested, she is depicted as an extraordinarily sexless coquette, whom it is more difficult to identify with Titian's comely Virgin than with *La Belle Dame sans merci* which Pater conjured up out of Leonardo's "La Gioconda."

As Shaw shows her to us, Candida is readily accessible, but impossible to please. Marchbanks's helplessness touches her. His poetry bores her. Judging by the samples provided, this is understandable. But she is even more deeply bored by Morell's efforts at social reform. As she sees her two lovers, the one is a child, the other a windbag. It is clearly not artistic creativity that impresses Candida, but something much more fundamental, the nature of which became clear to Shaw when he wrote *Man and Superman*.

In *Candida* the central figure of the Mother takes the place that Raina occupied in the plot-design of the earlier play. But where Raina had to choose between a romantic realist and a realistic romantic, Candida is given the choice, in Marchbanks's words, between "a wretched little nervous disease" and a "pig-headed parson." Neither is a worthy mate for so illustrious a figure. She deserves nothing short of divinity. Evidently that is what she looked for in Morell, and her dissatisfaction with him is based on the discovery, made long ago, that in him she has, not a father, but only another child.

It is not easy to say what Marchbanks desires in a lady constituted after this fashion. His own assertion in the play seems extravagant. "She offered me," he says, in reply to Morell's anxious question, "all I chose to ask for, her shawl, her wings, the wreath of stars on her head, the lilies in her hand, the crescent moon beneath her feet." But whatever it was she offered, in fact, she gave him nothing, and while Morell is led to imagine a passionate encounter, the scene in which Candida and Marchbanks are left alone together is idealistically pure.

For Marchbanks—and perhaps for Shaw also—Candida represents a child's image of the adorable and sexually unavailable mother, whose love can never amount to anything more than tenderness. But the identification is complicated by deeper considerations. Candida, like Raina, objectifies a psychic fact of some importance. Her rejection of the childish poet who recedes "into the night," and her acceptance of the manly, but unduly resonant preacher, seems to bear a significant relation to what happened to the author of the fantasy. The preposterous, but perhaps inescapable suggestion is that the Virgin Mother, lilies, crescent moon and all, is, at bottom, none other than Shaw himself. If this is so, the comedy of *Candida* becomes truly comic.

It is obviously possible, at any rate, and perhaps desirable, to consider *Candida* an autobiographical statement on some level of consciousness, and in this light the situation it sets up becomes in some measure comprehensible. Candida's choice, after all, is redundant. It was made long before the play began, when she married Morell. The action thus expresses her regret—and perhaps also Shaw's—in having lost the poet in choosing the preacher. But it is clear that the youthful Marchbanks, thus abandoned like his counterparts in Shaw's other plays, never quite vanishes from the scene. He hangs about insistently, haunting his more fortunate rivals—the Morells, the Tanners, and the Preacher Andersons of Shaw's fancy—from his secure domain in the night of the unconscious to which he has been relegated. Evidently it was not enough to banish Marchbanks into his darkness merely once. He had to be exorcized over and over; to his consistent intrusion on the author's sensibility we may, in all likelihood, attribute the stupendous creative vitality that in time exhausted the artist, but not the phantom that excited him.

The choice between happiness and blessedness which Marchbanks makes, with tragic emphasis, at the end of the play is, of course, gratuitous, since in fact the choice is made for him. For followers of Carlyle, nevertheless, the choice was mandatory. All Shaw's heroes make a point of it from *Candida* to *Heartbreak House*. The passage in *Sartor Resartus* is famous:

> . . . There is in man a HIGHER than Love of Happiness: he can do without Happiness, and instead thereof find Blessedness! Was it not to preach forth this same HIGHER that sages and martyrs, the Poet and the Priest, in all times, have spoken and suffered, bearing testimony, through life and through death, of the Godlike that is in Man, and how in the Godlike only has he Strength and Freedom? . . . On the roaring billows of Time, thou art not engulfed, but borne aloft into the azure of Eternity. Love not Pleasure; love God. This is the

Everlasting Yea, wherein all contradiction is solved, wherein whoso
walks and works, it is well with him.[26]

The echo of Teufelsdroeckh is quite perceptible in Eugene's parting
words to Morell: "I no longer desire happiness: life is nobler than that.
Parson James: I give you my happiness with both hands. . . ." But while
Shaw's heroes are in general, eager to abandon happiness as a bad business, Morell is not. Morell boasts repeatedly of his happiness—the more
so as it is necessary in the design of the play to contrast his happiness,
which depends on Candida, with the blessedness of Marchbanks, who
depends on nobody. Morell represents an unstable compromise. He has
chosen happiness without relinquishing his hope of blessedness. He seeks
his happiness in his marriage and his blessedness in his work, and it has so
far not occurred to him that he cannot have both. Until now, he has
wisely avoided introspection. Carlyle had written:

> The latest gospel in this world is Know thy work and do it. "Know
> thyself:" long enough has that poor "self" of thine tormented thee;
> thou wilt never get to "know" it, I believe! Think it not thy business,
> this of knowing thyself; thou art an unknowable individual: know
> what thou canst work at; and work at it like Hercules! That will be
> thy better plan.[27]

At the time of *Candida* it was apparently Shaw's belief that happiness
was not compatible with blessedness. As matters stand, Morell is especially vulnerable, and Candida deals him a blow calculated to make a less
durable man unhappy for the rest of his life. Whether, in these circumstances, Morell can at least find blessedness is a question which nothing
in the play helps us to resolve.

Candida is, nevertheless, a play of considerable depth and goes far
beyond the traditional patterns of domestic drama. Nineteenth-century
comedies of this cut, from the time of Augier's *Gabrielle* (1849) to
Ibsen's *The Lady from the Sea* (1888), invariably ended in the vindication of the prosaic, but reliable husband. Thus they represented an interesting middle-class reversal of the theme inherited from the romantic
poetry of a former age, in which it was customary for the lover to
triumph, not the husband. In *Gabrielle*, the heroine is about to elope
with her husband's attractive secretary when, in the nick of time, she
overhears her husband delivering a homily in alexandrines on the discomforts of an illicit relationship without a solid financial basis. This
oration brings Gabrielle instantly to her senses, and in the touching last
scene of the play, she celebrates the glamour of comfortable matrimony

by apostrophizing her husband in resounding verses, ending with, "O père de famille! O poëte, Je t'aime!"

Plays of the type of *Gabrielle* had been popular in England long before the time of *Candida* and continued to be so for long after it. Tom Taylor had great success with *Still Waters Run Deep* (1855), a melodrama in which the dull, but honest husband defends his marriage successfully against the dashing and dissolute Captain Hawksley. This play, indeed, was so popular that Taylor followed it up with *Victims* (1857), which depicts a similar contest between a stockbroker and a poet. The poetic aspects of the seemingly stuffy husband were developed more recently in *Divorçons* (1880) by Sardou and Najac, later by J. J. Bernard in *L'Invitation au voyage* (1924), later still by Noel Coward in *Private Lives* (1930), and, with appropriate irony, by Jean Giraudoux in *Intermezzo* (1933). All these are more or less straightforward plays which in one way or another defend marriage against the inroads of the romantic impulse. *Candida* obviously falls into the same category, but with a difference. The distance that separates *Candida* from *Gabrielle* takes in not only Ibsen's revolutionary doctrine but also Shaw's peculiar attitude with respect to the marital relation in general, which he had so far found congenial only when he was permitted, like Marchbanks, to invade it.

The ladies concerned in the conventional domestic *drame* were normally passive types longing for a passionate hero to rescue them from a life of domestic bliss. Candida is of another stripe. She is a person who can "manage people by engaging their affections." Her cunning, of course, is devoted to noble ends, and in this she much resembles Shaw. But it is not altogether clear what end is served by her flirtation with Marchbanks. As it is, she shatters her husband's self-confidence, frightens away her lover, and is left in the end mistress of the field, having affectively done in all the men in sight, save her husband's curate, in whom she is not interested.

It is impossible to say how Shaw explained Candida to himself. He explained her to others in a variety of ways. In a letter to Ellen Terry, Candida is once again said to be "the Virgin mother and nobody else."[28] On the other hand, in a letter to Huneker, which Huneker publicized, Shaw identified her, more realistically, with Ibsen's Nora. "Candida," Shaw wrote, "is as unscrupulous as Siegfried. No law will bind her. She is faithful not for conventional reasons but for rational ones. . . . It is just this freedom from conventional slop, this unerring wisdom on the domestic plane, that makes her so completely mistress of the situation."[29]

There is no doubt that in these allusions to Candida's sanctity, and her wisdom, there may be found some anticipation of Doña Ana and of Eve in *Back to Methuselah*, but at this point Shaw was inclined to stress her rational quality, in which she resembled Nora, rather than her mystical role as an instrument of the Life Force. It is possible to assimilate this rational Candida to the Holy Mother transfigured and poised for flight only on the theory that the flight to heaven is, like Don Juan's flight to Paradise, an intellectual leap, the modern counterpart of the upward flight of the lover in Bruno's *Gli eroici furori*. This would put Titian's painting in a Platonic light and, while it is not inconceivable that Titian had something of the sort in mind, it would be astonishing if Shaw, at this period of his life, had attained to so ample an insight into the symbolism of the Renaissance Platonists.

Candida's wisdom does not seem to be of so high an order. In the play it is only Marchbanks who sees her as the Virgin Mother poised for flight, and it would seem that he would like to enliven her heavenly voyage by joining her in a fairy shallop. From this viewpoint the assumption of Candida would suggest not so much Titian's painting as Rossetti's "The Boat of Love," which depicts two lovers setting off for an undisclosed destination in a shallop with an angel at the helm.

"The Boat of Love" was a well-known Pre-Raphaelite painting, but it does not help us to connect Candida with the Pre-Raphaelite movement. Shaw calls *Candida* a Pre-Raphaelite play. He understood the history of Pre-Raphaelitism as a dialectical process. "To distill the quintessential drama from pre-Raphaelitism, medieval or modern," he wrote,

> it must be shewn at its best in conflict with the first, broken, nervous, stumbling attempts to formulate its own revolt against itself as it develops into something higher. A coherent explanation of any such revolt, addressed intelligibly and prosaically to the intellect, can only come when the work is done. . . . Long before any such understanding can be reached, the eyes of men begin to turn towards the distant light of the new age. Discernible at first only by the eyes of the man of genius, it must be focussed by him on the speculum of a work of art, and flashed back from that into the eyes of the common man.[30]

The Pre-Raphaelite movement had begun, a half-century before, in 1848, as a reaction against English neoclassic art, with its underpinning of pagan mythology. For their method and subject matter the Pre-Raphaelites reached beyond the High Renaissance to the art of Giotto, Carpaccio, and Bellini, whom they considered representatives of the medieval spirit. Their painting thus combined a quaint absorption in exact representation of detail with a strictly Christian symbolism, relatively free of humanist influence. Since Pre-Raphaelitism from its inception had both literary and moral connotations, it was easy for Ruskin to infuse its disciples with social consciousness.

In the end, accordingly, the Pre-Raphaelite painters inclined to a socialist viewpoint with regard to contemporary problems, treating their subjects realistically, but without brutality. At the same time they developed their literary tendencies in the direction of symbolism, visual metaphor, and conceit. Pre-Raphaelitism thus became all-embracing as a movement, combining more or less illogically, socialist materialism with the mysticism and aestheticism of its earlier phases. It became possible for both Yeats and Shaw, whose views on most subjects had nothing in common, to acknowledge Pre-Raphaelite influence, and to reconcile their differences in the contradictory doctrines of William Morris of whom both professed to be disciples.[31]

In *Candida*, Titian's "Virgin" is prominently displayed on the wall above the hearth and so, in a manner, dominates the play. The painting can hardly be called medieval in spirit; but it is possible that in viewing it from an allegorical standpoint, as was his habit, Shaw may have considered it a forerunner of the Pre-Raphaelite mode. It was, in fact, one of his favorite paintings. He saw in it, "a union of the flesh and the spirit so triumphantly beautiful . . ." that Marchbanks might properly select it as a symbol of Candida, the perfection of womanhood.

The heaven toward which this transcendent figure is oriented would hardly be a wholly intellectual paradise. The phrases Marchbanks uses in connection with his love are rather symbolist than strictly Pre-Raphaelite in derivation, and the fairyland to which he desires to convey his beloved much resembles the Land of Heart's Desire where the young bride of Yeats's play is led to seek a refuge, through death, from the household drudgery which for her is synonymous with life. It is perhaps significant that *The Land of Heart's Desire* was not entirely alien to Shaw, since it had run as a curtain raiser in the same bill as *Arms and the Man* at the Avenue Theatre in 1894.

The allusion to death, if it is to be taken seriously, suggests a more sinister interpretation of Marchbanks's final lines than is usually given. It is far from clear what Shaw meant us to understand in having Marchbanks rush out "into the night." His words are unduly ominous:

MARCHBANKS (*with the ring of a man's voice—no longer a boy's—in the words*): I know the hour when it strikes. I am impatient to do what must be done.

What Marchbanks has it in mind to do is never made clear, but it does not occur either to Candida or Morell that he is contemplating suicide. His farewell speech to Candida, nevertheless, has an undeniably melodramatic ring:

MARCHBANKS (*turning to her*): In a hundred years, we shall be the same age. But I have a better secret than that in my heart. Let me go now. The night outside grows impatient.
CANDIDA: Good bye. . . .[32]

She kisses him, and he rushes out into the night. Then she and Morell embrace, but, we are told, they do not know the secret in the poet's heart. Neither do we.

In the first draft Shaw subtitled *Candida* "A Domestic Comedy," a phrase difficult to reconcile with any tragic interpretation of Marchbanks's last words.[33] It was doubtless as a tribute to the obtuseness of his audience that Shaw retitled *Candida* "A Mystery." This epithet has been generally explained as a reference to the poet's "secret." But it is more likely that Shaw had in mind the medieval mystery plays as a prototype of Pre-Raphaelite attitudes in the theater. Possibly he saw in the Candida situation an analogy to a play about Mary, Joseph, and their unruly son. In that case he might have done better to have called it a Morality, for its symbols, if symbols they are, come closer to the personification of the medieval moral plays than to the Bible stories enacted in the mystery cycles. At any rate the mystical aura with which Shaw invested *Candida*, with its ambiguities, its secrets, and its vague suggestion, brings the play somewhat closer to the symbolist drama which Lugné-Poë was popularizing at this time than to anything that had so far been seen in England. Save for Wilde's *Salomé*, banned by the English censor, but produced by Bernhardt in Paris in 1894, *Candida* may be considered the first symbolist play in England.

As an example of Pre-Raphaelite symbolism, however, *Candida* falls somewhat short of the mark. It is doubtful if anyone but a conscientious adherent of the movement would have understood the relevant passages in the preface of what Shaw called "a modern pre-Raphaelite play."[34] The case for symbolism is clearer in *The Master Builder*, which was published in 1892, at the height of Shaw's Ibsenist period. In that play the intruder is the young girl Hilde, as extraordinary a character in her way as Marchbanks, and her seduction of Solness results in his death. Shaw understood Ibsen's symbolism as well as anyone, and he was able to follow Ibsen in peopling *Candida* with figures reflecting his own inner dialectic, while at the same time he illustrated the evolution of Pre-Raphaelitism "as it developed into something higher" than art for art's sake.

By the time *Candida* was written, the Christian Socialism of Charles Kingsley had been succeeded by the medievalism of Anglo-Catholic pastors of the type of Stuart Headlam. Headlam made common cause with Ruskin and the Pre-Raphaelites. But the revolt of Pre-Raphaelitism against itself, of which Shaw speaks in his preface, was most clearly figured in the rise of a younger generation of socialists who, like Marchbanks, were impatient of pastoral efforts to repair the social structure from the pulpit. They desired, in the words of Zarathustra, to push over the leaning wagon and begin anew. It was in these terms that in *Candida* the conflict might be posed between "the higher, but vaguer and timider vision, the incoherent, mischievous, and even ridiculous, unpracticalness which offered me a dramatic antagonist for the clear, bold, sure, sensible, benevolent, salutarily shortsighted Christian Socialist idealism."[35]

In *The Master Builder* Solness is destroyed. We have no hint as to what happens to Marchbanks. Presumably he will serve some purpose, if only as a source of inspiration for others more durable than he. It is, however, the clear, bold, sensible—and by no means boring—Morell who does the social spadework, and it is appropriate that such characters should reap the more immediate rewards of virtue. In play after play Shaw indicates his admiration for Marchbanks, but it is Morell whom he invariably rewards. The suggestion is that in the one figure he saw himself as poet and martyr, and in the other as a worker in the vineyard, worthy of his hire. In this duality he strove to relate, though he could never reconcile, the two elements of the inner conflict which for him, judging by his work, was a modus vivendi.

In comparison with her two men, Candida seems remarkably opaque as a character. She has no conflict and is put under no strain. She remains objective, immutable, and mysterious throughout the action, and her participation in the passions she arouses appears to be minimal. The Candida-figure, though obviously of great importance to Shaw, is not completely realized in this or, indeed, in any other of Shaw's plays. Nevertheless, as the myth which was to order his fantasy little by little took shape in his mind, the mother-image at its core became progressively more vivid, and was eventually generalized philosophically in *Back to Methuselah* as Eve and as Lilith. In a letter to Trebitsch, his German translator, Shaw indicated clearly where it was that his interest centered in *Candida*. It was not at all in the Holy Mother, but in the conflict of

Father and Son: "Now the whole point of the play is the revelation of the weakness of this strong and manly man, and the terrible strength of the febrile and effeminate one." In Shaw's estimation, the key character of the play was Marchbanks, "a boy of genius, and—" he added in a letter to Mansfield, "a rattling good part."[36]

In a letter to the members of a play-reading club at Rugby who had ventured some conjectures as to the nature of the young man's secret, Shaw answered at some length in words reminiscent of Carlyle:

> The secret is very obvious, after all—provided you know what a poet is. What business has a man with the great destiny of a poet with the small beer of domestic conflict and cuddling and petting at the apron strings of some dear nice woman? Morell cannot do without it; it is the making of him; without it he would be utterly miserable and perhaps go to the devil. To Eugene, the stronger of the two, the daily routine of it is nursery slavery, swaddling clothes, mere happiness instead of exaltation—an atmosphere in which great poetry dies. To choose it would be like Swinburne choosing Putney. When Candida brings him squarely face to face with it, his heart rolls up like a scroll; and he goes proudly into the majestic and beautiful kingdom of the starry night.[37]

The explanation is interesting, but curiously beside the point. Shaw appears to have forgotten by this time that, in the play he had written, Marchbanks had no choice in the matter of his domestic engagements. It is Candida, not he, who makes the decision that sends him out into the starry night. When he is rejected, his heart, presumably, is broken. He does not go "proudly" into the night, but, we are told, he rushes out, with wild words of dire import. The explanation Shaw gave the Rugby youths, however, seems to have suited him better than anything he had offered so far as an interpretation, and he repeated it to Huneker. In this, no doubt, Shaw exhibited wisdom. The question of Marchbanks from a psychological point of view is complex. There is no reason to suppose that it was completely clear to Shaw. It was, in any case, best resolved simply. Marchbanks is, as Shaw repeatedly suggested elsewhere, a creature from another world. "He belonged to the night, to the world of dreams—." Probably he had no business on the stage. Indeed, for all his charm as a character, from the time of Granville-Barker nobody has been able to play Marchbanks convincingly save Granville-Barker, and few have been able to play him at all. The poet's secret, whatever it is, has been well kept in the theater. The secret that is revealed to Morell, however, is clear enough. It is not that a strong man is weak, for in truth

Morell is not weak; but that a woman always belongs to someone other than her husband, someone who inhabits the world of dreams and, if her husband is lucky, inhabits only that world.

The youthful Marchbanks, meanwhile, affords us a first glimpse of the superman. In the Shavian myth the superman is not a father, but a son. His province is the future; he is part of the world to come. At this stage of his development Marchbanks is a vague, disturbing figure barely detached from the romantic darkness to which he is ultimately relegated. It was evidently necessary for Shaw to bring him out into the light more clearly, and to this end he bent his efforts in his next plays. The task of defining the superman actually did not end for Shaw until he wrote *Back to Methuselah*. It began, however, immediately after *Candida*.

In the summer of 1895 Shaw wrote *The Man of Destiny*, a long one-act comedy involving Napoleon and the tricks of a young woman disguised as a man. The plot was quite conventionally contrived and highly amusing after the French manner. The play was Shaw's most obvious bid for commercial success, and there is nothing to indicate that he had a very high opinion of it as a work of art. "It is all stage business of the good old Napoleonic kind," he wrote to Janet Achurch, "hand in breast, hands behind back, trots up and down the room, curt speeches, and so on. The woman has a good comedy part. *She must be fascinating and she must look well in a man's uniform.*"

For the historical background he evidently depended on W. M. Sloane's *Life of Napoleon Bonaparte* which was running at this time as a serial in the *Century Magazine* in New York, but in his view the title role was purely a theatrical invention, without any special historicity: "The fun to me is that the character is not Napolean at all, but Mansfield."[38] Shaw did not offer the part of the Strange Lady to Miss Achurch. He had bigger things in mind. As soon as *The Man of Destiny* was finished, he began his courtship of Ellen Terry.

The wooing of Ellen Terry, at that time the most famous actress in England, provides an interesting instance of the adaptation of the Abelard-Héloïse myth to a contemporary setting. The Shaw-Terry correspondence, which makes delightful reading, actually centers on Shaw's efforts to get his plays produced at the Lyceum. These efforts lasted some five years and ended in disaster, but they resulted in a literary production which is, in many ways, quite as remarkable as the plays that engendered it.

As it turned out, the Shaw-Terry-Irving triangle was not essentially different from the situation Shaw had dreamed up in *Candida*. Ellen Terry and Henry Irving were not married, but in the theater they were allied as closely as Candida and Morell in their home. The Lyceum therefore gave Shaw an opportunity to exploit his favorite domestic situation, and he made preparations to move in at once on this august couple. But if the situation he sought to create in reality was a caricature of the situation he had imagined in *Candida*, the goal he had in mind was entirely realistic. Ellen Terry had to be won, but she was an intermediate goal. It was Irving he was after. In the beginning Shaw had no wish to destroy their relationship. He desired only to use it. It was only as a last resort that he attempted to demolish their partnership.

Shaw made two attempts to assault Irving's citadel. The first was in connection with *The Man of Destiny*, which had good parts for both Irving and Miss Terry. This venture would possibly have succeeded had Shaw pursued his advantage less vigorously. The second involved *Captain Brassbound's Conversion*. It was compromised by the antagonism which had by that time developed between Irving and Shaw. From a Machiavellian viewpoint, the entire affair was most lamentably mismanaged.

Very likely Shaw's attempt to enlist Ellen Terry's support in his campaign was doomed from the start, for their interests by no means coincided. Shaw was eager to break into the London theater at the summit. The summit was the Lyceum, where Irving reigned. In England the Lyceum was the only true temple of dramatic art, the citadel of good taste, and the pinnacle of the dramatic hierarchy. Its openings were brilliant social events. Its productions commanded the critics' respect and provided much serious discussion in the press. It was Shaw's greatest ambition in these years to have his work acted there. But to gain an entrance was no simple matter. Irving did not experiment with untried authors.

The Man of Destiny was devised as an entering wedge. It was in the current fashion, a much more commercial play than anything Shaw had so far written, short, and inexpensive to produce. If Shaw could induce Irving to perform it, it might well inaugurate his campaign to revise Irving's repertory, the substitution of Ibsen and Shaw for Shakespeare and Sardou, and ultimately it might mean the revolutionizing of the English theater. To this end, Shaw marshaled all his resources as critic, as author, and even as lover.

Shaw wooed Ellen Terry with all the ardor of a middle-aged Romeo— but he courted her exclusively on paper, keeping a sharp eye meanwhile on Irving. In the *Saturday Review* he played Irving like an experienced angler, alternately praising him to the skies as an actor, and reviling him mercilessly for his choice of plays. The campaign, conceived by Shaw as a holy war, included also the systematic disparagement of Shakespeare, Irving's principal dramatic resource. The full-scale attack on the Bard, however, did not begin until some years later. For the moment he concentrated on the gifted Ellen.

The move was well calculated. Miss Terry was anxious to secure her future by associating herself with the avant garde of the time. The old line was obviously played out, and Shaw's vigorous approach to the new drama gave promise of artistic rewards beyond anything else at hand in England. But Ellen Terry was too deeply rooted in tradition to make a new departure without serious misgivings. Shaw's plays had scenes which intrigued her, but they were not faultless plays. From the professional standpoint they were only too clearly the work of an amateur, and Terry's experienced eye saw much in them that gave her pause. She was, moreover, uncomfortably aware that as an actress she had passed her prime. Her embarrassment, accordingly, was extreme, and she dallied indecisively with Shaw from 1895 until 1900, unwilling to engage herself in his projects, and reluctant to give them up. After five years of fruitless negotiation, it became evident to both of them that they were not destined to be of use to one another, and their correspondence, together with the erotic mood they had sustained, dwindled into a desultory exchange of amicable notes.

In these years Shaw nourished great hopes for a revival of English drama, motivated by himself, and executed by these two great actors. It was for reasons beyond his control, including his own temperament, that the project failed. "And so, in the end," he wrote sadly in his notes to the published version of his correspondence with Ellen Terry, "my early vision of the two as ideal instruments for a new drama did not come true."[39] What came true was the correspondence itself, a minor masterpiece of epistolary art.

This correspondence had begun quite innocently in 1892, when Miss Terry wrote Edmund Yates, at that time editor of *The World*, to inquire about the talents of a young singer, a Miss Gambogi, in whom she was interested. The letter was referred to Shaw, as music critic, and Shaw dutifully reported to Miss Terry on Miss Gambogi's mediocre talents and prospects. After a short exchange of letters, the correspondence lapsed. Three years later, when Shaw was drama critic for the *Saturday Review*, and already an ambitious playwright, he resumed his correspondence, this time on a more intimate note:

To my great exasperation I hear that you are going to play Madame Sans Gêne. And I have just finished a beautiful little one act play for Napoleon and a strange lady—a strange lady who will be murdered by someone else whilst you are nonsensically pretending to play a washerwoman. It is too bad—I tell you you can't play a washerwoman.[40]

Miss Terry took the bait readily. Toward the end of the month, Shaw sent her a copy of *The Man of Destiny* to read during her American tour with Henry Irving. There ensued lengthy negotiations. By the beginning of March 1896, Shaw began to show signs of irritation. He redoubled his efforts to charm Miss Terry:

You will detect at a glance the adroit mixture of flattery and business in this letter. I am eager for business—keen on it—because it will be an excuse for more flattery—because I can gratify my desire to talk nonsense to you under cover of filling my pockets; I *must* attach myself to you somehow: let me therefore do it as a matter of business. Gold, be thou my idol henceforth.[41]

By this time he was protesting, with transparent hypocrisy, that he had never had any idea of offering the play to Henry Irving,

. . . Having no idea that His Immensity had any sort of interest in the play—having sent it to you, I swear, out of pure vanity, to steal another priceless millionth of an inch of your regard by shewing you what a clever fellow I am—I might at any moment have parted with it to Mansfield or another, both for England and America. . . . Will you therefore befriend me to the extent of letting me know seriously whether H. I. wishes me to hold the play for him, as its production by him would of course be quite the best thing that could happen to it.

He then proceeded to lay down stiff terms for its production, and concluded:

But it is all nonsense: you are only playing with me. I will go to that beautiful Mrs Patrick Campbell, who won my heart long ago by her pianoforte playing as Mrs Tanqueray, and make her head twirl like a chimney cowl with my blarney. *She* shall play the Strange Lady—she and the passion worn Forbes. Yes, it shall be so. Farewell, faithless Ellen![42]

It was, however, by no means farewell. Ellen Terry was not eager to play the Strange Lady; she wondered whether she might not play Candida instead. Shaw would not let her read *Candida*; he insisted he must read it to her himself. He was, in fact, not anxious to let her attempt Candida, which he had in a sense mortgaged to Janet Achurch. Yet it was impossible to keep the script of *Candida* from Miss Terry indefinitely, and, when at last he sent it to her, she did not respond properly. *Candida* made her weep, she wrote, but H. I. would not like it. He would laugh.[43]

In the meantime, curiously enough, the epistolary flirtation began to engender its own vitality, and for a time it lived a life of its own, more or less independent of the business in hand. Somehow these two self-centered people slipped into real intimacy. By the end of 1896, their temperature had risen appreciably. In a letter dated 8 December 1896, having briefed Miss Terry thoroughly on the progress of his courtship of Miss Payne Townshend, Shaw added, "I must stop: I have nothing to say, or rather no time to say it in. I love you. You are at liberty to make what use you please of this communication. Of course I will love you after Thursday; but the point is that I love you *now*."[44]

It was a strange business. They wrote one another very often, but in spite of the fact that they inhabited the same city, they did not meet for many years, and when they did, it was brief and perfunctory, and only once. For Shaw, Ellen Terry remained an abstraction, nightly visible in all the splendor of Irving's magnificent lighting at the Lyceum, but for the rest an utterly remote presence which became articulate with gratifying regularity in the morning post and nowhere else. As for her, the image Shaw created was attractive, evidently, but not altogether absorbing. It was not, and in the nature of their relationship could not be, a unified work of art. The Shaw he conjured up for her glimmered mysteriously through the mist of blarney with which he so efficiently shrouded it. He was incredible—and she did not believe him.

In the spring of 1896 his passion for her apparently exceeded all bounds. At this time he wrote Bertha Newcombe, with whom he was temporarily involved on a less exalted plane:

> My correspondence with Ellen Terry, the blarneying audacities of which would fill you with envy could you read them, has ended in an offer from Irving to buy the Napoleon play. On my refusing to sell, he offered to give me £3 a night for it. I stipulated for production this year; this was declared impossible & next year proposed, upon which I suddenly and elusively slipped away from business into a thousand wild stories and extravagances and adorations (I really do love Ellen), which are at present on the way to her. The fact is I suspect Irving regards my shewing her the play as a familiar means of securing my share of the bribery current in my profession: at least this is just as likely as not. He has no doubt bought many a play without the faintest intention of ever performing it. You must keep my counsel in these matters.[45]

This professional wooing might well have annoyed a less sturdy soul than Miss Terry. But the actress was inured to adulation, and these letters from an important drama critic evidently pleased her very much. She therefore responded suitably to his love-making, took no heed of his admonitions, and was patently resolved not to yield an inch to his blandishments. The correspondence soon crystallized into classic patterns, and it was maintained along these lines for some three years more. It was only when matters of business came up that its tone changed. Then the idiom altered with startling abruptness, and these lovers revealed themselves as hardheaded business people intent on their interests. Neither party seemed at all surprised by these sudden lapses. Their expressions of love were sincere, no doubt, but they were poetic abstractions, belonging to the fictions of a profession, the cutthroat tactics of which have always been sweetened by expressions of special warmth and intimacy.

Shorn of its frills, the correspondence is seen to be a canny negotiation conducted with the greatest astuteness on both sides, an excellent production, and only occasionally a little sickening. It would have been, perhaps, less tolerable had not Shaw been, as usual, disarmingly frank about his hypocrisy:

> I am fond of women (or one in a thousand, say): but am in earnest about quite other things. To most women one man and one lifetime make a world. I require whole populations and historical epochs to engage my interests seriously and make the writing machine (for that is what G. B. S. is) work at full speed and pressure: love is only a diversion and recreation to me. Doubtless, dear Ellen, you've observed that you can't act things perfectly until you've got beyond them, and so have nothing further to fear from them. That's why the women who fall in love with me worry and torment me, and make scenes (which they can't act) with me and suffer misery & destroy their health & beauty, whilst you, who could do without me as easily as I do without Julia (for instance) are my blessing and refuge, and really care more for *everybody* (including myself) than Julia cared for me. It is also, alas! why I act the lover so diabolically well that even the women who are clever enough to understand that such a person as myself might exist, can't bring themselves to believe that I am that person. My *impulses* are so prettily played—oh *you* know: you wretch, you've done it often enough yourself.

After this he had the effrontery to add: "I love you soulfully & bodifully, properly and improperly, every way that a woman can be loved. G. B. S."[46]

In thus inviting Ellen Terry's complicity in his efforts to deceive her, Shaw was perhaps underestimating her intelligence. She was a simpler and more straightforward person than he and had shown herself quite capable of love and sincere devotion. But Shaw was determined to display his intellectual prowess and willingly compromised his image as a romantic lover in order to cut a realistic figure as well. He was certainly capable of remarkable objectivity with regard to himself. In the preface he wrote in 1928 for the Ellen Terry correspondence he described himself, and his performance, with characteristic candor:

> Shaw was unlike Irving in all respects except that both of them were incorrigible actors. And unlike even there because Irving acted avowedly and in the theatre only, whereas Shaw made all the world his stage and was not supposed to be acting, in spite of his frequent clowning, and the mask of mountebankery which Ellen Terry saw through so easily.[47]

For one so incurably self-conscious as Shaw, the interesting question must have been what face he wore behind the mountebank's mask which he so willingly displayed. It is possible that, like Strindberg, he was not altogether sure of the nuance that distinguishes fantasy from reality, and that consequently he was not clear as to when he was acting and when he was not. At any rate, the duplicity of which he so readily accused himself was clearly mirrored in the characters he devised for the stage. Many of his plays culminate in a startling revelation of character, a more or less classical recognition of identity in which the character unmasks, or is unmasked by the event. These revelations seem in each case provisional. It is by no means certain that, when the mummery is over, the essential Blunstchli emerges, or Sergius, or Dudgeon, or Shotover. Even Joan is somewhat equivocal in her sainthood. Shaw had to a remarkable degree the ability to see through the superficial aspects of his personages, but it is seldom that he gives us the feeling of having probed to the heart of their mystery. His analysis stopped short of the ultimate, and his characters remain essentially impenetrable, like himself.

Save for the volume of letters which Miss Terry published in 1931, with an appropriately rhetorical introduction by Shaw, the Terry-Shaw affair had no substantial outcome. The book was perhaps enough. "Tout au monde," Mallarmé had written, "existe pour aboutir à un livre."

By the time Shaw embarked on his campaign to have *The Man of Destiny* performed at the Lyceum he had been a drama critic for rather more than a year. Irving was approaching sixty. When Ellen Terry brought him *The Man of Destiny*, he adopted a receptive posture, but he would not commit himself definitely to its production until he could find a place for a one-act play in his repertory, and a suitable piece to go with it. Nevertheless he offered Shaw fifty pounds per year for the option to produce it. Since Irving was in the habit of endearing himself to the critics by means of little douceurs of this sort, Shaw thought it unseemly to accept the advance. He insisted instead on a definite production date and a guarantee of minimum royalties. Along with these stiff conditions, he offered Irving the play for nothing, so he said, provided Irving would agree to produce Ibsen's *The Pretenders* or *Peer Gynt*.[48]

On 22 September 1896, Irving opened his new production of *Cymbeline*. In the customary curtain speech he said nothing about *The Man of Destiny*, but he announced that in the coming season he would appear in *Richard III*, and also as Napoleon in Sardou's *Madame Sans-Gêne*. The obvious inference was that he would not play Napoleon in Shaw's *The Man of Destiny*. Four days later, however, Irving asked Shaw to call at the Lyceum to discuss terms.

By this time he had probably read Shaw's account of *Cymbeline* in the *Saturday Review*. The notice was a masterpiece of critical tact. Shaw attacked the play and the production savagely. At the same time he lavished extravagant praise upon Irving's performance in the part of Iachimo. Irving was evidently flattered. He told Shaw he would produce *The Man of Destiny* the coming season along with *Madame Sans-Gêne*.

Shaw was writing now at top speed. By the beginning of 1897 he had finished *The Devil's Disciple*, and he sent it to Ellen Terry at once in the hope that she might induce Irving to read it. Nothing happened. Shaw then decided he would have to bludgeon Irving into paying attention to him. In April 1897, Shaw published a scathing review of Irving's *Olivia*. It was followed by an even more brutal attack on his *Richard III*, in which there was some suggestion that Irving was drunk on the opening night. The affront was inexcusable, and Irving's business manager, Bram Stoker, sent Shaw a curt notification that Irving had changed his mind about producing *The Man of Destiny*. Shaw wrote Ellen Terry: "I am in ecstasies: I have been spoiling for a row; and now I have Mansfield to fight with one hand and H. I. with the other."[49]

At this point, apparently, he decided that the time had come to mollify Irving. He wrote him that he had no intention of disparaging his performance in his criticism of *Richard III*. Irving was not mollified. He answered loftily:

I had not the privilege of reading your criticism—as you call it—of Richard. I never read a criticism of yours in my life. I have read lots of your droll, amusing, irrelevant and sometimes impertinent pages, but criticism containing judgement and sympathy I have never seen from your pen.[50]

With this their correspondence ended. Later that season Irving injured his knee and had to retire temporarily from the scene. The Lyceum had a ruinous season. Miss Terry wrote despairingly of her inability to reconcile her "two lovers," and the manuscript of *The Man of Destiny* was returned with a formal rejection.

Coupled with the withdrawal of *You Never Can Tell*, which had been in rehearsal at the Haymarket, this was a serious setback. Shaw's hopes for a commercial production seemed further off than ever. He wrote Ellen Terry: "I shall trouble myself no more about the theatre. I don't care and never did care who plays Napoleon (it was written for Mansfield); but I should have liked you to play The Strange Lady; and since your infant has put a stop to that, it may be played by Mrs. Pat's dresser for all I care."[51] The next day he wrote again: "Nevertheless you shall play for me yet; but not with him, not with him, not with him."[52]

Evidently Miss Terry was disappointed, if not distressed, by this turn of events. She replied testily: "Well, you are quite stupid, after all and *not* unlike other people. . . . Don't pity H. He thinks he has quite got the best of it in the recent altercation. The fact is he dont think the whole thing matters much. I do, and I'm angry with you."[53]

There was nothing further, and Shaw's disappointment was intense. He published several accounts of the matter over the years, all of them obviously biased, and eventually he accused Irving of having tried to buy him off as a critic with the promise of a production he had no intention of presenting.[54] Two years after his break with Irving he tried once again to win him over, this time in connection with *Captain Brassbound's Conversion*. Irving would have none of it. Shaw never forgave him. There the matter rested.

In the summer of 1897 when it became perfectly clear that Henry Irving would not produce *The Man of Destiny*, Shaw offered the play, as he had threatened, to Richard Mansfield. Mansfield, however, found Shaw's Napoleon distasteful. This character was in every way the antithesis of the heroic figures he liked to play, and he was revolted by Shaw's description of Napoleon's wolfish eating habits. One may, indeed, wonder at Shaw's naïveté in offering a part conceived after this fashion to an actor whose professional daintiness was proverbial. But Shaw felt sure he could revolutionize English taste through the sheer force of his will, and he did not slacken his efforts to force realism on those who were dedicated to romance. After receiving Mansfield's unequivocal rejection of *The Man of Destiny*, Shaw wrote him with his customary persuasiveness: "I was much hurt by your contemptuous refusal of 'A Man of Destiny,' not because I think it one of my masterpieces, but because Napoleon is nobody else but Richard Mansfield himself. I studied the character from you, and then read up on Napoleon and found that I'd got him exactly right."[55]

This obvious bit of blarney had an effect quite contrary to what was intended. Mansfield interpreted Shaw's flattery as a slur on his table manners and for a time refused to have further dealings with him. Meanwhile three performances of *The Man of Destiny* were given in the first week of July 1897 at the Grand Theatre, Croydon, with Murray Carson in the title role and Florence West as the Strange Lady. Shaw was greatly disappointed with the production, and for a time, despaired of the play.[56] It was not until March 1901 that *The Man of Destiny* was produced in London. It opened at the Comedy, with Granville-Barker as Napoleon, and was received with enthusiasm. Ellen Terry never played the Strange Lady and in this she showed wisdom. She was by no means suited to the part.

It is customary, in accounts of Shaw's dramatic career to pass over *The Man of Destiny* tactfully as a minor bid for public attention; no more than the "commercial traveler's sample" which Shaw called it in his letter to Ellen Terry. Nevertheless his immense disappointment when his plans for it miscarried indicates that he had a higher opinion of it than his comments suggest. It is, in truth, a farce of no great weight, full of the usual improbabilities of the genre, and chiefly interesting for the realistic portrayal of the hero, in whom it is far easier to recognize Shaw at the age of thirty-nine than Napoleon at twenty-six or Mansfield at thirty-eight. Shaw described his hero carefully and at length:

> He has prodigious powers of work, and a clear realistic knowledge of human nature in public affairs. . . . He is imaginative without illusions, and creative without religion, loyalty, patriotism or any of the common ideals. Not that he is incapable of these ideals; on the contrary, he has swallowed them all in his boyhood, and now, having a keen dramatic faculty, is extremely clever at playing upon them by the arts of the actor and stage-manager. Withal, he is no spoiled child. Poverty, ill-luck, the shifts of impecunious shabby gentility,

repeated failure as a would-be author, humiliation as a rebuffed time-
server . . . these trials have ground his conceit out of him, and forced
him to be self-sufficient and to understand that to such men as he is
the world will give nothing that he cannot take by force. In this the
world is not free from cowardice and folly, for Napoleon, as a
merciless cannonader of political rubbish, is making himself useful:
indeed it is even now impossible to live in England without sometimes
feeling how much that country lost in not being conquered by him as
well as by Julius Caesar.[57]

The Man of Destiny is written in the style of Scribe's La Bataille de
Dames and its plot in some measure resembles that of Sardou's Dora. It is
a contest of wits which seesaws through a succession of pleasant scenes
involving the handing about of a packet of letters, until Napoleon ac-
knowledges himself beaten by the superior strategy of the Strange Lady
and the letters at last are destroyed. The Lady has come, ostensibly, to
prevent him from reading a letter which compromises Josephine and
Barras. She does not in fact prevent him from reading it. She succeeds
only in furnishing him with a pretext for burning it—something he
would have done, we gather, in any case. There does not seem, therefore, to be much point in the Lady's intervention, aside from the occasion it affords her to coquette a little with her best friend's husband, the
General.

The plot is very brightly, but not very skillfully, contrived. It by no
means demonstrates Shaw's mastery of stage tricks, nor even of stage
logic. It does, however, provide a very agreeable hour's entertainment,
very suitable for amateur performance, in the course of which are suggested a number of ideas that must have been disturbing in the 1890's
and are still of considerable interest in the theater. Among them are some
clear insights into the nature of heroes, and the indication of a rational
approach to domestic relations, a theme later developed fully by Chiarelli and Pirandello. Napoleon says: "Do you suppose, little innocent,
that a man wants to be compelled by public opinion to make a scene, to
fight a duel, to break up his household, to injure his career by a scandal,
when he can avoid it all by taking care not to know?" Such speeches
lend sparkle to the dialogue, but not realism. Napoleon would very
likely have acted in accordance with this thought, but it is doubtful that
he would have expressed it. In this passage it is obviously the author, not
the character, who is speaking. The result of this technique is that we
sometimes lose sight of the character; we never lose sight of the author.

For all its flimsiness The Man of Destiny was an outstanding play for its time, and one wonders at the shortsightedness of those who refused to see its merits. No English dramatist of the period, not Wilde or Gilbert, could display so lively a sense of repartee and so clear an insight into human nature. Nor had anyone in England so far developed as showy a character part as that of the ingenious innkeeper in this play. Giuseppe is a type out of French comedy who had already seen some service on the English stage. Shaw managed him with unusual skill. The difficulty was that at this time it was hardly possible for a leading man to play a "character" unless he dominated the action—as does the Waiter in *You Never Can Tell*. It is consequently understandable that neither Irving nor Mansfield could see anything in the play that suited their particular talents.

On the contrary, both were convinced that *The Man of Destiny* was a risky venture, the drawbacks of which far outweighed its advantages. Romance was the order of the day. *The Man of Destiny* is essentially parodic, a "realistic" interpretation of romantic comedy, and openly subversive of the established tradition. In attempting to badger Irving into playing his Napoleon, Shaw gave evidence of truly Machiavellian shrewdness, though he was by no means skillful in seeing his venture through. But Irving had no idea of letting himself be compromised in this manner, and Shaw's bid for popular acceptance at the Lyceum thus suffered an inevitable setback. He had an even more discouraging experience at the Haymarket.

You Never Can Tell was begun in the summer of 1895. It was finished in the fall, and Shaw offered it at once to Cyril Maude, who accepted it with disconcerting alacrity. Unlike Irving, Maude was a specialist in character parts. He greatly fancied the role of William, the aged waiter, and his wife, Winifred Emery, quite fancied herself in the role of Dolly. The play went into rehearsal in April 1897 under Shaw's direction. After a few days the leading lady decided to play Gloria instead of Dolly. Jack Barnes and Fanny Coleman threw up their parts as impossible. There was nobody to play Valentine. Worst of all, the company made nothing at all of the play, and the author's explanations only served to confuse matters further. After some weeks of sterile argument, Shaw was faced with the prospect of rewriting the love scenes to suit the actors. He refused. He wrote Ellen Terry: "I have embraced the opportunity of escaping a 'brilliant success,' and now my one hope is that they are as much in earnest as I am; for I have had enough of wasting time on success that might have been employed in producing something real."[58]

The play was withdrawn, and with it Shaw's first encounter with the commercial theater came to an end. It was only after the Barker-Vedrenne seasons at the Court Theatre that London managers became aware of the popular interest in Shaw's comedies. By this time the theatrical revolution had already taken place, and Shaw was "commercial" everywhere save in England.

You Never Can Tell was domestic farce-comedy, a genre which Shaw had so far affected to despise, and it marked a change in his approach to the theater. He had begun as a writer of serious comedy in the French style. In this endeavor he had been uniformly unsuccessful. *Candida* was a venture into domestic comedy in the manner of Ibsen. It had received high praise in some quarters, but it had not yet been widely performed. His first success, *Arms and the Man*, had been an attempt at romantic comedy, but beyond its wry comment on military glory, it had no special significance and was of little use as a guide to future effort. *The Man of Destiny* was an interesting attempt to bridge the distance that still separated Shaw from the wide following to which he aspired, but the formula he had found for it, romantic farce with serious overtones, was evidently not quite what was needed. Once again he corrected his sights. *You Never Can Tell* was concocted with all the traditional ingredients of successful light comedy. In addition it had intellectual nuances and an Ibsenist orientation. This was as far as Shaw was prepared to go in the direction of popular drama. It was evidently not far enough.

In the preface to *The Pleasant Plays* Shaw wrote:

> ... Far from taking an unsympathetic view of the popular preference for fun, fashionable dresses, a little music, and even an exhibition of eating and drinking by people with an expensive air, attended by an if-possible-comic waiter, I was more than willing to shew that the drama can humanize these things as easily as they, in the wrong hands, can dehumanize the drama. But as often happens it was easier to do this than to persuade those who had asked for it that they had indeed got it. A chapter in Cyril Maude's history of the Haymarket Theatre records how the play was rehearsed there, and why I withdrew it.[59]

Shaw proposed to humanize the current stereotypes simply by giving them a realistic turn. This involved some difficulty. Conventional plot sequences could be made realistic only by peopling them with characters motivated by considerations that have validity in real life. Such considerations had, as a rule, little validity in the theater. In England in the 1890's, the facts of experience were not compatible with the "realities" of the stage. In a play such as Pinero's *The Profligate* (1889), for example, or Wilde's *An Ideal Husband* (1895), considerations of probability and common sense would obviously serve no useful purpose.

On the popular stage it was expected that conventional characters would do conventional things for conventional reasons. The fact that plays were expected to arouse admiration, but not thought, made it possible to concentrate on performance rather than idea, and the whole art of the theatre was conventionalized in accordance with age-old assumptions which it occurred to no one to question. The theatrical revolution which Shaw envisaged depended on questioning these very assumptions, as Ibsen had questioned them, in the light of human experience. "To me," Shaw had written, "the tragedy and the comedy of life lie in the consequences, sometimes terrible, sometimes ludicrous, of our persistent attempts to found our institutions on the ideals suggested to our imagination by our half-satisfied passions, instead of on a genuinely scientific natural history."[60]

It was his aim to manage a dramatic contrast between the sort of behavior that was thought of as ideal and the normal behavior of real people. But in a play composed of stock characters, it was virtually impossible to prevent these figures from playing out their roles in accordance with their ideal nature. In the ordinary course of playacting the lines of business were simple and rigid, and the actors who undertook them were both adept and inflexible. In causing his characters to explain their actions in ways unsuited to their traditional mentality, Shaw was proposing a dislocation of dramatic practice which was certain to throw his actors into a panic. In fact, they complained that Shaw provided them with neither laughs nor exits; but the simple truth was that once they ceased to function conventionally they no longer knew what they were doing and could neither get laughs nor manage exits.

You Never Can Tell, therefore, was all but impossible to produce in the current state of the commercial theater. In this it differed greatly from *The Importance of Being Earnest* which Wilde had offered two years before, in 1895. This farce was, in its way, equally advanced in its doctrine, but it was infinitely more subtle in its technique. Wilde's characters were quite as rational as Shaw's and equally outspoken; their motives were equally realistic and equally clear, but they were comic figures presented on a level of unreality, and stylized to the point of abstraction. Shaw's puppets, on the other hand, were humanized according to naturalistic principles. Thus, Mr. Crampton's ill temper, and his obstinacy, belong to the stereotype of the crabbed old gentleman, a

Dickensian figure, readily cast, and easily played by a "character man." But the attribution of his ill nature to the sufferings of a loveless marriage involves him in another type of drama, by no means comic and not particularly popular. His humanization thus required him to elicit sympathy and understanding rather than laughter and related him ideologically to complex personages quite foreign to the comic stage. Unlike the character types of domestic comedy which need neither justification nor etiology, Crampton invites careful attention and is expected to provoke discussion. What Shaw was aiming at, apparently, in elaborating this character was the type of tragicomic figure of which Ibsen had made a speciality. It was a great deal to ask of an English line-actor in the 1890's, and even more of an English audience long accustomed to simple entertainments in which everyone knew when to laugh and when to cry.

"To laugh without sympathy is a ruinous abuse of a noble function," Shaw wrote in a review of some London farces in 1896, "and the degradation of any race may be measured by the degree of their addiction to it. . . . Farcical comedy . . . is, at bottom, . . . the deliberate indulgence of that horrible, derisive joy in humiliation and suffering which is the beastliest element in human nature."[61] This dictum, obviously, mirrors the sensibility of a period which prided itself on its humanitarian attitudes. True comedy was of another sort. None of the classic masks calls for sympathy. In the classic forms exemplified by Terence and Plautus, and after them by Jonson and Congreve, the author takes an Olympian view of life which excludes any considerable degree of sentimental identification. Shaw, however, followed Diderot and the later writers of comedy, writers who ostensibly felt sorry for people, and therefore gave a pathetic bias to the comic. From Shaw's essentially romantic viewpoint true comedy was inhumanly aggressive, and laughter was evil unless it was tempered with understanding and counterbalanced by compassion. The result of this humanitarian attitude was, ultimately, to assimilate comedy to tragedy along lines which were, in Shaw's case, not so much sentimental as philosophical, that is to say, abstract. Thus farce was justifiable not because it made one laugh, but because it made one think.

What Shaw aimed at in *You Never Can Tell* was a level of comedy in which farcical situations would be given something like tragic weight. In some sense this was the contrary of Ibsen's method. The improbabilities of *You Never Can Tell*, its extraordinary encounters and coincidences, are acceptable only on the level of farce; but they were intended to have the force of parable. The *reductio ad absurdum* of the norms of social behavior would then have a moral connotation, and the jest would imply a sermon. Molière had done something of this sort in terms of the classic forms, tempered by the devices of popular comedy. Shaw proposed to do as much with the popular genres in use in his day. The consequence would be, he considered, not simple entertainment in the style of Morton's *Box and Cox* (1847), or the naughty Palais-Royal farces of which Albery's *Pink Dominos* (1877) was an outstanding English example, but a new and original form of intellectual drama.[62]

You Never Can Tell invited comparison with the current farcical comedy of the commercial theater. The seaside hotel, the comic waiter, and the masked ball were all normal fixtures of this genre. What was new in *You Never Can Tell* was the employment of these devices in the service of an idea. It was this which caused the difficulties of the play at the time it was written and this which assured its longevity thereafter. The play had recommended itself to Cyril Maude for quite obvious reasons. No living writer had so far demonstrated such sure mastery of comic characterization. In *You Never Can Tell* all the commonplaces of the genre were transformed as by a magic touch. The twins, Dolly and Philip, were transmuted from the mischievous children of conventional comedy into a pair of charming elves out of fairyland. The comic waiter became a benevolent minor deity. But unfortunately the traditional plot of domestic estrangement and reconciliation was completely subverted in the interests of a conflict not of passions or financial interests, but of ideas. This was more than the company at the Haymarket had bargained for.

You Never Can Tell has to do with the reconciliation of an estranged husband and wife in the interests of the children. It was a theme firmly rooted in the traditions of sentimental drama and difficult to free from the far-reaching influence of Kotzebue. Shaw managed it with a high hand, transposing its elements to a higher key. Mrs. Clandon, the errant wife, is a former member of The Dialectical Society, and a close spiritual relative of Ibsen's Nora. She is, accordingly, an Ibsenite, Millite, Darwinist, and feminist—a woman of very decided convictions, who has turned her ideas to account by publishing popular books about them. But she has been a long time away from England, and by now her radicalism is dated. In her absence the avant-garde has passed on to other considerations, so that she and her old friend McComas are lost in a limbo of aged causes. Over against these former radicals, the lady's husband, Mr. Crampton, represents the solidly conservative middle class, an organism which never ages. Between these two poles is placed the lovely Gloria, Mr. Crampton's daughter. She has been brought up by her mother in Madeira, far from England, in her mother's image, and is seemingly rational to the point of inhumanity. The action centers on the metamorphosis of Gloria under the influence of love, a force against which rational considerations are seldom effective.

Since Gloria represents a synthesis of the antithetical attitudes exemplified by her parents, the plot has the dialectical configuration of an Ibsenist drama without any of the seriousness which we normally associate with Ibsen. Both Mrs. Clandon and her self-righteous husband represent extreme viewpoints which must in time destroy one another. The future belongs to Gloria, in whom these viewpoints are reconciled through *force majeure*.

The action of *You Never Can Tell* involves a discussion of the patriarchal structure of the family and the sanctity of marriage. It therefore owes something to *A Doll's House*; perhaps something to *Ghosts*. In Gloria, the advanced woman of the future, and in Valentine, the bright, but commonplace Don Juan who captures her fancy, may be seen the spiritual descendants of Mrs. Clandon and Mr. Crampton renewing the duel of the sexes some steps further along the line of evolution. The love story which is the subject of the play is thus seen as a link in an endless chain of such encounters, one extremity of which is lost in the Stone Age and the other in some unimaginable utopia where all is eternally sweetness and light.

The conflict of mind and heart which Gloria experiences is defined by Valentine in the love-scene of Act Two.[63] This scene must have seemed wonderfully fresh and startling in the 1890's, and it still retains its freshness. The wooing of Gloria is delightfully arch. It pokes fun at the new rationalism which is Mrs. Clandon's specialty, while at the same time it represents comically the tension between romance and reason which all Shaw's early plays develop:

GLORIA: Excuse my reminding you that your reason and your knowledge and your experience are not infallible. At least I hope not.

VALENTINE: I must believe them. Unless you wish me to believe my eyes, my heart, my instincts, my imagination, which are all telling me the most monstrous lies about you.

GLORIA: Lies!

VALENTINE: Yes, lies. Do you expect me to believe that you are the most beautiful woman in the world?

GLORIA: That is ridiculous, and rather personal.

VALENTINE: Of course it's ridiculous. Well, thats what my eyes tell me. No: I'm not flattering. I tell you I dont believe it. Do you think that

    if you were to turn away in disgust from my weakness I should sit
    down here and cry like a child?
GLORIA: Why should you, pray?
VALENTINE: Of course not: I'm not such an idiot. And yet my heart tells
    me I should: my fool of a heart. But I'll argue with my heart and
    bring it to reason. . . .[64]

In this dialogue with its pleasant Victorian stuffiness, the experienced
reader will recognize clear traces of the love debates of the thirteenth
century, which were doubtless unknown to Shaw. The tradition is old,
but Shaw saw in this conflict something more than the traditional struggle of mind and heart. In *You Never Can Tell*, toward the end of Act
Two, quite suddenly the Life Force is manifested, and the frivolous
Valentine and the earnest Gloria are thrust instantly into their proper
roles in the cosmic drama.

The Life Force is manifested, it is true, in terms which are rather
chemical than biological. In this regard, Shaw's amorous young man was
anticipated some time before by Professor Remonin in *L'Etrangère*,
which Dumas *fils* had produced in 1876. It was Dr. Remonin's idea that
love and marriage are best understood in terms of chemical and physical
affinities and that Divine Providence itself is manifested as the workings
of the laws of science:

> The great lawgivers, the great religious leaders, the great philosophers
> who instituted marriage on the basis of love were thus working purely
> and simply in physics and chemistry in their most beautiful and most
> exalted forms for the purpose of extracting from marriage the idea of
> the family, morality, labor, and consequently the happiness of man
> which is contained in these three compounds.[65]

Valentine illustrates this thesis with the vigor of a young dentist working on a recalcitrant patient:

GLORIA: I hope you are not going to be so foolish—so vulgar—as to say
    love.
VALENTINE: No, no, no, no, no. Not love: we know better than that.
    Let's call it chemistry. You cant deny that there is such a thing as
    chemical action, chemical affinity, chemical combination: the most
    irresistible of all natural forces. Well, you're attracting me irresistibly.
    Chemically.
GLORIA: Nonsense![66]

Evidently the chemical action of which he speaks is quite pervasive. In
a very little while Gloria also feels its power:

GLORIA (*breaking down suddenly*): Oh, stop telling me what you feel:
I cant bear it.

VALENTINE (*springing up triumphantly, the agonized voice now solid,
ringing, and jubilant*): Ah, it's come at last: my moment of courage.
(*He seizes her hands: she looks at him in terror*). O u r moment of
courage! (*He draws her to him; kisses her with impetuous strength;
and laughs boyishly*). Now youve done it, Gloria. It's all over: we're
in love with one another. (*She can only gasp at him*). But what a
dragon you were! And how hideously afraid I was![67]

In Act Four, the Life Force finds its voice. It has not yet a full
vocabulary, and is not completely identifiable, nor is it yet metaphysi-
cally related to the action. But it speaks with authority.

VALENTINE: . . . You thought yourself very safe, didnt you, behind
your advanced ideas? I amused myself by upsetting t h e m pretty
easily.

GLORIA: Indeed!

VALENTINE: But why did I do it? Because I was being tempted to awaken
your heart: to stir the depths in you. Why was I tempted? Because
Nature was in deadly earnest in me when I was in jest with her.
When the great moment came, who was awakened? who was stirred?
in whom did the depths break up? In myself—m y s e l f. *I* was trans-
ported: you were only offended—shocked. . . .

In fact, Gloria is neither offended nor shocked. She is determined to
have him, just as in *Man and Superman* Ann Whitefield is determined to
have Tanner, and she prepares to overpower her lover, now recalcitrant,
in the same indomitable fashion. He has his moment of panic:

VALENTINE: Take care. I'm losing my senses again. (*Summoning all her
courage, she takes away her hand from her face and puts it on his
right shoulder, turning him towards her and looking him straight in
the eyes. He begins to protest agitatedly*). Gloria: be sensible: it's no
use: I havent a penny in the world. . . .[68]

At this point the lady develops the strength of Hercules. She kisses him
and he is lost. Quite suddenly the romance comes to an end, and life as
usual begins:

DOLLY: The matter's settled; and Valentine's done for. And we're missing
all the dances.

They all dance off, and Valentine is left alone, to savor by himself the
misery of the successful lover:

VALENTINE (*collapsing on the ottoman and staring at the waiter*): I
     might as well be a married man already.
WAITER (*contemplating the defeated Duellist of Sex with ineffable
     benignity*): Cheer up, sir, cheer up. Every man is frightened of mar-
     riage when it comes to the point; but it often turns out very comfort-
     able, very enjoyable and happy, indeed, sir—from time to time. . . .[69]

You Never Can Tell is the first of Shaw's tragic farces. It is perhaps
not his finest work but it includes all the elements of Shaw's future
greatness as a dramatist. It is clear that as early as 1897 he was mulling
over the metabiologic myth which was to find its ultimate expression
three years later in *Man and Superman*. The Life Force is not explicit in
You Never Can Tell, but without doubt it is at work here quite as
effectively as in the analogous scenes in the later play, of which this is
obviously the prototype. Possibly Shaw did not, at this point, realize
how good a play he had written. He knew it was funny, clearly, or he
would not have tried to palm it off on the Haymarket. Whether or not
he knew, as yet, how serious it was, is an open question. Seven years
after its first production in 1899, in answer to William Archer's unappre-
ciative review of its revival in the *Tribune* of July 1906, Shaw wrote
impatiently, "And you still talk about 'a farce.' The thing is a poem and
a document, a sermon and a festival, all in one."[69]

He was right. The play is a celebration of the rites of passage in use by
the English middle class of the 1890's, and of the human sacrifices they
entailed. In 1897, possibly, Shaw was not entirely aware of its importance. By 1906 *Man and Superman* was three years old. By then, Shaw
knew very well what it was he was getting at in *You Never Can Tell*,
and he was able to make it clear to anyone who would listen.

PLAYS FOR PURITANS

In England, next to romantic comedy, melodrama was the most popular dramatic genre of the 1890's. Its principal home in London was the Adelphi in the Strand, which had carried on the tradition of "Adelphi drama" since the days of Ben Webster and Madame Celeste. In Shaw's day, the resident company was headed by William Terriss. He had been its leading man since 1879 and was generally thought of as the greatest living exponent of the art. Shaw's first visit to the Adelphi took place some months after he assumed his duties on the *Saturday Review*. At that time he wrote:

> Last Saturday was made memorable to me by my first visit to the Adelphi Theatre. My frequent allusions to Adelphi melodrama were all founded on a knowledge so perfect that there was no need to verify it experimentally; and now that the experiment has been imposed on me in the course of my professional duty, it has confirmed my deductions to the minutest particular.
>
> Should anyone rush to the conclusion hereupon that my attitude towards the Adelphi Theatre is that of a superior person, he will be quite right. It is precisely because I am able to visit all theatres as a superior person that I am entrusted with my present critical function. As a superior person, then, I hold Adelphi melodrama in high consideration. A really good Adelphi melodrama is of first-rate literary importance, because it only needs elaboration to become a masterpiece. . . . Unfortunately a really good Adelphi melodrama is very hard to get.

He went on then to define the characteristics of a good Adelphi melodrama with all the assurance of an expert:

It should be a simple and sincere drama of action and feeling, kept well within that vast tract of passion and motive which is common to the philosopher and the laborer, relieved by plenty of fun, and depending for variety of human character, not on the high comedy idiosyncrasies which individualize people in spite of the closest similarity of age, sex, and circumstance, but on broad contrasts between types of youth and age, sympathy and selfishness, the maculine and the feminine, the sublime and the ridiculous, and so on. The whole character of the piece must be allegorical, idealistic, full of generalizations and moral lessons; and it must represent conduct as producing swiftly and certainly on the individual the results which in actual life it only produces on the race in the course of many centuries. All of which, obviously, requires for its accomplishment rather greater heads and surer hands than we commonly find in the service of the playhouse.[1]

The suggestion was clear, and Terriss was quick to draw the necessary inference. Shaw's commanding position as a superior person impressed Terriss so much that he proposed a collaboration and actually sent Shaw a synopsis of what he considered to be an ideal Adelphi melodrama. His conception was a bit heady for Shaw, but in September 1896 Shaw began work on an original melodrama for the Adelphi. By the end of the year *The Devil's Disciple* was finished. He offered it to Terriss for production in England, and to Mansfield for America. It was, he wrote Mrs. Mansfield, "just the play for America," but he quite despaired of having Mansfield play it.[2]

Mansfield saw its possibilities immediately. He bought it, put it at once in rehearsal, and opened it on 1 October 1897, in Albany, New York, with Mrs. Mansfield in the part of Judith Anderson. Three days later, he brought it to the Fifth Avenue Theatre in New York City, where it had a run of sixty-four performances. Then he took it on tour.

Its success could not have been more timely. It had been a miserable year for Shaw. His plans had gone all awry, and the leg injury he suffered that year had put him in desperate straits, both mentally and financially. Mansfield's production, however, brought Shaw £2500 in the course of the year; in his circumstances, it was a fortune. His leg healed slowly, but ultimately he regained his health. He even succeeded in publishing two volumes of his plays that year, at his own expense. The following year he married his Irish millionairess and ceased thereafter to worry about money.

The news of Mansfield's success with *The Devil's Disciple* vastly enhanced Terriss's interest in the play; but he had no opportunity to produce it, for in 1897 a madman brought the reign of Terriss at the Adelphi abruptly to an end by stabbing him to death as he left the theater. It was, in any case, by no means certain that Terriss, had he lived, would have produced *The Devil's Disciple* in London. It had all the earmarks of a good melodrama, to be sure, but it was much too abrasive to be a popular piece. For all his vaunted grasp of the medium, Shaw was far from certain, before Mansfield's production, that he had come anywhere near the mark. In November 1896 he wrote Ellen Terry:

> I want your opinion, for I have never tried melodrama before, and this thing with its heroic sacrifices, its impossible court martial, its execution (imagine W. T. *hanged* before the eyes of the Adelphi!) its sobbings and speeches and declamations, may possibly be the most monstrous piece of farcical absurdity that ever made an audience shriek with laughter. And yet I honestly tried for dramatic effect. I think you could give me a really *dry* opinion on it, for it will not tickle you like *Arms and the Man* and *You Never Can Tell*, nor get at your sympathetic side like *Candida* (the hero is not the heroine of the piece this time); and you will have to drudge conscientiously through it like a stage carpenter and tell me whether it is burlesque or not.[3]

Ellen Terry did not consider it burlesque. She was enthusiastic about the second act: "There has," she wrote, "never been anything in the least like it!" But she advised cutting the scenes between Burgoyne and Swindon as irrelevant interruptions. "Then too," she added, "three scenes in one act (and that the *last* act) is clumsy."[4]

She was not troubled, apparently, by the anti-British bias of the play. Others were. It was an unbreakable rule of military melodrama that British arms and British honor must be upheld at any cost, so that when Forbes-Robertson produced *The Devil's Disciple* at the Coronet Theatre, Notting Hill Gate, in September 1900, he proposed changing the last act so as to give Burgoyne the victory. Shaw declined. "I was not prepared," he wrote some years later, "to represent the battle of Saratoga as a British victory."[5]

The result of Shaw's intransigence was that *The Devil's Disciple* had no great success in England. It was first performed there on 26 September 1899 in Kennington, in the London suburbs, with Murray Carson playing the part of Dick Dudgeon, and ran a few weeks. The gallows speech was troublesome. As Carson mounted the cart, he cried, "Long live the devil and damn King George!" In the manuscript draft in the

British Museum, the line reads, "Amen, and God damn the King!"[6] But in the Forbes-Robertson production Dick Dudgeon says: "Amen. My life for the world's future!" It was this pious sentiment which appeared in the published version.

The question of the interpretation to be given this play was even more troublesome. From the preface first published in the volume entitled *Three Plays for Puritans* it might be concluded that the play was meant to be a parody of conventional melodrama and that the time-honored devices of this genre were consciously employed in a mood of Gilbertian topsy-turvydom. In melodrama it was indispensable that the prodigal son have a heart of gold. He was also required to love his mother and, above all, to honor his father. He must certainly rescue the heroine from a fate worse than death, especially at the risk of his life, and always for reasons of love.

In France these prescriptions furnished the customary pattern of melodrama from the time of Pixérécourt. In England they were best exemplified in Dickens's *A Tale of Two Cities*, which Tom Taylor had dramatized in 1860. The plot had more recently furnished the central episode of Boucicault's *Arrah-na-pogue* (1864), a play which Shaw probably had well in mind in framing *The Devil's Disciple*. There were innumerable examples of the genre, all more or less along the same lines.[7]

By the end of the nineteenth century the outlines of this brand of entertainment had crystallized into such rigidity that its rules could be formulated. The Sidney Carton-Chevalier de la Maison Rouge type of self-sacrifice was a favorite culminating episode. Scribe had ventured to present it comically in *La Bataille de dames*, which Tom Robertson adapted in 1851 as *The Lady's Battle*, but this was exceptional. Heroic self-sacrifice was customarily treated with the utmost seriousness and it was expected to elicit tears. Shaw had no idea of making fun of Dick Dudgeon. He was striving, as he had written Ellen Terry, chiefly for dramatic effect, and he was therefore content to preserve the heroic aspect of Dick Dudgeon's self-imposed martyrdom as far as was possible. The only change he made in the traditional formula was in his hero's motivation. Dick Dudgeon does not risk his neck for the love of a lady. He has motives of a higher order, the precise nature of which is not entirely clear to him or to anyone else. His action is by no means less romantic because its motives are mysterious. If anything, its romantic quality is enhanced, though its motives are, it is intimated, realistically presented.

This paradox gave Shaw some trouble but it was evidently intended to be the point of the play. In the Preface to *Three Plays for Puritans*, a real masterpiece of prefatory art, he wrote:

> The Devil's Disciple has, in truth, a genuine novelty in it. Only that novelty is not any invention of my own, but simply the novelty of the advanced thought of my day. As such, it will assuredly lose its gloss with the lapse of time, and leave The Devil's Disciple exposed as the threadbare popular melodrama it technically is. . . .[8]

The implication is that at some happier time in the future, when the romantic basis of melodrama had given way to more enlightened considerations, the motives proposed for self-sacrifice in *The Devil's Disciple* would be accepted so generally that the play would sink back to the level of melodrama from which it had been raised through the novelty of its ideas. The innovations of the present—Shaw had said more than once—are the commonplaces of the future.

If Shaw's prophecy has not yet come true, the fault is in some measure his, since his preface does nothing to clarify the advanced thought of his day with respect to Dick Dudgeon's motives. The passage in which these are discussed is interesting:

> But then, said the critics, where is the motive? *Why* did Dick save Anderson? On the stage, it appears, people do things for reasons. Off the stage they dont. . . . The saving of life at the risk of the saver's own is not a common thing; but modern populations are so vast that even the most uncommon things are recorded once a week or oftener. Not one of my critics but has seen a hundred times in his paper how some policeman or fireman or nursemaid has received a medal, or the compliments of a magistrate, or perhaps a public funeral, for risking his or her life to save another's. Has he ever seen it added that the saved was the husband of the woman the saver loved, or was that woman herself, or was even known to the saver as much as by sight? Never. When we want to read of the deeds that are done for love, whither do we turn? To the murder column. . . .[9]

The suggestion is ingenious, but the analogy is not especially cogent. Few instances are reported of policemen or firemen who, out of a sense of duty, offer their necks to the public executioner, as does Dick Dudgeon, in order to save a convicted insurgent. The extraordinary behavior of Dick Dudgeon in the circumstances does not come, however, as a surprise. His eccentricity is carefully planted from the first scenes of the play. Like Shaw, he is a superior person, contemptuous of middle-class hypocrisy, hardened by an unhappy childhood to the point where the wholesale extermination of his family leaves him sprightly and debonair. The death of his father does not grieve him in the least; nor is he troubled by his mother's curse; nor by the rest of the traditional sources of psychic discomfort. On the other hand, he is fiercely protective of the hapless Essie, whom he has not previously met, but whose distress he fathoms at a glance. Obviously he is a difficult and enthusiastic character, immune to conventional considerations, acutely sensitive to injustice, and irrationally headstrong in his reactions. He is, indeed, the modern version of the romantic scapegrace with the heart of gold, Karl von Moor in a New England setting.

What is chiefly remarkable in this character is his insistence on the freedom of his will and the law of his nature, considerations which would not have occurred to Schiller's idealistic hero. On this basis Dick fashions a code of behavior which lies well outside conventional imperatives. Nothing compels him to die for another. It is a magnificent but seemingly motiveless action, like the *acte gratuit* of the heroes of Gide, an act of will which serves to differentiate him from the mass of humanity. As in the case of Lavinia in *Androcles and the Lion*, and the Antigone of Anouilh's play, his offer of martyrdom is something that chiefly serves to affirm his superiority as an individual, a luxurious act which is exalted to sublimity because in affirming his own magnanimity he also affirms the potential greatness of the human race. He tells Judith:

> If I said—to please you—that I did what I did ever so little for your
> sake, I lied, as men always lie to women. . . . What I did last night, I
> did in cold blood caring not so much for your husband or for you as
> I do for myself. I had no motive and no interest: all I can tell you is
> that when it came to the point whether I could take my neck out of
> the noose and put another man's neck into it, I could not do it. . . .
> I have been brought up standing by the law of my own nature; and I
> may not go against it, gallows or no gallows. I should have done the
> same thing for any other man in the town, or any other man's wife.[10]

Not being of a philosophical turn of mind, like his author, Dick Dudgeon does not trouble to explain himself further. But there is nothing mysterious about his intellectual affiliations. He is an anarchist. Like Siegfried in *The Perfect Wagnerite*, he is "a totally unmoral person . . . the ideal of Bakoonin, an anticipation of the 'overman' of Nietzsche."[11] Shaw's omission to identify the sources of his hero's ideological orientation is attributable to his good sense in avoiding an embarrassing issue outside the Fabian pale.[12] At the time of the American Revolution, anarchism had not yet found its way formally into print. It was not until

1793 that William Godwin, in his *Enquiry Concerning Political Justice*, advocated the abolition of government in any form and laid down the blueprint for anarchistic egalitarianism. Dick Dudgeon does not go so far. His anarchism is not dogmatic. He is merely an extreme individualist.

Anarchism in the 1890's was based on the belief that men are naturally good but are perverted by the restrictions placed on their liberty by the social institutions they themselves engender, in short, by civilization. This idea had long ago found expression in the heretical writings of Pelagius. In Rousseau's formulation the idea was particularly congenial to the romanticists of the early nineteenth century, and it was closely involved with the wave of Satanism which swept over western Europe in the time of Byron. In the early nineteenth century the devil and his advocates had interesting political connotations, especially with relation to the problem of the freedom of the individual and the authority of the state and church, questions that were widely discussed in socialist circles.

Nineteenth-century socialism was far from a homogeneous movement. It developed along several more or less independent lines, the divergence of which resulted in fiery polemics. The doctrines of Saint-Simon furnished the basis for what came to be called social democracy, of which the Fabian Society was an offshoot. The ideas of Robert Owen resulted in the rise of trade unionism. The followers of Fourier founded cooperatives. It was out of the doctrines of Proudhon that modern anarchism developed.

The result of social democratic efforts to acquire power within the existing social structure was to stimulate state capitalism and the centralization of power in the government. Against this tendency were arrayed such revolutionists as Hess and Bakunin, who felt oppressed by the idea of governmental paternalism in any form. To their minds the only system that ensured social justice was a federation of free communes along the lines laid down in Proudhon's *The Federative Principle* (1873). After 1870 European thought was strongly influenced by German philosophy, and particularly by Hegelian ideas. The system of Marx and Engels thus came to be regarded as "scientific" and the anarchistic individualism of Bakunin was dismissed as utopian. At the Hague congress of the 1872 International, Marx went so far as to have Bakunin and his federalists excluded. The anarchist movement, however, did not die with Bakunin, nor did the terrorist methods which he favored. After Bakunin's death in 1876 the work of anarchist propaganda in England was taken over by Prince Pyotr Kropotkin, a most persuasive writer,

strongly inclined to communism but averse to the use of violence. His
evolutionary program was particularly congenial to Shaw.

"There is in mankind," Kropotkin wrote,

> a nucleus of social habits—an inheritance from the past, not yet duly
> appreciated—which is not maintained by coercion and is superior to
> coercion. Upon it all the progress of mankind is based, and so long as
> mankind does not begin to deteriorate physically and mentally, it will
> not be destroyed by any amount of criticism or of occasional revolt
> against it. . . .[13]

Anarchists did not anticipate overnight changes in social relations to be
brought about by means of terror. It was expected that the development
of free communities would be a long and arduous process, and that it
would involve the cooperation of outstanding individuals who would
bring out the best in man through their example:

> We understand also that the prevalent ideas concerning the necessity
> for authority—in which all of us have been bred—would not and
> could not be abandoned by civilized mankind all at once. Long years
> of propaganda and a long succession of partial acts of revolt against
> authority, as well as a complete revision of the teachings now derived
> from history, would be required before men would perceive that they
> had been mistaken in attributing to their rules and their laws what
> was derived in reality from their own sociable feelings and habits. We
> knew all that. But we also knew that in preaching reform in both
> these directions, we should be working with the tide of human
> progress.[14]

It is in this direction that Dick Dudgeon is working. The same may be
said of Parson Anderson, in whom Dick at once recognizes a kindred
spirit. It is an instance where the man of God and the devil's disciple
meet in a common cause. For this cause Dick is willing to die. He is by
no means, as he intimates, generally available for purposes of martyrdom.
He evinces no desire to suffer in place of any of his relatives. He is a
highly specialized fanatic, a moral patriot.

It was no great matter for Shaw to associate with the American Revolution the individualist's never-ending conflict with the state, a conflict
which, from an anarchist's standpoint, can be resolved only when society
is a federation of self-mastered individuals, voluntarily associated for the
common good in accordance with the dictates of nature. This was precisely the Ibsenist viewpoint.

It is in terms of Ibsen's professed anarchism that, in *The Master*

Builder, Solness plans to build "castles in the air on a firm foundation." The goal of the American war of independence, as both Anderson and Dick Dudgeon see it, is that very Kingdom of the Sun, the Third Kingdom, where freedom and responsibility are synonymous. A necessary step in this direction is independence from English authority and English capitalism.[15]

Against these enlightened attitudes, and the lighthearted characters who represent them in *The Devil's Disciple*, are ranged the dour Galileans, the traditional Puritans, with their outworn convictions, their hypocritical austerity, and their sadistic customs. Shaw accounts in some measure for their shortcomings on the ground of their unhappiness. Dick's mother, we are told, was forced by the local preacher to abandon the man she loved and to marry his more sensible brother, whom she disliked. As a result, she has inflicted her disappointment on all her dependents. Only Dick has managed to escape her vengeance and, considering that the God of the Puritans is an evil and oppressive power, he has joined the opposition, and he shocks everyone by calling himself a disciple of the devil. He is not, however, particularly convincing in this role. It is true that, for a romantic, he is enrolled quite early in the devil's charter but he shares with Lucifer only the spirit of revolt. In comparison with his colleagues in an era that was soon to become astonishingly rich in devil's disciples, he is not an impressive Satanist.

Shaw's attitude toward the Satanism of *The Devil's Disciple* was purely provisional. It was soon to be revised in *John Bull's Other Island*, and again in *Man and Superman*. Dick's diabolonian ethics serve his turn as a rebel against the Puritan God, but his devilish attributes are largely cosmetic. Hegel had stressed the role of negation as the source of every new thought. For the romantic age the devil was the symbol of negation and hence of originality. But Dick Dudgeon is not especially original. He is, in fact, a melodramatic character doing melodramatic things. It is actually Burgoyne who represents the devil and it was evidently with this charming cynic, and not with Dick Dudgeon, that Shaw mainly identified himself when he wrote the play.

The sketch of Dick Dudgeon which Shaw provides us in his stage directions does not in the least remind one of Shaw. What is memorable in it is only that Dick has "the eyes of a fanatic." The portrait of Burgoyne, on the other hand, is very carefully detailed:

> He is a man of fashion, gallant enough to have made a distinguished marriage by an elopement, witty enough to write successful comedies, aristocratically-connected enough to have had opportunities of high

military distinction. His eyes, large, brilliant, apprehensive, and intelligent, are his most remarkable feature: without them his fine nose and small mouth would suggest rather more fastidiousness and less force than go to the making of a first-rate general.[16]

Shaw's idea of Burgoyne was based on the account of Burgoyne's life in Edward de Fonblanque's *Political and Military Episodes in the Latter Half of the Eighteenth Century,* published in London in 1876. Beyond this, apparently, Shaw did not trouble to do any considerable research, and his account of the region in which *The Devil's Disciple* takes place bears less resemblance to the geography of New England than his portrait of Burgoyne to the Burgoyne of history.[17] The topography of the region did not, after all, matter very much in this instance, but Burgoyne served a distinct function in the play and had to be properly adapted to his purpose. As Shaw depicts him, Burgoyne has the aristocratic air, the suavity and wit which are traditionally associated with Mephistophelean characters, and he is loyal to the power he serves. He, Anderson, and Dick Dudgeon are initially represented as enemies, but like Trench, Sartorius, and Lickcheese in *Widowers' Houses,* they are birds of a feather and quickly recognize their similarity and common vocation.

In the end they go off together to dinner. Unlike the characters of *Widowers' Houses,* however, they are joined not by their common lack of principle, but by their devotion to the cause they serve, even though these causes are at war with one another. They are, all three, "superior persons," highly evolved individuals exempt from the rigors of ordinary morality and whatever their political commitments may be, they exemplify a chivalric style with which the matter-of-fact brutality of Major Swindon is sharply contrasted.

Shaw threw himself enthusiastically into the characterization of Burgoyne. In describing him he accentuated particularly the traits he considered they had in common, and their common difficulties as superior individuals:

> . . . his peculiar critical temperament and talent, artistic, satirical, rather histrionic, and his fastidious delicacy of sentiment, his fine spirit and humanity, were just the qualities to make him disliked by stupid people because of their dread of ironic criticism. Long after his death, Thackeray, who had an intense sense of human character, but was typically stupid in valuing and interpreting it, instinctively sneered at him and exulted in his defeat. That sneer represents the common English attitude towards the Burgoyne type. Every instance in which critical genius is defeated, and the stupid genius (for both

temperaments have their genius) "muddles through all right," is popular in England. But Burgoyne's failure was no work of his own
temperament but of the stupid temperament.[18]

As a political figure Burgoyne willingly served the cause of British
imperialism, in which Shaw also had confidence, considering that the
government of an established empire was superior to the petty tyrannies
of conflicting nationalistic groups. He served also to represent Shaw's
admiration for men of energy who are able to calculate a course of
action, and to navigate efficiently toward a goal, whatever it might be.
Burgoyne, it is true, seems somewhat lacking in humanity; evidently this
is the price that must be paid for efficiency in the management of people.
To some extent he shares this shortcoming with both Anthony Anderson
and Dick Dudgeon, both of whom have their eyes fixed on goals beyond
ordinary human considerations. In consequence Judith, who is presented
as the typically sentimental heroine of melodrama, is handed about like a
bundle from one man to the other without being consulted as to her
preference.

The implication is that Judith has fallen in love with the younger man.
This is understandable. It is less credible that Anthony should instantly
realize this, and perhaps this was not intended. He does, however, seem
to be quite ready to relinquish his pretty wife, along with his ministry,
in order to free himself for a more dynamic career as a captain of militia.
The shock which his sudden decision occasions contributes a good deal
to the freshness of the play, but also to its fictional character. Anderson
tells Burgoyne in the final scene:

> Sir: it is in the hour of trial that a man finds his true profession. This
> foolish young man boasted himself the Devil's Disciple; but when the
> hour of trial came to him, he found it was his destiny to suffer and be
> faithful to the death. I thought myself a decent minister of the gospel
> of peace; but when the hour of trial came to me, I found that it was
> my destiny to be a man of action and that my place was amid the
> thunder of the captains and the shouting. So I am starting life at fifty
> as Captain Anthony Anderson of the Springtown militia: and the
> Devil's Disciple here will start presently as the Reverend Richard
> Dudgeon, and wag his pow in my old pulpit, and give good advice to
> this silly sentimental little wife of mine. . . .

Nothing less convincing can be imagined than such an outcome to
Dick Dudgeon's diabolonian career. He is certainly given to sudden
displays of rhetoric, like all Shaw's heroic characters, but Shaw endowed
him with no other clerical attributes. On the contrary, he is depicted as

utterly contemptuous of the Westerbridge congregation, as they of him, and it would be something of a miracle if they accepted him as their spiritual guide.

As for Anderson, his inclination for the military life is apparently attested by the fact that he has married a pretty girl, contrary to local custom, and has, we are informed, sold the family bible in order to buy a brace of pistols. There is no other indication that he is qualified, save by temperament, to command a company of militia. The discoveries and peripeties of the third act might perhaps be made convincing by an actor who took care from the first to emphasize Anderson's military disposition. The inference would then be that Anderson's character does not change in his hour of trial, but that he continues to act in accordance with his nature, simply changing his uniform to suit his circumstances. But while a good actor can perhaps in a similar manner transform Dick Dudgeon into a saint, it is not easy to see what anyone can do to transform him into a parson.

The characterization of Dick Dudgeon needlessly enhances the difficulty of the role. Dick is not depicted as a passive man. He is hot-tempered and impulsive, energetically responsive to the promptings of his nature, and not much disposed to reason about them. If, as it seems, this temperament accords with Shaw's idea of a saint, then Dick belongs to the category of the militant saints, high-spirited people of more than normal vitality, single-minded in purpose and of extraordinary courage and fortitude. The suggestion that an individual of this sort would spend his time wagging his pow in a pulpit seems gratuitous, and one suspects it was motivated not by psychological considerations, but by some idea of dramatic symmetry. The exchange of roles that supposedly takes place, however, between the man of God and the devil's disciple is quite lacking in verisimilitude. Dick and Anderson do not represent contrary aspects of humanity like Morell and Marchbanks in *Candida*. They are different versions of the same temperament.

It is by no means suggested, however, that Dick is prepared to accept the role that Anderson has outlined for him, neither the cares of his ministry nor those of his wife, and Shaw wisely leaves this matter unresolved at the end of the play, contenting himself with the bit of prestidigitation which brings about the exchange of partners in the last act. The honesty of this sort of magic may be questioned, but aside from its dazzling effect, the trick has not much importance. What is important is the revelation that the devil's disciple is in reality in the service of humanity, that is to say, in the service of the living God; and that therefore he is associated with the forces of rebellion, of independence, of individualism, and of true morality, all the things which are hateful to the settled burghers of Shaw's New England.

In *The Devil's Disciple* Shaw rings a change on the *Candida* situation which is not entirely consistent with his usual postulate. Shaw's plays generally demonstrate that in a triangular situation the woman will always be drawn to the poet and dreamer, but that she will invariably choose for her mate the man of action. So it is in *Candida* and in *Man and Superman*. It is, of course, tempting to equate Dick Dudgeon with Marchbanks and Anthony Anderson with Morell. The result is then a situation in which the man of action willingly resigns his wife to a young rival who, for his part, gives no sign that he wants her. It is as if in this version of the *Candida* triangle, the two men combined to declare the lady irrelevant to their concerns. The emotional impact of the play is derived, accordingly, not from the agnitions and reversals of the third act, ingenious as they are, but from the normal workings of the melodramatic plot in which the hero sacrifices himself for a noble cause. Since this hero is, from a conventional viewpoint, a wicked character, it would be normal in this genre that his conversion should take place through love. The idea of the redeeming power of love is, of course, venerable. The conditions for the hero's conversion are invariable from the time of Boccaccio. They are all present in *The Devil's Disciple*.

In this play, however, Shaw hoped to explode what he considered an outworn romantic doctrine. Accordingly, Dick Dudgeon is motivated, presumably, not by the love of a woman, but by the love of humanity in general, a passion which, presumably, has even greater power to ennoble. Such an idea has everything to recommend it from an intellectual viewpoint, but for dramatic purposes it appears to be useless. In spite of the lines he is required to speak, and the author's repeated assurances, Dick Dudgeon is forever doomed to play Sidney Carton, and the idea that he chooses to be hanged for any reason other than his love for the beautiful Judith, whose happiness he is in duty bound to ensure, is merely puzzling.

As Shaw was to find once again in *Pygmalion*, the melodramatic forms are not amenable to tinkering. To engage oneself in melodrama is, willynilly, to abide by its rules. Shaw's plan to reform melodrama by means of common sense was doomed from the start. The audience's preconceptions were more vivid than the play, and whatever in the plot was incongruous with the audience's expectations was easily rationalized into conformity. "The critic," Shaw wrote, who discovered a romantic motive for Dick's sacrifice was no mere literary dreamer, but a clever barrister. He pointed out that Dick Dudgeon clearly did adore Mrs Anderson; that it was for her sake that he offered his life to save her beloved husband; and that his explicit denial of his passion was the splendid mendacity of a gentleman whose respect for a married woman, and duty to her absent husband, sealed his passion-palpitating lips. From the moment that this fatally plausible explanation was launched, my play became my critics' play, not mine. Thenceforth Dick Dudgeon every night confirmed the critic by stealing behind Judith, and mutely attesting his passion by surreptitiously imprinting a heartbroken kiss on a stray lock of her hair whilst he uttered the barren denial.[19]

It was, however, not the ingenious critic who rewrote the play to suit himself, but the audience, and the responsibility obviously rested with Shaw. Everything in the play affirms Shaw's romantic sensibility. The fascination that Dick has for Judith is foreshadowed in the first act, and it is made explicit in the second. The attraction that Judith has for Dick is expressed by himself, together with his regret that domestic happiness is not for the likes of him. In the beautiful environment that Judith creates Dick cannot so much as drink his tea, so deep is his awe of it:

RICHARD (*looking dreamily around*): I am thinking. It is all so strange to me. I can see the beauty and peace of this home: I think I have never been more at rest in my life than at this moment; and yet I know quite well I could never live here. It's not in my nature, I suppose, to be domesticated. But it's very beautiful: it's almost holy.[20]

It is only a few minutes later that he is arrested. If Shaw meant by this display of sentiment to lead his audience into a snare, it can only be said that he himself was caught in it. From this point onward the course of the love story is inevitable, and in straining later to disparage its design, Shaw succeeded only in confusing the issue. The Devil's Disciple is, accordingly, a first-rate example of Adelphi melodrama, among the very best the age produced, and none the worse for being a marvelously witty piece of writing. It demonstrated clearly what could be done in this genre by a writer of genius, and also the very limited extent to which one might tamper with the norms of fantasy. For Shaw the result must have been instructive. In spite of the intellectual pressure to which it was subjected, the plot of The Devil's Disciple sprang back into its original shape the moment the play left the author's hands, and the entire experiment indicated once again the extraordinary rigidity of the mythic patterns out of which drama is made. It was to be some time, however,

before Shaw was able to profit by this lesson. When he came to write
Pygmalion sixteen years later, he had to learn it all over again.

In France, Germany, Austria, and Scandinavia prose drama was a literary genre, and plays were regularly composed with a view to publication
prior to their performance on the stage. In England, on the contrary,
dramatic compositions were thought of as acting-vehicles. Unless they
were in verse, and could therefore be called poetry, plays were not often
deemed worthy of publication for the general trade. Moreover, for the
greater part of the nineteenth century the United States did not extend
copyright protection to foreign authors, and English dramatists were not
eager to make their work generally available for piracy. It was customary, therefore, for English publishers to print plays chiefly in paperback
"acting editions" for professional use. When, in 1891, it became possible
to copyright English publications in America, authors soon began to take
an interest in printing their works in a readable form. Henry Arthur
Jones published *Saints and Sinners* with a preface in which he encouraged dramatists to treat their plays as literature. Shortly after, Pinero
followed this suggestion by publishing a selection of his plays in a literary edition. It did not, however, find a ready market. The publisher,
Heinemann, let it go out of print. For a time play publication languished.

Shaw, however, was keenly interested in bringing his plays to the
attention of the general reader. In March 1897 he wrote to Grant Richards, a young publisher of his acquaintance, suggesting the publication of
the plays he had so far written:

> I wish we could get six plays in one volume. I propose to call the
> edition "Plays Pleasant and Unpleasant." Vol. I. *Unpleasant* 3/6, Vol.
> II, *Pleasant*, 5/-. Both together, half a crown. If we could get all six
> into one volume, I should have the unpleasant plays printed on light
> brown paper (Egyptian mummy color) in an ugly style of printing
> and the pleasant ones on white paper (machine hand made) in the
> best Kelmscott style. Nobody has ever done a piebald volume before,
> and the thing would make a sensation.[21]

Three months later the project was actually under way. He had by
now abandoned the idea of a volume in two moods, but he insisted on
"Morris margins" and special paper, the whole to be in the style of
Morris's *Roots of the Mountains*, typeset in Caslon Old Face and printed
at the Chiswick Press in 1892. The financing of the venture was managed
by the fall of 1897. By that time *The Devil's Disciple* was earning substantial royalties, and on October 8th, Shaw wrote Grant Richards that

he had now decided to pay the costs himself, allowing Richards a commission for attending to the details of publication and distribution. In the end, Shaw chose the type face and the paper, designed the title pages, and selected the green cloth binding, which promptly faded. With the shining example of William Morris before him, he went carefully into the question of the press work, emphasized words by spacing instead of italics, avoided apostrophes—though not consistently—and, in addition, adopted some unusual spellings, such as "shew" for "show," which he considered phonetically superior to the current usage. All this tended to give his books a look of singularity, which, together with the air of mystery which he cultivated even in his frankest utterances, was calculated to set him as far apart from other writers in the public eye as if he were a visitor from outer space.

Plays Pleasant and Unpleasant was published in the spring of 1898 in two volumes priced at five shillings each. The collection was extensively reviewed, on the whole not very favorably. William Archer, his intimate friend, published two long notices in the *Daily Chronicle*. He hardly knew what to make of Shaw as a dramatist and was by no means complimentary. The books enjoyed only a modest sale, but they achieved their purpose. "My plays broke into the publishing market as literature," Shaw wrote some time later, "And I, though unacted, made my mark as a playwright."[22]

The form in which the plays were presented was relatively original. They were composed as short novels suitable for staging, with extensive scene descriptions and character analyses, directed rather to the reader than to the actor or stage director. The prefaces generally had some relevance to the plays they accompanied but they ranged far beyond them in scope. They were rambling essays, including seemingly intimate biographical details which served not only to advertise the writer, but also to put his comedies before the reader in a curiously personal way.

Robertson had long ago initiated the practice of writing carefully detailed scene descriptions, and Jones had already published plays for the reading public. As for the discursive prefaces, which lengthened, as time went on, to the point where they overshadowed the plays to which they were prefaced, Shaw had the precedent of Dumas *fils*, who as we have seen, had assumed the role of social critic, reformer, and political prophet some twenty years before. In arrogating to himself a similar role, Shaw demonstrated once again his ability to innovate by imitating enthusiastically the innovations of others. But he was no simple imitator. He had style. And what he chose to imitate, he was able to surpass. The prefaces of Dumas *fils* were innovative at the time of their publication. They are now largely of antiquarian interest. Shaw's prefaces have lost neither their savor nor their sense. They are masterpieces of English prose, a joy for the ages.

The preparation of these volumes for the press occupied much of Shaw's time in the early months of 1898; but even before the proofs were corrected, and sometime before his marriage in June of that year, he had begun work on *Caesar and Cleopatra*. This play was intended, so he said, for Forbes-Robertson and Mrs. Patrick Campbell, his leading lady. With the exception of *The Devil's Disciple*, Shaw's earlier plays were all modestly conceived, with a small cast, and few scene-changes. *Caesar and Cleopatra* was designed on a grand scale, with lavish settings and mass effects requiring many extras. The result was a spectacle so costly that, although it was ready for performance in 1899, it was seven years before anyone had the courage to risk a production. When at last Max Reinhardt presented it in Berlin, in 1906, the play was so far successful that the following year Forbes-Robertson and his wife Gertrude Elliott decided to produce it in London.[23]

Caesar and Cleopatra departs widely from the Scribean formula which Shaw had so far employed in arranging a plot. Subtitled "An Historical Drama," this play is a series of episodes, ostensibly historical, linked chiefly by the presence of the principal characters, and by the relation of events during a comparatively short period of time. The narrative design is disarmingly simple. It depicts the arrival of Caesar in Egypt, in the year 48 B.C., some part of the details of his stay, and his departure at the end of the winter. What dramatic force it has is derived from the tensions aroused by the intrusion of Caesar's powerful personality into the complex situation posed by the rivalry of Cleopatra and her brother consort Ptolemy Dionysos for the throne of Egypt. At the beginning of the play, Caesar puts Cleopatra on the throne. At the end, he leaves her, under Roman tutelage, to await the coming of Antony. In the meantime, Cleopatra is transformed from a terrified child into a rather terrifying young woman.

In 1905 Shaw described *Caesar and Cleopatra* to Hesketh Pearson as "What Shakespeare called a history, that is, a chronicle play." He added that he had taken the chronicle without alteration from Mommsen, who had conceived Caesar as Shaw himself saw him.[24] In the program accompanying the copyright performance of March 1899, however, Shaw set forth an array of authorities worthy of a doctoral dissertation, from which were omitted, strangely enough, the two most obvious sources, the *History* of Dio Cassius and the *Civil Wars* of Caesar himself. He noted, "Many of these authorities have consulted their imagination, more or less. The author has done the same."[25]

Since Shaw had little Latin and less Greek, he had no direct contact with the classical sources. Shakespeare had relied heavily on Plutarch for his view of Caesar. Shaw drew largely on the tenth and eleventh chapters of the Fifth Book of Mommsen's *Roman History* in the English translation of 1862–66.[26] Mommsen's view of Caesar as "the only creative genius that Rome produced" suited Shaw's purpose admirably. The notes he took from the *Roman History* in 1898, now preserved in the library of the University of Texas, are considerably clearer with respect to Shaw's narrative scheme than is the play, in which the narrative thread is occasionally lost in the characterization. The Egyptian campaign was an episode in the Roman civil war, in the course of which Caesar pursued Pompey to Egypt, where Pompey was murdered. Three days later Caesar arrived. In his notes Shaw took account of the fact that Caesar, being in need of money, landed two legions at Alexandria for the purpose of collecting taxes. He was resisted by the Ptolemaic party, besieged in the palace of Alexandria by Achillas and the Pompeian army and was ultimately rescued by his ally, Mithridates of Pergamos. With the help of Mithridates, Caesar defeated the Egyptians at the Battle of the Nile, and soon after departed for Rome, leaving the Egyptian throne to Cleopatra and Ptolemy as joint rulers under the governorship of his lieutenant, Rufio.

Mommsen's Caesar was the reverse of Plutarch's. According to Plutarch, Caesar had planned to overthrow the Roman republic from the very beginning of his political career, and his premature aspirations to divinity made him an excellent example of a hubristic character actively inviting the attentions of Nemesis. Shaw wished to portray Caesar as a hero in the tradition of Carlyle. To this end he accepted all the reported evidence of Caesar's magnanimity and cannily smoothed over everything that was sordid in Caesar's career—his notorious debauchery, his cruelty, his ruthless ambition, and his shrewd maneuvers for power. He omitted also any mention of Caesar's amatory involvement with Cleopatra, and said nothing of the child she bore him, or of her attempt to see him in Rome after his departure from Egypt.

The result is a monumental figure, redeemed from rigidity by his humor and his humanity. This Caesar is a singularly engaging character, quite different from Shakespeare's would-be dictator. Shakespeare's Caesar is a sixteenth-century *condottiere*, a classic example of the Renaissance prince who acquires power by allying himself with the populace against the reigning oligarchy. Such figures were entirely familiar in the time of Shakespeare, and their methods had been carefully analyzed by Machiavelli and Guicciardini. In describing Caesar and his fall at the hands of his closest friend, Shakespeare had in mind contemporary situations analogous to that described by Plutarch, and he knew exactly the dramatic effect he desired to produce.

Shaw's Caesar is a Victorian empire-builder. He is a man of exceptional wisdom and shrewdness, irrepressibly vital, resourceful, and efficient, but it is not altogether clear what it is that he wants. Men instinctively desire power; but if Caesar wanted no more than that he would simply be involved in a power struggle with such people as Pothinus, Achillas, and Ftatateeta, ambitious creatures who inspire no respect. In fact, Caesar is depicted as a man of mystic vision, selflessly dedicated to an ideal of social progress which the petty politicians with whom he meddles in Egypt cannot even imagine. Were he endowed with supreme power, it is suggested, Caesar would organize the world in ideal fashion. But he is too far ahead of his time. The world is not yet evolved to the point where anything like an optimal organization is possible, and it stubbornly resists every effort to improve it. Thus Caesar is doomed to fail, and our foreknowledge of his failure in some sense colors this comedy, but in *Caesar and Cleopatra* there is no clear hint of his martyrdom. The play depicts one of his triumphs, and the end is appropriately comic and optimistic.

With this play Shaw declared himself in active rivalry with Shakespeare. In somewhat similar circumstances, Strindberg had declared war on Ibsen; but it was one thing to compete with Ibsen, quite another to try to supplant Shakespeare on the English stage. The extravagance of Shaw's claims to greatness was entirely consistent with his revolutionary posture. He deeply admired Shakespeare as a poet and fabulist; but Shakespeare was the sacred symbol of the theatrical interests which not only denied Shaw a foothold in the theater but which also stubbornly resisted every effort to introduce Ibsen to the commercial stage. To Shaw it seemed that if Shakespeare went, the entire edifice would crumble, and the way would open for the development in England of the new realism which it was his life's ambition to institute.

"The theatre," he wrote Ellen Terry, "is my battering ram as much as the platform or the press: that is why I want to drag it to the front. My capers are part of a bigger design than you think: Shakespear, for instance, is to me one of the towers of the Bastille, and down he must come."[27]

In *Julius Caesar* Shakespeare had stressed the tragic situation of Brutus. For this purpose Caesar was best portrayed as an ambitious politician who desired to become a dictator. Such was, indeed, the traditional view from the time of Livy. It did not recommend itself to imperialists who believed, like Dante, that the salvation of humanity depended upon the consolidation of temporal power in a world empire with a single head. From the Ghibelline standpoint Caesar was the instrument of cosmic order, and Brutus, the representative of the forces of disruption. Shaw inherited this idea. He regarded Caesar as a hero whose task it was to deliver society from the tyranny of a plutocratic oligarchy whose conflicting interests could result only in chaos. Shaw was interested, consequently, not in the poetic development of a tragic situation, but in the elaboration of a historical analogy with contemporary life, in the manner of Ibsen's *Emperor and Galilean*. For this purpose the format of a history play was clearly more appropriate than the well-made patterns Shaw had so far followed.

In 1896, when Shaw was vigorously promoting *The Man of Destiny*, Irving had preferred, no doubt wisely, to present *Madame Sans-Gêne*. Sardou thus became, along with Shakespeare, the special object of Shaw's displeasure. Since Sardou was the greatest living exponent of the Scribean system, Shaw felt it was necessary to annihilate him also, and it was to this end that he hit on "Sardoodledom" as an epithet with which to disparage the type of play which Sardou had inherited from Scribe.

The principal result of Shaw's attack was a significant change in his own dramatic style. After his vigorous campaign against the contrived play, it was no longer seemly for him to compete in the same genre. *The Man of Destiny* was an excellent example of the type of Sardoodledom Shaw affected to despise. With *Caesar and Cleopatra* he embarked on a new course. This play had no plot—nothing, at least, that could be called a plot in the Scribean sense. Nor was it based on an idea, in the sense that *Emperor and Galilean* developed an idea. It was a play based on a characterization.

The aromatic blend of shrewdness, flattery, and frankness which Shaw developed in the correspondence he was carrying on with Ellen Terry was displayed to advantage in his portrait of Caesar. Shaw's Caesar is the quintessential Machiavellian, a leader who combines perfectly the traits of the lion and the fox. An analogous sketch appears in *The Perfect Wagnerite*, with which Shaw was also occupied at about this time. In that extraordinary piece of interpretation he described Siegfried as a Protestant and an anarchist, an embodiment of

> the most inevitable dramatic conception . . . of the nineteenth century . . . that of a perfectly naive hero upsetting religion, law and order in all directions, and establishing in their place the unfettered action of Humanity doing exactly what it likes, and producing order instead of confusion thereby because it likes to do what is good for the race.[28]

Caesar will not bear comparison with the rambunctious hero of the Ring cycle. He is too old and too wily a warrior. His prototype is Wotan, and, like Wotan, he embodies that higher power which works, as Shaw put it, against the money-grubbing Alberics of this world. In this sense Caesar might well be said to be godlike. Shaw wrote in *The Perfect Wagnerite*:

> And these higher powers are called into existence by the same self-organization of life still more wonderfully into rare persons who may by comparison be called gods, creatures capable of thought, whose aims extend far beyond the satisfaction of their bodily appetites and personal affections, since they perceive that it is only by the establishment of a social order founded on common bonds of moral faith that the world can rise from mere savagery. . . .[29]

Like these Wagnerian heroes, Caesar achieves a high degree of virtue simply by following the dictates of his nature. He is subject to no other law and no other morality. He eludes even the erotic impulse of the evolutionary forces which, in Shaw's opinion, orient mankind toward its goal: he has no passions. In the Ring operas, Wotan suffers no such disability; but he has more apprehensions than Caesar, and also he has more time. Accordingly, he puts his daughter Sieglinde at the disposal of her brother Siegmund in order to engender the hero who is to save the world order he has appointed. Caesar, however, has no such far-reaching plan. Cleopatra's attractions are wasted on him. When he leaves her he promises to send her, not a mate with whom she can engender the superman, but a lover with whom she may amuse herself.

Shaw's Caesar seems entirely absorbed in his own devices. These presumably are of value to mankind because in order to fulfill himself properly it is necessary for him to reshape the world in his own image. Like Shaw he is a highly original genius. Shaw wrote:

> Originality gives a man an air of frankness, generosity, and magnanimity by enabling him to estimate the value of truth, money, or success in any particular instance quite independently of convention

and moral generalization. . . . His lies are not found out: they pass for candors. . . . Hence, in order to produce an impression of complete disinterestedness and magnanimity, he has only to act with entire selfishness; and this is perhaps the only sense in which a man can be said to be *naturally* great. It is in this sense that I have represented Caesar as great. Having virtue, he had no need of goodness. He is neither forgiving, frank, nor generous, because a man who is too great to resent has nothing to forgive; a man who says things that other people are afraid to say need be no more frank than Bismarck was; and there is no generosity in giving things you do not want to people of whom you intend to make use. This distinction between virtue and goodness is not understood in England: hence the poverty of our drama in heroes. Our stage attempts at them are mere goody-goodies. Goodness in its popular British sense of self-denial, implies that man is vicious by nature, and that supreme goodness is supreme martyrdom.[30]

In accordance with these ideas, Shaw's Caesar is depicted as an *eiron*, the deceptively simple man of whom Socrates is the classic prototype. His wisdom is so distinctly a middle-class wisdom that it is difficult to think of him as other than an astute businessman involved with military matters. As an administrator he is very much the realist. He considers that men are primarily egotists, like himself, and he is therefore able to plot a course efficiently in terms of their self-interest. Highly endowed with common sense, incapable of love, hate, or sentimentality, he easily conquers a world which, apparently, asks nothing better than to be conquered by him. His reward is self-fulfillment. Caesar does not desire riches. He needs money only because he needs power, and he needs power only in order to realize himself fully. He has an irresistible urge to expend energy to some purpose. He is the greatest living manifestation of the will to live.

Shaw was at no time a rationalist. In his desire to put his doctrine on a scientific basis, he followed Mill; but he could not accept a materialistic position, neither the positivism of Comte, nor the logic of Marx, and least of all the concept of mass pressure as the dynamic principle in the evolution of social organizations. The masses did not inspire Shaw with respect. He had a horror of poverty, ignorance, and brutality, and he wasted no sympathy on those who were willing to suffer these indignities. In his view the spiritual forces which work for the betterment of mankind are embodied not in the common man, but in outstanding examples of humanity, heroes who normally endure martyrdom at the hands of those less generously endowed than they. Caesar was an example.

By the time he wrote *Caesar and Cleopatra* and *The Perfect Wagnerite*, Shaw had come to see heroic effort as the manifestation of a universal spirit working through the consciousness of the individual toward a goal which could only be defined as an eternal desire for improvement. Historical evolution was, in his judgment, neither a mechanical process of adaptation in the Darwinian sense, nor something subject to artificial acceleration through such social organizations as those imagined by Fourier. The reform of social institutions was the visible result of spiritual processes working obscurely at the very heart of humanity. Evolution was the slow operation of a vital principle resident in all living things but most clearly manifested in those extraordinary individuals who represent the cosmic organism at its growing tip.

These individuals constitute the aristocracy of nature and, by reason of their superior endowment, are exempt from the moral restrictions of lesser folk, which represent the order of a former stage of progress. Such men must be free to follow their impulses, in which is manifested the unconscious will. The gifted man is a law unto himself. He achieves virtue simply by doing as he pleases. Thus Caesar is an immoralist at the same time that he exemplifies the highest morality of his age.

Such ideas had gained considerable currency in Europe by the time Shaw took them up. In *Crime and Punishment* Raskolnikov argues:

> . . . The "extraordinary" man has the right . . . to permit his conscience to overstep . . . certain obstacles, but only in the event that his ideas (which may sometimes be salutary for all mankind) require it for their fulfillment. . . . All . . . the lawgivers and regulators of human society, beginning with the most ancient, and going to Lycurgus, Solon, Mahomet, Napoleon, and so on, were, without exception, transgressors, by the very fact that in making a new law they *ipso facto* broke an old one, handed down from their fathers and held sacred by society; and, of course, they did not stop short of shedding blood provided that the blood (however innocent and however heroically shed in defence of the ancient law), was shed to their advantage. It is remarkable that the greater part of these benefactors and lawgivers of mankind were particularly bloodthirsty. . . . In a word, I deduce that all of them, not only the great ones, but also those who diverge ever so slightly from the beaten track, those, that is, who are just barely capable of saying something new, must, by their nature, inevitably be criminals—in a greater or less degree. . . .[31]

These ideas came to Russia by way of the newspaper *Golos*, which had published a summary of the *Saturday Review*'s analysis of the views of Napoleon III, in his *Life of Julius Caesar*, on the right of exceptional people to shed blood. Apropos of such people Raskolnikov remarks, in words that Shaw might have written:

> There is, however, not much cause for alarm: the masses hardly ever recognize this right of theirs, and behead them or hang them (more or less), and in this manner quite properly fulfill their conservative function, although in following generations these same masses put their former victims on a pedestal and worship them (more or less). . . . The first preserve the world and multiply; the second move the world and guide it to its goal. Both have an absolutely equal right to exist.[32]

Shaw's idea of the superman was not a systematic concept. It was patched together from various sources, but mainly from Schopenhauer, Nietzsche, and Samuel Butler. In projecting the highly evolved man, Butler had emphasized the merging of practical intellect with the instinctive impulse, but he was inclined to minimize the role of speculative thought in the development of the human psyche.[33] Shaw's Caesar follows this prescription. He is a practical man who trusts his impulses and is able to justify them rationally if need be. He has no more use for philosophy than he has for literature.

Such a man, Butler had indicated, finds it hardly necessary to think, since the natural faculty, untroubled by irrational desires, is automatically efficient. For Caesar there is no distinction between mind and heart, desire and reason. He desires and enjoys what is good for him, and since he desires only what reason indicates as desirable, he denies himself nothing, obeys no external law, and is blessedly free from feelings of guilt and sin. He is, as Shaw conceived him, a healthy man, "above fear, sickliness of conscience, malice, and the makeshifts and moral crutches of law and order which accompany them."[34]

Ibsen, too, had found the Nietzschean hero admirable, but Ibsen's Viking types are seldom central characters in his plays. What interested Ibsen as a subject for drama was not the Viking, but men of the type of Solness, powerful men half-mad with guilt. Such men are capable of suffering. Caesar does not suffer. He is resourceful and amusing, but his is a character part, and it is invariable. Cleopatra is dwarfed by him, but she develops, and it is upon her development that the action centers.

Like Caesar, Cleopatra desires power. She desires, above all, the power to do as she pleases, to be herself, the more so as she has been under tutelage all her life. Her natural impulses, however, are not trustworthy. By nature she is cruel, willful, vengeful, and vain, and it is only through fear that she is induced to behave properly. Shaw's Cleopatra is a child. Shakespeare's heroine, a character Shaw professed greatly to admire, is depicted as a mature and exquisitely voluptuous woman, ruined by passions she has no wish to restrain. She is an excellent example of the sort of woman the Renaissance associated with Eve, the temptress, and doubtless it was the magnificence with which she fulfilled her role as *femme fatale* that fascinated Shakespeare. In comparison, Shaw's Cleopatra is minuscule. She is poised between desire and passion, but neither has as yet any decisive claim upon her, and the contrast in scale between her petty concerns and Caesar's vast designs provide the comic background of the action.

The historical Caesar, three times married, the man Suetonius contemptuously called "every woman's husband and every man's wife," obviously has no place in Shaw's play. Shaw's hero is properly presented in the first act as a man normally susceptible to the charms of woman, but his relation to Cleopatra from first to last is clinically pure. He is mainly her tutor; in effect, he supplants Ftatateeta as the queen's nurse. According to the best authorities, Cleopatra was twenty-one years old when Caesar came to Alexandria. It is possible that Shaw was misled as to her age by Froude's account of Cleopatra, or perhaps by Mommsen; but it is altogether more likely that he wished to avoid the problem of managing his Caesar prudently in the neighborhood of a young woman whose amorous proclivities were legendary. In a rather tedious prologue, the hawk-headed god Ra prepares us for the consequent situation in the biblical dialect presumably in use at Memphis in the time of the Ptolemies:

> Are ye impatient with me? Do ye crave for a story of an unchaste woman? Hath the name of Cleopatra tempted ye hither? Ye foolish ones; Cleopatra is as yet but a child that is whipped by her nurse. . . .[35]

The God is impressive; but it cannot be denied that in side-stepping the romantic issue in this manner, Shaw prevented Caesar and Cleopatra from taking part in what might well have been a dramatic masterpiece.

In this historical setting Shaw's Caesar is less of an anachronism than is Britannus, who is obviously a visiting Englishman from the nineteenth century. Shaw attempted to justify in summary fashion whatever might be found amiss in the historicity of his play on the ground that times have not changed since Caesar's campaign in Egypt:

> in truth, the period of time covered by history is far too short to allow of any perceptible progress in the popular sense of Evolution of

the Human Species. The notion that there has been any such Progress since Caesar's time (less than 20 centuries) is too absurd for discussion. All the savagery, barbarism, dark ages and the rest of it of which we have any record as existing in the past, exists at the present moment. . . .[36]

But whatever may be said in disparagement of Britannus as a Roman slave, Caesar is entirely acceptable as a Roman general. His portrait accords excellently with the cliché of the *homo humanus* of Cicero, and he comes as close to the Renaissance ideal of manhood as any character might whom Forbes-Robertson was intended to impersonate. The well-adjusted man of the sixteenth century, the *euphues* of the humanists, was one whose soul was in health and in command of a healthy body. The Aristotelian soul, which Christianity inherited, was trinitarian, a pousse-café of interrelated faculties. In the well-ordered soul, the appetites were controlled by the will, which was in turn at the service of the intellect. In Renaissance theory, any disruption of this arrangement was a sign of psychic illness and likely to have dramatic consequences. Shaw's hero represents the man of ideal constitution in whom will and reason are synonymous, and appetite is always controlled. In Caesar, Shaw depicted, therefore, not only the perfection of Irish gentility in the nineteenth century, but also the great man in the classic tradition, a composite of the hero according to Plutarch, and the statesman according to Cicero.

Aside from the magnificent characterization of Caesar, the play has no very definite outline. In the fourth act, the action for the first time shapes itself into a plot. Pothinus accuses Cleopatra of trying to rid herself of Caesar, and Cleopatra avenges herself by having Pothinus murdered by her nurse, who is in turn murdered, for prophylactic reasons, by Rufio. This reminiscence of Renaissance revenge-drama is the only theatrical episode in the play. The action, apart from this, is a series of interesting incidents chronologically arranged for the purpose of displaying Caesar in various demanding situations. Shaw's hero, however, comes somewhat short of his historic prototype. The Caesar of history is said to have slaughtered a million souls in Gaul and enslaved another million. He was determined to be a god in his own lifetime and had his statue set up in the temple of Quirinus for public worship. Such a Caesar is far from Shaw's ideal, but as a human being he has scale; in comparison, Shaw's athletic middle-aged general seems merely wise.

As for Cleopatra, it is recorded that, after having borne Caesar a son in Egypt, she lived happily in Rome until the year that Caesar was killed; that she fled the capital at once; that three years later Antony, middle-aged, fat, and bearded, came to Egypt with an army; and that Cleopatra bore him twins and married him four years later. These feminine involvements, far from being serpentine, represented simply the efforts of an attractive and quite practical female statesman to survive in a world torn apart by powerful men. It might seem, in consequence, that reality in the first century B.C. was more imaginative than Shaw, twenty centuries later, and a good deal more dramatic. In comparison with its historical basis the situation depicted in *Caesar and Cleopatra* seems simple, reasonable, and relatively comprehensible. Perhaps this is its chief shortcoming as drama.[37]

Early in May 1899 Shaw began a new play. It was written, if we may take him at his word, expressly for Ellen Terry, and with her character in mind. Since Shaw knew Miss Terry only through their correspondence, her character must have been for him largely a matter of conjecture. Ellen Terry was, in fact, at this time quite fifty years of age, and already a grandmother. The new play—*Captain Brassbound's Conversion*—had an excellent part for her. It provided no comparable role for Henry Irving, and perhaps, in offering the play to Miss Terry at this point, Shaw hoped at last to drive a wedge between the great man and his leading lady.

Though the plot of *Captain Brassbound's Conversion* centers on the story of Black Paquito, the principal character is Lady Cicely. She had, to begin with, the title role. Shaw had first called the play *The Witch of Atlas, a Melodramatic Comedy*; when he revised the title to its present form, the subtitle became simply *An Adventure*. Both descriptions were apt. *Captain Brassbound's Conversion* has a romantic setting, brigands, Arabs, a ruined tower, an abduction, a bloodthirsty sheikh, a trial, an eleventh-hour acquittal. It is furnished with all the outward trappings of melodrama, and with some of the inward elements as well. It also has an idea and thus bears the same relation to the popular genre as *The Devil's Disciple*: it is a melodrama with a difference.

An alliance with Henry Irving, even at this late date, would have been of inestimable value to Shaw, and it might well have proved of value to Irving. Unhappily, the division between the two men was fundamental. For Irving a play was a device designed so as to offer an actor an opportunity to exhibit his talents. Shaw, on the other hand, wrote plays designed to exhibit the playwright. Irving had no intention of being used for any such purpose. As an actor-manager he employed writers for his own use; he was not in the habit of being employed for theirs.

His objection to Shaw was therefore rooted in something deeper than personal dislike. In resisting this newcomer's attempted invasion of his theater Irving was defending the dramatic tradition which he served against something that actually menaced its existence; and it is likely that he realized much better than Shaw the danger of giving the nontheatrical a foothold in the theater. In Irving's judgment, the theater had no need of ideas, least of all of controversial ideas. What it required was strong scenes, magnificent effects, fine words, and great gestures. Plays should act well and look beautiful. The rest was irrelevant to the actor's art.

As we can see from her letters to Shaw, Ellen Terry thoroughly concurred in these notions. Shaw's campaign to inaugurate a new order in the theater seemed to her a doubtful undertaking, all the more doubtful since Shaw desired his very talky plays to be interpreted flamboyantly in the old-fashioned style of Ristori and Barry Sullivan, whose work he had admired as a boy in Dublin.

In fact, what Shaw had in mind for the new theater was not at all the relatively restrained style that had come into fashion for comedy, still less an acting style that purported to be a faithful imitation of "life as it is." At this time Shaw was experimenting with a type of play which displayed the wildest romantic behavior on the part of the characters as a foil to the common sense of the playwright. Such plays required the full rhetorical resonance of which the old line-actors were capable. Shaw wished to rationalize melodrama. For this he needed actors who could really play melodrama. Terriss and Forbes-Robertson were better suited to this end than Irving, but Irving ruled the Lyceum, and in the case of *Captain Brassbound's Conversion* he seemed to be—at least from a tactical viewpoint—an ideal choice. Once again Shaw returned to the fray.

Early in May 1899 he began making tentative casts in Miss Terry's direction. She rose to the bait this time with calculated reluctance. She would like very much to see the first act of the play: "*What* play? If you mean a Play for me all depends upon whether I like it, or don't like it. I'm pretty nearly sure to—but!"[38] Some weeks later Shaw's repeated advances elicited an even greater show of diffidence: ". . . I don't think that play of yours will do for me at all! You suggest it is a one-part play! I loathe that sort of thing."[39] She had not yet seen the script, but she already disliked it: ". . . I don't like the play one bit. Only *one* woman in it. How *ugly* it will look, and there will not be a penny in it."[40]

At the beginning of August Shaw sent her the manuscript with a covering letter calculated to melt a heart of stone:

> There's your play—Ellen's play. My conscience was so burdened with the infamy of having written plays for other people about whom I

dont care a straw (thank my stars they cant act them) and made no
play for you, that it had to be done. Now it *is* done . . . the only thing
on earth in my power to do for you. And now no more plays—at
least no more practicable ones. None at all, indeed, for some time to
come: it is time to do something more in Shaw-philosophy, in politics
and sociology. Your author, dear Ellen, must be more than a common dramatist.[41]

But in spite of these flattering sentiments Miss Terry did not like "the
Play." Her answer was courteous, but entirely negative:

No one but Shaw could have written the last Play Cap. B's Conversion (?) but it's not the sort of play for me in the least. The three I
think finest are Arms and the Man, Mrs Warren's Profession and the
Cleopatra thing. I couldn't do this one, and I believe it would never
do for the stage. The two parts, the man and the woman, are right;
but that *bore* Drinkwater! Mrs Pat. for Lady C! I couldnt do it. Mrs
Potter would revel in the part, but it is surely for Mrs Pat. *Not* for
me. . . .

And she added, with a touch of mercy:

I enjoyed reading it up to the hilt . . . but the expressions: "There's
not a penny in it—" "More fitted for the closet than the stage," occur
to me when one has finished it. Also, after reading it comes a great
refreshment to the tired spirit, but it would not be so when it was
acted! (And it would not "*Act*" well.") Shall I send it back to you?[42]

Shaw's answer was prompt, at once sharp and touching, and quite
possibly sincere:

Alas! dear Ellen, is it really so? Then I can do nothing for you? I
honestly thought Lady Cicely would fit you like a glove, that I had
sacrificed everything to make the play go effectively from second to
second, even that Drinkwater was a tragi-comic figure worthy of
Robson. And now you tell me it is a play for the closet, and that
Lady Cicely would fit Mrs P. C.—all of which proves that either I am
mad, or you are mad, or else there is an impassable gulf between my
drama and your drama.
    . . . No: it is clear that I have nothing to do with the theatre of to-
day: I must educate a new generation with my pen from childhood
up—audience, actors and all, and leave them my plays to murder
after I am cremated. Captain B. shall not be profaned by the stage: I
will publish it presently with the D's D and Caesar, and preach a nice
sermon in the preface.
    And so farewell my project—all fancy, like most projects. Send me

back the script when you are done with it: I will send you the printed
volume when it is ready.

Silly Ellen![43]

This had the sound of finality, but Shaw was not so readily put off,
and Ellen Terry, for her part, was not so eager to foreclose the relationship. At fifty, she had an understandable yearning to play the role of a
young girl. She wrote Shaw again, manifesting an abiding interest in the
roles of Vivie and Cleopatra. Shaw answered at very great length, em-
ploying, in his effort at salesmanship, all the wiles of the bazaar. It now
developed that Lady Cicely far transcended the ordinary limits of stage
presentation. She was intended to celebrate Ellen Terry's genius on a
cosmic scale:

> I—poor idiot!—thought the distinction of Ellen Terry was that she
> had this heart wisdom, and managed her own little world as Tolstoy
> would have our Chamberlains and Balfours and German Emperors
> and Kitcheners and Lord Chief Justices and other slaves of false
> ideas and imaginary fears manage Europe. I accordingly give you a
> play in which you stand in the very place where Imperialism is not
> believed to be necessary, on the border line where the European
> meets the fanatical African. . . . Here then is your portrait painted on
> a map of the world—. . . . In every other play I have ever written—
> even in Candida—I have prostituted the actress more or less by
> making the interest in her partly a sexual interest: only the *man* in
> the Devil's Disciple draws clear of it. In Lady Cicely I have done
> without this, and gained a greater fascination for it. And you are
> disappointed. Oh wretch, wretch, wretch! It is true that the record of
> the play as a book written by me for you is worth a thousand
> Lyceum successes; but its publication with 'Repudiated by Miss Ellen
> Terry as unworthy of her professional eminence' across it—do you
> think I intended that? Oh Ellen, Ellen, Ellen. This is the end of
> everything.[44]

It was only the beginning. Early in October she offered Shaw £500 in
cash for all the rights to *Brassbound*.

> And if you don't think £500 is fair, then you must tell me what else
> (and *less* than you would perhaps stipulate for because of your
> getting the *immediate* advantage of the money!) . . . I've studied
> Lady C. now, and am *transported*. The tragic end I go over again and
> again and—*see* it. A triumph for us both. I love the whole thing and
> am certain I could do it.[45]

Irving was of another opinion. He considered Shaw's terms exorbitant.
In the meantime, Mrs. Shaw spirited her husband off on a Mediterranean

cruise, and he answered his "ever-cherished" Ellen's letter from the S. S. *Lusitania* on the way to Sicily, which, he wrote, he disliked intensely. In this letter he adduced many examples of Irving's "stupendous ignorance" of the drama and displayed his own vast familiarity with the business end of playwriting. There followed a disquisition on the iniquity of the author's landlordism in collecting royalties on his property while sweating the working actor to pay them:

> It is not a fair way of securing the author's living any more than it is fair that a charwoman should get eighteen shillings for a much harder week than ever Patti got £500 for; but is the way we authorize at present. And its iniquities—literally its inequities—are the real secret of the rebellion of the actor—the protests of Henry. But I take a grim delight in exploiting Henry. . . . And as entrepreneur and manager, he does not see that what I do to him he does to the carpenter and check taker. Ask him, and he will tell you that he is generous to his dependents. So am I: I take 10% when I might exact 15.

Having savored his triumph in this manner, he added: "To be immediately practical, there is one thing rather lacking between us: and that is a signed agreement. However, keep my letters and depend on them for the present."[46]

The following week, Ellen's mood changed again. She had played the copyright performance and it had depressed her. The audience loved the play, but "They all loathe Lady Cecily. . . . Edy . . . doesn't think lady C is shown to be either very clever or humorous or vital, and certainly not of great humanity. I should have to get you to know more about Lady C's *inside* before I did her! (Or did for her!)."[47] Shaw replied promptly from the *Lusitania*. He detested the Grecian archipelago and Athens "with its stupid classic Acropolis and smashed pillars," and he rejected her offer of £500 for the rights to *Brassbound* as too little in case of success, and too much in case of failure. The enterprise now bogged down completely. Toward the end of January 1900, four months later, Miss Terry wrote from Toledo, Ohio, that she had decided not to leave the Lyceum or Henry Irving for the next season. She was now thinking she might have to give up *Brassbound* entirely for her next American tour, and she recommended Mrs. Fiske for the part.

Shaw once more gave up his role of astute man of business. He reassumed his Olympian mask:

> Very well, dear Ellen: we cry off Brassbound. I wrote Brassbound for you merely for the sake of writing it for you, without any faith in your ever being able to produce it, knowing that the existence of the

play would strengthen your hold on H. I. (by making you independent of him if you chose to abandon his ship)—obviously if he
wants you to stay, stay you must. Consequently, I am in no way
disappointed or surprised: destiny has fulfilled itself exactly as I
foresaw it would if affairs took their normal course. . . . So out of the
window you go, my dear Ellen, and off goes my play to my agent as
in the market for the next highest bidder. . . .[48]

Ellen answered five weeks later, expressing regret for the whole affair,
and shouldering off the blame on the self-centered Irving. The
correspondence dwindled. After 1900, letters continued to be exchanged
at lengthening intervals until May 1922, when it ended completely, six
years before Miss Terry's death. These letters included becoming allusions of personal regard, but with her refusal to play Lady Cicely in
1900, the courtship of Ellen Terry came to an end.

The preface which Shaw wrote in 1928 in connection with the publication of the Ellen Terry correspondence made no bones as to his intentions, but it put the matter on a somewhat more exalted plane than the
letters seem to warrant:

This correspondence shows how, because Irving would not put his
peculiar talent at the service of this new and intensely interesting
development of the drama which had begun with Ibsen, and because
he wasted not only his own talent but Ellen Terry's, I destroyed her
belief in him and gave shape and consciousness to her sense of having
her possibilities sterilized by him. Then her position became untenable; and she broke loose from the Ogre's castle.[49]

It is impossible to doubt Shaw's sincerity in this account of his relations
with Irving and Ellen Terry. He was by this time seventy-two, and the
self-portrait he had devised for the contemplation of posterity was virtually complete. Doubtless he believed by this time that it had all happened
as he said. At any rate, there was now no one left to contradict him, and
perhaps, after all, what he remembered was in some sense true.

On 16 December 1900 *Captain Brassbound's Conversion* was performed at the Strand in London by The Stage Society with Janet
Achurch in the part of Lady Cicely. Miss Terry attended the performance, and there for the first time she met Shaw face to face. The
meeting took place under the stage, in the passage to the dressing rooms.
It was brief and distant. Shaw bowed. A word of greeting passed between them. They never met again.

Ellen Terry was nevertheless destined to play Lady Cicely, and to her
heart's content. In July 1902 her connection with the Lyceum company

came to a close. She went on to play an engagement at Beerbohm Tree's theater, Her Majesty's, which had by this time replaced the Lyceum as the center of fashion. Then she undertook a final tour of the provinces with Henry Irving. It was the end of their long association. Irving enjoyed a great ovation in London in June 1905 at the Drury Lane. Four months later he was taken ill on the stage at Bradford while playing in Tennyson's *Becket*. He finished his performance, took his bows, and died a half hour later in the lobby of his hotel. It was then October 1905.

The preceding June, during the highly successful Barker-Vedrenne season at the Court Theatre in London, it was decided that the time had come to try a new production of *Captain Brassbound's Conversion*. By this time Ellen Terry's popularity had begun to wane, but Shaw still felt that her presence would add something to the play's chance of success, and once more he dangled the part before her eyes. This time the conditions were less attractive, and once again she declined. She could not afford, she wrote, to work under such conditions.

The following year, however, in November 1905, she agreed to play the part with Frederick Kerr, at the Court. *Brassbound* went into rehearsal toward the end of February 1906, but the production did not go altogether well. Ellen Terry was now fifty-eight, and she was uncertain of the role. "I think," she wrote Shaw in May 1906, "we are nearly all of us going astray in your play, some way or another." James Carew, who was playing Captain Kearney, nevertheless, seemed very right to her, and that year she took him to America with her under Charles Frohman's management. In March 1907 they were married secretly in Pittsburgh. A year later they were still playing *Captain Brassbound's Conversion* together. By that time the play was an established success, and the author was famous.

In the notes to *Captain Brassbound's Conversion* Shaw wrote that he had taken his local color from Cunninghame Graham's travel book *Moghreb-al-Acksa*, "Morocco the Most Holy," and that his own experience with North Africa was limited to a morning's walk through Tangier some time after the play was written. He had evidently read more widely on the subject, however, than he admitted, for he indicated elsewhere some acquaintance with Mary H. Kingsley's *Travels in West Africa* (1899) and H. M. Stanley's *In Darkest Africa* (1890). In any case, the Arabian background of the play is strictly theatrical. The local color is rather less convincing than the Bulgarian environment of *Arms and the Man*; and there is no attempt to deal realistically with the Arabs, the missionary, the U.S. Navy or anything else, save Lady Cicely.

Plays set in romantic Arab surroundings were by no means uncommon in the 1890's. Ouida's *Under Two Flags* had been dramatized repeatedly since its first publication in 1867. It was followed by a host of imitations, and very soon, desert-plays with camels, sheiks, and lost patrols became a regular feature of the popular stage. The handsome officer, the savage sheik, and the lovely lady made an excellent triangle for a melodrama. They have remained a useful fixture of the cinema to this day.

Interesting parallels have been noted between the thrilling incidents of *Captain Brassbound's Conversion* and those of Rowe and Harris's *Freedom* (1883), a play in which the beautiful lady is kidnaped by Arabs, rescued by a handsome officer, recaptured with her rescuer, and at last delivered from the power of the sheik by the brave bluejackets of a passing gunboat.[50] Into a narrative frame of this order, Shaw introduced a legal anecdote he had heard involving a West Indian planter who had once left a sugar plantation in the hands of an unscrupulous agent, only to have the agent convert the estate to his own use with the help of the resident judge. The additional details—the dispossessed widow who is driven to madness, and the tale of the avenging son—were apparently Shaw's own contribution to the plot.

Shaw's workmanship in fitting together these random elements was of the rough-and-ready sort appropriate to a type of drama not intended for close scrutiny. *Captain Brassbound's Conversion* is sheer melodrama. The coincidences necessary to enable the characters to assemble in one place at one time, the recognitions and reversals which advance, complicate, and resolve the intrigue are all frankly theatrical. Despite some pleasantly realistic touches, the minor characters—among them Drinkwater, Marzo, and the Reverend Mr. Rankin—are all stock types. The play does not suffer in the least from this, or from its lack of realistic detail. It rests principally on the relation of Lady Cicely, Captain Brassbound, and Sir Howard Hallam, and the plot is devised so as to bring these characters into a suitable collocation. Once this is done, the action goes more or less by itself and would work equally well in almost any environment.

Captain Brassbound's Conversion involves questions of justice and retribution, illusion and reality, but, like *Caesar and Cleopatra*, it is primarily a characterization. It depicts the way in which an exceptionally gifted person is able to solve a seemingly insoluble problem through the application of good will and good sense and thus illustrates the infallible triumph of reason over emotion. Beyond this, the action is essentially a demonstration of the power of genius to organize its environment according to the principles of its nature. Thus its formula comes very close to that of *Caesar and Cleopatra*, which in many ways *Captain Brassbound's Conversion* parallels.

Shaw's vaunted realism was not at all a matter of careful documentation. In outward matters he conformed quite closely to the dramatic stereotypes of his time. The difference between his practice and that of his contemporaries in the theater is that, while they used theatrical artifice as an end in itself, he used it for purposes that went some distance beyond the customary limits of drama.

Thesis plays in the nineteenth century were ordinarily formulated in terms of plots contrived to demonstrate a proposition. They seldom made use of naturalistic methods and did not purport to be "slices of life." Plays like the younger Dumas's *Le Fils naturel* or Ibsen's *Ghosts* were not expected to be rigorously realistic. For their purposes it was necessary only that the narrative be logically arranged; and the logic of the theater normally accommodated a wealth of coincidence. It was generally understood that, however serious its thesis, a play was a fantasy dealing with events well outside the norms of everyday experience, a remarkable happening which proved a point. It was paradoxical that these fictions, no matter how improbable, were invariably advanced on the level and in the style of anecdotes derived from reality, and not at all as creations of the imagination.

In using materials patently derived from farce and extravaganza in order to demonstrate a point, Shaw followed in the path of Molière rather than of Dumas *fils* or Ibsen; but until relatively late in his dramatic career, Shaw did not relinquish the artifices of the Scribean dramatists. On the contrary, in a period which was profoundly influenced by naturalism, he inclined more and more to a style of comedy which was deliberately stagey and emphasized its staginess by means of alarming coincidences, improbable twists, and surprises. Shaw did not tamper, as Brecht did later, with the dramatic illusion. His plays were conceived frankly as plays, and touched reality only in its essential aspects. The degree of realism with which he characterized his figures was, therefore, in the main, cosmetic; and his secondary characters, in particular, rarely make the impression of individuals modeled in the round and surrounded by space.

Shaw's naturalism was largely concerned with linguistics, a field in which he fancied himself expert. He insisted his American naval officer should have a "Chicagoan" accent.[51] In the case of Drinkwater, the attempt to transcribe the speech of a London cockney is tedious by any standards, and oppressively so on the printed page. The play is an early example of that passion for the realistic transcription of dialectical forms which makes it all but impossible to read such poems as Tennyson's "Northern Farmer," or such plays as Stanley Houghton's *Hindle Wakes*. In spite of the phonetic difficulties with which he has to cope, Drinkwater is nevertheless as memorable in his way as Robertson's Eccles, and quite as fictitious a character.

In the case of Brassbound and Sir Howard, there is an obvious attempt to "humanize" characters that belong to the stockroom of melodrama. The consequence is an interesting mixture of styles. In *Captain Brassbound's Conversion* the action is conventional; the characterization is not; and this discrepancy makes a curious effect. Between what generically Brassbound is, and what in fact he does and says, there is an area which belongs neither to the stage nor to the world outside the theater, but to something in between, which combines the two. It is in this uncertain region that Shaw habitually set his stage.

Melodrama traditionally affords a view of people doing extraordinary things for quite ordinary reasons. Since the variety of extraordinary things available for exploitation in the theater is necessarily limited, melodrama occasions astonishment only when its surprises fall outside the traditional boundaries. Such departures are necessarily rare in a dramatic framework designed to reassure the spectator in his faith that, in a universe created in accordance with principles of right and justice, the good will invariably triumph.

Shaw's world is not, however, an established structure but an evolving organism developing through trial and error. In his melodramas, consequently, the characters do the things appropriate to melodramatic characters, but they are made to examine their motives in the light of reason, and thus to explain themselves more or less intelligently to themselves and to one another. The source of dramatic surprise is not what they do, but what they discover, and their development as characters is manifested in the disparity between their assumptions regarding themselves and the conclusions to which they are driven. Thus, what is demonstrated in Shaw's melodrama is not the infallible triumph of good, but the unexpected triumph of reason. Instead of trying to make us aware of the permanent outlines of the moral creation underlying the seeming chaos of existence, as is usual in this genre, Shaw aims at a description of the structure of the world at one of the transitional points in its development. It is in this respect that he considered himself a realist.

Aside from its dynamic aspect, Shaw's world is substantially the world of Restoration comedy, transformed by a romantic belief in the spiritual capacity of exceptional individuals to transcend self in the service of a moral principle. It is to such a principle that the extraordinary behavior of Dick Dudgeon, Julius Caesar, and Lady Cicely is referred, and it is through its operation that the conversion of Brassbound is accomplished. Presumably, once he becomes aware of the workings of this principle in another, Brassbound becomes conscious of its existence in himself and, in this realization, as if by an act of grace, is instantly transformed into a higher being.

Brassbound's conversion involves both a revelation—in which he is made aware of the follies of his past—and an intuition through which he has a glimpse of his future. Lady Cicely is the source of both. It is evidently her function to illuminate in this fashion all the fortunate souls with which she comes in contact: such is the source of her power over men. In the beginning, Brassbound is the slave of his illusions. When Lady Cicely dispels the fantasies that have both enslaved and sustained him, he is for the moment pathetically helpless and disoriented. Lady Cicely mercifully spares him any further servitude and restores him to himself with his manhood more or less intact. He is now free, self-mastered, and restored, we assume, to the service of humanity and the universal principle which is his reality. His release from illusion is thus seen from a very different viewpoint than that of Dr. Relling in Ibsen's *The Wild Duck*, whose therapeutic function it is to supply illusions for the ill to live by. For Ibsen illusions are necessary to make life tolerable. For Shaw the dispelling of illusion is the indispensable preliminary to a meaningful existence.

Brassbound is thus required to come a certain distance, psychically speaking, in the course of the action, and it is questionable whether his conversion could be accomplished by a being less attractively contoured than Lady Cicely. In spite of Shaw's assurances to the contrary, she is pictured as a very caressable saint. Her beauty, however, constitutes a danger. In Shaw's world, as in the world of Dante, the first step in the direction of the Absolute is the beauty of woman. But woman's beauty is not only a signpost, it is also a trap. In the Platonic system that Shaw inherited it was necessary for man's salvation that he be oriented toward the good by the beauty of woman, but it was absolutely essential that he pass on to higher things. Thus Morell is hopelessly ensnared in the beauty of Candida, and this is his limitation as a human being. Brassbound, like Marchbanks, escapes and may thus achieve the blessedness which, we are assured, transcends happiness.

The conversion of Captain Brassbound involves a comic reappraisal of the grounds of justice and contrasts the workings of private and public vengeance, to the obvious detriment of both. But the play has rather more to do with the question of vocation than with justice and therefore comes somewhat closer in its way to *Brand* than to *Hamlet*. The conclusion is altogether ambiguous. It is hardly likely that Shaw meant to suggest that it is better to pursue a false aim than none at all, but there is nothing to prevent one from drawing such an inference if one wishes.

In this play the hero is a high-minded young man in revolt against what he conceives to be a corrupt and evil system. His whole life has been shaped by his gnawing sense of evil, and it is in order to signalize his dissatisfaction with the current state of affairs that he has turned into an outlaw. This much he has in common with Dick Dudgeon and Shaw's other brigands—including Blanco Posnet—all of whom seem to trace their ancestry more or less directly to Karl von Moor in Schiller's *The Robbers*. Brassbound, however, has, like Hernani and the other idealized brigands of literature, a special role in life. He is an avenger.

When the facts of Brassbound's life are examined in the cold light of reason, it turns out, however, that he is an avenger without a motive. The villain he is pursuing is not a villain; the stolen plantation was worthless; the oppressed mother was a woman unworthy of sympathy. Thus all the traditional elements of robber-melodrama are comically disintegrated, and Brassbound's mission in life is reduced to absurdity. His misguided efforts to set matters right result in a mischievous situation which requires the intervention of the United States Navy for its resolution. At the end of the play, saved from the consequences of his evil-doing by Lady Cicely's shrewd tactics, the would-be avenger is faced with the need to find a new justification for his existence. He does so through a denouement which leaves much to the imagination; but the tragic undercurrent in this presumably comic situation is too close to the surface to be altogether comfortable, and the play for all its comedic elements does not end on a comic note.

In the absence of any clear statement on the author's part, it is difficult to say what his intention was in framing the play in this manner. *Brassbound* has interesting existentialist implications. The hero was doubtless called Brassbound in token of his single-minded dedication to his mission. It is in this engagement to a mistaken cause that he finds his being and defines himself as a man. Until he is disabused of his idée fixe he is, like Sartre's hero in *Les Mains sales*, a man with some business in the world, and by reason of his dedication he has self-confidence, dignity, and strength: he has become not only a man, but a leader of men. The play describes his liberation from the idea that enslaves him, but once he is free of it he is lost. Thus the last scene places him in a situation similar to that of Ibsen's Brand when he is liberated from the merciless God who sustains him up to the moment when Gerd brings down the avalanche with her gun.

The gunshot that recalls Brassbound to his duty is an even more ambiguous symbol than Ibsen's, and the play ends with a question for which Shaw had perhaps no answer. "The wretched leading man," Shaw wrote in a letter to Miss Terry, "has nothing in the last act but ignominious dumbness and ridicule until the final scene, in which he gets a consolation prize."[52] Indeed, even when one makes suitable allowances for Shaw's obviously tendentious appraisal of Brassbound's situation in this letter, it is evident that at the end of the play Brassbound is woefully diminished from his former state. Thus the practical result of the action is the partial destruction of the hero—a process in which Lady Cicely plays a leading part. It is understandable that so experienced an actress as Ellen Terry might not, at first blush, fancy such a role.

The disintegration and reconstitution of Captain Brassbound is so rapidly accomplished that the play derives its principal interest less from the dispelling of his illusions than from the tension that develops between him and Lady Cicely. She is at first his adversary; then she becomes his conqueror and finally his savior, thus achieving his complete subjection. The contestants are less fairly matched than is usual in this type of plot. In spite of Brassbound's evident virility, Lady Cicely makes a child of him, very much as Candida makes children of her men: such is the power of these Virgin Mothers. And as Candida shows Marchbanks the hard road to manhood, so Lady Cicely sets Brassbound on the proper path. In his moment of agony Brassbound cries out:

> I'm a stupider man than Brandyfaced Jack even; for he got his romantic nonsense out of the penny numbers and such like trash; but I got just the same nonsense out of life and experience. . . . It was vulgar, v u l g a r. I see that now, for you've opened my eyes to the past; but what good is that for the future? What am I to do? Where am I to go?

Lady Cicely answers:

> It's quite simple. Do whatever you like. That's what I always do.[53]

For Brassbound this poses a problem. He no longer knows what he wants to do and in his confusion he yearns to take service again under a trustworthy commander. Lady Cicely, however, has no ready employment for him: her methods preclude the use of lieutenants. Brassbound was interesting to her as an adversary. Defeated, he is an embarrassment both to her and to himself. It is at a most opportune moment, therefore, that he blunders on the secret of command and is rescued from moral disaster.

He is rescued by the sudden realization that a commander must renounce the comforts of servitude. Leadership is an austere and lonely occupation. It must do without friendship, and it must do without love; for to love is to serve, and the true leader serves only his will and expects nothing for his pains. Like Caesar, Lady Cicely loves no one, and needs no one to love her. She tells Brassbound: "How could I manage people if I had that mad little bit of self left in me? That's my secret." This is the bitter lesson that converts Captain Brassbound. Thus far his illusions have sustained him. In comparison, reality seems to have no substance. It gives him no foothold, and nothing to live for. Seemingly he is lost. It is at this point that he finds himself.

Like *Caesar and Cleopatra, Captain Brassbound's Conversion* belongs to the category of pedagogical drama: it describes an education. The same may be said of a number of Shaw's other plays, *Candida, Pygmalion, Heartbreak House* and, in a more general sense, *Back to Methuselah*. In each of these plays the teacher is a more or less lovable person who is himself incapable of love, a Socratic character whose power is derived from a purely intellectual identification with those he influences. Lady Cicely, however, is attractive and, like Candida, evidently not beyond temptation. But she knows that to surrender any part of herself is to abdicate her state completely, and she saves herself from love by an austere act of self-control. Even so, it is suggested that, were it not for Brassbound's realization of the advantages of emulating rather than serving her, she might have been lost. The situation is not very different from that in *Pygmalion*. The five plays in question are thus seen to have a common mold. Each consists of a series of pedagogical demonstrations, and in each, save perhaps the last, the romantic relation of master and pupil is brutally dispelled. Evidently this type of drama gave Shaw an opportunity to play the schoolmaster, a role in which he particularly fancied himself. In each play the lesson is the same and involves some degree of heartbreak. The result, however, in each case, is freedom, and if this leaves the recipient somewhat confused at the final curtain it is because freedom, doubtless, is confusing.

In spite of their loveless outcome, the tendency of these plays is actually romantic in the extreme. In *Caesar*, *Pygmalion*, and *Heartbreak House* the central character is male, and the situation is obscured by the reversal of the traditional roles of lover and beloved. In *Captain Brassbound's Conversion* the central character is Lady Cicely. She is the star on which Captain Brassbound's life is centered. Lady Cicely shines upon Brassbound as Beatrice upon Dante. Her splendor is the flame that refines and exalts her lover: the relationship is traditional.

For this process of refinement through the fires of Eros to be carried to completion it is vital that the relationship be free of physical contact. The indispensable condition of pure love is that the flesh be frustrated: it is out of his bodily suffering that the poet's soul develops. This situation, a major stereotype of Renaissance literature, recommended itself highly to the poets of the nineteenth century, and the fact that Shaw fixed upon this romantic cliché in the name of "scientific natural history" indicates to what an extent his scientific attitudes were rooted in tradition. The ideal posture of the lover as poet or hero, sublimating his ungratified passion in song or in deeds of valor, evidently suited Shaw's psychic configuration extremely well. It certainly provided the erotic element of the Ellen Terry correspondence which glosses this group of plays much as Petrarch's *Secretum* glosses the songs to Laura. Thus, perhaps as a result of his Pre-Raphaelite affiliation, Shaw presented his plays in accordance with a conception altogether different from the middle-class patterns of conventional nineteenth-century comedy, in which lovers are regularly united in the last act.

In this group of plays Shaw attempted to ring a change on the type of melodrama in which the happy ending is synonymous with a union of lovers. He did not, of course, succeed. All the comedies he designed along these lines end sadly. It is quite in vain that the author tries to mollify his readers with cheerful epilogues and witty explanations. At the dawn of the Renaissance it was still possible for Dante to sublimate a tragic love into a "comedy," but the comedic traditions which Shaw inherited did not admit of such feats of metaphysical legerdemain. In Shaw's time it was altogether necessary that, in a comedy, lovers should be united. In these circumstances it is easy to understand why Ellen Terry considered the end of *Captain Brassbound's Conversion* to be tragic.

In his effort to persuade Miss Terry to play Lady Cicely, Shaw mightily stressed the heroic nature of the role. Lady Cicely is, indeed, in some sense a superman, governing others through the sheer power of her will, that is to say through cunning and moral suasion. Her methods are unashamedly devious. She views the world with the naïveté of a sensible child and thus manages to get directly to the heart of every problem that confronts her. Unlike her brother, the judge, she believes that men are naturally good, and will revert to their native goodness the moment they are free to do so. It is evidently for this reason that she undermines authority whenever she encounters it.

Sir Howard instinctively plays the judge wherever the occasion offers; his sister judges no one. She goes her way in the world with the air of an experienced kindergarten teacher. Accordingly, she has—as Shaw intimated in a letter to Ellen Terry—the qualities of the Virgin Mother in a higher degree even than Candida.[54] Candida is quite conscious of her desirability as a woman and is therefore not above coquetry. But Lady Cicely has an open love affair with all the world and has no need for lesser flirtations. It is by appealing to her maternal instinct—or perhaps to the administrative faculty which underlies it—that Brassbound is able to sway her toward himself in the moment of his helplessness, and thus to focus on himself the love that is meant only for all. Their relation is, nevertheless, quite as implausible as that of Candida and Marchbanks, and it is doubtless well that Brassbound heeds the call of the open sea, a more engaging environment than the night which is impatient for Marchbanks.

Lady Cicely is one of Shaw's most successful characters. While her brother is forced by his temperament, and the narrow-mindedness characteristic of his profession, to chip away at human nature, and thus to encounter resistance at every blow, Lady Cicely manipulates people as deftly as clay in the hands of a potter. Her methods in *Captain Brassbound's Conversion* are thus a charming version of the very methods by which Shaw attempted to manipulate Ellen Terry to his ends. They demonstrate, if nothing more, the advantage of exercising one's artistic talents in regions where reality does not unduly assert its lamentable resistance to the shaping hand of the artist.

Captain Brassbound's Conversion was written during the period that marked the turn in Shaw's life from poverty to affluence. Mrs. Bernard Shaw insisted on making a substantial settlement on her husband. He did not demur, but in the circumstances it was hardly possible for him to nourish decently the sense of social injustice which had so far inspired his efforts as a dramatist.

The composition of *Captain Brassbound's Conversion* at precisely this point of Shaw's career cannot have been without significance. It is unseemly for rich men to complain of social injustice: in the field of social protest it is, above all, necessary to fail. It is a proof of Shaw's extraordinary resilience of character that success troubled him no more than failure, but at this time he must have experienced some embarrassment. Very likely the *reductio ad absurdum* of Black Paquito's unjustified quarrel with the social order in some measure reflects Shaw's need to reappraise the socialist cause. It is certainly possible to see, if one wishes, in Brassbound's moment of agony some projection of Shaw's predicament when he felt himself suddenly deprived of his personal grievance against the world; and in the shot that recalls Brassbound to his ship, the imaginative reader may perhaps see the symbol of Shaw's resolution to continue the socialist struggle on a higher plane than the purely economic issue.

In any case, the cannon shot from the schooner *Thanksgiving* unequivocally punctuates Shaw's dramatic career. In the year 1898 he reached a modus vivendi with the middle class, and his hatred of its hypocrisy was in some measure tempered by his pity for its stupidity. He saw himself, as time went on, less as a literary terrorist dedicated to the destruction of an infamous social organization, than as one whose mission it was to guide society along the tangled paths of evolution.

His social attitudes also showed some alteration. As he boasted to Ellen Terry in a mood of obvious exaltation, he could now join the ranks of those who could exploit the labor of others. As an author he was in a position to sweat the actor, and now that he was enabled to collect his rents he had no intention of sparing those who worked his properties for their livelihood.[55] In his eyes poverty, which formerly he had considered a crime of the rich, rapidly took on the aspect of a disease of the poor. Shaw at no time renounced Proudhon's radical tenet, but his attitude was now touched with cynicism. Property was robbery—but it was obviously more agreeable to rob than to be robbed. It was also healthier.

It is difficult to avoid the conclusion that as Shaw grew prosperous, and poverty became more and more a loathsome memory, he tended to shift the guilt for this sort of social inadequacy from the privileged to the deprived. While he was poor, he had decided that it was morally reprehensible to endure poverty, and he had in fact endured it not a moment longer than was necessary. He had acquired riches on reasonable terms. It seemed to him now that it rested with the afflicted to rid themselves of their afflictions, like himself, by an act of will. A continued state of poverty argued a lack of energy. It was possible for the poor to acquire property, and for the downtrodden to rebel. If they did not, they had best perish so as to make way for a less passive race. Those who helped to maintain wretchedness by making it possible for the poor to survive through an insidious philanthropy were as much to blame for poverty as the poor. It was this viewpoint that was ultimately asserted in *Major Barbara*, Shaw's final attempt to reconcile his socialism with his capitalism.

Shaw's great plays were all written after 1898. Before this time he was an activist, and the note of protest that he sounded was understandably shrill. Now his mood underwent a subtle change. His later plays and his prefaces display not so much a desire to tinker with the existing patterns of society as the need to supersede them entirely in the fullness of time. Wealth did not diminish his revolutionary ardor. All his life he continued to advocate the redistribution of property, but seldom in such a way as to arouse a passionate response in any but the most inflammable minds. The distaste for democracy and the rule of the masses, which he shared with Ibsen, Strindberg, and Nietzsche, became increasingly evident in the Olympian attitudes which characterized the long period of his maturity. In the decade preceding the outbreak of the First World War, his radical views were widely publicized; but there was no great immediacy about his revolutionary program. After *Man and Superman* Shaw became popularly acceptable as a philosopher, like Ibsen; someone vaguely disturbing, but worthy of respect, whom it was increasingly unnecessary to comprehend.

As the theoretical basis of his plays became progressively more abstract, their urgency as social documents was lessened in proportion. His evolutionary doctrines were obviously not dangerous, and his theology was received with the formal courtesy that all religious ideas, no matter how bizarre, were accorded in nineteenth-century England. A half-century after their initial promulgation his ideas remained as fresh and provocative as ever, but he had somehow passed, with his age, beyond controversy. Others took up his notions and with them made a great show of radicalism. As for Shaw, by this time he had long ceased to be thought of as dangerous and was accorded the respectful indifference due to a classic.

Dick Dudgeon was a disciple of the devil and invited hanging. Captain Brassbound, however, was a disciple of Lady Cicely Wayneflete and became a very acceptable pirate. He did not die young. One is afforded a view of him in his age, majestically at home in *Heartbreak House*, magnificently bearded, drunk as an owl, as tragic as Lear, and as mad. Undeniably there is something pathetic in this transition. It is of a different order from the pathos of Ibsen's Brand or Rubek, men who require an avalanche to quench them; but Shotover, also, needed a world cataclysm to silence him, and it is true that nobody since his time has spoken with that voice.

MAN AND SUPERMAN

The first part of Shaw's career as a dramatist was a period of unbelievably intense activity. In the course of six years, in the intervals between his many chores—his journalistic duties, his work at the Fabian office, his research at the British Museum, his meetings and conferences with socialist colleagues, the workingmen's lectures to which he devoted his spare evenings, and the staggering load of correspondence he carried—he had somehow managed to write ten plays, jotted down piecemeal in shorthand in pocket notebooks, mostly while he was riding on trains and buses on the way to some engagement.

His labors brought him virtually to the edge of death. In 1901 nothing came from his pen but *The Admirable Bashville*, a dramatization of *Cashel Byron's Profession*. This play, written in blank verse of the utmost banality, was intended chiefly to preserve the stage copyright of the novel and has since served no useful purpose. But in 1903 Shaw finished *Man and Superman* and with this he entered upon his greatness.

In England the 1890's were a time of unusual spiritual fervor, evidenced, on the one hand, by a powerful renewal of Christian faith and, on the other, by a significant reawakening of interest in mysticism, magic, astrology, and the occult. This revival of arcanic lore was strongly influenced by the Paris school of mages, the groups associated with Sâr Péladan and Eliphas Lévi. Essentially these movements, intimately related to the ascendancy of symbolism in literature and the arts, were the result of a widespread reaction against the positivistic tendencies of the earlier part of the century. In France, the reaction was in some measure signalized by the enthusiastic reception of Paul Bourget's *Le Disciple*, but there is no doubt that the antecedent wave of materialism had generated its counterwave some time before Bourget made it official in 1889.

It is to this movement toward a revitalization of spiritual values that *Man and Superman* must be referred. Even before the composition of *The Devil's Disciple*, possibly as early as *The Philanderer*, Shaw had been working toward the formulation of a general idea of religious nature, something which would arrange his metaphysical notions in a meaningful pattern. In *Man and Superman* the design was for the first time unfolded in all its complexity, exemplified by a dramatic action, explained in a lengthy preface, symbolically extended through the philosophic dialogue interpolated in the third act, and supported by an appendix and a glossary of maxims in the style of La Rochefoucauld. Whatever may be thought of this performance as philosophy, it is certainly a very complete exposition of a dramatic idea, the most ambitious that anyone had so far put forth in the theater.

The action of *Man and Superman* is frankly exemplary. It involves a love story played in comic style, with episodes of melodramatic extravagance and a more or less conventional conclusion. The heart of the play is the dream sequence, a lens through which the love story is magnified to cosmic proportions, so that the characters are exhibited *sub specie aeternitatis*, or somewhere near it. The method marks a decisive change in Shaw's approach to comedy. With this play he departed from the type of realism he had learned from Ibsen, Becque, and Brieux. In *Candida* he had experimented with symbolism. *Man and Superman* was a full-scale example of symbolist drama.

By 1903 symbolism had undergone a full development on the Continent, and its influence in England was already strong. Maeterlinck had furnished the new movement with a striking manifesto, but symbolism had deeper roots than Maeterlinck imagined. The consequence of the movement against realistic representation became apparent first in literature and painting, then in music and the decorative arts. In the theater the strictly mimetic approach to drama that the naturalists professed in the name of "science" evoked a decided reaction. Plays of the type of Villier's *Axël* and Maeterlinck's *La Princesse Maleine* had given early symbolism a medieval coloring which blended readily with English Pre-Raphaelitism; but *L'Intruse* and *Intérieur* indicated other paths to the Maeterlinckian *au-delà*, and, soon after Ibsen, writers such as Hauptmann and Hofmannsthal showed what could be done to reveal the psychic landscape that the naturalistic viewpoint obscured. By the end of the century every major dramatist on the Continent was a symbolist.

It was to be some time before anyone in England showed an interest in symbolism, but before the end of the century Yeats, Synge, and later

Barrie began experimenting with the new techniques. Meanwhile, in Sweden, Strindberg was developing the methods of French symbolism into what came, some decades later, to be called expressionism. *To Damascus I* (1898) and *The Dream Play* (1902) clearly indicate the course of symbolist drama in the twentieth century: with these plays Strindberg laid the foundation of what is modern in the modern theater.

Shaw had seen several examples of symbolist drama when Lugné-Poë's Théâtre de l'Oeuvre came to London in March 1895, but he does not seem to have been aware at the time of the importance of the new movement. By this time both Walkley and Yeats were deeply concerned with symbolist ideas. Shaw, however, seems to have thought of this movement as an aspect of Pre-Raphaelitism unworthy of any special attention. In the lengthy preface with which he introduced *Man and Superman* he gave no evidence of being aware of the fact that with this play he was breaking new ground in English drama.

Symbolist drama was designed to afford an intimation of the spiritual reality which lies, presumably, beyond sensual experience. To become aware of this plane of being is to perceive the significant pattern, the Idea, which orders the seeming chaos of the material world. In this connection the nineteenth-century symbolists were greatly impressed by the theory of signatures and correspondences in which the symbolists of the seventeenth century had seen a secure basis for poetry. They did not, for a time, relish Blake or Donne but they read Swedenborg avidly and, in connection with Swedenborg, Poe.

The theory that underlay their art depended, of course, on the assumption that beyond the visible world there is in fact a suprasensual reality of which the artist becomes aware when he is properly sensitized, and the nature of which he is able to suggest through a special vocabulary of symbols, that is to say, through images of unusual potency. For Swedenborg this reality was none other than the cosmic structure long ago described by Philo Judaeus and Dionysius the Areopagite, defined by Thomas Aquinas, and realized poetically by Dante.

Swedenborg was a scientist who in his later life saw visions. The symbolists who were influenced by him, however, were poets. For them, the Beyond was less clear and less rational than it seemed to Swedenborg. It had a Platonic look; but there was no agreement whatever as to its nature, or the nature of the Idea at its core, and their visionary experiences were notably mysterious. In later times when the artist peered into the depths of his soul he was likely to find there, like Rilke, chiefly himself. The narcissistic nature of these psychic adventures led quite naturally to the probing of the unconscious by way of dream and myth; but a quest that turned in this manner upon itself left something to be desired. The symbolists had embarked on a mystic errand, much like the knights in search of the Sangreal. Their failure to find anything substantial to symbolize drove some into the church and others to despair, but their efforts nevertheless resulted in a body of exceedingly interesting literature and art.

Shaw was doubtless attracted briefly by the mystical aura of French symbolism, and he gave voice to this variety of religious experience through Father Keegan in *John Bull's Other Island*; but evidently he distrusted this poetic strain and ultimately rejected it in favor of a more energetic faith, the basis of which he found in the writings of Samuel Butler. It was through this heady blend of science and religion that ultimately he found his true vocation as a writer.

In the 1890's a sense of vocation was indispensable to a writer of serious leanings, and particularly to one who fancied himself a poet. Shelley had fixed the type of latter-day apostle in the popular imagination, and many a romantic young man believed himself to be marked, like the unknown poet in *Adonais*, with the sign of Cain or Christ. The problem of *l'homme engagé* had concerned Ibsen deeply. It was debated in his plays from *Brand* to *When We Dead Awaken*. In the circumstances a writer like Shaw could hardly avoid the need for a reliable cause to serve. In the absence of God, however, it was not easy to find an idea capable of sustaining a lifetime of dedication. There was, of course, the cause of humanity which Shaw had early adopted, but the concept of humanity was vague, and at best provisional. It was in his search for God that Shaw at last came upon the Life Force, which henceforth monopolized his efforts.

The workings of the unconscious will, which Schopenhauer had so dramatically described in *Die Welt als Wille und Vorstellung* (1818), furnished a basis considerably more interesting from a philosophic viewpoint than the vague imagery of the symbolists or the stark materialism of Marx.

Schopenhauer began to be read extensively in England only after the middle of the nineteenth century. In April 1853 John Oxenford published an account of Schopenhauer's philosophy in the *Westminster Review* under the title "Iconoclasm in German Philosophy," but it was only in 1833 that *The World as Will and Idea* became available in English.[1] The idea that the will and the passions determine the life of the intellect was intolerable to those who insisted on the traditional primacy of the reason; but it found favor with many who disliked the bureaucratic disposition of the Platonic soul, as well as with those who were frightened by the specter of materialism, to which the rationalistic theories of the time infallibly led. The utilitarian notion that prudence is the essence of morality was particularly offensive to those who looked to a higher principle with which to justify the social concept. Schopenhauer's Will, though blind and aimless, had romantic glamor, and a spiritual quality which the dry rationalism of the positivists obviously lacked.

In spite of the fact that Coleridge and, after him, Carlyle, were strongly influenced by German ideas, German metaphysics played no great part in shaping English thought in the first half of the nineteenth century. Toward the beginning of the century there had been in Germany a growing reaction against Kantian rationalism, the result of which was a gradual shift in emphasis within the classic framework of German idealism. For Kant, as for Plato, the intellect was the primal reality. Fichte and Schelling, however, deeply influenced by such writers as Cabanis and Helvetius, saw the vital principle of reason as something immanent in the will and therefore looked to the individual, rather than to some external essence, for the sources and formative principles of belief. Such attempts to reach back of the intellect in the quest for an ultimate reality culminated in Schopenhauer's formulation of being in terms of Will and Idea.

Schopenhauer argued that reason could do no more than to arrange and classify the data of sensual perception. Science dealt only with phenomena; but behind the material world apprehended by the senses, it was possible to intuit the existence of an urge which was neither rational nor intelligible and which defied explanation. This was life itself, the vital principle. Schopenhauer called this urge the will to live. The resulting metaphysics seemed—in contrast to the idealism of his contemporaries—realistic. Its consequence in the latter part of the century was a mounting attack against rationalism and the supremacy of the scientific method which had so far dominated nineteenth-century thought. One aspect of this reaction was the symbolist movement.

It is unlikely that Shaw came directly to a knowledge of Schopenhauer's system, and even less likely that he thoroughly understood its implications, but the theory of love in *Man and Superman* seems to rest quite firmly on a Schopenhauerian basis, and it is evident that Shaw's thinking at the time of its composition was influenced by ideas that could have had no other source. For Schopenhauer the principle of life is an irrational and motiveless energy which in time develops consciousness. This is the underlying reality in which we find our kinship with whatever lives that is not man. Ideas have no creative function. Reality is revealed to us in our sense of the Will immanent in ourselves. Life is both painful and senseless. One may find palliatives, but while there is consciousness there is no escape from pain.

Schopenhauer's pessimism suited Strindberg very well, and after *Master Olaf* it furnished the groundwork of his drama until he turned in his later life once again to God. It was wholly unsuited to Shaw's temperament. What appears in Schopenhauer's system as the driving, senseless, and motiveless will is in Shaw's view motivated, sensible, and sacred. It is God, effectively dynamic in every living being, a soul of infinite potentiality striving for fulfillment through its creatures.

What the ultimate goal of its endeavor might be, aside from the attainment of perfection, Shaw was not able to imagine. It was only in *Back to Methuselah* that he attempted to come to grips with the ultimate; and the conclusion there is indeterminate. Nevertheless it is arguable that the goal of the spiritual effort which Lilith exemplifies is, in Hegelian terms, freedom, that is to say, freedom of the will. This is seemingly attainable through the development of mind. In *Man and Superman* the blessed are engaged in an apparently endless intellectual effort. Conceivably the aim of this process is the liberation of the spirit from its material entanglements to the point where it is self-conditioned and self-determined. That is certainly the direction indicated for the human adventure in *Back to Methuselah*. Shaw's idea thus appears to approximate Hegel's assumption much more closely than Schopenhauer's. For Schopenhauer the evolution of the will to live ends in extinction; for Shaw it ends in omnipotence.

Shaw doubtless passed through a period of godless materialism, but his mother was a spiritist, and he himself was in considerable need of God. By his early thirties he had read Bunyan, Blake, Butler, and Bradley, as well as other writers in the B volumes of the British Museum catalogue; doubtless he had read Schopenhauer in translation and some account of Hegel's system. In these writings he found both a basis for faith and a way to establish himself personally in the Messianic tradition. In 1889 he wrote his fellow Fabian Hubert Bland of the price one has to pay in material prosperity in order to arrive at a consciousness of one's spiritual self "as a vessel of the Zeitgeist or Will or whatever it may be." "You and I," he concluded,

have followed our original impulse, and our reward is that we have
been conscious of its existence and can rejoice therein. The coming
into clearer light of this consciousness has not occurred to me as a
crisis. It has been gradual. I do not proceed by crises. . . . My
tendency is rather to overlook change in myself, and proceed on
absolute assumptions until the consequences pull me up with a short
turn.[2]

Shaw was at that time thirty-three, and well on the way to something
like a definition of his "spiritual self." He had reviewed Butler's *Luck or
Cunning?* two years before for the *Pall Mall Gazette*, in 1887, without
giving any indication that it held any special meaning for him. But its
influence on his thinking was evidently immense. Twenty years later he
was so sure of his metaphysical position as to declare with pride that he
was "implacably anti-rationalist and anti-materialist."[3]

In reaching this position Shaw followed the major trend of the time.
In the 1880's materialism was no longer in vogue. Comte had long ago
come to the conclusion that, since in the nature of things the search for
final causes was fruitless, society could do no better than to abandon the
quest for ultimate truth in order to seek out such knowledge as might be
immediately useful. From this viewpoint the philosophical method of the
future would necessarily be empirical rather than speculative, and the
systematic establishment of data would constitute a necessary prerequisite to any formulation of the laws that govern human relations. It was
Comte's intention to emancipate his age in this manner from the tyranny
of religion. Instead he condemned it to the despotism of science. In
France the positivists, after having, with considerable fanfare, abandoned
the search for the ultimate, proceeded to advance improbable generalizations ostensibly derived through scientific procedures. The result was a
form of authoritarian dogmatism more arbitrary, less credible, and much
less agreeable than that of the church.

In England, Mill had already attempted in a similar fashion to apply
empirical methods to social phenomena, but, as he was the first to admit,
without success. Though supernaturalism had been by this time effectively banished from the laboratory, it continued to haunt the minds of
all but the most confirmed rationalists. In the case of Mill it was evident
that his approach to philosophy was seriously hampered by his unwill-
ingness to accept a rigorous determinism. In an age that had reluctantly
accepted Darwin without quite giving up God, the need to affirm the
free will of man was felt to be of critical importance, and the ability of
humanity to perfect itself through its own efforts seemed especially

demonstrable. Thus Mills's essay *On Liberty*, published in 1859, was vastly more influential than any of his more closely reasoned theses; and his faith in the essential goodness of man, the infallibility of reason, and the fundamental morality of mankind had—as his last essays indicate—more religion in it than logic. Even John Morley, a most determined agnostic, found it impossible to give up his quite unscientific belief in the sanctity of human nature, although he was unable to see Comte's deification of humanity as other than an empty metaphor.

The school of idealistic thought that was associated with Oxford in this period, together with the influence of such antipositivist works as W. H. Mallock's *The New Paul and Virginia* (1878) and *Is Life Worth Living?* (1879), opened the way for a developing anti-intellectualism of respectable proportions, and in England many were impelled to look beyond logic for an acceptable spiritual principle. For a socialist of Shaw's temper it was no great feat to discover somewhere in the vicinity of the Schopenhauerian Will and the Hegelian *Weltgeist* a congenial principle of divinity. In spite of the absence of any demonstrable basis for such an assumption, the idea of an evolving spirit immanent in its creatures, blind to begin with, but ultimately all-seeing, seemed to him to afford a ready avenue to a believable religion.

In 1881 Frederic Harrison, the most articulate and most prolific of the English positivists, instituted the Positivist Church in London at Newton Hall in Fetter Lane. It was in this church that Cyril Sykes's parents are said to have been wed in Shaw's *Getting Married*.[4] This notable experiment in adult education was organized around a library selected by Comte himself. It was intended to develop the idea of "man's dependence on the human Providence which surrounds him from the cradle to the grave." Harrison's position was staunchly positivistic, but he was deeply concerned also with the search for a general idea, a synthesis which might serve as a rational basis of faith. As the religious views which Harrison sought to develop involved the worship of humanity as the *grand être* of Comte, it reconciled a strictly rationalistic idea of the human enterprise with a mystical outpouring of veneration for the vital principle at its core. It was this kind of thinking that Shaw had in mind in speaking of the "new theology."[5]

In the 1860's Schopenhauer's work was tolerably well known in England, but it took some years more for the Victorians to become aware of Hegel. In 1865 J. M. Stirling published *The Secret of Hegel*, a valiant attempt to interpret *The Phenomenology of the Spirit* (1807). Soon thereafter an influential school of English writers headed by F. M. Bradley and T. H. Green heralded a strong idealistic reaction against Millite rationalism and the vestiges of Bentham. Mill, like the humanists of an earlier age, had concluded that pleasure is the highest good, but in his view the individual's pleasure lay in the pleasure of others. This charitable concept, which Mill himself eventually abandoned, Bradley scorned as a utilitarian remnant and in his *Ethical Studies* of 1876 he asserted the view that pleasure, in the utilitarian sense, was an empty abstraction. To Bradley it seemed that the only reality was the life of the mind, and that the goal of evolution was the Absolute, the highest determination achievable by a self-creating and self-subsistent God. With this Absolute the intermediate human self in its truest reality could be identified through faith and, in this manner, man might attain to an immediate intuition of God. Faith meant, in Bradley's judgment, both the belief in the reality of an object and the will that this object be real. Thus the active principle in evolution was neither intellect nor desire, but will in its creative aspect. The implication was that mind is a self-creating entity in continuous development.[6]

Bradley's system departed in some ways from the usual interpretations of Hegel, but essentially they reached the same conclusions. The Hegelian dialectic is a spiritual process in which, taking account of the contradiction inherent in every finite statement, the intellect strives to overcome this contradiction by an appropriate synthesis on a higher level of understanding. Knowledge thus unfolds through the inner stress of its own contradictions, proceeding from the simplest formulations through progressively more complex stages of comprehension until it reaches its fulfillment in the Absolute. The development of the human spirit is thus seen to be the progressive revelation of God, whose reality as intelligence is manifested in the human self-consciousness alone as it develops into complete and perfect self-awareness.

It is obviously more sensible to relate Shaw's conception of the Life Force to the English idealists of the 1870's—the more so as Bradley wrote a brilliant style—than directly to Hegel's *Geist* or to the *élan vital* which Bergson described in *L'Evolution créatrice* of 1907. Without doubt, Shaw's ideas differ a great deal from Bradley's in ways that are of significance to specialists, and even more from Hegel's, but to the unaided eye they might seem remarkably similar. Shaw was certainly no philosopher, though he struck philosophical poses, and still less a scientist, though he liked to think of himself as one, but he was well abreast of the principal thought of his time. The idea of an aspiring element at the heart of being was widespread in the speculative fancies of an age that was deeply infected with evolutionary concepts. Motion and change were indispensable factors in the etiological patterns of the time, as indeed they are now, and Bergson's substitution of durational values for the fixed forms of classical philosophy came at a moment when it could shock nobody. Hegel's system had special validity for Shaw, as the basis of Marxism, and Bergson's notions seemed so congenial that Shaw claimed them for his own without even troubling to examine them. Fully committed as he was to an evolutionary pattern of change, it was natural for him to agree with Bergson that time is of the essence of being. After *Man and Superman* time plays a leading role in all Shaw's plays, but even in *Back to Methuselah* it is not definitely characterized: it is simply duration, the measure of the process through which the Will develops.

The consequence of the metaphysical attitudes which Shaw adapted to the stage was a view of man as a transitional phase in the development of a superior level of being, from which humanity as such might perhaps be ultimately excluded. The essential element in the characterization of Shaw's heroes is therefore their awareness of responsibility as agents of the Life Force, an entity which is not altogether distinguishable from the Hegelian *Weltgeist*. These characters are all, therefore, more or less conscious of a vocation in life to which all other considerations must be subordinated. This they have in common with Ibsen's great characters, from Brand to Rubek. But while Ibsen invariably stressed the sacrificial side of dedication and thus developed the tragedy of the engaged individual, Shaw magnified the cosmic element to the point where the individual's protest becomes, in the minuteness of its scale, an appropriate subject of comedy. In the crucial scene of *Man and Superman*, Tanner's personal uneasiness, as he surrenders to the onslaught of the Life Force in the guise of an attractive girl, is hardly calculated to make one weep in sympathy. He makes us grin. But Ibsen's John Gabriel is a deeply tragic figure, and in Brand, Rosmer, Solness, and Rubek there is not much that is funny.

Both Shaw and Ibsen were primarily comedic writers, typically concerned with the plight of the individual in his relation to society. If their drama is so widely dissimilar it is because of the different emphasis placed on the elements of the inner conflict their plays depict. In the interplay of psychic pressures, Shaw stressed the universal impulse as the significant reality, in relation to which the individual's concerns seem trivial. For Ibsen, however, drama was centered in the soul's loneliness. Beyond the individual consciousness there was only the unfathomable mystery of existence, of which nothing whatever could be said with confidence. For Ibsen drama took place in the individual; for Shaw the play of the individual was comprehensible only in terms of the universal comedy. The difference between them was thus chiefly a matter of scale.

Both were essentially skeptics. "In taking your side," Shaw had written, "don't trouble about its being the right side—north is no righter than South—but be sure that it is really yours, and then back it for all you're worth."[7]

Shaw backed the Life Force for all he was worth. By 1903 he had apparently convinced himself that what he felt as an urgency within himself was the manifestation of a universal impulse which it was his high privilege to serve. This conviction gave him a delightful sense of freedom. The Life Force was, above all, original, and its originality was demonstrable in the behavior of those rare individuals who stood, like himself, in the forefront of the evolutionary process, and thus prefigured, at each stage in its development, the superhumanity of the future. From Shaw's viewpoint, these were the proper subjects of drama.

Since the Life Force is essentially dynamic and progressive, the superior individual is always at odds with a society that tends to perpetuate each stage of its career as if it were ultimate and eternal. The price of genius is incessant conflict; and the tension between the extraordinary individual and the mass of undifferentiated humanity he is destined to influence, though comic when viewed under the aspect of eternity, is in the temporal frame the subject of tragedy. God and the individual are in eternal opposition, while at the same time they are inseparable and completely interdependent expressions of one another. At the dawn of the twentieth century this paradox was neither new nor by any means peculiar to Shaw. Rilke was writing at about this time:

> Was wirst du tun, Gott, wenn ich sterbe?
> Ich bin dein Krug (wenn ich zerscherbe?)
> Ich bin dein Trank (wenn ich verderbe?)
> Bin dein Gewand und dein Gewerbe,
> mit mir verlierst du deinen Sinn.[8]

Possibly in English:

> What wilt thou do, God, when I die?
> I am thy jug (when smashed am I?)
> I am thy drink (when I run dry?)
> Thy dress, thy trade—when I go hence
> wilt thou continue to make sense?

Shaw began working on *Man and Superman* in 1901. It took him two years to finish it and obviously it represented an enormous investment of creative energy. The reward was not immediate. Robert Loraine produced it successfully in New York in September 1905. In London The Stage Society gave it two performances. Then on 23 May 1905 it opened a run of twelve matinees at the Royal Court with Granville-Barker as Tanner and Lillah McCarthy in the role of Ann Whitefield. The play was received with politeness, and the production was praised, but though the play had been in print for a year, in England the importance of *Man and Superman* was not yet generally apparent.

Man and Superman is subtitled *A Comedy and a Philosophy*. Of the two the comedy is by far the less interesting component. The plot is a love story, in Shaw's words, "a trumpery story of modern London life, a life in which, as you know, the ordinary man's main business is to get means to keep up the position and habits of a gentleman, and the ordinary woman's business is to get married."[9] The result is a well-made play of conventional shape, founded upon a *méprise*, centered upon a love chase, embellished with melodramatic incidents involving brigands and rescuers, and resolved, in accordance with the usual tenets of romantic comedy, in the happy union of young lovers.

It is chiefly in the dream sequence of the third act that its symbolism becomes apparent. This act was considered dispensable even by the author. Yet it is John Tanner's dream, and only this, that gives the play its extraordinary scope and grandeur. The rest is, as Shaw indicated in the introduction, simply the story of the conquest of an eligible, but reluctant young man by a girl who has set her cap for him. The dream makes it clear that the play, as a whole, is a conceit intended to suggest the nature of the attraction that draws the sexes together—in short, an attempt to define love in cosmic terms.

The pattern of the action is conventionally Scribean. There are four acts, and, as usual in plays of this sort, two plots which converge toward the climax and are simultaneously resolved in the final scenes. The main plot is of the A loves B loves C variety and has the itinerant quality of romantic sequences traceable to the sixteenth-century epic. As in *Candida*, the heroine has a choice of men, but the heroine of *Man and Superman* makes a choice different from Candida's. She chooses the man who needs her least. For the rest, the situation is not markedly different from that of the earlier play. The poet, Tavy, is a pale reflection of Marchbanks. Tanner is a younger version of Morell. As between the two candidates for the hand of Ann it becomes evident that it is Tanner who is predestined to be the husband, while it is Tavy's lot to be the broken-hearted lover who creates poems instead of children. There is also Mendoza, his comic counterpart, the high quality of whose poetry it is possible to judge, since we are favored with a sample. He is evidently fated to be a brigand.

The *méprise* stems from the fact that, while Ann is supposedly in love with Tavy, who is solemnly warned against her wiles by Tanner, it is actually Tanner whom she is resolved to marry. This comes as a surprise to nobody except the men most nearly involved. When the situation is made clear to Tanner, however, he is terrified and makes off in his high-powered car, with Ann in hot pursuit. The chase takes them all halfway across Europe, to the Sierra Nevada in Spain. There Tanner is captured first by the brigand Mendoza, himself a hapless victim of love, and afterwards by Ann, who turns up with an armed escort and all the panoply of Eros, the police force and the Life Force.

The action could not.be simpler. It is a love chase, the originality of which consists in the reversal of traditional roles. In this case, the lady is aggressive; the gentleman is coy; what gives the play its comic tone is that in this unconventional situation everyone tries to preserve appearances. The lady plays the coy maiden; and the gentleman, as the seemingly aggressive male, finds himself engaged in a rear-guard action against impossible odds.

In this play the main plot is concerned with courtship, the subplot with marriage; but there is little in it that can be called romantic. It is all extremely businesslike. Ann's sister Violet is supposedly bearing the child of an unknown lover, whose identity she refuses to disclose. In fact she is secretly married to Hector Malone, whose father opposes the match. It is the conquest of the father, and the father's millions, which principally occupies Violet; the conquest of Tanner is Ann's principal concern; and in the ruthless efficiency of the two young women in organizing their lives, the play makes its wry point: *amor omnia vincit.*

While *Man and Superman* is principally about love and marriage, it is also concerned with a closely related topic, the conflict of youth and age. The principal characters are all in their early twenties. *The Revolutionist's Handbook* appended to the play, as the work of John Tanner, is what one might expect from a bright young firebrand of the 1890's, and its radicalism inevitably conflicts with that of the still-smoking embers of an earlier age, such as Roebuck Ramsden. In the contrast between the former radical, who will not grasp the fact that the times have passed him by, and the young enthusiast, who is still somewhat ahead of his day, Shaw is able not only to indicate the relativism of accepted beliefs at successive stages of social evolution, but also to prefigure in the pathetic figure of the older man the sad destiny of the younger. The inevitable transformation of the fiery radicalism of each age into the pompous conservatism of the next is the natural order of a developing society. The contrasts are comic in their effect, but the implications of this dialectic are not altogether funny.

The contrast of generations, in the case of the ladies, is less emphatic, but no less striking. The female character, it is intimated, is more stable than the male, if only because her function in life is more clearly defined. Mrs. Whitefield, having fulfilled her role as mother, is no longer an agent of the Life Force, but her vital energy has passed in full measure to her daughter, Ann, whose femininity she fears, dislikes, and serves. The elderly Miss Ramsden, on the other hand, is the prototype of Violet, the supremely self-confident English gentlewoman, the backbone of the British Empire, the feminine principle upon which English manhood depends.

Shaw's purpose in juxtaposing the successive elements of a family history in this manner could not be more clear. In his view, the laws of heredity are irrefrangible. A chain of inexorable causation links each generation to the next. Just as the matrimonial choices of the generation that is departing has determined the shape of the generation that is taking its place, so the young people's love affairs of the moment are destined to shape the generation yet unborn. From the evolutionary viewpoint, love, the selective principle, is the essential biological determinant.

In the comedy of Tanner, Ann, and Tavy it is therefore possible to symbolize the eternal comedy of the husband, the lover, and the lady, and the triangle of romantic comedy is thus transformed into an exemplum of impressive magnitude. The situation in *Man and Superman* is assimilated to the myth of Don Juan, the legendary lover, in somewhat the same manner as James Joyce assimilated the itinerary of the peripatetic Mr. Bloom to the journeyings of Ulysses, the legendary wanderer. In the case of Shaw, also, the conceit is not especially apt, since the mythical Don Juan is an incorrigible philanderer, whereas John Tanner has no special interest in women, yet is fated for matrimony from the start. For Shaw's purposes, though, the analogy, however strained, was useful. John Tanner is what, in the course of evolution, Don Juan has become. The idea sprang, undoubtedly, from Shaw's experiences during the relatively brief period of his sexual flowering, the years from 1881 to 1898. Like *The Philanderer, Man and Superman* is both autobiographical and apologetic.

From what Shaw tells us of himself it seems plain that as a youth he was unusually susceptible. His early years were marked by a series of half-imaginary romantic attachments, the details of which are carefully posted in his diaries behind concealing asterisks, among notes of his engagements and current expenses. The painful shyness of his early twenties, his extensive poverty, and the morbid irritability which caused him to bicker periodically with the women he fancied kept him away from any serious involvement until the fateful evening in July 1885 when, on the occasion of his twenty-ninth birthday, Mrs. Jane Patterson induced him to spend the night in her house in Brompton Square. This initiated a period of amatory activity which Shaw never permitted himself or his public to forget.

"Jenny" Patterson was a widow some fifteen years his senior, quite wealthy, not especially beautiful, and of an unusually passionate and jealous disposition. She sang. Her relations with her singing teacher's son were for the most part stormy, but they were maintained over a period of fully seven years, a time marked by frequent and feverish displays of hysteria on her part, while her lover, on the other hand, hardly troubled to conceal his growing restlessness. In the meantime he worked assiduously at the complex system of interlocking flirtations with which he appears to have defended himself against the depredations of individual women while maintaining a receptive, and even aggressive, attitude toward the sex in general.

Of the half-dozen women with whom he achieved some intimacy during this time only Jenny Patterson seems to have involved him seriously. The nature of his amatory interests in this period is, of course, a matter of conjecture, but his state of mind is perhaps sufficiently indicated in a letter he wrote in October 1888 to Alice Lockett, a really pretty girl, judging by her photograph, with whom he had carried on a quarrelsome and fruitless love affair since first they met in 1881, when he was twenty-five:

> My season is commencing: my nights are filling up one by one. I am booked for a half-dozen lectures within the next month. I shall be out tonight with Stepniak and the underdone. My DR (Dramatic Review) copy must be done to-day, to-morrow an article is due for the Magazine of Music. On Saturday my contribution to Our Corner must be written. On Sunday there is a lecture ("The Attitude of Socialists Toward Other Bodies"), not one idea for which have I yet arranged. Meanwhile To-day is howling for more copy. See you this week! Avaunt, Sorceress: not this month—not until next July. Not,

in any case, until I am again in the detestable humor which is the only one to which you minister. Remember, I am not always a savage. My pleasures are music, conversation, the grapple of my intelligence with fresher ones. All this I can sweeten with a kiss; but I cannot saturate and spoil it with fifty thousand. Love making grows tedious to me—the emotions have evaporated from it. This is your fault: since your return I have seen you twice, and both times you have been lazy and unintelligently luxurious. I will not spend such evenings except when I am for a moment tired and brutish. . . . Do not forget that I cannot esteem the most beautiful woman for more than she is. I want as much as I can get; there is no need to force it upon me if it exists; I am only too thirsty for companionship. Beware. When all the love has gone out of me, I am remorseless: I hurl the truth about like destroying lightning. G. B. S.[10]

Shaw cherished the belief all his life that he was interested in women primarily for literary purposes.[11] The naïveté of this excuse for philandering need not obscure the ambiguity of Shaw's amatory proclivities, out of which he fashioned the doctrine of *Man and Superman*. Everything indicates that he was personally a most attractive man, witty, charming, amusingly unpredictable, but from a sexual viewpoint uncomfortably ambivalent. Like many men who are excessively aware of their talent, he was demanding in his relationships and frankly selfish in his aims. Married women principally interested him, or women who had been married: he evidently found the Candida situation particularly to his liking and reconstructed it among his acquaintances whenever he could. For all his ready fund of blarney, he was an essentially honest man and he made no secret of the fact that he had no intention of being trapped into matrimony, or even into lovemaking on any permanent basis. Even after he was married he declared, at least half-seriously, that he had been lured into domesticity only at the point of death.

The love letters he wrote Mrs. Patrick Campbell in 1913, when he was fifty-seven, are particularly revealing. It is clear that, while he longed for a passionate relationship with a woman that would fulfill his need for love, the prospect of a thorough physical involvement threw him into a panic, so that in almost every case his love affairs essentially amounted, as Mrs. Campbell noted, to "a carnival of words." It is possible that at this time he was sexually impotent, but his need for love was great. The letter that he wrote "Stella" in answer to an only mildly inflammatory letter from her, has, for all its rhetoric, an almost tragic tone:

Oh, if only you were alarmed, and could struggle, then I could struggle too. But to be gathered like a flower and stuck in your bosom frankly! to have no provocation to pursue, and no terror to fly! to have no margin of temptation to philander in! to have a woman's love on the same terms as a child's, to have nothing to seize, nothing to refuse, nothing to resist, everything for nothing . . . to draw the sword for the duel of sex with cunning confidence in practised skill and brass breastplate, and suddenly find myself in the arms of a mother—a young mother, and with a child in my own arms who is yet a woman; all this plunges me into the wildest terror. . . . Yet here I am caught up again, breathless, with no foothold, at a dizzy height, in an ecstasy which must be delirious and presently end in my falling headlong to destruction. And yet I am happy, as madmen are. . . .[12]

From the available facts, a psychologist might reasonably conjecture that in the women he courted Shaw sought, unconsciously, the unattainable mother of his infancy, the Virgin Mother around whom his fantasies unceasingly revolved. It is understandable, in these circumstances, that the establishment in adult life of a satisfactory sexual relationship was of prime importance to him, and also that he could not admit it as a possibility. In point of fact, whatever Shaw attempted along sexual lines seems to have been attended by profound feelings of guilt, and in the end he settled for a loveless marriage comfortably grounded upon friendship.

His courtship of Mrs. Pat Campbell was predicated on the knowledge that she was engaged to marry another and younger man. This fact only served to increase his ardor. He wrote her:

I want my plaything that I am to throw away. I want my Virgin Mother enthroned in Heaven, I want my Italian peasant woman. I want my rapscalliony fellow-vagabond. I want my dark lady. I want my angel—I want my tempter. . . . I want my inspiration, my folly, my happiness, my divinity, my madness, my selfishness, my final sanity and sanctification, my transfiguration, my purification, my light across the sea, my palm across the desert, my garden of fresh flowers, my million nameless joys, my day's wage, my night's dream, my darling and my star.[13]

Beyond any doubt there was a heartbreaking sincerity in the love letters Shaw wrote to Stella: it was his last chance at romance, and perhaps his first. But there was as much rhetoric in them as longing. It is impossible to say how much of Shaw's passion was mere literature. What is clear is the neurotic element in all of his philanderings, the desire to be over-whelmed and to suffer rather than to enjoy his loves. John Tanner exhibits unusual insight:

> Of all human struggles there is none so treacherous and remorseless as the struggle between the artist man and the mother woman. Which shall use up the other? that is the issue between them. And it is all the deadlier because, in your romanticist cant, they love one another.[14]

The idea that an artist exploits the feelings of women in order to have something to write about has some savor of reason, but it is hardly realistic. The normal sexual curiosity of an adolescent may well be trans-formed into the professional voyeurism of the artist, but the idea that the dramatist makes love in order to write love scenes is less convincing than the idea that he writes plays in order to sublimate his love-making. In the case of *Man and Superman* it seems evident that the love story was not commensurate with the psychic needs of the author. It was necessary to supplement it with an elaborate philosophical system which would place the action on a plane of universality. Luckily, the material was at hand:

> The ultimate end of all love affairs, whether they are played in sock or cothurnus, is really more important than all other ends of human life, and is therefore quite worthy of the profound seriousness with which everyone pursues it. That which is decided by it is nothing less than *the composition of the next generation.* The *dramatis personæ* who shall appear when we are withdrawn are here determined, both as regards their existence and their nature, by these frivolous love affairs.[15]

This striking passage from the essay "Metaphysics of the Love of the Sexes," which Schopenhauer appended in 1844 to *The World as Will and Idea*, appears to have furnished the necessary basis for Shaw's meta-physics of sex in *Man and Superman*. The idea was, indeed, far-reaching in its implications. Schopenhauer had come under Eastern influence rela-tively early in his career. The Upanishads teach that a simple reality underlies the apparent multiplicity of the phenomenal world. The true self is not the individual consciousness, but the formless and voiceless being within each person, the impersonal spirit of life, the Atman. This divinity lies beyond the reach of the intellect, which is therefore power-less to arrive at the ultimate significance of being. It can be reached only by that final act of dissolution which comes with the relinquishing of both form and individuality, in short, in nirvana.

In accordance with this conception Schopenhauer advocated the view that individuality is an illusion, and that the individual will is simply a manifestation of the universal will. Man's intense preoccupation with love can therefore be justified on the basis of the imperiousness of the instinct through which the will to live combines the available biological forms so as to ensure the persistence of the species in its most perfect possible form. Schopenhauer wrote:

> . . . The will of the individual appears at a higher power as the will of the species . . . and what presents itself in the individual consciousness as sexual impulse in general . . . is simply the will to live. But what appears in consciousness as a sexual impulse directed to a definite individual is in itself the will to live as a definitely determined individual. Now in this case the sexual impulse, although in itself a subjective need, knows how to assume very skilfully the mask of an objective admiration, and thus to deceive our consciousness; for nature requires this strategem to attain its ends.[16]

In Schopenhauer's view, the future generation is

> already active in that careful, definite, and arbitrary choice for the satisfaction of the sexual impulse which we call love. The growing inclination of two lovers is really already the will to live of the new individual which they can and desire to produce, a future individuality harmoniously and well composed. . . . They feel the longing for an actual union and fusing together into a single being in order to live on only as this; and this longing receives its fulfillment in the child which is produced by them, in which the qualities transmitted by them, fused and united in one being, live on.[17]

Since the future child is a new Platonic idea, and "ideas strive with the greatest vehemence to enter the phenomenal world," the mutual passion of the future parents is simply the expression of the desire of the potential child to come into being.[18] Schopenhauer saw the Will as chiefly operative in the father, and the intellect in the mother. Since the child's corporization comes from both parents, the degree of harmony in these elements is the measure of the attraction between the individuals who embody them. "The more perfect the mutual adaptation of two individuals to each other . . . the stronger will be their mutual passion," while aversion is the sign of an inharmonious set of physical and mental qualities.

In these biological combinations the individual actually counts for little: "Egotism is deeply rooted—but the species has a greater claim on the individual than the perishable individuality itself." Since nature

strives to maintain in the progeny a mean between the extreme manifestations of sexual differences, it is natural for manly men to seek out
womanly women as their mates. The lover imagines that in his choice
he serves his own inclinations. In fact he is serving the interest of the
species "which presents what is of benefit to it to the will which is here
become individual." Thus the individual is actually the dupe of the
species, insofar as its interests differ from his own; and what he experiences as love is no more than his sense of the suitability of his mate to
join with him in procreating, as well as possible, the being which is to be
produced.[19]

In the 1890's, when these ideas had percolated English thought, the
question of love and marriage came once again under careful scrutiny. A
number of radical writers, among them Belfort Bax, Edward Carpenter,
Grant Allen, and Havelock Ellis, took up the cudgels for a rational
approach to the problems of sex. Schopenhauer's idea of love as a manifestation of the unconscious wisdom of the species now became the basis
for a full-scale discussion of eugenics, and the desirability of accelerating
the evolutionary process through artificial selection. The group that
called itself neo-Malthusian publicized the idea that poverty was the
result of indiscriminate breeding. Grant Allen and Havelock Ellis both
argued that inequalities of class and wealth put unnecessary obstacles in
the way of eugenic marriages, and Belfort Bax—a Marxist and an ardent
Schopenhauerian—published a series of papers advocating the regulation
of marriage, divorce, and birth control from the viewpoint of social
policy rather than that of property and religion.[20]

The effect of these discussions was to emphasize more and more
strongly the role of women in carrying on what Schopenhauer had called
"the affairs of the species." In an essay translated by Bax in 1891,
Schopenhauer had written: "It lies therefore in the nature of women to
regard everything solely as a means to win the man, the interest in
anything else being never more than a simulated one."[21]

It was evidently from such sources that Shaw derived the theoretical
basis of *Man and Superman*. Schopenhauer provided whatever was
needed to formulate a love story as "scientific natural history;" but
evidently in Shaw's estimation, this theory did not account properly for
all the facts. Schopenhauer subordinated everything in the love story to
the urge for producing children. In his view the unborn child, as Idea,
presided over each sexual union, and the child's insistence on being
brought into being was the source of the urgency and intensity of the
lovers' passion. Thus far, the metaphysics of sex was acceptable to Shaw,
but Shaw was an individualist who thought of himself as an amatory

freebooter. He had no desire to beget progeny and found the deterministic tendency of Schopenhauer's doctrine oppressive. Before this system became entirely acceptable to him it was necessary that the will to live be reconciled with the freedom to philander.

The image of Don Juan provided the necessary means. Don Juan is the culture hero who best embodies for our time the idea of freedom without responsibility. He is the archetypal philanderer, eternally available, and eternally inconstant, resisting no temptation save the temptation to be localized in marriage.

The original Don Juan, as Tirso de Molina conceived him, is of quite another sort. He is a prankster who plays practical jokes, and whose ambition it is to be thought the greatest trickster in Spain. He is not a lover of women, but the contrary of a lover. His sexual exploits are athletic, aggressive, and cruel, a form of manly prowess which is at the other pole from the ways of true love. He is, in fact, the seventeenth-century version of the medieval *losengier*, a deceiver who apes the lover in order to gain his ends, and it is his special pleasure to dishonor women. As Tamburlaine was the scourge of kings, sent by heaven to humble their pride, Don Juan is the scourge of women and serves a similar purpose. It is appropriate that he is damned for his pains.

Shaw did not have this figure in mind. His Don Juan belongs to a later age and plainly shows the influence of Molière. He is a romantic figure, a rebel who refuses to be bound by convention, dominated by his passions and determined to have his will at any cost. Shaw evidently found this figure fascinating. In the great cynic, duelist, and wit, particularly in the operatic form which Mozart had given him, Shaw doubtless saw much of himself, and in his early life he made valiant efforts to emulate this irresistible figure. In the Epistle Dedicatory to *Man and Superman* he gives evidence of having researched the subject thoroughly. He mentions all the major versions of the myth from *El Burlador de Sevilla* to *Don Giovanni*, all, that is, but the one most apposite to his purpose, Zorilla's *Don Juan Tenorio* (1844). There is, however, a certain difference between the romantic figure which Da Ponte devised for Mozart's opera and Shaw's Don Juan. In Shaw's view Don Juan is not an exploiter of women. He is their victim.

The turn given to the Don Juan myth in *Man and Superman* developed the theme of a short story which Shaw had written a dozen years earlier, in 1887. In this story, entitled *Don Juan Explains*, the ghost of Don Giovanni appears to the narrator in a railway carriage in order, as he says, to correct through him the current misconception of his charac-, ter and purposes. Don Giovanni begins by explaining that, while his friends considered him devoid of moral fiber, he was in truth an exceptionally evolved individual who, having come into existence long before his time, was not properly appreciated by his contemporaries. In fact, he was a preternaturally shy young man whose sexual maturity was deferred until at last a widowed lady threw herself into his arms and conquered his timidity so far as to permit him to possess her. Unhappily, after a month with this lady, he found the romantic side of the affair "tedious, unreasonable and even, except at rare moments, forced and insincere." This uncomfortable indoctrination into the mysteries of love rendered him immune to the attraction of sex. Neither Doña Ana nor Zerlina interested him in the least, and his passion for Elvira was simply a figment of her imagination. After his experience with the statue of the Commander, he was dragged off to a hell made up of well-intentioned nonentities who despised the saints in heaven as unfeeling snobs of frightfully boring character and disposition.[22]

One needs no great acumen to locate the autobiographical elements in this story. The relation to the scene in hell in *Man and Superman* is equally clear. These identifications have a certain importance. They justify the inference that Don Juan in Hell essentially represents Shaw in hell, and that the dialogue with the Devil and the Statue is interpretable as a transcription of the author's inner debate with regard to issues of the deepest personal interest.

In Tanner's vision, hell is an eternity of pleasure. It is peopled by such souls as prefer to live in a state of perpetual illusion, bemused by such idle fancies as youth, beauty, love, and romance, together with the arts through which such fantasies are given a semblance of reality. This aesthetic dream world is fittingly presided over by the master illusionist, the Devil. To those who prefer reality, however, an eternity of pleasure is an eternity of boredom, the worst of all possible torments. For these elect, salvation is to be found only in the useful expenditure of energy, that is, in work. Heaven, accordingly, is a state of constant striving.

In a program note written by Shaw for the first performance of *Don Juan in Hell* at the Court Theatre on 4 June 1907, he explained that

> modern theology conceives heaven and hell, not as places, but as states of the soul; and by the soul it means, not an organ like the liver, but the divine element common to all life, which causes us "to do the will of God" in addition to looking after our individual interests, and to honor one another solely for our divine activities and not at all for our selfish activities.

This "higher theology" moreover, held that

> this world, or any other, may be made a hell by a society so lacking
> in the higher orders of energy that it is given wholly to the pursuit of
> immediate individual pleasure, and cannot even conceive the passion
> of the divine will. Also that any world can be made a heaven by a
> society of persons in whom that passion is the master passion, "a
> communion of saints" in fact.[23]

The identification of the Schopenhauerian Will with the divine principle, and the assimilation of the *état d'âme* of the individual with the
condition of society at a given time, had already been made in the
prefatory material published with *Man and Superman* in 1901. This preface was in the form of a dedicatory letter addressed to A. B. Walkley
who, after having seen service on the *Speaker*, the *Observer*, and the
Star, had lately taken over the post of drama critic on the *Times* and was
in this period the most discriminating and most respected theater critic
in England. The Epistle Dedicatory went some way beyond dedication.
It not only fathered the play upon Walkley, it also involved him tacitly
in its ideology on the basis *qui facit per alium facit per se.*

It was characteristic of Shaw to confer intellectual partnership upon
people whose opinions he valued, particularly with regard to ideas that
stood in some need of support. The connection between Walkley and
Man and Superman was largely imaginary. In 1902 there had appeared a
volume of Walkley's collected articles which included a review, written
in February 1890, of John Buchanan's version of a French dramatization
of *Clarissa Harlowe*. In this article Walkley had written, apropos of the
characterization of Lovelace:

> . . . No doubt the Don Juans of real life are often poor, empty
> creatures. Women have strange taste. But if you bring a Don Juan on
> the stage, you must make him a Don Juan who satisfies my imagina-
> tion. There must be a magnificence about the fellow; he must be a
> virtuoso in the Fine Art of Don Juanism; must have *maestria*: must
> be a philosopher like the Don Juan of Molière; a heroic figure that
> will not make Leporello's catalogue sound ridiculous; a host not too
> puny to invite the statue of the commander to supper. How else will
> you satisfy a generation that (if it does not read "Clarissa Harlowe")
> is very familiar with Feuillet's M. de Camors and Daudet's Duc de
> Mora? I recognize the dramatist's difficulty here. A character of this
> complexity is not easily rendered by the simple method of the stage.[24]

It is possible that Shaw had this passage in mind in connecting his Don
Juan play with Walkley. The Epistle Dedicatory of *Man and Superman*
begins with the remark that Walkley had once asked Shaw why he did

not write a Don Juan play. After considering with some archness the various implications of this question, which he interprets as a request, Shaw decides that what Walkley required of him was "a Don Juan in the philosophic sense." Philosophically, Don Juan is "a man who, though gifted enough to be exceptionally capable of distinguishing between good and evil, follows his own instincts without regard to the common, statute, or canon law . . . and therefore . . . finds himself in moral conflict with existing institutions. . . ."[25]

These institutions, he continues, are no longer those of the sixteenth or the eighteenth century, but the beliefs of the ubiquitous middle class, as a result of which women of all classes have become equally dangerous, so that, if they are wronged, "they grasp formidable legal and social weapons, and retaliate. . . ." As a result,

> Man is no longer, like Don Juan, victor in the duel of sex. . . . His thousand and three affairs of gallantry, after becoming, at most, two immature intrigues leading to sordid and prolonged complications and humiliations, have been discarded altogether as unworthy of his philosophic dignity. . . . Instead of pretending to read Ovid he does actually read Schopenhauer and Nietzsche, studies Westermarck, and is concerned for the future of the race instead of for the freedom of his own instincts. . . . he is now more Hamlet than Don Juan. . . .[26]

Through this line of reasoning Shaw manages somehow to relate Don Juan's legendary exploits to his own relatively modest achievements as a philanderer and thus arrives at a conception of the arch-seducer as one more sinned against than sinning. In *The Philanderer* Shaw does not make out a very strong case for Charteris as a lover of women, nor does he do much better for Valentine, the sex duelist in *You Never Can Tell*. It is in *Man and Superman* that these characters are finally developed, and here, for the first time, the pursuer turns out to be the pursued. The difficulty with the characterization is, however, that while Charteris and Valentine are both depicted as woman-chasers, John Tanner gives no indication of being at all interested in the opposite sex.

The ingenious turn upon which *Man and Superman* depends was doubtless suggested by Shaw's own sense of being ruthlessly hounded by adoring females. It was a feeling—judging by his diaries—barely supported by the facts, but one which he evidently cherished and strove mightily to realize in his manifold flirtations with Fabian ladies. From Shaw's viewpoint, Don Juan is a man irresistible to women, who occasionally condescends to one or another while he keeps his mind resolutely fixed on the higher things of life.

Apart from the similarity of their names, it is difficult to see what John

Tanner has to do with Don Juan Tenorio in Zorilla's play, or in Mozart's opera. It is with astonishment that we learn in Act One of *Man and Superman* that in some mysterious manner Tanner is descended from Don Juan, and even when we realize that their relationship is purely spiritual, the analogy seems strained. In fact, Don Juan, as he appears in hell, represents only the fugitive aspect of John Tanner; the rest of the similitude we must take on faith. In John Fletcher's comedy, *The Wild Goose Chase* (1621), it is the hero's elusiveness which makes him especially attractive to the ladies of the play. It is certainly not Tanner's recalcitrance which appeals to Ann Whitefield. It is his forthright maleness that attracts her, while the soft romanticism of Tavy makes him, in her opinion, undesirable as a mate.

Tavy has only the vaguest relation to Don Ottavio in the Mozart opera. Like Marchbanks in *Candida*, he is not marriageable. He is the eternally frustrated lover, the poet who idealizes, but never possesses the lady, a vestige of the Petrarchan tradition. It is his destiny to create works of art, not children, and it is precisely because he never possesses the lady that he is able to idealize her in his fantasy. John Tanner, on the other hand, has no illusions about the lady in question. He sees through her wiles perfectly in everything save what concerns himself and, believing himself to be immune from her machinations, he thinks only of protecting his friend. This is not the cream of the jest. The practical joke, of which he is the victim, is of cosmic magnitude.

Tanner is not, like Hector Malone, *l'homme moyen sensuel*, whose business in life is merely to perpetuate the species on its present cultural level. He is a superior being, intellectually advanced and physically apt above the other men in his circle, and he appeals to Ann for reasons more cogent than she knows. He attracts her precisely because, whether she is aware of it or not, it is his child she desires to create, one who will bring the species a step closer to its entelechy. Therefore she hastens to unite with him in obedience to high behests, which she heeds without in the least identifying them, and is willing to sacrifice everything to bring about this union—her modesty, her integrity, even, if need be, her life.

Tanner is the darling of the Life Force and for that reason destined for sacrifice. In the cut of his mind, and the cut of his clothes, he serves as a modern counterpart of that *kalokágathia* which the ancients prized in their young men. He is strong, but in the hands of the implacable power that pre-empts his energies, he is helpless. His position thus approximates that of the tragic hero of classic drama, and if we are disposed to laugh at his plight instead of feeling the appropriate measure of pity and terror, it is only partly because we lack imagination. In our social framework, marriage with a pretty woman cannot really be considered a fate worse than death, and the fact that Tanner sees the matter in this light gives a comic turn to a situation which on another scale might well fulfill the conditions of tragedy.

It is doubtless in order to suggest this higher level of interpretation that the Dialogue in Hell precedes the scene in the garden—one might say of Eden—in which the sacrifice of Tanner is celebrated. The upshot, as in *Candida*, is an interpretation of the age-old story of the wife, the lover, and the husband in a manner that seems original with Shaw. In his view, the cosmic Will asserts its biologic choices through the female, so that every woman knows instinctively the man best fitted by nature to serve her procreative function. The artist, the thinker, the poet—self-engrossed, meditative types primarily interested in creative activity along intellectual or aesthetic lines—are parthogenetic organisms not properly fitted for the task of bisexual procreation. The woman may find such men to her liking, but in her instinctive wisdom, she rejects them no matter how attractive they may seem. Nor is the ordinary man much to her liking, though she may have to settle for him, for she can do no more than to perpetuate his mediocrity. The truly desirable man is one who is developed beyond the generality, but not to the point where he is beyond the possibility of domestication. Such is John Tanner. In him, as Mrs. Whitefield remarks, Ann meets her match.[27]

For Strindberg also, marriage was a form of martyrdom; but the purpose of marriage, as he saw it, was quite other than eugenic reproduction. In *To Damascus*, and *The Dream Play*, and in *The Dance of Death*, marriage is the refining flame through which the spirit is purified. Shaw takes another view of the matter. Tanner's martyrdom is real enough, but the dance into which Ann leads him is not the dance of death. It is the dance of life. His agony is measured by the extent to which the life to which marriage condemns him falls short of the ideal existence of which he dreams, but his sufferings are by no means unendurable. "I never was master in my own house, sir," the Waiter tells Valentine at the end of *You Never Can Tell*. "My wife was like your young lady: she was of a commanding and masterful disposition, which my son has inherited. But if I had my life to live twice over, I'd do it again, I assure you."

In Shaw's view, the good life is a constant labor and is consequently never a happy experience. Happiness implies stasis, which negates the vital principle. Heaven is a state of eternal dissatisfaction. Presumably the blissful moment which will lure Tanner into crying "*Verweile doch!*" will thrust him instantly into hell. For the dedicated revolutionist in particular domestic happiness constitutes a mortal danger. Shaw's attitude in this regard was not especially original. "He that is unmarried," St. Paul admonishes, "careth for the things that belong to the Lord, how he may please the Lord, but he that is married careth for the things that are of this world, how he may please his wife."[28]

In this manner Shaw, after a prolonged detour through the most advanced thought of his day, found a safe harbor in the traditional tenets of his youth. His aspiring geniuses, the Marchbanks, Dudgeons, and Brassbounds—to say nothing of the saints who already populate his heaven—are humanity's priests and, by reason of their vocation, are exempt from carnal involvements. They are, at most, philanderers, lovers for whom woman is a point of departure, never a stopping place. So it was with Don Juan also; and now, like the archetypal lover of the *Symposium*, he desires to relinquish the delights of hell.

The denizens of his hell are romantics, diligently torturing themselves in the endless pursuit of pleasure; but Don Juan has found no happiness in pleasure. Happiness, as Aristotle noted, "does not lie in amusement; it would, indeed, be strange if the end were amusement, and one were to take trouble and suffer hardship all one's life in order to amuse oneself."[29] Don Juan's horror at the prospect of an eternity of pleasure corresponds to the misgivings of a highly evolved individual in this life who has nothing to do but to amuse himself as long as he lives. For such a man happiness is an impossible will-o'-the-wisp. The alternative is the quest for blessedness, the realistic substitute for happiness. It is this which Don Juan, like Marchbanks, hopes to find among those who are engaged in the eternal life of contemplation that is their heaven.[30]

The Dialogue in Hell is obviously meant to be read metaphorically. It takes place in the mind of man, specifically in the mind of a certain man and is, in this sense, autobiographical. In the critical position in which Tanner is placed at the end of the second act, he finds himself torn by contrary impulses, doubts, and fears. It is this state of mental turmoil which the dream sequence represents. In the portion of *Man and Superman* which takes place on the plane of contemporary reality, this critical moment is effectively dramatized in terms of freedom and the loss of individuality. But in the aspect of eternity the problem of marriage is seen to center on much wider issues, on the nature of men and the purpose of life.

Practically the discussion in hell involves the choice between the carefree life of the senses, self-justified, and a life of intellectual labor, justified by an ideal. The alternatives had long ago been allegorized as "The Choice of Hercules," the subject of a celebrated painting by Rubens, and it had furnished Carlyle also with a congenial theme. In *Man and Superman* the Devil is a romantic. He speaks eloquently for the sensual life. Don Juan argues for the life of the intellect. Neither is the victor, for the issue is beyond resolution, and the conflict is never-ending.

In hell there are no hard facts, only agreeable enchantments. It is a *locus amoenus* of the order of the Bower of Bliss or the Garden of Armida, a pleasant place to be, but bad for the soul: one would imagine hell was Shaw's idea of a resort hotel on the Riviera. Heaven, on the contrary, is a never-ending contemplation of reality. Unlike the sensual life, which is aimless, the life of the mind has a goal. It aims at the extension of knowledge; it represents the desire of life to know itself. It is to the furtherance of this taste that Don Juan, having grown weary of pleasure, now resolves to devote his eternity. These activities, the Statue remarks, are not universally amusing. They require a special aptitude, which he no longer shares. He himself has decided, after a long sojourn in heaven, to spend some aeons in hell.

Between these two spirits who meet at the crossroads of the infinite—the Statue who is bored with heaven, and the sensualist who is weary of hell—the Devil plays an equivocal role. He is a suave and convincing personage, well-suited to manage the sort of luxury hotel which hell seems to be, and naturally anxious not to lose his clientele to the competition. Doña Ana is no match, intellectually speaking, for these gentlemen among whom her lot is cast, but she is impressively single-minded: she is eternally in search of fruition. Doña Ana belongs neither to heaven nor to hell. She embraces both. As the vehicle of life she is neutral and anonymous, but indispensable.

The Devil has no use for Doña Ana, but Don Juan sees clearly that squalling brats and household chores are the price humanity must pay for the perpetuation of the race. The Statue adds that a life without responsibility, while seemingly attractive, leads only to an endless demand for entertainment, and at last to the discomforts of old age and impotence. As an ancient hedonist, he himself has amply experienced the disadvantages of the sensual life. "I confess," he remarks, "that if I had nothing to do in the world but wallow in these delights I should have cut my throat." In these circumstances, his decision to settle in hell does not seem particularly logical. But the Devil understands it. Men tire of everything, he says, of heaven no less than hell. History is nothing but the record of the oscillations of the human spirit between these extremes. Under the aspect of eternity, Don Juan and the Statue continually change places, for Don Juan will weary of the life of reason just as surely as he has wearied of the life of pleasure. What appears to be progress is nothing but change, and all that can be said of this is "*vanitas vanitatum.*" Life has neither aim, nor end.

It is at this point in the discussion that Don Juan loses patience, for the hit is shrewd. He has an answer. If life has no purpose, one will be found. The Life Force has devised consciousness in order to know itself. It is even now at work developing means for discovering its purpose and its destiny. The means is the philosophic mind. The philosopher is nature's pilot, "And there you have our difference," Juan tells the Devil, "To be in hell is to drift: to be in heaven is to steer." The Devil answers: "On the rocks, most likely." To which Don Juan answers: "Pooh! which ship goes oftenest on the rocks or to the bottom—the drifting ship or the ship with a pilot on board?" In the absence of precise statistics, the question remains unresolved; but the indication is that Don Juan means to take a course in navigation: he proposes to spend eternity in developing his mind.

The Devil sees no reason to develop the human mind any further. Man has shown himself, he points out, chiefly ingenious in devising means of destruction. What best captures his imagination is not life but death: "There is nothing in Man's industrial machinery but his greed and sloth: his heart is in his weapons. This marvellous force of Life of which you boast is a force of Death: Man measures his strength by his destructiveness." In our day, nearly three-quarters of a century after *Man and Superman* was written, the Devil's argument seems even more cogent than it was when it was first propounded:

> Nowadays the chronicles describe battles. In a battle two bodies of men shoot at one another with bullets and explosive shells until one body runs away. . . . Over such battles the people run about the streets yelling with delight, and egg their governments on to spend hundreds of millions of money in the slaughter, whilst the strongest Ministers dare not spend an extra penny in the pound against the poverty and pestilence through which they themselves daily walk.[31]

The argument, however, does not unsettle Don Juan. He answers that, while men seem to be bold and bad, they are really cowards and will undergo every humiliation in order to live. Man becomes heroic only in the service of an idea: "I tell you, gentlemen, if you can shew a man a piece of what he calls God's work to do, and what he will later on call by many new names, you can make him entirely reckless of the consequences to him personally."[32] The task of the saints is, accordingly, the creation of ideas for men to live by, vital ideas. It is to this work that Don Juan proposes to devote his energies. The transition from hell is simple. When we think, we are in heaven. The Devil, for his part, wishes him joy of his undertaking. His reward will be, "in a word, the punishment of the fool who pursues the better before he has secured the good." Don Juan replies, "But at least I shall not be bored. The service of the Life Force has that advantage, at all events."

Thus Don Juan and the Devil part company in a manner reminiscent of the scene toward the end of Strindberg's *To Damascus III* (1901), and they leave Doña Ana to vanish by herself in the void. She has just acquired an idea. She has overheard the Devil remark that to the superman—something conceived by a German-Polish madman named Nietzsche—the human race will seem an inferior species. Her mission suddenly becomes clear to her and, as she vanishes, she cries, apparently to the universe, "A father! a father for the Superman!"

On this note the dialogue ends. It is perhaps not entirely satisfactory from the viewpoint of philosophy, but it is beyond doubt a great masterpiece of English literature. It might seem that Don Juan's decision should hang on something more solid than the thought that an eternity of work is the only alternative to an eternity of boredom. But the *taedium vitae* he fears is a more potent threat to the Life Force than any other. Boredom is the one illness the will to live cannot survive. The final argument helps also to justify Shaw's position as a realist—and also Don Juan's—for his line of reasoning brings him very close to an idealistic conclusion, and he has no way of disproving historically the Devil's paraphrase of Ecclesiastes. To the observation that all is vanity an honest man can oppose nothing but the faith which perhaps in time moves mountains.

It is in *The Revolutionist's Handbook* that we most clearly sense the nature of Shaw's faith. He is, insofar as the present race of men is concerned, entirely pessimistic. His efforts are not directed to the immediate amelioration of the human lot. As humanity is presently constituted, he considers it hopeless. Socialism is therefore mainly an instrumentality intended to facilitate the creation of a new species which will be capable of leading a rational existence. The Third Kingdom which the sage Maximus describes in Ibsen's *Emperor and Galilean* is not, in Shaw's opinion, a kingdom of this world. The ideal anarchy of which

Ibsen dreams is, for Shaw also, a castle in the air. The necessary basis of our future felicity is eugenic. In the world as it is, all is hopeless; save only hope. Tanner writes:

> . . . if you know the facts and are strong enough to look them in the face, you must admit that unless we are replaced by a more highly evolved animal—in short, by the Superman—the world must remain a den of dangerous animals among whom our few accidental supermen, our Shakespears, Goethes, Shelleys, and their like, must live as precariously as lion tamers do, taking the humor of their situation, and the dignity of their superiority, as a set-off to the horror of the one and the loneliness of the other.[33]

The idea of comedy implied in this passage does not adequately suggest the source of Shaw's comic vein. It does not take into account Shaw's innate sense of fun which so often leads him into slapstick. But it indicates how close to the tragic his sense of comedy came. There is no doubt that Shaw felt himself to be one of the "accidental supermen" condemned to a precarious life among beasts who must be frightened into civility. He saw himself brandishing his thunderbolts from the height of his genius, saddened by the uncouth antics of his contemporaries, but more amused than saddened.

If the effect of *Man and Superman* is not quite that of classic comedy, it is because Shaw was both incurably romantic and essentially sentimental, and because also he was in some degree restricted by the comedic patterns of his time. In current practice, the sympathetic role, incidental to classic comedy, was indispensable. The result is that Tanner, whose role as raisonneur is comic, becomes pathetic as a principal in the action. Very likely that is what Shaw intended. At any rate, Tanner is caught in the trap of the Life Force very much as Oedipus is caught in Apollo's snare. It takes the Theban King some time before, at the very end of his life, he becomes aware of the injustice of his position. In the case of Tanner the irony of the situation is apparent to him at once, since he can hardly avert the sacrifice to which his own reasoning condemns him:

> Enough, then, of this goose-cackle about Progress: Man, as he is, never will nor can add a cubit to his stature by any of its quackeries, political, scientific, educational, or artistic. . . . Our only hope, then, is in evolution. We must replace the man by the superman.[34]

The tragic element in Tanner's destiny was by no means something apparent only to Shaw. The sacrifice of the individual in the interests of the race is an idea common to all dramatic systems based upon an evolutionary concept. Tanner's sad fate is not precisely comparable to the destiny of the three sisters in Chekhov's play, but they too are sacrificed in the evolutionary process. *The Three Sisters* is perhaps a comedy, as Chekhov insisted; but the comic element in *Man and Superman* leaps to the eye, and the salt of the jest is that, in inviting personal annihilation, Tanner faithfully fulfills his own prescription for the survival of humanity:

> And so we arrive at the end of the Socialist's dream of "the socializa-
> tion of the means of production and exchange," of the Positivist's
> dream of moralizing the capitalist. . . . The only fundamental and
> possible Socialism is the socialization of the selective breeding of
> Man: in other terms, of human evolution. We must eliminate the
> Yahoo, or his vote will wreck the commonwealth.[35]

The implication is that the irresistible physical attraction which Ann concentrates upon Tanner, her charm and her youthful beauty, are, ultimately, nothing more than an expression of the racial need to elimi-nate the Yahoo. The mysterious power of love is a political force more potent than any man-made revolution, and, for reasons which at the moment escape him, Tanner is forced to unite in marriage with a woman he neither likes nor trusts, but merely loves.[36] Schopenhauer had re-marked, "in the case of difference of disposition, character and mental tendency, and the dislike, nay, enmity proceeding from this, sexual love may yet arise and exist; when it does, it blinds us to all that; and if it here leads to a marriage it will be a very unhappy one."[37]

It would be a mistake to identify Shaw's theory of love too closely with this idea. In a play written from the strictly Schopenhauerian standpoint Tanner and Ann Whitefield would be drawn together by a mutual passion. In Shaw's plan, Ann tracks down her quarry with the implacability of a Javert in pursuit of Jean Valjean, while Tanner eludes her with comparable resolution. It is thus necessary for the success of the play that the *scène à faire* in the last act be played with extraordi-nary intensity. When the play was first performed at the Court Theatre, Shaw directed it so that Tanner—who was actually made up to resemble Shaw—seemed to be drawn little by little into a web over which Ann presided spiderlike, radiating chiefly animal magnetism until she darted in for the kill. Such an effect is not quite in accordance with what one might expect of the workings of the Will. Very likely Schopenhauer had something quite different in mind.

Man and Superman leaves Doña Ana in an equivocal position. In her maternal character she is the basis of the evolutionary process; but there is no doubt as to the intellectual superiority of Don Juan. Shaw's attitude toward Ann in *Man and Superman* seems hardly accordant with the feminist doctrine of *Mrs Warren's Profession*. As socialist, Ibsenite, and Millite, Shaw was certainly committed to the movement for the equality of the sexes, but his advanced views were not always consistently applied, and it is by no means easy to say on which side of the woman's cause he actually stood.

By the end of the nineteenth century the *querelle des femmes* had reached warlike proportions. For four centuries it had been raging, more or less as a literary pastime, but it had its serious side, and now it reached its crisis. In England, in the first half of the century, Mary Wollstonecraft, Shelley, Godwin, and J. S. Mill, among others, had directed attention to the unhappy plight of woman in Western Europe. After 1860 the "woman question" came more and more sharply into focus, and in the course of the next decades women gradually achieved civil equality in most branches of the social structure. Actually, women were not enfranchised politically in England until 1918, and then only partially; but by 1882 married women had acquired legal capacity to own and dispose of property, and in 1893 the right to make contracts, to sue, and to be sued. These changes, which went far to unsettle what had so long been a securely established patriarchal culture, were obviously not won without a considerable display of energy on both sides of the issue. The results were soon manifested on the stage.

The storm of critical protest which marked the first production of *A Doll's House* and *Ghosts* in England revealed the depth of the emotions stirred by the radical conceptions these plays were thought to embody. Over against these revolutionary stereotypes, there were advanced the corresponding idols of the reaction, the various romantic versions of the medieval Eve, the temptress, the vampire, the serpent, the parasite, and the adultress. These formidable types moved easily into the new realistic literature of the latter half of the century. After 1860 the literary mode in France was predominantly misogynistic. The role of woman as a destructive influence, the chosen vehicle of the evil powers, appealed enormously to an age that was fascinated by Satanism, and which discovered in the amiable face of the Gioconda

> the unfathomable smile, always with a touch of something sinister in it, which plays over all of Leonardo's work . . . the animalism of Greece, the lust of Rome, the reverie of the middle age with its spiritual ambition and imaginative loves, the return of the Pagan world, the sins of the Borgias.[38]

The type of sexual fantasy that was congenial to the nineteenth century resulted in a series of memorable female figures representing sexuality in its more disquieting aspects. *La femme bête-féroce* was a by-product of romanticism, but obviously her roots went deep into the psychological substructure of Western culture, and the complex fascination of the dangerous woman, with her capacity to evoke the image of the bad mother, had significant repercussions in the literature of the time. In France the delectable destroyer of men's lives became an indispensable ornament of *la belle époque*. To be magnificently ruined by a lovely courtesan was no ordinary privilege. It was a voluptuous experience which only the rich could afford, but the poor, particularly if they had some claim to distinction, might aspire to disaster of this sort on a lesser scale. In her myriad guises—as Justine, Carmen, Hérodiade, the Iza of the younger Dumas's *L'Affaire Clemenceau*, Ibsen's Hedda Gabler, Strindberg's Laura, the Goncourts' Manette Salomon, Daudet's Sapho, Wilde's Salomé, Maugham's Mildred—the list is endless—the *femme fatale* haunted the imagination of a public that was avid for proofs of the predatory nature of woman in an age when women were for the first time vying with men for a foothold on the earth.

In the preface to *L'Ami des femmes* Dumas *fils* had written:

> Woman is a limited being, passive, instrumental, expendable, a being in perpetual expectation. She is the only uncompleted work of creation that God has permitted man to take in hand and finish. She is a rejected angel. . . . She has invented nothing, discovered nothing, to increase her collective value; she is forever at the stage of seduction, forever with the apple which gives her only a personal and limited value, and even there it is the serpent who showed it to her. There alone is all her genius in the past, the present and the future. . . . Her liberation would be her death.[39]

This conception of the passive role of woman was widely illustrated in the contemporary novel, but woman in her aggressive aspect was considerably more interesting. The tensions which might be expected to arise between woman in her creative capacity and the artist in his seemed especially fascinating in this period of awakened aestheticism. The image of the artist sucked dry by the beautiful vampire was an apt subject for dramatic treatment. Strindberg made it a specialty and, in France, the divine Sarah, for whom Dumas *fils* had written *L'Etrangère* in 1876, and to whom Wilde in 1893 offered *Salomé*, became for her time the epitome of the beautiful lady whose natural prey is the man of genius. In the theater the conflict between the sexes was by no means one-sided. Complementary images took shape in the tableaux of Ibsen's Mrs. Alving, mercifully reaching for the morphine in the last scene of *Ghosts* (1881), Strindberg's Laura presiding over the destruction of her husband in *The*

Father (1887), and Suderman's *Magda* asserting her emancipation from parental authority (1893).

The Father preceded *Man and Superman* by fifteen years. There was ample time for Shaw to become aware of the battle of the sexes which it described. Zola had not been impressed with *The Father* as an example of naturalism, but he had been struck by the manner in which Strindberg had pictured "*la vraie femme* in the unconsciousness and the mystery of her qualities and faults." Nietzsche related Strindberg's idea to his own conception of love, "with war as its means and the deathly hatred of the sexes" as its root. In the 1890's much of the advanced thought of the day was swinging once again toward antifeminism, and there were those who were disposed to agree with Strindberg that the "woman's cause" was in the hands of an international conspiracy, the purpose of which was to undermine the virile basis of our culture. The *femme fatale* was thus magnified into a social menace, and the Gioconda smile took on alarming political connotations.

In the atmosphere of this reaction Shaw's feminism seems both complex and confusing. Ostensibly he made no social distinctions on sexual grounds. But from *Widowers' Houses* to *Back to Methuselah*, his plays clearly reveal his mistrust of women as women. Even his Virgin Mothers have in them some hint of that Mona Lisa on whose enigmatic charms Pater had dwelt so impressively in his essays on the Renaissance. The portrait which Pater undertook to describe in jeweled prose was certainly not Pre-Raphaelite; but the description was. Shaw did not describe Candida or Mrs. George in any such terms. It is a pity; for nothing could have been more apt. Shaw's heroines are all ambiguous women, dangerous to men in a thousand ways, desirable, but seldom entirely available, or else too much so; alluring, but never wholly absorbed in the object of their allurements; smiling seductively at their lovers with eyes that look beyond him for someone who is not there.

In *Man and Superman* the relation of the sexes is posed in terms that closely approximate the classic antithesis of form and matter. Man represents the spiritual principle; woman, the material component. Man is light; woman, darkness and mystery. In procreation man transmits form; woman receives it: she contributes only her warmth and her desire. Don Juan is self-sufficient. It is in the nature of spirit to be self-sufficient; but woman—judging by Doña Ana—represents the craving of matter for form in order to come into being. It is for this reason that woman is always the pursuer, and man the pursued.

In the last part of *Back to Methuselah* these distinctions have vanished, along with the other characteristics of sex which the race of the future relinquishes in infancy; therefore the views put forward in *Man and Superman* may be thought of as provisional. Save for their evolutionary aspect the sexual attitudes which Shaw developed in this play did not depart very far from the traditions which after the time of Gregory the Great were accepted by most clerical writers on the subject. The church approved—if with some reluctance—of cohabitation for utility, but never of cohabitation for pleasure, so that the love of woman was in every case suspect, since it distracted the soul from the proper object of its desire, which was God.

One might perhaps have had some difficulty in persuading Thomas Aquinas that women bring men happiness, and even greater difficulty in convincing him that women are the stronger sex, as Shaw seems to indicate. But by the end of the nineteenth century, the concept of Mother Eve had been considerably extended. Biological research had by this time gone so far as to suggest to the American sociologist Lester Ward, for example, that since single-celled organisms have the power to reproduce themselves by simple mitosis, the Life Force must be a female principle which at some stage of its development devised the male in order to secure for itself the advantages of biological variation, "and through variation the production of better and higher types of organic structure—in a word, organic evolution." In the scale of forms the male, Ward concluded, is a Johnny-come-lately who somehow managed to get out of hand and thus developed the strength and mental capacity to dominate its creator. In this endeavor, the male, obviously, was not always successful. The plight of the male spider, for instance, moved Dr. Ward's sympathy, although he recognized its sacrifice as "perfectly natural and normal."[40]

In *The Father*, Strindberg's Captain is bitter at the thought of how thoroughly the woman he married has subjected him to her own interests. But Ward's ideas found a less pessimistic reflection in *Man and Superman*. Don Juan says:

> Man is Woman's contrivance for fulfilling Nature's behest in the most economical way. She knows by instinct that far back in the evolutional process she invented him, differentiated him, created him in order to produce something better than the single-sexed process can produce. . . . But how rash and dangerous it was to invent a separate creature whose sole function was her own impregnation! For mark what has happened. . . . He has become too strong to be controlled by her bodily, and too imaginative and mentally vigorous

to be content with mere self-reproduction. He has created civilization
without consulting her, taking her domestic labor for granted as the
foundation of it.[41]

For Shaw the Virgin Mother was a figure of the greatest significance,
but she plays no role in *Man and Superman*. Presumably in this play
Shaw's attitude is realistic, and significantly post-Raphaelite. The difference between the woman who leads Dante upward through the spheres
of heaven and the woman who runs John Tanner to earth in a rented
garden in Granada in some sense measures the cultural abyss that separates the idealistic fantasies of the Middle Ages from those appropriate to
the time of Shaw. The beauty of the unattainable Beatrice mirrors the
splendor of Dante's God, an ineffable abstraction majestically enthroned
beyond the bounds of human thought. The divine element in Ann
Whitefield is not so clearly discernible, yet she too is fashioned in the
image of the divinity she serves. Shaw's comedy is at the other pole from
the *Comedy* of Dante; nevertheless there are some points of similarity in
the conception. Don Juan needs no woman to show him the way to
heaven. He knows the way by himself. But for John Tanner, his earthly
counterpart, the way to God lies through woman, and—such is the
implication—she leads him there through hell.

THE VINTAGE YEARS

B y the time *Man and Superman* was finished, Shaw's work was attracting considerable attention on the Continent. In 1902 Siegfried Trebitsch, a young Austrian who had come upon Shaw's plays through William Archer, asked permission to translate his dramatic works into German. At first Shaw manifested some reluctance to authorize the work, but in the end Trebitsch secured the right to translate three plays. He then set about getting productions for them in Vienna.

It was usual at this time for authors to revise their plays in accordance with the manager's suggestions before their works reached the stage. This form of collaboration, indispensable to the producer's ego, Shaw firmly resisted. When the question of revision came up, he wrote Trebitsch in a spirit which many a playwright has envied:

> I wont have a line omitted or a comma altered. I am quite familiar with the fact that every fool who is connected with a theatre, from the call boy to the manager, thinks he knows better than the author how to make a play popular and successful. Tell them, with my compliments, that I know all about that; that I am forty-six years old, that I know my business and theirs as well; that I am quite independent of tantièmes and do not care a snap of my fingers whether they produce my plays or not. . . .[1]

On this point Shaw remained inflexible all his life. In the course of the next years he was usually his own stage director. When he was not, he permitted no one to tamper with his text without his express permission, so that whatever was done to alter his intention in the course of production was usually done without verbal changes, and never without the strongest protest.

He was now on the very threshold of success. In 1904 J. H. Leigh, a

wealthy amateur actor, leased the Royal Court Theatre for a series of
"Shakesperian Representations." His business manager, John Vedrenne,
persuaded Granville-Barker, whose work he had seen at The Stage Society's productions, to direct *Two Gentlemen of Verona* at the Court. In
turn he agreed to assist Barker in presenting six matinee performances of
Candida, with Barker in the role of Eugene. To everyone's astonishment,
the matinees, secretly subsidized by Mrs. Shaw, made a profit. With
Leigh's help, a partnership was formed and, under the joint management
of Barker and Vedrenne, a season of plays was offered at the Court in
the fall of 1904 along the lines of the art-theater which Grein had established some years before. Barker had planned to include *Captain Brassbound's Conversion* in his repertory; but Ellen Terry declined to work
at the Court, and Shaw would not permit the production of *Man and
Superman* at this time. The season opened with the *Hippolytus* of Euripides in Gilbert Murray's version. Its reception was disappointing.

Meanwhile Shaw was finishing a comedy which Yeats had bespoken
for his Irish Literary Theatre in Dublin. It was to be a play which,
unlike *The Colleen Bawn*, would afford a candidly realistic view of
contemporary Ireland. It was first called *Rule Britannia*, but Shaw
thought better of this, and renamed it *John Bull's Other Island*.

He finished it sometime before September 1904 and sent it to Yeats.[2]
It was a very long play with very long speeches, and its themes were not
at all in accord with the neo-Gaelic movement which Yeats was promoting. The Abbey Theatre returned the manuscript with regrets. Shaw
promptly handed it over to Barker, with instructions—quite contrary to
his usual custom—to cut the text to the bone.

The casting posed unusual problems, since Shaw insisted on finding
authentic types and accents. In the end, it was done; Barker was dra-
gooned into playing Father Keegan, and the play went into rehearsal
under Shaw's direction. It opened at the Court in November 1904 for
the customary run of six matinees and was an immediate success. The
prime minister, Lord Balfour, came to see it, brought other dignitaries
and eventually arranged a command performance at which, it is indispensable to note, Edward VII laughed so heartily that he broke a chair.
The question of what there is in this melancholy little play to provoke
laughter of such Olympian proportions is well worth pondering.

John Bull's Other Island is, in fact, a dour comedy, the irony of which
is enlivened by broad caricature in the style of Dickens, and a good deal
of slapstick suitable for low comedians. It depicts with a pungent blend
of disgust and compassion the continuing conquest of Ireland by the

British invader, specifically the conquest of an Irish village by an English land developer who plans to convert a bankrupt Irish estate into a tourist resort. The view of Ireland which is unfolded in the course of these operations is flattering to nobody. Both the English and the Irish are scoundrels, each according to his bent, and both seem singularly inept in their attempts to overreach one another. Irish cunning is the cunning of the serpent; in comparison, English shrewdness seems elephantine. But there is no doubt where the advantage lies. In the end the Englishman wins. He wins, indeed, all the things the Irishman does not want, but in general he has his way in everything and is despised as a fool for getting it.

As Shaw depicts them, the Irish villagers are small men, mean-spirited, stingy, and self-centered, and quite incapable of extricating themselves from the economic slough into which they have fallen, or of comprehending their national problem in any but its most trivial aspects. The Englishman, for his part, is stupid, obvious, and entirely humorless, but he has the vigor and the efficiency of a bulldozer. In comparison with Irish two-facedness, English hypocrisy seems embarrassingly transparent; but it has the merit of innocence—it is a form of deceit which principally deludes the deceiver. Both sides are Machiavellian in their dealings. The Englishman prides himself on the nobility of his motives, which justify every deceit, while the Irish are completely realistic in making use of him for what they conceive to be their advantage. Thus the Irish, with all their native cleverness, fall with the utmost eagerness into the Englishman's trap; and the Englishman, for all his stupidity, carries on the work of exploitation with the enthusiastic cooperation of the exploited.

These generalities are documented by means of a pleasant anecdote. The village of Roscullen is poor. Its people are wretched and niggardly, difficult and suspicious. Many of them have suffered great injustice at the hands of their former landlords, and their past sufferings are a rich heritage which they exhibit on all occasions. Roscullen furnishes an apt illustration of the brutalizing effects of a long tradition of oppression and exploitation, a tradition the residents secretly respect and hope to emulate when they are sufficiently advanced themselves.

The English syndicate which has undertaken to transform Roscullen into a paying venture is represented by two partners, only one of whom is English. The other is an expatriate Irishman, a native of the village. The Englishman, Broadbent, is a stock character so broadly drawn as to approach abstraction. He is a likeable man of unusual obtuseness, a romantic idealist, as thick-skinned and serviceable as a tame elephant, and quite as capable of working up momentum. He is, in addition, earnest, sentimental and good-humored, complacent, and utterly unprincipled.

His partner, Larry Doyle, belongs at the other end of the human spectrum. He is a passionate man, as subtle, finicky, and perceptive as Broadbent is clumsy and insensitive. Doyle is painfully honest, and congenitally afflicted with the melancholy mistiness of his native climate, from which eighteen years of self-imposed exile have only partly emancipated him. It is easy to identify him with Shaw. Few of his characters speak so sincerely for him:

> . . . your wits cant thicken in that soft moist air . . . on those hillsides of granite rocks and magenta heather. Youve no such colors in the sky, no such lure in the distances, no such sadness in the evenings. . . . An Irishman's imagination never lets him alone, never convinces him, never satisfies him; but it makes him that he cant face reality nor deal with it nor handle it nor conquer it: he can only sneer at them that do. . . . And all the while there goes on a horrible, senseless, mischievous laughter. . . . eternal derision, eternal envy, eternal folly, eternal fouling and staining and degrading, until, when you come at last to a country where men take a question seriously and give a serious answer to it, you deride them for having no sense of humor, and plume yourself on your own worthlessness as if it made you better than them.[3]

The earnestness of this speech is exploded at once:

> BROADBENT: Never despair, Larry. There are great possibilities for Ireland. Home Rule will work wonders under English guidance.
> DOYLE: Tom: why do you select my most tragic moments for your most irresistible strokes of humor?

With all his scorn for the English mentality, Larry is quick to admit that England has made a man of him. He tells Broadbent: ". . . in the main it is by living with you and working in double harness with you that I have learnt to live in a real world and not in an imaginary one. I owe more to you than to any Irishman."[4]

In these circumstances, Larry is happy to be carried along, constantly protesting, by his more vigorous partner. It is clear that he is full of misgivings, but he has the outward confidence of one who rides an armored tank into battle. Broadbent has no misgivings. He has only the characteristic optimism of his race, and its ability to muddle through whatever mess it blunders into.

Since Broadbent's idea of the Irish is derived exclusively from the theater, he is easily taken in by a Glasgow man named Tim Haffigan who, with the aid of a stage brogue and some vocal mannerisms in the style of Boucicault, bilks him out of an advance on a salary he has no intention of earning. Yet when Broadbent actually arrives in Ireland he is unable to see the difference between the reality and its stage version, and he acts as if he himself were a character in an Irish comedy. The Irish landscape intoxicates him almost as quickly as the punch he drinks, and he proposes marriage to the first Irish girl he meets five minutes after first setting eyes on her. Obviously the caricature of Broadbent is as broad as can be, and the scales most unfairly weighted. They are unfairly weighted on both sides; but while Larry Doyle is constantly on hand to explain the Irish to the Englishman, there is nobody in the play to explain the Englishman to the Irish. Broadbent speaks for himself. Perhaps nothing more is needed.

In his notice of the revival of Boucicault's *The Colleen Bawn* (1860) in January 1896, Shaw had written:

> The occupation of the Irish peasant is mainly agriculture, and I advise the reader to make it a fixed rule never to allow himself to believe in the alleged Arcadian virtues of the half-starved drudges who are sacrificed to the degrading, brutalizing, and, as far as I can ascertain, entirely unnecessary pursuit of unscientific farming. The virtues of the Irish peasant are the intense melancholy, the surliness of manner, the incapacity for happiness and self-respect that are the tokens of his natural unfitness for a life of wretchedness. His vices are the arts by which he accommodates himself to his slavery—the flattery on his lips which hides the curse in his heart, his pleasant readiness to settle disputes by "leaving it all to your honor," in order to make something out of your generosity in addition to exacting the utmost of his legal due from you. . . . Of all the tricks which the Irish nation have played on the slow-witted Saxon, the most outrageous is the palming off on him of the imaginary Irishman of romance.[5]

The stereotype to which Shaw objected was established quite early in the nineteenth century. In *John Bull, or The Englishman's Fireside* (1803), by George Colman the Younger, the engaging Irish innkeeper Dennis Brulgruddery appears to have initiated the long tradition which provided such talented actors as John Brougham, Tyrone Power, Dion Boucicault, and Edmund Falconer with their principal line of work. The charm of the jolly stage-Irishman depended largely on the contrast he made with his English foil, so that the characterization of the archetypal

Irishman involved, by a kind of reflex, a corresponding characterization of the English. In the case of *John Bull*, the Englishman John Thornberry and the genial Irish innkeeper are in much the same relation to one another as Broadbent and Tim Haffigan in the first act of *John Bull's Other Island*. The difference is that, in Colman's play, Brulgruddery is passed off as the genuine article, while in Shaw's version the stage-Irishman has never set foot in Ireland.[6]

The idealization of the Irish peasant was due not so much to those who worked up this character for the theater as to the Irish novelists of the first part of the century, writers of the type of Charles Lever and John and Michael Banim. The Irishman who emerges from their books is a wild figure with a heart of gold, the charming type exemplified by such high-spirited ne'er-do-wells as Myles-na-Coppalean in *The Colleen Bawn* and Conn in *The Shaughraun*. These romantic stereotypes were much too valuable to be destroyed by a single act of sabotage such as *John Bull's Other Island*. Matthew Haffigan might come closer to a real peasant than such magnificent inventions as the shaughraun, but he served no useful purpose in the theater. He was merely realistic; and realism as such has never been a prime consideration in the drama. In spite of Shaw's sensible admonitions, therefore, Tim Haffigan the stage-Irishman, remains a valuable theatrical commodity, while his uncle Matthew serves only to remind us of the plight of Ireland at the beginning of the twentieth century. In Shaw's play, Larry Doyle holds him in no great respect: ". . . I say let him die, and let us have no more of his like." Very likely most Irish character actors would be of this opinion; at any rate, the Abbey Theatre would have none of Matthew Haffigan.

The question of whether or not Shaw's characters represented the Irish temperament better than Boucicault's is a matter of opinion. They were certainly different, a selection of caricatures intended to represent a less engaging view of Ireland than that which the Irish had so far advanced in their own interests. The problem of how far one might safely go in an effort at realistic portrayal was evidently not entirely resolved in Shaw's mind. *John Bull's Other Island* is not without its sentimental side. It is Father Keegan, not Matthew Haffigan, who provides the memorable role in the play; and Nora Reilly is depicted with charming delicacy, in spite of the question as to the sufficiency of her diet. Both with respect to her extravagant innocence and her wit, she seems closer to the lovely figure of Irish womanhood which Claire Ffoliott represents in Boucicault's *The Shaughraun* than to anyone we might conceivably meet in the streets of Cork or Limerick. Shaw certainly

rendered a more just account of Ireland and the Irish than did Boucicault; but in Shaw's play, also, the characters with rare exceptions, are
stage types and as such neither real nor unreal, but merely more or less
apt for their special uses. It is this aptitude which gives them, in each
case, their verisimilitude. As for their truth, it is impossible at this point
to assay it.

In *John Bull's Other Island*, Broadbent comes to Ireland bursting with
missionary zeal, eager to survey, absorb, and transform the object of his
attentions. The natives regard him as a gullible idiot and are happy to
mortgage their lands to him for more than their value, little realizing that
they are being pauperized in the process. Doyle knows the game well
and detests his part in it. But he is powerless to stop the wheels of
progress, and he adopts a neutral position in this process which he knows
must end in the destruction of a class which is incapable of maintaining
itself. The result is that Broadbent comes miraculously into Doyle's inheritance. At a single stroke he acquires his influence, his Irish heiress,
his seat in Parliament, and also his Irish cause, all the things of which
Doyle desires to divest himself.

The mood in which these events are represented lies somewhere between comedy and farce, but it has also an unmistakable undercurrent of
pathos which undoubtedly reflects Shaw's deeper feelings with relation
to his native land and its destiny. In his play the *raisonneur* at first sight
not even remotely resembles Shaw. It is Father Keegan. He has reput-
edly gone mad, has consequently been defrocked, and is superseded in
the community by the powerful and very orthodox Father Dempsey.
Like Larry Doyle, Keegan has long been an expatriate, but, while Doyle
is uncomfortable in Ireland, Keegan has found peace there and is at home
with the people, the landscape, and even the insects.

By association with the English, Doyle has become vital, able, militant,
and useful, and also something of an anomaly. He is a permanently
displaced person. To a cosmopolitan of this sort, the dreaminess of Ireland is alien and dangerous, an opiate, the effects of which he dreads.
Keegan is more truly cosmopolitan. He has trudged the roads of Europe,
and studied at all the great centers of learning. Now, full of wisdom, he
has subsided into contemplation and become a sage. He is evidently a
pantheist and sees God everywhere. Thus he finds it amusing, and doubtless instructive, to communicate with the local grasshopper, who evidently understands him better than the native population, and he feels
equal compassion for Haffigan and Haffigan's pig, both of whom he
looks upon as near kinsmen.

It is reasonable to suppose that in Father Keegan Shaw meant to depict not merely the essence of the Irish spirit but also the highest manifestation of current humanity. But this magnificent being is by no means a practical person. He is hedged in by his wisdom and the passivity it engenders. His vision is too keen and his horizons too wide for him to be of much use to his generation. His figure is regal. He is the consummate version of Marchbanks; but his kingdom is not of this world, and his vision of a better world seems utterly foolish both to Broadbent and to Larry Doyle, the practical men of affairs.

As matters stand, Keegan can make at most a gesture in the direction of salvation, and he is quite aware that for the time his efforts are futile and his words are wasted. He is resigned to play the only role in this world for which he is suited, the role into which Shaw, for all his reformist zeal, was gradually subsiding: he is a seer. Father Keegan thus occupies a place somewhere between Julius Caesar and Captain Shotover, but he has not Caesar's energy and is pathetic in a different way than Shotover. He is a romantic figure in the style of Blake, but he has an oriental coloring, and for him—as for Strindberg—this world is a horror explicable only in terms of an expiation of its past crimes, its karma:

> This world, sir, is very clearly a place of torment and penance, a place where the fool flourishes and the good and wise are hated and persecuted, a place where men and women torture one another in the name of love; where children are scourged and enslaved in the name of parental duty and education; where the weak in body are poisoned and mutilated in the name of healing; and the weak in character are put to the horrible torture of imprisonment, not for hours but for years, in the name of justice. It is a place where the hardest toil is a welcome refuge from the horror and tedium of pleasure, and where charity and good works are done only for hire to ransom the souls of the spoiler and the sybarite. Now, sir, there is only one place of horror and torment known to my religion, and that place is hell. Therefore it is plain to me that this earth of ours must be hell, and that we are all here, as the Indian revealed to me—perhaps he was sent to reveal it to me—to expiate crimes committed by us in a former existence.[7]

With Father Keegan the role of the *raisonneur* in Shaw's plays emerges in its full splendor. Since Keegan has nothing to do, it is natural that he should have a great deal to say. He is, indeed, an orator of more than ordinary resonance, and it is unfortunate that his talents are not always under control. His final speech, though often admired, is doubtless overinflated; but his summary of the human condition in Act Four is a magnificent piece of sermonic oratory, quite "the genuine pulpit article."[8]

Since Shaw's prefaces were in most cases written some time after the plays for which they were intended, it is to the preface of *Man and Superman* that one looks for what is apposite to *John Bull's Other Island*. Moreover, it is clear that, while Shaw was writing his Irish play, the ideas that were to culminate in *Major Barbara* were already taking form within his mind. Broadbent's Gladstonian liberalism is as old-fashioned in *John Bull's Other Island* as Roebuck Ramsden's mid-century radicalism in *Man and Superman*; but it is possible to sense in Broadbent some foreshadowing of the vastly more impressive figure of Andrew Undershaft. Keegan finds Broadbent little to his liking; yet he is aware of the usefulness of such men:

KEEGAN: Sir: I may even vote for you.

BROADBENT: You shall never regret it, Mr Keegan, I give you my word for that. I shall bring money here; I shall raise wages: I shall found public institutions: a library, a Polytechnic (undenominational, of course), a gymnasium, a cricket club, perhaps an art school. I shall make a Garden city of Roscullen: the round tower shall be thoroughly repaired and restored.

KEEGAN: And our place of torment shall be as clean and orderly as the cleanest and most orderly place I know in Ireland, which is our poetically named Mountjoy prison. Well, perhaps I had better vote for an efficient devil that knows his own mind and his own business than for a foolish patriot who has no mind and no business.

BROADBENT: Devil is rather a strong expression in that connexion, Mr Keegan.

KEEGAN: Not from a man who knows that this world is hell. But since the word offends you, let me soften it, and compare you simply to an ass.[9]

Obviously Keegan cannot be said to mirror the astonishing personage that Shaw had by this time become. He reflects specifically neither the writer nor the active reformer. Keegan is saintly. He is, if anything, the sublimation of Shaw; and thus resembles Shaw the Socialist in the same way that Don Juan resembles Shaw the Philanderer. Don Juan leaps up the *scala amoris*, as Shaw conceived it, three rungs at a time, to the top. Keegan represents Shaw's highest reach in religion; thus the two characters converge. If Keegan's mysticism is more convincing than Don Juan's, it is because, like everything else to which Shaw set his hand, it has its practical side. Father Keegan is not merely a mystic. He is also a

Fabian, with a sound head for business. Along with the *eironeia* of his classical prototype, he exhibits the necessary practical foresight of the philosopher king:

> KEEGAN: . . . believe me, I do every justice to the efficiency of you and your syndicate. You are both, I am told, thoroughly efficient civil engineers, and I have no doubt the golf links will be a triumph of your art. Mr Broadbent will get into Parliament most efficiently, which is more than St Patrick could do if he were alive now. You may even build the hotel efficiently if you can find enough efficient masons, carpenters and plumbers, which I rather doubt. (*Dropping his irony and beginning to fall into the attitude of the priest rebuking sin.*) When the hotel becomes insolvent (*Broadbent takes his cigar out of his mouth, a little taken aback*) your English business habits will secure the thorough efficiency of the liquidation. You will re-organize the scheme efficiently; you will liquidate its second bankruptcy efficiently; . . . you will get rid of its original shareholders efficiently after efficiently ruining them; and you will finally profit very efficiently by getting that hotel for a few shillings in the pound. . . .[10]

And having traced this cycle to its logical conclusion, Father Keegan unexpectedly reveals his apostolic side. His charity, like Shaw's, encompasses all forms of sin:

> . . . Standing here between you and the Englishman, so clever in your foolishness, and this Irishman, so foolish in his cleverness, I cannot in my ignorance be sure which of you is the more deeply damned, but I should be unfaithful to my calling if I opened the gates of my heart less widely to the one than to the other.[11]

Only to this extent does Father Keegan permit these intruders to invade the privacy of his dream. It is the dream which, in one way or another, underlies all of Shaw's literary work, the dream of the Third Kingdom which Ibsen preached from the time of *Emperor and Galilean*, that same vision which lit up the last days of the nineteenth century, and which still faintly illumines the bitter disillusionments of our time. Father Keegan may seem unduly rhetorical at this juncture, more so than poor Vershinin, who indulges similar fancies in *The Three Sisters*; but Shaw was never more serious. What he describes is an earthly paradise that is neither Marxist nor Christian, yet is something of both:

> In my dreams it is a country where the State is the Church and the Church the people: three in one and one in three. It is a common-

> wealth in which work is play and play is life: three in one and one in
> three. It is a temple in which the priest is the worshipper and the
> worshipper the worshipped: three in one and one in three. It is a
> godhead in which all life is human and all humanity divine: three in
> one and one in three. It is in short, the dream of a madman.[12]

Shorn of its numerology and its Catholic embellishments, it is the vision
of Don Juan in hell.

Immediately after *John Bull's Other Island*, Shaw dashed off a short
three-character play called *How He Lied to Her Husband*. It was no
great thing. Arnold Daly had been using *The Man of Destiny* as a
curtain-raiser for *Candida*. He found the combination strenuous and
asked Shaw to write him an easier piece to fill out the evening. It is said
that Shaw wrote *How He Lied to Her Husband* during four days of
continual rain in Scotland. Nothing is more likely; but he would have
been better off playing bridge. The play is a bit of nonsense which he
would have done well to destroy, and the fact that it has survived, was
revived, and has been several times reprinted, indicates to what a degree
Shaw lacked the fatal gift of self-criticism.

In the course of the next spring, however, he was engaged on *Major
Barbara*. This was finished by summer and was given a memorable production at the Court Theatre in November 1905 under the Barker-
Vedrenne management, with Louis Calvert in the part of Undershaft
and Granville-Barker playing Cusins. The play attracted great attention
in its first production and has been the object of increasing interest since,
the more so as it deals with what has become one of the most urgent
issues of our time.

By the first years of the nineteenth century the problem of poverty
was already a matter of concern to many who were not poor. The
literary history of Britain from the time of Gray and Burns vividly
reflects the growing dissatisfaction of British writers with the social
system they had inherited, and the influence of the French Revolution
on the social conscience of England in this period was inescapable. This
is perhaps the most significant aspect of romanticism in the time of
England's great prosperity.

In the 1870's the rapid industrialization of the English economy immeasurably widened English horizons until they encompassed a good
part of the world. The expansion of trade had, of course, been going on
for many years. England had not been self-sufficient for centuries. In the
time of Disraeli its increasing dependence on foreign markets and for-

eign materials resulted in imperialist attitudes which quickly took on the attributes of a national cult. In these circumstances everything conspired to minimize the urgency of the internal difficulties of England; and the popular press, particularly, labored to shift public interest from the social evils which the radicals were trying to reform to the thrilling adventures of the expanding empire.

The growing radicalism of the period, however, kept pace with the growing complacency of the jingoists. The editor of the *Fortnightly Review*, John Morley, characterized the England of his time as a system of "hollow shams disguising the coarse supremacy of wealth," and a conspiracy of silence on the part of the powerful classes aimed at preserving England as "a paradise for the well-to-do, a purgatory for the able, and a hell for the poor."[13]

Morley's rhetoric distinctly belongs to the 1870's, but this strain of Protestant eloquence welled up repeatedly in the succeeding decades. In 1907 Shaw wrote, in the preface to *Major Barbara*:

> Here am I, for instance, by class a respectable man, by common sense a hater of waste and disorder, by intellectual constitution, legally minded to the verge of pedantry, and by temperament apprehensive and economically disposed to the limit of old-maidishness; yet I am and have always been, and now shall always be, a revolutionary writer, because our laws make law impossible; our liberties destroy all freedom; our property is organized robbery; our morality is an impudent hypocrisy; our wisdom is administered by inexperienced or malexperienced dupes, our power wielded by cowards and weaklings, and our honor false in all its points.[14]

There is no reason to distinguish Victorian complacency from the smugness of the present day, although quantitatively there may be some difference, nor is there much point in distinguishing Shaw's dissatisfaction with the state of things—or Morley's—from our own. Apart from matters of detail, the social struggle of the 1890's is completely comprehensible in terms of current patterns and contemporary events. Even present-day pessimism has its counterpart in the previous century. In the 1890's it was prophesied that the day of doom was certainly at hand and would be presaged in the year 1896 by the assumption to heaven of 144,000 selected Christians.[15] In our day such prophecies—though often reiterated—ordinarily meet with some skepticism: it is certain, at any rate, that the lunacies of the 1890's seem singularly lighthearted in comparison with the apocalyptic visions of the post-Hiroshima era. In spite of the various manifestations of apprehension and disgust which characterize the critical literature of the period, the Victorian mood seems, in general, to have been hopeful. The manifold defects of middle-class industrialism were certainly evident to many, particularly to many among the liberal clergy which marked out the *appetitus divitiarum infinitus* of the wealthy classes as its particular target, and there was also the chorus of social protest to which such writers as Ruskin and Morris gave ample expression. But in 1890 it was impossible to contemplate without some satisfaction the many social advances which had come about since the accession of Victoria. At the close of her reign there was every reason to suppose that what remained to be done might well take place in time through orderly legislative process. The world was certainly not perfect, but it was improving visibly every day.

The idea of progressive organic development underlay much, if not all, the thought of the later nineteenth century and, after Herbert Spencer, few people doubted that progress was a normal consequence of the passing of time. A handful of writers—among them T. H. Huxley—had expressed the disagreeable idea that social progress was not necessarily automatic; but in the light of history, most Victorians appear to have rejoiced, like Tennyson, in the expectation that in the end it would be well.

It is this optimistic attitude which is reflected in *Major Barbara*, a dramatic discussion with narrative passages in which the technique, as well as the subject matter, of the Dialogue in Hell is developed into something like a dramatic action.

Major Barbara makes an impression of considerable originality, but Shaw did not invent the form. He merely extended the technique which Dumas *fils* had sketched out in *Le Demi-monde*. This involved the dramatization of an issue which is first debated, then tested through a critical experiment. *Major Barbara* may be said to mark a very late stage in the development of the thesis play. The action, as in most plays of this type, takes place in a controlled environment, so to speak, *in vitro*. The play has two plot lines, convergent, but logically independent of one another. The first centers on the question of who is to inherit the Undershaft munitions works, a vast industrial complex reminiscent of the Krupp empire. The second culminates in Barbara's decision to leave the Salvation Army and to take service in the arms factory.

The Krupp works were attracting considerable interest at this time. Friedrich Alfred Krupp died in 1902, after greatly extending the workers' welfare program initiated by his father, with its model villages at Essen and its many social benefits. His daughter Bertha then assumed the direction of the firm and its 43,000 employees. In 1906—the year after the publication of *Major Barbara*—she married Dr. Gustav von Bohlen und Halbach, who later assumed the name of Krupp, and took over the management of the Krupp combine, thus fulfilling in reality the role of Dr. Cusins in Shaw's play.

The battle for the soul of Barbara which principally motivates the action in *Major Barbara* is in the nature of a psychomachia, the visible projection of the spiritual ambivalence of a conscientious Fabian, and in this light the play takes on the exemplary character of a medieval morality. The contest is won by Barbara's father, the Mephistophelean munitions magnate, a fascinating personage characterized in rather more detail than is customary in personifications of this type. Nevertheless, the plot obviously transcends the limits of the action. It suggests the agelong struggle between God and the devil for the soul of man; and as one might expect, it is the devil who wins.

The moral implications of the situation are, accordingly, of considerably greater interest than the events which generate them. *Major Barbara* is a play intended to provoke discussion, and the sentimental involvements of the characters, indispensable to a comedy designed for a wide public, are beggared by the importance of the theme. This is developed principally in two scenes—the colloquy between Undershaft and Cusins in the Salvation Army shelter, and the triangular discussion in the munitions plant in the last act. The rest of the play is no more than the dramatic armature on which these scenes are mounted.

The first act is mainly expository and derives humor from the ironic treatment of the return of the prodigal father to the bosom of his family. Lady Britomart is presented as a caricature of the upper-class matriarch, a more earnest version of Lady Bracknell in *The Importance of Being Earnest* (1895). It is probable that in devising this character Shaw had in mind Gilbert Murray's mother-in-law, Lady Rosalind Howard, the countess of Carlisle. Lady Rosalind was an influential crusader, prominent in the temperance movement, whose imperious nature and indomitable spirit elicited both admiration and terror among the members of her considerable retinue. Lady Britomart, however, plays no great part in *Major Barbara* after the first act. She is an interesting character, but the play is not about her; and in developing her so fully in the expository part of the play and making so little use of her thereafter, Shaw demonstrates how far he had departed by this time from the economy of the well-made play.

In the opening scene Lady Britomart has assembled her brood—her son Stephen, her two daughters, Sarah and Barbara, and their respective young men—in order to force her erring husband, from whom she has long been separated, to settle an income on her daughters and to ensure the inheritance to her son. There is obviously some reminiscence here of the situation in *You Never Can Tell.*

The husband turns out to be a very eccentric gentleman. Andrew Undershaft is a millionaire. The first to bear that name was a foundling left on the steps of the church of St. Andrew Undershaft, so called, it is said, because of the Maypole customarily set up in front of it in the spring. The munitions works which the first Undershaft established has since been handed down, together with his name, to a succession of foundlings, each of whom has selected and adopted his successor for reasons of aptitude alone. The present incumbent is the seventh in the line of succession. His daughter Barbara is a major in the Salvation Army, and it is to her management that he proposes to entrust the Undershaft works at St. Andrew's.

She is by no means amenable to the suggestion. She is dedicated to the idea of preaching salvation through faith and good works and is revolted by the idea of manufacturing the means of destruction. The issue between Barbara and her father thus takes shape instantly in the first act. At the end of their discussion, he agrees to visit her army shelter provided she will come directly afterwards to see his cannon factory. These two visits comprise the action of the play.

The characterization is equally simple. Barbara is young. She has the moral fervor of youth, and she does what she can to spread the gospel from her headquarters in a miserable shelter in the East End. Her father easily demonstrates what should have been at once evident to a less innocent militant, that a philanthropic organization depends for its existence on the social system under which it operates. When Barbara understands at last that her beloved Army is, at bottom, a poorly subsidized instrument of middle-class capitalism, designed mainly to keep the poor in order, she indignantly resigns her commission. For a time she is plunged into moral and emotional bankruptcy, but this existentialist crisis lasts scarcely a day. The next morning she visits her father's arms factory at St. Andrew's, and there she finds faith and work, and a surer way to salvation. Thus the major action of the play depicts a discovery and a reversal, in the course of which Barbara turns from the service of the Christian God to the service of his demonic counterpart, and thus becomes, like Dick Dudgeon, a devil's disciple.

The manner of Barbara's conversion involves a simple demonstration.

Undershaft is neither benevolent nor philanthropic. He is a merchant of death. His factories thrive on bloodshed and are dedicated to the idea of making war profitable. To this end he keeps his labor supply stable by making his workers happy, not through visions of a better life in the future, but by the tangible realities of a good life in the present—precisely the idea of Friedrich Albert Krupp in developing the workers' villages at Essen. The contrast between the agreeable living arrangements of the Undershaft factories and the squalor of the West Ham Salvation Army shelter is only too apparent. As between these two enterprises the one that serves the Prince of Peace is infinitely less successful than the one that serves the lords of war: the moral is plain.

The question for Barbara thus becomes painfully clear—is it better for society to keep its slaves under sedation, or to provide the means through which they may win their freedom? Is it better to beguile the poor with dreams of heaven, or to wake them to the grim reality of life on earth? The question is not altogether simple; but as it is posed in *Major Barbara* it seems to answer itself at once, and most of what is said in the course of the third act seems a needless elaboration. The result is that, for all practical purposes, the play is over a good while before it ends, and it is only by a series of tricks that the action is prolonged until the curtain descends.

Shaw's *raisonneurs* are among the very best the drama affords, but they have a tendency to keep talking long after their points are made. Their wisdom is impressive; but they are luxurious creatures, opulent in their discourse, and as self-indulgent as schoolmasters. Undershaft is no exception. He is as voluble as Father Keegan. In *Major Barbara*, nevertheless, the argument is exceptionally interesting, and the paradox most ingeniously posed. Whatever we may think of the play from a technical viewpoint, there is no doubt of its value as a dramatic essay. The demonstration, it is true, is not always rigorous. The scene in which Barbara stirs up Bill Walker's conscience is sheer melodrama, and his pathetic effort to square his accounts with God through the payment of a small fine does not contrast properly with Bodger's offer to buy out the whole operation. Moreover, if Undershaft is to be associated with the dark powers, as the play suggests, we cannot logically exclude Bodger from his company: both the gunsmith and the brewer are in the service of Bacchus. The difference is that while Bodger traffics in drunkenness, and inspires disgust, Undershaft deals in death and inspires terror.

The syllogism on which *Major Barbara* is grounded is deceptively simple. Once it is granted that poverty is the root of all evil, it follows that the elimination of poverty is the most pressing of human needs. To bring about a better world it is first of all necessary to manage a more equable distribution of the world's wealth. But in the nature of things it is unthinkable that the rich will willingly part with their possessions. Social justice is attainable, consequently, only through force. It is only when the socially minded are in control of the armed forces that the government can be induced to do what is necessary to secure a good life for all. The way to salvation lies through the arms factory. Such is the gospel according to Andrew Undershaft.

For the religion of submission, Undershaft proposes to substitute the religion of power. It is his faith that the union of power and conscience —Cusins and Barbara—will in time bring about the earthly paradise which the Christian fantasy indefinitely postpones. The assumptions on which his argument is based are, of course, questionable, but neither Barbara nor Cusins attack them seriously. These assumptions involve the customary preconceptions of Millite utilitarianism, supplemented by idealistic notions borrowed not overcritically from a variety of sources, including Marx, Hegel, Butler, and Bradley. They constitute a spicy philosophic purée which will hardly suit every palate. As the action is arranged, however, the effect of this doctrine upon the characters is spectacular. The demonstration, indeed, is so devastatingly conclusive that, from a dramatic standpoint, it very nearly ruins the play.

It is the characterization that saves it. The personages are memorable. Barbara, as the archetypal idealist, would be particularly vulnerable to ironic treatment, but Shaw portrays her without a trace of malice. Her power manifests the cosmic force that drives her; and to the extent that she is driven, she is mad. Her lover, Adolphus Cusins, is equally mad in his way, and her father, the empire builder, willingly admits his own irrationality. All three—the poet, the millionaire, and the evangelist—are excessive characters acting under the spell of a force that transcends reason. They move among men therefore with the conscious grace of superior beings. "What have we to do," says Undershaft, "with the common mob of slaves and idolaters?"[16]

What makes these three beings so closely kin is their energy. The force that animates Barbara is not intellectual. She understands no more than most people and is not remarkably articulate. It is her moral passion, not her mind, that Undershaft wishes to place at the service of the cannon factory. Cusins is bright, but for Undershaft the acquisition of Cusins is secondary to the acquisition of Barbara. Cusins has no special conviction, aside from his faith in Barbara; but he has intellect. There-

fore his decision, which is essentially Barbara's decision, is quite explicitly reasoned out, although, like John Tanner, he is actually stampeded
by a force beyond his ken. He tells Undershaft, in words reminiscent
of Tanner's protestations:

> I dont like marriage: I feel intensely afraid of it; and I dont know
> what I shall do with Barbara or what she will do with me. But I feel
> that I and nobody else must marry her. Please regard that as settled.
> —Not that I wish to be arbitrary; but why should I waste your time in
> discussing what is inevitable?[17]

Cusins is a professor of Greek whose specialty is Euripides. The analogy with Gilbert Murray was originally quite explicit, and Shaw made
no secret of it. Murray was more Irish than Shaw; an avowed disciple,
also, of Shelley; a radical reformer; and, like Shaw, a vegetarian. In his
opinion, which was given wide currency, Euripides was the spiritual
ancestor of Ibsen, and Murray's oft-quoted characterization of the
Greek dramatist might be taken to apply equally well to the Norwegian.
Doubtless, Shaw applied it also to himself, and not without reason:

> His contemporary public denounced him as dull, because he tortured
> them with personal problems; as malignant, because he made them
> see truths they wished not to see; as blasphemous and foul-minded,
> because he made demands on their spiritual and religious natures
> which they could neither satisfy nor overlook.[18]

The unusual reverence with which Cusins's scholarship is displayed in
the course of the action attests to the respect in which Shaw held the
classics. In truth, Murray's rhymed translation of *The Bacchae* owes
almost as much to Shelley as to Euripides, and his versions of *An-
dromache* and *The Trojan Women* seem quite as apposite to the antiwar
sentiment in England during the Boer campaign of 1899–1901 as to the
pacifist reaction in Athens during the war with Sparta. Shaw's occasional
displays of classical erudition are not impressive; their purpose is mainly
cosmetic; but in hailing the production of Murray's Greek plays at the
Court Theatre as "modern masterpieces" he showed real insight. Unfortunately, he carried Murray's methods of translation some steps further
than Murray. The versions of the chorus from *The Bacchae* which
Cusins quotes in Act Two of *Major Barbara* and which Shaw attributed
to Murray in the notes prefaced to the play, might well have caused a
scholar some embarrassment had he taken the attribution seriously. Apparently Murray took it good-humoredly as a joke.[19]

The characterization of Cusins is enthusiastic, but apart from his single-minded devotion to Barbara, he remains mysteriously aloof from the action; he appears to be a young man deeply concerned with matters that have nothing to do with the play. Like most classical scholars he talks shop a good deal, but the insistence with which he drags his Hellenic interests into everything he touches is in the end almost as embarrassing as the tiresome pedantry Shaw exhibits in reproducing phonetically the dialect of his cockney characters. It is in these touches that we become uncomfortably aware of the literary parvenu in Shaw.

Cusins is witty, ironic, and sensitive to every nuance in the dialogue. He is also unbearably arch. In the scene in which he haggles with his Mephistophelean adversary over the terms of his proposed servitude, he exhibits a precocious insight into the methods of the bazaar, but one imagines he would have done better to postpone the negotiations until after he had decided to sell his soul. Neither these peccadillos nor the Gilbertian revelation concerning Cusin's technical status as a foundling do anything to impair seriously the dramatic force of the play. This depends almost entirely on the characterization of Undershaft.

Undershaft is one of Shaw's authentic masterpieces. Shaw perhaps did not understand Cusins very well. He understood Undershaft as well as he understood himself. The self-made millionaire presents a new aspect of the Shavian hero—the poet as captain of industry. In Shaw's conception this figure is necessarily mystical in character and Satanic in mood. Like Dick Dudgeon, he is essentially a romantic figure, a glamorous brigand in the service of a higher power. Like Caesar, he is both Machiavellian and simple-hearted, at the same time majestic and genuinely humble. An aristocrat without traceable lineage, he appears to have sprung full-armed from the brow of Zeus, without the usual biological amenities. He is, like Shaw, a miracle of nature.

Undershaft's kingdom is wholly of this world. He is wise and, without formal schooling, learned. He is strong with the energy of the earth. He is, in short, Dionysian; and it is this quality that recommends him to Cusins. Through Undershaft, Cusins at last makes connection with the life-current that has eluded him in his academic cloister. "What drives this place," Undershaft remarks as he proudly displays his cannon factory, "is a will of which I am a part." Henceforth, we are to understand, Cusins also will be part of this will.

Undershaft is a source of power. His function in the body politic corresponds to that of the intermediary faculty described in the *Republic* of Plato, the pugnacious faculty which may be exerted in accordance with the dictates of the higher or the lower faculties of the soul, depending on which is in control of the organism. His motto, "Unashamed," indicates his neutrality as a provider of weapons to all who desire them. But Undershaft is not really neutral. Underlying his motto is the gospel of the sixth Undershaft: "Nothing is ever done in this world until men are prepared to kill one another if it is not done"; and his sense of moral justice is evidenced by his choice of Barbara as the priestess of the house of power. Cusins, the future Undershaft, is necessarily committed to the forging of weapons; but Barbara, presumably, will know what must be done if humanity is to be saved, and it is into her hands that Undershaft entrusts the spiritual direction of his works.

Major Barbara reflects very clearly the mood of *Man and Superman*. Don Juan had said in the earlier play:

> . . . It is not death that matters, but the fear of death. It is not killing and dying that degrades us, but base living, and accepting the wages and profits of degradation. Better ten dead men than one live slave or his master. Men shall yet rise up, father against son and brother against brother, and kill one another for the great Catholic idea of abolishing slavery. . . .[20]

This is the point made in *Major Barbara*. If it is granted that men are naturally devoted to destruction, it follows that evolution must make its way through force. The normal consequence of man's natural cowardice is submission and slavery; but men become heroic, as Don Juan says, when they have faith in an idea. It is through its energy, not its passivity, that the human race evolves into something better than itself. Cusins takes a distinctly radical position:

> As a teacher of Greek I gave the intellectual man weapons against the common man. I now want to give the common man weapons against the intellectual man. I love the common people. I want to arm them against the lawyers, the doctors, the priests, the literary men, the professors, the artists, and the politicians who, once in authority, are more disastrous and tyrannical than all the fools, rascals, and impostors. I want a power simple enough for common men to use, yet strong enough to force the intellectual oligarchy to use its genius for the general good.[21]

The nature of this power is not in doubt. It is not moral suasion that Cusins has in mind. Undershaft describes it tersely: "Your pious mob fills up ballot papers, and imagines it is governing its masters; but the ballot paper that really governs is the paper that has a bullet wrapped up in it."[22]

In his *Réflexions sur la violence* (1906), published the year after *Major Barbara* was written, Georges Sorel wrote:

> . . . capitalism plays a part analogous to that attributed by Hartmann to the Unconscious in nature, since it prepares the coming of social reforms which it did not intend to produce. Without any co-ordinated plan, without any guiding ideas, without any idea of a future world, it is the cause of an inevitable evolution . . . it performs in an almost mechanical manner whatever is necessary in order that a new era may appear. . . .
>
> Socialists should therefore abandon the attempt (initiated by the Utopians) to find a means of inducing the enlightened middle class to prepare the *transition to a more perfect system of legislation*. Their sole function is that of explaining to the proletariat the greatness of the revolutionary part it is called upon to play. . . .
>
> Proletarian violence not only makes the future revolution certain, but it seems also to be the only means by which the European nations—at present stupefied by humanitarianism—can recover their former energy. This sort of violence compels capitalism to restrict its attentions solely to its material role and tends to restore to it the warlike qualities it formerly possessed. . . .[23]

It is this line of reasoning that *Major Barbara* follows in dramatizing the contrast between the Salvation Army and the cannon factory. But while Cusins agrees with Sorel in advocating a sharpening of the class struggle, he by no means shares his faith in the role of the proletariat. In Cusins's opinion, it is by forcing men of genius to serve them that the masses will succeed in bringing about an improvement in the social organism and not by taking the direction into their own hands. Cusins thus reaffirms Shaw's essentially aristocratic position. Nevertheless it is clear that at this time Shaw—by nature, physically timorous and much inclined to peace—was not at all averse to violence as a matter of theory. In this respect *Major Barbara* is the most explicit of his plays.

In some measure, no doubt, the revolutionary posture which Cusins adopts reflects Shaw's own energetic temper, with which the patient and painstaking methods of the Webbs provided an interesting contrast. The primitive vitality of Undershaft, which Cusins finds irresistible, reflected a trend which Nietzsche had defined in his celebrated work *Die Geburt der Tragödie* (1870–71). In the opening years of the new century, Dionysos was much in vogue both in his creative and his destructive aspect. "This spirit that I call Dionysos," Murray wrote, "this magic of inspiration and joy, is it not also the great wrecker of men's lives?"[24]

It was not difficult to sanctify the duality of Dionysos to the uses of socialism. All that was necessary was to enlist this unreasoning power in the service of society. Thus in *Man and Superman*, Tanner speaks of the youthful destructive urge which he turned into socially useful channels when he grew up. Undershaft describes a similar process, but he attributes his transformation to the struggle to survive:

> I moralized and starved until one day I swore that I would be a full-fed man at all costs; that nothing should stop me except a bullet, neither reason nor morals nor the lives of other men. I said, "Thou shalt starve ere I starve," and with that word I became free and great. I was a dangerous man until I had my will: now I am a useful, beneficent, kindly person. That is the history of most self-made millionaires, I fancy. When it is the history of every Englishman we shall have an England worth living in.

Therefore, in contradistinction to the Christian doctrine which inspires the Salvation Army, Undershaft advocates war to the death against hunger and misery: "I had rather be a thief than a pauper. I had rather be a murderer than a slave. I dont want to be either; but if you force the alternative on me, then, by Heaven, I'll choose the braver and more moral one. I hate poverty and slavery more than any other crimes whatsoever."[25]

It is along such lines that Undershaft's topsy-turvy morality is justified. Once it is granted that poverty is the worst of evils, the individual is justified in defending himself against it in whatever way he can, and a wholly new system of morality develops foreign alike to the classic and the Christian conception. If poverty is evil, it is sinful to be poor. In the preface to *Major Barbara* Shaw wrote, in words that oddly recall the Ragpicker's wry speech in Giraudoux's *La Folle de Chaillot*: "Money is the most important thing in the world. It represents health, strength, honor, generosity and beauty as conspicuously and undeniably as the want of it represents illness, weakness, disgrace, meanness and ugliness."[26]

While Undershaft has no scruples about the manner in which wealth is acquired, Barbara has. Like Trench, in the first two acts of *Widowers' Houses*, she has idealistic notions concerning the quality of money, and she refuses to accept Bill Walker's expiatory sovereign because it is impure. She tells Walker: "There is bad blood on your hands; and nothing but good blood can cleanse them. Money is no use. Take it away." She is badly shocked, in consequence, when Mrs. Baines eagerly accepts Bodger's offer of money, as well as Undershaft's gift for the preservation of her organization. Barbara, evidently, is a romantic idealist; Mrs. Baines, a realist. Like Undershaft she subordinates the means to the end, and she has an administrator's keen eye for contributions, whatever their source. She marches out therefore with Undershaft and Cusins in an unholy trinity not altogether different from that of Trench, Sartorius, and Lickcheese in the earlier play, and the ironical implication is the same. But the play has a very different aim from *Widowers' Houses.* That play was written by a poor man with a great desire to settle a score with the rich. When *Major Barbara* was written, Shaw himself was rich, and he had come to see that money is a desirable commodity regardless of its source.

Undershaft looks forward to a time when every poor man in England will rise above his poverty in the same way as himself. Meanwhile his aims are unashamedly selfish. As he remarks astutely, for the moment the Salvation Army is good for business and he supports it cheerfully:

CUSINS: I dont think you quite know what the Army does for the poor.
UNDERSHAFT: Oh yes I do. It draws their teeth: that is enough for me as a man of business.
CUSINS: Nonsense. It makes them sober—
UNDERSHAFT: I prefer sober workmen. The profits are larger.
CUSINS: —honest—
UNDERSHAFT: Honest workmen are the most economical.
CUSINS: —attached to their homes.
UNDERSHAFT: So much the better: they will put up with anything sooner than change their shop.
CUSINS: —happy—
UNDERSHAFT: An invaluable safeguard against revolution.
CUSINS: —unselfish—
UNDERSHAFT: Indifferent to their own interests, which suits me exactly.
CUSINS: —with their thoughts on heavenly things—
UNDERSHAFT (*rising*): And not on Trade Unionism nor socialism. Excellent.[27]

This duet need not confuse us. Undershaft is a paradox. He is, precisely like Shaw, both capitalist and socialist, both egotist and altruist, and he is also original in being a disconcertingly honest man. His views accordingly involve a contradiction which can be resolved only on a higher dialectical plane. As an individual, Undershaft is ruthless and selfish; as an antagonist, he is formidable. But the universal Undershaft is the hope of mankind. When all men are like Undershaft, honest and explicit in the assertion of their desire, and determined to do their best for themselves, poverty and slavery will no longer be possible, for no man will tolerate subjection. Undershaft militant is a danger to all the world, but Undershaft triumphant is a benevolent deity shared by all, the very spirit of evolving mankind.

The source of revolution, Shaw believed, is "rich men and aristocrats with a developed sense of life—men like Ruskin and William Morris and Kropotkin." But, however it may have been with Ruskin in his later years, or with Morris, it is not at all clear to what degree Shaw himself—as distinct from Undershaft—was actually committed to the idea of violent revolution. For all the bluster of the preface he wrote to *Major Barbara*, or the heroic utterances of Don Juan in hell, Shaw was singularly circumspect in his advocacy of force, and even Old Hipney in *On the Rocks*, and the Judge in *Geneva*, seem doubtful of its efficacy in the present condition of mankind.

Shaw's Fabian gradualism was certainly not founded on any moral objection to the use of force. Its basis appears to have been his distrust of the masses, and his conviction that those who are given power must first be educated in its use. In Shaw's view a violent revolution would be as ineffective ultimately in altering the social balance as was the Great Revolution of 1789, unless those who directed the battle were able to administer properly the fruits of their victory.

In the early *Fabian Essays* catastrophism was explicitly rejected as a socialist method. Twenty years later, in the preface to the 1908 reprint, published three years after *Major Barbara* was written, Shaw took care once again to repudiate force as a political instrument. He accused Marx of being a liberal fatalist: "did he not say that force is the midwife of progress without reminding us that force is equally the midwife of chaos, and chaos the midwife of martial law?" He continued:

> The one thing that is politically certain nowadays is that if a body of men upset the existing government of a modern State without sufficient knowledge and capacity to continue the necessary and honest part of its work, and if, being unable to do that work themselves, they will not let anyone else do it either, their extermination becomes a matter of immediate necessity.

As for violence as such, he added:

> The Fabian knows that property does not hesitate to shoot, and that now, as always, the unsuccessful revolutionist may expect calumny, perjury, cruelty, judicial and military massacre without mercy. And the Fabian does not intend to get thus handled if he can help it. If there is to be any shooting, he intends to be at the State end of the gun. And he knows it will take him a good many years to get there.[28]

It is not altogether easy to reconcile these eminently sensible utterances with the headier passages in the gospel of Undershaft; but Undershaft, after all, reflects the pugnacious aspect of the Life Force, the blind will which must enlist the intellectual and moral faculties in its service if it is to avoid destroying what it has created. The Undershaft works in themselves are a mine of energy, as aimless and as dangerous as the lightning, and as potentially useful. Left to itself, the cannon factory is excellent evidence of what the Devil in *Man and Superman* says of humanity's self-destructive tendencies. But directed to a moral purpose it can help to bring about the seemingly impossible miracle of a super-humanity. For this reason, if for no other, it is necessary that Undershaft secure the succession in the proper line. When Barbara is in command of the cannon factory, and the Fabians are at the state end of the gun, we may look, presumably, for an end to slavery and exploitation. Power in itself is neither good nor evil. It may be the source of either. In *Major Barbara* it is a hopeful sign that the cannon factory is actively in search of the soul that will orient it toward the good, the Undershaft who will at last fulfill its destiny.[29]

The astute scholar will have no difficulty in finding a wealth of contradictions in Shaw. He wrote too much, too often, and too quickly to assure himself of complete consistency, and perhaps also he changed his mind. Yet at no time can he be said to have been a pacifist. An important advantage of Fabian gradualism was in the leisure it afforded in the preparation of the future; but as Shaw saw it, violence was very likely unavoidable, and it was always justifiable as a last resort. The cannon factory was an unfortunate, but necessary adjunct to social progress. Shaw had long ago insisted on adding a final warning to the Fabian "Manifesto" of 1884: "We had rather face a civil war than another century of suffering as the present one has been." In *Major Barbara*, Undershaft says: "Poverty and slavery have stood up for centuries to your sermons and leading articles; they will not stand up to my machine guns. Dont preach at them: dont reason with them. Kill them."[30]

Undershaft's religion is militant in an extreme degree, and in this regard he is in complete accord with the Salvation Army. Undershaft desires to devote his energies to the destruction of evil, but he has no faith in the weapons of the Prince of Peace, nor has he time to use them. It is his faith, he tells Cusins, that there are two things necessary to Salvation:

UNDERSHAFT: The two things are—
CUSINS: Baptism and—
UNDERSHAFT: No. Money and gunpowder.

CUSINS: (*surprised, but interested*): That is the general opinion of our governing classes. The novelty is in hearing any man confess it.

UNDERSHAFT: Just so.

CUSINS: Excuse me: is there any place in your religion for honor, justice, truth, love, mercy and so forth?

UNDERSHAFT: Yes: they are the graces and luxuries of a rich, strong, and safe life. . . .

There is a pause for reflection. The discussion resumes:

CUSINS: Barbara wont stand that. You will have to choose between your religion and Barbara.

UNDERSHAFT: So will you, my friend. . . .[31]

The rejoinder defines the shape of the play. The Undershaft who figures in this scene, however, is not the ultimate Undershaft. He is the realistic aspect of the hero, the capitalist, the egotist and money-maker. The mystic, the idealist, the socialist, develop later—the first scenes barely foreshadow them. Together they make the whole man, a resplendent figure too vast to be seen all at once, and by no means readily comprehensible. The difficulty of the characterization is not merely conceptual. It is in some degree the consequence of the poverty of the theater in providing the means of evoking anything beyond a conventional reality. Nevertheless in this respect the theater far exceeds the capacity of life itself.

It is certainly arguable that in *Major Barbara* Shaw came to terms, in some measure, with capitalism, conceding that great industrial empires developed in the pure self-interest of their managers may create for their employees the very conditions which are the goal of socialist activity. In this manner, enlightened capitalism and socialism may be thought to converge; and in such enterprises the management may properly be expected to come into the hands of those best fitted to direct. The result would be an aristocracy based on ability which—once the purely parasitic elements were screened out—would approximate the conditions of state capitalism, and, on a sufficiently extensive basis of ownership, would in fact be state capitalism. Such seems to be the intimation in *Major Barbara*.

In this process of evolution, Undershaft represents an intermediate stage. His business, financed by the gentle but astute Lazarus, is the service of the Life Force in its destructive aspect. But the essential character of the Life Force is not destructive. It is creative. The primal Will is the will to live, and the will to live implies the will to live properly. In Shaw's view, material well-being is the necessary condition of spiritual health. The Salvation Army manifests its recognition of this truth by doing what it can to alleviate the hunger pangs of its converts. Undershaft goes further. He provides his employees with all the attributes of the good life, save freedom, which perhaps they neither need nor want, but without which they are less than completely human. It is for their spiritual liberation that he needs Barbara: presumably it is where his work leaves off that her work begins. The way of life, as at last she sees it, lies through the factory of death: "Yes, through the raising of hell to heaven and of man to God, through the unveiling of an eternal light in the Valley of the Shadow."

The rhetoric is vague, as well as sonorous, but there is surely some glimmer of meaning in the context. Barbara says:

> I was happy in the Salvation Army for a moment. I escaped from the world into a paradise of enthusiasm and prayer and soul saving; but the moment our money ran short, it all came back to Bodger: it was he who saved our people; he and the Prince of Darkness, my papa. Undershaft and Bodger: their hands stretch everywhere: when we feed a starving fellow creature it is with their bread, because there is no other bread; when we tend the sick it is in the hospitals they endow; if we turn from the churches they build, we must kneel on the stones of the streets they pave. As long as that lasts, there is no getting away from them. Turning our backs on Bodger and Undershaft is turning our backs on life.[32]

Major Barbara's conversion is thus, like Captain Brassbound's, a matter of turning from illusion to reality. When her ideals are shattered, she is forced to a realistic appraisal of the facts, the necessary preliminary to a course of effective action. A comparison of her father's works with those of the Army in which she has served forces the realization that the salvation of humanity as it is presently constituted lies not in the rejection of material values, but in their acceptance.

For Barbara this idea opens a new career of evangelism. Henceforth, her work will be done among the strong, not the weak. Henceforth she will save, she says:

> . . . not weak souls in starved bodies, sobbing with gratitude for a scrap of bread and treacle, but fullfed, quarrelsome, snobbish, uppish creatures, all standing on their little rights and dignities, and thinking that my father ought to be greatly obliged to them for making so much money for him—and so he ought. That is where salvation is really wanted. My father shall never throw it in my teeth again that my converts were bribed with bread (*She is transfigured*). I have got rid of the bribe of bread. I have got rid of the bribe of heaven.[33]

The idea that physical well-being is a prerequisite to spiritual health is not traditionally Christian. It is a pagan idea, classic and humanistic, and from a Christian viewpoint it has only the merit of common sense. In hell Don Juan scorns the material amenities of his environment in favor of a life of eternal meditation. But Don Juan in hell has no food problems. Shaw nowhere denies the ascendancy of the spirit. *Major Barbara*, however, is concerned not with the eternal life, but with the life of the body, and it suggests an interesting way to combine the service of God and Mammon. In 1906 the war against poverty was society's primary concern. So it is still; and the wisdom of Shaw's idea becomes increasingly clear as time dispels the illusions of the past. Doubtless Shaw hoped that the war against poverty might be carried on along classic lines without the need for bloodshed. Such too is Undershaft's hope. But Undershaft appraises the nature of the future conflict realistically. From his viewpoint the factory of death is indispensable. The only question is, how much violence will be needed, and how long the sojourn with death must be before the new life begins.

In the meantime Undershaft remains in command, and doubtless will remain so, though it is clear he looks forward to the day when he can abdicate his kingship. When his son Stephen protests against having the government of his country insulted, Undershaft sets him straight with brutal realism:

> The government of your country! *I* am the government of your country: I and Lazarus. Do you suppose that you and half a dozen amateurs like you, sitting in a row in that foolish gabble shop, can govern Undershaft and Lazarus? No, my friend: you will do what pays us. You will make war when it suits us, and keep peace when it doesnt. You will find out that trade requires certain measures when we have decided on those measures. When I want anything to keep my dividends up, you will discover that my want is a national need. When other people want something to keep my dividends down, you will call out the police and military. And in return you shall have the support and applause of my newspapers, and the delight of imagining that you are a great statesman. . . .

> STEPHEN (*actually smiling and putting his hand on his father's shoulder with indulgent patronage*): Really, my dear father, it is impossible to be angry with you. . . . It is natural for you to think that money governs England; but you must allow me to think I know better.

> UNDERSHAFT: And what d o e s govern England, pray?
> STEPHEN: Character, father, character.[34]

The scene is funny; but the serious undercurrent is obvious. Undershaft and Lazarus are so deeply entrenched in the social structure as to escape the notice of the innocent, yet without doubt theirs is the decisive influence in the management of society. It is the recognition of this fundamental political fact that impels Barbara to take her place at the source of power, alongside her father, rather than in the stagnant depths of humanity.

The anarchist Victor Serge, after his long imprisonment in France during the Great War, in the preparation of which Undershaft was presumably busy in 1906, wrote in terms which fully express the socialist viewpoint of *Major Barbara*:

> In the class war which is like the other kind, but stripped of hypocrisy, the greatest humanity must be combined with the most decisive use of force. The class that wants to build a new world, forever cleansed of killing machines, must learn how to kill in battle so as not to be killed. . . . But it must learn as well—along with all those who turn resolutely to the future—to abolish a past which has put such arms into its hands. . . .[35]

As Undershaft sees it, the future conflict will very likely be grim. It may end in total disaster. But it is not humanity, it is the Life Force that is important. "Let God's will be done for its own sake," Barbara says at the end of the play, "the work he had to create us to do because it cannot be done except by living men and women." Presumably if humanity blows itself up in its efforts to evolve, other means will be found to advance the vital energy that animates us. Such an outcome would be tragic for mankind, but hardly of importance when viewed under the aspect of eternity; and, at the age of fifty, Shaw, like Undershaft, was able to contemplate this possibility without undue excitement.

Early in the summer of 1906, Barker asked Shaw for a new play with which to open the forthcoming season at the Court Theatre. Shaw decided to try his hand at a comedy about the medical profession. The new play was *The Doctor's Dilemma*.

The theme is said to have been suggested by a story Barker told Mrs. Shaw about a physician of his acquaintance who had been treated for tuberculosis at a London hospital, and Mrs. Shaw's subsequent comments on the trouble involved in treating people who, unlike Barker's friend, were useless to society.[36] There is also an anecdote regarding Shaw's friend, Sir Almroth Wright, a famous immunologist. During a visit to

Wright's clinic at St. Mary's hospital, Shaw heard an assistant reporting that a tubercular patient in one of the wards wished to be added to the list of those on whom Dr. Wright was testing his new opsonic treatment. The treatment was difficult, and Wright is said to have impressed Shaw by asking, "Is he worth it?"[37]

Whatever the immediate source, *The Doctor's Dilemma* demonstrates Shaw's lifelong interest in medical things, and it illustrates his curiously paradoxical attitude toward those who practise the art. For one who openly professed his scorn of the medical profession, Shaw was on friendly terms with a surprisingly large number of physicians. It is said that Almroth Wright advised him on the technical aspects of *The Doctor's Dilemma*. If this is true, it cannot be assumed that Shaw followed his counsel closely, for the medical discussions in the play, particularly those that touch on the physiology of the opsonin treatment, are rather more reminiscent of the kitchen than the laboratory. Aside from Ridgeon, Shaw's doctors appear to be a singularly amateurish lot, even for the time, and, from a technical viewpoint, any of the current medical melodramas of television would put *The Doctor's Dilemma* to shame.

The play was begun 11 August 1906 and was finished that year in the first week of October.[38] Barker opened it at the Court on 20 November 1906. It was generally taken to be an attack on the medical profession, just as *Major Barbara* had been taken as a criticism of the Salvation Army, and for this reason, if no other, it excited a good deal of attention in the press.

The Doctor's Dilemma belongs to the tradition of *Le Malade imaginaire*, but, while Molière was seriously ill and had therefore good reason to make light of the medical practices of his time, Shaw had no obvious motive for poking fun at doctors. He was an exceptionally healthy man, and his rare ailments had been very adequately treated. It is true that he had once been vaccinated and, in spite of that, caught smallpox, but his skepticism appears to have had deeper roots than this. Judging by his intense preoccupation with matters of health and exercise, his finicky dietary habits, and his exaggerated personal fastidiousness, one might suspect that his interest in medicine had in it some tinge of hypochondria.

In this play, at any rate, Shaw treats the science of medicine with appropriate respect. His irony is reserved for its practitioners, especially those impelled to abandon science for magic by the economic pressures of a society which refuses to subordinate the interest of the individual to the common good. The lengthy preface which Shaw added to this play in 1911 is concerned chiefly with the question of socialized medicine, and the urgency of recognizing the administration of medical care as a primary concern of the state. It ends with a list of useful admonitions to the reader, for example, "Treat the private operator exactly as you would treat a private executioner—" a maxim which, if generally followed, would justify a considerable increase in surgeon's fees. Such statements —considering the peculiar sensitiveness of the medical profession— apparently affected the drawing power of the play so much that Shaw felt it necessary to issue a flysheet along with the theater program for the first New York performance, explicitly denying any intention to malign the practice of medicine.

The Doctor's Dilemma has nothing at all to do with the problem of socialized medicine. It centers on the question of the relative value to society of two sharply distinguished human types, the irresponsible genius on the one hand, and the earnest plodder on the other, and is thus another example of the dramatic pattern of Candida. In The Doctor's Dilemma, Shaw sets up the problem in terms of an opposition so extreme that the details in some measure obscure the issue. Louis Dubedat is a brilliant young artist. As a man he is thoroughly untrustworthy. He demonstrates very exactly the single-minded nature of the artist as Tanner described it for Tavy's benefit in Man and Superman. On the other hand, Blenkinsop is a wretchedly unsuccessful slum physician, barely able to keep either his patients or himself alive. He is, however, both honest and reliable, the faithful servant of an ungrateful community. As it happens, both the artist and the doctor are gravely ill and in need of Dr. Ridgeon's attention.

In order to bring the social question sharply into focus Shaw arranged the situation so that one of the two, and only one, can be given the special treatment that will save his life. It is assumed that Dr. Ridgeon's opsonic technique is infallible, while Sir Ralph Bloomfield-Bonnington's professional ministrations are certain to be fatal. Matters turn out precisely as predicted. Sir Ralph stimulates Dubedat's phagocytes at the wrong time, and Dubedat obediently dies as a result.

The action holds no surprises. In spite of the delightful skepticism displayed in the preface, the play exhibits a perfectly orthodox faith in the miracles of modern science. Ridgeon is a scientist; Bonnington is an ass; and Nature for once takes proper account of the distinction. There is also the observation—scarcely astonishing—that in the medical profession the proportion of asses to scientists is impressively large. Nothing is said to disparage the cause of science. Dubedat falls into the wrong hands; and that is all.

The question posed in *The Doctor's Dilemma* is a problem of artificial selection: assuming that it is possible to select for survival one or another type of human being, which type is it advisable to preserve? Such an issue cannot be resolved in terms of any existing social policy. Utilitarian principles provide no way of determining whether society is better served by the honest mediocrity who labors in its vineyard, or by the genius who lives at its expense. The decision is purely subjective. The situation of *The Doctor's Dilemma* offers no satisfactory alternative. Once Dr. Ridgeon is caught up in this affair, he is doomed.

Shaw subtitled this play "A Tragedy," but the problem is posed in terms appropriate to a thesis play, and much of the play is funny. There is nothing noteworthy about Dr. Blenkinsop, save the principle he embodies, but the man has a certain sanctity which Dubedat has not. Blenkinsop is an average man, of no special importance to the social order. Why then, is it unthinkable that he should be left to die? To Ridgeon he is particularly sympathetic by reason of their long acquaintance, his personal goodness, and the close trade-unionism of the profession. But from the point of view of the race he has not much to recommend him save his moral integrity; and in giving him a degree of importance which seriously challenges the splendor of Dubedat, Shaw not only sharpens the horns of Ridgeon's dilemma, but also demonstrates his own sentimentality as a writer.

Dubedat is a genius. If it is to the advantage of society to cherish men of outstanding ability, the choice as between Blenkinsop and Dubedat is simple. But Dubedat is a blackguard. This complicates the issue. It is by no means certain that the Life Force is better served by cherishing men of genius who are scoundrels than by helping mediocre men of good moral character to survive. *The Doctor's Dilemma* thus raises the question generally of the privilege of men of genius. More particularly, it raises the problem of the sanctity of art, and the relation of the artist to the rest of the world.

In the early years of the twentieth century the relation of art to morality was still debatable. The aesthetic which Ruskin had formulated before 1855 was by no means unacceptable in 1906. Ruskin had felt that his age could make no true approach to art until it clarified its moral and social objectives. It is a viewpoint which is still widely held in socialist countries, and it was this very attitude which caused both Ruskin and William Morris to turn eventually from art to politics.

From Ruskin's standpoint, art has value only in its relation to the realities of human experience. It is neither an amusement for the rich, nor a refuge for the artist. In the social milieu the artist has a privileged position only because he serves an exceptionally useful function, the manifestation of the universal spirit which motivates our existence. Great art is the expression of great ideas. It is the revelation of truth, transmissible only through those specially clear-sighted individuals who are able to perceive truth and to communicate their perceptions to others. Consequently the artist must be, in the moment of artistic creation, a completely integrated personality, living in perfect harmony with nature and, in this sense, perfectly moral.

The artist's morality, however, is not measurable in terms of his private life. It is revealed in the seriousness and depth of his work, and in the honesty of his workmanship. It is necessary for him to be, as an artist, a man of the highest integrity. Outside of his art, his personal behavior is a matter of concern chiefly to his family or his creditors. It has nothing whatever to do with his value as an artist.[39]

It is in these terms that Dubedat is depicted. In *The Doctor's Dilemma* Shaw is careful to distinguish between Dubedat's integrity as an artist and his worthlessness as an individual. But in 1906 the question of the artist's morality was still confused by the aestheticism of the 1880's, and the controversy over the cult of decadence which the Ruskin-Whistler libel suit of 1878 had stirred up in England. The actual question in that trial had, of course, nothing to do with the artist's personal morality. After seeing a group of Whistler's paintings at the Grosvenor gallery, Ruskin had written that he had "never expected to hear a coxcomb ask two hundred guineas for flinging a pot of paint in the public's face." The subsequent lawsuit went far to ruin Whistler financially, but the farthing which the court awarded him as damages seemed to Ruskin to imply an official rejection of everything he stood for as a critic, and he resigned his professorship at Oxford in consequence. In fact what Whistler was defending was the honesty of his workmanship and the financial value of his work by current standards. But the trial brought more general questions to the fore, and the consequent publicity, together with Oscar Wilde's resounding espousal of the cult of *l'art pour l'art* stimulated the younger English aesthetes to formulate a religion of beauty, the effect of which was to elevate the artist above ordinary morality.

Shaw was as hostile as Ruskin to the idea of art for art's sake.[40] With respect to the religion of beauty *The Doctor's Dilemma* is obviously ironical. But Shaw's irony was not of the same brand as Gilbert's in *Patience.* Shaw was willing to mock the fashionable bohemianism of his time. He was not at all willing to relinquish the special privilege of the artist as priest of the Life Force. He had made fun of Morell in *Candida*. In *The Doctor's Dilemma* it was Marchbanks's turn to be satirized. Both these characters represented essential elements of his own psychic pattern. They were perhaps irreconcilable; they were not destructible.

Shaw had stated the case for Dubedat quite clearly three years before in *Man and Superman*. In that play Tanner warns Tavy that as an artist he has a purpose as peremptory and as unscrupulous as a woman's purpose in life:

OCTAVIUS: Not unscrupulous.
TANNER: Quite unscrupulous. The true artist will let his wife starve, his children go barefoot, his mother drudge for his living at seventy, sooner than work on anything but his art. To women he is half vivisector, half vampire. . . . He steals the mother's milk and blackens it to make printer's ink to scoff at her and glorify ideal women with. . . . Since marriage began, the great artist has been known as a bad husband. But he is worse: he is a child-robber, a blood-sucker, a hypocrite and a cheat. Perish the race and wither a thousand women if only the sacrifice of them enable him to act Hamlet better, to paint a finer picture, to write a deeper poem, a greater play, a profounder philosophy! For mark you, Tavy, the artist's work is to shew us ourselves as we really are. Our minds are nothing but this knowledge of ourselves, and he who adds a jot to such knowledge creates new mind as surely as any woman creates new men. In the rage of that creation he is as ruthless as the woman, as dangerous to her as she to him, and as horribly fascinating. . . .[41]

Evidently it is this formidable figure that Shaw meant to portray in *The Doctor's Dilemma*. The play is therefore, in some sense, a refutation of the antifeminism of works of the type of the younger Dumas's *L'Affaire Clemenceau*, in which woman was regularly depicted as a vampire whose natural prey was the artist. It also includes, in the person of Dubedat, as resolute an attempt at self-caricature as the sketch of Marchbanks in *Candida*. But Dubedat goes well beyond what was strictly necessary to advance the author's creative purpose. He is as completely unrestrained in gratifying his desires as was Richard Wagner, and as unscrupulous in attaining his ends.

His desires are, in any case, in no way remarkable. He wants money, women, fame, and pleasure—entirely normal desires in a young man of twenty-three. But Dubedat is evidently prepared to go beyond normal lengths in order to get what he is after, and it is the natural conclusion of the staid Victorian gentlemen with whom he comes in contact that he is a moral leper who should be sequestrated before he does some serious mischief. The question is put squarely—how far is moral turpitude to be tolerated in a man of genius? It is, of course, impossible to answer a question put in such terms, and the issue is merely indicated, since it cannot be resolved.

As between Dubedat and Blenkinsop, the problem of survival might most fairly be settled, in these circumstances, by tossing a coin. Ridgeon, however, follows his own convictions. He lets Dubedat die so that Jennifer may not discover that he is a scoundrel. That, at least, is his rationalization. As for Jennifer, her faith is such that, while Dubedat's guilt is obvious to everyone, in her eyes he is a pure and noble creature, a saint, whose actions cannot be measured by ordinary standards. There is in fact no way of proving that he is not a saint; the problem of Dubedat is far from simple. In Jennifer's opinion, Dubedat is godlike. But it is society that judges him.

Ridgeon's rationalization is well based. He is sure that sooner or later Jennifer's illusions will be dispelled and that she will see her husband in his true light. Since she has threatened to kill herself if she loses her faith in Dubedat, Ridgeon resolves to perpetuate her faith by permitting her saint to die in the odor of sanctity. These are motives borrowed from melodrama, and it would be unthinkable for Shaw to permit Ridgeon to be rewarded for so broadly romantic a gesture. For the sake of realism it is necessary that Ridgeon's motives be misunderstood, and that Jennifer should despise him as the murderer of her beloved. In this situation, as elsewhere, virtue is its own reward. The matter is therefore treated with appropriate irony, and the last act is bitterly comic.

Shaw had written Ibsen's obituary for the *Clarion* that very June, and in it objected to Ibsen's preoccupation with scenes that depend on "a morbid terror of death."[42] Archer replied in the *Tribune* the following month in a column entitled "Bernard Shaw and Death" that the ability to deal with death on the stage was the real test of dramatic genius. In following this up, Shaw announced that his next play would be about death, and also the most amusing play that he had ever written.[43]

These journalistic japes have little to do with *The Doctor's Dilemma*. It is not a play about death, although there is a death-scene in it. The death scene, indeed, is a masterpiece. It is at the same time solemn and funny and conceived on a level of comedy which nobody so far had attempted. Jennifer moves through the absurdities of Dubedat's last hour with the majesty of a priestess, making sacred whatever she touches, and her deep veneration for the pompous image her husband is constructing almost succeeds in ennobling it, just as Solveig's love almost succeeds in ennobling the life of Peer Gynt.

Dubedat's death is, presumably, his supreme artistic achievement. It is a work of cheap overstatement which casts serious doubts on the artistic value of the other masterpieces Dubedat is said to have produced. His final tableau, in fact, is so badly composed and in such lamentable taste that it is difficult to avoid the conclusion that Shaw was deliberately inflating the scene of Pre-Raphaelite absurdity which B. B.'s orgy of misquotation at the end could not fail to explode. In any case, this scene, with its reminiscences of the final moments of *La Traviata*, does not rise far enough above melodrama at any point to warrant any considerable emotional involvement on the part of the audience. It is a magnificent spoof, the effect of which is somewhere between grand opera and slapstick, a sublime manifestation of irreverence.[44]

It is entirely possible, as it has been suggested, that in composing Dubedat's death Shaw borrowed some details from the death-scene staged by the socialist lecturer Edward Aveling. Aveling, memorable chiefly through his association with Karl Marx's daughter, whose suicide he is said to have caused, was personally as ambiguous a character as Dubedat. It is reliably reported that he staged his own death-scene with appropriate ceremony, including beautiful quotations from Shelley, and a poem composed especially for the occasion.[45] But Aveling, however unscrupulous he may have been as a man, could hardly have served as a model for the frail and pretty, "though not effeminate," young artist that Shaw had in mind.

Dubedat is made of sterner stuff than Aveling. It is no accident that he reminds us of Marchbanks, the strange, shy youth of nineteen, "slight, effeminate, with a delicate childish voice, and shrinking manner that show the painful sensitiveness of very swift and acute apprehensiveness in youth, before the character has grown to its full strength." Dubedat is Marchbanks five years grown, no longer an obstreperous teen-ager, but a young man with his strength fully developed and his weakness painfully evident. Apparently in Shaw's mind twenty-three was the total life-expectancy of this character. In Shaw's plays, art and youth are generally synonymous, so much so that in *Back to Methuselah* the artistic phase of life is outgrown by the age of four.

Dubedat dies at twenty-three, but it is not the fact of his death, so much as the circumstances that surround it, that carries the real pathos of the play. Whatever is tragic in this situation inheres in the discrepancy between the manifest realities and the illusions the characters cherish. As an artist Dubedat is as much of an enigma as is Marchbanks as a poet. Ridgeon represents the type of successful physician who collects art; he appraises Dubedat's work as Lewis Carroll appraised Tenniel's drawings—with the aid of a magnifying glass—and he values it at so many strokes per square inch. Jennifer, however, needs no glass to magnify her husband's work. She is completely convinced of his greatness and, in her innocence, she is able to make what we must assume is a truer aesthetic judgment than Ridgeon's.

It must be assumed that Jennifer sees in Dubedat what the others cannot see, just as they see in him what is hidden from her. She adores Dubedat with the fanaticism of a martyr. His image is as necessary to her as is the idea of God. She may forgive Ridgeon for killing Dubedat. She cannot forgive him for trying to destroy her faith in the cause that glorifies her life. It is impossible for Ridgeon to understand this, for he does not see the fanatic in Jennifer. He sees only the woman.

The woman in Jennifer is extremely visible. She raises false hopes in the middle-aged doctor in much the same way that Candida coquettes with Marchbanks, but from a less charitable impulse. Her scornful rejection of Ridgeon in the last act as an "elderly man" is both heartless and insensitive. In some measure it disfigures her character. Evidently Jennifer is as incapable of understanding Ridgeon as he of understanding her. Thus the play, far from being a tragedy, is a drama of misunderstandings, in the nature of classic comedy, and it exhibits its characters with the objectivity appropriate to that genre. With the exception of old Sir Patrick, who has the role of *raisonneur*, and the unfortunate Blenkinsop, *The Doctor's Dilemma* has no truly sympathetic characters. The author's viewpoint is objective, and the conclusion is simply "What fools these mortals be"—a conclusion that is quite surprising in what promises to be, in the beginning, a thesis play.

In the time of Molière, comedy of this sort might have seemed funny; but some centuries of sensibility have influenced our attitudes in this respect. A view of life which is less than compassionate often leaves us with a feeling of depression which may be mistaken for the feeling of tragedy. It is likely that in calling his play a tragedy, however, Shaw had something else in mind. "The most tragic thing in the world," Ridgeon remarks in the fourth act, "is a man of genius who is not also a man of honor."[46]

Apparently Shaw meant this phrase to be taken seriously. The inference is that he considered it supremely tragic for humanity to evolve supermen who are not morally advanced in proportion to their genius. A race of highly skilled technicians devoid of social responsibility might readily spell disaster for the human species. Such fears had already served to provoke in the 1870's a reaction against science and reason similar to that which colors the thought of many in the 1970's. Long before the date of *The Doctor's Dilemma* a group of prominent writers, including John Morley, Leslie Stephen, Frederic Harrison, W. H. Mallock, and Charles Kingsley, had expressed misgivings on the subject of science and "progress," and there were many who sought a means of withdrawal from the spiritual emptiness of contemporary life. Sensitive souls like Gerard Manley Hopkins took refuge in the church. Others lost themselves in the labyrinths of symbolism or followed the dubious paths of the occult sciences. There were also those who sought a refuge from life in art.

It was at this point that *The Doctor's Dilemma* touched upon the current controversy as to the autonomy of art and the artist's position in society. This was evidently not Shaw's main concern in the play, but it was not a theme he could easily overlook. Shaw depicts Dubedat as being single-minded in his calling to the virtual exclusion of all other considerations. His deathbed speech, colored by his exaggerated concern for his posthumous press notices, affirms not only the current aesthetic creed in its most obvious form, but also the dying man's sense of martyrdom and sainthood:

> I know that in an accidental sort of way, struggling through the unreal part of my life, I havnt always been able to live up to my ideal. But in my own real world I have never done anything wrong, never denied my faith, never been untrue to myself. Ive been threatened and blackmailed and insulted and starved. But Ive played the game. Ive fought the good fight. And now it's all over, theres an indescribable peace. (*He feebly folds his hands and utters his creed*): I believe in Michael Angelo, Velazquez and Rembrandt, in the might of design, the mystery of color, the redemption of all things by Beauty everlasting, and the message of Art that has made these hands blessed. Amen. Amen. (*He closes his eyes and lies still.*)[47]

The difference between this impressive declaration, adapted seemingly from the deathbed speech of a poor musician in a short story by Richard Wagner, and Father Keegan's more eloquent credo in *John Bull's Other Island* indicates to what an extent Shaw felt the limitations of the religion of art.[48] Shaw was certainly interested in art, but like the adolescents in *Back to Methuselah*, he was quite willing to relinquish such toys in favor of more serious things and, in the light of his own high vocation, Dubedat seemed to him pathetically limited. Possibly all gospels glorify the same truth. But to Shaw, at this time of his life, Undershaft's message seemed incomparably more valid than the message of the artist and, in dying for art, Dubedat provokes at best a smile.

From *Brand* to *When We Dead Awaken*, Ibsen had gone at length into the question of a man's vocation, and he had found the sense of mission insufficient to justify a lifetime of single-minded endeavor. Both Brand and Rubek, and the long line of Ibsenist protagonists between them, are depicted as deeply unhappy men, whose excessive absorption in their work has ruined their lives and the lives of those who love them. It is likely that Shaw had a similar idea in his representation of Dubedat. Like Ruskin and Morris, Shaw had not much use for art divorced from human concerns. It was his idea that the moral ethos is a function of the awakening self-consciousness of the Life Force; consequently it is inexcusable to retreat from one's social obligations, as the aesthetes professed to do, into the ideal world of art, with its absence of morals, and its traditional libertinism.

In fact, the aesthetic climate of the *fin de siècle* in England was nothing like that of the Parisian *bohème* which Osvald so pathetically longs for in *Ghosts*. In the 1890's English aestheticism was dandified, ostentatious, and aristocratic, the expression of a professedly superior sensibility. Its purpose was to exalt the artist far above the conventions of the mercantile society that supported him into a rarefied atmosphere which was incompatible with the life of tradesmen and shopkeepers. This atmosphere was entirely conformable with the popular caricature of the superman which resulted from a casual reading of Nietzsche. As Whistler described it in his *Ten O'Clock* of 1888, art was the exclusive concern of the professional artist and was "selfishly preoccupied with her own perfection only, . . . having no desire to teach, . . . seeking and finding the beautiful in all conditions and in all times." The artist, accordingly, was no reformer. His world was completely severed from that of his fellow mortals. The grandeur of art was quite independent of the virtues of the state and had no relation whatever to the virtues and vices of the artist.[49]

For Shaw this was an untenable position. He considered himself by temperament to be both artist and reformer. He was the one on condition of being also the other and was entirely unwilling to relinquish either identification. Nevertheless the question of which of his two selves took precedence in his personality evidently troubled him a good deal, for this is the most obvious aspect of the Marchbanks-Morell dialectic which his drama so often reflects, and of which *The Doctor's Dilemma* furnishes so convenient an example. It can occasion no surprise, therefore, that the doctrine of this play is ambiguous, quite as ambiguous as that of *Candida*.

Shaw was by profession a man of advanced views, but while he neglected no opportunity to proclaim his proud superiority to middle-class convention, he never actually relinquished the puritanism of his Protestant upbringing. A superman who in theory transcended bourgeois morality was entirely acceptable to Shaw and completely defensible in Nietzschean terms, but not a superman who picked his friends' pockets in the interests of art, or blackmailed his acquaintances in order to write even first-rate poetry. In *Candida* the character of young Marchbanks was clearly a source of joy for its author. It was also a source of terror, and it is reasonable to suppose that Shaw was more closely identified in that play with the unfortunate Morell than with the *enfant terrible* with whom he was contrasted. At any rate, Marchbanks is consigned to the night and the fog, while Morell abides at home more or less cozily with his wife, his adoring secretary, and his feelings of inferiority.

In *The Doctor's Dilemma*, Shaw found Dubedat quite as fascinating a character as Marchbanks, but he had no hesitation in packing him off as summarily to another world. Ridgeon, however, is not fated to inherit Jennifer. Shaw was too partial to Ridgeon to inflict Jennifer upon him, for if there is anything harder to bear than a genius, it is the widow of a genius. Marchbanks's personal disadvantages are fully matured in Dubedat. At twenty-three he has found a Candida of his own age, more innocent, more gullible, and much less practical than her prototype in the earlier play, one who is avid to be his handmaid and his apostle among the gentiles. He has also found his own proper function, which is to die with appropriate splendor, leaving the world some samples of his greatness, while at the same time he relieves it of the embarrassment of his presence.

The Doctor's Dilemma thus turns out to be a clear elaboration of the *Candida* formula, but its doctrine—if it has one—is quite as elusive as that of *Major Barbara*, and doubtless for the same reason. In exaggerating Dubedat to the point where he is socially impossible, Shaw avoided taking sides explicitly on the question of *l'art pour l'art*. In *The Sanity of Art* he had taken the position that genius and morbidity have no necessary connection. In the preface to *Misalliance* he ridiculed the worship of artists by those who know nothing of art.[50] In *The Doctor's Di-*

lemma Dubedat is treated with something less than reverence. Nevertheless it is assumed that he is a scoundrel of genius, and in his premature death there is a deep sense of waste.

There is no doubt that all his life Shaw believed that art should serve humanity. The idea that humanity must serve the cause of art was entirely foreign to his thought; but the waste of genius had tragic implications for him, both personally and in a general sense. The man of genius represented the special effort of the Life Force, was its chief artistic achievement, and its primary thrust into the future. It was the duty of society, therefore, to cherish genius wherever it might be found. But genius must be a force for good. In combination with evil tendencies, genius constitutes a danger in proportion to its greatness and must be considered a disease of the vital principle. It is this reflection, undoubtedly, which prompted Shaw's remark that a man of genius who was not a man of honor is the most tragic thing in the world.

The tragic element in *The Doctor's Dilemma* thus has little to do with the characters themselves, or the love story in which they are entangled. It is an abstraction. If Jennifer is involved in tragedy, she is not overly conscious of it. She is conscious mainly of her mission, which is to bring to the world the message of beauty for which Dubedat lived and died; and in this task she rejoices. Dubedat's death does not crush her. On the contrary, it liberates her in his service, to which his life would have enslaved her. It is entirely consonant with this outcome that Dubedat is depicted as being quite impervious to suffering. He feels no more pain than she, neither in his body nor his soul. He is above mortality, as befits one who knows that death is no more than a condition of the Life Force. This he has on indisputable authority. He is—as he tells us—a disciple of George Bernard Shaw, "the most advanced man now living."[51]

His death, in these circumstances, is essentially ceremonial, a ritual in which he forces the others to take part. It can hardly be taken seriously, for it is certain that he will emerge periodically from under his purple pall to plague with insufferable wit whatever living rival he may have acquired in the course of time. In spite of Ridgeon, Dubedat survives in the pure form which humanity can manage only through death. Jennifer tells her would-be lover: "You did not paint those pictures which are my imperishable joy and pride: you did not speak the words that will always be heavenly music in my ears. I listen to them whenever I am tired or sad. That is why I am always happy."[52]

It is true that Jennifer is not depicted as an especially sensible person, but she serves as the lens through which the fundamental issues of the play are brought into focus. These issues have little to do with the abstractions which the characters discuss and demonstrate. As in all great drama, what is essential in *The Doctor's Dilemma* remains implicit in the action, is operative on a level somewhat below the intellectual plane, and is therefore perceived without being understood. It is certainly not in its sardonic commentary on the medical profession, nor in its half-hearted effort to evaluate the rival claims on society of the artist and the merely useful man, that this play achieves its greatness. It is in bringing into a perceptible relation the inner forces which determine a personality.

The Doctor's Dilemma is, like *Candida*, at bottom a psychological study, and in this sense the difference between the two plays indicates the general direction of Shaw's development as a dramatist in the course of the intervening years. *Candida* is rather precise in its conception, a grouping of figures with definite contour in an exact relationship to one another. It is a play of classic design, smooth and elegant in its working, but without nuance, and of no great profundity. *The Doctor's Dilemma* rehandles the theme, but in its ambiguity, allusiveness, and wealth of possible implication, it is infinitely more capacious. There is really not much to say about *Candida*: the poet's secret is hardly worth pondering. In *The Doctor's Dilemma* we touch upon a deeper mystery.

It is likely that by the time he wrote *Candida* Shaw was beginning to see that his true power as a dramatist lay less in his doctrines than in himself. Both *Candida* and *The Doctor's Dilemma* are attempts at self-analysis. The one is the reverse of the other; and it is noteworthy that in each case Shaw pronounced judgment in the guise of a beautiful woman capable of great love and great cruelty. This woman is not quite the same in the two plays, but in each case she is "the Virgin Mother" whose charms Shaw evidently found irresistible. It is characteristic of this charming figure that those she loves best cannot be hers. The young poet belongs to the night. The young artist belongs to death. Other men can have her at their peril; but she does not forgive those who stand between her and her beloved.

From a psychological viewpoint, this woman is a familiar figure. She represents the infinitely desirable and completely unattainable mother, and in one guise or another, she haunted Shaw's fantasy, so it would seem, all his life. If *The Doctor's Dilemma* has in fact some color of tragedy, evidently this has little to do with the moral question or the metaphysical conception. Genius without honor is certainly unpleasant to contemplate; but the roots of tragedy reach down far beneath adult considerations, down to the hidden depths of sensibility, into the life of the child in us. On this plane of sentiment Jennifer's choice, like Candida's, has universal poignancy; but the emergent fantasy, and the work of art which results from it, have a lighter effect. It is of the essence of the dramatic fantasy that what is most deeply felt is most often manifested as comic. If *The Doctor's Dilemma* had been subtitled "A Comedy," the point would have been immediately apparent.

The year that saw the production of *The Doctor's Dilemma*, Shaw joined the English squirearchy, which all his life he had affected to despise. In 1906 the Shaws bought the New Rectory in the little town of Ayot St. Lawrence and established themselves in the country, well away from the apartment they continued to maintain at Whitehall Court in London. The principal innovation in their new quarters was a revolving summer house built so that it could be turned to face the sun. This retreat was dubbed Shaw's Corner.

The following year the Barker-Vedrenne company moved from the Court Theatre to the Savoy. In the course of its four seasons of repertory from 1904 to 1907, this company had performed eleven of Shaw's plays, most of them directed by Shaw himself. On the whole these plays had proved profitable, thus demonstrating the existence of a paying public, small, but sufficient to support the new drama of which Shaw was still the principal proponent.

The Euripidean translations by Gilbert Murray, with which Shaw's plays were often alternated, were not financially successful. In the end, the Barker-Vedrenne company found itself in financial straits, and the deficit had to be made up by Barker and Shaw personally. By this time Shaw was beginning to look to America for the future of the venture. Toward the end of April 1907 he wrote to Barker:

> The game is up at the Court: it has not yet begun at the Savoy. Four years is enough to give to any one move in the way of high art. . . . Debating societies, which always begin on a wave of public interest in something, begin to die after four years; and the Court is nothing but a debating society. The Shaw boom, in its novelty phase, cannot last longer.[53]

He was right. The boom was over for the time. In the early part of 1908 he wrote *Getting Married*, a curious experiment in plotless comedy. It was first performed by the Barker management at the Haymarket in May 1908, and its failure in the West End brought the Barker-Vedrenne company to the verge of bankruptcy. Eight years later, William Faversham presented this play at the Booth Theatre in New York with somewhat better results, but *Getting Married*, though interesting as a play, was never a profitable enterprise. It was, nevertheless, an interesting dramatic experiment.

Shaw had called *Major Barbara* "A Discussion in Three Acts." *Getting Married* was first subtitled "A Conversation," and, later, "A Disquisitory Play." With these two plays, and the later *Misalliance, A Debate in One Sitting*, Shaw seemed to be initiating a new dramatic form, something closer to Plato than to Scribe.

It would be idle to argue the question of whether *Getting Married* is a play or not. Though there is something like a narrative progression in it, its action hangs upon a dialectical rather than a narrative thread, and it is not a well-planned composition from any standpoint. The dialogue does not develop as an orderly inquiry, nor does it end in conclusive fashion. It is rather a juxtaposition of ideas than a debate; a display of attitudes, sometimes convergent and sometimes opposed, in an arrangement that suggests free association. The ultimate source of such entertainments, no doubt, is the Platonic dialogue; but *Getting Married* comes closer to Castiglione than to Plato. Doubtless Shaw was encouraged to attempt this form by the success of *Don Juan in Hell* and *Major Barbara*, both of which are plays of discussion. But while *Major Barbara* makes its points through a dramatic action, in *Getting Married* there is no action. There is only movement.

The type of thesis play developed by Dumas *fils* centered on a debate calculated to discharge the dramatic situation in which the characters are involved, through a critical decision. In such plays the debate is normally the result of a carefully contrived plot designed to bring the issues to a head in the *scène à faire*. Dumas's plays, accordingly, demonstrate rather the ingenuity of the playwright than the originality of his ideas, and the same may certainly be said of the plays of Sardou, who followed in his footsteps.

Sardou's *Divorçons* (1880), in a wretched adaptation entitled *The Queen's Proctor*, enjoyed a spectacular success in London, and it is possible that its popularity suggested to Shaw the idea of writing an "Instructive Conversation" on the problems of marriage. It certainly did not suggest the technique. *Divorçons* hinges on the astuteness of a husband who woos his errant wife away from a dangerous rival by tricking her into a clandestine rendezvous in which his own charms become apparent. It belongs therefore to the tradition of Augier's *Gabrielle* and depends for its interest on a farcical situation rather than on a serious discussion of marriage and divorce. Shaw intended his play to develop the technique of *Man and Superman*. Unhappily, *Getting Married* has neither the magnitude of *Man and Superman*, nor the advantage of the love story which symbolizes the relations of the characters in their universal aspect. It is simply a discussion.

Getting Married takes place in the Bishop of Chelsea's Norman kitchen on the morning when the last of his daughters—Edith—is to be married to a young man called Cecil Sykes. The marriage is delayed by an unexpected obstacle. Someone has sent Sykes a copy of Belfort Bax's *Essays on Men's Wrongs*. Another well-wisher has presented Edith with an analogous work on the tribulations of married women. The result is that neither the bride nor the groom now wishes to enter into matrimony, and their doubts precipitate a long and frequently interrupted discussion on the disadvantages of marriage.

The ladies who take part in the conversation form a spectrum of female types. The unmarriageable spinster called Lesbia would like to fulfill her social obligations as a mother, but she cannot tolerate the thought of having a man around the house, particularly one who smokes. The Bishop's wife, Alice, appears to be the perfect spouse: she has no problems and expresses no opinions. A lady called Leo has been granted a preliminary decree of divorce but is unwilling to let her husband go, though she feels the need of another man to amuse her. The mayoress, Mrs. George, represents the eternal feminine. She is strong and passionate, completely devoted to her husband on condition that he tolerate her every infidelity, a charming example of constant inconstancy.

Over against these ladies is set a group of gentlemen of various ages. They are not so clearly defined as the ladies. General Bridgenorth is the Bishop's brother. He is a lovelorn bachelor whose "natural desires" are unalterably fixed upon the unavailable Lesbia. Soames, the Bishop's chaplain, is a Paulist celibate. Hotchkiss is a libertine, a professed snob, whose morality is founded solely on his sense of honor. Rejjy, whom Leo has divorced, is the conventionally lonely husband of fiction. The Bishop appears to have made the only successful matrimonial bargain. He has proven himself eminently capable both of work and of love and is evidently the ideal husband married to the perfect wife.

The Bishop has fathered four daughters; in other respects he much resembles Bernard Shaw. He is described as

> a slim, active man, spare of flesh and younger by temperament than his brothers. He has a delicate skin, fine hands, a salient nose with chin to match, a short beard that accentuates his sharp chin by

bristling forward, clever humorous eyes, not without a glint of mischief in them, ready bright speech, and the ways of a successful man
who is always interested in himself, and generally rather pleased with
himself.[54]

This lively character takes charge of the discussion, but he contributes
little to it save his controlling presence. A good deal of the incident with
which the dialogue is enlivened occurs spontaneously, seemingly without
plan or preconception of any sort. The effect is bizarre, not to say
surrealistic, and for this reason the play in our time has an unusually
modern flavor.

At a certain point in the action, Mrs. George, who is not only the
mayoress of the town but also the wife of the local coal merchant, goes
unexpectedly into a state of trance, and transmits from the transcendental plane to which she is mysteriously exalted a rhetorical declamation of
sybilline character. Her speech, which has been much admired, is in fact
an *arioso* passage which takes the play some distance into the Maeterlinckian *au-delà*.[55] Through her lips the Life Force addresses mankind in
an effort to reorient the path of evolving humanity. Consequently she
speaks for the female principle in its cosmic aspect, saying things in the
Bishop's kitchen which it did not occur to Doña Ana to say in hell. Since
she speaks for the future on the level of prophecy, it is to be expected
that nobody among her listeners will be able to comprehend. In fact,
only the Bishop understands her.

Mrs. George speaks of the liberation of woman. Woman, she says, has
done her part for the race in giving man the momentary ecstasy of love,
and in bearing his children. It is altogether unreasonable to require her to
add to that sublime function a lifetime of domestic drudgery and sexual
captivity. The argument is irrefutable, and also she speaks with the
tongues of men and of angels; but her listeners are evidently not yet
sufficiently evolved to profit by the admonitions of the Power that is in
temporary possession of the handsome mayoress. The upshot of the
discussion appears to be, therefore, that, since in the present condition of
humanity marriage is inescapable, the best that can be done to alleviate
its miseries is an arrangement in the nature of a *ménage à trois*. In this
manner an assistant-husband of pleasant conversation can be made regularly available both to lessen the boredom of the official husband and to
give scope to the wife's domestic captivity. It is purely an interim arrangement, obviously; the Life Force is certain in time to evolve something better.

This ingenious disposition, for which Shelley had furnished the precept in *Prometheus Bound*, and something of an example in his own

domestic situation, had in fact been Shaw's preferred solution to his domestic difficulties in the years before Miss Payne Townshend rescued him from his celibacy. It was after this fashion that he had maintained pleasant relations with several of his female friends and their husbands over considerable periods of time—with Janet Achurch and Charles Charrington, May Morris and Henry Sparling, Edith Nesbit and Hubert Bland, and Kate Joynes and Henry Salt, among others. In *Getting Married*, Leo and Rejjy, her former husband, effect a dramatic reconciliation on the basis that the philandering Mr. Hotchkiss is to maintain a permanent bridgehead in their home. In addition, Hotchkiss undertakes to assuage his passion for Mrs. George at the cost of undertaking the amusement of Mr. George, presumably in the intervals of duty at his other post.

The suggestion that domestic arrangements of this sort involve psychic relationships of considerable intricacy will seem gratuitous in a day when well-nigh a century of clinical experience has made us embarrassingly aware of the nature of the unconscious. It is now hardly possible for any but the very pure in heart to react innocently to Shaw's suggestion for a stable domestic situation. It is significant that two decades after the production of *Getting Married*, Noel Coward produced a play called *Design for Living* which explores rather thoroughly the situation proposed in Shaw's play, with a certain emphasis on its homosexual implications.

It is to be expected that with the current increase of insight into the psychology of personal relations, dramatic situations which formerly seemed to border on abstraction may now be seen to involve motives of considerable depth. It is doubtless unnecessary to comprehend the motives which are at work in *Candida*, for example, in order to feel their force; but, as our insight deepens, plays of this sort are seen to have interesting dimensions. The solution to the matrimonial problem proposed in *Getting Married* does not, in fact, work out in *Candida*. The first scenes of that play depict what appears to be a relatively comfortable domestic arrangement. The manly husband is drawn to the effeminate young man, who is drawn to the pretty wife who mothers them both. But the young man evidently envies his friend's position and attempts to supplant him, so that the domestic balance is upset, and we now have the two men in active competition for the woman. The result is that the wife's latent aggressiveness is brought into play to the detriment of both men, and the patriarchal structure of the Morell establishment is officially transformed into a matriarchy.

It requires no great degree of sophistication to rationalize Candida's symbolic castration of Morell. The reflection that it is in this manner that she avenges herself for what might be considered his unfaithfulness to her in bringing Marchbanks into the house, gives a satisfactory basis to a play which, in the absence of some such awareness, might seem impossibly abstract. Thus, the inner logic of a dramatic situation, upon which its acceptability depends, may be quite different from the rationalization advanced by the author through the characters.

Intimations of this sort, dynamically effective in spite of the fact that they were perhaps not present in the author's consciousness and are only dimly apprehended by the spectator, may nevertheless be essential to the workings of a play, may constitute its real emotional basis, and should certainly be implied in any really serious production in the theater. It would be an error to make them explicit, for it is in the ability to perceive and to suggest motives below the level of conscious comprehension that the genius of the dramatist lies. In *Man and Superman*, Tanner's protest against marriage is not based on the loss of his independence as a revolutionist. What he bewails is that, in appropriating him to herself, Ann is curtailing his sexual possibilities, a polite way of saying that in marrying him, she is in a measure unmanning him. Doubtless it is the fear of losing his manhood in this manner that underlies Cyril Sykes's sudden panic in *Getting Married* and Valentine's sudden depression in *You Never Can Tell*.

In *Getting Married*, the ostensible motives for the unexpected decision which resolves the central situation of the play are shamelessly frivolous. Sykes's doubts are set at rest by an insurance policy covering actions for libel arising from Edith's outspoken social views, and Edith's misgivings are assuaged by Cyril's promise to give her grounds for divorce in the event that he is found guilty of some crime. The implication is that since marriage cannot be avoided, the best that can be done is to establish safeguards against its more obvious disadvantages.

Such a conclusion may seem less than brilliant and, in truth, *Getting Married* seems uninspired from any viewpoint. Apparently, Shaw was not eager at this point in his life to shock anyone with the originality of his ideas on marriage. He had by this time been married some ten years, and he was apparently content. Whatever his personal life may have been in his salad days, he had by now come to terms with domesticity, and he had no idea of disparaging its comforts. It is significant that, aside from the melodramatic behavior of General Bridgenorth, the relations among the characters in this play, even when they are professedly adulterous, are curiously circumspect, as if they were perpetually poised on the threshold of some sexual imprudence which nothing in the world would induce them to commit.

In arranging the discussion which is the action of *Getting Married*, Shaw evidently intended to represent every viewpoint which must be taken into account in a disquisition on the subject. The result is something less amusing than a play, but far more entertaining than the panel discussions of our time. Shaw professed to have derived this form of intellectual entertainment from *A Doll's House*. In the expanded version of *The Quintessence of Ibsenism* he wrote:

> Formerly you had in what was called a well-made play an exposition in the first act, a situation in the second, an unravelling in the third. Now you have exposition, situation, and discussion, and the discussion is the test of the playwright. The discussion conquered Europe in Ibsen's Doll's House, and now the serious playwright recognizes in the discussion not only the main test of his highest powers, but also the real centre of his play's interest.[56]

This is a clear case of wishful thinking. The discussion in the last act of *A Doll's House* is indeed the *scène à faire* of the play, but it is not the climax of the action. It is the epilogue. The actual tendency of European drama in the period of *Getting Married* was, in fact, toward intimation and suggestion rather than discussion. In the time of Dumas *fils*, and for some years in the time of Ibsen, an intellectual approach to life's problems was in fashion on the stage, but, save for brief intervals, the current of drama in the course of the twentieth century was not predominantly intellectual. Shaw was actually fighting a rearguard action.

It is possible that in these years he actually believed he was in the van of the current trend, and that the drama of the future would be increasingly designed as a basis for discussion. He later told Henderson: "Both authors and audiences realize more and more that the incidents and situations of a play are only pretences, and that what is interesting is the way we should feel and argue about them, if they were real."[57] It was not, however, along the lines of *Getting Married* that the drama of social problems was to develop. The problem play, as it was conceived by Dumas, was intended to explore a *dubbio*, first through the establishment of a dramatic situation, then through a discussion of its possibilities, finally through a crucial scene in which the doubt is resolved. It was along such lines that Ibsen developed the modern play of ideas. The type of discussion play which Shaw initiated with *Getting Married* was, however, rather an extension of the Renaissance interlude, an entertainment in which opposing ideas were represented by characters who were little more than voluble viewpoints. In *The Perfect Wagnerite* Shaw had written: "There is only one way of dramatizing an idea; and that is by putting on the stage a human being possessed by that idea, yet none the less a human being with all the human impulses which make him akin and therefore interesting to us."[58] Apparently by the time he wrote *Getting Married* he was ready to abandon the notion that ideas must be dramatized in action and was willing instead to risk a dramatization through characterization alone.

The technique of Shaw's discussion plays was certainly not unprecedented in his time. After 1848 Octave Feuillet began publishing in the *Revue des deux mondes* a series of *Scènes et proverbes* which he later adapted for the stage. *Le Cheveu blanc* and *Le Pour et le contre* are salon dialogues set in a very slender narrative frame in imitation of Musset's *Caprice*. These, however, are moral discussions revolving around prurient topics, and, if Shaw had them in mind in devising *Getting Married*, he adapted the form very freely indeed.

In any case, his detail in the discussion plays owed a great deal to contemporary farce. But while the farces current in his day were normally based on an ingenious plot, pleasantly contrived and full of surprises, Shaw dispensed almost completely with the element of design, and made use of a very loose narrative structure which he evidently improvised as he went along. The disquisitory plays are therefore full of unpredictable and improbable occurrences, surprising entrances, and a variety of tricks, arranged in a setting detailed with such precise realism that the effect borders upon absurdity.

It was evidently Shaw's intention in these plays to minimize the actual to the point where the degree of emotional identification with the characters would be thoroughly subordinated to the vividness of the intellectual interchange. He had already explored the possibilities of melodrama as a method of engaging his audience's attention in an abstract question. Since farce was even further removed from reality, he expected, it would seem, that this form would provide a narrative frame so insubstantial as hardly to obtrude itself on the play of ideas. Unfortunately, the intellectual genre which Shaw meant to inaugurate with his disquisitory plays did not result in works of art of great distinction. Despite Shaw's efforts to develop this form of drama further, *Don Juan in Hell* remains the masterpiece of this genre, the first and the only one.

It is possible that the cool reception of *Getting Married* discouraged Shaw for the moment from further efforts in this vein. In March 1909 he finished a short play which he described as "a crude melodrama in one act—the crudity and the melodrama both intentional."[59] It was entitled *The Shewing-Up of Blanco Posnet: A Sermon in Crude Melodrama.* Later the subtitle was simplified to "A Melodrama," and in the preface he called the play "A religious tract in dramatic form." It is an apt description.

Apparently Shaw expected Beerbohm Tree to produce this piece in London. It ran afoul of the Lord Chamberlain, however, and was denied a license on grounds of immorality and heresy. Shaw offered it next to Lady Gregory in Dublin. After some difficulties with the government, she gave it a production at the Abbey Theatre. It played there to capacity audiences for the week beginning 25 August 1909 and was later given two private performances at the Aldwych in London. The banning of the play made somewhat more of a stir than the play itself. Shaw devoted to the question of dramatic censorship a preface which is rather more than twice the length of the comedy, and also considerably more interesting. This treatise included a noteworthy personal statement:

> I am not an ordinary playwright in general practice. I am a specialist in immoral and heretical plays. My reputation has been gained by my persistent struggle to force the public to reconsider its morals. In particular, I regard much current morality as to economic and sexual relations as disastrously wrong; and I regard certain doctrines of the Christian religion as understood in England today with abhorrence. I write plays with the deliberate object of converting the nation to my opinions in these matters. I have no other effectual incentive to write plays, as I am not dependent on the theatre for my livelihood. If I were prevented from producing immoral and heretical plays, I should cease to write for the theatre, and propagate my views from the platform and through books. . . . I object to censorship not merely because the existing form of it grievously injures and hinders me individually, but on public grounds.[60]

The censor's objection to *Blanco Posnet* was entirely comprehensible, though hardly sensible. Even by the most conventional standards this is a deeply moral play. It is perhaps not acceptably orthodox in its theology. The God who works through Blanco is apparently neither omniscient nor omnipotent, but, judging by the results, He is trying hard and may perhaps achieve ideal stature in the fullness of time. In the meantime He manifests himself in the mining camp where the play takes place in all the splendor He can muster, and it must be admitted that, considering His limited resources, He makes an excellent impression.

Blanco's sermon at the end of the play is certainly not couched in terms suitable to an Anglican clergyman, but his intentions are of the purest, and his approach to the problem of evil has, at the least, biblical authority. That the God of the Old Testament occasionally makes a mistake is indicated by the story of the Fall, and the idea that God hastens to rectify his errors is quite amply attested in the story of the Flood. The seeming blasphemy of *Blanco Posnet* is in reality a consequence of its allegory. Blanco sees God not as a supremely self-confident being secure in his omniscience but as an earnest artisan trying hard to get things right. From this viewpoint it may well be considered that, while Blanco's remarks are crudely familiar, and consequently unseemly, they are not at all out of character with the type of faith he professes. The Life Force in *Man and Superman* is, theologically speaking, perhaps too abstract to be the subject of blasphemy, but in this play Blanco is a rough preacher, interpreting scripture according to his lights, and, in the 1900's, his pulpit style might well have given offense to those for whom the forms of religion were of greater concern than its substance.

For the rest, the play is hardly objectionable save on dramatic grounds. Shaw was certainly not an even writer, and his self-esteem prevented him from being rigorously self-critical. As an exercise in amateur theology, *Blanco Posnet* certainly has its points. It brings the Life Force down to the level of the mining camp with the kind of frontier bluffness that enlivens *The Girl of the Golden West*. As a play it seems singularly inept.

Evidently, in *Blanco Posnet*, Shaw meant to write the equivalent of the sort of peasant play which Tolstoy's *The Power of Darkness* (1886) had popularized in Paris and Berlin, a work coarse in texture, brutal and vigorous in its impact, but rich in its religious implications. In Tolstoy's play the young peasant Nikita is led through a maze of wrongdoing step by step until his conscience unexpectedly explodes in a burst of moral splendor. The *raisonneur* of the play, Akim, is an exceptionally inarticulate man, by profession a cleaner of cesspools. He explains: "You keep turning things your way, you know, the way you think it's going to be best for you, but then, you see, God turns them all back his way, that's how it is. . . ."

AKIM: . . . You know how it is, you keep trying to get ahead, you know, and you forget all about God. You feel like you're getting ahead fine, all by yourself, you know, and then all of a sudden you find the load's on your own shoulders. We think we're getting ahead fine, you know, and then, you see, all of a sudden it's not good, because we left out God—

PIOTR: That's right. We can't leave out God.

AKIM: No. So, all of a sudden, it's no good, you see, no matter how good it is. But if you act according to what's right, you know, the way God wills, you know, then, you see, everything turns out fine—then, you see, it makes you feel happy all over. . . .[61]

Blanco Posnet's conversion comes about in as unexpected a fashion as Nikita's access of grace. Having stolen a horse, Blanco meets a poor woman on foot who is carrying a sick child to town. The child puts its arms around Blanco's neck. At once, Blanco's heart is touched. Knowing that he will be caught and hanged, he gives the woman the horse and walks off, crying, laughing, and singing dirty words to a hymn tune. When the story of his sudden conversion is told at his trial all those who hear it are touched also, and they conspire to save Blanco. The outcome causes him some embarrassment:

BLANCO: . . . Why did I go soft myself? Why did the Sheriff go soft? Why did Feemy go soft? Whats this game that upsets our game? For seems to me there's two games bein played. Our game is a rotten game that makes me feel I'm dirt and that your all as rotten dirt as me. T'other game may be a silly game; but it aint rotten. When the Sheriff played it he stopped being rotten. When Feemy played it the paint nearly dropped off her face. When I played it I cursed myself for a fool; but I lost the rotten feel all the same.[62]

While the traces of Tolstoy in this speech seem evident, Blanco Posnet's idea of God is not quite the same as Akim's. His approach to the problem of evil is realistic. As Blanco sees it, God is as fallible and as resourceful as man. The child Blanco tried to save dies of the croup in spite of Blanco's sacrifice; yet God turns this death to advantage. Apparently God created the croup, thinking it was a good idea. When he discovered his error, he made a man who would try to undo the evil:

BLANCO: . . . It was early days when He made the croup, I guess. It was the best He could think of then; but when it turned out wrong on His hands He made you and me to fight the croup for Him. You bet He didnt make us for nothing; and He wouldnt have made us at all if He could have done His work without us. By Gum, that must be what we're for! . . .[63]

The inference is that God proceeds by trial and error His wonders to perform. Blanco is reasonably articulate on this point. By causing some men to suffer, God arouses pity in others. Thus we are reclaimed from our indifference and become better men. In the case of Blanco, God contrived the death of the child in order to soften the hearts of the local community, which badly needed softening. Very likely because of this death the mining camp will be a better place—for a time, at least. Thus, willy-nilly, we play God's game, to our own advantage and also his. Such is Blanco Posnet's conclusion.

The picture Shaw painted in this play of the workings of the divine principle in a frontier town is perhaps not altogether convincing. It has the realism of the early cinema, no more, and this is probably the level of drama that Shaw desired to reach. Strindberg had spoken in his foreword to *Miss Julie* of the drama as a *Biblia pauperum*, a comic-strip version of reality for the edification of those who do not read. It is in this spirit that *Blanco Posnet* was conceived, and evidently it was directed to an audience not yet sufficiently evolved to receive the gospel according to Don Juan save in the form of "crude melodrama," with a liberal infusion of sentimentality. *The Shewing-Up of Blanco Posnet* thus differs from the usual Western melodrama of the time only in the character of its sermon.

In melodrama the chief dramatic principle is the elemental contest of good and evil exemplified in the struggle of good men and bad men. In the land of saloons and fancy women, where the fast draw is the criterion of intellectual superiority, the badness and goodness of men is very clearly visible and the underlying allegory can be made clear even to the least perceptive. Perhaps for this reason the frontier melodramas that Bret Harte showed in London in the early years of the century were marvelously successful, and plays like Belasco's *The Girl of the Golden West* (1905), and Moody's *The Great Divide* (London, acted, 1909), were accounted classics of the stage. It was Shaw's idea to make use of the popular genres for the dissemination of ideas. There was nothing more popular than the type of melodrama which *Blanco Posnet* exemplified.

At this time, Shaw knew less of the Wild West than he had known of New England when he wrote *The Devil's Disciple*, or of North Africa when he wrote *Captain Brassbound's Conversion*. But his documentation was better in the earlier plays. In writing about Serbia he had the advantage of Stepniak. *Blanco Posnet* was based on nothing more substantial than the novels of Bret Harte, and even as caricature it comes short of the mark. The play has nevertheless aroused some scholarly interest. As a character Blanco has been likened to Robert Macaire, the grotesque hero of *L'Auberge des Adrets* adapted into English by Stevenson and Henley as *Macaire, A Melodramatic Farce* (1885). The resemblance is not striking. It would be more reasonable to trace Blanco's ancestry to Karl von Moor, the good brother in Schiller's *Die Räuber*, the more so as the bad brother is represented in the person of Elder Daniel.

Shaw did not need to go this far for Blanco's prototype. The hero of the mining camp is obviously a first cousin of Dick Dudgeon. Like him, he believes himself to be a disciple of the devil, until at a crucial moment he is betrayed into the good deed which reveals to him the master whom he truly serves. But while Dudgeon discovers in the end—or so we are told—that he is more the preacher than the warrior, he does not feel the need, happily, to preach a sermon before the final curtain. Blanco Posnet does. He might have done better not to have indulged himself in this respect, but Shaw, as time went on, increasingly felt the need for fuller explanations.

In a letter to Tolstoy, who had manifested some interest in *Blanco Posnet* as a religious work, Shaw set forth his doctrine somewhat more clearly than Blanco could: "To me God does not yet exist, but there is a creative force constantly struggling to evolve an executive organ of godlike knowledge and power: that is, to achieve omnipotence and omniscience: and every man and woman born is a fresh attempt to achieve this object."[64]

Tolstoy did not agree. He approved neither of Shaw's doctrine, nor of his flippancy in propounding it. For Shaw, as for the later existentialists, there was no distinction between becoming and being. The individual was what he made of himself; things were what they became; and there was no a priori determinant to limit the direction of their development. Where Will is the essential motive, morality can only be a concept of relative character, arrived at by the individual in terms of his idea of what is good for all. In the existentialism of Sartre there is, of course, no teleological principle; but Gilbert Marcel assumed the existence of a divine purpose which, through a leap of faith, becomes knowable to the individual, who may then establish moral values in accordance with his knowledge. This identification of man with God takes place in anguish, for the honest action can never, in the nature of things, occur in an atmosphere of certainty. It is something of this sort that takes place, apparently, in *Blanco Posnet.*

Existentialist doctrine has not much room for an evolving deity; but while Shaw did not anticipate in any significant fashion any variety of the existentialist doctrine of the next generation, it is possible that Blanco Posnet, in his innocence, did.

The surprising *succès d'estime* of the Barker-Vedrenne seasons at the Court Theatre gave the enterprising American producer Charles Frohman the idea that a repertory of "advanced" plays under really professional management would do well financially in the West End. The year after the demise of the Barker-Vedrenne company Frohman announced a season of repertory at the Duke of York's Theatre. This was to include Granville-Barker's *The Madras House*, John Galsworthy's *Justice*, and two plays by Shaw. The first was *Misalliance*. The second was a one-act comedy entitled *Overruled*. This was to run in a triple bill with plays by Barrie and Pinero.

With *Misalliance* Shaw returned once again to the technique of *Getting Married*. It opened 23 February 1910 and was played eleven times, after which the entire repertory was scrapped for lack of popular support, and Frohman hastened to recoup his losses by putting on *Trelawney of the Wells*. Seven years later, William Faversham revived *Misalliance* in New York at the Broadhurst. It failed. But in 1953, it was once again performed in New York, with Barry Jones in the role of the energetic underwear magnate, and this time it enjoyed a long run.

It is, in truth, a tolerably dull entertainment based on an aimless narrative. The dialogue has some sparkle but on the whole it marks a low point in Shaw's career. The play includes, however, an interesting gallery of portraits and can therefore be sustained by a good cast in the flamboyant style appropriate to what was obviously intended as a comically unreal fantasy.

In *Misalliance* Shaw developed further the type of semifarcical discussion play which he had initiated two years before with *Getting Married*. The theme is not quite the same. There the subject under discussion involves principally the conditions under which marriage is endurable. In *Misalliance* the problem of selecting a husband is presumably under consideration; but what is chiefly examined is actually the relation of parents and children, and it is to this topic that the lengthy preface is addressed.

The artless narrative that supports the dialogue is unfolded in a rambling sequence of unlikely happenings. Hypatia, an exceptionally energetic girl, is the daughter of a millionaire named John Tarleton, a linen draper who has made a fortune in the underwear business. She is engaged to an effete young man named Bentley, the son of Lord Summerhays, a highly placed civil servant, now retired. Lord Summerhays has endeavored in vain to marry his son's fiancée. This situation is enlivened by unexpected guests, the first of whom fall from the sky in a flying machine which crashes into the Tarleton's greenhouse. A beautiful circus acrobat called Lina Szczepanowska steps out of the wreckage with her companion, a college friend of Bentley's named Joey Percival. All the gentlemen hasten to make more or less indecent overtures to Lina.

Hypatia immediately engages in the pursuit of Joey. There appears also a young clerk of socialist views, who comes to assassinate Tarleton for having seduced his mother and ends by being put to bed by Tarleton's wife.

The play was originally subtitled, "A Debate in One Sitting," but there is neither a debate nor a sitting, nor any clear-cut subject of discussion. The incidents are all familiar expedients borrowed from popular comedy or farce, and there are also some reminiscences of Ibsen's *Love's Comedy*. Chiefly at issue is the relation of youth and age.

In the latter half of the nineteenth century the tensions between the younger and older generations was already the subject of wide discussion. Such notable works as Turgenev's *Fathers and Sons* (1862), Ibsen's *Ghosts* (1881), and Butler's *The Way of All Flesh* (1903) served in some measure to define the issues, but the sociological problem was in fact beyond the scope of literature, a symptom of the accelerated erosion of the patriarchal family-structure in this period, and the deterioration of the vestiges of the religious and feudalistic system which had survived the Great Revolution.

In 1908 the first International Psychoanalytic Congress met in Salzburg. There is not the slightest evidence that Shaw had any inkling of what was being said there. His position on the antagonism of fathers and sons was stated in evolutionary terms without benefit of Freud. In *Misalliance* the parents do not at all inspire their children with that reverence which Ibsen's Pastor Manders regards as essential to the health of the family. On the contrary, the children in Shaw's play consider themselves more adult than their parents and criticize them with the utmost freedom. The parents, for their part, look upon their children as a punishment for their sins. Tarleton is willing to pay £1500 a year to get Hypatia off his hands, no matter, so he says, to whom.

These domestic antagonisms, in Shaw's view, are the consequences of the historical process which makes it natural and desirable that each generation should relinquish its hold on life promptly so as to make room for the next. In the preface to *Misalliance* it is urged that the old should welcome death as the earnest of rebirth in a new and better life: "Death is for many of us the gate of hell; but we are inside on the way out, not outside on the way in. Therefore let us give up telling one another idle stories, and rejoice in death as we rejoice in birth; for without death we cannot be born again...."[65]

Misalliance does not, however, in any way illustrate this invigorating thought. A good deal of witty talk goes on in the Tarleton ménage, but the generations are really not on speaking terms. The old men are quite pathetic in their sexual aspirations; the young seem to have neither passion nor romance; and the abyss that separates the children from their parents is no less profound than that which separates the young from one another. In his desire to minimize the romantic, Shaw makes Hypatia's acquisition of Joey Percival a purely mercantile operation. There is much talk of love between them, but no love.

The Tarleton house is by no means a bower of bliss. Nevertheless the incomparable Lina, presumably an example of the superwoman, finds the place so oppressively erotic in its atmosphere that she cannot abide there the night:

> LINA: Old pal: this is a stuffy house. You seem to think of nothing but making love. All the conversation here is about love-making. All the pictures are about love-making. The eyes of all you are sheep's eyes. You are steeped in it, soaked in it: the very texts on the walls of your bedrooms are the ones about love. It is disgusting. It is not healthy. Your women are kept idle and dressed up for no other purpose than to be made love to. I have not been here an hour; and already everybody makes love to me as if because I am a woman it is my profession to be made love to. . . .[66]

Lina is evidently an exceptionally touchy woman. The idea of marriage revolts her even more than the idea of love:

> LINA: . . . And this Englishman! this linendraper! he dares to ask me to come and live with him in this rrrrrrabbit hutch, and take my bread from his hand, and ask him for pocket money, and wear soft clothes, and be his woman! his wife! Sooner than that, I would stoop to the lowest depths of my profession. . . . And so you may tell your Johnny to buy an Englishwoman: he shall not buy Lina Szczepanowska; and I will not stay in the house where such dishonor is offered me. Adieu.[67]

The title of the play evidently refers to the proposed marriage of Hypatia, the vigorous middle class heiress and the exhausted aristocrat, Bentley Summerhays. It might apply with equal validity to Hypatia's marriage to Joey Percival. These two seem tolerably well suited to one another as animals, but hardly in any other fashion. Finally, it might refer to the forthcoming alliance of Bentley and Lina, who proposes to fly off with him in her reconstructed aircraft for reasons and for parts unknown. Perhaps in bringing together in this inexplicable manner the effete male and the masculine woman the Life Force is projecting some biological operation the purpose of which is not immediately apparent.

As matters stand, it would appear that any combination of its characters would result in a misalliance, and perhaps this is the intimation.

Misalliance might well have convinced a less resolute writer than Shaw that, while the forms of melodrama were hospitable to the discussion of ideas, the farcical genres were not. Shaw was not so easily deterred. After a short piece called *The Dark Lady of the Sonnets* (1910), written for the benefit of the Shakespeare Memorial Theatre, he turned, the following year, once again to the dramatic essay. The new work was called *Fanny's First Play* and subtitled "An Easy Play for a Little Theatre." It was in fact first performed at the Little Theatre in the Adelphi in London on 19 April 1911. The author was identified as Mr. XXXXXXX XXXX. Shaw called the play a potboiler which did not merit a preface. He did, however, endow it with an Induction and an Epilogue and, taken together, these provide an amusing frame for what is, in truth, a very slight piece of work.

Fanny's First Play is in three short acts. The play itself is supposedly performed privately for a group of critics whom Count O'Dowda has invited, for a fee, to appraise it for the benefit of his daughter, its authoress. The critics are thinly disguised caricatures of some actual members of the contemporary press and were chosen so as to constitute a cross section of critical opinion in 1911. Gilbert Cannon of the *Star* appears as Gunn; A. B. Walkley of the *Times*, as Trotter; E. A. Baughan of the *Daily News*, as Vaughan; and there is a young man called Flawner Bannal, who apparently represents the general run of drama reviewers. The critical framework around Fanny's first play is gay and witty, and pleasantly impudent. The intention was to satirize the critical reception of Shaw's plays, particularly the reaction to *Misalliance*, which had recently evoked exceptionally bad notices.

Shaw did not attempt here to justify his plays. He contented himself with caricaturing his critics. In the Epilogue he has them attributing Fanny's play to Pinero and Barker, as well as to himself, for a variety of reasons, both real and fanciful. Apart from the unblushing effort at self-advertisement, what is significant in the Induction is Shaw's insistence on the validity of the type of discussion-drama he was attempting to naturalize in the English theater:

> TROTTER: I am aware that one author, who is, I blush to say, a personal friend of mine, resorts freely to the dastardly subterfuge of calling them conversations, discussions, and so forth, with the express object of evading criticism. But I'm not to be disarmed by such tricks. I say

they are not plays. Dialogues, if you will. Exhibitions of character, perhaps: especially the character of the author. Fictions, possibly, though a little decent reticence as to introducing actual persons, and thus violating the sanctity of private life, might not be amiss. But plays, no. I say NO. Not plays. . . . I must ask you, Miss O'Dowda, before we go a step further, Do you or do you not claim that these works are plays?

FANNY: I assure you I dont.

TROTTER: Not in any sense of the word?

FANNY: Not in any sense of the word. I loathe plays.[68]

In sober fact, Fanny's first play is worthy neither of Barker nor Pinero, nor even of Shaw: it is worthy only of Fanny. The thesis it is intended to demonstrate is Shaw's thesis. This has to do principally with the lack of communication between parents and children; but it ranges wider—into the question of freedom and order, and the degree of permissible deviation from the accepted norms of society.

The play concerns two very respectable families, the heads of which are partners in a shop and desire to become even more closely related. For this reason Mr. Gilbey's son is engaged to Mr. Knox's daughter. Through a coincidence, both the young people have spent a fortnight in jail—the boy, for showing disrespect to a policeman who was assaulted by a young prostitute; the girl, for resisting arrest during a raid on a dance hall full of riotous students. This experience has evidently had a remarkably exhilarating effect on them. They are now resolved to throw off the trammels of respectability once and for all and to assert their individuality as free people.

The upshot of the situation is that Bobby Gilbey decides to marry the young prostitute, and Margaret Knox becomes engaged to Juggins, the Gilbey's footman, who is suddenly discovered to be a former Guards' officer and the younger son of a duke. The doctrine which this light-hearted bit of comedy propounds is not as clear as it might be. On the surface it appears to follow in the wake of *Mrs Warren's Profession* and *Getting Married*, but it goes a good deal further than either of these plays. The idea seems to be that, if each generation is to progress in its own way toward a higher cultural level, it is necessary for it first to liberate itself from the plane on which its predecessors are established. Respectability means conformity with current standards; consequently, the cult of respectability results in a static society in which any departure from the established norms is reprehensible.

In order to evolve freely society must endure the periodic revolt of its children. Those of the young who are specially qualified to free their generation from the bondage of tradition must therefore be encouraged to defy authority whenever the spirit moves them, to shock their elders, and to get into difficulties with the police. Since it is the traditional task of the police at every stage of evolution to maintain the state of things as they are, progress is always made in the teeth of law and order. Peace and progress are antithetical ideas, and it is only at the expense of the one that the other is maintained. Evolution implies a continual destruction of existing forms. Presumably its dialectic results in each case in a synthesis which will in turn invite attack.

There are, however, significant qualifications to this revolutionary doctrine. Not everyone is fitted by nature to defy the existing order. For that it is necessary to be self-sufficient in a very special sense. Those who are not conscious of representing the Life Force in its evolutionary aspect are not fitted to act for themselves and had best conform to the accepted cultural modes of the day; otherwise they risk disaster. In *Fanny's First Play* Mrs. Knox, as *raisonneur*, represents the middle-class puritanism which is respectable for her time. She is nevertheless aware of the joyful spirit which animates and liberates the race:

> MRS. KNOX: . . . I say that if youve happiness within yourself, you dont need to seek it outside, spending money on drink and theatres and bad company, and being miserable after all. You can sit at home and be happy; and you can work and be happy. If you have that in you, the spirit will set you free to do what you want and guide you to do right. But if you havent got it, then youd best be respectable and stick to the ways that are marked out for you; for youve nothing else to keep you straight.[69]

From Mrs. Knox's viewpoint the power that guided her daughter Margaret into an act of violence and then saved her from its dire consequences, was a power for good, in the nature of divinity. There is also a power for evil which leads men into wanton actions from which nobody benefits. These two forces are distinguishable only by the moral conscience of the individual. Luckily there is such a thing:

> MRS. KNOX: I dont say she was ignorant. But I do say that she didnt know what we know: I mean the way certain temptations get a sudden hold that no goodness nor self control is any good against. She was saved from that, and had a rough lesson too; and I say it was no earthly protection that did that. But dont think, you two men, that y o u l l be protected if you make what she did an excuse to go and do as y o u d like to do if it wasnt for the fear of losing your characters. The spirit wont guide y o u , because it isnt in you; and it has never been: not in either of you.[70]

The result of such a doctrine is to distinguish from the rest of society an elite endowed with a special moral sensibility which frees them from the laws of the collective. These individuals in whom the Will is especially active constitute the forefront of civilization, and it is essential that they be free to follow their impulses. Such individuals constitute a community of the elect, responsive to a higher law than that which the police enforce.

Presumably Margaret Knox belongs to this race of super-beings. She somehow discovered her special talent immediately after her first conflict with the law, and is henceforth independent of the imperatives which customarily guide ordinary people. Such people must be respectable, for respectability means conformity with established rules, which are serviceable for those who have no intimation of the morality of the future. For such people, however, there is sometimes a rude awakening:

> MRS. KNOX: . . . We dont really know whats right and whats wrong. We're all right as long as things go on the way they always did. We bring our children up just as we were brought up; and we go to church or chapel just as our parents did; and we say what everybody says; and it goes on all right until something out of the way happens: there's a family quarrel, or one of the children goes wrong . . . And then you know what happens. . . . We find out then that with all our respectability and piety, weve no real religion and no way of telling right from wrong. Weve nothing but our habits; and when theyre upset, where are we?[71]

Obviously, Mrs. Knox is extending here, in terms appropriate to her station in life, the truisms which Shaw had long ago set down in *The Quintessence of Ibsenism* and exemplified in a number of plays. Ibsen had pointed out in *Ghosts* that we are haunted by dead truths, ideals which perhaps had validity in their time, but are no longer suited to the realities of the present. "As a general rule," says Dr. Stockmann in *An Enemy of the People,*

> a normally constituted truth has a life span, let us say, of some seventeen or eighteen years, at the most twenty; seldom longer. Truths as old as that have rarely much flesh on them. Yet it is not till then that the majority will take them up and recommend them as wholesome fare. . . . The truths the masses acknowledge today are the very truths held by advanced thinkers in the days of our grandfathers. We who constitute the advanced guard of today no longer acknowledge them as true. In my opinion, only one truth is certain always: and that is, that no society can live a healthy life on the dry bones of outworn ideas.[72]

Mrs. Knox is more keenly aware of the dangers of following one's natural inclination in moral matters than is Dr. Stockmann, for in her view not everyone is cut out to be an individual. In the case of Mr. Knox, who is evincing an unaccountable taste for whisky and soda, she sees no alternative save to condemn him to the ideals of his fathers:

MRS. KNOX: I blame nobody. But let him not think he can walk by his own light. I tell him that if he gives up being respectable he'll go right down to the bottom of the hill. He has no powers inside himself to keep him steady; so let him cling to the powers outside him.[73]

It would seem that the spiritual guide which directs Margaret Knox, but not her father, is a pre-eminently English impulse. In *Fanny's First Play* the French lieutenant Duvallet speaks enthusiastically of the turbulence of English family life, and the degree to which the young cast off the bonds of filial servitude in England. He is impressed by "the exhilarating, the soul-liberating spectacle of men quarrelling with their brothers, defying their brothers, refusing to speak to their mothers. In France, we are not men: we are only sons—grown-up children. Here one is a human being—an end in himself."[74]

Unfortunately, the special endowments of the younger generation of Knoxes and Gilbeys do not lead in this play to an impressive conclusion, and the narrative is resolved in a series of improbabilities which need not be taken seriously. In a situation that borders so closely on extravaganza, it is doubtless acceptable that the noble footman should marry the shopkeeper's daughter, while the partner's son marries a congenial prostitute, but this outcome—while apt as a foreshadowing of the coming obliteration of class frontiers—is convincing only on the plane of make-believe.

It was one of Shaw's favorite propositions that marriages should be made in accordance with eugenic considerations, regardless of the restrictions of caste or wealth. In *Fanny's First Play* the question of misalliance is taken up much more thoroughly than in *Misalliance*, but in both cases the plot is treated with such carelessness as to suggest an irrelevancy to be got out of the way as speedily as possible. In these plays Shaw wished, evidently, to stress his argument, not his narrative; and very likely he went to some trouble to make his story so improbable that his audience would not be drawn into it.

The silliness of the anecdote in these plays is, in fact, so great as to produce the type of alienation which Brecht thought necessary to a dispassionate argument. But experience shows that in the theater the narrative and the discussion are not readily separable, so that careless workmanship in the one invariably results in the derogation of the other. In spite of the engaging Induction and the interest of its theme, *Fanny's First Play* is no longer likely to be a rewarding experience in the theater. In its day, however, it had great topicality, and in its initial production at the Little Theatre in London it was received with gratifying enthusiasm, the more so as the secret of its authorship was carefully guarded. Before the year was up, it had a total of 624 performances.

Overruled is dated 1912. In the preface Shaw wrote:

> Of one thing I am persuaded: we shall never attain to a reasonably healthy public opinion on sex questions until we offer, as the data for that opinion, our actual conduct and our real thoughts instead of a moral fiction which we agree to call virtuous conduct, and which we then—and here comes in the mischief—pretend is our conduct and our thoughts. . . .[75]

One might conclude from this language that in *Overruled* Shaw would restate the position which he had so earnestly advanced two decades earlier in his Ibsenist period. In fact, *Overruled* is a particularly innocuous farce involving the relations of two married couples who contemplate infidelities of which they are incapable. The subject under discussion in this little play is, accordingly, no longer misalliance but adultery. In *Overruled*, the respective spouses are properly married and quite fond of one another, but they also enjoy, presumably, occasional lapses from their mutual devotion, or at least, they enjoy the prospect of such lapses. The play does not go very deeply into this matter. While the problem of adultery obviously includes emotional profundities which are beyond the scope of farce, the assumption in conventional situations of this type is that, underlying their comic complications, there is an undercurrent of passion of which the farcical situation is the comic indication, so that the subject of farcical treatment might, if taken seriously, quite easily become tragic.

The situation in *Overruled*, however, is such that it could not be taken seriously in any circumstances. The revolt of the young people in *Fanny's First Play* is meaningful as comedy only if we can assume that it costs them something, psychically speaking, to break with the traditions which confine them. But since it was important for Shaw to disparage the sentimental relationship of parents and children, the play has not a sufficiently deep emotional basis to support the type of abstraction which farce entails. The same may be said of *Overruled*. It is simply an exercise in wit.

Farce operates on the margin of traditional morality. Its world is a makeshift Arcadia in which everything that is normally forbidden is readily attainable. It depends, nevertheless, on the assumption that the real world is there, doing business as usual in an atmosphere of absurdity from which the characters of the farce are temporarily exempted. In farce the usual inhibitions which limit social behavior are not negated. They are, on the contrary, affirmed constantly, but in an atmosphere of permissiveness which makes it both sensible and delightful to disregard them, the more so as the characters involved are eager to transgress the social norms, and experience no sort of inner conflict in the process. Thus the author, the audience, and the characters of the fantasy enter into an implicit conspiracy to cheat the psychic censor, and it is, apparently, in this connivance of individuals at the expense of the collective idea that the naughtiness of farce consists.

In the atmosphere of farce, life may be caricatured to the point of unreality, but the action generally has the logical solidity of a game of chess, so that all happenings are credible provided they conform to the rules of the game. Such fantasies are, however, permissible in a rigidly organized social environment only on the assumption that they need not be taken seriously. Farce, accordingly, is the most relaxed of the dramatic genres and the most rational. It represents an area of the imagination in which the reality principle is least assertive while at the same time the logical framework is flawless. For this reason, farce is most hospitable to purely hypothetical situations but, because of the nature of the fantasy, it is less amenable to a discussion of ideas than is comedy. In farce, ideas are suggested; normally they are not discussed.

In Shaw's farces, unlike those of Labiche or Courteline, social conventions are neither eluded nor disparaged. They are subjected to a frontal assault, and an attempt is made to destroy them. The result is to dissipate the peculiar atmosphere in which farce ordinarily functions and to place the action, however preposterous, in a serious light.

The assumptions of *Fanny's First Play* negate the idea that there is any natural bond between parent and child. The break in normal domestic relations simply affirms these assumptions, and the only element of comedy results from the surprise of Knox and Gilbey when the naughtiness of their children is brought to their attention. There is no naughtiness whatever in *Overruled*. There the beautiful Mrs. Lunn is cruelly bored by the amorous protestations of Mr. Juno, while the susceptible Mrs. Juno appears to have only contempt for her diminutive husband with his waxed moustache and his fussy ways. The consequence is a *reductio ad absurdum* of the idea of romantic love, domestic bliss, its adulterous corollaries, and the associated social postures. This rather inclines one to sadness than to laughter, for normally it is the circumvention of an idea that is comic, not its destruction. The mood of *Overruled* is grim, not gallant; and in general the result of Shaw's technique in these plays is to reduce the characters to dimensions more meager even than those of farce—virtually, to points of view—and the narrative, to a witty repartee relieved by an occasional flash of humor. It may be concluded that farce was not Shaw's strong point. He was too earnest to be successful in a genre in which it is above all important not to be earnest.

In January 1912 Shaw wrote Pinero that he was working on a religious play, something like *The Sign of the Cross*, with a part for a lion, and he asked Pinero if he knew of anyone who could play a lion. Shaw had reviewed Wilson Barrett's *The Sign of the Cross* sixteen years before, in January 1896. At that time he had written:

> The play is a monument of sacred and profane history. The influence of Ibsen is apparent throughout, the Norwegian keynote being struck by Mr. Barrett himself in the words: "How many crimes are committed under the cloak of duty!" With scathing, searching irony, and with resolute courage in the face of the prejudiced British public, he has drawn a terrible contrast between the Romans ("Pagans, I regret to say," as Mr Pecksniff remarked of the sirens), with their straightforward sensuality, and the strange perverted voluptuousness of the Christians, with their shuddering exaltations of longing for the whip, the rack, the stake, and the lions. The whole drama lies in the spectacle of the hardy Roman prefect, a robust soldier and able general, gradually falling under the spell of a pale Christian girl, white and worn with spiritual ecstacy, and beautiful as Mary Anderson. As she gradually throws upon him the fascination of suffering and martyrdom, he loses his taste for wine; the courtezans at his orgies disgust him; heavenly visions obsess him; undreamt of raptures of sacrifice, agony and escape from the world in indescribable holiness and bliss tempt him; and finally he is seen, calm and noble, but stark mad, following the girl to her frightfully voluptuous death. It is a tremendous moral lesson; and though I am pagan enough to dislike most intensely the flogging and racking and screaming on the stage (I am really such a bloodless creature that I take no delight in torture), yet no doubt it helps to drive the irony of the theme home.[76]

This seemingly ingenuous account misrepresents Wilson Barrett's intentions in *The Sign of the Cross* so far that it might well have given the author a cause of action. The play is in fact a perfectly conventional Christian melodrama, with a full complement of Christian martyrs, pagan sadists, brutal gladiators, and the usual menagerie, as well as the pure Christian maiden dressed, in spite of all her difficulties, in white robes always fresh from the laundry, a virgin of such overwhelming purity as to cause any right-minded lion to cringe in terror. The spectacle was lavish and richly sentimental in tone. It was framed to point the inevitable triumph of Christian piety over the dissolute forces of paganism in the time of Nero. The interpretation which Shaw published in the *Saturday Review* must have been infuriating.

In 1912 the censorship of religious plays was already much relaxed, but in 1896 religious melodrama was still a venturesome genre, attended by some of the exciting hazards which add zest to the outspoken sex-drama of our day. In the climate of religion in England at that time, plays on biblical subjects ran a constant risk of official censure, and great tact had to be exercised in avoiding the more sensitive areas of church doctrine. Three years before the production of Barrett's play, in 1893, Oscar Wilde's *Salomé* had been refused a license. The veto precipitated a considerable discussion in the press as to the propriety of treating sacred subjects in the theater in any form.[77]

The controversy was not new. Bulwer-Lytton's novel, *The Last Days of Pompeii* (1834), had been dramatized both by Buckstone and Fitzball immediately after its publication, and it was adapted for the stage many times thereafter, always in the face of clerical opposition. The latest version, George Fox's *Nydia*, was an opera. This was produced the year before *The Sign of the Cross*, and Shaw gave it a cruel review.[78] But *The Last Days of Pompeii* and its numerous derivatives were not, strictly speaking, on a scriptural subject. The story concerns the love of the blind flower girl Nydia and the proselytizing zeal of the saintly Olinthus, who converts the principal characters to the new faith. It is a thrilling story about Christians and pagans which has something in common with stories about cowboys and Indians, but nothing to do with the Bible.

In 1880, however, Lew Wallace's *Ben Hur, a Tale of Christ*, took the bull, so to speak, by the horns and firmly established religious melodrama as a popular genre. The viability of this formula was amply attested to by Sienkiewicz's *Quo Vadis?* (1896). This was dramatized in 1900, again in 1902, and yet again in 1912. The resulting plays were frankly based on scriptural themes, and all were vastly successful. Nevertheless, the topic was delicate and continued to be so for some time.

The Sign of the Cross does not touch directly on a scriptural topic, and while the divine influence is manifested in it, there is no direct use of the image of Christ, or even of his name, which was changed to Chrystos to avoid offending the more sensitive ears in the audience. Nevertheless it is in the name of Christ that the lovely Mercia converts the prefect Marcus Superbius to a view of life inaccessible to infidels and, after his mystical illumination, leads him to martyrdom, and presumably to glory. In the somewhat heady blend of *eros* and *agapé* which envelops these lovers, there is nothing even vaguely reminiscent of Ibsen, save perhaps the phrase "Chrystos has conquered," which may have been suggested by *Emperor and Galilean*.

This play was enormously popular in London in spite of the scathing comments of the more literate critics. Archer called it a "salvationist pantomime."[79] Shaw's interpretation was, as we have seen, more imaginative. Nevertheless, when Shaw came to write *Androcles and the Lion* sixteen years later, he did not develop the interesting contrast between Christian masochism and pagan voluptuousness which Ibsen had dramatized in *Emperor and Galilean*, and which Shaw himself had played on sardonically in his review of *The Sign of the Cross*. In 1912 Ibsenist themes were no longer uppermost in Shaw's mind. What chiefly interested him at this time was the evolutionary aspect of early Christianity, considered as a stage in the progressive development of the vital spirit.

In dramatizing the transitional period between the Roman Empire and the Christian Middle Ages Ibsen had intended to represent the Emperor Julian's tragic attempt to institute a perfect state in which freedom with responsibility would be the birthright of every individual, and all men would be self-mastered, free of external constraint. But in Ibsen's play, Julian goes about his mission the wrong way round. He tries to restore paganism by force. It is out of Christianity that the Third Empire must develop:

> MAXIMUS: . . . You have tried to make the youth a child again. The empire of the flesh is swallowed up in the empire of the spirit. But the empire of the spirit is not final, any more than the youth is. You have tried to hinder the growth of the youth—to hinder him from becoming a man. Oh, fool, who have drawn your sword against that which is to be—against the third empire, in which the twin-nature shall reign!
>
> JULIAN: And he—?

MAXIMUS: The Jews have a name for him. They call him Messiah, and they await him.

JULIAN (*slowly and thoughtfully*): Messiah?—Neither Emperor nor Redeemer?

MAXIMUS: Both in one, and one in both.

JULIAN: Emperor-God: God-Emperor. Emperor in the kingdom of the spirit—and God in that of the flesh.

MAXIMUS: *That* is the third empire, Julian![80]

Julian is unable to achieve this ideal, and on the eve of his crucial battle, he has a vision of his enemy and of the manner of his victory:

JULIAN: . . . Then I looked down at my own earth—the Emperor's earth, which I had made Galileanless—and I thought that all I had done was very good.

But behold, Maximus—there came a procession by me, on the strange earth where I stood. There were soldiers, and judges, and executioners at the head of it, and weeping women followed. And lo!—in the midst of the slow-moving array, was the Galilean, alive and bearing a cross on his back. Then I called to him, and said, "Whither away, Galilean?" But he turned his face toward me, smiled, nodded slowly, and said, "To the place of the skull."

Where is he now? What if that at Golgotha, near Jerusalem, was but a wayside matter, a thing done, so to speak, in a passing, in a leisure hour? What if he goes on and on, and suffers, and dies, and conquers, again and again, from world to world?[81]

Translated into Ibsenist terms, *The Sign of the Cross* barely resists the sort of interpretation Shaw gave it. It demonstrates the passage of a presumably normal citizen from one type of sensuality to another, from the robust appetites of a healthy pagan to the voluptuousness of asceticism and death, that is to say, from the world of the Emperor to the Empire of the Galilean. In *Androcles and the Lion* Shaw forebore to involve his characters in this kind of spiritual transformation. Shaw's Roman captain stoutly resists conversion. He is seduced from his native paganism neither by Lavinia's beauty nor by the contemplation of the more or less resolute martyrs he has marched into the circus. He is an estimable young man without faith and preserves his common sense in the face of every temptation. It is Lavinia who sheds her illusions in the hour of trial:

THE CAPTAIN: . . . What you are facing is certain death. You have nothing left now but your faith in this craze of yours: this Christianity. Are your Christian fairy stories any truer than our stories about Jupi-

ter and Diana, in which, I may tell you, I believe no more than the
Emperor does, or any educated man in Rome?

LAVINIA: Captain: all that seems nothing to me now. I'll not say that
death is a terrible thing; but I will say that it is so real a thing that
when it comes close, all the imaginary things—all the stories as you
call them—fade into mere dreams beside that inexorable reality. . . .[82]

The stout Ferrovius also is faced with a choice of faith. Lavinia gives
him sensible advice in his critical hour:

LAVINIA: Nothing but faith can save you.

FERROVIUS: Faith! Which faith? There are two faiths. There is our
faith. And there is the warrior's faith, the faith in fighting, the faith
that sees God in the sword. How if that faith should overwhelm me?

LAVINIA: You will find your real faith in the hour of trial.[83]

What Ferrovius finds in his hour of trial is not peace, but a sword. He
has not, as he had hoped, the ability to let himself be butchered by
gladiators. In the face of the enemy he turns naturally to the strength of
his arm, where his true faith lies, and his victory affirms the gospel of
Undershaft, not the gospel of the Prince of Peace.

Like Spintho, who is terrified by the prospect of death, Ferrovius loses
his illusions in the moment of truth and discovers himself as he really is.
His victory does not, however, constitute a defeat for Christianity, any-
more than does the victory of the reformed pugilist who foreshadows
him in *Major Barbara*. On the contrary, he affirms its militant element,
which does him honor. With relation to the propagation of the faith,
Ferrovius stands in the same relation to Christianity as Undershaft to
socialism. He is an available instrument of power; but as a force he is
essentially neutral. He embodies the vital energy of the will to live: it is
obvious therefore that in his hour of trial he will exert himself to the
utmost in order not to die.

The conversion of Ferrovius, under these conditions, is of the same
order as that of Blanco Posnet, but it is rather more readily comprehensible, and, of course, it is much more spectacular. It is so spectacular,
indeed, that from a dramatic viewpoint it quite overshadows the conversion of Lavinia, which is accomplished more subtly. In her hour of trial,
Lavinia too discovers her real faith:

THE CAPTAIN: Are you then going to die for nothing?

LAVINIA: Yes: that is the wonderful thing. It is since all the stories and
dreams have gone that I have now no doubt at all that I must die for
something greater than dreams or stories.

THE CAPTAIN: But for what?

LAVINIA: I dont know. If it were for anything small enough to know, it would be too small to die for. I think I'm going to die for God. Nothing else is real enough to die for.

THE CAPTAIN: What is God?

LAVINIA: When we know that, Captain, we shall be gods ourselves.

THE CAPTAIN: Lavinia: come down to earth. Burn the incense and marry me.

LAVINIA: Handsome Captain: would you marry me if I hauled down the flag in the day of battle and burnt the incense? Sons take after their mothers, you know. Do you want your son to be a coward?

THE CAPTAIN (*strongly moved*): By great Diana, I think I would strangle you if you gave in now.

LAVINIA (*putting her hand on the head of Androcles*): The hand of God is on us three, Captain.[84]

This is the sheerest melodrama, but it has a serious implication. The implication is that in her critical hour Lavinia finds it imperative to affirm above all the inviolability of her will, which constitutes her dignity as a human being and is the transmissible quality which ensures the vitality of the species. Fortitude is a good in itself, worth dying for even in the abstract; for if, through a process of artificial selection, only the submissive were allowed to survive, humanity must be irretrievably impoverished in the process. It is paradoxical that only the strong brave the lions; but it is part of the miracle of life that somehow the strong survive in spite of the lions, and, surviving, impart their strength to their children. The union of Lavinia and the handsome Captain, in case it takes place, is supervised, in true Schopenhauerian fashion, by the Idea of the child who so far exists only *in posse*. That Idea is precise, and is defined by the special qualities they embody, which is the source of their mutual attraction. The child which they are to realize must be brave. No other children need apply.

Thus *Androcles and the Lion* extends the doctrine of *Major Barbara*, the theme of which it in part recapitulates. When Lavinia loses her faith in Christ and the myth of salvation, she discovers the God within herself, and this God she cannot deny without a complete sacrifice of her personality, that is, without the complete annihilation of her will. On the threshold of death, she understands what it is in her that can survive death. She is then no longer loyal to Christ, but she is loyal to the divine principle within herself, and for that principle she is willing, if need be, to die.

As between Caesar and Lavinia, the issue involves, ultimately, not freedom of worship, but the freedom of the will. For Lavinia, as for Androcles, this above all is sacred. To Ferrovius's strength and to Androcles's lion, Lavinia owes her life. Her dignity is her own affair, and that she defends by herself. In the hour of trial the hand of God is, as she says, upon them: their victory is God's victory. The play celebrates, therefore, not the victory of the Galilean over the paganism of Rome, but the victory of the Life Force over the powers that conspire to resist it—tradition, passivity, obedience, and fear.

Androcles and the Lion is not only one of Shaw's most amusing plays, it is also one of his most successful attempts to combine the *utile* with the *dulce*. Thematically, it develops the doctrine of *Major Barbara* and *The Devil's Disciple*, both of which are designed to provide hours of trial in which the hero may find himself. Dick Dudgeon is an anarchist: it is possible that Shaw found him faintly ridiculous, as Ibsen found Dr. Stockmann; but in one respect Shaw identified himself completely with this unruly character. Dick Dudgeon is willing to die for a concept of human dignity, inseparable from the freedom of the individual, which is the vital principle of existence. With Dick Dudgeon, as with Lavinia, the struggle, at bottom, is between the forces of life and death.

The situation in *Androcles and the Lion* is not similar to that developed in Anouilh's *Antigone* (1944), but the analogy is striking. The problem under discussion in *Antigone* touches the theme of *Misalliance* more closely than that of *Androcles and the Lion*, that is to say, the conflict of generations; but in her insistence on dying "for nothing," in the face of Creon's patient and practical opposition, Antigone exemplifies—perhaps self-consciously—something of the existentialist posture which Lavinia innocently assumes in Shaw's play, written thirty-two years before. Lavinia, indeed, has none of Antigone's aggressiveness. She is not a militant teen-ager, nor does Shaw reproach her with masochism. She has nothing in common with the heroine of *The Sign of the Cross*. Lavinia hears no voices. She is in no sense mad. But in her insistence on having her will she demonstrates once again the doctrine that Mrs. Knox announces in *Fanny's First Play*, that social progress is possible only insofar as the gifted are willing to outrage the established conventions of their time. It is in this conviction, by no means entirely rational, that Lavinia affirms her intention of exerting herself in the service of the God who is not yet.[85]

The goal toward which the emperor Julian strives in Ibsen's *Emperor and Galilean* is an ideal anarchy, a condition which Ibsen tried to define both in sociological and psychological terms in all his works. Lavinia is not so definitely oriented. She is resolved to live—or if need be to die—not for any special religion, but for religion. It is her belief that all creeds are in essence the same and embody common principles of charity, generosity, justice, and mercy. Like Major Barbara, she is a creature in search of God, and her conversion in the Coliseum precisely parallels the conversion which Barbara undergoes in the factory of death. From *The Devil's Disciple* to *Androcles and the Lion* the underlying concept is perfectly consistent. If one listens closely, it is possible to hear in all these plays the voice of Father Keegan enunciating in terms of varying solemnity and amplitude, but with quite astonishing clarity, his vision of the godhead in which all life is human and all humanity divine, in short, the dream of a madman.

Androcles and the Lion, which Shaw called "A Fable Play," is a notable example of Shaw's use of a popular genre for a serious purpose. Its subject matter is far from simple. It is in some ways one of Shaw's most serious plays, but its technique was derived from the Christmas pantomime—in form it is a play for children.

Following the vogue of J. R. Planché's "fairy extravaganzas," the Christmas pantomimes specialized in fairy stories and popular fables treated in more or less comic fashion, with elaborate settings and marvels of stage engineering. Stage animals were an essential element of these shows, and there were highly paid specialists in animal-clowning who devoted themselves to these roles. *Androcles and the Lion* is not a typical example of this sort of entertainment. It is, in fact, a high comedy sandwiched between two scenes of extravaganza, one in the prologue and one at the end. It seems unlikely that a serious theme might be developed under these conditions, but in this genre Shaw's talent found its fullest scope. He was himself a genius sandwiched between layers of extravagance, and the mood of *Androcles and the Lion* suited him perfectly. It is very arguable that this was Shaw's highest achievement in the comic genre. It certainly does not have the provocative quality of *Major Barbara*, nor anything like the comic perspective that is unfolded in *Man and Superman*; but it is difficult to find anything quite so delightful in all the literature of the theater, and beyond doubt it is one of the great masterpieces of the modern stage.

In turning from the tight realism of his early plays to the techniques of melodrama and extravaganza, Shaw evidently meant not only to reach a wider public but also to compensate for the polemic character of his plays through the greater freedom which these forms permit. They had another advantage. Maeterlinck had attempted in plays of the order of *Pelléas et Mélisande* to reach a higher level of abstraction than the realistic drama permitted by setting his narrative in the long ago and far away, as far from current reality as possible. In much the same way, Shaw found it convenient to remove his situations further and further from the everyday world in order to emphasize the parabolic nature of his narrative. His technique in this respect recalls the efforts of the postimpressionist painters to withdraw their art as far as possible from the representation of external nature in order to touch a reality which sensual observation obscures.

Gay and Fielding had long ago demonstrated the possibilities of burlesque as a medium of political comment, and Meilhac and Halévy in France, and in England, W. S. Gilbert, had amply illustrated the uses of extravaganza as social satire.[86] Shaw, however, in spite of his professed antipathy to Gilbert, to whom he obviously owed much, was to develop the Gilbertian method far beyond the limits of Gilbertian satire. In *Androcles and the Lion* he made use of the fable of Androcles, but the play is not a fable; nor is it, in the usual sense of the word, an extravaganza. It is a new dramatic form which has no precise parallel in English drama, nor even in the drama of Shaw. Although many of the plays of his senescence from *The Apple Cart* (1929) to *Geneva* (1938–39) were in the nature of extravaganza, nothing that he achieved along this line approached either the charm or the cogency of *Androcles and the Lion*. It remains the classic, and unique, example of the merging of the extremes of drama—the serious and the farcical—in a unified plot structure.[87]

The preface to *Androcles and the Lion* includes an exhaustive interpretation of the New Testament from a Fabian point of view. This essay touches on most of Shaw's favorite topics and may well be considered a compendium of his political and social ideas. As might be expected, the full-length description of Jesus which it includes bears a strong similarity to the self-portrait which Shaw was still diligently retouching.[88] According to Shaw, Jesus advocated:

> communism, the widening of the private family with its cramping ties, into the great family of mankind under the fatherhood of God, the abandonment of revenge and punishment, the counteracting of evil by good instead of by a hostile evil, and an organic conception of society in which you are not an independent individual but a member of society, your neighbor being another member, and each of you

members one of another, as two fingers on a hand, the obvious conclusion being that unless you love your neighbor as yourself and he reciprocates you will both be the worst for it. He conveys all this with extraordinary charm, and entertains his hearers with fables (parables) to illustrate them.[89]

From this, and similar passages it might be concluded that Jesus was in a manner the precursor of Shaw, much as John was the precursor of Jesus. The essay, indeed, is Shaw's most elaborate commentary on traditional religious beliefs, and, while it has only the vaguest relation to the play, it indicates that *Androcles and the Lion* was intended to be a parable illustrating the workings of the evolutionary principle in religion generally, that is to say, of faith in its largest aspect. In this respect both the preface and the play are consonant with Shaw's oft-stated views. On the essential question of religious faith Father Keegan and Lavinia are in complete accord.

Androcles and the Lion was first produced in Berlin at the Kleines Theater in November 1912, shortly after it was finished. Granville-Barker produced it in London the following year, in September, with Lillah McCarthy in the part of Lavinia. After the outbreak of hostilities in Europe, Barker took it to New York and opened it on Broadway in January 1915. Shaw may have thought of it as a romp when he first wrote to Pinero about it, and even when he described it to Trebitsch later that year. Three years after, he was disposed to take it more seriously. The program note which accompanied the first New York production included a comment on the deeper meaning of the work:

> The author of *Androcles and the Lion* received one of the worst shocks of his life when an American editor published its text under the heading "A Comedy." It is not a comedy: it is precisely what its author calls it, A Fable Play: that is, an entertainment for children on an old story from the Children's books, which nevertheless contains matter for the most mature wisdom to ponder.[90]

The epilogue which Shaw appended to the play in its published version brought its doctrine as close to that of *Fanny's First Play* as its subject matter would permit. The play dealt essentially, he wrote, with the process of social evolution:

> In this play I have presented one of the Roman persecutions of the early Christians, not as the conflict of a false theology with a true, but as what all such persecutions essentially are: an attempt to suppress a propaganda that seemed to threaten the interests involved in

the established law and order, organized and maintained in the name of religion and justice by politicians who are pure opportunist Have-and-Holders. . . . My martyrs are the martyrs of all time, and my persecutors the persecutors of all time. . . . All my articulate Christians, the reader will notice, have different enthusiasms, which they accept as the same religion only because it involves them in a common opposition to the official religion and consequently in a common doom. . . . In short, a Christian martyr was thrown to the lions not because he was a Christian, but because he was a crank: that is, an unusual sort of person.[91]

These explanations served to bring *Androcles and the Lion* further into the mainstream of Shaw's drama, but it was difficult to erase the first impression the play made. It was generally thought of, and doubtless always will be, as a pleasant prank two steps removed from the children's theater. The case was quite different with Shaw's next play, the first of his plays to be genuinely successful, and the first to provoke general discussion as really serious comedy.

In a letter to Ellen Terry, written in 1897, Shaw had expressed his desire to cast Forbes Robertson and Mrs. Patrick Campbell in a future play: " 'Caesar and Cleopatra' has been driven clean out of my head by a play I want to write for them in which he shall be a West End gentleman and she an East End dona in an apron and three orange and red ostrich feathers."[92] It was sixteen years before Shaw could realize this ambition. The result was *Pygmalion*. He called it the last of his potboilers.

Pygmalion was finished in 1913. In order to forestall the bad notices that Shaw's plays usually elicited in London, it was first produced in German at the Hofburg Theater in Vienna in October of that year, and its success impelled Herbert Beerbohm Tree to produce it in London the following year at His Majesty's. Tree took the part of Higgins; Mrs. Patrick Campbell, who was now under contract to him, played Eliza; and Philip Merivale played Colonel Pickering. The play opened in London on 11 April 1914 and was hugely successful. It is said that in London alone, under Tree's management, it earned £13,000 in three months. It was soon performed everywhere in Europe in a variety of languages, and by the end of its run Shaw was established as the foremost living dramatist, as well as the richest.

The magnitude of this success must have astonished Shaw as much as anyone. He took it in his stride. The short preface he added when the

play was published is largely a description of Henry Sweet, the phoneti-
cian, with whom he vaguely connects his hero. In this preface, Shaw
wrote:

> I wish to boast that Pygmalion has been an extremely successful play
> all over Europe and North America as well as at home. It is so
> intensely and deliberately didactic, and its subject is esteemed so dry,
> that I delight in throwing it at the heads of the wiseacres who repeat
> the parrot cry that art should never be didactic. It goes to prove my
> contention that art should never be anything else.[93]

This impressive declaration is not altogether cogent. *Pygmalion* has to
do, of course, with the relation of speech to class status, but it is not a
play about linguistics, any more than *The Wild Duck* is a play about
photography. It is a love story. It is also a play of *déclassement*, a theme
which had already generated excitement when Augier popularized it,
three-quarters of a century before, with *Le Gendre de M. Poirier*.

For the nineteenth century the classic prototype of the hero tragically
displaced by a superior education was, without doubt, Julien Sorel in
Stendhal's *Le Rouge et le noir* (1831). That too is a love story. In the
interval, the topic of *déclassement* had been exhaustively developed in
the French theater in every possible genre from the melodrama of San-
deau's *Mademoiselle de Serglière*, Curel's *Les Fossiles*, and Bernstein's *Le
Detour* to the grim naturalism of Brieux's *Blanchette* (1892). In England,
which had to some extent been spared the social upheavals of the Great
Revolution, the theme was less seriously exploited, but there were a good
many plays of the order of Robertson's *Caste* which were occupied in
one way or another with the problem of class. By the time of *Blanchette*,
the problem was of urgent importance on both sides of the Channel, but
it was now no longer principally a question of domestic relations. What
troubled Brieux was the upper-class monopoly of social opportunities.

Blanchette centers on the predicament of a highly educated girl, the
daughter of a village innkeeper, who because of her low birth is unable
to secure the academic position for which she is qualified and is therefore condemned to choose between an unworthy marriage and a life of
sin. The situation was by no means funny, and the state of affairs which
it uncovered provoked much discussion, and even some measure of reform.

Like *Blanchette*, *Pygmalion* touches upon the vexing problem of finding a place in the social structure for exceptional individuals of lower-
class origin emancipated by the widening trends of popular instruction,

and educated beyond the capacity of society to absorb their services. In the time of *Pygmalion* this question was still under much discussion in France, and it had recently been the subject of several influential novels, among them Edouard Estannié's *Le Ferment* (1899), and Paul Bourget's *L'Etape* (1901). In his discussion of Stendhal's portrait of Julien Sorel, Gustave Lanson wrote:

> . . . He is told that the Revolution has established equality among all the French, and, suppressing all privilege, has proportioned the individual's rights to his merits. People are taught this beautiful principle from their earliest youth; they learn that ability leads to everything: they have ability; they learn that social superiority follows intellectual superiority: they have intellectual superiority.
>
> And when, at the age of twenty, they are loosed into society, with the ambition and the assurance necessary to reach every goal, they find all the places taken. . . . But the energetic natures . . . the strong ones . . . what will they do? . . . they will rush into the fight . . . they will make their way, boldly, brutally. They will be crushed, or they will conquer.[94]

The problem was grave, but Shaw's evident awareness of its gravity did not incline him to give the subject serious treatment. *Pygmalion* is certainly among the most engaging of Shaw's plays. It is also among the lightest and most carefree. As the action is arranged, the question of the ultimate disposition of the displaced Eliza looms more and more insistently on the horizon, but from beginning to end Higgins remains blissfully indifferent to the predicament into which his ministrations have placed his protégé and to his own responsibility for her future. This is the joke upon which the action turns.

As the play progresses, Mrs. Higgins tries to make her son aware of the seriousness of the situation he is creating, and Mrs. Pearce, his housekeeper, constantly admonishes him of the need to think what he is about. Higgins refuses to look beyond his nose. At the end of the third act, the curtain speech brings the problem sharply into focus. The expectation is, therefore, that the situation will be dramatically detonated in the last act, and this is the principal source of suspense in the latter part of the play. In fact nothing of the sort happens. Instead of staging a luxuriously explosive scene ending in a reversal, *Pygmalion* fizzles out in a *Doll's House* type of discussion which is never resolved. The play ends, indeed, with the heroine slamming the door on the hero, as in Ibsen's play, but in so deliberate a manner as to warrant the suspicion that the scene is a parody of the celebrated Ibsenist ending.

Doubtless Shaw considered that in deferring the resolution of his plot indefinitely he was following in the footsteps of the master, who also had left the *Doll's House* plot unresolved at the final curtain. But the difference between the two plays is obvious. Ibsen framed his play along the lines of conventional domestic drama, so that his final situation seemed both unusual and shocking. *Pygmalion*, on the other hand, was based on a fairy tale. It is, of course, possible to accord the patterns of myth with the facts of life through the normal methods of symbolism. This is done, for example, in Giraudoux's *Ondine*, where the realistic and the mythical are consciously related within a single statement. Naturalism is another matter. It is difficult to imagine anything artistically more inept than a rationalistic conclusion of the Cinderella story. This is, however, precisely what Shaw had in mind in the last act of *Pygmalion*.

By the time *Pygmalion* was written there were in existence innumerable stage versions of Cinderella. The fable offered an excellent basis for plays of *déclassement*. In all likelihood the direct ancestor of *Pygmalion* was Boucicault's melodrama, *Grimaldi, or the Life of an Actress* (1862), in which a Covent Garden flower-girl is educated, brought to fame, and finally adopted by a broken-down actor, who turns out to be a duke in disguise. Many other analogies have been collected.[95] It seems clear that Shaw intended to follow in *Pygmalion* the traditional formula of such plays—the discovery, the education, the preliminary test, the crucial scene, and so on—up to the point at which the prince and the beggar maid are finally united. Shaw said of the traditional scene of the ball, which *Pygmalion* omits:

> The obligatory scene, the scene in which Eliza makes her successful début at the Ambassador's party, was the root of the play at its inception. But when I got to work I left it to the imagination of the audience, as the theatre could not afford the expense, and it made the play too long. Sir James Barrie spotted this at once and remonstrated. So when the play was screened, I added the omitted scene.[96]

The scene of the ball which Shaw added to the screen version of the play was not, however, obligatory. It was merely decorative. A love scene at the end of the play was really obligatory. It was therefore regularly supplied by the actors from the time of Beerbohm Tree, in the teeth of the author's peremptory instructions to the contrary. The discussion which, in the fifth act, serves the purpose of a denouement therefore constitutes a serious embarrassment in the development of the action. This scene, which is actually the *scène à faire*, advances the plot not a jot further than the fourth-act curtain and is therefore both superfluous and repetitious. It is in any case quite irrelevant to an anecdote which admits of only one acceptable solution.

A myth is ordinarily an organism of very precise form. Such durable fantasies come into being as the result of a subtle interplay of psychic forces and are in every case living things carefully designed to subserve a necessary function. For this reason, myths, like trees, are constructs of limited elasticity, and any serious attempt to distort their structure will encounter resistance. No application of logic will serve to transform the myth of Cinderella into anything other than what it is. Once the fairy godmother has waved her wand and the girl's magical transformation has been effected, it is absolutely indispensable that the Prince should seek out the resulting Princess, marry her, and live happily with her forever after.

In fact, Shaw was too canny a writer to spoil his play by tampering with the vital elements of the fairy tale. It is reasonably clear in the third act that Higgins, for all his protestations, is in the toils of the Life Force, very much as Tanner is in *Man and Superman*, that he would rather die than part with Eliza, and that she is destined to live with him, more or less happily, all the rest of his life in the flat in Wimpole Street. In this regard the play is neither perverse nor inept. The epilogue is another matter.

The epilogue is a prose narrative, offered provisionally for the edification of those who insist on having the story resolved. From every point of view the proposed resolution is unsatisfactory; nevertheless it indicates a good deal about Shaw's attitude toward his characters and his play and thus affords some insight into the influences which gave the play its shape. In the epilogue it is demonstrated that Higgins belongs to the category of the unmarriageable, along with such characters as Marchbanks, Tavy, and those others whose destiny it is to produce ideas, but not children. The demonstration depends, of course, on the depiction of Higgins as a cranky and egotistical genius, whose good qualities do not include a capacity for sympathy. As Shaw portrays him, Higgins is not lovable; he is overwhelming. His single-mindedness is impressive, and it is amusing, but it is not an endearing trait. The normal expectation is that the author will manage his redemption through love. He does not. From beginning to end, his hero is as hard as nails, a sacrificial offering to the cause of realism.

Like *Caesar and Cleopatra*, *Pygmalion* is a play about education, a subject with which Shaw was more than ordinarily concerned, and in both plays the problem includes the precarious business of managing the transference when the pedagogical relation is at an end. After her period of schooling under Caesar's tutelage, Cleopatra has learned, presumably, how to be a queen. In *Pygmalion* Eliza learns not only how to produce upper-class sounds, but also, as a necessary by-product, how to be a self-sufficient and self-reliant person, traits for which she has already shown extraordinary native aptitude. But while Cleopatra never becomes worthy of Caesar, Eliza is in the end pre-eminently worthy of Higgins. His rejection of her in the circumstances is, from the point of view of drama, hardly acceptable.

In both these plays the comedy is predicated on the mutual relations of an unemotional man and an emotional woman. The difference in their temperature is the consequence in each case of the hero's intense preoccupation with his work, to which the heroine's emotional needs have no relevance. Thus the difference in sexual response boils down to the disparity between the biological functions of men and woman according to the doctrine of Shaw. This is also the theme of *Man and Superman*. Don Juan wants to think; Doña Ana, to breed. When they are thrown together, their relationship is not necessarily comic, but Shaw makes it a source of comedy.

In *Man and Superman* Tanner is forced by Ann into the normal domestic compromise of familial life; but neither Caesar nor Higgins is willing to relinquish any part of his psychic autonomy in this manner. Both are indifferent to the blandishments of the flesh. For this reason these plays, while provocative of reflection, seem somewhat lacking in human values, that is to say, in realism. In the abstract, Don Juan makes a good case for the intellectual life; but nobody—so long as he remains in the flesh—is wholly indifferent to the demands of the flesh, least of all Don Juan.

Pygmalion does not make a clear statement as to Higgins's sexual interests. They would seem to be nonexistent. The implication is that it would be indecent of an upper-class Englishman of the period to take any special notice of women save as domestic conveniences. Such is the suggestion also in plays of the order of Barker's *The Madras House* (1910), and it is perhaps in the light of these Islamic attitudes that *Pygmalion* should be interpreted. In our enlightened age it would be tempting to direct the play with some intimation of the homosexuality latent in these social arrangements, and this might result in a very interesting performance. It would have nothing to do with Shaw's intentions, of course; but it is only in the epilogue that we discover what these are, and there the disparity between Shaw as a dramatist and Shaw as a novelist becomes painfully apparent. If the epilogue were dramatized as a sixth act, it would doubtless be intolerable on the stage.

On the question of caste the play is clearer in its doctrine. Shaw assigns to each individual his exact specific gravity in the social order. In the epilogue to *Pygmalion* the Eynsford Hills, who cling desperately to their upper-class status in spite of their poverty, are brought down to the level of small shopkeepers. In the play itself Eliza is accepted by Mrs. Higgins as a social equal; but Higgins is willing to accept her as such only when she indicates her potentialities as a professional competitor. The astonishing rise of Mr. Doolittle is, like the elevation of Mr. Lickcheese in *Widowers' Houses*, somewhat more improbable than the other improbabilities of the play: it is this sort of imaginative leap that causes so much of Shaw's comedy to approximate extravaganza. But, however unrealistic they may be, these unexpected reversals are refreshing, and certainly they serve a useful function. For Shaw caste is essentially a matter of character and ability, not of birth, so that once the individual is cut free of the restrictions of class, he tends to find his own level in the human hierarchy. Social mobility is indispensable to the evolutionary process.

While such is, beyond doubt, the conclusion to be drawn from the play, the epilogue suggests a contrary inference. Here Shaw declined to imagine the easy rise of his gifted heroine, even as the owner of a flower shop. On the contrary, he found it necessary, in the name of realism, to punish Eliza and her hapless spouse, Freddy Hill, by putting them through an obstacle course of economic vicissitudes as arduous as his own had been before fortune favored him.

The proposed solution of Eliza's economic problem therefore seems dismally novelistic. Experience indicates that in reality beautiful girls of exceptional ability do not marry impecunious Freddies. They marry industrial magnates of a certain age and are eventually widowed or divorced with stupendous financial settlements. The meager destiny which Shaw metes out to his Galatea in the name of realism must therefore be accounted an unpardonable intrusion of common sense not only upon the myth but also upon that aspect of the myth which is normally thought of as reality.

In fact, the mythological pattern which includes such stories as *The Ugly Duckling*, *Cinderella*, *Beauty and the Beast*, *King Cophetua and the Beggar Maid*, and *The Patient Griselda*—all of which depend on the ultimate recognition of the superior merits of a disprized individual—is a compensatory mechanism of the greatest efficacy in the management of feelings of inferiority. For this reason, if no other, it is indispensable that Cinderella have her prince at the end of her story, and any other culmination is in the nature of a betrayal. Happily, Shaw had the good sense to leave the way open in his play for an inference of fulfillment according to the rules of romance, and *Pygmalion* has always been played in this manner. In the end, in spite of the author, Jack has his Jill. The epilogue may therefore be dismissed as an unfortunate irrelevancy, interesting chiefly because of the insight it affords into the mentality of the author.

The myth upon which *Pygmalion* is based has, of course, nothing to do with the legend of Pygmalion and Galatea. The Pygmalion story was treated most perceptively by Pirandello in *Diana e la Tuda* (1927) fourteen years after Shaw's play was written, and it had already furnished the basis for Ibsen's *When We Dead Awaken* (1899) fourteen years before. It is possible that Shaw had Ibsen's play in mind in devising *Pygmalion*, but the relation is not very close. Higgins does not create Eliza. He merely revises her. His relation to her is not artistic, but surgical. In *When We Dead Awaken*, the sculptor Rubek is destroyed because he has preferred his creation to the living woman who informed it, and toward the end of his life he realizes with regret that in his eagerness to work he has forgotten to live. Higgins has no such difficulty. For him work and life are synonymous. He has no need of love and is quite willing to sacrifice Eliza to his career, though he obviously finds her presence more convenient than her absence.

The final scene of *Pygmalion* is in some sense a realization of the scene—which in *When We Dead Awaken* Ibsen forbore to write—in which Rubek lets Irene go after he has finished with her as a model. For Irene the epilogue is prostitution and afterwards madness. For Rubek it is disillusion, regret, and eventually death. But in *Pygmalion* Eliza parts company with Higgins long before any of these operatic developments take place. Eliza may or may not look after Higgins's shopping list after the final curtain. It is no great matter: the sequel is not likely to be tragic. From the time of Brand, Ibsen's heroes invariably live to regret their single-minded dedication to their vocation. Shaw's heroes revel in it.

Ibsen came to the conclusion relatively early in his career that the sense of vocation is a special form of madness, and that life is justified mainly by love. Shaw thought of love as a physical urge which must at all costs be prevented from interfering with a creative man's work, in which chiefly his salvation lies. The two viewpoints are diametrically opposed and reflect the profound difference in temperament between the master and his foremost disciple in the drama. In Ibsen's plays, characters like Higgins are monomaniacs who come invariably to a tragic end. Shaw, however, found his professor singularly congenial, and he gave him a distinctly comic turn.

In Higgins we are invited to see more of Henry Sweet than of Shaw, but he has a good deal of Shaw's shamelessness, his impudence, and his gift of blarney. There is, moreover, something ungainly in Higgins's insistence on the virtues of the intellectual life. He tells Eliza:

> If you cant stand the coldness of my sort of life, and the strain of it, go back to the gutter. Work til you are more a brute than a human being; and then cuddle and squabble and drink til you fall asleep. Oh, it's a fine life the life of the gutter. It's real: it's warm: it's violent: you can feel it through the thickest skin: you can taste it and smell it without any training or any work. Not like Science and Literature and Classical Music and Philosophy and Art. You find me cold, unfeeling, selfish, dont you? Very well: be off with you to the sort of people you like. Marry some sentimental hog or other with lots of money, and a thick pair of lips to kiss you with and a thick pair of boots to kick you with. If you cant appreciate what youve got, youd better get what you can appreciate.[97]

In such passages one uncomfortably senses the intellectual snob. It would be charitable to suppose that Shaw expressed through Higgins not his own intellectual smugness, but what he imagined a character like Higgins might feel, but there are too many echoes of this attitude in Shaw's personal correspondence to make the supposition likely. In any case the passage is unfortunate, and confirms one's opinion that Higgins is not a particularly pleasant man. Even for a stage professor, he seems relatively bloodless, and there is little indication that he feels any premonition of that sudden craving for warmth that overwhelms Brand in the precincts of the Ice Church. Nevertheless Higgins's desperate search for Eliza in the last act, his manifest jealousy of Freddy, and his exaggerated posturings in the final scene suggest that he feels some emotional need for the girl he so scornfully rejected, and that ultimately he means to get her, like an astute man of business, on his own terms.

As Shaw describes him, Higgins comically suggests madness. He considers himself to be a modest, diffident, shy, and soft-spoken man of irreproachable manners. He is in fact a brash and tyrannical egotist, generous, but rude and totally inconsiderate of others. Evidently Shaw found this type of superman a little awesome. In his epilogue he says of Eliza that she may sometimes imagine

> Higgins making love like any common man. . . . But when it comes to business, to the life that she really leads as distinguished from the life of dreams and fancies, she likes Freddy and she likes the Colonel; and she does not like Higgins and Mr Doolittle. Galatea never does quite like Pygmalion: his relation to her is too godlike to be altogether agreeable.[98]

This observation, though witty, belies the play. If Eliza did not find Higgins likeable she could have no real emotional involvement with him, and the contrast which Shaw meant to dramatize between her romantic illusions and his cold realism could not be demonstrated. One may wonder why Shaw found it so necessary to stress Higgins's aversion from sexual involvements with so attractive a girl as Eliza. His reasons are interesting:

> When Higgins excused his indifference to young women on the ground that they had an irresistible rival in his mother, he gave the clue to his inveterate old-bachelordom. The case is uncommon only to the extent that remarkable mothers are uncommon. If an imaginative boy has a sufficiently rich mother who has intelligence, personal grace, dignity of character without harshness, and a cultivated sense of the best art of her time to enable her to make her house beautiful, she sets a standard for him against which very few women can struggle, besides effecting for him a disengagement of his affections, his sense of beauty, and his idealism from his specifically sexual impulses. This makes him a standing puzzle to the huge number of uncultivated people who have been brought up in tasteless homes by commonplace or disagreeable parents, and to whom, consequently, literature, painting, sculpture, music and affectionate personal relations come as modes of sex if they come at all. . . .[99]

Shaw thus introduced into the Higgins-Eliza discussion what appears to be a deeply personal note. Mrs. Higgins is a personification of the ideal mother according to Shaw—a beautiful woman, charming, intelligent, and rich. She is a person of impeccable taste. Her apartment is described in detail. It is spacious, uncluttered, and decorated in accordance with the best Pre-Raphaelite standards. They contrast sharply with the Victorian jumble to which her son is committed. Mrs. Higgins wisely keeps him at some distance, but there is no doubt that she finds him amusing as well as exasperating, and she manages him adroitly like a willful child. There is no suggestion in the play of any sort of rivalry between Mrs. Higgins and Eliza. It is suggested, on the contrary, that she would make the most desirable of mothers-in-law.

The rationalization of Higgins's sexlessness in the epilogue was in all likelihood an afterthought, but it has the advantage of affording us another glimpse of the motives which underlie the play. Shaw's dependence on his mother during the early part of his life, and her habitual indifference to his concerns, were, as we have seen, amply reflected in his early novels. It is easy to discern in these fantasies the injury to his ego which her indifference caused him, and it is even possible to perceive, if we wish, something of the sort in several of the early plays, particularly in *Mrs Warren's Profession*.

The need to idealize the imaginary mother, in contrast to the real one, on the other hand, may well have influenced the characterization of the Virgin Mother in *Candida*, who rejects the young poet in terms acceptable to his narcissism, and to have led, by way of Lady Britomart in *Major Barbara* to the genial matriarch of *Pygmalion*, who unwittingly inhibits her son's sexual activity. "We cannot help suspecting," Shaw concluded, "that the disentanglement of sex from the associations with which it is so commonly confused, a disentanglement which persons of genius achieve by sheer intellectual analysis, is sometimes produced or aided by parental fascination."[100]

The extent to which Shaw himself was subject to parental fascination must remain, in the circumstances, a matter of conjecture. What we know is that in the fullness of time this resolute bachelor married a lady who answered, in some respects, the description he gives of Mrs. Higgins, and who mothered Shaw, sometimes to his annoyance, as long as she lived. There is no special need, nor beyond a certain point is it desirable, to connect the intimate circumstances of Shaw's life with the works of his imagination. Art is a sublimation, not a reproduction of life. But there is certainly reason to suppose, if we wish, that Shaw's special brand of Don Juanism, along with the metaphysical basis assigned to it in *Man and Superman*, in short, Shaw's entire philosophic structure, was an elaborate rationalization of his own psychic situation.

The idea that class-distinctions are primarily a matter of linguistics seems fantastic at first blush, but such a notion might have made sense at a time when upper-class speech was still a monopoly of the upper classes. It is conceivable that in a classless society everyone will speak the same language. Shaw apparently took this idea with some seriousness, since in his will he left a sizeable bequest to further a system of phonetic spelling. He wrote in the preface to *Pygmalion*:

> The English have no respect for their language, and will not teach their children to speak it. They spell it so abominably that no man can teach himself what it sounds like. It is impossible for an Englishman to open his mouth without making some other Englishman hate or despise him. . . . The reformer England needs today is an energetic phonetic enthusiast: that is why I have made such a one the hero of a popular play.[101]

In *Pygmalion* there is nothing to suggest that Higgins is a socialist, and he has apparently no idea of leveling the classes under a common phonetic system. But the implication is that what could be done with Eliza Doolittle can be done, more or less successfully, with anyone who shows the necessary aptitude. Shaw himself had learned upper-class English ways in somewhat the same manner as Eliza, and he evidently liked the idea that in order to transform a clever garbageman into a prime minister all that is necessary is a course in speech. Such ideas were certainly current in the early decades of this century, and the vast proliferation of speech courses in those years attests to the influence of the theory.

Eliza observes very justly that what makes a lady is the manner in which she is treated. The idea that all those who make estimable sounds will be treated as ladies and gentlemen, so that socialism will spring up by itself in the wake of Wyld's *Pronouncing Dictionary*, depends, however, upon a strictly Victorian concept of the hierarchy of classes. In the 1870's, possibly, Higgins might feel some sense of the futility of his profession; but in 1913 he has the professional ardor of a true revolutionist. He tells his mother: "you have no idea how frightfully interesting it is to take a human being and change her into a quite different human being by creating a new speech for her. It's filling up the deepest gulf that separates class from class and soul from soul."[102]

The suggestion that, if Eliza behaves like a duchess, she may well become a duchess is—however one calculates the probabilities—immediately acceptable in the theater. Consequently the intermediate stages in the assumption of Eliza are fascinating. The incongruity between what Eliza says at Mrs. Higgins's at-home, and the manner in which she says it, provided Mrs. Pat Campbell with an incomparable opportunity to display her comic talents, and the effect of Eliza's elegant rendition of "Not bloody likely" is said to have been the talk of London all during the first run of the play. Clara Hill, on the other hand, illustrates a tendency contrary to that which motivates Eliza's rise in the world. She is quite ready to affect lower-class speech patterns if they are considered fashionable. In Shaw's day the attrition of the King's English was evidently already a cause for concern:

PICKERING: . . . Ive been away in India for several years, and manners have changed so much that I sometimes dont know whether I'm at a respectable dinnertable or in a ship's forecastle.

CLARA: It's all a matter of habit. Theres no right or wrong in it. Nobody means anything by it and it's s o quaint, and gives such a smart emphasis to things that are not in themselves very witty. I find the new small talk delightful and quite innocent.[103]

Possibly for Shaw these indications of the tendency to obliterate class distinctions presaged the classless society of the future, but it is more likely that he saw in this process a salutary movement of individuals to take their proper places in the social hierarchy regardless of the class into which they were born. *Pygmalion* is a play of exceptional people. Eliza, like her father, is a highly evolved individual whose potentialities would normally be stifled by the limitations of a rigidly stratified social environment. But even when she is artificially freed from the restrictions of her social class, her economic possibilities are a matter of chance and, in her time, she is in a predicament much the same as that of the general's daughter in *Hedda Gabler* or the general's daughters in *The Three Sisters*. Mr. Doolittle, on the other hand, is emancipated not by education but by money, with the result that he joins the middle class and is cursed with the need for respectability all the rest of his life.

The intimation is that social displacement is both perilous and uncomfortable no matter how it is brought about: nevertheless it is indispensable to the evolution of society. In *Pygmalion* it is accident that determines the extraordinary rise of Eliza and her father; but the rapid development of mass education in England in this period was already making it possible for the underprivileged to become privileged as a matter of course. What *Pygmalion* describes is the process by which exceptional people find their way into the upper reaches of society, and from this point of view it is perhaps a satire. But its satirical intention does not obscure the underlying idea. The evolutionary principle involves a constant displacement of individuals within the class structure. The result is doubtless of benefit to the species, but it is not uniformly pleasant for the individual. Chekhov had dwelt more or less humorously on the tragic aspects of this process in *The Three Sisters*, a very sad sort of comedy. *Pygmalion*, on the contrary, is very funny; but it too has its pathetic side. Nature is insensible to suffering. Its obtuseness is mirrored in the insensitivity of Higgins, who identifies with nobody and is therefore inhuman to a degree that is not altogether agreeable. But the fact is that Eliza, as she repeatedly points out, has her feelings like anyone else; and it is in keeping this poignant consideration constantly before his audience that Shaw, for all his realism, shows his worth as a dramatist.

Shaw's mother died the year that *Pygmalion* was first offered for production, in 1913. She was then eighty-two years old and had finally given up her position as choirmistress at Sophia Bryant's North London

Collegiate School for Girls. She had long been in communication with the other world through automatic writing. Shaw was respectful of her literary achievements. He wrote:

> When I was an elderly man, my mother amused herself with a planchette and a ouija, which in her hands produced what are called spirit writings abundantly. It is true that these screeds might have been called wishful writings (like wishful thinkings) so clearly were as much her own story-telling invention as the Waverly novels were Scott's. But why am I doing essentially the same as a playwright? I do not know. We both got some satisfaction from it or we would not have done it.[104]

Lucinda Shaw was duly cremated. Her son attended the ceremony in the company of Granville-Barker and apparently was vastly entertained by the whole performance, which he described in detail in an amusing letter to Mrs. Pat Campbell. Barker remarked later on Shaw's extraordinary gaiety on an occasion which most people take with ritual solemnity: ". . . He was delighted with the spectacle of his mother's body enveloped in garnet flames, and imagined her spirit anxiously regarding the workmen who separated her ashes from the remains of the coffin as if she feared they might make a mistake."[105]

Lucinda's death appears to have released her son for a last fling at romance. He had been flirting with Mrs. Patrick Campbell for some time, more or less in a professional capacity. When *Pygmalion* was ready for production, he was determined that she must play Liza, and he went to work in earnest to charm her. Mrs. Campbell was at this time thinking of marrying George Cornwallis-West, an actor with high social connections, but she was not above encouraging a flirtation with a notoriously attractive man who could be of value to her in her profession. She warmed quickly and charmingly to Shaw's advances, and before long Shaw found himself experiencing emotions of which he had not so far considered himself capable. The two met often, and their correspondence soon took on a fervently erotic tone.

Mrs. Campbell was in every way an exceptional woman, highly gifted, at forty-eight still beautiful, notoriously difficult, and unusually intelligent. Her given names were Beatrice Stella. Shaw addressed her habitually as Stella, and was in turn dubbed Joey. He began his courtship by warning her of his bad character:

> Shut your ears tight against this blarneying Irish liar and actor. Read no more of his letters. . . . His notion of a woman in love with him is one who turns white and miserable when he comes into the room,

and is all one wretched jealous reproach. O dont, dont, DONT fall in
love with him; but dont grudge him the joy he finds in being in love
with you, and writing all sorts of wild but heartfelt exquisite lies—
lies, lies, lies, lies to you, his adoredest. G. B. S.[106]

Meanwhile his rival was much in evidence. Shaw could not deny that
it would be sensible for Mrs. Campbell to marry him, but he wished to
have his pleasure of her first:

> . . . Though I like George (we have the same taste), I say he is young
> and I am old; so let him wait until I am tired of you. That cannot in
> the course of nature be long. I am the most faithless of men, though I
> am constant too: at least I dont forget. But I run through all illusions
> and trample them out with yells of triumph. And about you I am a
> mass of illusions. . . . You cannot really be what you are to me: you
> are a figure from the dreams of my boyhood—all romance, and
> anticipation of the fulfillment of the destiny of the race, which is
> thousands of years off. . . . I promise to be tired as soon as I can so as
> to leave you free. I will produce *Pygmalion* and criticize your acting.
> . . . I will run after other women in search of a new attachment; I
> will hurry through my dream as fast as I can: only let me have my
> dream out.[107]

Mrs. Campbell did nothing to interfere with his dream. On the contrary, she encouraged it pleasantly without changing her own plans in
the slightest. She had a mordant wit and an uncontrollable temper. There
was steel in her character, and when she disagreed with Shaw, she did
not hesitate to set the great man straight. Thus when he sent her the
proofs of his new edition of *The Quintessence of Ibsenism* she did not
dissimulate her displeasure:

> Your "Hedda" makes me very sad—not one little bit do you under-
> stand Hedda—your interpretation of "do it beautifully" positively
> made me scream—her love—her shame—her physical condition—
> her agonizing jealousy—even the case of pistols—you're wrong at all
> points—did you think about it at all—or is it just your adoration for
> bl——y plain facts that makes you so indifferent to all the poetry, the
> universal truths and beauty that lie behind and beyond?—
>   —You miss it all dolefully in *Little Eyolf*—the fact is you write
> carelessly sometimes—And with whom are you quarrelling? Be calm,
> dearest, be gentle with fools—And why take it for granted that your
> reader doesn't know what you know, and isn't agreeing with you?
>   You seem to have a simpleton always in your mind's eye.[108]

The affair with Mrs. Pat Campbell took a very different turn from the
involvement with Ellen Terry. It had begun, as always, with words; but

the words soon evinced a desire to be made flesh. Shaw and his Stella began meeting surreptitiously at the home of Shaw's sister Lucy, who was not well, and the temperature of their relationship rose rapidly. Charlotte was not amused by this turn of events. Her nature was far from passionate, but her sense of property was strong, and she proved to be as jealous of intruders as Jenny Patterson. Shaw could not resist the temptation to stir her up from time to time, if only to enhance his self-respect. Shortly before *Pygmalion* opened in the spring of 1913, she overheard a telephone conversation between her husband and his leading lady which greatly upset her. There was a scene. Shaw immediately reported the painful incident to Stella with every sign of satisfaction, and some observations indicating his intellectual superiority to this sort of thing:

> . . . If I could be human and suffer with a suffering of my own, there would be some poetic justice in it, but I cant; I can only feel the suffering of others with a pain that pity makes, and with a fierce impatience of the unreasonableness of it—the essential inhumanity of this jealousy that I never seem to escape from.[109]

In August 1913 Mrs. Campbell went to the Guildford Hotel in Sandwich for a rest and a stretch of solitude at the seaside. To her consternation, Shaw decided to join her. It was his professed intention to spend a week in her company, but the affair turned out badly. He spent only three days in Sandwich. On the morning of the second day, by his account, he walked eight miles and wrote a scene of a play. In the afternoon he was sleepy and she was bored. She had already written him: "Please will you go back to London today—or go wherever you like but don't stay here—if you don't go, I must—I am very very tired and I oughtn't to go another journey. Please don't make me despise you. Stella."[110] The next morning, when he came to look for her, Mrs. Campbell was gone. She had settled her bill the night before. Shaw was outraged. He wrote, in godlike wrath:

> Very well, go. The loss of a woman is not the end of the world. . . . But I am deeply, deeply, deeply wounded. . . . You are an owl, sickened by two days of my sunshine: I have treated you far too well. . . . Go then: the Shavian oxygen burns up your little lungs: seek some stuffiness that suits you. . . . You have wounded my vanity: an inconceivable audacity, an unpardonable crime. . . .[111]

Later that day he wrote again in an even more melodramatic vein. He was now fifty-seven years old, he said:

... Of that 57 years I have suffered 20 and worked 37. Then I had a moment's hapiness: I almost condescended to romance. I risked the breaking of deep roots and sanctified ties: I set my feet boldly on all the quicksands: I rushed after Will o' the Wisp into darkness: I courted the oldest illusions, knowing well what I was doing. . . . I said "for myself I want seven days." They began; and I held back: I was not greedy: for I wanted the last to be the best. And you yawned in my face, and stole the last five to waste in some desolate silly place with your maid and your chauffeur. . . .[112]

It was two days before Stella answered. She was now safely established at Littlestone:

You, with your eighteenth century ribaldry habit. You lost me because you never found me.—I who have nothing but my little lamp and flame—you would blow it out with your bellows of self. You would snuff it out with your egotistical snortings. . . . Do you think it was nothing to me to hurt my friend?[113]

The rest went by itself. Stella was tender and conciliatory. The rift was soon healed. But the love affair was over. In the fall of 1913 Shaw was whisked off to France by his wife on a motor tour. He wrote heartbreaking letters to Stella and continued to provoke scenes with his wife. When he returned to London for the rehearsals of *Pygmalion* he had further cause for wrath. The rehearsals were interrupted by Stella's marriage to George West and her subsequent honeymoon. When they were resumed Shaw was cold, biting, and businesslike. Tree proved to be immensely difficult. Stella was impossible. In these circumstances the rehearsals were stormy; but the spectacular success of the play restored everyone's good will.

Pygmalion opened in April and closed at the end of June. War was declared in August. In September Mrs. Campbell took the play to New York. It ran at the Park Theatre until the spring of 1915. Then she took it on tour with George West, who had come to join her in America on furlough from the British army. When she returned to England times had changed. She had some further successes on the stage, but before long it became evident that she was no longer in favor with the public. Her marriage turned out badly, and in the 1920's she began to know adversity.

Shaw declined to cast her in *Heartbreak House*, and her relations with him rapidly became pathetic. In her need of money, she proposed to publish his letters; but Shaw refused to have his love letters published during Charlotte's lifetime, and his correspondence with Stella became acrimonious. In the end he authorized their publication only in 1950, ten years after Stella's death.

The last of her letters to Joey was dated 28 June 1939 from a hotel in the Rue des Capucines in Paris, where she and her dog Moonbeam shared a room *en pension*. She wrote: "I am getting used to poverty and discomfort, and even to the very real unhappiness of having no maid to take a few of the little daily cares for me, and give me an arm when I cross the street carrying "Moonbeam" through the terrifying tearing traffic.[114]

She died in Pau on 9 April 1940 at the age of seventy-five. Shaw gave no sign of emotion. He wrote to his old friend Mrs. Ada Tyrell:

> She made a great success for Pinero and another for me, but though we both wrote plays afterward containing parts that would have suited her to perfection, we did not cast her for them. . . . She enchanted me among the rest; but I could not have lived with her for a week; and I knew it; so nothing came of it. . . . Orinthia in *The Apple Cart* is a dramatic portrait of her.   R. I. P.[115]

On 28 June 1914 the archduke Franz Ferdinand was assassinated at Sarajevo. Five weeks later all Europe was at war. Shaw took sides at once. In 1900, at the time of the Boer War, he had declared himself in favor of British imperialism. ". . . the fact remains," he had written,

> that a Great Power, consciously or unconsciously, must govern in the interests of the world as a whole; and it is not to these interests that such mighty forces should be wielded by small communities of frontiersmen. Theoretically, they should be internationalized, not British-Imperialized; but until the Federation of the World becomes an accomplished fact, we must accept the most responsible Imperial federation available as a substitute for it.[116]

At that time, accordingly, he had favored a strong British army created "by giving to the whole male population an effective training in the use of arms, without removing them from civilian life." This declaration was accompanied by a proposal for a thorough reform of the professional army, which was to be given status and pay on a basis equal to other public institutions. Needless to say, nothing of the sort took place.

On 7 November 1914 Shaw published, in the *Nation*, "An Open Letter to the President of the United States of America," and a week later, a pamphlet entitled "Common Sense About the War" appeared as a supplement to the *New Statesman* for 14 November 1914. It was a surprisingly sensible appraisal of the current situation, patriotic in tone, but far from jingoistic. In it Shaw called attention to England's proud political tradition, the dangers of Prussian imperialism, and the need to crush it. At the same time, he launched a bitter attack against Sir Edward Grey, whose devious diplomacy, he wrote, had served only to confuse the issue. He pointed out, besides, that Junkerism was not confined to the Junkers, and that militarism was by no means a German monopoly. It was, he said, rampant in England, as well as in France: "Unless we are all prepared to fight militarism at home as well as abroad, the cessation of hostilities will last only until the belligerents have recovered from their exhaustion."[117]

The pamphlet was mainly a protest against militarism, but it included some remarks in defense of German culture, in the course of which Shaw argued that the arrogance of the Prussian military establishment could hardly be attributed to the influence of Wagner, a revolutionist, or of Nietzsche, a Pole. More than half a century after the fact, Shaw's attitudes seem irreproachably temperate; but in 1914 the times were not suited to temperate statements, and his tone was hardly appropriate to the occasion. The sentiment which must follow the war, he wrote, must establish

> a Hegemony of Peace, as desired by all who are really capable of high civilization, and formulated by me in the daily Press in a vain attempt to avert this mischief whilst it was brewing. Nobody took the smallest public notice of me; so I made a lady in a play say, "Not bloody likely," and instantly became famous beyond the Kaiser, beyond the Tsar, beyond Sir Edward Grey, beyond Shakespear and Homer and President Wilson, the papers occupying themselves with me for a whole week. . . . I concluded then that this was a country which really could not be taken seriously.[118]

All this went down badly with his readers, even with those who were generally disposed to agree with his political views. The pamphlet sold 75,000 copies and was evidently not considered worthy of discussion. But Shaw had not reckoned with the Germans. As a playwright, he had been far more successful in Germany than in England, and his views on the war, the War Office, English Junkerism, and Belgium were seized on gratefully by the German propaganda agencies, which proceeded to feed them back to the English with tasteful embellishments.

The effect upon Shaw was disastrous. For the first time in his life he learned what it is to feel the full weight of public disapproval. He was called a traitor. His plays were blacklisted. Many of his friends turned against him. The Dramatists League declared him persona non grata. Henry Arthur Jones, with whom he had once been on warm terms, published an open letter in which he called Shaw a "freakish homonculus, germinated outside of lawful procreation." All Shaw's eccentricities were now thrown at his head, and what had formerly been interpreted as an amusing madness was cited as evidence of a dangerously subversive personality. He protested feebly: "I find that most of the writers who differ with me are perfectly reckless of the effect of their statements on the war provided only they can damage me for my insufferable airs of intellectual superiority."[119]

He was in fact deeply hurt. He had rather fancied himself in the role of an elder statesman, and his attack on Grey, though richly deserved, was perhaps motivated by a secret desire to supplant him, at least in popular estimation, at the helm of state. Possibly he aspired to a ministerial post. It may be that in the emergency he was as well qualified as anyone; but he was not a political figure, and his cold rationalism was completely out of accord with the public mood. He learned painfully that it is not by being sensible that one governs people in time of war, but by capturing their imagination and directing their emotions. In the circumstances, Shaw had no idea how to rehabilitate his diminished fortunes. He did not retire from the fray. He was brusquely pushed aside, and all through the war he savored the indignity of being right when it was wise to be wrong. He had written, in terms which, nearly sixty years later, seem singularly prophetic:

> The one danger before us that nothing can avert but a general raising of human character through the deliberate cultivation and endowment of democratic virtue without consideration of property or class, is the danger created by inventing weapons capable of destroying civilization faster than we can produce men who can be trusted to use them wisely. . . . It is therefore undeniably possible that a diabolical rhythm may be set up in which civilization will rise periodically to the point at which explosives powerful enough to destroy it are discovered, and will then be shattered and thrown back to a fresh start with a few starving and ruined survivors. H. G. Wells and Anatole France have prefigured that result in fiction, and I cannot deny the strength of its probability. . . .[120]

He continued to write in these terms; but he gained no ground, and his unpopularity in these years was not alleviated by his behavior in the matter of Roger Casement, on whose behalf his assistance was solicited. Casement was an Ulsterman who had spent the first years of the war in Germany in a pathetic effort to engineer a coup in Ireland. On 30 April 1916, a U-boat landed him, with two companions, on the coast of Kerry to initiate an Irish insurrection, which was to be followed by a German invasion of Ireland. Casement, however, was immediately arrested and taken to London to stand trial for his treason.

He was ill, and his desperate plight aroused much sympathy among the English. Petitions were circulated, and funds solicited, and many rose to his support. Alice Green, the wife of the eminent historian, headed a campaign to finance his defense. Shaw helped to draft some of the petitions, but he refused to sign any, and he also refused to contribute to the fund, which he considered a waste of money. At a luncheon with Mrs. Green and Beatrice Webb, however, he offered to write a speech for Casement to deliver at his trial which would, so he said, bring down the house and thunder through the ages. It was remarked at the time that he seemed less interested in saving Casement's life than in staging his trial. In the end, he wrote the speech, the gist of which was that Casement was not an English traitor but an Irish patriot. This eminently sensible distinction did not please Casement, who preferred to rest his case on a general denial. The consequence was a verdict of guilty, after which Shaw's speech was carefully read to the jury. The speech was much admired, and Casement was hanged.

Shaw's attitude on this occasion added perceptibly to the displeasure he had long inspired in the wife of Sidney Webb, his closest friend. Beatrice Webb was a humorless woman of utter sincerity and the highest principles. She was convinced from the first that Shaw was a vain and flighty man whose brilliance was not to be trusted. After the Casement trial, she wrote in her diary:

> The man is kindly and tolerant, but his conceit is monstrous, and he is wholly unaware of the pain he gives by his jeering words and laughing gestures—especially to romantics like Alice Green. . . . If everyone were as intellectual and unemotional as he is—as free from convention in thought and feeling—his flashes might alter the direction of opinion. There would remain his instability of purpose. He is himself always in a state of reaction from his last state of mind or generalizing from his most recent experience. A world made up of Bernard Shaws would be a world in moral dissolution.[121]

However biased this appraisal might be on the part of a lady who was notoriously unable to relish a joke, there is something to be said for its justice. It was, of course, by no means the general impression among his colleagues that Shaw was untrustworthy. As he grew older and more successful, there were those, indeed, who regarded him as a saint; but it is not clear that this sort of adulation was much nearer the mark. As for

Mrs. Webb, her estimate of him as intellectual and unemotional would probably have been acceptable enough to him, and he probably would not have bothered to deny his conceit, which he held to be justified, but the idea that he was unstable in his views would have shocked him deeply. In his mind, he was the most stable of men.

The war years were hardly a proper time for the sort of play Shaw wished to write, but he did what he could to keep himself in the public eye. *Great Catherine* was produced in November 1913, the year before the outbreak of hostilities. It is an amusing and reasonably useful skit based on the notion that an English gentleman of traditional cut belongs in a museum among the respected vestiges of antiquity. Of the short plays he wrote during the war—*O'Flaherty, V.C.* (1915), *The Inca of Perusalem* (1917), *Augustus Does His Bit* (1917), and *Annajanska* (1918)—the last three are certainly trash. The first must be treated with the respect due to a comic masterpiece.

O'Flaherty, V.C. centers on a discussion between a young Irish soldier just back from the front, where he has greatly distinguished himself for bravery, and his landlord, Sir Pearce Madigan, an Irish baronet who has invited him to tea. Sir Pearce is wearing the uniform of a general, but he has evidently not seen combat in some time and is now engaged in recruiting Irishmen for the British army. The two heroes are joined by O'Flaherty's mother. She has been, until quite recently, under the impression that her son was away fighting their natural enemy, the British. There is also his fiancée, who thinks only of the money she can squeeze for herself out of her hero's pay. Faced with the young man's refusal to be exploited any further, the women begin to quarrel among themselves, and the play ends in a desperate hassle which is calmed only when the warring ladies are pushed forcibly indoors. When peace once again descends upon the General's garden, the young soldier is moved to some sage reflections:

> O'FLAHERTY (*idyllically*): . . . Only a month ago, I was in the quiet of the country out at the front, with not a sound except the birds and the bellow of a cow in the distance as it might be, and the shrapnel making little clouds in the heavens, and the shells whistling, and may be a yell or two when one of us was hit, and would you believe it, sir, I complained of the noise and wanted to have a peaceful hour at home. Well: them two has taught me a lesson. . . . Some likes war's alarums; and some likes home life. Ive tried both, sir, and I'm all for war's alarums now. I always was a quiet lad by natural disposition.

SIR PEARCE: Strictly between ourselves, O'Flaherty, and as one soldier to another (*O'Flaherty salutes, but without stiffening*), do you think we should have got an army without conscription if domestic life had been as happy as people say it is?[122]

This little play, written in very trying circumstances, is, in a small way, among the best that Shaw produced in the comic genre, and a worthy corollary to *John Bull's Other Island*. The play had been solicited by the War Office as an aid in its efforts to recruit troops in Ireland. If we can credit the preface, Shaw went about his task sincerely and realistically in the belief that an appeal in these terms was the most effective way of getting Irishmen to fight for England. The play, however, was considered an unpardonable piece of effrontery on Shaw's part, and the War Office, as Shaw blithely noted in his preface, judged it "utterly inadmissible" for the purpose intended. In the circumstances, it is hardly possible to say whether *O'Flaherty, V.C.* was an egregious bit of Irish impudence, an earnest disquisition on Irish character, or a cunning appeal to the practical good sense of the Irish male. It was perhaps all of these, as well as a refreshing display of Irish humor under exasperating conditions. Whatever it was, it does not adequately represent Shaw's mood during these unhappy years. That is most fully revealed in *Heartbreak House*, the major play of the First World War.

HEARTBREAK HOUSE

Heartbreak House was begun in 1913. Clouds were gathering in the East, but in England there was no thought of a general war. There had been nothing of the sort since the time of Napoleon, when the Congress of Vienna settled the affairs of Europe seemingly for always. In the national alignments that took place in 1870, there was, nevertheless, some cause for anxiety, and in March 1913 Shaw joined with those who advocated a triple alliance of Britain, France, and Germany as a method of averting any future European conflict.[1]

By the time the last act of *Heartbreak House* was finished, in 1916, the carnage at Verdun was at its height, and there was reason to anticipate the end of civilization in Europe. Nevertheless, there is no mention of conflict in the play, nobody is in uniform, and, until the final scene, there is no allusion of any sort to the war that was in everybody's thoughts at the time. *Heartbreak House* takes place in an atmosphere of peace, boredom, and unreality. The action transpires in the course of a day, but there is no way of dating this day. It is a day out of eternity. There is only the mysterious drumming in the air in the last act, and a series of explosions, which occasion more excitement than fear.

Bombs had in fact fallen on England by the time this play was finished. Not far from Shaw's house in Ayot St. Lawrence a workman had been killed by an explosion while he was lighting a flare, it was said, to attract enemy aircraft. The bombs were German; but Shaw resolutely declined to see an enemy in Germany. The enemy, in his view, was the stupid egotism of mankind, and this was equally at work everywhere. The fire from heaven was not so much the work of the Kaiser's war-machine as the consequence of the self-destructive impulses of humanity. Man was a dead end in the evolutionary process. The species could progress no further in the line that was mapped out for it. The Life Force had therefore actuated in it an organic instrument of self-destruction which was about to be detonated. If the superman was to evolve, he would evolve from some source other than man. Such was the implication.

In calling the play "A Fantasia in the Russian Manner on English Themes," very likely Shaw meant to allude to its musical construction; but the musical analogy is not striking. In form it is a salon comedy set, as usual, in a country house during a week-end party. But after his experiments with melodrama, farce, and extravaganza, Shaw evidently thought of developing further for his purposes the type of symbolism with which he had experimented earlier in *Man and Superman*. In *Heartbreak House* it was his intention to exhibit symbolically the unhealthy state of England in the post-Victorian era, and to indicate at the same time the nature of the disaster which this England was inviting. To this end, a group of more or less representative English types are assembled in a villa in Sussex. The detail is represented realistically. But the techniques of symbolism, as they had been developed from the time of Maeterlinck, made it necessary to remove the events of the play, as well as its characters, as far as possible from actuality, and thus to bathe the action in the atmosphere of mystery which was considered indispensable to the genre. Had Shaw intended to present a cross-section of English life in the ordinary way of comedy, it would have been simple to devise a plot laid in an ordinary country house peopled with ordinary people. Captain Shotover's house is altogether extraordinary. It is situated on the borders of the Maeterlinckian Beyond. Its inhabitants are all exaggerated well beyond the ordinary. With the exception of the servants, they are all of the stuff of dreams.

The August offensive of 1914 took place, apparently, after a good part of *Heartbreak House* was written, yet there is nothing to indicate that Shaw undertook any extensive revision to bring the end of the play into a closer relationship with the beginning. Shaw's antiwar sentiments had been by this time thoroughly aired, and he continued to express them even at a time when pacifist views were considered to be seditious. In *O'Flaherty, V.C.* the hero asks Sir Pearce:

> . . . Why should I read the papers to be humbugged and lied to by them that had the cunning to stay at home and send me to fight for them? Dont talk to me or to any soldier of the war being right. No war is right; and all the holy water that Father Quinlan ever blessed couldnt make one right. There, sir! Now you know what

O'Flaherty, V.C. thinks, and youre wiser so than the others that only knows what he done.[2]

These words were written at about the time that Shaw was engaged on the last act of *Heartbreak House*; but nobody in *Heartbreak House* talks in such terms. "War cannot bear the terrible castigation of comedy," Shaw says in the preface he wrote for *Heartbreak House* in 1919.

> When men are heroically dying for their country, it is not the time to shew their lovers and wives and fathers and mothers how they are being sacrificed to the blunders of boobies, the cupidity of capitalists, the ambition of conquerors, the electioneering of demagogues, the Pharisaism of patriots, the lusts and lies and rancors and bloodthirsts that love war because it opens their prison doors, and sets them in the thrones of power and popularity. . . . Truth telling is not compatible with the defence of the realm.[3]

Heartbreak House is built in the form of a ship and may thus be thought to symbolize the ship of state, the British Empire, the human race, and other abstractions of that order. It may also figure the transitory quality of the planet or the transitional nature of the evolutionary process. The play is not an allegory. Its symbols are not precise. They suggest analogies which do not work out consistently and make intimations which serve to orient our thought without defining an idea. This is, in fact, the proper style of nineteenth-century symbolism. It is allusive, not definitive.

It is hardly possible to work out anything like a precise correlation between the sloppy bohemianism of the Shotover ménage in *Heartbreak House* and the condition of England in the early twentieth century. The play clearly manifests Shaw's impatience with the indifference of the cultural classes to the political concerns of the nation. The same reproach was later leveled against the indifference of the intellectual class in Germany at the time of the rise of the Nazis to power. But in *Heartbreak House* the action does not turn on this point. The play is a sequence of love stories, all of which turn out badly. Perhaps this is meant to suggest the condition of England at this time. If so, *Heartbreak House* has, from a formal viewpoint, more in common with *The Lower Depths* than with *The Cherry Orchard*.

The suspicion that all those who are assembled at Captain Shotover's villa in Sussex are ill with a mysterious sickness does not begin to take form until quite late in the action. At first they seem merely peculiar, and the plot seems aimless. The characters are bored and feverish. They seem to be awaiting something; but it is not until the bombs begin to fall that the play acquires a definite outline. We see then what it is the play depicts. It is the last paroxysm of a dying culture.

To what extent this effect was calculated, it is impossible to guess. At this time Shaw was thoroughly distasted with plot and plot-contrivance. He said later that he let the play write itself without premeditation, and that he hardly kept one speech ahead of himself as he wrote. The advantage of this method of composition is apparent in the liveliness of the dialogue and the spontaneous nature of the action. The disadvantages are equally clear. The action has no necessary sequence. It depends on the juxtaposition of units arranged so as to make a pattern. The pattern is discernible; but since the relations are not causally determined, whatever happens in the play need not have happened and might just as well have happened otherwise. The effect is kaleidoscopic, but as the sequences are accidental, in the end, the effect is both disturbing and confusing.

In *Heartbreak House* the narrative sequence is less important than the mood in which the action takes place. This is initiated by Ellie Dunn, a young singer, who comes to Captain Shotover's villa at the invitation of his daughter, Hesione Hushabye, in order to be dissuaded from making an unsuitable marriage with Boss Mangan, her father's employer. It develops that she has meanwhile fallen in love with a romantic character named Marcus Darnley whom she encountered by accident at the National Gallery. Darnley is a dashing young man of fifty, of heroic temper, with magnificent mustaches and a background of thrilling adventure. She has hardly finished describing this Don Juan, when the man himself walks in. He turns out to be Hesione's philandering husband Hector. Ellie's heart breaks on the instant.

There are further disenchantments in store for her. The rich man she is now resolved to marry no longer wishes to marry her. He has seen the incomparable Hesione, who despises him, and has instantly fallen in love with her. He soon discovers, unhappily, that everyone despises him. His heart breaks. About this time Hesione's beautiful sister Ariadne arrives, only to find that after an absence of twenty-three years she is no longer welcome in her father's house. She makes herself at home, nevertheless, and at once falls in love with the irresistible Hector, who cannot endure her. But her heart is more durable than the hearts of others. It does not break, and she compensates for her discomfort by being particularly rude to her lover, a functionary called Randall, whose heart is periodically broken. In this manner, these gentlefolk wander about the house, with hearts broken or breaking, until suddenly bombs fall from the sky, and people are killed. Nobody breaks his heart about that.

These characters, their idiosyncracies, and their erotic involvements are purely artificial creations. Only Ellie and Captain Shotover make the impression of living beings. Hector, Hesione, Ariadne, Mangan, and Mazzini Dunn are scarcely more than well-detailed caricatures, archetypal characters motivated in accordance with principles which do not need to be psychologically valid. Played by competent actors, in the unaffectedly theatrical atmosphere of the play, they function perfectly, without being in the least believable.

The degree of abstraction this technique necessitates, however, involves some difficulty. In this play Shaw brings his characters together quite regardless of probability in a manner that foreshadows the methods of surrealism. If we assume that drama is the art of the improbable, the coincidences of *Heartbreak House* will cause no embarrassment, for they are obviously intended to evoke, not an illusion of life, but a succession of surprises and shocks. In such plays only extraordinary things happen. *Heartbreak House* is thus at the other pole from the "Russian manner" of Chekhov, who makes us marvel at the ordinary. If we consider it from the point of view of what is said, it is eminently rational and edifying. From the standpoint of what is done, it is the sheerest lunacy.

This may not reflect Shaw's intention when the play was first conceived. *Heartbreak House* appears to have been designed not at all on the pattern of *The Cherry Orchard*, with which Shaw invites comparison, but in imitation of *The Master Builder*. Shotover's house, like the house of Solness in Ibsen's play, is of peculiar construction, the brain child of a symbolist rather than of an architect. There is, of course, a difference. Solness's house points upward; Shotover's onward: in each case, the construction reflects the character of the designer. Both Solness and Shotover are exhausted men, who have survived their greatness but not their dreams. Both are visited unexpectedly by a brisk young woman, with whom they have an inexplicable spiritual affinity, who makes impossible demands upon them. Solness is a builder; Shotover, an inventor. Both are mad. But while Solness is not yet too old to have a last fling at romance, Shotover is already in his dotage. He is no longer available sexually, and his alliance with Ellie is a purely spiritual engagement, a symbolic passing on of the torch without the usual physical amenities.

It is possible to see, also, if one desires, in the curious exaltation with which disaster is invited at the end of *Heartbreak House*, some reminiscence of the final scene of *The Master Builder*. The end of *Heartbreak House* is spectacular. The neighboring rectory is blown up, along with the two frightened characters who take refuge in the Captain's gravel pit. Mrs. Hushabye is delighted:

> MRS HUSHABYE: But what a glorious experience! I hope they'll come again tomorrow night.
> ELLIE (*radiant at the prospect*): Oh. I h o p e so.

One would say the ladies feel the sort of excitement with which Hilde witnesses the fall of Solness from the top of his tower. They hear, it is true, no harps in the air. But they hear a drumming in the sky, and the rest of the music is presently furnished by Randall and his flute.

Heartbreak House may be considered a montage of dramatic improvisations designed to demonstrate the spiritual decay of cultured England. It is the portraits, not the plot which give the play its interest. Shotover and Hushabye are, in a curious way, counterparts. They are men of action whom life has reduced to passivity, the one through age; the other, through marriage. Both are now entangled in dreams which they can barely distinguish from reality. Shotover has outlived his time. Hushabye has not lived at all. Each is, in his way, pathetic, and, in his way, ridiculous. They are, in the manner of Ibsen, tragic characters playing comic roles.

Mangan is typical of the managerial class, an empty man who handles the property of others without much benefit to himself, a cipher in the economic system, who is destined to be supplanted eventually by a computer. Mazzini Dunn is a touching vestige of the romantic past, an idealist groping through mists of illusion. Hector is a figure in a dream; Randall, a petulant child. The ladies are dangerously attractive and serve no purpose save to ensnare men who should be better occupied elsewhere. In this exhibition of decadent types, only Ellie Dunn seems vital, and it is on her disillusionment and her subsequent illumination that the action hinges.

The air of mystery which surrounds Shotover, his family, and his house in Sussex belongs to the tradition of Maeterlinck and Villiers de l'Isle Adam. In *Heartbreak House* symbols confront us at every turn. Shaw understood allegory better than symbolism; nevertheless, it is in its allegory that the play is bewildering. Nothing in the Shotover establishment really seems to invite destruction. The inmates seem to be kindly and well disposed, though their meals are haphazard and the service poor. They are said to be wasting their lives in dreams and love-making;

but these are, after all, the normal occupations of mankind, and it is difficult to sustain the thought that the social uselessness of these characters has anything to do with the final convulsions of the Austro-Hungarian Empire, and its disastrous consequences for Europe.

It is implied that, if cultured people in England had taken a proper interest in politics, Britain, at least, might have been spared the horrors of a World War. It is entirely possible; but as the play is framed, the suggestion has no particular basis. The Shotover establishment is not sufficiently representative to warrant the assumption that what is true of its inhabitants would be true, in the aggregate, of the English people. Heartbreak House is a unique phenomenon. Ostensibly it is a microcosm in which we may discern in miniature the elemental forces which are preparing the crack of doom; but the generalization is not compelling. Judging by the last scenes of the play, in the rarefied atmosphere of Captain Shotover's country house the crack of doom would cause no more of a stir than the snap of a party favor.

Captain Shotover's villa has other than allegorical connotations. It is a place where people are forced, for some reason, to tell the truth about themselves. This compulsion to strip away the pretenses of civilized society seems indecent, and particularly so to Boss Mangan. Nevertheless he too takes part, willy-nilly, in this orgy of truth-telling, although the effort leaves him physically exhausted and morally bankrupt. Shaw evidently considered this technique of dramatic unmasking a characteristic of Ibsenite drama, and some type of psychic anagnorisis is, as we have seen, a prime element in his early plays.[4] In *Heartbreak House* the truth game is played to its limits. The maskers are very thoroughly unmasked. In the end they are all stripped naked, and their shortcomings are embarrassingly visible. From a critical viewpoint this is the most compendious and also the most cruel of Shaw's comedies.

It is possible to see in Shotover some reminiscence of Shakespeare's Lear, but the analogy has little interest. The portrait of the old buccaneer subsiding into senility was perhaps suggested by the character of Captain Laroque in a play adapted from Octave Feuillet's five-act drama, *Le Roman d'un jeune homme pauvre* (1858).[5] This play has some interesting points of resemblance with *Heartbreak House*, but while Shotover perhaps recalls Laroque, his resemblance to Shaw is even more striking.

Shaw was actually no more than sixty years old when *Heartbreak House* was written; yet it is easy to see in the aged captain something like a caricature of the aging author. Doubtless in these years Shaw was subsiding into contentment, a state he dreaded worse than death. The idea of suffocating in happiness horrifies Shotover also: "I cant remember what I really am. I feel nothing but the accursed happiness I have dreaded all my life long: the happiness that comes as life goes, the happiness of yielding and dreaming instead of resisting and doing, the sweetness of the fruit that is going rotten.[6]

Shotover is Shaw's most memorable character, but as a symbol he has Protean vitality and stoutly resists precise definition. He is Shaw in a valetudinarian mood. He represents the decline of English greatness. He is impressively heroic in the style of Carlyle, a highly evolved individual whom the Life Force has exhausted, ready for the scrap heap, but still alive and active. None of this puts the imagination to rest. Like Hector Hushabye and Andrew Undershaft, his name obviously carries a suggestion, but it is not certain what that suggestion is. He has evidently overshot his mark, though it is difficult to say in what sense. It must suffice that he is a persistent spirit haunting a time that is no longer congenial to his temper and is unable to utilize his genius. Yet the younger generation finds him fascinating, and the play suggests that through his union with Ellie Dunn the bold spirit of the past will somehow be transmitted to the future.

Shotover has no great hope for this future. He tells Ellie:

> I can give you the memories of my ancient wisdom: mere scraps and leavings; but I no longer really care for anything but my own little wants and hobbies. I sit here working out my old ideas as a means of destroying my fellow creatures. I see my daughters and their men living foolish lives of romance and sentiment and snobbery. I see you, the younger generation, turning from their romance and sentiment and snobbery to money and comfort and hard common sense. . . .[7]

For Shotover money and comfort and common sense mean stagnation and death. The health of the human spirit is in its sense of purpose and its willingness to serve; for it is only in the pursuit of an aim that life is blessed. Shotover speaks nostalgically of a time of striving long gone by, of the divine discontent which he no longer feels, and which perhaps is no longer felt. Ellie understands his meaning, and for her it opens an avenue of hope. She tells Hesione Hushabye: "Life with a blessing! that is what I want. . . . There is a blessing on my broken heart. There is a blessing on your beauty, Hesione. There is a blessing on your father's spirit. Even on the lies of Marcus there is a blessing; but on Mr Mangan's money there is none."[8]

What Ellie has in mind is the blessing of the vital force which advances itself through pain, through intellect, through imagination, through beauty, through all the things that enhance the human spirit.

Life, and the will to live is the basis of evolution, as Butler defined evolution, and those who feel its vitality are blessed. But property is a sterile pursuit, involved not with doing, but with having. Such endeavors advance nothing and are not blessed. The realization of this truth is, presumably, the salvation of Ellie Dunn.

In order to be blessed it is first necessary to dispel the delusions that hinder the progress of the soul. *Heartbreak House*, like the Quarantine Station in Strindberg's *The Dream Play*, is a psychic cleaning establishment, where souls are purified of illusion. But the house itself is not proof against the process it engenders. In the merciless light that is shed upon it, the glamorous villa, with its handsome inmates, is seen to be an ill-regulated abode, peopled by shoddy characters—a mad old man, sodden with rum, a young singer bent on making a rich match, "a sluttish female trying to stave off a double chin and an elderly spread," a member of His Majesty's government whom everybody considers an ass, a stupid administrator, a sentimental dupe, and a romantic gentleman whose only occupation is a handsome wife. From a realistic viewpoint it is a sorry collection:

HECTOR: All heartbroken imbeciles.

MAZZINI: Oh no. Surely, if I may say so, rather a favorable specimen of what is best in our English culture. . . .[9]

It is because these people come to see themselves as they really are that they suffer heartbreak, but it is not clear that what they see is their ultimate reality. In Mazzini's eyes they are "very charming people, most advanced, unprejudiced, frank, humane, unconventional, democratic, free-thinking, and everything that is delightful to thoughtful people." Mazzini is too sentimental a man to be a trustworthy judge; the others are too cruel. They have all been disillusioned in turn, and the loss of illusion is an unpleasant experience which one is inclined to share with others: the disillusioned are vindictive. Yet, it is intimated, heartbreak is the indispensable prerequisite to a meaningful existence. It is the only sure method of producing a realist:

CAPTAIN SHOTOVER: Heartbreak? Are you one of those who are so sufficient to themselves that they are only happy when they are stripped of everything, even of hope?

ELLIE (*gripping the hand*): It seems so; for I feel now as if there was nothing I could not do, because I want nothing.

CAPTAIN SHOTOVER: Thats the only real strength. Thats genius. Thats better than rum.

ELLIE (*throwing away the hand*): Rum! Why did you spoil it?[10]

The Captain spoils it because he is not a wholly admirable old man. He no longer has faith in anything, not even in despair, not even in rum. There are no wholly admirable characters in *Heartbreak House*. It is all ready for the fire. But while Shaw depicted these personages in a most unflattering light, he was not disposed to destroy them utterly. The burglar and Mangan, neither of whom has any real substance, are annihilated. The others, with the exception of the brutally caricatured Randall, preserve their humanity and our sympathy to the end. In order to give tragic color to the final scene, it is necessary that the passing of this culture should evoke some measure of regret.

Heartbreak House is intended to represent the cultured element of English society. The English squirearchy is said to consist of two classes, the neurotic intellectuals—interested only in themselves—and the equestrian boobies, who live their lives luxuriously in the odor of the stable. Neither class is much concerned with the national interest; hence the management of the nation is left to professional politicians, incapable of pursuing any goal aside from their own personal aggrandizement. In *Heartbreak House* Boss Mangan exemplifies the type of expert manager who is chiefly skillful in preventing anyone from getting anywhere. In these circumstances, the nation drifts aimlessly, and in the gathering storm it is certain to founder. It is on this metaphor that the play, in its political aspect, is based:

HECTOR: And this ship that we are all in? This soul's prison we call England?

CAPTAIN SHOTOVER: The Captain is in his bunk drinking bottled ditchwater; and the crew is gambling in the forecastle. She will strike and sink and split. Do you think the laws of God will be suspended in favor of England because you were born in it?

HECTOR: Well, I dont mean to be drowned like a rat in a trap. I still have the will to live. What am I to do?

CAPTAIN SHOTOVER: Do? Nothing simpler. Learn your business as an Englishman.

HECTOR: And what may my business as an Englishman be, pray?

CAPTAIN SHOTOVER: Navigation. Learn it and live; or leave it and be damned.[11]

It is far from certain, however, that Hector will learn his business as an Englishman. He lives in the world of fiction. His mind is an adventure story; his vitality is diverted into useless channels; his motivations are rooted in the sheerest fantasy. He has, in short, all the qualities of an irresponsible officer and may be counted on to invite disaster just as surely as Mazzini Dunn courts failure, and Boss Mangan the inevitable heart-attack. In Ellie Dunn, there is some glimmer of hope; but Heartbreak House itself is hopeless, and the best that can be done with it is to blow it up without delay so that a fresh start can be made on its ruins. This is, indeed, what everyone seems to desire in the last scene of the play. It is an urgent and joyous manifestation of the need to die.

The last scene is, indeed, magnificent, and might well remind one of a Beethoven symphony, as Ellie somewhat inopportunely suggests, had it the benefit of a full orchestration. But, aside from the dialogue, its music is meager; there is only percussion and the squeak of an ailing flute. It is marvelously sardonic to have the abject Randall in his pyjamas piping up the conflagration with "Keep the Home Fires Burning," but it is also somewhat out of character for him to turn up unexpectedly with a flute at this juncture and even more so for his mistress to make him play it. Here, as elsewhere, Shaw makes use of a purely arbitrary turn in order to secure an effect. In the turmoil of the final scene only Shotover and Hector preserve their integrity as characters, and even Hector seems unduly enthusiastic in his desire to bring destruction upon them all.

As the play is conceived, there is no way to work out a convincing allegory, and this is doubtless an advantage. *Heartbreak House* is only vaguely suggestive of the disease which Shaw felt to be at the root of English society. Yet this suggestion is infinitely more effective than any precise allegory could be. The magic of the play is in its power of evocation, which is immense, and not at all in its line of reasoning, which is debatable. The action and the dialogue, inconsequential as they are, have the capacity to intimate what is not defined, so that the sense of doom, anticipated and even longed for, is pervasive as the scene lights up for the final effect.

This effect is all the more extraordinary since the end is, in contrast with the mood of despair which it generates, singularly lighthearted and joyous, an example of the power of disaster to relieve discomfort. The psychic basis of *Heartbreak House* is, in short, the death wish, and from this the play derives its romantic charm and all its cogency as drama.

In the end, it is clear that Ellie's union with the aged Captain is no more than a metaphor. The Captain is going to die. Nobody in Heartbreak House is going to learn navigation. What Hector desires is not time to chart a safe course for his people, but a signal with which to call down fire from the skies. There is a wonderful exhilaration in this yearning for a general explosion. It manifests the spirit of romance in its deepest and purest form, and it is not unlikely that, at this stage of his career, Shaw, who had resolutely resisted a masochistic tendency all his life, now for a brief period, succumbed, at least in fantasy, to its enchantments.

The mood in which this *Götterdämmerung* was composed was by no means characteristic of Shaw, nor was it at all peculiar to him in this period. The Victorian era, though officially optimistic in tone, had not been uniformly complacent. Many had been aware in these years of formidable obstacles to progress in the unparalleled prosperity of the mid-century. At that time, two generations before the time of *Heartbreak House*, such writers as G. R. Porter had already taken account of the ills of the machine-age in terms which, save for the sententiousness of his style, might have been written a century later: "It must be owned," Porter wrote,

> that our multiplied abodes of want, or wretchedness, and of crime— our town populations huddled together in ill-ventilated and undrained courts and cellars—our numerous workhouses filled to overflowing with the children of want—and our prisons (scarcely less numerous) overloaded with the votaries of crime, do indeed but too sadly and too strangely attest that all is not as it should be with us as regards this most important branch of human progress.[12]

Sixty-five years later, the great "storm-clouds of the nineteenth century," which Ruskin had marked on the horizon in his day, were filling the skies with lightning. The year after Shaw began *Heartbreak House*, Beatrice Webb noted in her diary: "I am haunted with the fear that all my struggles may be in vain, that death and disease are moving with relentless certainty."[13] The mood of pessimism had long ago been anticipated in France, especially by the more decadent of the Catholic writers. "Nous sommes," Barbey d'Aurevilly had written, "une race à sa dernière heure." There had been many who believed, for one reason or another, that the world would not survive the century.

But the First World War came to a close without bringing the human race to an end; the prophecy of *Heartbreak House* did not come true; and its warning remained unheeded. Its publication in 1919 came at an unauspicious time. There was no immediate English production. *Heartbreak House* was first produced by the Theatre Guild in New York in November 1920 and had a successful run. It fared worse in London. It was staged in October 1921 at the Court Theatre under the direction of James Fagan and was speedily withdrawn; but Barry Jackson revived it, some ten years later, at the Queen's Theatre in 1932, and at this time it was received with the respect due to an English classic.[14]

Had Shaw not invited comparison with Chekhov, it is doubtful that anyone would have considered *Heartbreak House* a play "in the Russian manner." By 1913, Shaw had seen *The Cherry Orchard, Uncle Vanya,* and *The Sea Gull.* He is reported to have said that, after seeing *The Cherry Orchard,* he felt like tearing up all his plays and starting afresh. It was an impulse he wisely resisted, for he had nothing in common with Chekhov.

Evidently what Shaw most admired in *The Cherry Orchard,* aside from its theme, was what he considered to be Chekhov's principle of dramatic construction. Ibsen's social plays had been carefully composed in the tradition of the Second Empire dramatists, and Shaw had followed these models faithfully, save in his "Disquisitory Plays," as late as the time of *Pygmalion.*

Chekhov's masterpieces were not so obviously well made. They had a novel quality which was entirely foreign to French drama. To Shaw, Chekhov's plays seemed to be the result of a spontaneous linking of associations very lightly controlled by a preconceived design. From a technical viewpoint this method of composition was new also to the type of art which passed for symbolism in England. It was pointillistic, a series of seemingly random touches which at a certain distance sprang together to make a design. Chekhov's dialogue did not seem to serve the plot, as dialogue does in a well-made play. His characters spoke in a curiously inconsequential fashion, as if they were not listening to one another. Yet their speeches were strangely suggestive of what lay behind in the mind of the speaker, so that the dialogue seemed to proceed on two levels, one spoken and the other wordless. All this gave Chekhov's plays a lifelike quality in comparison with which Ibsen's work seemed theatrical and old-fashioned.

Shaw did not respond to the pictorial tendencies of Chekhov's style. He interpreted his method musically. *The Cherry Orchard* in his estimation was an improvisation on a theme which admitted of many variations. Thus, while Chekhov departed widely from Ibsen's technique, his purpose was the same. He was, as Shaw saw him, primarily a writer of social plays; therefore the key to his method was to be sought in *The Quintessence of Ibsenism,* the only rational guide to the drama of the new age. The same might be said of Tolstoy, whose *Fruits of Enlightenment* also seemed to Shaw to be a satire of European upper-class culture, an independent exploration of "the house in which Europe was stifling its soul." Chekhov was a fatalist who "had no faith in these charming people extricating themselves from their predicament." They would,

Shaw believed, be sold up and sent adrift by the bailiffs; therefore Chekhov had "no scruple in exploiting and even flattering their charm."[15]

It is clear that, while Chekhov in the main eluded Shaw's comprehension, Shaw found quite enough in him to suit his purpose, and he cheerfully adapted Chekhov's viewpoint to his own frame of reference, very much as he had formerly adapted Ibsen's. In Chekhov he saw chiefly the socialist. *The Cherry Orchard* showed the truth behind the pleasant pretenses of middle-class culture. This truth was grim. The destruction of Madame Ranyevsky's villa, and the dispersion of her family, symbolized the end of Heartbreak House everywhere in the world. In Chekhov's play it was with regret that Lopakhin presided over the work of demolition, but he was only partially aware of the cosmic purpose he served in sweeping the debris of the past into the dustheap. The young people were more clearly conscious of the dialectic of history than their elders, and the destruction of their home and their orchard seemed to them a joyous and exciting prelude to the future.

So too it seemed to Shaw, but for Chekhov the transition from the past to the future was tinged with sadness. It was necessary that the past, and the beauty of the past, should give way to the life of the future; but it was by no means certain that the future would fulfill the hopes of those who looked forward to it. What was certain was the transitory nature of human life and human values, and the passing of all gracious things. Shaw was unwilling to waste a moment brooding over such sentimentalities. The past inspired him neither with nostalgia nor regret, only with a desire to get on with things, and at this time he had no confidence in the future of civilization. Therefore he took macabre pleasure in the prospect of a world that smashed itself up out of sheer stupidity. As betwen him and Chekhov the difference in viewpoint is evident in the endings of the two plays. *The Cherry Orchard* ends with old Firs, ill, alone, and forgotten, lying down to his last sleep in the deserted house, with the bell of the departing troika fading in the distance. *Heartbreak House* ends in a series of explosions accompanied by the tootlings of an uncertain flute played by a frightened fool.

Two years after *Heartbreak House* was finished, and two years before its first production in New York, Shaw began what he considered to be his major work, the play that was to sum up everything he had so far written. In this period his only other important writings were *Doctor's Delusions*, published in installments from December 1917 to March 1918 in the *English Review*, and *Peace Conference Hints*, a brochure published in 1919, which he later reprinted in *What I Really Wrote About the War* (1930).

The first was a carefully reasoned diatribe aimed at the abuses of organized medicine. Both the arguments and the abuses they deal with are curiously the same as those which in the 1970's we recognize as contemporary. The other had to do with the management of the post-war situation in Europe after the defeat of Germany, and the formation of a League of Nations with sufficient police power to ensure the world order. Neither of these estimable pieces appears to have had any influence anywhere.

Early in 1918, directly after finishing *Doctors' Delusions*, Shaw took up "The Gospel of the Brothers Barnabas." He worked at the play steadily until May of that year. By that time he had finished "The Thing Happens" and had begun "The Tragedy of an Elderly Gentleman." Apparently he put these scenes aside at this point in order to write the brochure on the peace conference. When he took up his play again, he decided to extend his plan of composition to include the story of the Garden of Eden. The two scenes of "In the Beginning" were completed in February 1919. In July 1919 he wrote to Trebitsch: "I am working at a huge tetralogy (like Wagner's Ring) called *Back to Methuselah*. First Play, Garden of Eden. Second Play the present day. Third Play, 300 years hence. Fourth Play, 1000 years hence."[16]

About a year elapsed, however, before he took up this work again. "The Tragedy of an Elderly Gentleman" was finished in mid-March of 1920, and immediately after it Shaw began "As Far As Thought Can Reach." The cycle of five plays was actually completed toward the end of May 1920, and the preface was written shortly after. In all, *Back to Methuselah* took a year and a half to complete.[17] It was produced in its entirety by The Theatre Guild at the Garrick Theatre in New York beginning 27 February 1922. The play took three nights to perform, even with drastic cuts in Part IV. It was presented in cycles of a week, ran nine weeks, and then closed. Its reception was extremely respectful; but it cost the Theatre Guild $20,000, a ruinous loss in the 1920's.[18]

As Shaw had foreseen, *Back to Methuselah* was not a popular success anywhere. It was first produced in England on 9 October 1923, by Barry Jackson at the Birmingham Repertory Theatre with a cast that included Edith Evans and Cedric Hardwicke, both at that time—in Shaw's phrase —provincial nobodies. It was played there four times with great acclaim and lost £2500.[19] The following year it was brought briefly to the

Court Theatre in London and, in 1927, it was recalled for some additional performances. In 1958—after Shaw's death—a condensed version was produced by the Theatre Guild in New York, with neither profit nor critical approval. On the whole, it was among the least successful of Shaw's great plays.

Shaw was awarded the Nobel Prize for literature in 1925. Nineteen years later, Oxford University Press asked him to select one of his works for publication as the 500th volume of its series of World's Classics. Shaw chose *Back to Methuselah*. In the postscript to the Oxford edition he wrote that this play was his masterpiece and, with becoming modesty, he ascribed its composition to a superior power:

> I do not regard my part in the production of my books and plays as much greater than that of an amanuensis or an organ-blower. An author is an instrument in the grip of Creative Evolution, and may find himself starting a movement to which in his own little person he is intensely opposed. When I am writing a play, I never invent a plot: I let the play write itself and shape itself, which it always does, even when up to the last moment I do not see the way out. Sometimes I do not see what the play was driving at until quite a long time after I have finished it; and even then I may be wrong about it just as any critical third party may.[20]

It may be assumed that in this semimystical identification with the Life Force Shaw had in mind a process analogous to that through which his mother had produced some volumes of automatic writing. The difference was that, while his mother considered her sprirtual guidance to be supernatural, Shaw considered his to be supremely natural, an elemental intelligence communicating through his agency tidings of exceptional urgency. *Back to Methuselah* was, he intimated, the latest effort of the Life Force to make itself intelligible, a supreme attempt of the vital spirit to achieve self-consciousness. As such it was holy, a work of scriptural importance which was destined to supplement the Bible.

For a twentieth-century writer to speak seriously of an external power as the source of his writings seems quaint, if not downright mad, but Shaw had not only excellent literary precedents, but by this time very likely he had complete faith in himself as an agent of the Creative Will. His was the outstanding voice of the time, of this everything combined to assure him. In the circumstances it was with a certain humility that he presumed to speak with the voice of God.

Milton had called upon the Holy Spirit for inspiration in writing *Paradise Lost*. Shaw had equal reason to believe that the Life Force would take a hand in the composition of *Back to Methuselah*. In an approving reference to Lorenz Oken's *Nature Philosophy* (1809), Shaw assimilated the Life Force to the Holy Ghost—with which, apparently, he associated Hegel's *Weltgeist*—and thus brought his evolutionary theory into a positive relation with acceptable Christian doctrine. Similar feats of syncretism had long ago been achieved in the early efforts at promoting Darwin's hypothesis. Oken, whom Weismann cited approvingly in his *History of Evolution*, had defined natural science as "the science of the everlasting transmutations of the Holy Ghost in the world." Shaw commented: "The man who was scientific enough to see that the Holy Ghost is a scientific fact got easily in front of the blockheads who could only sin against it."[21]

The preface to *Back to Methuselah* employs, together with some very convincing arguments, all the artifices of the hard sell, and the vehemence of the discourse gives cause for wonder. Shaw's motives are seldom entirely lucid. At sixty-five he was certainly in no need of money, and his position as a literary figure was enviable. On the other hand, he was a man of boundless ambition, and his longing for power had been cruelly thwarted. For one who aspired to be a world leader it was hardly enough to have been elected Vestryman of St. Pancras at the age of forty-one and nothing more. Evidently even at the last the dream of political preferment was difficult for him to relinquish. In the postscript he composed at the age of eighty-eight for the Oxford edition of *Back to Methuselah*, he wrote, only half-humorously:

> Physically I am failing: my senses, my locomotive powers, my memory are decaying at a rate which threatens to make a Struldbrug of me if I persist in living: yet my mind still feels capable of growth; for my curiosity is keener than ever. My soul goes marching on; and if the Life Force would give me a body as durable as my mind, and I knew better how to feed and lodge and dress and behave, I might begin a political career as junior civil servant and evolve into a capable Cabinet Minister in another hundred years or so.

But while he was too old, even at sixty-five, to dream of governing a nation, he was certainly not too old to aspire to be the spiritual guide of those who governed. The age requirements for the divine apostolate have never been fixed; indeed, age is an ornament to the successful seer. Very likely, Shaw more than half believed that *Back to Methuselah* had been dictated to him as the Koran had been dictated to Mohammed, and that one day it would be appointed to be read in churches.

Regardless of the source of his inspiration, Shaw's description of the spontaneity of his method is more justly applicable to his later works than to his earlier comedies. It was in the series of "disquisitory plays" culminating in *Heartbreak House* that Shaw put aside the calculated effects of the well-made play in favor of the freewheeling methods of his later compositions. Doubtless his growing faith in the creative ingenuity of the Life Force induced him to abandon himself so completely to its dictation that any preconceived plan of composition might be considered an obstacle to its influence. In these plays, accordingly, he came close to those writers who, under symbolist influence, felt that the unconscious is the surest guide to truth and that the artist's principal function is simply to describe the stream of images which are presented to his consciousness.

Accordingly, such plays as *Heartbreak House* in some ways anticipate the methods of surrealism without actually making use of surrealistic idioms. With regard to the association of ideas Shaw willingly relaxed the principle of logical sequence, the more so as he considered that any restraint was unjustified in a man of genius. Nevertheless, he never completely relinquished his rational control over the fancies that came into his mind. What he abandoned was the tight blueprint which was generally thought to be indispensable to sound dramatic construction. In his later plays the sequence of incidents often defies logical analysis, but the material itself is always under the control of the intellect.

In *Back to Methuselah* the result of this method is disappointing. It is by no means the worst of Shaw's plays. That honor must be divided among such potboilers as *Augustus Does His Bit* and the *Inca of Perusalem*. But while *Back to Methuselah* includes some of Shaw's best writing and some of his most vivid scenes, it is, on the whole, a dramatic composition so tedious as barely to support the spectator's attention in the theater. It is certain that Shaw was aware of its shortcomings as drama. Some time before the New York opening, he wrote to Granville-Barker of the contrapuntal scheme which governed the disposition of characters in *Back to Methuselah*: "To this end I may have to disregard the boredom of the spectator who has not mastered all the motifs, as Wagner had to do; but I daresay I shall manage to make the people more amusing, some of them more poetic, and all of them more intelligible than they are now in this first draft."[22]

Far more important, however, than the effect of the play as drama was its spiritual message, and it was this which made it, in Shaw's opinion, a great literary masterpiece. *Back to Methuselah* was not intended to amuse, but to edify. The usual sugar-coating, with which didactic comedy was made palatable, was of secondary importance in a work of such serious import. The play was intended to be a symphony, an opera, a gospel, and a prophecy. In the 1944 postscript, Shaw wrote: "The history of modern thought now teaches us that when we are forced to give up the creeds by their childishness and their conflicts with science we must either embrace Creative Evolution or fall into the bottomless pit of an utterly discouraging pessimism. . . ."[23]

Shaw was by this time using the word "discouragement" in the sense of a heart-withering ailment. To those afflicted with it the play was to bring new hope, as *Faust* had done in its day:

> Goethe rescued us from this horror with his "Eternal Feminine that draws us forward and upward" which was the first modern manifestation of the mysterious force in creative evolution. That is what made *Faust* a world classic. If it does not do the same for this attempt of mine, throw the book into the fire; for Back to Methuselah is a world classic or it is nothing.[24]

To the original preface of 1920, Shaw added some paragraphs in the nature of an apology, which provide a clue to his intentions both in the play and in his later work. Here he explicitly rejected the Horatian idea of a poetic work as a combination of the *utile* and the *dulce*. Such an idea was suitable, Shaw intimated, for a writer in the exuberance of youth; but one who has entered, like the ancients in his play, upon the stern disciplines of adult life, no longer has much taste for the *dulce*, nor any desire to sweeten his thought for the delectation of others. This is, he added, as true of himself as of his time, which has also achieved maturity in the theater:

> In 1901, I took the legend of Don Juan in its Mozartian form and made it a dramatic parable of Creative Evolution. . . . The effect was so vertiginous, apparently, that nobody noticed the new religion in the centre of the intellectual whirlpool. . . . Since then the sweet-shop view of the theatre has been out of countenance; and its critical exponents have been driven to take an intellectual pose which, though often more trying than their old intellectually nihilistic vulgarity, at least coincides with the dignity of the theatre. . . .
>
> I now find myself inspired to make a second legend of Creative Evolution without distractions and embellishments. My sands are running out; the exuberance of 1901 has aged into the garrulity of 1920; and the war has been a stern intimation that the matter is not one to be trifled with. I abandon the legend of Don Juan. . . . I exploit the eternal interest of the philosopher's stone which enables men to live forever. . . .

He added, a bit wistfully: "I am doing the best I can at my age. My powers are waning; but so much the better for those who found me unbearably brilliant when I was in my prime."[25]

He had, in fact, thirty years more to live.

As a play for the theater, *Back to Methuselah* leaves much to be desired; as an illustrated lecture on Creative Evolution it is unsurpassable. The play is a sequence of brightly colored vignettes animated chiefly by the ideas they develop, linked together by a group of recurrent type-characters, each of which is meant to be played by a single actor. Shaw did not see history, like Yeats, in terms of cycles of recurrence; but it is possible that he believed in something like reincarnation. At any rate, in *Back to Methuselah* the same types recur in generation after generation; possibly they are the same souls in successive manifestations. The characters that manifest them—Cain, Burge, Lubin, Haslam among others—are woven into the design of the play like threads in a tapestry. Each serves to represent a mode of thought. The resulting pattern is predominantly pictorial, but Shaw undoubtedly thought of it as an interweaving of Wagnerian *Leitmotiven* in a musical design.

The narrative hardly conceals the underlying tract. This is addressed to a world that has barely avoided crashing on the rocks and is once again drifting dangerously near them. In preaching his sermon, Shaw did not relinquish his customary role as socialist, economist, and statesman. He simply invested himself with his new priesthood, under which all these callings were subsumed. Without any special transition, he moved from the service of humanity into the service of God.

These were, at bottom, the same; but from this time forward, Shaw took on the guise of an evangelist preaching salvation in more or less traditional fashion, along with the threat of hell-fire for the unredeemed. His role was henceforth both saintly and prophetic. In the preface to *Saint Joan* he spoke with evangelical vehemence of "our shameless substitution of successful swindlers and scoundrels and quacks for saints as objects of worship, and our deafness and blindness to the calls and visions of the inexorable power that made us, and will destroy us if we disregard it."[26]

This transition from political economy to theology necessarily put a different complexion on Shaw's work as a dramatist. He now proclaimed himself the "conscious iconographer of a religion" and instituted an attack on his principal literary competitors on the basis of their lack of genuine significance. As he saw it, Shakespeare had neither a religious viewpoint nor a consistent philosophic outlook. The same was true of Ibsen and Strindberg:

> The giants of the theatre of our time, Ibsen and Strindberg, had no greater comfort for the world than we: indeed much less; for they refused us even the Shakespearean-Dickensian consolation of laughter at mischief, accurately called comic relief. . . . Goethe is Olympian: the other giants are infernal in everything but their veracity and their repudiation of the irreligion of their time: that is, they are bitter and hopeless. It is not a question of mere dates. Goethe was an Evolutionist in 1830: many playwrights, even young ones, are still untouched by Creative Evolution in 1920. Ibsen was Darwinized to the extent of exploiting heredity on the stage much as the ancient Athenian playwrights exploited the Eumenides; but there is no trace in his plays of any faith in or knowledge of Creative Evolution as a modern scientific fact. True, the poetic aspiration is plain enough in his Emperor or Galilean; but it is one of Ibsen's distinctions that nothing was valid for him but science; and he left that vision of the future which his Roman seer calls "the third Empire" behind him as a Utopian dream when he settled down to his serious grapple with realities. . . .[27]

If Ibsen was not able to grasp the idea of Creative Evolution, it was because this concept was not, in Shaw's judgment, a rational inference, but an intuition of which Ibsen was simply not capable. For Shaw this intuition, however, was of critical importance. Happiness was an illusion he had long since abandoned in the service of the Will; but in the absence of an understandable aim such service would be no more than slavery. Its aim, however, is evident. The Will develops intellect in order to attain self-consciousness, that is to say, in order to know itself. Consequently man is impelled to strive unceasingly for self-knowledge. Thus, while the Will remains inscrutable, its goal is clearly manifest to the elect. It is nothing less than the attainment of unlimited wisdom, and with it, unlimited power. In short, its end is godhead.

As it seemed to Shaw each age defines God in terms of its own limitations. The God of the Old Testament was once a useful concept. He is no longer serviceable in the age of science and must give way to a more accurate representation of the primal energy. Since the Will is immanent in man, the progressive intuition of truth takes place in the most intellectually advanced members of the species, for truth is nothing other than the knowledge attained by human minds, which in the aggregate are the mind of God. These elect must be heeded by the rest of humanity at its peril, for it is through them that the Will directs the course of its evolution. Since this evolution, apparently, cannot stop short of the absolute, the will to live is eternally operative as the mainspring of the cosmic process. The science of this process Shaw called metabiology:

> I had always known that civilization needs a religion as a matter of life and death; and as the conception of Creative Evolution developed, I saw that we were at least within reach of a faith that complied with the first conditions of all the religions that have ever taken hold of humanity: namely that it must be, first and fundamentally, a science of metabiology. . . .[28]

From the assumptions of this science it follows that evolution does not take place by chance, nor wholly through trial and error. It is through a conscious act of will that mankind transcends into higher forms of life. To this end great works are written, for all great art is fundamentally religious, and it is its high function to promote as far as is possible the impulses of the vital principle.

Metabiology is, obviously, no laughing matter, and cannot be presented in comic terms. *Back to Methuselah* is comic only in the sense that Dante's *Comedy* is comic. It exhibits Shaw for once in sober earnest, writing not in the guise of a bright and bellicose young man, but as the wise, stern, and all-seeing father, heavy with the need to admonish and to guide. It was a posture he had so far assumed chiefly in his prefaces and treatises.

The solemn nature of the preface to *Back to Methuselah*, with its show of erudition and its very plausible discussion of evolutionist theory, cannot obscure the fact that the play is essentially a work of science-fiction based on the improbable assumption that human life can be prolonged by a certain effort of the will. Underlying this assumption was Shaw's often expressed conviction that mankind, as it is presently constituted, is neither fit to govern itself, nor capable of being governed, so that any substantial advance in social conditions must await the evolution of a superior race of men. In *Man and Superman* the breeding of such a race is left to the Life Force operating through the beauty of woman. It is in this manner that the Eternal Feminine leads us upward, and from this standpoint Creative Evolution is an erotic adventure appropriately represented by the loves of John Tanner and Ann Whitefield.

In *Man and Superman*, these characters, in their universal aspect, are not depicted as being entirely in accord with the evolutionary pressures to which they are subjected. While Doña Ana is evidently eager to bring the superman into being through the usual channels, Don Juan somewhat perversely declines to lend his collaboration, and he withdraws at the first opportunity into the spiritual realm where sexuality has no meaning. In *Back to Methuselah* this disparity of purpose is further developed in the evolution of humanity, and the sexes are ultimately assimilated by the abandonment of sex as a means of reproduction. In contrast to *Man and Superman*, the amatory content of *Back to Methuselah* is minimal. For the will to live, love is a temporary expedient, which science in time supersedes.

In *Back to Methuselah*, the superman comes into being not through artificial selection, but through mutation. Genetic changes are motivated and realized in each case by an act of volition. Shaw ascribed this idea to Samuel Butler upon whose writings he had already drawn for the theoretical basis of *Man and Superman*. Butler's evolutionary hypothesis was teleological. In amplification of Lamarck's thesis, Butler had written: "I am insisting that important modifications of structure have always been purposive. A bird learns to swim . . . by trying to swim . . . but without exactly knowing what it is doing."[29] In similar fashion, Shaw reasoned, a man would learn to live longer by desiring to live longer. It was a conclusion which Butler had fully anticipated. Through an examination of the workings of the racial memory passed on from parent to offspring, Butler wrote:

> . . . a new light is poured upon a hundred problems of the greatest delicacy and difficulty. Not the least interesting of these is the gradual evolution of human longevity—an extension, however, which cannot be effected till many generations as yet unborn have come and gone. There is nothing, however, to prevent man's becoming as long-lived as the oak if he will persevere for many generations in the steps which can alone lead to this result.[30]

Passages of this sort provided the plan for *Back to Methuselah*. The actual working out of the system, however, necessitated a more complex concatenation of ideas. In formulating "The Gospel of the Brothers Barnabas," Shaw combined the Lamarckian theory of use and disuse with the Schopenhauerian will to live, the Hegelian World Spirit, and the theory of mutation recently developed by De Vries. The result was a heady "scientific" cocktail which only faith could make palatable and which, accordingly, might well be called a religion.[31]

From a philosophic viewpoint the Life Force approximated Nietzsche's will to power more closely than Schopenhauer's will to live; but in order to bring Nietzsche's idea into a fruitful relationship with the Lamarckian concept, Shaw assumed that the will to power was normally expressed as the individual's will to have power, not so much over others, as over himself—that is to say, in self-mastery. Thus the She-

Ancient of Part V explains to the children she is looking after, who are still involved with their dolls and drawings and their sex, that the object of a mature art is oneself and only oneself:

> . . . When I discarded my dolls as he discarded his friends and his mountains, it was to myself I turned as to the final reality. Here, and here alone, I could shape and create. When my arm was weak and I willed it to be strong, I could create a roll of muscle on it; and when I understood that, I understood I could without any greater miracle give myself ten arms and three heads.[32]

An ideal humanity, however, implies complete self-mastery. By the year 31,920, Shaw's ancients have not yet attained to that blissful state, but they have made some progress toward it. They have quite freed themselves of political concerns. Society has ceased to exist. There are only individuals and, apparently, not many; for birth, among other things, is under effective control.

As they are constituted in our time, it is suggested, men and women are ungovernable not because they are depraved, but because their lives are short. They have hardly passed beyond childhood when death takes them. The evolution of the superman depends, therefore, upon the prolongation of life long enough for the individual to attain intellectual maturity. In "The Gospel of the Brothers Barnabas" the optimal life span is considered to be 300 years. Such an extension of life is attainable, it is thought, through an act of volition sufficiently intense to communicate the necessary impulse to the unconscious forces at the service of the will. When this occurs a change may be expected to take place in the genetic substance, as a result of which mutants will come into being which will engender a long-lived race.

These new people will have leisure to attain wisdom through experience and study; the consequence will be a society in which individuals will be able to order their lives rationally. The state will then wither away as a useless framework, and an ideal anarchy will result. This is, indeed, the political situation that Shaw depicts in the year 31,920. By this time old age has ceased to be a burden, and life is enjoyable throughout its duration. There remains the risk of accidental injury. The social problem is solved; but not the vital problem. As yet nobody lives at will. The world spirit is still some distance from the freedom toward which it strives.

Nineteenth-century literature was rich in science-fiction, but as yet nobody had ventured to put anything serious of this sort on the stage.

What was performed in this genre was chiefly extravaganza of the type of W. S. Gilbert's *The Happy Land*, or *Utopia, Ltd*. Shaw was very willing to have his later utopian fantasies thought of as extravaganzas— evidently he fully intended to adapt this genre to serious purposes. *The Apple Cart* (1929), *Too True to Be Good* (1931), and *Geneva* (1938-39) are all three subtitled "Political Extravaganza." *Back to Methuselah*, however, has only the vaguest affinity with this sort of play, and it has no subtitle. Shaw was certainly familiar with such classics as the *Republic*, *Utopia*, and *The City of the Sun*. In writing *Back to Methuselah* he had in mind, also, the utopist writings of Swift, Samuel Butler, H. G. Wells, and William Morris, and he levied specifically on Bulwer-Lytton's *The Coming Race*. But *Back to Methuselah* differs both in scope and in purpose from any of these works. In a curious way, it rather recalls *Paradise Lost*.

"The Gospel of the Brothers Barnabas" was written very soon after the end of the Great War, so that this play and "The Thing Happens," which was written immediately after it, clearly reflect Shaw's wartime attitudes. Burge is a broad, but unmistakable caricature of David Lloyd George, the rough and ready Welshman who succeeded Asquith in the war ministry. Asquith is represented by the genial Lubin, elegantly educated and, aside from party intrigue, completely out of touch with political realities. Since both these statesmen were alive at the time of composition, and Lloyd George was still prime minister of England, these plays dealt polemically, and even daringly, with critical questions which now seem vital only by analogy. As social satire *Back to Methuselah* thus occupies a position somewhere between *The Acharnians* and *Gulliver's Travels*, but it is doubtful that either Aristophanes or Swift would have afforded himself the luxury of such an assault on the reader's patience as Shaw evidently felt his subject warranted.

In contrast to Burge and Lubin who, as practical men of affairs, decline to look an inch beyond their noses, the Barnabas brothers are endowed with the kind of foresight which is indispensable to political navigation. Conrad Barnabas is a biologist. Franklyn, his brother, is a statesman of clerical background. Together they typify the kind of politician that nations never entrust with the actual conduct of affairs; their work looks to the future, not to the present state of things. They are, indeed, involved not with politics but with metabiology, a science of which biology, religion, and statesmanship are necessary elements.

In the seemingly hopeless situation of contemporary Europe, it is their idea to perpetuate a race of men who will ensure the future of mankind. To this end, Conrad has published a work which suggests the possibility of achieving longevity by concentrating the will. The actual mechanics of the exercise are not entirely clear, but apparently it is enough to plant the possibility in people's minds in order to have it realized in time.

The thing happens some 250 years later, along with some other things forecast in the Fabian prospectus. At this time, mankind as a whole has not reached anything like its maturity, but social pressures have brought about some pleasant political changes. In the year of our Lord 2170 there is no longer any thought of war. In England there is communism, and the economic problem is solved. There is an equal distribution of wealth. Children are maintained and educated at the public expense up to the age of thirteen, after which they are required to work for the community for the next thirty years. The workers are retired at forty-three, with their maintenance guaranteed for the rest of their lives, and their pensions are calculated on the basis of an average life expectancy of seventy-eight years. It is through an infraction of this statistic that the actuarial authorities discover the secret presence of some unusually long-lived members in the community.

At this time communication is by television, and transportation takes place generally by air, but the British are still incapable of governing themselves. Parliament is an assemblage of harmless lunatics. The head of state, Burge-Lubin, is a pleasant figurehead, elected by popular vote, who hardly differs from his ancestral prototypes of 1918. The actual management of public affairs is in the hands of Chinese and Negro bureaucrats. The state is efficient, but soulless; it suffers from the disadvantages pointed out by Raznaikhin in Dostoevski's *Crime and Punishment*: "The phalanstery is ready, but nature is not ready for the phalanstery; it wants life; the living process is not yet fulfilled."

In these circumstances it is suddenly discovered that the Bishop of York and the Domestic Minister have lived quietly through several lifetimes and are now in the third century of their age. These long-lived people are, indeed, none other than the scatterbrained parson and the parlor maid of Part II. Much to their own surprise, these unlikely beings have demonstrated the validity of the gospel of the Brothers Barnabas, and to the consternation of the short-lived ministers, once they became aware of one another's existence, they rush off together to breed the super-race.

By the year 3000 the new strain of long-lived people is firmly established in the Western Isles, and the British capital, with its short-lived inhabitants, has moved eastward to Baghdad. A deputation of these eastern Britishers has come to Ireland to consult the oracle of the long-livers. The delegates are accompanied by an elderly tourist of exceptional inquisitiveness, and also by a Napoleonic figure strongly reminiscent of Cain. The contrast between the childishness of these visitors and the calm maturity of the super-race so discourages the Elderly Gentleman that he wishes to die and is mercifully killed by a glance of the Oracle's eye.

Shaw was consistent in ascribing death, as well as life, to an act of will. In his authoritative work, *The Evolutionary Theory*, August Weismann had written that death is a device of nature to prevent the unnecessary accumulation of exhausted organisms from cluttering up the earth. Weismann was a staunch Darwinian. He considered that death was no more than a convenient method of weeding out, in the ordinary course of natural selection, such individuals as were no longer adapted for survival.[33]

The difficulty with this idea, from Shaw's standpoint, was its determinist bias. Shaw found the sense of free will absolutely necessary to his comfort. In his view, accordingly, in the absence of accident, death also is the result of an act of volition, a measure taken freely by man in the beginning as a relief from the burden of everlasting existence.

In the treatise entitled "Parents and Children," prefaced to *Misalliance* (1910), Shaw had written:

> The Life Force either will not or cannot achieve immortality except in very low organisms. . . . With all our perverse nonsense as to John Smith living for a thousand million eons and for ever after, we die voluntarily, knowing that it is time for us to be scrapped, to be remanufactured, to come back, as Wordsworth divined, trailing ever brightening clouds of glory. We must all be born again, and yet again and again. . . . There is only one belief that can rob death of its sting and the grave of its victory; and that is the belief that we can lay down the burden of our wretched little makeshift individualities for ever at each lift toward the goal of evolution . . .[34]

The intimation that the time has come to die, Shaw called "discouragement." He had read travelers' accounts of the morbid despondency of primitive people who are suddenly exposed to the marvels of civilization, and he accounted on this basis for the rapid extinction of primitive races such as the Indians of North America. In *Everybody's Political What's What* (1945), he wrote of feeling something of the sort in his youth in the presence of a venerable Jew whose spiritual power made him feel insignificant:

> I was simply discouraged by him. . . . Since then, my observation, and the stories I have read about the dying out of primitive tribes at the impact of civilized invaders, have convinced me that every living

person has a magnetic force of greater or less intensity which enables those in whom it is strong to dominate those in whom it is relatively weak, or whose susceptibility to its influence, called shyness, is excessive.[35]

The idea that the mechanism of discouragement operates through magnetic pressure in all likelihood came to him through Strindberg. The experiments of Charcot with hypnosis at the Salpetrière, and Bernheim's experiments at Nancy in the 1880's, had convinced Strindberg that every meeting of individuals implied a psychic conflict to establish the mastery. This soul-conflict was the spiritual aspect, he thought, of the physical struggle for survival which Darwin had described in *The Descent of Man*. The conditions of existence were thus under constant adjustment through psychic encounters by means of which the stronger forced the weaker souls into subservience or, if need be, destroyed them. This idea of psychic murder is central in Strindberg's *Creditors*, *The Father*, and *Crime and Crime*.[36]

Shaw readily adapted the idea of soul-murder into his system. "Discouragement" was a humiliation of the will to live which might be so intense as to extinguish it in the individual soul. "You cannot converse with persons of my age for long without bringing on a dangerous attack of discouragement," the Woman tells the Elderly Gentleman in the year 3000. "Do you realize that you are already shewing grave symptoms of that very distressing and usually fatal complaint?"[37] The Elderly Gentleman does not realize it, but he does not feel as well as he might, either; and, in the end his discouragement becomes altogether too intense to be borne. The implication is that intellectual discrepancies of this magnitude cannot be endured for very long, and that the colonization of the short-lived by the race of supermen must end, sooner or later, in the extinction of mankind as we know it.[38]

By the year 31,920, in Part V, this process is concluded, and the very aspect of humanity is altered. The cycle of growth has by this time been vastly accelerated. People are hatched, fully developed, from the egg. In infancy they make love, dispute, and dance. Their alimentary organs have vanished. They no longer require sustenance, and there are no longer animals, nor birds, nor fish, for the Life Force has passed beyond such fruitless biological experiments. Sexuality is now a pastime which ceases at about the age of four; at this time people lose their secondary sex characters, and the sensual life rapidly gives way to the life of the intellect. But while there is no limit to the duration of life the body is still vulnerable to injury, and accidental death is, in the course of time, a certainty. The goal of humanity at this stage of its development is therefore the complete divestiture of the spirit from its bodily vehicle.

Even at this advanced stage of evolution, such an idea is not agreeable to the young. But since the period of youth is compressed into the first three years of a life of prodigious duration, the opinions of the young do not greatly concern the ancients. The revolt of youth which was to perturb the world in the 1960's and 70's is pleasantly anticipated in Shaw's account of the gerontocracy of the future. In Part V, there is a brief dialogue between a newly born girl and her nurse which comically foreshadows the campus dialogues of the present day:

THE NEWLY BORN: But I want power now.

THE SHE-ANCIENT: No doubt you do; so that you could play with the world by tearing it to pieces.

THE NEWLY BORN: Only to see how it is made. I should put it all together again much better than before.

THE SHE-ANCIENT: There was a time when children were given the world to play with because they promised to improve it. They did not improve it; and they would have wrecked it had their power been as great as that which you will wield when you are no longer a child. . . .[39]

This passage measures the distance that separated the Shaw of 1920 from the young radical of the early street-corner days. The scene is, indeed, not unduly prolonged. The She-Ancient is a patient schoolmarm, but not indefatigable:

THE NEWLY BORN: What is being tired?

THE SHE-ANCIENT: The penalty of attending to children. Farewell.[40]

Shaw's disillusionment with contemporary politics, which these passages reflect, is paralleled by the disenchantment implied in the Festival of Art which follows. The children amuse themselves with an exhibition of pictures and statues, but there is a discordant note which curiously anticipates the situation in Pirandello's *Diana e la Tuda* (1927). The aging sculptor in Shaw's play, at the age of four, has smashed his statues because he is unable to give them life and is now turning his attention to more important things than dolls. He is at this point pretty well grown-up and is therefore in a position to give his junior the benefit of his experience as an artist: "In the end the intellectual conscience that tore you away from the fleeting in art to the eternal must tear you away from art altogether, because art is false and life alone is true."[41]

It is, indeed, to life alone that the Ancients look for their creative activity, for they have discovered that ultimately one can create only oneself. This takes time. It is for this reason that death has been postponed indefinitely. The question of a convenient life span has been decided only after extensive experimentation. In Part I of *Back to Methuselah*, Adam, in a mood of discouragement, sets his life-span at 1000 years: it is all he can bear. But while Adam, in the beginning, invents death as a precaution against boredom, he continues to be troubled by the possibility of an inopportune accident. The possibility of such a thing is brought home to him at the very beginning of his life in Eden, when his destruction would necessarily involve the annihilation of all humanity; and it is in order to obviate any such possibility that the serpent imparts to Eve the secret of reproduction. But while reproduction, which at first Eve finds distasteful, ensures the survival of the race, it does nothing to ensure the persistence of the individual. Even after the life span has been indefinitely extended by the ancients, the fragility of the body continues to be a matter of concern, and the dualism of matter and spirit remains as a principal obstacle to the progress of those who survive to the imaginable limits of human longevity. Thus, in the year 31,920, the He-Ancient tells his class:

> THE HE-ANCIENT: That, children, is the trouble of the ancients. For whilst we are tied to this tyrannous body we are subject to its death, and our destiny is not achieved.
> THE NEWLY BORN: What is your destiny?
> THE HE-ANCIENT: To be immortal.
> THE SHE-ANCIENT: The day will come when there will be no people, only thought.
> THE HE-ANCIENT: And that will be life eternal.[42]

The idea of a bodiless existence seems both unattractive and improbable to the children of this era, but the grown-ups fervently anticipate the delights of becoming a vortex of pure energy:

> THE SHE-ANCIENT: None of us now believe that all this machinery of flesh and blood is necessary. It dies.
> THE HE-ANCIENT: It imprisons us on this petty planet and forbids us to range through the stars.
> ACIS: But even a vortex is a vortex in something. You cant have a whirlpool without water; and you cant have a vortex without gas, or molecules or atoms or ions or electrons or something, not nothing.
> THE HE-ANCIENT: No: the vortex is not the water nor the gas nor the atoms: it is a power over these things.[43]

Shaw's ancients aspire to power, not to Nirvana. They have no desire to relinquish individuality. They desire, on the contrary, to preserve their self-consciousness and to exert their will so far as is possible. Adam found the burden of life too heavy to bear for very long. Not the ancients. The difference is that Adam knew only the life of the body, while the ancients have already gone a long way toward the pure vitality of the spirit. They represent the finite aspect of the Don Juan of *Man and Superman*, but, like him, they are engaged in an infinitely extended intellectual adventure.

There is, of course, some question as to the purpose of a spiritual enterprise which ends about where it began. In *Back to Methuselah*, the author's optimism is overshadowed by a sense of futility which no rhetoric can conceal, and, in the end, Adam thinks the whole thing a piece of foolishness in which he would as soon not have taken part. But, at the last, Eve is content. The offspring of Cain, her bad son, have vanished. Only her good children have survived. Man was never really evil. He was merely childishly aggressive; and this is a fault that time has cured. As with Schopenhauer's saints, salvation lies in "joyfully forsaking the world," and this the ancients appear to have done with all possible alacrity. In Eve's opinion, a good time has been had by all, or nearly all, and the results have amply justified the effort.

In the end, however, Lilith, who has brought life into the world out of her own being, seems as uncertain as Adam as to what the whole thing was about. She has infused life into matter and brought a semblance of order out of chaos. The experience has been interesting:

> I am Lilith: I brought life into the whirlpool of force, and compelled my enemy, Matter, to obey a living soul. But in enslaving Life's enemy I made him Life's master; for that is the end of all slavery; and now I shall see the slave set free and the enemy reconciled, the whirlpool become all life and no matter. And because these infants that call themselves ancients are reaching out towards that, I will have patience with them still; though I know well that when they attain it they shall become one with me and supersede me, and Lilith will be only a legend and a lay that has lost its meaning. Of Life only there is no end . . . and though its vast domain is as yet unbearably desert, my seed shall one day fill it and master its matter to its uttermost confines. And for what may be beyond, the eyesight of Lilith is too short. It is enough that there is a beyond.[44]

Thus Lilith, as the source of being, remains enigmatic. She is the Life Force, but she is neither life nor force. She is the principle through which the two are combined and progressively ordered, an entity whose existence is purely inferential. Samuel Butler had written: "Von Hartmann personifies the unconscious and makes it act and think—in fact, deifies—whereas I only infer a certain history for certain of our growths and actions in consequence of observing that often repeated actions come in time to be performed unconsciously.[45] Such an abstract conception of the Will behind evolution was perhaps suitable for the preface of *Back to Methuselah*, but it was obviously useless for dramatic purposes. If the Unconscious is to be represented on the stage, it must be personified. Thus, while Shaw has Lilith say that she represents the primordial Will through which life is embodied in matter, he is careful not to identify her with life itself. She is, in Shaw's conception, a phase in the development of the vital energy, but, in the light of eternity, a provisional phase, like everything else that lives.

Back to Methuselah is perhaps unduly didactic, but it displays a perspective of truly Wagnerian grandeur. As a poetic statement, obviously, it does not bear comparison with the great epic works, neither with *Faust*, nor *Paradise Lost*, nor *The Divine Comedy*, with all of which it has some affinity. These are myths completely realized as works of art, poetic entities based on a total conviction of truth, and what was once their truth is now their beauty. *Back to Methuselah* is a tract in epic form. Like Dante's *Comedy* and Milton's *Paradise Lost*, it bears the stamp of its time and country and is shaped, like both these works, in accordance with the author's political and social preconceptions. It has some fine poetic passages, but neither the universality nor the sublimity of a poetic synthesis. It belongs, therefore, not with the great masterpieces which abstract the essence of an age, but with the type of utopian literature which satirizes the unhappy present, while at the same time it affords a provocative glimpse of a more agreeable future.

Judging by his prose writings, Milton had no doubt that Adam and Eve once actually existed, and that Satan, having deprived them of the joys of Eden, was still busy in his efforts to discommode their progeny. Doubtless the sincerity of his belief has much to do with the extraordinary power which his work still exerts over the imagination. But for Shaw, Adam was no more than a convenient symbol, and the myth of the Garden was useful principally for its poetic value. In the preface to *Back to Methuselah*, it is true, the theory of Creative Evolution is advanced as scientifically valid and is accordingly bolstered up with much documentation and a great show of authority. There is no reason to doubt that at the time this preface was written Shaw believed in his facts as fervently as Dante believed in the love that moves the sun and the other stars. But by 1944 Creative Evolution appears to have taken on the guise in his mind of a myth of government, part of the necessary religious framework of an orderly state. "It is through such conceits," he noted, "that we are governed and governable."[46] Evidently his faith in the supremacy of the Life Force was subject to change. Like everything else in an essentially mutable universe, his religion had by this time become a useful metaphor, and his fervor, however sincere, was now to be considered in the light of a promotional effort.

For these, and other reasons, *Back to Methuselah* is unlikely to occupy so high a place in the estimation of posterity as Shaw bespoke for it. But the greatness of his conception cannot be denied. In spite of the chattiness of the early scenes, the perspective the play affords of the vital force developing blindly through a series of progressively complex material forms, including humanity, towards its entelechy as pure intelligence is an impressive example of nineteenth-century romantic thought.

The fact that it appears to be a tardy example of neo-Aristotelian doctrine should not obscure the glamor of the conception. In attempting to integrate, in the manner of Dante, Milton, and Goethe, the most advanced thought of his time with the philosophic tradition he found personally most congenial, Shaw accepted a challenge normally taken up only by the major poets of our culture. Unhappily, he was not of their company. He was an exceptionally gifted journalist with a genius for dramatic writing. In the circumstances, his pretensions to prophetic vision seem, like everything else about him, magnificently extravagant, but their magnificence is more impressive than their extravagance. When we compare his vision with the vision of Yeats they even seem reasonable.

Both Dante and Milton stood on secure theological ground. The science they interpreted was sanctified by authority and was, in their time, beyond controversy. On the other hand, Yeats permitted his imagination to roam luxuriously through a jungle of cabalistic imagery. He did not trouble to support his cosmology in *A Vision* (1937) with even a semblance of empirical testimony, and it is far from clear to what extent he himself was convinced by the universe he had created. Shaw, however, had unbounded confidence in the scientific basis of his conception and, at least for a time, complete faith in the accuracy of his intuition. He lived, however, in a skeptical age, when no dogma, theological or scientific, was safe, and he was forced to promote his views with unseemly vigor. In speaking of their gospel, the Barnabas brothers reach a height of enthusiasm more suitable to the marketing of a patent medicine than to the exposition of a philosophic system:

> CONRAD: . . . Ever since the reaction against Darwin set in at the beginning of the present century, all scientific opinion worth counting has been converging rapidly upon Creative Evolution.

FRANKLYN: Poetry has been converging on it: philosophy has been converging on it: religion has been converging on it. It is going to be the
religion of the twentieth century: a religion that has its intellectual
roots in philosophy and science just as medieval Christianity had its
intellectual roots in Aristotle.[47]

In their understandable enthusiasm the brothers Barnabas seem a
bit over-emphatic. Creative Evolution had no more secure basis in
twentieth-century science than theosophy or anthroposophy, and scientific writers such as Julian Huxley declined to take it seriously.[48] The
evidence against the inheritance of acquired characters was at this time
overwhelming. There was absolutely nothing to indicate that the course
of evolution was ever directed by an act of volition, either conscious or
unconscious: nothing, that is, but common sense, the conclusions of
which ordinarily carry little weight in the laboratory. In the time of the
brothers Barnabas, neither poetry nor philosophy nor scientific opinion
could be said to converge upon anything; and least of all upon Creative
Evolution. Shaw's religion, however attractive, had at no time any discernible future as a popular creed save in Shaw's imagination and, for all
his urging, he was unable to will it into anything like general acceptance.
If the alternative to Creative Evolution was despair, as Shaw believed,
humanity evidently preferred despair. In the 1950's, existentialism
emerged as a dominant influence on twentieth-century thought. It was a
far cry from Shaw's optimistic faith.

Thus, from every viewpoint, save the aesthetic, Shaw's "world classic"
might be judged a failure. He was, by all odds, the most important
English dramatist since Shakespeare, and possibly the most influential
spirit of his time, but his genius did not extend to an epic conception. If
Back to Methuselah proves anything, it is that great ideas do not—as
Shaw believed—make great drama. But great drama can make great
ideas. It was perhaps some intimation of this truth that motivated Shaw's
next major work. *Saint Joan* was neither a discussion nor a tract. It was
an attempt at a tragedy of ideas, and as such it was splendidly successful.

At sixty-five Shaw was sufficiently sure of himself, and sufficiently in
honor, to blame the failure of *Back to Methuselah* on the obtuseness of
the public rather than on the shortcomings of the play. Nevertheless,
soon after its composition, he told his biographer, St. John Ervine, that
he felt he was finished as a dramatist.[49] It was fully two years before he
got over his discouragement. Then he began work on *Saint Joan*.

The theme had some immediacy. In 1920 Joan of Arc was at last canonized by Pope Benedict XV. The decision to exalt her to sainthood, motivated by a variety of considerations, reflected church policy with respect to the postwar resurgence of faith in Catholic countries. In France Joan had played a significant part in the war effort. She had been seen on posters fighting magnificently in the trenches alongside her poilus. She was an invaluable symbol of French military prowess, and her belated canonization gave Shaw a golden opportunity to express his views on the subject of war, religion, patriotism, and sainthood. The subject had long ago captured his imagination. In a letter to Mrs. Patrick Campbell, written from Orléans in the fall of 1913, he had already expressed a warm interest in the story of Joan of Arc.

Nevertheless when it was suggested to him seriously, ten years later, that he write a play about her, the project did not move him to enthusiasm. To fit the story of Joan into his system would involve, necessarily, a rather more subtle manipulation of history than had been required with the story of Julius Caesar, his other venture into historical drama. When he had taken up the matter of Caesar twenty-five years before, Shaw's world view was still in the process of crystallization. By the time of *Saint Joan* it had been formulated and revised and was perhaps in need of further revision. The legend of Joan was quite apt for the purpose, but evidently it took Shaw some time to realize its possibilities.

There was no lack of available documentation. The record of the trial of Jeanne d'Arc in 1431 has been carefully preserved. The original manuscript, bearing vestiges of the seal of Pierre Cauchon, is treasured in the library of the Chamber of Deputies in Paris. There exists, in addition, a contemporary account of the trial, drawn up by Thomas de Courcelles of the University of Paris, one of the more obnoxious judges in Shaw's play. This model of Latin eloquence, proving that the trial was conducted in accordance with the most meticulous procedural technique, was widely circulated to the chancelleries of Europe by the English government as part of its campaign to discredit the French crown. Five copies are still extant.

Charles VII made no effort to rebut the evidence against Joan until after his conquest of Normandy, but in 1450 he considered it politic to institute an inquiry into the legality of Joan's sentence and the justice of the verdict. His first attempt failed. Some years later, under Calixtus III, the case was reopened, ostensibly at the insistence of Joan's mother. As a result of the testimony offered during this inquiry twenty-five years after the fact, the Grand Inquisitor of France, Jean Bréhal, published a memorandum establishing Joan's orthodoxy. On 16 June 1456, the original judgment was annulled, and the blame for the manifest irregularities of the first trial was laid at the door of Pierre Cauchon. He had died in honor, some years before, as Bishop of Lisieux. He was promptly removed from the magnificent tomb he had provided for himself in his Cathedral and was cast into the public sewer. Thus Cauchon became the villain, and Jeanne d'Arc the heroine of a melodrama of some importance for the history of France.

The story of Joan's life was first extricated from the myths that grew around it by Edmund Richer in the seventeenth century; but this biography remained in manuscript in the Bibliothèque Nationale until 1911. In the meantime, Jules Quicherat collected, transcribed, and published the records of both trials, as well as the other evidence adduced in the case, in five volumes of painstakingly documented history (1841–49). Quicherat's scholarly work was translated into English in an abridged edition by T. Douglas Murray in 1902. In 1921 Pierre Champion published the text, together with a French translation of the *Procès de condamnation*, in an excellent edition with an introduction and notes. There is no evidence that Shaw knew this book. In all likelihood he based his play on Murray's English translation.

This was brought to his attention early in 1923 by Sydney Cockerell, at this time Curator of the Fitzwilliam Museum at Cambridge, with the suggestion that there might be a play in it. Shaw evinced no interest in the idea. But Mrs. Shaw was deeply interested, and she contrived to keep the subject warm until at last it captured her husband's imagination. According to Rattray, his chronicler, Shaw wrote a good part of the play in Ireland, threading his way through the tangle of ecclesiastical lore with the aid of a couple of friendly priests. It is said that he modeled his heroine upon Mary Hankinson, a lady who managed the Fabian summer schools. The suggestion is supported by the inscription in a copy of the play which Shaw presented to her. It reads: "To Mary Hankinson, the only woman I know who does not believe she was the model for Joan, and also the only woman who actually was."

It is difficult, however, to understand in what way Miss Hankinson, a pleasant, middle-aged woman of firm disposition, could have served as a model for Saint Joan: or, indeed, how any woman of our time could possibly represent this embattled teen-ager of the fifteenth century. The real Jeanne d'Arc was, it is said, the daughter of a well-to-do farmer, the *doyen* of the village of Domrémy, situated just across the Meuse from Burgundian territory. God first spoke to her when she was thirteen. In consequence she vowed to remain a virgin and to consecrate her life to

His service. Thereafter she had visions several times a week and enjoyed long conversations with Saint Michael, Saint Catherine, and Saint Theresa.

At sixteen, Joan, now a full-grown girl, began to importune Baudricourt, the commander of the local French garrison, for permission to go to the Dauphin Charles at Chinon in order to tell him that God had ordered her to crown him king of France in the cathedral at Reims.

Meanwhile the English, with Burgundian aid, were assembling an army in Champagne for the invasion of Charles's territories south of the Loire. In July 1428 the armies began to move. Domrémy was burnt, and Orléans was soon invested. The situation at Orléans was not at all desperate. The city was besieged by an English force of 10,000, but the French garrison, under the command of Dunois and La Hire, was constantly reinforced with French troops. There were 250 pieces of ordnance mounted on the ramparts. The English held the bridgehead on the Loire, and they had built a dozen bastilles around the city walls, which were constantly manned.

In these circumstances, Joan at last succeeded in getting Baudricourt to give her a sword and a horse, and to send her to the castle of Chinon to see the Dauphin. To test her powers, Charles hid himself among his courtiers. She recognized him immediately and gave him a sign which, it is said, at once convinced him of her divine authority. Nevertheless, he had her thoroughly examined by a committee of clerics from the University of Poitiers, after which it was decided to send her to Tours to take up arms against the English. Preceded by a procession of French priests, Joan then solemnly led a column of 4000 French troops to the relief of Orléans.

Dunois met her before the city walls. Her troops crossed the Loire with a favorable wind and entered the city without incident. On April 30, she formally ordered the English to depart. They paid no attention. Five days later, she stormed one of their bastions; and two days after that, she led an assault on the tourelles at the bridgehead, took it after a sharp struggle in which she suffered a wound and drove the English from the city. In two months' time, on 16 July 1428, after an uninterrupted series of victories, she presided over the coronation of the Dauphin at Reims, exactly as she had promised. She had further plans. She was now resolved to unify all of France under the newly crowned king.

The time, indeed, was ripe for an immediate march on Paris, which was still held by the English under Bedford. But Charles was reluctant to commit his troops to so hazardous a venture, and he wasted a month in negotiating a truce with Burgundy. On August 26, Joan marched upon St. Denis, in the vicinity of Paris, signed an armistice with the Burgundians, and, early in September, led an assault on Paris at the Porte St. Honoré. The assault failed. Once again Joan was wounded. By the time she recovered, Charles had disbanded his troops and the campaign was over.

When the armistice came to an end the English resumed their alliance with Burgundy and proceeded to invest Compiègne. Joan took a small force to its relief. On 23 May 1429, she led a sortie against the besiegers. Her force was driven back into the city. The drawbridge was closed before she could get in, and she was taken prisoner by the Burgundians.

Jean de Luxembourg, the Burgundian commander into whose hands she had fallen, could have put her to death at once; but Bedford, considering that it would be advantageous to discredit her first and to kill her afterwards, requested the ecclesiastical authorities to put her to trial as a witch. On July 14, Pierre Cauchon, an ambitious priest who had been bishop of Beauvais and now aspired to the see of Rouen, offered to conduct the trial under English auspices. Jean de Luxembourg then sold her to the English for 10,000 livres, and she was held at the English military headquarters at Rouen in the custody of the Earl of Warwick, pending the constitution of the court.

On 3 January 1431, Warwick handed her over to Cauchon for trial. The tribunal was carefully picked. It consisted of ten members of the Faculty of Paris, twenty-two canons of the Cathedral of Rouen, and a few monks. The interrogation began 21 February 1431. Three weeks later, the Vice-Inquisitor appeared, accompanied by a Dominican friar, and joined himself to the investigation. Twelve points were charged against Joan. The main offense was her declaration that she was responsible only to God, and not to the church.

Joan held out manfully throughout most of the trial, but toward the end of May she began to show signs of exhaustion. On May 23 she was taken to the cemetery of Saint Ouen to have a sentence read to her in which she was condemned to the stake unless she signed an abjuration. In great fear, fainting, she signed the paper. The court then sentenced her to life imprisonment. Warwick, however, was not satisfied. He insisted that she be burnt, and Cauchon was ordered to visit her in her cell in an effort to elicit new grounds for action.

Finding that Joan had resumed her male dress, Cauchon decided that she had relapsed into heresy. It was determined, consequently, to deliver her at once to the secular arm for execution. On 30 May 1431, after receiving communion in her cell, she was dressed in woman's clothes and led to the stake in the Old Market Place in Rouen. There, after listening to a long sermon, she had her sentence read to her a second time and was then burned to death. Her ashes were raked up and thrown into the Seine.[50]

These were the ascertainable facts when Shaw sat down to write his play. He arranged his narrative in six scenes, beginning with Joan's visit to the garrison at Vaucouleurs. The first three scenes are brisk and busy. They depict her meeting with Baudricourt, her presentation to the Dauphin, and her rendezvous with Dunois before Orléans. The fourth scene develops a long negotiation between Cauchon and Warwick in a tent in "the English camp," in the course of which the two powers, military and ecclesiastical, come to an accord with regard to Joan's ultimate fate, though she is still at the height of her power and prestige. The following scene is set in the Cathedral of Reims, immediately after Charles's coronation. It is at this point that the hopelessness of Joan's position becomes apparent. In the sixth scene, the blow has fallen. The trial at Rouen begins and ends with marvelous celerity; and Joan is rushed off to the fire.

These scenes, vivid and realistic in conception, are followed by a seventh, a dream sequence in quite a different style. This takes place twenty-five years later in the royal bedchamber in one of Charles's castles. In the course of Charles's dream, all the principal themes of the play are recapitulated, and Joan's canonization five centuries later is foreshadowed. It is with this epilogue that Shaw sets his cachet on the story of Joan.

The amount of invention necessary to carry forward the action of the play might seem to be minimal, since the indispensable events are a matter of history, and quite precisely fixed in time. But in a period when historical drama in England was either poetic in the manner of Browning, Tennyson, or Stephen Phillips, or impossibly melodramatic in the style of Bulwer-Lytton, it was no inconsiderable feat to arrange a narrative sequence in such a way as to make a point, establish a character, and evoke a mood, without a wholesale falsification of the record.

In his historical plays Ibsen had departed widely from the romantic style of Schiller, and even further from that of Victor Hugo and Dumas *père*. *Saint Joan* however, inaugurated a new tradition. It was a work of art of essentially modern design based on an unmistakably modern interpretation of history, peopled with characters conceived so that they were entirely intelligible in contemporary terms. As historical drama it was completely different from the Elizabethan history plays, which in their fashion had also brought history up to date. There was nothing in English since the time of Shakespeare that was equally impressive in this genre.

The subtitle of *Saint Joan*, "A Chronicle Play in Six Scenes and an Epilogue," has some flavor of antiquity. Chronicle plays, obviously, belong to the sixteenth century. By the time of Shakespeare they had given place to a kind of historical drama plotted so that it is not always distinguishable from tragedy. History plays of the type of *Richard III* and *Edward II* have normally a didactic tendency; but their exemplary character is usually of a very simple sort, and the philosophic basis, if any, is the normal assumption that history is the record of man's sins and God's judgments. The subtitle Shaw gave *Saint Joan* was obviously fanciful. It is in no sense a chronicle play, nor is it in the usual sense a history play, although it makes use of a narrative sequence derived from historical sources. In the preface it is actually presented as a thesis play. Shaw speaks of it elsewhere as "classical tragedy." There is reason to believe, also, that it was intended to be a comedy. No great purpose is served by trying to allocate it to a specific category. What is clear is, that of all Shaw's plays, this comes closest to the heroic genre.

Saint Joan was produced first in New York at the Garrick Theatre, on 28 December 1923, with Winifred Lenihan in the title role. The New York critics, with characteristic acumen, found the play tiresome, talky, and overlong, but the audience received it with enthusiasm, and it was soon moved to the Empire, a larger house.[51] In London it opened the following March with Sybil Thorndike in the part of Joan, and settings and costumes designed by Charles Ricketts. The production had a run of 244 performances, and the London critics received it with the greatest respect. It was no longer fashionable in England to sneer at Shaw.

In March 1936 Katherine Cornell revived the play in New York. She was already a famous actress, and this time the New York press was respectful. Percy Hammond, thirteen years before, had thought *Saint Joan* "just another example of Mr. Shaw's gift for interminable ragchewing." He now wrote reverently of the final scene: "I said to myself, here is the theatre in one of its most consecrated moments." Alexander Woollcott saw some trace of greatness in it also, though he deplored a tendency "to falter and go astray." Kenneth Macgowan felt that Shaw had aged: "the inspiration and divinity of Shaw have departed."[52] A

Nobel laureate was not to be brushed off lightly. Those who had never seen any sign of greatness in Shaw now lighted happily on his confession of oncoming age and hastened to bewail the fact that his greatness had passed. Yet in spite of critical disapproval, expressed or implied, *Saint Joan* proved to be among Shaw's most durable contributions to modern drama. In the following years, it was played many times, and the trial scene in particular was screened, broadcast, televised, and exhibited in every possible way. At the end of his life Shaw had the satisfaction of knowing that he had in fact written one of the world's classics.

According to Lawrence Langner, his American manager, Shaw said that the play was written under the direct inspiration of Joan of Arc. "As I wrote," he said, "she guided my hand, and the words came tumbling out at such speed that my pen rushed across the paper and I could barely write fast enough to put them down."[53] If this was true, one can only marvel at the literary aptitude of his saintly muse. The legend of Jeanne d'Arc, carefully nurtured over the centuries, had so far been hopelessly sentimentalized in the theater. Its heroine, a handsome, brave, and splendidly patriotic maid, betrayed by her friends and destroyed by her enemies, could hardly be managed on the stage without melodramatic extravagance. All that was lacking to fill out her story according to the traditional patterns was a love affair, and this had been regularly supplied by all those who had handled her story for the theater in the past.

Shaw omitted the love interest and stressed the political and religious aspects of the situation. In the course of his research, which was extensive, he rummaged over everything that might be deemed significant in the literature of the subject. His preface, a marvel of critical writing, includes estimates of Shakespeare's *Henry VI*, Voltaire's *La Pucelle d'Orléans* (1762), and Schiller's *Die Jungfrau von Orleans* (1801), all of which he found quite lacking in truth. The work of Quicherat is mentioned with appropriate respect, and there are brief comments also on Anatole France's *La Vie de Jeanne d'Arc* (1907), *The Maid of Orleans* by Andrew Lang (1908), and Mark Twain's novel, *Personal Recollections of Joan of Arc* (1896). Most of these works are dismissed summarily either because of the author's special bias, as in the case of Voltaire, or because of his frivolousness and lack of historical understanding. The clear intention of this survey was to indicate the need for a work of art on the subject of Joan of Arc which should be unbiased, realistic, and authoritative, and the intimation is that *Saint Joan* is that work.

Actually there is no evidence in the preface or elsewhere that Shaw had any special insight into the history of the fifteenth century. Happily ignorant of the complexity of his subject matter, Shaw was able to view both Joan and her times strictly in terms of nineteenth-century concepts. He could therefore argue that the martyrdom of Joan would have taken place in the course of the First World War in much the same way as it had five centuries earlier, and for very similar reasons; and he cited the martyrdom of nurse Edith Cavell and the execution of Roger Casement in support of his contention. This argument brought Joan pretty well up to date. The assumption was, as in the case of *Caesar and Cleopatra*, that human nature does not change perceptibly in the course of a few centuries, and that the social and national pressures that were operative in 1431 are still operative and, in similar circumstances, would bring about similar consequences today.

Shaw's anachronisms would, of course, warrant little comment if his display of scholarship did not put one off the track as to his intentions. Very likely he did his play some disservice by insisting on the accuracy of his historical conclusions. He had, however, excellent precedents for his method. In *Emperor and Galilean* (1872), Ibsen had succeeded brilliantly in fitting the Emperor Julian into a modern historical pattern, and in *Master Olaf* (1872, 1877) Strindberg had redesigned Swedish history in even more striking fashion. The vicissitudes of the history of Joan of Arc were, however, much more varied than those of the history of Julian the Apostate or the story of Gustav Vasa and his Pastor Primarius. In arranging his narrative Shaw had his choice of a host of misinterpretations.

For the English statesmen of the fifteenth century, the obstacle presented by a rambunctious teen-age girl to the territorial ambitions of the Crown could admit of only one solution. It was impossible for the English government to agree that Joan was a great general, much less a saint. She had to be either an impostor, a witch, or a whore, or all of these together, and so it is that she appears in Holinshed's *Chronicle* on which Shakespeare based the *Henry VI* cycle of plays. In *Henry VI, Part I*, Joan is represented as an agent of the devil, very much as such disruptive ladies as Alcina and Armida are depicted in the Italian *romanzi*. This was not, however, a viable cliché, and it soon gave way to a much more engaging image.

At the time of Joan's martyrdom, France was just beginning to emerge from the *épaisse nuit gothique* of which Rabelais was to complain a century later. The Sorbonne was not only pro-Burgundian but also rigidly orthodox in its opinions, which at that time had the force of law. The impudence of an unlettered girl who insisted that her authority be acknowledged by the church was therefore most offensive to Paris, and it was equally offensive to Rome, which was already reacting to the divisive forces—humanistic in Italy; in Bohemia, Hussite; and Lollard in England—which were to culminate eventually in Luther's Reformation. She was, for her age, an intolerable threat to authority.

It was precisely in this fashion that Shaw conceived her. But for a united France, a generation later, Joan was chiefly valuable as a saint, and the first steps toward her canonization were taken long before her beatification in 1909. From a political standpoint, the legend of a simple peasant girl who by the grace of God had crowned a king and unified a nation was obviously a national treasure to be cherished along with the crown jewels. The myth of Jeanne d'Arc thus reflects both the fortunes of the church and the monarchy in France during the centuries that separate her martyrdom from her canonization. After being the puppet of history in her own time, Joan became the puppet of the historians of later ages. This is perhaps the really tragic aspect of her story and, in some respects, it is the most interesting.

Jeanne d'Arc played a significant role in French literature from the time of François Villon. For many years she was an object of sympathetic curiosity, a kind of natural wonder. In the wave of anticlerical sentiment that characterized the age of Voltaire, it became important to minimize her religious importance. In *La Pucelle d'Orléans* Jeanne is a pretty minx with influence at court, and her seduction becomes an essential element of English military policy. In this interpretation Voltaire was evidently under the spell of Ariosto, and he ended his poem very plausibly with Jeanne's marriage to Dunois, thus making an interesting detour around the facts of history.

The anticlerical bias which influenced Voltaire is even more clearly evident in Michelet's classic treatment of Jeanne d'Arc. This was first published in 1841 in the fifth volume of his *Histoire de France*. By the time he reached this point, Michelet had suffered considerable hardship at the hands of the clerical party that had long been in power, and his personal resentment found expression in his treatment of the medieval clergy. Michelet cast his heroine in the conventional mold of Senecan tragedy, and she emerged from his marvelously readable account as the innocent victim of the bigots of the Sorbonne and the Holy Inquisition. This unforgettable portrait of the Maid served to characterize her for all subsequent ages.[54]

It was against this cliché that Shaw reacted in his intrepretation of the story of Saint Joan. He had been in some degree anticipated by Anatole

France, whose sober and scholarly *Life of Jeanne d'Arc* makes out the Maid to be the innocent dupe of the French military party, which employed her, not as the leader, but as the mascotte of their forces. This was a realistic approach. The romantic viewpoint had been fully developed in Schiller's tragedy, which shows the unmistakable influence of Tasso. Like the warrior maid Clorinda, in the *Gerusalemme liberata*, Schiller's Joan falls in love with her enemy, in this case the knight Lionel. The love-honor predicament, indispensable to romantic tragedy, is further complicated, in this instance, by Joan's need to maintain her purity in God's service. Schiller mercifully extricates his heroine from her embarrassment by causing her to die heroically on the battlefield, thus neatly avoiding the disagreeable aspects of the historical fact.

With the exception of Charles Péguy's excellent *Jeanne d'Arc* (1897), a play which Shaw gives no indication of having read, all the more recent plays on this subject, both in France and in England, were in the nature of conventional melodrama. There was nothing in Tom Taylor's very popular *Joan of Arc* (1871) which could possibly have been of use to Shaw. Percy Mackaye's *Jeanne d'Arc* (1906) was of more ambitious cut. It was based on Murray's abridged translation of the work of Quicherat; but the play Mackaye wrote was in the vein of Stephen Phillips, a romantic tragedy, poetically conceived, studiously medieval in the Pre-Raphaelite manner, with a self-sacrificial heroine whose sentimentality Shaw found pitiable.[55] So far as English drama was concerned, Shaw—as he intimated in his preface—had a clear field. He desired to maintain his play, he wrote, "on the level of high tragedy," and characteristically, he chose an approach that brought him close to Ibsen.[56]

In the type of modern tragedy which Ibsen developed, the stage is set at a turning-point in world history, so that it becomes possible to demonstrate, in the person of the tragic hero, the conflict of cosmic forces in the historical dialectic. In *Emperor and Galilean* Ibsen posed his hero dramatically in the transition from paganism to Christianity, and caused him to go down, more or less heroically, as the last great representative of the ancient world. In *Rosmersholm*, similarly, the tragedy of the apostate pastor exemplifies the clash of Christian faith and scientific revelation in the age of Darwin. It was in such fashion that Shaw conceived the conflict in which Joan was destroyed, and for this purpose he associated her directly with the coming Reformation on the one hand, and the end of feudalism, on the other.

The Reformation, of course, awaited the coming of Luther, and the monarchic idea in France took shape in the time of Louis XI. But from Shaw's standpoint, Joan was the precursor of both Protestantism and nationalism and, in his play, it is chiefly because of their premonition of the coming danger that the nobility, in the person of Warwick, and the prelacy, in the person of Cauchon, reluctantly resolve that the Maid must be discredited and destroyed. In fact, as the play itself demonstrates, the burning of Joan had no effect whatever on the progress of history. Within a quarter-century of her death, both church and state found it necessary to affirm her righteousness and her orthodoxy and, once her sentence was annulled, the way was opened for the very contingencies which Warwick and Cauchon were resolved at all costs to forestall. Thus Joan became a symbol of progress, and Warwick and Cauchon came to represent the forces of reaction in their time. The play in these terms fitted admirably into Shaw's philosophic scheme.

Shaw had no idea of using the story of Jeanne d'Arc for purely dramatic purposes. He wished to write a tragedy with universal connotations. Joan, in her sacred aspect is, accordingly, a spectacular realization of the Life Force, a genius precariously balanced on the threshold of the future, and therefore especially vulnerable to the forces of reaction. In accordance with Marxist theory, Shaw felt that it was necessary for social organizations to pass through a nationalistic phase on the way to world socialism. Hence Joan's voices, doubtless the same voices which in *Back to Methuselah* guided Adam in his initial explorations in the Garden, cause her to will into being the idea of France as a national entity, something which had not so far existed, and which was, in fact, not to exist for some time.[57] In Shaw's play, Joan's will prevails to the point where the Dauphin is crowned king of France. Here, however, her nationalistic ambitions come into sharp conflict with the interests of the feudal barons and the universal church, and the dialectic opposition is set up which eventually destroys both Joan and her enemies. The resulting synthesis is then manifested in the next phase of social development, the Renaissance, with its obsessive dream of world unity.[58]

"In genuine tragedy," Hegel wrote,

> there must be powers, both equally moral and justifiable, which from this side and that, come into collision. . . . Two opposed Rights come forth, the one smashes itself to pieces against the other: in this way both suffer loss, while both are equally justified: not as if this were right, the other wrong.[59]

There was not, in this view of the matter, any question of the injustice of the gods, or the tyranny of kings. Hegel's view of tragedy was relativistic. From his viewpoint dramatic art is an attempt to illustrate the workings of the dialectic by exhibiting some phase of the contradictions involved in the passage from the actual to the ideal. Tragic characters represent actual ethical forces in conflict. Their struggle represents, not the conflict of good and evil, but the collision of two incompatible goods, and the tragedy of such characters is the consequence of their inflexible partisanship. In the struggle to achieve a synthesis, both contradictory forces are necessarily annihilated, and those who cling to them most closely are destroyed with them. Accordingly in tragedy both protagonist and antagonist are doomed to perish. Only those survive who represent the dialectical synthesis which results from the tragic clash. In simplest terms, tragedy results from the resistance of the individual to the harmonious development of the World Spirit, and his refusal to conform with the changes which this development entails. In a dynamic universe it is tragic to stand firm.

It is from this idea that *Saint Joan* derives its magnitude. The source of its tragedy is not merely the agony of Joan—which is treated ironically, since she is ultimately triumphant—but the eternal agony of a race that burns its saints. Shaw's saints are all rebels who fight against the established order and are therefore particularly vulnerable at the hands of its defenders. "The law of evolution," Shaw wrote, "is Ibsen's law of change. All improvement is founded on tolerance of change. The law of God is change—and churches that set themselves against change are against the law of God."[60]

But while Shaw regularly paid lip service to the relativism of Ibsen, which Ibsen had, at least indirectly, from Hegel, he actually inclined to absolute ideas of right and wrong. The sense of injustice was, in Shaw's judgment, inseparable from the idea of tragedy.[61] The tragedy of Joan illustrates the injustice of mankind, which is always ready to consign its revolutionary saints to martyrdom, and Shaw's purpose in writing *Saint Joan* was, he wrote, to furnish an object lesson for his time, which had recently inflicted martyrdom on hundreds of honest people who were guilty only of following the inner promptings of their spirit: ". . . the question raised by Joan's burning is a burning question still, though the penalties involved are not so sensational. That is why I am probing it. If it were only a historical curiosity I would not waste my readers' time and my own on it for five minutes."[62]

Thus, in his preface, Shaw introduced *Saint Joan* not as a tragedy, but as a *pièce à thèse*. He had the example of Ireland particularly in mind:

> Thousands of women, each of them a thousand times less dangerous and terrifying to our Governments than Joan was to the Government of her day, have within the last ten years been slaughtered, starved to

death, burnt out of house and home . . . in the course of Crusades far more tyrannically pretentious than the medieval Crusades which professed nothing more hyperbolical than the rescue of the Holy Sepulchre from the Saracens.

In our day, he added, Joan would have had "no trial and no law except a Defence of the Realm Act suspending all law; and for judge she would have had, at best, a bothered major, and at most a promoted advocate in ermine and scarlet to whom the scruples of a trained ecclesiastic like Cauchon would seem ridiculous and ungentlemanly."[63]

These allusions belong only to the preface. In the play the tragic intention is clear, and it is made doubly clear in the Epilogue: in the nature of man, as he is presently constituted, there is no remedy for the injuries inflicted by society upon its revolutionary avant-garde. The time is not foreseeable when saints will be welcome on this earth. As matters stand, the mutants from which the race of supermen will develop must wait for the rest of the species to catch up before they can manifest their superiority. Otherwise they must suffer the nasty consequences of social displeasure.

The discomfort of the extraordinary individual in the world of ordinary people was a favorite theme of Strindberg. Like Shelley, Strindberg thought of himself as one marked with the brand of Cain or Christ, and he nourished a useful paranoia which permitted him to feel that, as a superior being, he was doomed to be a pariah among those who were capable of envy and hatred, but not of understanding. This idea, generalized into a theory of the eternal antagonism of the aristocratic mind and the plebeian mentality, was publicized vigorously in two articles he wrote in 1888, De sma and De stora, and in numerous stories and articles thereafter; and it played an important role in shaping his plays from the time of Comrades and The Father (1886–88). The idea was most congenial to Shaw. It not only flattered his vanity, it also justified him in his favorite posture of unhonored prophet.

In the preface to Saint Joan he wrote: "it is not easy for mental giants who neither hate nor intend to injure their fellows to realize that nevertheless their fellows hate mental giants and would like to destroy them."[64] Joan of Arc was not ordinarily thought of as a mental giant; but in his efforts to rationalize her legend, Shaw was quite willing to attribute her voices to a mental quirk by which she was able to objectify her genius so that her ideas became audible and visible to her, robed in celestial garments and speaking with angelic voices.

Shaw found the scientific basis for this assumption in Francis Galton's studies of people with exceptional powers of memory and calculation. Galton called such people "visualizers," on the theory that they actually could bring before their eyes what ordinary people could only think about.[65] Shaw thus found it possible to consider Joan a genius who humbly referred her superior powers to agencies external to herself but was ready and able to support her ideas rationally whenever it was necessary to do so. She was also, in Shaw's opinion, a saint, and worthy of membership in that communion of saints which included Socrates, Shelley, and Mohammed, at least two of whom had had visions.

The members of this elite through whose efforts mankind is progressively exalted toward its perfection were, in Shaw's opinion, the instruments of impersonal forces which are miraculous without being in any way supernatural. Saints, Shaw suggests, perform miracles; but their miracles are the miracles of nature. They themselves are individuals driven by an appetite which most people neither feel nor comprehend:

> . . . that there are forces at work which use individuals for purposes far transcending the purpose of keeping these individuals alive and prosperous . . . is established by the fact that men will, in the pursuit of knowledge and social readjustments for which they will not be a penny the better, and are indeed many pence the worse, face poverty, infamy, exile, imprisonment, dreadful hardship, and death. . . . There is no more mystery about this appetite for knowledge and power than about the appetite for food . . . the difference between them being that the appetite for food . . . is a personal appetite, whereas the other is an appetite for evolution, and therefore a superpersonal need.[66]

It is likely that Shaw arrived by way of Carlyle at the idea of a communion of saints testifying to the natural supernaturalism of the world order; but since for Shaw the Life Force in nature was synonymous with the Holy Spirit, the will that moved Joan was actually what she said it was: it was the will of God. Her martyrdom therefore represents the agony of the individual whose need to advance the species transcends the need for self-preservation.

Whether or not the historical Joan was actually a saint in this sense is obviously of no consequence to the dramatic conception. For Shaw's purposes it was necessary that his heroine be inspired in this very manner. His Joan had to be eminently sane, rational and far-sighted, brave to the point of recklessness, and also a military genius of Napoleonic scope, far ahead of her time in the management of artillery, and highly talented as a strategist and statesman. That such a combination of qualities could be found in a sixteen-year-old girl who had so far hardly set foot outside her native village was credible only on the assumption that she was a miracle of nature. Luckily, such things were readily explicable in terms of the theory laid down in *Back to Methuselah*. The conception of Joan as an extraordinary natural phenomenon was thus entirely consistent with Shaw's philosophic scheme, and, after all, hardly at variance with the recorded facts.

As Shaw conceived her, Joan is a simple country lass, and therefore speaks—at least in the opening scenes—a provincial English dialect, presumably the English equivalent of her French patois. The effect is neither realistic nor especially sensible. It is simply an embarrassment for the actress. All the extant documentation indicates that the historical Joan, though unlettered, was well spoken, extremely articulate, courteous in her manner, and fastidious in her dress. She had, it appears, no liking for rough clothes. On the contrary, we are told that she was fond of sumptuous apparel, splendid armor, and fine horses. The trial record includes evidence that she was prudish in her habits, and particularly disliked bad language. At a time when military oaths were especially imaginative, she was heard to swear only "en nom Dé!" or "par mon Martin!"

What has been preserved by way of portraiture, if it can be credited, indicates also that Joan was a very handsome girl, but Shaw was determined to exclude whatever in her legend was even remotely romantic. In contrast to the eloquence attributed to her by Schiller, Shaw made her out blunt and plain spoken, and in order to avoid the question of her traditionally romantic involvement with Dunois, he clothed her in rough clothes and made her entirely impervious to the demands of sex.

In his preface Shaw likens his heroine to the type of militant female associated with the activities of Sylvia Pankhurst. At court and in the camp, she is a gadfly, an earnest, urgent woman of mannish cut, logical, businesslike, and efficient in the pursuit of her goals. It was not a novel characterization in Shaw's canon. Joan is an advanced version of Vivie Warren, ritually pure, and wholly dedicated, a career girl with no nonsense about her. The danger of having such a character played by a handsome actress with a good figure does not seem to have troubled Shaw. Nevertheless the part presents a problem. It would be naïve to expect that a beautiful woman, becomingly dressed in tight-fitting clothes, would deliberately obscure her femininity on the stage. Consequently, Joan's trial takes place in a perversely erotic atmosphere which no amount of serious discussion can dispel. Regardless of the author's intention, it is virtually impossible to disguise the sadistic nature of the proceedings, and the play, no matter how tactfully it is directed, will always fall into the traditional mold of Senecan horror tragedy. Doubtless it is to this, as much as to anything, that his play owes its popularity.

In a radio speech commemorating the 500th anniversary of Joan's death, Shaw begged his audience to forget that Joan was burnt at the stake. But the fact cannot be glossed over. It is because Joan was actually burnt to death on the Place du Vieux Marché in Rouen that her story has its extraordinary poignancy. Shaw, however, wished at all costs to avoid a melodramatic confrontation of heroes and villains. He centered his play on the trial. This was intended to be a conflict of ideas, not of people, the sort of discussion scene which he considered indispensable to modern drama. In *Saint Joan*, therefore, the difference between Joan and her persecutors is mainly a matter of historical perspective. It is their ignorance of the course of history, not their evil nature, that motivates her enemies. They see nothing beyond the immediate interests of the institutions they represent. Joan sees further. She sees God. Had her opponents shared her visual acuity, they would have followed her joyfully instead of bringing about her death. The keen-sighted fare badly among those who do not see. Such, it is implied, is the unhappy destiny of those who are the chosen instruments of the Life Force.

The formulation, from this viewpoint, is faultless; but the consequence, insofar as it is effective, is in some measure to depersonalize the characters of the play. To the extent that they symbolize forces and principles, they become abstract to the point where, in the theater, we tend to lose touch with them. The process is the opposite of medieval allegory, which commonly personifies concepts, instead of conceptualizing persons; but the result is not altogether different. Considered in the light of the preface, *Saint Joan* becomes a kind of morality play in which the characters are conscious of the abstractions they symbolize and therefore remain, on the whole, personally neutral and passionless. It is, then, difficult to enter into the agony of Joan, for it is not so much Joan who is rushed into the pyre, as the principle she represents, and as this principle is not combustible, it may be expected to emerge from the refining flames none the worse for the experience.

The last act of *Saint Joan* is magnificent, both as drama and as literature, but it is a relatively bloodless piece of work. At the end there is no scream of anguish to chill the blood, no smell of the fire. There is only the semicomic horror of Stogumber. It may be argued by those who do not approve of this sort of drama, that plays that deal primarily with ideas rather than with emotions may well evoke acquiescence, and even understanding, but not the sort of spiritual resonance that is the attribute of the greatest poetry. If *Saint Joan* is an exception, it is for reasons extraneous to Shaw's purpose in writing it. For in spite of his painstaking effort to present the trial of Joan as a clash of cosmic forces in which both tyrants and victim are tragically enmeshed, the logic of the situation is lost in the overwhelming fact that, no matter what is being said, in the end a young woman will be burnt alive. On this point the drama is centered, and in the light of this tremendous fact, the reasoning hardly matters. Shaw wished to make drama of the reasons, not the facts; but the fact sweeps all before it. For the trial, with all the elegant intricacy of its procedure, its delicate and forceful show of logic, and the manifest inevitability of its conclusions, is actually no more than the ritual attending a human sacrifice, and there the drama resides.

It is evident that in the end Shaw was aware of what was happening to his play, and his use of the chaplain Stogumber to point the horror of the climax is ingenious. It is not effective. The chaplain's hysteria is too childish and too light to carry the necessary weight, just as the trial is too heavy to justify its conclusion, and the story ends in a piece of wanton brutality. Thus *Saint Joan*, after skirting with circumspection the borders of tragedy,. plunges suddenly into melodrama. Shaw could hardly stop there. The comic epilogue was inevitable.

The passion of Joan provides all the necessary materials for the type of ritual which Mallarmé, and Artaud, his disciple, deemed proper to drama. Shaw did not exploit them. In his view the execution of Joan was a regrettable but thoroughly understandable measure taken by upright men in the full confidence of their judgment. "It is what men do at their best, with good intentions," he wrote,

> and what normal men and women find they must do and will do in spite of their intentions, that really concern us. . . . If Joan had not been burnt by normally innocent people in the energy of their righteousness her death at their hands would have no more significance than the Tokyo earthquake, which burnt a great many maidens. . . .[67]

There is, nonetheless, a world of difference between the elegantly sophisticated idiocy of Cauchon and Lemaître and the coarse brutality of Stogumber and Estivet. The Vice-Inquisitor is described in Shaw's preface as a mild, scholarly and fair-minded old man. He closely resembles the Inquisitors involved in the extirpation of Catharism as Lea depicts them in his *History of the Inquisition*.[68] He is convinced that it is his sacred duty to discredit Joan at any cost, but he is not a sadist. In his opinion, order, authority, and proper procedure are the prime tenets of the church, and their maintenance is the peculiar charge of the Holy Office. The rigidity of his position—reminiscent of the ironclad Marxism of our time—indicates to what an extent his institution is sclerotic: "Heresy at first seems innocent and even laudable; but it ends in such a monstrous horror of unnatural wickedness that the most tender-hearted among you, if you saw it at work as I have seen it, would clamor against the mercy of The Church in dealing with it."[69]

Shaw meant to emphasize Lemaître's sincerity: he wrote a magnificent speech in defense of his position, and it is possible that Shaw's own fear of anarchy found some reflection in Lemaître's horror of it. Nevertheless, the Inquisitor's zeal seems excessive. He plays unmercifully on the fears of his audience; he is shrewd; and the ironic intention is clear. In discussing the Inquisitor later with Henderson, Shaw remarked that he thought Lemaître "a most infernal old scoundrel."[70] This is far from the view he takes of him either in the preface or in the play; doubtless it is another example of Shaw's impish conversational manner, for the Inquisitor's viewpoint is crucial for the understanding of the play, and Shaw did not confuse it in the least.

At the bottom of the clerical problem posed by Joan's disobedience there is an important psychological consideration. She is an individualist, and between her and Lemaître the fundamental opposition is the opposition of the individual and society, a question of freedom. What is being judged, fundamentally, in Joan's trial is the problem of order and liberty, the irreconcilable elements in any social organization short of an ideal anarchy.

In the Inquisitor's opinion, Joan's most grievous sin is pride: in setting her individual will above the will of the church she reflects the sin of Satan. But Joan's pride is merely a manifestation of her faith in the rightness of her cause, which the church took 500 years to confirm. Obviously in time the church changes its opinion. Joan does not. She is at all times quite sure of herself, for, in Shaw's words, she is self-elected by the Holy Ghost. In this sense, as the archbishop points out, she is hubristic and is therefore subject to nemesis.[71]

In qualifying his play as "classical tragedy," Shaw evidently intended to invite comparison with such models as *Prometheus*, *Antigone*, and *The Trial of Socrates*, all of which turn also on the question of freedom and order. But the tragedy of Joan arises, in part, rather from another classic motive, the realization of human helplessness in the face of destiny. Nobody really desires the martyrdom of Joan, not even her enemies, and nobody is able to avert it, not even her friends. *Ananké*, not *hubris*, is at the core of her agony. Tragedy is characteristic of the Life Force at each turning point in its development. In the case of Joan it results from an embarrassment so profound that its memory has afflicted us for centuries. It was from this idea that Shaw derived the dramatic epilogue which crowns the play.[72]

The world is never ready for its saints: such is the tragic conclusion. The development of the Will is commensurate with the sufferings of those who are subject to it. It is out of the world's pain that the saints are born. Through its chosen instruments, self-elected like Joan, the Will strikes out constantly in new directions, and each advance is marked by cries of anguish, each step entails the blood sacrifice, each revolution entails a conflict and a defeat. The martyrdom of the individual concentrates the pain of the race, its growing pains. For Shaw, quite as much as for Strindberg, this is the kernel of tragedy. But Shaw could not overlook the comedic implications of the situation: "The tragedy of such murders is that they are not committed by murderers. They are judicial murders, pious murders; and this contradiction at once brings an element of comedy into the tragedy: the angels may weep at the murder, but the gods laugh at the murderers."[73]

From an Olympian standpoint, the spectacle of dignified men solemnly making asses of themselves is undoubtedly a comic sight. In the long perspective of history, the clumsy somersaults of humanity have a clownish look, and they look even more absurd if we accelerate their tempo as Shaw does in his epilogue. It is in the light of the problem it raises that the saint's tragedy seems funny. In the development of the race the revolutionary martyrs are indispensable; but there is no denying that so long as they are present among us and actively busied about their sacred tasks, the saints are a nuisance to everybody. Saints work miracles, and miracles are subversive of the natural order. As history amply demonstrates, those who perform such feats are inflammable and must handle themselves with the greatest tact lest they be injured in the process.

In the case of Joan, the difficulty is manifest even to her judges. If she is neither mad nor wicked, it must be that she is divinely inspired, in which case her voice is God's voice, and her authority is superior to that of popes and emperors. The very thought of permitting a nineteen-year-old village girl to aspire to such eminence gives the bishop of Beauvais a bad moment:

> What will the world be like when The Church's accumulated wisdom and knowledge and experience, its councils of learned, venerable pious men, are thrust into the kennel by every ignorant laborer or dairymaid whom the devil can puff up with the monstrous self-con-

ceit of being directly inspired from heaven? It will be a world of blood, of fury, of devastation, of each man striving for his own hand: in the end a world wrecked back into barbarism. For now you have only Mahomet and his dupes, and the Maid and her dupes; but what will it be when every girl thinks herself a Joan and every man a Mahomet? I shudder to the very marrow of my bones when I think of it.[74]

From the ecclesiastical viewpoint, the case against Joan is clear. Left to herself, Joan would wreck the church. The time for divine interference in the affairs of men is past. It is comforting to know that God remembers us, but intolerable to have Him tinkering interminably with His establishment. The best saints, in the bishop's opinion, are the least obtrusive. It is for this reason that the Inquisitor hastens to neutralize Joan while there is time.

From a secular standpoint, Joan's case is equally clear. She was a formidable weapon in the hands of the French while they were engaged against the English. But with an army at her back, she was also the dominant power in France, and the king himself was in a sense her vassal. After the coronation she was therefore a woeful embarrassment to those she had saved. The grateful French had no recourse but to follow the example of those Italian states which could never sufficiently reward an oversuccessful condottiere and were therefore forced to have him assassinated in order to immortalize his memory with a fitting monument.

The situation is not entirely comic. Generally speaking, there is something uncanny about genius. It is indispensable, but the sooner it is got out of the way, the better. The thought is depressing. In *Saint Joan* the point is not made very gracefully, but it is made very clearly. Joan's last words to her judges are surely Shaw's last significant words to his countrymen: "I am His child, and you are not fit that I should live among you."[75]

The Epilogue takes a broader view of the matter. In King Charles's dream, the principal characters of the play, after addressing a truly wretched litany to the saint at whose martyrdom they have collaborated, excuse themselves politely, one by one, when they are asked if they would like to have her once again among the living. They would not. They sincerely revere her spirit, but they want nothing more to do with Joan in the flesh. The paradox of sainthood is inherent in the concept of sainthood. The earth will be ready to receive its saints only when there is no longer any need for them. It is in the nature of humanity that its choicest spirits are also its fiercest critics; therefore they have their reward mainly in heaven.

The idea is obviously interesting. Whether or not it is of value in the theater is a matter of opinion. For many people the drama of the intellect is absorbing; but there are those who think the springs of tragedy lie elsewhere. Upon this question hangs the matter of Shaw's shifting popularity.

In the opinion of Renaissance critics tragedy was a moral exercise. In romantic times it became an emotional experience. As we have seen, it was Shaw's cardinal principle that the pleasure of drama, as distinct from theater-going, is primarily an intellectual pleasure. It is from this standpoint that *Saint Joan* was written.

The difficulty with this view is that it attributes to tragedy the degree of emotional detachment which is the traditional attribute of comedy, and the consequence is a type of tragedy that makes us laugh. This was certainly not Shaw's intention in writing *Saint Joan*. It was his idea, often expressed, that the deepest human passion is intellectual passion, and that the sharpest conflict is the conflict of ideas. This view antedates romanticism by some centuries. It is based on the idea of the soul as an entity in which the specifically human faculty is the intellect, which we share with God. It follows that the appetites of the mind are stronger, and its passions deeper, than those of the inferior faculties. Consequently, the drama of ideas is the only drama worthy of serious attention, and those who are not capable of an intellectual experience are simply not capable of enjoying drama at its best.

In the preface of *Saint Joan* Shaw wrote:

> Nobody says straight out that genuine drama is a tedious nuisance, and that to ask people to endure more than two hours of it (with two long intervals of relief) is an intolerable imposition. Nobody says "I hate classical tragedy and comedy as I hate sermons and symphonies. . . . And whatever superior people may pretend, I cannot associate pleasure with any sort of intellectual activity; and I dont believe anyone else can either." Such things are not said; yet nine-tenths of what is offered as criticism of the drama in the metropolitan Press of Europe and America is nothing but a muddled paraphrase of it. If it does not mean that, it means nothing.
>
> I do not complain of this, though it complains very unreasonably of me. But I can take no more notice of it than Einstein of the people who are incapable of mathematics. I write in the classical manner for those who pay for admission to the theatre because they like classical comedy or tragedy for its own sake. . . . These are the patrons on whom I depend for my bread.[76]

The extravagance of this statement need not obscure its significance. In the 1920's Shaw felt that he could afford to write intelligent plays for an intelligent audience; indeed that he could afford to do nothing less. But in asserting that he was writing drama in the classical manner, he was either imposing on the ignorance of his readers or betraying his own. Shaw's comedies are, in general, romantic plays with realistic observations, and those that are most romantic have proved to be the most successful. In the line of tragedy, he wrote only *Saint Joan*. Its connection with classical tragedy is vague. Insofar as it depicts the persecution of a beautiful heroine by a cruel tyrant it accords with the Senecan pattern; but it is not likely that this is what Shaw had in mind.

By the time of *Saint Joan*, Shaw's dramatic theory was completely influenced by the Hegelian concept of drama as a conflict of antitheses. In Shaw's view, drama was a dialectic which marked, tragically or comically, a step forward in the development of the vital spirit. In this sense drama is seen to be the chronicle of human development, and a play is significant in proportion to the degree in which it clarifies a specific human situation in cosmic terms. The great plays are, from this standpoint, mainly iconographical—pictures which illustrate the history of mankind. Their vividness and their beauty are, of course, important, but their function is, essentially, to illumine the text.

With regard to the play of Joan of Arc, Shaw asserts first of all his superior sense of history, and therefore his ability to make clear what Shakespeare and Schiller had muddled:

> I write in full view of the Middle Ages, which may be said to have been rediscovered in the middle of the nineteenth century after an eclipse of about four hundred and fifty years. The Renascence of antique literature and art in the sixteenth century, and the lusty growth of Capitalism, between them buried the Middle Ages; and their resurrection is a second Renascence.[77]

The truth is that Shaw had not a very full view of the Middle Ages, and his view of the Renaissance was not overly perceptive. His ideas of these very indefinite periods were derived from writers who, like Carlyle and Morris, had formulated their notions of the past largely as a reflection of their dissatisfaction with the present. In the nature of things, it is impossible for even the most learned medievalist to afford himself, much less anyone else, a "full view of the Middle Ages." The spectrum of medieval thought is wide. It ranges from Boethius to Bacon and encompasses both St. Bernard and Abelard. Shaw did not identify his thinking with any recognizable stream of medieval thought. He was, doubtless, widely read, but he was not a specialist. The consequence is that *Saint Joan* falsifies history most appallingly. It is a brilliant interpretation of a period the author knew next to nothing about, and was thus able to explain with perfect clarity.

From every point of view, *Saint Joan* comes somewhat short of perfection. But the drama it suggests quite staggers the imagination. It is arguable that the great masterpieces of the theater are great not so much in themselves as in their power to intimate what cannot be written, but can perhaps be played. In this sense, one might reasonably assert that *Saint Joan* is a world classic as secure in its own right as *Don Quixote* or *Faust*, though a good deal more comprehensible than either.

Saint Joan was the last of Shaw's great plays, and he lived long enough to see it accepted internationally as a masterpiece of dramatic literature. Its success did not dispel his feeling of bitterness at the cool reception of his work in England, nor did the Nobel Prize for literature with which in 1925 *Saint Joan* was rewarded go far to mollify him. Shaw accepted the prize money and with it established the Anglo-Swedish Foundation, for the purpose of making Swedish works, and particularly the works of Strindberg, available in English translation. The following year he received an official letter from the German government congratulating him on his seventieth birthday. In his reply, he complimented the German people on being the cultural leaders of Europe. He added: "The sole notice taken on my seventieth birthday by the British government was its deliberate official prohibition of the broadcasting of any words spoken by me on that occasion."[78]

Two years later, in 1928, Barry Jackson proposed the establishment of a Drama Festival to be held each year at Malvern. Shaw was enthusiastic. He set to work at once on a play with which to inaugurate the festival. The play was *The Apple Cart*.

This comedy best illustrates the character of Shaw's slow decline as a dramatist. It was begun in November 1928 and was finished before Christmas of that year. Like *Geneva*, which was written ten years later, it is the elaboration of a situation suggested in *Back to Methuselah*. It takes place somewhere about the year 2000 and illustrates a political crisis in the transition between the Burge-Lubin type of constitutional monarchy and the future welfare state in the period of "The Thing Happens."

The plot is tenuous. It has to do with the struggle for power between a wily prime minister and a wily king at a time when the populace, manipulated by the press, is completely at the mercy of the great capitalist adventurers who really rule the nation. Into the suave conflict between the very attractive King Magnus and the very artful prime minister Proteus are projected several ideas for discussion—the danger of having England swallowed up into the American union, the role of Breakages, Ltd. in fostering industrial obsolescence, and the role of love and marriage in the life of a busy man. These themes have little relevance to the main narrative, so that the play makes the impression of a series of discussions, enlivened by the sparkle of the dialogue and the interest of the portraiture.

The Apple Cart is, on the whole, a very pleasant entertainment, with topical allusions which time has blurred. It is said that Mr. Boanerges, the pro-Soviet minister, was intended to be reminiscent of John Burns, and that Proteus was a recognizable caricature of Ramsay MacDonald: at this remove of time, it hardly matters. The theme of the play, however, remains with us in all its complexity—it is the problem of democracy. In *The Apple Cart* the basis of power is, more than ever, the huge mass of ignorant voters, whose preferences are controlled by a corrupt press and the personal appeal of amusing candidates who beguile them with songs and mimicry. The defense of the state against the stupidity of its rulers, when these rulers are the untutored populace, is the principal task of the monarchy.

Machiavelli had written convincingly of the devolution of states from autocracy to anarchy in an endlessly recurring cycle. Shaw sets his stage in *The Apple Cart* at the point where democracy is on the verge of anarchy, and a strong hand is necessary to avert disaster. It is, as Machiavelli had pointed out, the classical moment for a dictatorship. The Florentine secretary had not foreseen a time when a huge mass of voters would be manipulated by powerful groups of industrialists for their own benefit. Shaw, however, was able to open a perspective, based on modern history, at the end of which may be glimpsed a political utopia founded on despair. In the meantime, King Magnus wins an agreeable victory, but his triumph is not more than provisional. In a state arranged along the lines of King Magnus's Britain, no victory can be permanent.

The Apple Cart was first produced in Warsaw in June 1929, and later by Reinhardt at the Deutsches Theater in Berlin. Barry Jackson inaugurated the Malvern Festival with it that August with Cedric Hardwicke in the role of King Magnus and Edith Evans as Orinthia. Its success was modest; nevertheless, *The Apple Cart* furnished Shaw with a pattern for all his future serious comedy. He subtitled it "A Political Extravaganza." In fact, it had little in common with extravaganza. It was a political tract, admirably managed, quite amusing, and thoroughly pessimistic. Thus Shaw's dramatic development reached a logical conclusion. *Widowers' Houses* was a tract in the guise of a comedy of the 1850's. *The Apple Cart*, and its successors in this genre, dispensed with the narrative tricks which were normally considered indispensable to comedy and concentrated forthrightly on the intellectual core of the matter under discussion. At the age of seventy-three Shaw pinned his future as a dramatist on a technique that was manifestly undramatic.

Henceforth the action of his plays became progressively more abstract and more frankly improbable. Their doctrine elaborated ideas which are traceable to earlier plays, principally to *Back to Methuselah*. His later plays may seem, in consequence, somewhat repetitious; but they are redeemed from dullness by flashes of brilliance far beyond the capacity of more amenable writers. They are, clearly, the work of a failing genius; nevertheless they are works of genius.

The views set forth in *The Apple Cart* were amplified the following year in the preface to the new edition of *Fabian Essays* (1930). In this preface Shaw pointed out that European culture had outgrown its capitalist phase, and that the arm of free enterprise and "rugged individualism" must inevitably give way to government regulation. The party system, he argued, was doomed. Government must be put into the hands of experts. It is clear that the situation in which he saw the Europe of his own time was the very same he had imagined for the year 2190 in *Back to Methuselah*.

At this time Shaw was seventy-four. He was to live another two decades, through the Depression of the 1930's and through another World War far greater and more terrifying than the first. Perhaps he remembered Goethe's lines:

> Wer immer strebend sich bemüht
> Den können wir erlösen.

Between 1929 and 1950 he published seventeen titles. Most of these were plays, and nearly all of them were performed. The works of his senescence might well have made the fortune of a lesser man. In the case of Shaw, they did nothing to magnify his stature nor anything to diminish it: he had by this time attained heroic proportions, and the last twenty years of his life were in the nature of an apotheosis.

By the time Shaw was gathered to his fathers, he had become the world figure he had dreamed of becoming. His face looked back at him sardonically from every newspaper; his every word was newsworthy; he ranked with Einstein, Gandhi, Tolstoy, and Charlie Chaplin as one of the great spirits of the age, perhaps the greatest. It was by no means an unrewarding experience, but he sometimes complained of it.

The list of his works was by now unconscionably long, yet he kept writing as if under a compulsion. *Too True To Be Good* (1931) was first produced in New York, later at Malvern. It was not a success. *The Village Wooing* (1933) had a modest production by the Theatre Guild and was afterwards done at Tunbridge Wells. *On the Rocks* (1933) was a more ambitious effort. It was, like *The Simpleton of the Unexpected Isles* (1935), an animated tract which afforded a bleak view of unregenerate humanity. The most successful play of this period was *The Millionairess*. He finished this in 1935 at the age of seventy-nine. He was eighty when he began *Geneva* (1938) and eighty-three when he wrote *Buoyant Billions* (1947); at ninety-three he wrote *Far-Fetched Fables* (1949). It was not his last play. That same year he wrote a puppet play called *Shakes versus Shav* and saw it produced at Malvern that August.

Not much need be said of these last plays. They are, in general, facile and overexhibitionistic works, the final affirmations of an irrepressibly vital personality, and they make us think sadly of Captain Shotover. Almost all of them give the effect of being variations on earlier themes. In 1944 Shaw had attributed his works to a superior power whose high behests he served. It was a characteristic expression of humility. It also relieved him of the responsibility for careful workmanship.

In his declining years his plays did not shape themselves properly. He had never had a really secure sense of dramatic form. His genius was impatient of restraint, and he was inclined, even at his best, to indulge himself as a craftsman. From the first he had been loathe to let a phrase go forth without a retinue of attendant phrases. Now he became really garrulous. His mighty voice showed no strain. It was simply that it could not keep still; and after *Saint Joan* there was really no more to be said.

It would be a mistake, however, to conclude that, like so many gifted men, he outlived his greatness. His dotage was magnificent, and luxuriously protracted. His plays were constantly revived; his royalties multiplied; his wit was echoed more frequently than that of Chesterton or Wilde; his pose became classic. The world caught up with him at last, though, as always, too late. The image he had labored so long to fix in the public mind had long ceased to amuse him. Now he made faces mechanically. He had, besides, other causes for complaint. The author of *Geneva* was powerless to compete with the man who had written *Pygmalion*. Thus Shaw found, to his cost, what every great man learns in time—that among human afflictions success is quite as hard to bear as failure.

Mrs. Shaw died quite suddenly in September 1943, after a long period of invalidism. She had been her husband's staunchest supporter, and he was very fond of her. But he was too busy and too self-centered a man to feel any emotion intensely, and now he was too old to feel sorrow. In the last years of his life he was under intense scholarly scrutiny. It was as if he were being anatomized while still alive. These attentions do not seem to have troubled him. He took a cheerful part in his own post-mortem, issuing instructions and admonitions, and even anticipating the flood of posthumous literature by publishing his memoirs as *Sixteen Self-Sketches*, a compilation of reminiscences, letters, and other materials of biographical nature. He was evidently anxious to leave a definitive portrait of himself for the contemplation of future ages and he labored steadily to complete it. He had sat for innumerable portraits. None of them, not even the bust Rodin had modeled after much persuasion and at great expense, had really pleased him. The anecdote reported by the photographer Yousuf Karsh is apt:

> George Bernard Shaw told me that the best caricature he had ever seen of himself was one night at a dinner party. His hostess was in the act of greeting him when he became aware of a picture beyond her and thought, "Ah, Here I am at last." It was cruel, but the best portrait of himself he had ever seen. Said Shaw: I went toward it and the nearer I got, the better it became, until it dawned on me that I was looking in a mirror.[79]

Shaw was well aware that the mirror that best revealed him was his work, and he was grimly determined to fix his image in it before it faded. In August 1950 he was at work on a new play entitled *Why She Would Not*. He did not finish it. That autumn he suffered a fall in his garden. His leg was broken. He was taken to the hospital at Luton. There were complications. The old showman played his part gallantly, as always; but he was ninety-four, and the effort was more than he could manage. On 2 November 1950 he died. His body was cremated, and the ashes were mingled with those of his wife and scattered in the garden of their house at Ayot St. Lawrence.

It was already a museum.

THE CART AND THE TRUMPET

Dramatic art consists, according to Shaw, in the truthful representation of reality and results in a picture of ourselves as we really are. This is not a very useful definition, but, in the light of his plays, it serves to indicate what Shaw meant in calling himself a realist.

Aristotle seems to have thought that the chief concern of the dramatist is drama. Shaw considered that the principal business of the dramatist is truth. The dramatist, in his opinion, is a philosopher. He does not create illusions; he dispels them. He is an observer and a thinker, concerned primarily with reality, and reality is what is perceived when the essential design of things becomes visible. A work of art based on such premises will be, above all, meaningful, and result in an aesthetic experience founded on comprehension. The pleasure of the theater is the pleasure of understanding.

But, in spite of Shaw's convictions and his manifest intent, what we miss in his comedies is precisely that sense of reality on which he prided himself. His characters are memorable, but they are partial, they cast no shadow. In his plays there are no bad people. There are stupid people, mistaken people, romantic people comically contrasted with the enlightened, the skeptical, and the wise. Shaw's characters, even the least admirable, are rational beings. They are moved, it is true, by varying degrees of intelligence, but they are all explicable and subject to analysis, motivated by their own ideas of self-interest toward goals which they consider desirable. The remedy against their shortsightedness, when they are shortsighted, is enlightenment; and enlightenment is the result of education. Thus, all Shaw's comedies are in some sort pedagogical exercises.

The dark side of human nature, which has increasingly absorbed the attention of the dramatists of our time, did not interest Shaw. What impressed him was not the madness of mankind, but its stupidity. Shaw's plays exhibit, accordingly, a view of life which is so far from reality that one thinks of them as fables. It is evident that in presenting them as authentic "natural history," Shaw was thinking of the underlying motives rather than the realism of the demonstration. These motives are rooted in a purely philosophic conception, for Shaw made no effort to sound the depths of the soul below the rational threshold. His comedies therefore go only a little way beyond common sense; but on this level, they have their truth; and in comparison with what ordinarily passes for truth in the theater, it is at first sight dazzling.

Generally speaking, the great dramatic characters belong to tragedy. In comedy there is not much room and little occasion for profound character analysis. In choosing the lighter genres of drama, Shaw wisely avoided the intricacies of a type of introspection for which he had no taste, and possibly not much aptitude. If we agree that Shaw's plays are fabulistic, it must be granted that they have all the reality of fables, and it is not reasonable to require more of the fabulist than the measure of reality a fable can accommodate.

In Shaw's opinion, great drama is directed first of all to the intellect and results in an intellectual experience to which all the other pleasures of the theater are ancillary. Judging by his own comments he took little pleasure in theater as theater. While he was still employed as a drama critic, in 1895, he wrote:

> Put an end to my professional interest in the theatre and I shall stop going there. Put an end to Archer's, and he will still, as he says, "find a melancholy satisfaction in the glare of the footlights." For him there is illusion in the theatre; for me there is none. I can make imaginary assumptions readily enough; but for me the play is not the thing, but its thought, its purpose, its feeling, and its execution.[1]

In these circumstances, it was natural for Shaw to identify his method as a dramatist with that of Brieux, whom he much admired:

> . . . The great dramatist has something better to do than to amuse either himself or his audience. He has to interpret life. . . . It is the business of Brieux to pick out the significant incidents from the chaos of daily happenings and arrange them so that their relation to one another becomes significant, thus changing us from bewildered spectators of a monstrous confusion to men intelligently conscious of the world and its destinies.[2]

As early as January 1895, the year in which Shaw wrote *The Sanity of Art*, as well as *You Never Can Tell*, he wrote to Henry Arthur Jones: "The best established truth in the world is that no man produces a work of art of the very first order except under the pressure of a strong conviction and definite meaning as to the constitution of the world."[3] At this time, in all likelihood, Shaw had not yet formulated in detail the general idea which was to serve him as the basis of all his major works. It was not until he wrote *Man and Superman*, a half-dozen years later, that he was able to define his conviction as to the constitution of the world clearly enough to warrant the composition of a work of art of the first order. By that time he was ready to exhibit a dramatic conceit of such amplitude that it was capable of transforming a quite commonplace love story into an event of cosmic significance.

In the love of Ann Whitefield and John Tanner, Shaw found it possible to exemplify the eternal romance in its deepest significance. Similar things might be said of the love of Bradamante and Ruggiero in the *Orlando furioso*, or of the marriage of Aeneas and Lavinia in the *Aeneid*. This symbolism was standard in Renaissance epic and had been thoroughly exploited from the time of Dante to that of Goethe and Wagner. In *Man and Superman*, however, the symbolic framework was made to rest on a semiscientific basis. For Virgil the motive force of the narrative was the will of the gods; for Dante and for Ariosto it was the will of God; for Shaw it was the will to live, which he later identified, quite seriously, with the Holy Spirit.

After *Man and Superman* the demonstration of the Life Force as the motivating principle in human affairs became an increasingly absorbing element in Shaw's dramatic system, and his characters acquired magnitude in proportion to the degree to which they seemed to embody the divine principle. His themes became progressively more abstract. Unlike the contemporary symbolists in France and England, Shaw was not content simply to contemplate the mystery of being. The metaphors on which his plays are based are all decipherable; and he himself abundantly provided whatever was necessary to unravel his conceits. While the symbolists retreated from external reality deeper and deeper into their inner solitude, Shaw advanced his symbols fearlessly into the hurly-burly of the times. Insofar as his drama was a public act, it suggested not an *état d'âme*, but a mode of action.

Shaw considered himself for a time an Ibsenist; but the difference between Shaw's approach to the theater and Ibsen's soon became apparent. Ibsen's idea of drama was essentially poetic and contemplative. Shaw had something to sell. Among other things, he had to sell himself, the sage whose living presence guaranteed the authenticity of the prophecy.

After the production of *A Doll's House*, a dramatist without a sense of mission could hardly expect to be taken seriously by serious people, and even theatrical artisans of the type of Sardou, Jones, and Pinero found it convenient to emphasize their earnestness as social critics. Shaw had before his eyes, in addition to Ibsen—whose crusading zeal he greatly overestimated—the stirring examples of Mill, Carlyle, Ruskin, and Morris, who were real crusaders. It was, accordingly, in the guise of a dedicated evangelist that Shaw presented himself in the theater, and this posture, first assumed in *Widowers' Houses*, he maintained to the end. In the course of time, he found occasion to speak, in the manner of Wagner, of the theater as a cathedral, and the drama as a rite. Eventually, like Yeats, he devised a new religion and became its hierophant. But from first to last his stage was set in the market place, and his methods were those of a huckster peddling his wares from the tail of a cart. It was chiefly on his proficiency as a salesman of ideas that he based his claim to greatness as a dramatist. Very early in his career he wrote:

> . . . like all dramatists and mimes of genuine vocation, I am a natural-born mountebank. . . . I am ashamed neither of my work nor of the way it is done. I like explaining its merits to the huge majority who dont know good work from bad. It does them good; and it does me good, curing me of nervousness, laziness, and snobbishness. I write prefaces as Dryden did, and treatises as Wagner, because I *can*; and I would give half a dozen of Shakespear's plays for one of the prefaces he ought to have written. I leave the delicacies of retirement to those who are gentlemen first and literary workmen afterwards. The cart and trumpet for me.[4]

This is the most obvious aspect of Shaw, but it would be naïve to conclude that there is nothing more. We do not ordinarily think of him as a poet. It is rarely that we find in his plays the kind of poetic atmosphere that gives *John Bull's Other Island* its peculiarly elegiacal mood. For a time, Shaw's tastes, like his talents, inclined rather to the hard-edged type of drama with which Brieux was assaulting the conscience of the middle-class French. In this period, Shaw was instrumental in developing in England, along with Hankin, Barker, and Galsworthy, a genre of serious comedy which had nothing to do with poetry.

It is not until the last years of the nineteenth century that we become aware of drama which is intended to make poetry out of science. Such plays are normally associated with the naturalist movement. In *Le Naturalisme au théâtre* Zola argued for a return to the classical tradition. The naturalist precept, *faire simple, faire grand, faire vrai*, could hardly be bettered as a poetic principle, and it is clear that, for all its professed realism, it was along the lines of classic tragedy that *Thérèse Raquin* was designed.

Shaw's comedies, however, were not arranged along naturalistic lines. His youthful plays were extensions of Second Empire drama. The formal structure of the plays that followed these was derived from the popular theater. It was in the utilization of these popular forms as a framework for an intellectual exercise that Shaw demonstrated the extraordinary originality of his talent.

In his assault on the theater he soon found himself in opposition to the poetic drama which he aspired to displace. The Shakespearean tradition had made the stage a vehicle, like the opera, for displays of the personal *virtù* of the actor. For Shaw the play was mainly in the text, not in the performance; and from a textual viewpoint, he found the plays of Shakespeare wanting in doctrine, and of little utility. To invite comparison with the greatest of dramatic poets required a singular display of effrontery; but Shaw did not carry his boasting so far as to suggest that he wrote better poetry than Shakespeare. On the contrary, he willingly conceded Shakespeare's pre-eminence as a poet and contented himself with urging his own superiority to the Bard as a thinker.

The attack on the Lyceum was ill timed and poorly calculated, but to Shaw it seemed mandatory to turn the course of English drama from aesthetic into utilitarian channels. He did not succeed, obviously, in destroying Shakespeare, or even in displacing Sardou. But his own success in the theater indicates how much more accurately than Irving he interpreted the signs of the times.

Whether this result, and the attendant changes, could have been brought about with less fanfare and fewer casualties, is questionable. Shaw's full-throated salesmanship had, after all, a solid foundation in truth. In the history of English drama Shakespeare and Shaw stand at the extremes of the spectrum. Shakespeare had summed up his age poetically in a manner it was useless to emulate. Shaw was ambitious to do as much for his own time. The manner was necessarily different. The difficulty was that the audience was the same. If the nineteenth century was to get a hearing, the Renaissance must in some measure be displaced: here, as elsewhere, the past must make room for the present. For Shaw the urgency of this need was aggravated by the fact that there was apparently not room in the contemporary London theater for both Shakespeare and Shaw. It was, in fact, a long battle. As late as 1949, Shaw still felt that Shakespeare was inordinately slow to move over. His puppet play, *Shakes versus Shav*, ends with Shav's pathetic blank verse:

> We both are mortal. For a moment suffer
> My glimmering light to shine.

The type of dramatic fantasy to which Shaw inclined depended on a rational appraisal of the world he lived in. His style, on the other hand, was operatic. From Mozart and Rossini he adapted a manner of composition which approximates the alternation of recitative and aria and, through purely verbal means, suggests musical effects such as duets and choral passages. Ruskin had spoken of a "Gothic style." Apparently it was something of this sort also that Shaw wished to achieve in the theater. This style is Pre-Raphaelite insofar as it is ideal in its conception and specific in its detail, a blend of modes which the early Elizabethan drama also quaintly suggests. It was, perhaps, in elaborating this style that Shaw became aware of the mystical tendency which first became manifest in *Candida*.

Shaw's ventures into contemporary mysticism were extremely circumspect. As an active socialist he found it necessary to keep his sense of material reality at a safe distance from his intimations of the supernatural. He greatly cherished his sharp eyesight and often boasted of his ability to view the world in the light of reason, a radiance which illumines without dazzling the eye. In this manner he tried to perceive and to explain everything. There remained the inexplicable.

Contemporary mysticism addressed itself to the reality beyond reason, but it was closely related to aestheticism. Nothing was further from Shaw's mind. In his judgment, the justification of art was its capacity to facilitate the transmission of useful thoughts. In this idea, it seemed to Shaw, he was at one with Tolstoy. As their correspondence indicates, Tolstoy was not at all of his mind; nevertheless Shaw does seem to have come closer to him in theory than to any of his other contemporaries. In his later life Tolstoy was convinced that great art was necessarily religious, and great in proportion to its ability to transmit religious ideas. Since it was just so that Shaw defined his art also, he could not see where, precisely, he and Tolstoy differed and evidently considered that he understood Tolstoy better than Tolstoy understood himself.

The poetic element in Shaw's drama is often a matter of suggestion rather than one of direct statement. It was his method to develop an obviously unrealistic situation in order to draw a realistic inference: the effect is invariably astonishing. But the demonstration of a proposition was not usually his major concern as a dramatist. That, or something near it, may often be found in his prefaces. What is generally exemplified in his drama is not so much a doctrine as an attitude. It was only in his later years that he became dogmatic.

In the early plays, Shaw's viewpoint is vaguely Hobbesian. His characters demonstrate a high degree of self-interest, and the egotism of such figures as Trench, Charteris, and Vivie Warren is set down to the author's realism in the portrayal of human types. By the time of *The Devil's Disciple*, however, egotism takes on a more complex character. Self-interest develops to the point where it transcends the uses of the self and is put at the service of humanity. The hero now responds to the impulses of a being more abstract than himself. This being rather evades definition. But obviously it represents an overwhelming need to associate oneself with a meaningful principle, a point of reference in the seemingly senseless flux of existence. It is at this point that Shaw's realism begins to shade into poetry, and his poetry into mysticism.

The consciousness of serving a purpose, profoundly selfish, but immensely wider than one's immediate advantage, gives Dick Dudgeon a quite novel quality as a dramatic character. He is, in other respects, a very ordinary, decent young man. What makes him a hero is his consciousness of an appetite beyond the usual, which Shaw later called the evolutionary appetite. He identified it, in accordance with the latest fashion, with the diabolic, that is to say, the spirit of negation; but it soon became associated in his mind with the Holy Spirit. It became God.

In this manner, having rejected in the name of realism, all the traditional values of romance, Shaw retrieved them one by one as realistic expressions of the Life Force. By shifting his axis from the self-interest of the individual to the self-interest of the species, he was able to reconcile individualism with socialism, and realism with idealism, and thus to place his characters on a level where their extravagance could be justified in terms of a higher morality. Lady Cicely's will to power would be an intolerable nuisance were it not consecrated to the service of humanity; and Caesar might seem oppressively intrusive did he not embody an ethical principle. Similarly, in *Androcles and the Lion*, Lavinia's determination to be eaten by lions might be interpreted as the sheerest masochism were she not serving the cause of freedom, and in *Pygmalion* Higgins might seem unbearably egotistical were he not justified by his devotion to science. In each case it was by treating the equivocal realities of this life as symbolic of a higher and more intelligible reality that Shaw was able to suggest through the idiosyncracies of exceptional people the workings of a universal principle. The result of his method is a type of drama which aims at revelation rather than at revolution, so that it is with pleasure that we discover that in the course of the action we have somehow been converted to a view we have never questioned.

Shaw's technique clearly foreshadows the method of Pirandello; but Shaw did not share Pirandello's analytic zeal, and he had no desire to disintegrate reality. In Italy the tendency of the school of the grotesque was to stress the antithesis of forma and vita, the ideal and the real, the outer face and the inner truth. For Pirandello the face which the individual wears in public is a construct fashioned in accordance with the demands of the collective. It is behind this mask that one must look for the life of the individual, his truth, just as it is behind the face which nature presents to our eyes that we must look for whatever reality it may have. This reality, for Pirandello, remained enigmatic. In all likelihood he suspected that beyond the process of becoming and passing away there is nothing, and that in reality there is no reality. At any rate it was enough for him that things are not what they seem, and he evinced no desire to go beyond this consoling thought.

Shaw, however, could not stop short of certainty. Like most militant skeptics he had an urgent need to be sure, and in his need to know he differed much from Pirandello, for whom Pyrrhonism was a refuge. He differed from him mightily also in his choice of subject matter. Pirandello, as a dedicated realist, specialized in the analysis of ordinary people. Shaw was interested mainly in the extraordinary and the extravagant, and his heroes are all exceptionally gifted people in whom it is easy to catch a glimpse of the author. The author is a little more difficult to find in the characters of Pirandello, but it is easy to measure in them the depth of his disillusionment and his despair. Pirandello makes the impression of one leaning amiably out of a window in hell; but all his life Shaw lived within earshot of paradise.

Like the Italian *grotteschi*, particularly Chiarelli and Pirandello, Shaw made the unmasking of his characters a central motif in his dramatic system. It is very usual for his personages to appear in romantic guises which ultimately they discard, either voluntarily or under compulsion. There is no reason to suppose that Pirandello was especially indebted to Shaw for this useful notion: it was Ibsen who principally influenced both writers in this respect.

Ultimately this tendency toward a radical analysis of character was a product of the skeptical current which followed the disillusionments of the Great Revolution of 1789. The consequence was to bring under closer scrutiny the assumptions on which middle-class values are based. It is a process which has obviously been continued with unabated vigor to the present day and is still of perennial interest in the theater. But, unlike those who now follow this trend in the drama, Shaw had no wish to discard the moral framework of his time. He wished, on the contrary, to strengthen it wherever it was possible to do so.

The pretenses of society, and the pathetic efforts of the individual to adapt himself to them, filled Pirandello sometimes with amusement and sometimes with horror. In the end they resulted in a calm skepticism which had no outcome. For Shaw, however, the disparity between appearance and reality had enormous metaphysical significance. Behind the mask of the individual, Shaw discerned the expression of the race: in the face which humanity showed him, he saw the dimly defined features of the evolving God.

It was in this intuition that Shaw found the faith that was to serve him as a substitute for Christianity. Pirandello's vita is not, at bottom, much more than Schopenhauer's aimless Will. Shaw's vital spirit is of another sort. It has purpose and something like direction, and the world it makes is quite different from the ever-changing flux which is the world of Pirandello. For Pirandello the function of art is to reveal the essential absurdity of life. But in Shaw's view, absurdity is an attribute only of the world of pretense; he was concerned about revealing this absurdity only in order to make manifest the splendor of the truth it obscures. Shaw's comic effects depend upon the ridiculous postures which men assume in their ignorance, but nature itself inspired him with reverence and awe, and the play of contradictions in which Pirandello saw only the absurdity, Shaw perceived as the indispensable dialectic through which the spirit achieves its fulfillment.

Among the various truths with which Shaw battered the ears of his listeners, the gospel of Creative Evolution was at first the least strident. But in time, everything he had to say seemed to depend upon it, and his evangelical task took on great urgency. The amalgam of progressive socialism and biological theory which he called metabiology was by no means entirely ridiculous from a philosophical viewpoint; but it gained no ground as a religion, and it was barely acceptable as a basis for drama. From the standpoint of Creative Evolution, Shaw's plays, though seemingly sharp and clear, take on the look of a phantasmagoria behind which invisible forces meet and merge in deadly combat. Most of Shaw's admirers prefer to see his comedies in a less metaphysical light. They take them simply and wholly for what they seem to be, a series of comic situations revolving around a mildly shocking inversion of what usually passes for truth.

But in Shaw's later plays, as in the later plays of Strindberg, every dramatic situation implies a spiritual conflict, and every resolution includes a future commitment, for in the light of Shaw's theory the characters must be viewed not only in themselves but as aspects of the developing spirit, progressive, inert, or retrograde, and the situation which relates them, however frivolous, has its serious side. It is mainly in this general sense that Shaw's plays are didactic. Even when, as in the case of *Pygmalion*, they seem to teach us little or nothing, a moment's reflection will reveal their relation to the doctrine of *Man and Superman*.

In this regard, once again, Shaw comes close to Strindberg; and again there is a difference. Fulfillment, in Strindberg's world, is an individual problem. Each man strives toward it as best he can. For Shaw it is a collective effort, motivated by the cosmic Will, which the individual will subserves. Strindberg's God is external to mankind, a stern father whose caresses are mainly blows and curses. Shaw's divinity is a spirit immanent in its creatures and indistinguishable from them. Thus, even the individual will has creative power: it is necessary only to wish hard in order for the wish to come true. A realist could hardly consider such an idea matter of fact. It is matter of faith.

Shaw's work may thus be regarded as a phase of the agelong process of reconciling science with religion. It may be objected that in *Man and Superman* and *Back to Methuselah* there is to be found neither reliable science nor sound theology. Doubtless this is true, but the search for certainty in both these fields is, at best, a dubious quest, and it was no small achievement to have found, on any terms, a believable doctrine in a skeptical age. Jacques Maritain remarked in his *Notes on Modern Poetry*, that symbolist poets, groping about their void, sometimes to their surprise find God there. Something of the sort happened to Shaw. He did not follow the path of Claudel, or Eliot, nor did he come upon the same God as they. His symbolism, like his poetic, was singularly his own; he found his God, naturally where most he sought Him, in science, or something like it. It was also characteristic of Shaw that, once he had gained what he thought to be a fundamental insight, he hastened to incorporate it into the program of public instruction which he had undertaken as his special mission in life. Marx had proposed to educate the working classes into full consciousness of their power. Shaw's aim was wider. He made it his task to educate mankind into an awareness of its divinity. It is in this sense that he spoke of his work as religious iconography.

After Darwin, orthodoxy in religious matters became increasingly difficult for many, but the need for faith was especially poignant in those who had really lost it. In 1875 Arnold wrote that we can neither do with Christianity nor do without it. The long preface to *Androcles and the Lion* which Shaw wrote in 1915 indicates the degree to which he too was committed to Christian doctrine, and his need to reconcile the teachings of Jesus with the moral system he had evolved for himself. It was not at all difficult to maintain that Jesus advocated "communism, the widening of the private family with its cramping ties into the great family of mankind under the fatherhood of God, the abandonment of revenge and punishment, the counteracting of evil by good instead of by a hostile evil, and an organic conception of society. . . ."[5] But it was difficult to find Christian roots for the doctrine of Creative Evolution. Shaw might have done better to have looked elsewhere than to the Bible for a theological basis for the new faith. But even from a theological viewpoint, if one is constrained to that, Shaw's principle of divinity would probably not be utterly repugnant to those who, following Tillich, Bultman, and Bonhoeffer, take comfort in a wider conception of godhead than traditional Christianity affords.[6]

From the dramatic standpoint, however, it is the poetic side of Shaw's theology that is interesting. In the theater his idea of the Life Force seems magnificently fruitful. It provides a theoretical basis for conflict which exalts drama far above the monotonous struggle of good and evil, and it provides a teleological framework for situations which, in our present state of faith, quite defy resolution. The fact that this teleology is wholly conjectural can hardly trouble those for whom reality has, in any case, become increasingly a matter of conjecture. What Shaw provided was a dramatic system which has enormous possibilities if one is willing to grant its assumptions, and, if one is not willing, it is at least sufficiently logical within its framework to support the necessary illusion. In a period when much of our drama consists of miniature transactions which scarcely repay the effort of attention, Shaw's plays at least have scale. In the major plays, beyond the immediate situation, the canvas is so vast as to encompass the whole reach of human destiny. Not all of Shaw's drama, of course, does so much. But of the two-score plays that have come from his shop, at least a half-dozen must be accounted of the first importance. With the exception of Shakespeare, not so much can be said of any English dramatist.

Shaw took some time to attain this order of greatness. At the time he was writing *The Man of Destiny* he was still some way from a general idea. Even after he found his certainty, much more was needed to frame a work of art of "the very first order." The Hegelian idea of history suggested a useful method for the dramatic confrontation of conflicting ideas. But art is a sublimation of thought, not thought itself. The Greek tragedies had been written in the light of the Homeric world-view; Shakespeare had framed his drama within the cosmic outlines of Renaissance Christianity. Neither Sophocles nor Shakespeare needed to define the cosmic ambience in which their plays took place, but by 1895 the intellectual horizon had widened beyond the reach of man's vision, and the *certezze* of the Renaissance artist had dwindled into nothing. Shaw's drama had to be provided with a cosmic frame based on philo-sophic concepts which must be defined and justified in the course of the action. The necessary exposition could well be relegated to the reading matter appended to the play; but on the stage the invisible must be suggested through symbols. Before a work of art of the very first order could be achieved in the ordinary way of the theater, the symbols had to be found, and also the symbolism.

Shaw's early drama was bounded by the materialistic considerations of a Social Democrat of the 1880's, but he had before him the example of Goethe. In *Faust*, and especially the second part of *Faust*, Goethe had shown the possibilities of drama conceived so that the destiny of human-ity could be prefigured in the fate of a single individual. It is, of course, possible to interpret the Faustian adventure as a romantic version of *The Pilgrim's Progress*, but the difference in magnitude is striking. Bunyan's work is sheer allegory, childlike in comparison with the rich symbolism of Goethe. Shaw revered Bunyan; but in Shaw's youth, Goethe was still very much in fashion. More than anyone he had inflamed the imagina-tion of Lamartine and Hugo, and through them of a whole generation of interesting writers. It was precisely to this time that Shaw looked for a point of departure in his artistic enterprise.[7]

The influence of Goethe upon Shaw is plainly perceptible in *Man and Superman*; but in all likelihood Shaw had come somewhat earlier under symbolist influence. French symbolism, with its secondary attributes of decadence, aestheticism, and alienation, had no attraction for Shaw: he had no patience with the affectations of Wilde or Whistler, and no great admiration for Yeats. One looks through Shaw's critical writings in vain for any indication that he was aware of symbolism as a cult. He occasionally makes mention of Maeterlinck, Yeats, or Joyce, but not as symbolists, and there is no evidence that he felt the slightest interest in the exotic ideas recently imported from France by Arthur Symons and George Moore. Probably he would have repudiated energetically any imputation of French symbolist influence. He called *Candida* a Pre-Raphaelite play; but it would be a wise man that could distinguish between the symbolism of the last Pre-Raphaelites, Holman Hunt or William Morris, and the symbolism of the symbolists.[8]

In France, after the production of *La Princesse Maleine* in 1889, Maeterlinck had been hailed as a genius greater than Shakespeare. The publication of *L'Intruse* and *Les Aveugles* the following year, and the production in 1892 of *Pelléas et Mélisande*, enormously enhanced his reputation. In the years when Shaw was perfecting his style, Maeterlinck, not Ibsen, was considered the greatest living dramatist, and when he was awarded the Nobel Prize in 1911, his literary position seemed monumental.

Shaw had come in contact with Maeterlinck's work as early as 1895, in the line of duty, and he soon had an opportunity to see what was going on in the symbolist theater which Lugné-Poë had recently founded. Maeterlinck's work does not seem to have impressed him. He praised the stage-management of *L'Intruse* and *Pelléas*, and the décor, which he said "produced a true poetic atmosphere" and triumphed "easily over the shabby appointments and ridiculous incidents." But if he was aware of what Maeterlinck was getting at in these plays, he did not impart his insights to his readers.[9]

In *The Celtic Element in Literature* Yeats wrote:

> The symbolist movement which has come to perfection in Germany in Wagner, in England in the pre-Raphaelites, in France in Villiers de l'Isle Adam and Mallarmé, and in Belgium in Maeterlinck, and has stirred the imagination of Ibsen and D'Annunzio, is certainly the only movement that is saying new things."

Like Yeats, Shaw evidently thought that Pre-Raphaelitism and symbolism were synonymous. *Candida* was very far from the sort of symbolist drama which Maeterlinck was developing; and further still from the kind of drama Yeats had in mind; nevertheless there is no doubt that Shaw went to some trouble to stress its symbolist attributes, and that by this means he meant to ally himself so far as possible with the new movement.

Yeats had gathered from Mallarmé and Maeterlinck that drama was—or should be—a religious exercise; but he went further afield than the French symbolists in search of appropriate rituals. The French had looked to pagan rites and Christian liturgy for the sacrificial basis of their art. Yeats preferred Celtic mythology and eventually devised a private mythology of his own. Shaw was very willing also to give a religious tone to his plays, but he had no idea of aping ancient ceremonials in the modern theater. Since the theater was, admittedly, a temple, he enshrined the Life Force in it, but he did not insist on rites of worship. In *Candida* he had made little more than a gesture in the direction of the new symbolism; but with *Man and Superman* Shaw brought symbolism into the English theater as decisively as Villiers had brought it to France a decade earlier. It is possible that he was not entirely aware of the implications; but there is no reason to suppose that he did not know what he was about.

The nineteenth-century symbolists had founded their church upon Swedenborg, but they acknowledged their obligations to Coleridge, Blake, Poe, Wagner, and especially to Baudelaire. For Swedenborg, a scientist whose latter days were enlivened by conversations with angels, symbolism was mainly a matter of allegory. The visible universe, in the eyes of this seer, was a vast conceit, a complex metaphor of interrelated signs which might be deciphered, code book fashion, by means of the Bible. The Word of God furnished the adept with the key to the whole mystery of creation. The spiritual world, in which resided the causes of things, and the material world, in which the senses perceived the effects, were precisely correspondent. Consequently, the unraveling of the enigma, impossible for man without the direct revelation of God, was a purely deductive process.

The result of this process was to unveil the reality of nature, which was now seen to be a moral structure, substantially similar to the cosmos of Dante or Aquinas. Its function was the ultimate reconciliation of man with God. In this process, the motivation on every level of man's intellectual ascent was love—the love of natural things, first of all; then the love of the spirit; finally, divine love. It was under these auspices that the symbolists operated, from Balzac to Strindberg.[10]

Baudelaire, writing a century after the publication of Swedenborg's *Heaven and Its Wonders, and Hell,* found this account of the invisible universe completely convincing, but he could not accept Swedenborg's idea of symbol as a simple allegorical reference. In the correspondences by which the visible world was bound to the spiritual reality beyond it,

Baudelaire caught glimpses of a transcendental hierarchy of Platonic forms; but he forebore to define his insights any more precisely than did Emerson or Poe. In this regard his followers were even more indefinite than he. The later symbolists are seldom clear. In general they cherished their obscurity and showed no desire to dispel the mystery in which their poetry was enveloped. On the contrary, they made mystery their stock in trade.

Symbolism is not, and never has been, a term of precise connotation. Strictly speaking, it suggests the literary movement which, in the decade 1885–95, was associated with *La Revue wagnérienne*, and the contributors to *La Vogue*, *Le Symboliste*, *La Revue indépendante*, and *La Décadence*. In the drama it suggests the plays of Villiers de l'Isle Adam, Maeterlinck, Verhaeren, and their German imitators, all of whom attempted to convey a supernatural experience in terms of visible things. The central years of its development were actually 1870–75. It was in this period that Rimbaud's *Illuminations* were written, and in this period Mallarmé's major poetry was completed.

These works came into prominence only after 1886. In the meantime symbolist theory had already been shaped through the critical reception of Verlaine's *Romances sans paroles*, together with the personal influence of Mallarmé and the efforts of Gustave Kahn and the symbolist reviews with which he was associated. The influence of symbolism was, however, vastly greater than these names suggest. It was the most important literary trend of the 1890's and continued to have an incalculable effect on the art and literature of the following century. In the drama its influence was pervasive. By the end of the century, every major dramatist in Europe was a symbolist.[11]

The essence of symbolism is the assumption that beyond the material world there is a reality which poets can know and can perhaps reveal. The process of revelation is seldom definable, and it always involves some suprarational influence. It may take place through inspiration, through meditation, through the exploration of the soul by means of free or partially controlled association, through an emptying of the mind, or through the intoxication of alcohol or drugs. Whatever the means, the goal is the same. It is an opening of the psychic gateway to the truth beyond the reach of the intellect.

The essential difference between the symbolists of the Middle Ages and those of the time of Mallarmé and Valéry is that the medieval symbolists knew what they were looking for, and the nineteenth-century seers did not. It was possible for Dante to embark on his voyage through the spheres in the full confidence that in due course he would witness all the wonders described in the celestial travel-guides. After Darwin the psychic voyager no longer knew what marvels he might encounter in the beyond. Doubtless in the progress of the soul he hoped to be afforded some glimpses of the hierarchy of ideal forms which had furnished the basis of so much mystical thought in the past; but normally he found nothing in the psychic labyrinth save himself, and occasionally not even that. Apart from its artistic results, which are impressive, symbolism, until the time of Freud, proved to be a blind alley of impressive dimensions. Ultimately its convergence with Eastern mysticism developed its current manifestations, together with the musical silence, the blank page of verse, and the untouched canvas, symbols of the ineffable beauty of the incommunicable truth.

Tidings of the emerging patterns of French symbolist drama came early to England. The best and most authoritative account of it was the "second chronicle" published by Mallarmé in June 1893 in the London *National Observer*. The new writers, Mallarmé reported, conceived of drama as an expression of the inner life, *la scène intérieure*. They sought to create a theater of atmosphere and dream, representing a spiritual action free of the limitations of the actual. For this purpose they devised, like Goethe, plots designed to suggest the eternal plot of humanity, so that a play would depict not merely the action of an individual in a single anecdote, but of man in the eternal anecdote. Thus, the new dramatists refrained from the literal representation of an action, and aimed, through a more abstract representation of actions, at an evocation of the sense of the mystery of being. Among the representative poets of this new drama, Mallarmé singled out Maeterlinck as the moving spirit.

A dramatic action conceived along these lines would obviously not be explicit. In the drama, as in poetry, symbolism was concerned not with events but with the spiritual effect of events. Symbolist drama was therefore at the other pole from naturalism. It rejected, along with a literal mimesis of outer reality, all practical purpose, and had nothing to do with the *pièce à thèse*. It was closely related to music. At its best, it was music.

The relation of poetry to music, an essential consideration of symbolist theory, had first been described by Wagner. In a *Letter on Music*, addressed to François Villot, Wagner made it clear that the relation of poetry to music was a matter of sound: music began where poetry left off. For Wagner the power of poetry was mainly suggestive. The meaning of words was far less important than their power to evoke images and to stimulate moods. Since poetry, like drama, was at bottom an incantation, its relation to music was clear. At the point where music was most articulate, and poetry least so, the two become one. Wagner wrote:

> . . . In his diction the poet seeks . . . through a rhythmic arrangement of his verse, and finally through the almost musical adornment of rhyme, to ensure for his phrase an effect that shall take the feeling captive and control it as by a spell. In this tendency of the poet, essential to his very being, we see him arrive at last at the limit of his art, where he comes already into immediate contact with music; and thus that work of the poet must rank as the most excellent which in its final consummation becomes entirely music.

In the theater the double effect of music and poetry put the soul into an especially receptive state:

> . . . The atmosphere of the theatre and the legendary tone combine to place the mind in that dreamlike state wherein it presently shall come to feel clairvoyance, and thus perceive a new coherence in the world's phenomena, a coherence it could not detect in the waking eye of every day.[12]

This was the idea that shaped the current of symbolism in the nineteenth century. Since the sense of beauty was essentially the perception of the workings of the ideal on each level of being, music was the clearest expression of the harmonic correspondences which poets attempted to suggest verbally through the use of similitude, metaphor, and rhyme. It was therefore through the agency of music that the dramatic poet could most readily communicate the universal harmonies which it was the function of all art to reveal, but especially the function of poetry.

The theory of correspondences was venerable in Italy and in England, less familiar in nineteenth-century France. The moment, however, was ripe for its revival, and it was seized upon eagerly in the current reaction to the subjectivism of the romantics, the objectivity of the Parnassians, the materialism of the naturalists, and the relativism of the Impressionists—in short, to all the aesthetic creeds which the followers of Baudelaire disliked. The new ideas could hardly be called revolutionary; but in the circumstances they offered a providential opportunity to affirm the existence of the eternal verities, and with them the substantial reality of the order of nature, a concept which was forever eluding those of little faith. These ideas, unfortunately, were not entirely comprehensible and required vivid promotion. At the time no man alive captured the imagination more vividly than Wagner, who seemed to have done, and even stated, everything that the new poets aspired to do and state.

Rumors of Wagner's genius had filtered into Paris for more than a decade when in 1861 the scandalous reception of *Tannhäuser* at the Paris Opera brought Wagner directly to the attention of the Paris intellectuals. It was through Baudelaire's celebrated essay "Wagner and Tannhäuser in Paris" (1861), republished in 1869 in *L'Art romantique*, that Mallarmé first came to know of Wagner's revolutionary theory of the drama.[13]

By the time he became aware of the German composer, Baudelaire had been an admirer of Poe for some fifteen years. He understood at once that Wagner's music-drama, like Poe's verse, was neither music nor poetry, but a fusion of both and, accordingly, more potent than either in its power to evoke the spiritual awareness which Baudelaire conceived to be the goal of art. The idea accorded perfectly with Mallarmé's idea of poetry, and he agreed heartily also with Wagner's estimate of the poet's calling as a priesthood. Moreover, Mallarmé found particularly congenial Baudelaire's idea of drama as religious ritual and of the theater as a place of worship. By 1876, after prolonged meditation on these subjects, Mallarmé formulated for himself the idea of drama as a sacred rite in which the masses participate, a rite the totality of which manifests "le colossale approche d'une Initiation." The impact of these ideas on the musical literature of the following period may be judged from the manner in which Stravinsky's *Le Sacre du printemps* gained acceptance after the shock of its first performance in Paris in 1913.

At the time of Wagner's death in 1883 Baudelaire had been dead for sixteen years. His followers, groping about hopefully in the forest of correspondences where he had lost them, were now calling thmselves *symbolistes*, and, however dissimilar their individual practice as poets, they were resolved to make a common cause and to organize themselves into a literary movement. Their program at this point was hardly explicit. The basis was their common opposition on the one hand to the vestiges of romanticism—with its stress on emotion, and its cult of the ego—and, on the other, to the realists of the 1880's, with their emphasis on the literal representation of nature as it appears to the senses. Wagner, whose dramatic theories were both nebulous and awe-inspiring, provided a welcome rallying-point for an aesthetic movement which was having trouble in defining its aims in other than negative terms. The symbolists gratefully acknowledged him as their master, and adopted his viewpoint, whatever it might be.

In this manner Wagner became the father of symbolism. In 1884 *La*

Revue wagnérienne was founded as the official organ of the symbolist movement, with Villiers, Mallarmé, and Edouard Dujardin as its principal contributors, and Wagnerian studies became the starting point for the developing theories of the new poetry. But in spite of the initial intensity of the effort, the relation of Wagner's work to that of the new poets remained vague. Few of the symbolists had heard Wagner's music-dramas, and those who journeyed to Bayreuth to hear them experienced some perplexity in squaring their experience with their anticipation of it.

It was, however, Wagner's emphasis on the power of music to afford such insights as elude direct communication through language that seemed particularly significant in France, and in this respect Wagner's operas were not disappointing. In contrast to the current drama of literal representation, Wagner had created, through the utilization of all the arts of the theater, and especially through music, a type of dramatic composition that spoke eloquently to the sense of mystery which the symbolists especially savored. As to what precisely it said, there was no general agreement. In Mallarmé's opinion, Wagner's technique resulted in a *théâtre de sortilège* which, through atmosphere, suggestion, and mystery, by means of a complex fusion of sound, movement and color, succeeded in arousing in the spectator an awareness of the reality beyond sensual experience. It was with this reality that the symbolist drama was particularly concerned.

Mallarmé, however, was too jealous of the autonomy of poetry to admit of the need for music in the drama. His article in the *National Observer* stressed the fact that poetry makes its own music. Maeterlinck's *Pelléas* is "un drame réglé par les conflits melodiques," to the point where even the sound of a violin would be intrusive. These melodic conflicts were developed, apparently, not in terms of sound, but in the relation of symbols and ideas, a silent spiritual counterpoint for the mind to decipher.[14]

Accordingly, Mallarmé took issue with the usual Wagnerite view of the time, which stressed not so much the musical element in the libretto as the literary content of the score. Wagner's father-in-law, Liszt, had written in March 1861, the very year of the disastrous performance of *Tannhäuser* in Paris:

> Wagner enables music to address itself to our minds, to stimulate thought, to appeal to our reflective faculties; he gives it a moral and intellectual meaning. . . . His melodies are, as it were, personifications of ideas; their recurrence announces the return of feelings which the words uttered do not explicitly indicate; Wagner entrusts them with the revelation of the heart's secrets.

This description of Wagner's use of *Leitmotiven* has, obviously, not much bearing on symbolist theory. Melodies which represent ideas, or identify characters, play a symbolic role in the opera score, but they do so with quasi-mathematical precision, resulting in a kind of musical algebra. The juxtaposition, subordination, or interweaving of such motifs may suggest the corresponding relation of the ideas these melodies represent. Essentially this is the method of allegory applied to music. In the *Ring* operas, Wagner's use of musical symbols is as precise as Spenser's symbolism in Book One of *The Faerie Queen*. For the symbolists, however the word was creative in proportion to its capacity to suggest the inexpressible. In 1895 Mallarmé wrote: "It is not by means of the elemental sonorities of the brasses, the strings, the woodwinds, undeniably, but from the intellectual spoken word at its apogee that, with plenitude and clarity, in token of the existent harmony of all creation, music will result."[15] The year before, in the course of his talk at Oxford on "Music and Letters," he had said: "Music and letters are the two faces, here stretched toward the darkness; and there, shining with certitude, of what I called a single phenomenon, the Idea."[16]

Mallarmé is not the clearest of writers, but in this case his meaning is clear. The music of poetry is audible to the mind, not to the ear; it must be comprehended in order to be heard. It results from the spoken word in its highest significance, which is its power to suggest the hidden correspondences that constitute the divine harmony, the Idea. At the point where the word becomes revelatory its effect is indistinguishable from music.

In Wagner's music-drama it is not the text but the score that is the primary source of the total experience. It is because words, though rhythmically arranged and adorned with rhyme, are symbols that fail to convey a sufficient meaning that music is necessary to the composition. If the text were sufficient, the orchestration and the melody would be superfluous. As it is, the score speaks a language that communicates thought more effectively than the sound of words.

Mallarmé's opinion was thus the reverse of Wagner's. For Mallarmé the music of poetry was not a matter of verbal sonority. Thoughts sing together in the mind of the poet. The correspondences of nature come to him as audible chords. Ideas vibrate harmonically in the soul, and the poet accords them very much as the composer does. The difference is that sounds are more primitive than words and thus speak chiefly to the intuition, while words are sonorities of more precise signification, more difficult to accord, but far more effective as music when properly composed. Thus, poetry is the highest form of music, for words which resonate in sympathy with the Word make music such as no concert of strings and brasses can do more than dimly suggest.

There was, indeed, no reason why the concept of synaesthesia, essential to the symbolists' theory of correspondences, should not be extended in this manner to the intellectual faculty. The notion that ideas are audible as music requires only the assumption that thought is a sensation akin to sight or hearing, and that ideas are perceived by the mind in the same way as objects by the senses. For a symbolist such an assumption presented no difficulty.

The consequence of this reasoning was the rejection of Wagner's synthesis of music and poetry, the ground on which the symbolists had originally based their doctrine. Since the poet was a composer, there was no need, in Mallarmé's view, for poetry to be set to music. Poetry was music, and, as such, incomparably more effective in awakening the soul to the perception of reality than the sounds of drums and trumpets. Thus when Debussy told Mallarmé that he had turned *L'Après-midi d'un faune* into music, Mallarmé is said to have answered coldly that he had thought he had done this already himself.

It is hardly possible to say how much of all this came to Shaw's attention. In 1894 Mallarmé had lectured to some sixty people at Oxford, and to a score of listeners at Cambridge. He was known in England only to a small number of intellectuals such as York Powell, and to a few critics such as Sir Edmund Gosse. Shaw cultivated the avant-garde assiduously, but in all likelihood he understood little of Mallarmé, whose prose, indeed, quite pointedly defies interpretation. The symbolist jargon, if he ever read symbolist writings, must have seemed to Shaw so much gibberish; but he evidently understood enough of what was being said in France on the subject of symbolism to write *The Perfect Wagnerite*.

Here he undertook to do for Wagner what he had done for Ibsen some years before, that is to say, to explicate him in Fabian terms. It is perfectly clear that he associated symbolism with Wagner, whom he took to be a symbolist because the symbolists said he was one. In writing his guide to the *Ring* cycle, Shaw had the advantage of Hans von Wolzogen's *Thematic Guide to "The Ring of the Niebelungen"* (1876). He followed it, but he himself understood Wagner in a very special way.

The first part of *The Perfect Wagnerite* describes Wagner as an allegorist deeply involved with ideas of social justice. A most improbable allegory is then traced in detail through the *Ring* operas: the net result is to transform the affair of the Rhinegold and the Niebelungs into a socialist tract. It is clear, nonetheless, from his discussion of Wagner's method, that Shaw saw the music-drama in the same light as Liszt and Mallarmé, that is, as a quasi-literary composition in which the music plumbs depths too deep for words to fathom. "After the symphonies of Beethoven," Shaw wrote, "it was certain that the poetry that lies too deep for words does not lie too deep for music, and that the vicissitudes of the soul, from the roughest fun to the loftiest aspiration, can make symphonies without the aid of dance tunes."[17]

In *The Perfect Wagnerite*, however, Shaw does not illustrate this idea. What distinguishes Wagner from Beethoven, in his opinion, is the intellectual content of the music, the significance of which is made perfectly explicit in the *Ring* operas through the use of symbols. All their meaning is in the allegory set forth in the text. For the rest, if the score suggests meanings beyond the power of language to transmit, the suggestions are well hidden, and Shaw says nothing about them. On the contrary, he feels that the words add immeasurably to the significance of the music:

> A Beethoven symphony (except the articulate part of the Ninth) expresses noble feelings, but not thought: it has moods, but no ideas. Wagner added thought and produced the music drama. . . . The libretto of *Don Giovanni* is coarse and trivial: its transfiguration by Mozart's music may be a marvel; but nobody will venture to contend that such transfigurations, however seductive, can be as satisfactory as tone poetry or drama in which the musician and the poet are at the same level.[18]

Since Shaw was committed to an evolutionary concept which envisaged the progessive intellectualization of all mood and feeling, it followed that the development of music would lead from "the exquisitely beautiful gothic traceries in sound" of Bach to a completely articulate intellectual expression which would surpass language as a means of communication. Presumably such a process would transform music into poetry, a result analogous to that anticipated by Mallarmé.

In insisting on the musical structure of his plays Shaw meant something rather different from Mallarmé, but there are points of similarity. The arrangement of ideas and images in patterns reminiscent of music was a cardinal principle of symbolism; but in contrast to the "instrumentation" of those symbolists who followed Verlaine in the elaboration of verbal sonorities, Mallarmé saw in musical construction the possibility of a poetic design of thematic character which, while entirely logical, would surpass the limits of language through its capacity for indirect communication.

This idea, which he elaborated in *L'Après-midi d'un faune*, and to which T. S. Eliot gave currency in *The Waste Land*, was perhaps the most fruitful of the symbolist theories. Whether it came to him by way of Mallarmé or through Wagner, who had first suggested it, Shaw gives evidence in *The Perfect Wagnerite* of being quite familiar with the method:

> The other and harder way of composing is to take a strain of free melody and ring every variety of change of mood upon it as if it were a thought that sometimes brought hope, sometimes melancholy, sometimes exultation, sometimes raging despair, and so on. To take several themes of this kind, and weave them together into a rich musical fabric passing panoramically before the ear with a continually varying flow of sentiment is the highest feat of the musician.[19]

This describes perfectly the technique of *L'Après-midi d'un faune*, but Shaw obviously had in mind variations on musical, not poetic themes. It is quite likely, nevertheless, that he intended *Heartbreak House* to be apprehended in this manner. Whether or not the result in that case is musical is a matter of opinion, but it seems tolerably clear that in his insistence on the musical construction of his plays, Shaw was joining his voice to the chorus of the avant-garde across the Channel.

In his later life, Shaw spoke often of the dramatic method he had developed through the study of symphonic scores. In claiming Mozart as his master in the drama, however, he proposed a riddle which his admirers have found it difficult to solve. It was clearly not the wretched libretti of Da Ponte and Schikaneder that Shaw had in mind. He himself remarked more than once on the foolishness of *Don Giovanni* as a play. But the manner in which Mozart juxtaposed, supported, and contrasted melodic themes and tonal coloring, the design and arrangement of arias, the relation of arioso passages to recitative, and the witty use of melody to characterize and to caricature, suggested a musical technique in playmaking which nobody had so far consciously developed. "My method, my system, my tradition," Shaw said at the Malvern festival of 1939, "is founded upon music. It is not founded on literature at all. I was brought up in music. I did not read plays. . . . If you study operas and symphonies, you will find a useful clue to my particular type of writing."

Some of Shaw's critics have been moved by such provocative statements so far as to look for symphonic construction and chamber-orchestration in his plays, as well as for harmonic and contrapuntal effects in the management of vocal lines. Such interpretations, while stimulating, do not seem to be especially fruitful. Shaw was, without doubt, well versed in music, but from his writings one may conclude that for him music had not primarily a musical significance. He was deeply moved by the beauty of sound and was certainly aware of musical design; but design, for him, suggested idea: without idea, music ceased to have utility and fell within the category of art for art's sake. What chiefly impressed him in the *Ring* operas, therefore, was the verbal allegory, which the score supported: he interpreted the Niebelungen cycle very much as if it had been composed by John Bunyan.[20]

For Shaw the essence of drama was the argument, not the incantation. The power of spoken dialogue was its capacity to distinguish and define; to inform, convince, disprove, and persuade—precisely those things that music does not, and cannot, do. The influence of Mozart on Shaw's writings must therefore be looked for chiefly in his developing sense of rhetorical patterns, the rhetoric of action as well as of words, the arrangement of conflicting or conforming ideas, and the *numérotage* of scenes and entrances in a carefully ordered pattern of geometrical nature. This was the method also of the series of symbolist writers from Mallarmé to Joyce and Beckett.

By 1900 symbolism had so far swept over Europe that it was indispensable for poets to associate their work with music, whether they understood the connection or not. Shaw attributed his method to Mozart; Strindberg was partial to Beethoven and spoke of himself as a composer of prose sonatas and chamber pieces. It is as difficult to define the sonata in *The Ghost Sonata* as it is to discover the symphonic poem in *Heartbreak House*, but it is impossible to deny to these works some musical connotation. Wagner's use of *Leitmotiven* was, after all, a sublimation of the thematic underscoring which Pixerécourt had developed for melodrama; but in a play without orchestral accompaniment there is no way of making a musical comment on the text except through the text itself. In *Easter*, Strindberg tried to combine three movements of Haydn's "Seven Words of the Redeemer" with his dramatic action, so that the musical preludes create a suitably unearthly atmosphere for the spiritual purgation which the play demonstrates. Shaw, however, appears to have relied on the "conflits melodiques," which Mallarmé identified in *Pelléas et Mélisande*, in order to give his plays their musical structure. This was evidently a matter of vocal antiphony and the interweaving of lines of thought and character. Mallarmé had called Banville's *Forgeron* an "ode aux plusieurs voix." In somewhat the same sense, apparently, Shaw thought of his comedies as prose cantatas, which must be heard, and hardly needed to be seen. "All that is necessary for you to do," he once told his actors, "is to say my lines so slowly and clearly that the audience can understand every word; as long as they can hear my lines you can act or not, as you please."[21]

In the end, Shaw came to the conclusion that his players were simply voices for delivering lines, and that the musical effect of the delivery was far more important than anything else. The cast was a choir trained to perform the score that was written for it. There was no need for the actors to display operatic bravura. That was the author's province. What was chiefly necessary was that the actors should not obscure the author's meaning. This was, of course, especially true of radio broadcasts. Here the actors were in fact nothing but voices, and this was the ideal toward which all playacting tended. In 1950 Shaw wrote in the *Strand Magazine*, apropos of radio plays:

> In selecting the cast no regard should be given to whether the actors understand the play or not (players are not walking encyclopedias), but their ages and personalities should be suitable, and their voices should not be alike. The four principals should be soprano, alto, tenor and bass. Vocal contrast is of the greatest importance and is indispensable for broadcasting. . . .

If in Shaw's plays the association of drama with music seems at times uncertain, it is doubtless because his plays demand a very different mental attitude than that which music usually requires. Even ordinary conversation involves an element of polyphony, if only because of the interrelation of the voices. Ordinarily there is no reason to call these interrelations musical. But the conditions of the theater transform conversation into a performance, and when the speeches are consciously devised so as to approximate melody, and even counterpoint, the musical analogy becomes apt. In the nineteenth century Shakespeare's plays were still being declaimed in a style that suggested the opera.

In the case of such quasi-dramatic compositions as *Hérodiade* and *L'Après-midi d'un faune* the relation to music is inescapable, but for quite other reasons than the rhetorical structure or the style of performance. Here the text so far eludes comprehension as to induce a state of reverie which the poem controls in such a way as to approximate the conditions of a musical experience. Such, indeed, was the mood which Maeterlinck sought to create in *Pelléas*, an intensely receptive psychic state on the border of dreams.

Shaw did not write in this vein. His plays, whatever their formal structure, are perfectly articulate and completely comprehensible. The type of reverie that might be induced in an active mind through the instrumentality of *Man and Superman* is actually developed fully in *Man and Superman.* The fantasy suggested by the action of the play is completely discharged in the dream of John Tanner, and after it nothing is left to the imagination. The Epilogue of *Saint Joan* forestalls any tendency one might have to meditate on the tragedy of Saint Joan. It has all been done for us, the event and the dream; when the curtain falls, the experience is complete.

The atmosphere of Shaw's comedies is not dreamlike, not even in the plays that include dreams; for these dreams are Shaw's dreams, not ours, and they have all been thoroughly screened through the intellect before they reach us. The dream in *Man and Superman* is sharper than the play. The do-it-yourself element in Shaw's drama is at all times minimal, for Shaw seldom trusted his audience to carry on his train of thought: even when the play is over, the author is still bustling about with explanatory epilogues and postscripts. It is perhaps for this reason that his plays occasionally seem to lack alcohol. We become aware of the poetry in them chiefly in the intervals when the author is silent, and the author is seldom silent. In general, the mood of Shaw's plays is as far removed as possible from that of symbolist drama. His mood is, on the contrary, the mood of the gymnasium, alert, athletic, and aggressive. Nevertheless, in the major part of his career he was a symbolist. If this seems to involve a paradox it is only because here, as elsewhere, Shaw transformed what he borrowed into something that was peculiarly his own.

In *Le Tragique Quotidien* Maeterlinck had hailed Ibsen as a precursor of modern symbolism and, in truth, *The Master Builder* is curiously enveloped in the atmosphere of mystery which the symbolists claimed as their special habitat. The mystery surrounding *Heartbreak House* is another sort of mystery; but Shotover's house is poised on the brink of the abyss quite as precariously as the house of Solness or the house of Usher. It was Maeterlinck's purpose, both in *L'Intruse* and in *Pelléas*, to suggest the mystery which underlies the commonplace. Neither of Maeterlinck's plays gives any inkling of the nature of the supernatural aura which pervades the action. It was not until he published *La Sagesse et la destinée* in 1898 that Maeterlinck's readers were afforded some insight into the character of the Maeterlinckian Beyond, and it cannot be said that even then it became intelligible.

Shaw was inclined to mysticism, perhaps from the first, but mystery made him uneasy. He was ambitious to solve every riddle with which he was confronted, even the riddle of life. Accordingly he organized the elements of his philosophy as one arranges a bowl of flowers. The idea of the all-embracing Life Force had been developed by the *philosophes* of the eighteenth century. For Shaw it remained only to define it in accordance with the system of beliefs he cherished. When this was done all became simple and clear. The bad name which the vital principle had acquired through Schopenhauer and von Hartmann obviously could have no part in Shaw's philosophy. His thinking was dominated by the idea of progress; it required an acceptable teleology, and a divinity that inspired respect. Once he found it, his way was clear. By the time he came to write *Man and Superman* Shaw could feel that the riddle of life was, for all practical purposes, solved.

He had, up to this time, assumed the energetic posture of a literary workman with no nonsense about him. As time went on, however, he felt himself more and more inclined to play the *voyant*, the revealer of mysteries. Jean Paul had long ago described the visionary poet in appropriate terms:

> The real poet, in writing, is only the auditor, not the master of his characters; that is to say, that he does not compose the dialogue by piecing together the answers according to a spiritual stylistic which he has acquired painfully. But as in a dream he watches his characters come to life, he *listens*. . . .[22]

In his later years, as we have seen, Shaw insisted that his plays were not the product of a conscious plan:

> When I write a play, I do not foresee or intend a page of it from one end to the other: the play writes itself. I may reason out every sentence until I have made it say what it comes to me to say; but whence or how or why it comes to me, or why I persisted, through nine years of unrelieved market failure, in writing instead of stockbroking or turf bookmaking, or peddling, I do not know. You may say it was because I had a talent that way. So I had: but that fact remains inexplicable.[23]

Among the romantics, after the time of Tieck, poetic composition was often thought of as a dreamlike revelation, and dreams were said to afford sudden glimpses into a world absolutely impenetrable to the waking eye. For Swedenborg dreams were simply a refinement of conscious thought by means of which the mind intuitively apprehended clearly the spiritual realities which normally elude the logical faculty. From the time of Baudelaire this was the view that recommended itself most strongly to the new poets of France and Germany. That reality which was imperceptible to the senses might be apprehended by the intellect in the ordinary way through intelligible symbols. Revelation was, accordingly, a matter of inference. Shaw spoke often of the automatic character of his writing, but it was evidently from the symbolist, not the spiritist viewpoint that Tanner's dream in *Man and Superman* was written. The Dialogue in Hell, with its musical prelude and its logically developed discussion is very far removed from the freely associated imagery of Strindberg's *The Dream Play*, or the Freudian jungle of later dream sequences. It is a carefully composed intellectual exercise through which the dreamer is afforded a rational insight into the nature of his destiny with relation to the destiny of mankind in general.

From the time of *Candida* Shaw's major plays are generally interpretable in terms of the effort of the Life Force to develop itself through its creatures. This effort is manifested in each case in the spiritual tensions experienced by the individual in the crucial moments of his life, and the enhanced awareness of his reality which results from his crisis. These plays may be considered to center, accordingly, on a psychomachia which reflects the struggle that is of the very essence of the Life Force, its need to live. In this struggle the adversary, ultimately, is death. The will to live develops power in despite of death, in the face of the longing of Adam for peace and an end of striving.

The romantics had specialized in the poetry of death. By Shaw's time the symbolist poets were reacting valiantly against the romantic *I* with all its implications, but, for all their aversion from romanticism, they were unable to resist the seductions of *le néant*: "To him who has looked upon the night of death, and known its sweet secrets," Thomas Mann had written, "to him day can never be other than vain, nor can he know any longing save for night, eternal, real, in which he is made one with love."[24] In the twentieth century, after World War I, everything suggested the longing of mankind to extinguish itself. When Freud published his celebrated paper on the conflict of Eros and Thanatos, his idea, though wholly without clinical foundation, found instant resonance everywhere in the world of letters.[25]

In the early 1900's the death wish was not yet established as a popular stereotype, so that the end of *Heartbreak House* was not so readily comprehensible as it has since become. In the early years of the century the desire for death still seemed a gentle twilight thing, in the mood of the Nightingale Ode, and not at all consonant with the blaze of lights and the shouts of enthusiasm with which Hector Hushabye and his friends invite annihilation from the skies.

Perhaps in the bitterness of the war years, with the spectacle of death and destruction constantly before his eyes, Shaw experienced briefly something like despair. If so, he expressed his feelings in *Heartbreak House* with his customary energy and more than a touch of caricature. In those years it was especially clear that men have always marched out with drums and trumpets in search of death, and that they celebrate destruction with such pomp as no other human activity seems to warrant. Shaw had developed the idea long before in *Man and Superman*, and again in *Major Barbara*; but in 1918 the note of optimism was conspicuously missing. At the time of *Heartbreak House* the will to live perhaps seemed to him also a futile and senseless impulse, and the longing of mankind to desist at length from its aimless task of self-perpetuation seemed exceptionally sensible. The mood, if it existed, did not last long. In *Back to Methuselah* the will to live was once again triumphantly asserted.

It was, indeed, against the call of death that Shaw consistently put forward his strength as a writer. He was deeply aware of the transitory condition of individual existence, and it troubled him not at all, for, in his view, the individual was merely a passing manifestation of the universal Will in which all that lives has its being. For this very reason, the desire for death was a betrayal, a treason to be avoided at any cost. For Shaw the Gospel of Life implied a kind of patriotism. He had fled for his life from romantic Ireland, where everything spoke to him of death and dreams; but even in England, where life asserted itself in all its brashness, the death-wish was manifest in the apathy of the masses and the aimlessness of the governing classes; and the war years emphasized the tragic stupidity of a race that above all desired to smash itself up in glory.

It was in the guise of universal critic that Shaw had first presented himself to the English, as a gadfly sent to awaken them from their stupor. It was long before they thanked him; and the war gave him a bad setback. When it was over, and the world was quiet, he gathered his forces once again and returned to the attack, only to find himself once again shouting into deaf ears. But in spite of everything, he felt it his duty to guide and to advise as long as he had breath left in his body, and he published vast quantities of persuasive literature on both sides of the Atlantic. Perhaps he had some immediate influence, but by this time his eyes were firmly fixed upon the future, and his horizons were very wide. He was no longer occupied with strictly temporal matters. He was occupied with the eternal, and while he amused himself occasionally with contemporary things, he no longer set great store by them.

Because of the singularity of Shaw's plays, and the polemical character of his prefaces, the formal principles of his dramatic system are easily overlooked, and, of course, there is also the possibility that they are not there. But since in all his plays the result is, in the end, a clarification, it may be said that his method is analytical. His plays normally set up a situation that is confused through misunderstandings, misconceptions, and pretenses. These are cleared away in the course of the action, so that at last the truth of the matter is in some measure manifest. Insofar as the characters are concerned, this process consists in first establishing the individual as he thinks he is, as a preliminary to the discovery of what he is in fact. Generally speaking, this discovery is climactic, an *anagnorisis* accompanied by a peripety, after which the play ends quickly. The method may properly be considered classic; but Shaw's comedies, unlike the ancient comedies, or their Renaissance versions, turn on spiritual recognitions and mark stages in the slow progress of self-discovery and self-knowledge. Such is the result not only of mature plays like *Heartbreak House*—which consists essentially of a series of such recognitions—or of earlier plays like *Blanco Posnet, The Devil's Disciple*, and *Captain Brassbound's Conversion*—each of which depicts a single crucial revelation—but also of Shaw's earliest comedies, from the time of *Widowers' Houses*. The process through which individuals come to know themselves may thus be regarded as representative of the evolution of the universal consciousness as it progressively dispels the illusions in which it is enveloped and achieves a more perfect self-awareness. From the viewpoint of *Back to Methuselah* each of Shaw's plays illustrates a phase in the process of Creative Evolution.

In the nature of things, self-knowledge cannot come about on a general scale purely as a spiritual development. The vital spirit is inextricably involved with matter, consequently the preconditions for spiritual progress include material considerations such as health and social reform. As men are presently constituted, mind and body are too intimately associated for the one to grow while the other is starved. Social and economic improvement are the indispensable prerequisites of spiritual enlightenment. However, it seemed unlikely to Shaw that anything substantial could be achieved along these lines until a superior order of humanity was engendered. "For remember:," he wrote, "what our voters are in the pit and gallery they are also in the polling booth. We are all now under what Burke called 'the hoofs of the swinish multitude.' "[26]

Necessary steps in the procreation of a superior humanity were the extension of the present life span, and the abandonment of love as a guide to human relations. In this regard Shaw found himself in accord with the latest literary currents. The symbolists had rejected love, along with nature, as vestiges of an outworn romanticism. For Shaw, love was the intellect of the mindless, an irrational desire to unite physically with the beautiful and the good; but it was useless to the superior mentality which forms such associations outside the physical realm. The consequences of this idea for Shaw's later comedies is most clearly apparent in *Pygmalion*.

With respect to love, Shaw's major characters are depicted in austerely classic fashion. For Vivie Warren, Dick Dudgeon, Lady Cicely, Caesar, Higgins, Lavinia, and Joan, love is a nuisance: they have other fish to fry. Love is the ruin of Hector Hushabye. It brings Dr. Ridgeon sorrow; and heartbreak to Ellie Dunn. Even in the few plays in which love plays an agreeable role, *Candida*, *Major Barbara*, and *The Doctor's Dilemma*, it appears to be a highly refined influence, a spiritual bond as intangible as that which unites Ellie to the aged Shotover, or King Magnus to his dull, but comfortable Jemima.

But while love is dispensable, eugenic marriages, and the weeding out of inferior individuals, are in Shaw's opinion, absolutely requisite to the evolution of a superior society. The fact that such is the manifest tendency of the universal Will is evident in the instinctive preferences of healthy people, but this process cannot work efficiently as a blind response to instinctual impulses. It must be made subject to intellectual guidance. In the same way, the social organism must be made subject to rational control by those best qualified to rule it, more or less as in the *Republic* of Plato the government is placed in the hands of philosopher-kings. The dream of a self-governed democratic society dwindles in the distant and mythical future; meanwhile, what is indicated for the guidance of humanity is an aristocracy of the best minds available, the very thing in which present-day democracy is most conspicuously lacking.

Shaw's crucial scenes are all in the nature of unresolved discussions. From the evolutionary viewpoint these may be considered indicative of the uncertainty of the creative Will, whose various aspects and possibilities the characters represent, in the process of developing a higher stage of intelligence. In this process, truths are necessarily relative, conclusions provisional, and their proponents only temporarily serviceable:

> I shall perhaps enjoy a few years of immortality. But the whirligig of
> time will soon bring my audiences to my own point of view; and then
> the next Shakespear that comes along will turn these petty tentatives
> of mine into masterpieces final for their epoch. By that time my

twentieth-century characteristics will pass unnoticed as a matter of course, whilst the eighteenth century artificiality that marks the work of every literary Irishman of my generation will seem antiquated and silly. . . . Reputations are cheap nowadays. Even were they dear, it would still be impossible for any public-spirited citizen of the world to hope that his reputation might endure; for this would be to hope that the flood of general enlightenment may never rise above his miserable high-water mark. . . . We must hurry on; we must get rid of reputations: they are the weeds in the soil of ignorance.[27]

Since in most of his plays Shaw very wisely did not insist unduly on the workings of the divine principle, we see in each play only the effic_nt causes of the action; we are only occasionally made aware of the final cause. But the prefaces often serve to make the point clear where the action obscures it: mankind is a developing entity which constantly renews and restates itself, and in so doing defines God at each stage of his being. Taken as a whole, Shaw's plays were evidently intended to constitute something akin to Balzac's *Livre mystique*, a description of the workings of the Holy Spirit on the material plane; but the effect could hardly be more different. Balzac had a firm groundwork in Christianity and was, at least for a time, deeply imbued with Swedenborgian zeal. Shaw's mysticism had other sources.

In the 1890's God could no longer be taken for granted. Science had given the Victorians a rude shock from which it was not easy to recover. Many gave up in despair and retired into empty agnosticism, or else took up atheism with a zeal which approximated the fanaticism of faith. There were others who found it impossible to relinquish their trust in an external principle working for good. The spiritual struggle which is reflected in Tennyson's *In Memoriam* was wholly characteristic of the age of Shaw. It is significant that Tennyson voiced his own faith in an apostrophe which Shaw might have written:

> O Living Will that shalt endure
>   When all that seems shall suffer shock,
>   Rise in the spiritual rock,
> Flow thro' our deeds and make them pure,
> That we may lift from out the dust
>   A voice as unto him that hears. . . .[28]

In Shaw's plays the carnival is so engrossing that it is easy to overlook its significance. Of all those who have attempted an interpretation, doubtless Chesterton came closest to the truth. He made Shaw out a Puritan and organized all that he knew of him around his Protestant compulsions. But Chesterton's brilliant study was written in 1909, at a time when Shaw had not yet defined himself completely, and Chesterton had no opportunity to revaluate him in terms of a broader concept. Nor is it, at this remove of time, an easy thing to do.

Shaw was by nature a critic. He sought to revise the world as one edits a book, penciling out its errors in conformity with an inner aesthetic which he considered unquestionable and which he called moral passion. This led him early into socialism, but he was at no time a proper socialist. He was by temperament an evangelist. As such, he was remarkably effective in spreading the Fabian gospel, but he had very little actual communication with the working classes and no sympathy with their activities. Doubtless he sincerely longed for a social revolution. He wrote much on the subject, but he exposed himself on the barricades no more than Ibsen: he had a horror of tumult. He was, for all the vehemence of his opinions, a prudent man who balanced his accounts with care, made careful investments, and signed his name with circumspection. Moreover, it must be remembered, he was an old man the greater part of his life.

Very likely, all true reformers are sentimentalists at heart. Shaw was not sentimental. He neither loved nor hated his fellow men, nor trusted them. He was generous and could be sincerely friendly; but he had no faith in the capacity of people to receive unsolicited benefits with grace. His generosity was whole-hearted but, as he described it in his portraits of Dick Dudgeon and Lavinia, quite abstract, a luxury which he savored thoughtfully by himself. His convictions were sincere, but they did not include a need for martyrdom. By nature he was an insurgent as other men are tennis players or sports-car fanatics and he struck out manfully with his pen for the sheer luxury of the sport, disclaiming responsibility for his excesses by ascribing them to an inscrutable power whose energy he shared but whose designs he did not fully comprehend. It was thus possible for him to assign his confusions as well as his insights to the dawning intelligence of an external divinity. Sometime late in his life he recognized the features of this God to whose service he was committed. They were his own.

He had long suspected something of the sort. At the age of thirty-six he had written to Florence Farr, whose connivance was necessary to him at the time:

> There are two sorts of geniuses in the world. One is produced by the
> breed throwing forward to the godlike man, exactly as it sometimes
> throws backward to the apelike. The other is the mere monster pro-

duced by the accidental excess of some faculty—musical, muscular, sexual, even. . . . The first order . . . is immature at thirty, and though desperately in need of education . . . can find nothing but misleading until it laboriously teaches itself. I am a genius of the first order; and so are you. . . .[29]

Two years later he was even more deeply convinced of his preeminence among men. He wrote to Jones, at that time considered by many the outstanding dramatist of the age: "Do you now begin to understand, oh Henry Arthur Jones, that you have to deal with a man who habitually thinks of himself as one of the great geniuses of all time?—just as you necessarily do yourself."[30] The degree of seriousness with which he advanced this idea publicly in 1894 is questionable, but we cannot doubt that by 1950 he was entirely comfortable in his megalomania. In his moments of exaltation he felt not merely that he was godlike, but actually that he was God. The idea would have been the sheerest lunacy had he not also seen God elsewhere; in fact, everywhere.

It takes some little thought to realize how deeply religious Shaw was, and how closely associated his plays are with the idea of a divine principle at work in the universe. Shaw did not doubt the reality of the material world any more than did Dr. Johnson in his day; but Shaw's reality lacked the stabilizing influence of Dr. Johnson's faith in the traditional beliefs of a Christian. For Shaw faith of this sort was no longer possible. He had to create a plausible substitute for Dr. Johnson's God in terms of an organizing principle whose embodiment he felt himself to be. The result was a somewhat diminished and indefinite divinity, but one endowed with possibilities of advancement which were denied to the God of the eighteenth century. Immanent in every living creature, and especially manifest in Shaw, this emergent God required no special cult. He required only service; and if the type of *latria* that was His due involved an excessive measure of self-esteem in those who were signally honored by His presence, it also implied a proportionally high degree of self-criticism.

The recognition of the divinity that surged in his veins caused his chosen vessel to flex his muscles in earnest. In Shaw's later years the task he had long ago set himself of improving the world he inhabited appeared to him in a clearer light. It was his mission to make men aware of the god within and among them. In pursuance of this goal he set aside his more immediate concerns as formerly he had put aside his critical duties. He knew now that it was a divine, not a human task in which he was involved. It had scope, and would take many centuries to accomplish, and many hands. He did not shrug off the burden as too heavy for one lifetime; but he no longer exaggerated the urgency of his mission. Practically it was a matter of asserting leadership in an environment peopled as yet largely by clods and madmen. To summon up the god in such creatures it was necessary to knock hard and often. He did so as long as his strength held out; even longer. His power, of course, was only the power of the word. But the Word, after all, was the principle of creation.

In *The Book of the Flower*, the fourteenth-century playwright Zeami speaks of the essence of drama as the beauty dimly perceived beneath the surface of the play, the result of the distillation of experience into its essential forms. This sense of life in its eternal aspect, colored by the sadness of its passing, is the flower which it is the high function of the poet to pass on to those who are able to receive it, even as Buddha held it out silently to his disciples in the Flower Sermon.

Yeats was deeply sensitive to this poetry, and he tried to emulate the mystery of the Nō plays in the alien idioms of the English theater. Shaw arrived at it by quite another route and with other motives. His plays make no use of the usual expedients of the poet in the theater, neither dance nor incantation, to induce a mood in which the flash of revelation may be expected to occur. The way to the heart of his drama is direct. All his teaching turns ultimately on the single concept of self-knowledge. To know oneself is to become aware of the vital current through which all things have their being. It is to become sensible, moral, just, and even beautiful. It is to be blessed in the knowledge of our oneness with humanity, and beyond humanity, with all living things, with the angels, and with God.

The sense of God as the vital stream from which we emerge as individuals, and with which, after brief differentiation, we inevitably merge, is only dimly adumbrated in Shaw's early drama. In his later plays it becomes explicit, and ultimately it is central in his work. This idea, the nucleus of his thinking, represents a curious synthesis of Eastern and Western thought. It is easy to see how Yeats arrived at such a point, or Strindberg: one wonders precisely how Shaw came by it, though this is of no particular consequence. The idea is the sheerest poetry and comes as close to truth as one needs to come in order to write plays.

As a writer, Shaw was by no means reserved; but he had his reticences. The mood he creates, as a rule, is an unquiet mood, typically Western, intended to induce action, not meditation. Shaw blasts his way into our consciousness with the insistence of a jackhammer, awakening every tonality of response from acquiescence to wrath. But occasionally his thunder is hushed. We become aware then of something unspoken which is not his message, but which dictates it and shapes it, a strain of poetry which eludes definition and even localization, but which is somehow at the core of everything in his work. It is at such times that we are conscious, not without astonishment, of the passing on of the flower.

NOTES

REFERENCES to *Collected Letters* are
to *Bernard Shaw, Collected Letters, 1874-1897*, edited by Dan H. Laurence,
New York, 1965. References to *Collected Works* are to *The Collected Works*
translations, unless otherwise credited, are mine.
of Bernard Shaw, Ayot St. Lawrence edition, 30 vols., New York, 1930-32. The

THE GREEN YEARS

1. Letter to M. E. McNulty, 3 June 1876, *Collected Letters*, p. 19.
2. St. John Ervine, *Bernard Shaw: His Life, Work and Friends*, London, 1956, p. 27.
   On Shaw's mother, see further pp. 12–19, and Shaw, *Sixteen Self-Sketches*, London, 1949, p. 69.
3. The standard reference: R. H. Tawney, *Religion and the Rise of Capitalism*
   (London, 1926), 8th ed., London, 1948, pp. 222 ff.
4. Karl Marx, *Das Kommunistische Manifest*, New York, 1918, pp. 27 f.; see also
   Charles Kingsley, "Letters to the Chartists" in *Politics for the People*, London,
   27 May 1848, p. 58; 17 June 1848, pp. 136 f.
5. John Morley, "Lancashire," *Fortnightly Review*, XXX (1878), 5.
6. See Shaw, Letters of 13 June 1880 et seq., *Collected Letters*, pp. 31 ff.
7. *Sixteen Self-Sketches*. See also *Immaturity*, Preface (1921), *Collected Works*, Vol.
   I, p. xliii.
8. Letter to Pattie Moye, 18 December 1881, *Collected Letters*, pp. 44 f.
9. To Ethel Southam, 31 July 1882, *Collected Letters*, pp. 50 f.
10. In "Who I am and What I Think," Part I, *The Candid Friend*, 11 May 1901,
    quoted in Archibald Henderson, *George Bernard Shaw, Man of the Century*
    (hereafter referred to by subtitle), New York, 1956, p. 219. See also *Major Barbara*, Preface, *Collected Works*, Vol. XI, p. 218.
11. Letter to Archibald Henderson, 17 January 1905. In Henderson, *Man of the Century*, p. 222.
12. See Shaw, *The Fabian Society, Collected Works*, Vol. XXX, pp. 129 ff., and
    Fabian Tract no. 70 (1896). See also "Fabian Essays Twenty Years Later," *Collected Works*, Vol. XXX, pp. 299 ff., and E. Bentley, *Bernard Shaw*, New York,
    1947, pp. 16 ff.
13. *Immaturity*, Preface, *Collected Works*, Vol. I, p. xxiii.
14. *Everybody's Political What's What*, London, 1944, p. 49.
15. Quoted in Maurice Colbourne, *The Real Bernard Shaw*, New York, 1949, p. 203.
16. Letter to Pattie Moye, 18 December 1881, *Collected Letters*, p. 46.

17. To Ellen Terry, 27 January 1897, *Collected Letters*, p. 722.
18. Charles Archer, *William Archer, Life, Work, and Friendships*, New Haven, 1931, p. 135.
19. *The Sanity of Art*, *Collected Works*, Vol. XIX, p. 303.
20. Jacob Epstein, *Let There Be Sculpture*, London, 1940, p. 99
21. See J. Percy Smith, *The Unrepentant Pilgrim*, Boston, 1965, pp. 67 f.
22. See Eric Blom in Sir George Grove, *Dictionary of Music and Musicians*, 5th ed., New York, 1954, Vol. VII, p. 743. See also B. H. Haggin, "A Music Critic Looks at Music Criticism," *Yale Review*, XLV, no. 3 (March 1959), 338.
23. *Music in London*, Vol. I, p. 54, *Collected Works*, Vol. XXVI, p. 54.
24. See Henderson, *Man of the Century*, p. 203.
25. *How To Become a Musical Critic*, edited by Dan H. Laurence, New York, 1961, pp. 310–11; "Am I An Educated Person?" in *Sixteen Self-Sketches*, p. 69.
26. See Henderson, *Man of the Century*, pp. 198 ff.
27. Review of 6 June 1877, *The Hornet*. See also *How To Become a Musical Critic*, Preface, p. xix; William Blissett, "Bernard Shaw, The Imperfect Wagnerite," *University of Toronto Quarterly*, XXVII, no. 2 (January 1958).
28. *Collected Works*, Vols. XXIII–XXV.
29. *Our Theatres in the Nineties*, "The Author's Apology," *Collected Works*, Vol. XXIII, p. vii.
30. "Valedictory," *The Saturday Review*, 21 May 1898.

SHAW'S THEATER

1. H. A. Jones, Preface, *The Renascence of the English Drama*, London, 1894, pp. vi, 171.
2. Augustin Filon, *The English Stage*, trans. by Frederic Whyte, Introduction by H. A. Jones, London and New York, 1897, pp. 10, 15 ff.
3. See M. Willson Disher, *Winkles and Champagne*, London, 1938, pp. 3–11; George Rowell, *The Victorian Theatre*, Oxford (1956), revised edition, 1967, pp. 6–12.
4. Letter to Ellen Terry, 10 March 1897, *Collected Letters*, p. 734.
5. *Our Theatres in the Nineties*, Vol. III, p. 175, *Collected Works*, Vol. XXV, p. 175.
6. Thomas Purnell, *Dramatists of the Present Day*, London, 1871, p. 93.
7. James Boaden, *Memoirs of Mrs. Siddons*, Philadelphia, 1827; one-volume ed., pp. 141 ff., 334.
8. Boaden, *Memoirs of the Life of J. P. Kemble*, 2 vols., London, 1825, Vol. I, pp. 92 ff., 175 f.; H. M. Hillebrand, *Edmund Kean*, New York, 1933; Philip Beck, "Realism," in *The Theatre*, VII (September 1883), 127–31; E. B. Watson, *Sheridan to Robertson*, Cambridge, Mass., 1926, pp. 342 ff. See also Archer, *The Old Drama and the New*, Boston, 1923; Cecil Armstrong, *A Century of Great Actors, 1750–1850*, London, 1912; J. A. Hammerton, *The Actor's Art*, 2nd ed., London, 1897; Joseph Bertram, *The Tragic Actor*, London, 1959; Clement Scott, *The Drama of Yesterday and To-day*, London, 1899; Alan Downer, "Players and Painted Stage: 19th Century Acting," in *PMLA*, LXI (June 1946), 522 ff.; Montague Summers, *The Playhouse of Pepys*, London, 1935, pp. 45 ff. A great deal has been written about acting style in this period, much of it not especially informative. In the absence of film records, nothing is more difficult to determine than the actual practice of actors on the stage.
9. See *Saturday Review*, 22 December 1888, 741 f.
10. For an excellent general discussion see G. Rowell, *The Victorian Theatre*, Oxford, 1967. See also W. J. Lawrence, *Elizabethan Playhouses, First Series*, Stratford-Upon-Avon, 1912, p. 171; *Second Series*, Stratford-Upon-Avon, 1913, pp. 165, 176; Montague Summers, *The Restoration Theatre*, London, 1934, pp. 97 ff.; Richard

Southern, *Changeable Scenery, Its Origin and Development in the British Theatre*, London, 1952, pp. 162 ff. On the use of the curtain, see A. Nicoll, *A History of English Drama*, Vol. I, *Restoration Drama, 1660–1700*, Cambridge, 1923, p. 54; Vol. II, *Early Eighteenth Century Drama 1700–1750* (1925), p. 28; Vol. III, *Late Eighteenth Century Drama 1750–1800* (1925), p. 32; Vol. V, *Late Nineteenth Century Drama* (1959), p. 30. See also G. Bapst, *Essai sur l'histoire du théâtre*, Paris, 1893, p. 598; Julien Lefèvre, *L'Electricité au théâtre*, Paris, 1894.

11. Sidney Dark and Rowland Grey, *W. S. Gilbert, His Life and Letters*, London, 1923, p. 59; *Mr. and Mrs. Robertson On and Off Stage, Written by Themselves*, 2 vols., London, 1888, Vol. I, pp. 118 f. See also T. E. Pemberton, *The Life and Writings of T. W. Robertson*, London, 1893; Maynard Savin, *Thomas William Robertson; His Plays and Stagecraft*, Providence, 1950.

12. W. S. Gilbert, "A Hornpipe in Fetters" in *The Era Almanack* (1870), p 91.

13. Ibsen, Letters to Georg Brandes, 20 December 1870, and 4 April 1872, in E. Sprinchorn, *Ibsen, Letters and Speeches*, New York, 1964, pp. 105, 121 ff.

14. Cf. H. A. Jones, *The Renascence of the English Drama*, London, 1895, pp. 96 f.; Shaw, *Saturday Review*, LXXXI (14 March 1896), 273.

15. Alexandre Dumas *fils*, *Un Père prodigue*, Préface, in *Alexandre Dumas, fils, Théâtre complet*, Paris, 1890–1918, 8 vols., Vol. III, p. 210.

16. Barrett Clark, *A Study of the Modern Drama*, New York and London, 1938, p. 222.

17. *Le Fils naturel*, Préface, in *Alexandre Dumas, fils, Théâtre complet*, Vol. III, p. 27.

18. *L'Etrangère*, Préface, in *Alexandre Dumas, fils, Théâtre complet*, Vol. VI, p. 223.

19. Cf. René Doumic in Petit de Julleville, *Histoire de la littérature française*, Paris, 1899, Vol. VIII, pp. 92 ff.

20. Ibsen, Letter to Brandes, 20 December 1870, in Sprinchorn, *Ibsen, Letters and Speeches*, p. 106.

21. Ibsen, Letter of 4 April 1872, in Sprinchorn, *Ibsen, Letters and Speeches*, p. 122.

22. Ibsen, Letter of 15 July 1869, in Sprinchorn, *Ibsen, Letters and Speeches*, p. 85.

23. See also Watson, *Sheridan to Robertson*, pp. 434 ff.; J. R. Planché, *Recollections and Reflections*, 2 vols., London, 1872, Vol. I, pp. 147 ff.; See also Shaw, Letters to Jones, 20 March 1894, and 24 April 1894, *Collected Letters*, pp. 421, 429.

24. Statues of 3 William IV, c. 15.

25. *The Extravaganzas of J. R. Planché*, 5 vols., London, 1879, Vol. II, p. 66. See also "The Author's Preface," ibid., Vol. I; H. Granville-Barker, "Exit Planché— Enter Gilbert" in *The Eighteen Sixties, Essays by Fellows of the Royal Society of Literature*, edited by John Drinkwater, Cambridge, 1932.

26. H. A. Jones, *The Renascence of the English Drama*, Preface, p. vii.

27. See Richard A. Cordell, *H. A. Jones and the Modern Drama*, New York, 1932.

THE UNPLEASANT PLAYS

1. Henderson, *Man of the Century*, p. 110.

2. W. Archer in *The World*, London, 4 May 1893.

3. W. Archer, "Mr. Shaw and Mr. Pinero" in "Study and Stage," *The Morning Leader*, London, 22 August 1903.

4. Archer, Letter to Shaw, 22 June 1921, in C. Archer, *William Archer*, p. 376.

5. W. Archer in *The World*, 14 December 1892, reprinted by Shaw in *Widowers' Houses*, London, 1893, Appendix I. See also *Pen Portraits and Reviews, Collected Works*, Vol. XXIX, pp. 1–32; C. Archer, *William Archer*, p. 119.

6. *Widowers' Houses*, Independent Theatre Series, No. 1, edited by J. T. Grein, London, 1893, p. xii.

7. W. Archer, *English Dramatists of To-day*, London, 1882, p. 9.

8. For Archer's review of *Breaking a Butterfly*, see *Theatre* (London), 1 April 1884.
9. *Pall Mall Gazette*, 13 June 1889.
10. C. Archer, *William Archer*, p. 156. See also W. Archer, "Ibsen as I Knew Him" in *The Monthly Review*, London, June 1906; "Henrik Ibsen," in *The Critic*, July 1906.
11. *Our Theatres in the Nineties*, Vol. III, p. 189, *Collected Works*, Vol. XXV, p. 189.
12. Shaw, "Ibsen," *The Clarion*, 1 June 1906.
13. Philip Wicksteed, *Four Letters on Ibsen*, London, 1891. See also Wicksteed, "Henrik Ibsen's Poems," *Contemporary Review*, September 1891.
14. *The Quintessence of Ibsenism*, Preface, 1st ed., *Collected Works*, Vol. XIX, p. 13.
15. *The Daily Chronicle*, London, 13 August 1890.
16. Ibid., 28 August 1890.
17. W. Archer, *New Review*, November 1891.
18. *Collected Works*, Vol. XIX, p. 134.
19. For Henrietta Lord's *Ghosts*, see *To-Day*, III, London, 1885, pp. 29 ff., 65 ff., 106 ff. See also *Major Barbara*, Preface, *Collected Works*, Vol. XI, p. 208.
20. *Fortnightly Review*, July–December 1891, 663 f.
21. See N. H. G. Schoonderwoerd, *J. T. Grein, Ambassador of the Theatre, 1862–1935*, Nijmagen, 1963. See also Alice A. Grein (Michael Orme), *J. T. Grein: The Story of a Pioneer, 1862–1935*, London, 1936.
22. The MS. copy is in The Berg Collection, New York Public Library.
23. Letter to Charles Charrington, 14 December, 1892, *Collected Letters*, p. 372. See also the review in *The Era*, 29 December 1892.
24. P. J. Proudhon, "La Baigneuse" in *Du Principe de l'art et sa destination sociale*, *Oeuvres complètes*, Paris, 1923–52, Vol. XV, pp. 179 f. For Louis Geofroy see Larousse, *Grand Dictionnaire universel du XIXe siècle*, Paris, 1865, Vol. X, p. 344.
25. Cited in Jules Coulin, *Die sozialistische Weltanschauung in der französische Malerei*, 1909, p. 61; Emile Zola, *La République et la littérature*, Paris, 1879.
26. *Thérèse Raquin*, Preface (1873) in Emile Zola, *Oeuvres complètes*, edited by Le Blond et Fasquelle, 50 vols., Paris, 1927–29, Vol. XXXVIII: *Théâtre, I*, p. 48.
27. Proudhon, *Oeuvres complètes* (1926), Vol. V, p. 132.
28. *Plays Pleasant and Unpleasant*, New York (Brentano's), 1919, pp. xxxi f.
29. *Widowers' Houses*, Preface, *Collected Works*, Vol. V, p. xxv.
30. For a full exposition, see Mario Praz, *La Carne, la morte, e il diavolo nella letteratura romantica*, trans. as *The Romantic Agony* by A. Davidson, New York and London, 1954, Chap. IV.
31. Eugène Sue, *Les Mystères de Paris*, 1st American ed., New York, 1844, Vol. II, p. 181.
32. See *Plays Pleasant and Unpleasant*, Preface, Vol. I, p. xiii, *Collected Works*, Vol. VII, p. xiii. Shaw's diary indicates the play was begun March 1893 and revised in July of that year. Brit. Mus. Add. MS. 50596 A-C includes an unpublished draft of a third act which takes place after Julia's marriage.
33. Letter to Ellen Terry, 28 August 1896, *Collected Letters*, p. 644; to J. H. McCarthy, 12 October 1896, *Collected Letters*, p. 678; to Ellen Terry, 5 December 1896, *Collected Letters*, p. 709; to Mrs. Patrick Campbell, 5 February 1913, in *Bernard Shaw and Mrs. Patrick Campbell: Their Correspondence*, edited by Alan Dent, London, 1952, p. 86.
34. *Plays Pleasant and Unpleasant*, Vol. I, p. xiii, *Collected Works*, Vol. VII, p. xiii; see also Letter to Richard Mansfield, 27 February 1895, *Collected Letters*, p. 488.
35. Mansfield, Letter to William Winter, 22 March 1895, in Paul Wilstach, *Richard Mansfield, The Man and the Actor*, New York, 1909; Shaw, to Mansfield, 27 February 1895, *Collected Letters*, p. 488.
36. *Plays Pleasant and Unpleasant*, Preface, *Collected Works*, Vol. VII, p. xxv.

37. *Advice to a Young Critic and Other Letters*, edited by E. J. West, New York, 1955; Letter to Golding Bright, 10 June 1896, *Collected Letters*, p. 632.

38. See also *Plays Pleasant and Unpleasant*, Preface, *Collected Works*, Vol. VII, p. xxvii.

39. *The Quintessence of Ibsenism*, *Collected Works*, Vol. XIX, pp. 28–31 and 133 f.

40. Letter to Florence Farr, 28 January 1892, *Collected Letters*, p. 332.

41. See Shaw's Diary entry for 4 February 1893, quoted in *Collected Letters*, p. 296. Letter to Florence Farr, 4 May 1891, *Collected Letters*, p. 298; to Florence Farr, 12 October 1896, *Collected Letters*, p. 674; to Janet Achurch, 29 January 1896, *Collected Letters*, p. 591. See also Stanley Winsten, *Jesting Apostle, The Life of Bernard Shaw*, London, 1956, p. 85.

42. See Henderson, *George Bernard Shaw, His Life and Work*, Cincinnati, 1911, Chap. X; W. Archer, "Mr Bernard Shaw's Plays" in *Study and Stage*, London, 1899; A. Filon, "*M. Bernard Shaw et son théâtre*," *Revue des deux mondes*, 15 November 1905; Ervine, *Bernard Shaw: His Life, Work, and Friends*, pp. 164 ff.

43. *Plays Pleasant and Unpleasant*, *Collected Works*, Vol. VII, p. xiii.

44. Ibid., p. vii.

45. Ibid., p. v.

46. *Pall Mall Gazette*, July–November 1885. See also A. S. Dyer, *The European Slave Trade in English Girls: A Narrative of Fact*, London, 1880, 9th ed., 1885.

47. See Shaw, Letter to *The Daily Chronicle*, 30 April 1898. See also G. Bullough, "Literary Relations of Shaw's Mrs. Warren," *Philological Quarterly*, XLI (January, 1962), 339 ff.

48. *Mrs Warren's Profession*, Act II, *Collected Works*, Vol. VII, p. 211. In general stage-directions are omitted, save where they seem indispensable for the interpretation of the text.

49. Ibid., p. 216.

50. *Mrs Warren's Profession*, Act III, *Collected Works*, Vol. VII, p. 233.

51. Ibid., p. 232. See also Letter to Golding Bright, 4 November 1895, *Collected Letters*, p. 566.

52. *The Quintessence of Ibsenism*, *Collected Works*, Vol. XIX, pp. 130 f.

53. Letter to Golding Bright, 10 June 1896, *Collected Letters*, p. 632.

54. "A Dramatic Realist to his Critics," *The New Review*, II, 1894.

55. *The Humanitarian*, VI, May 1895. Reprinted in *Shaw on Theatre*, edited by E. J. West, New York, 1958, p. 68.

56. Ibsen, "Speech to the Norwegian Society for the Woman's Cause," 26 May 1898, in Sprinchorn, *Ibsen, Letters and Speeches*, p. 337.

57. *Sixteen Self-Sketches*, p. 89.

58. *Misalliance*, Preface, *Collected Works*, Vol. XIII, p. 105.

59. *Mrs Warren's Profession*, Act IV, *Collected Works*, Vol. VII, p. 244.

60. See also *Plays Pleasant and Unpleasant*, Preface, *Collected Works*, Vol. VII, p. xvii.

61. J. T. Grein, "Mrs. Warren's Profession" in *Dramatic Criticism 1902–3*, London, 1904, p. 7. See also Henderson, *Man of the Century*, pp. 460 ff.

62. *Music in London, 1890–94*, Vol. III, *Collected Works*, Vol. XXVIII, pp. 146.

PLEASANT PLAYS

1. Letter to G. R. Foss, 12 January 1894, *Collected Letters*, p. 452.

2. A. B. Walkley in *The Speaker*, 28 April 1894; W. Archer in *The World*, 25 April 1894. See also Shaw, Letter to Archer, 23 April 1894, *Collected Letters*, pp. 425, 428.

3. Letter to Mansfield, 9 June 1894, *Collected Letters*, p. 441; undated letter, October 1894, in Wilstach, *Richard Mansfield*, quoted in *Collected Letters*, p. 458.

4. Brit. Mus. Add. MS. 50601 A-C.

5. *Pall Mall Budget*, 19 April 1894.

6. G. J. Wolseley in *The Fortnightly Review*, I (August 1888), 279 ff.; Horace Porter in *The Century*, XXXVI (June 1888), 246 ff.

7. Shaw, "A Word about Stepniak," *To-Morrow*, February 1896. See also letter to C. T. H. Helmsley, 17 April 1894, *Collected Letters*, p. 424.

8. See A. J. Tschiffeley, *Don Roberto: The Life of Robert Bontine Cunninghame Graham*, London, 1937.

9. *Sixteen Self-Sketches*, p. 42. Reprinted from "The Days of My Youth" in *Mainly About People*, 17 September 1898.

10. Ibid., p. 6.

11. Preface, *Plays Pleasant and Unpleasant*, Vol. II, p. xv, *Collected Works*, Vol. VIII, p. xv. See also Denis Diderot, "De la Poésie dramatique," in *Le Père de famille* (1758).

12. *Sixteen Self-Sketches*, p. 89. See also Henderson, *Man of the Century*, p. 59.

13. *Arms and the Man*, Act II, *Collected Works*, Vol. VIII, p. 28.

14. See also Praz, *The Romantic Agony*, pp. 74 ff.

15. *Arms and the Man*, Act II, *Collected Works*, Vol. VIII, p. 36.

16. Ibid., p. 71.

17. *Plays Pleasant and Unpleasant*, Preface, Vol. I, p. xxvi, *Collected Works*, Vol. VII, p. xxvi.

18. The first draft is dated 2 October 1894. Brit. Mus. Add. MS. 50603.

19. Letter to Mansfield, 22 February 1895, *Collected Letters*, p. 484.

20. To Mansfield, 16 March 1895, *Collected Letters*, p. 498.

21. Mansfield, Letter to Shaw, 18 April 1895. Reprinted from *Drama*, (new series) no. 2 (Autumn 1946), pp. 8–10, in Henderson, *Man of the Century*, p. 438.

22. C. E. Raven, *Christian Socialism*, London, 1920; C. W. Stubbs, *Charles Kingsley and the Christian Socialist Movement*, London, 1899, pp. 24 ff.

23. *Water Babies*, in *Life and Works of Charles Kingsley, ed. by His Wife*, London, 1901–3, 19 vols., Vol. XIX; see R. B. Martin, *Dust of Combat*, New York, 1960.

24. *Candida*, Act I, *Collected Works*, Vol. VIII, p. 79. See also Letter to Mrs. Patrick Campbell, 20 March 1913, in *Bernard Shaw and Mrs. Patrick Campbell*, p. 106.

25. *Candida*, Act I, *Collected Works*, Vol. VIII, p. 93.

26. *Sartor Resartus*, Chap. IX, in *The Works of Thomas Carlyle*, London, 1903–4, 30 vols., Vol. I.

27. *Past and Present*, London, 1843, Book III, "Labour," p. 264.

28. Letter to Ellen Terry, 6 April 1896, *Collected Letters*, p. 623.

29. J. Huneker, "The Truth About Candida" in *The Metropolitan Magazine*, August 1904; "The Quintessence of Shaw," in *G. B. Shaw*, edited by L. Kronenberger, New York, 1953, pp. 18 ff.

30. *Plays Pleasant and Unpleasant*, Preface, Vol. II, *Collected Works*, Vol. XIII, p. ix.

31. See also Elsie B. Adams, "Bernard Shaw's Pre-Raphaelite Drama," *PMLA*, LXXXI (October 1966), 428 ff.

32. *Candida*, Act III, *Collected Works*, Vol. VIII, pp. 145 f.

33. Brit. Mus. Add. MS. 50603.

34. *Plays Pleasant and Unpleasant*, Preface, Vol. II, *Collected Works*, Vol. VIII, p. viii.

35. Ibid., p. x.

36. MS. letter to Trebitsch, 7 January 1903, Berg Collection; to Mansfield, 22 February 1895, *Collected Letters*, p. 485.

37. George A. Riding, "The Candida Secret," in *The Spectator*, no. 185 (17 Novem-

ber 1950), p. 506. See also the excellent discussion of *Candida* in Louis Crompton,
Shaw the Dramatist, Lincoln, Nebraska, 1969.

Unwin, 27 August 1895, *Collected Letters*, p. 551; to Janet Achurch, 16 August
38. Letter to Janet Achurch, 31 August 1895, *Collected Letters*, p. 553; to Fisher
   1895, *Collected Letters*, p. 544.
39. *Bernard Shaw and Ellen Terry: A Correspondence*, edited by Christopher St.
   John, New York, 1932, p. xxvi.
40. Letter to Ellen Terry, 1 November 1895, *Collected Letters*, p. 564.
41. To Ellen Terry, 9 March 1896, *Collected Letters*, p. 610.
42. Ibid.
43. To Ellen Terry, 28 August 1896, *Collected Letters*, pp. 643 f.; Letter of 19 October 1896, in *Bernard Shaw and Ellen Terry: A Correspondence*, New York,
   1931, p. 80.
44. To Ellen Terry, 8 December 1896, *Collected Letters*, p. 712.
45. To Bertha Newcombe, 31 March 1896, *Collected Letters*, p. 620.
46. To Ellen Terry, 8 September 1897, *Collected Letters*, p. 801. See also Shaw's letter of 8 November 1912, to the same effect to Mrs. Patrick Campbell, in *Bernard Shaw and Mrs. Patrick Campbell*, p. 54.
47. *Bernard Shaw and Ellen Terry*, p. 14.
48. Letter to Mrs. Mansfield, 8 August 1896, *Collected Letters*, p. 640; to Ellen
   Terry, 20 (?) August 1896, *Collected Letters*, p. 645.
49. To Ellen Terry, 17 April 1897, *Collected Letters*, p. 747.
50. To Henry Irving, 29 April 1897, *Collected Letters*, p. 751; to Shaw, in Laurence
   Irving, *Henry Irving, The Actor and His World*, London, 1951, p. 604.
51. To Ellen Terry, 12 May 1897, *Collected Letters*, pp. 760 f.
52. To Ellen Terry, 13 May 1897, *Collected Letters*, p. 763.
53. Letter to Shaw, n.d. (c. 13 May 1897), *Bernard Shaw and Ellen Terry*, p. 150.
54. *The Observer* (London), 26 October 1930.
55. Shaw's letter to Mansfield of 8 September 1897 is not extant. An extract was
   published in Wilstach, *Richard Mansfield*, p. 264. It is quoted in *Collected Letters*,
   p. 803.
56. Letter to Ellen Terry, 4 July 1897, *Collected Letters*, p. 778.
57. *The Man of Destiny*, *Collected Works*, Vol. VIII, p. 149.
58. Letter to Ellen Terry, 27 April 1897, *Collected Letters*, p. 750; to Ellen Terry, 12
   April 1897, *Collected Letters*, p. 742; to Mrs. Mansfield, 21 October 1899, in Henderson, *Man of the Century*, p. 474.
59. *Plays Pleasant and Unpleasant*, Preface, Vol. II, *Collected Works*, Vol. VIII, p. xi.
   I quote the revised version of this preface (1898).
60. Ibid., p. xix.
61. *Our Theatres in the Nineties*, Vol. II, p. 118, *Collected Works*, Vol. XXIV, p. 124.
62. Ibid., Vol. II, p. 120, *Collected Works*, Vol. XXIV, pp. 125 f. For a collection of
   examples of farces in this period, see Martin Meisel, *Shaw and the Nineteenth
   Century Theater*, Princeton, 1963, pp. 285 f.
63. *Collected Works*, Vol. VIII, pp. 254 ff.
64. Ibid., p. 258.
65. A. Dumas *fils*, *L'Etrangère*, Act II, sc. I, *Théâtre complet*, Vol. VI, p. 265.
66. *You Never Can Tell*, Act II, *Collected Works*, Vol. VIII, p. 257.
67. Ibid., p. 259. The stage directions are indispensable to this quotation. I have included them.
68. Ibid., pp. 301, 302.
69. Ibid., p. 305.
70. Letter to Archer, 10 July 1906. In C. Archer, *William Archer*, p. 295.

PLAYS FOR PURITANS

1. *Our Theatres in the Nineties*, Vol. I, p. 195; "Two Bad Plays," 20 April 1895, *Collected Works*, Vol. XXIII, pp. 97 f.
2. In a letter to Ellen Terry, Shaw indicates that *The Devil's Disciple* was almost ready to be read 30 November 1896; see *Bernard Shaw and Ellen Terry*, p. 97. The MS. in the British Museum (Add. MS. 50606 A-D) dates the beginning at 10 September 1896, and the end at 31 December 1896: "Stage business finished 20/2/97."
3. Letter to Ellen Terry, 30 November 1896, *Collected Letters*, p. 705.
4. From Ellen Terry, 7 March 1897, *Bernard Shaw and Ellen Terry*, p. 120.
5. *The Observer* (London), 24 August 1930. See also Letter to Ellen Terry, 30 April 1899, *Bernard Shaw and Ellen Terry*, p. 235; and *Our Theatres in the Nineties*, Vol. III, p. 357, *Collected Works*, Vol. XXV, pp. 378 f.
6. Brit. Mus. Add. MS. 50606 D, f. 58.
7. For a most useful collection of analogues, see Meisel, *Shaw and the Nineteenth Century Theater*, pp. 194 ff.
8. *Three Plays for Puritans*, Preface, p. xxiv, *Collected Works*, Vol. IX, p. xxvii.
9. Ibid., p. xxix.
10. *The Devil's Disciple*, Act III, *Collected Works*, Vol. IX, p. 54.
11. *The Perfect Wagnerite*, "Siegfried," *Collected Works*, Vol. XIX, p. 212.
12. Shaw, "The Impossibilities of Anarchism" (1891), *Fabian Tract no. 45* (1893), *Collected Works*, Vol. XXX, pp. 67 ff.; see also *The Perfect Wagnerite*, *Collected Works*, Vol. XIX, p. 235.
13. Prince Pyotr Alekseyevich Kropotkin, *Memoirs*, Boston and New York, 1899, pp. 401 f. The *Memoirs* were published in *The Atlantic Monthly*, in serial form, from September 1898 to September 1899 under the title, *The Autobiography of a Revolutionist*.
14. Ibid., p. 400.
15. For an interesting passage associating anarchism with state capitalism as an intermediate step, see ibid., p. 401.
16. *The Devil's Disciple*, Act III, *Collected Works*, Vol. IX, p. 55.
17. See H. Woodbridge, *G. B. Shaw, Creative Artist*, Carbondale, 1963, pp. 45 ff.
18. *The Devil's Disciple*, Notes, *Collected Works*, Vol. IX, p. 82.
19. *The Devil's Disciple*, Preface, *Collected Works*, Vol. IX, pp. xxix f.
20. *The Devil's Disciple*, Act II, *Collected Works*, Vol. IX, p. 38.
21. Letter to Grant Richards, 27 March 1897, *Collected Letters*, p. 740.
22. *Drama* (London), Winter 1946.
23. See Letter to Trebitsch, 18 June 1906, Berg Collection.
24. To Hesketh Pearson, in Hesketh Pearson, *Bernard Shaw, His Life and Personality*, London, 1942, p. 212.
25. See also Henderson, *Man of the Century*, p. 555.
26. Theodor Mommsen, *History of Rome*, Berlin, 1854–56, trans. by William Dickson, New York, 1908, Vol. V, pp. 324 ff. See also "Shaw's Mommsenite Caesar" in *Anglo-German Cross-Currents*, edited by P. A. Shelley and others, Chapel Hill, 1962, Vol. II, pp. 259 ff.
27. Letter to Ellen Terry, 27 January 1897, *Collected Letters*, p. 722.
28. *The Perfect Wagnerite*, "Siegfried as Protestant" (1898), *Collected Works*, Vol. XIX, p. 228.
29. *The Perfect Wagnerite*, "First Scene," *Collected Works*, Vol. XIX, p. 186.
30. *Three Plays for Puritans*, Notes to *Caesar and Cleopatra*, *Collected Works*, Vol. IX, p. 211.

31. Dostoevski, *Crime and Punishment*, trans. by Jessie Coulson, London and New York, 1953, pp. 249 f.
32. Ibid.
33. C. F. M. Joad, *Samuel Butler*, London, 1924, p. 165; cf. Philip Furbank, *Samuel Butler*, New York, 1958; M. Muggeridge, *The Earnest Atheist*, London, 1936.
34. *The Perfect Wagnerite*, "Siegfried as Protestant," *Collected Works*, Vol. XIX, p. 225.
35. *Caesar and Cleopatra*, Prologue (1912), *Collected Works*, Vol. IX, p. 93.
36. *Caesar and Cleopatra*, Notes, *Collected Works*, Vol. IX, p. 204.
37. See also Gordon W. Couchman, "Here was a Caesar: Shaw's Comedy Today," *PMLA*, LXXII (March 1957), 272 ff.
38. Letter to Shaw, 31 May 1899, *Bernard Shaw and Ellen Terry*, p. 236.
39. To Shaw, 10 July 1899, ibid., p. 240.
40. To Shaw, 12 July 1899, ibid., p. 241.
41. To Shaw, 1 August 1899, ibid., p. 244.
42. To Shaw, 3 August 1899, ibid., p. 245.
43. To Ellen Terry, 4 August 1899, ibid., p. 246.
44. To Ellen Terry, 8 August 1899, ibid., p. 247.
45. To Shaw, 2 October 1899, ibid., p. 260.
46. To Ellen Terry, 30 October 1899, ibid., p. 261.
47. To Shaw, 11 October 1899, ibid., p. 264.
48. To Ellen Terry, 9 February 1900, ibid., p. 271.
49. *Bernard Shaw and Ellen Terry*, Preface, p. xxv.
50. See Meisel, *Shaw and the Nineteenth Century Theater*, p. 209.
51. See Shaw's letter to Granville-Barker, 6 December 1900, in *Bernard Shaw's Letters to Granville-Barker*, edited by C. B. Purdom, New York, 1957, p. 6.
52. Letter to Ellen Terry, 7 July 1899, *Bernard Shaw and Ellen Terry*, p. 240.
53. *Captain Brassbound's Conversion*, Act III, *Collected Works*, Vol. IX, p. 296.
54. Letter to Ellen Terry, 8 August 1899, *Bernard Shaw and Ellen Terry*, p. 247.
55. To Ellen Terry, 3 October 1899, ibid., p. 263.

MAN AND SUPERMAN

1. Arthur Schopenhauer, *The World as Will and Idea*, trans. by J. Kemp and R. B. Haldane, London, 1883.
2. Letter to Hubert Bland, 18 November 1899, *Collected Letters*, p. 228.
3. "Mr. Bernard Shaw Explains His Religion"; see also "On Going to Church," *The Savoy*, January 1896, both cited in Henderson, *Man of the Century*, p. 52.
4. *Getting Married*, *Collected Works*, Vol. XII, p. 302.
5. See Frederic Harrison, *The Creed of a Layman*, London, 1907, and his *De Senectute*, London, 1923. See also J. S. Mill, *Auguste Comte and Positivism*, new ed., London, 1908, and E. S. Beesley's commentary on Comte's *Discours sur l'esprit positif* (1844), published in Beesley's English translation, London, 1905.
6. F. H. Bradley, *Ethical Studies*, London, 1876, and *Appearance and Reality*, London, 1893. See also Richard Wolheim, *F. H. Bradley*, Baltimore, 1959.
7. Letter to Ellen Terry, 27 January 1897, *Bernard Shaw and Ellen Terry*, p. 110.
8. R. M. Rilke, *Das Stunden-Buch, Erstes Buch* (1905), Leipzig, 1920.
9. *Man and Superman*, "Epistle Dedicatory," p. xiv, *Collected Works*, Vol. X, p. xviii.
10. Letter to Alice Lockett, 8 October 1885, *Collected Letters*, pp. 42–43.
11. See also letter to Frank Harris, published in *Sixteen Self-Sketches*, No. 15; *Man and Superman*, Act I, *Collected Works*, Vol. X, p. 24.

12. Letter to Mrs. Patrick Campbell, 3 March 1913, *Bernard Shaw and Mrs. Patrick Campbell*, p. 104.
13. To Mrs. Patrick Campbell, 27 February 1913, *Bernard Shaw and Mrs. Patrick Campbell*, p. 96.
14. *Man and Superman*, Act I, *Collected Works*, Vol. X, p. 24.
15. *The World as Will and Idea*, trans. by Kemp and Haldane (1883), 6th ed., London, 1909, Vol. III, p. 340.
16. Ibid. See also Sarvepalli Radakrishna, *Indian Philosophy*, New York, 1931, Vol. I, pp. 236 ff.
17. *The World as Will and Idea*, Vol. III, p. 342.
18. In *Major Barbara* Andrew Undershaft has his doubts regarding the metabiological acumen of his son Stephen. He tells Lady Britomart: "He has indeed induced us to bring him into this world, but he chose his parents very incongruously, I think; I see nothing of myself in him, and less of you." *Major Barbara*, Act III, *Collected Works*, Vol. XI, p. 315.
19. *The World as Will and Idea*, Vol. III, pp. 336–57.
20. See Grant Allen, *The Woman Who Did*, London, 1895; Belfort Bax, "From Phallicism to Purism," in *Outspoken Essays on Social Subjects*, London, 1897; "Marriage," in *Outlooks From the New Standpoint*, London, 1891; Edward Carpenter, *Love's Coming of Age*, London, 1896; Grant Allen, *Falling in Love, With Other Essays on More Exact Branches of Science*, London, 1889; Havelock Ellis, *Man and Woman*, Boston and New York, 1929, particularly pp. 481 ff. See also Stephen Winsten, *Salt and His Circle*, London, 1951, pp. 112 f.
21. *Selected Essays of Arthur Schopenhauer*, trans. by Belfort Bax, London, 1891, p. 343.
22. "Don Giovanni Explains" in Shaw, *Short Stories, Scraps and Shavings*, New York, 1934, p. 105.
23. *Man and Superman*, Program Notes (1907), reprinted in Mander and Mitchenson, *Theatrical Companion to Shaw*, London, 1954, 88 f.
24. A. B. Walkley, *Playhouse Immpressions*, London, 1902, pp. 160 f.
25. *Man and Superman*, "Epistle Dedicatory," *Collected Works*, Vol. X, p. xii.
26. Ibid., p. xvi.
27. *Man and Superman*, Act IV, *Collected Works*, Vol. X, p. 167.
28. I Cor. 7.32.
29. *Nicomachean Ethics*, X, 5, 1176 b.
30. Ibid., X, 8, 1178 b.
31. *Man and Superman*, Act III, *Collected Works*, Vol. X, pp. 106 f.
32. Ibid., pp. 109 f.
33. Ibid., p. 207.
34. Ibid., p. 209.
35. Ibid., p. 210.
36. See also Havelock Ellis, *Man and Woman*, Boston and New York, 1929, p. 481.
37. "Metaphysics of the Love of the Sexes," in *The World as Will and Idea*, p. 345.
38. Walter Pater, *The Renaissance*, London, 1901, p. 124.
39. *Théâtre complet d'Alexandre Dumas fils*, Paris, 1876–1892, Vol. IV, p. 43.
40. Lester Ward, *Pure Sociology, A Treatise on the Origins and Spontaneous Development of Society*, London, 1903, 2nd ed., New York and London, 1907, Chap. XIV, pp. 309 ff.
41. *Man and Superman*, Act III, *Collected Works*, Vol. X, p. 110.

THE VINTAGE YEARS

1. MS. Letters to Siegfried Trebitsch (1902–1950), Berg Collection.
2. Letter to Ellen Terry, 9 September 1904, *Bernard Shaw and Ellen Terry*, p. 209.

See also letters of 4 August 1904 and 18 August 1904 to Granville-Barker, in Purdom, *Bernard Shaw's Letters to Granville-Barker*, pp. 22, 23.

3. *John Bull's Other Island*, Act I, *Collected Works*, Vol. X, pp. 86 f.

4. Ibid., p. 89.

5. *Our Theatres in the Nineties*, Vol. I, *Collected Works*, Vol. XXIV, p. 31.

6. For a summary view of the long line of nineteenth-century stage-Irishmen, see Meisel, *Shaw and the Nineteenth Century Theater*, pp. 275 ff.

7. *John Bull's Other Island*, Act IV, *Collected Works*, Vol. XI, p. 155.

8. Ibid., p. 100.

9. Ibid., p. 176.

10. Ibid., p. 177.

11. Ibid., p. 180.

12. Ibid., p. 181.

13. John Morley, *Critical Miscellanies*, London, 1923, pp. 74 ff.; see also J. H. Buckley, *The Victorian Temper*, New York 1951, Chap. VI, pp. 109 ff.

14. *Major Barbara*, Preface, *Collected Works*, Vol. XI, p. 243.

15. Grant Richards, *Memoirs of a Misspent Youth*, New York, 1933, p. 112.

16. *Major Barbara*, Act II, *Collected Works*, Vol. XI, p. 294.

17. Ibid., p. 293.

18. G. Murray, *A History of Ancient Greek Literature*, New York, 1897, p. 250; see also *Euripides and His Age*, New York, 1913.

19. The relevant passage: *Bacchae*, ll. 898–911. Murray's version reads ". . . one and another/ In gold and power may outpass his brother." The last lines of the strophe, in Murray's text are: ". . . To hold a hand uplifted over hate./ And shall not Loveliness be loved forever?" See also *Major Barbara*, Act II, *Collected Works*, Vol. XI, p. 292; G. Murray, *Euripides* (1902), 5th ed., New York, 1915, p. 26.

20. *Man and Superman*, Act III, *Collected Works*, Vol. X, p. 109.

21. *Major Barbara*, Act III, *Collected Works*, Vol. XI, pp. 346 f.

22. Ibid., p. 340.

23. Georges Sorel, *Réflexions sur la violence* (Paris, 1906), trans. by T. E. Hulme as *Reflections on Violence*, New York, 1941, pp. 85–90. My translation.

24. Murray, *Euripides and His Age*, p. 187.

25. *Major Barbara*, Act III, *Collected Works*, Vol. XI, pp. 339 f.

26. *Major Barbara*, Preface, *Collected Works*, Vol. XI, p. 219.

27. Ibid., pp. 295 f.

28. "Fabian Essays Twenty Years Later" (Preface to the 1908 reprint), *Collected Works*, Vol. XXX, p. 302. See also *Major Barbara*, Preface, *Collected Works*, Vol. XI, p. 218.

29. See also *Man and Superman*, Act III, *Collected Works*, Vol. X, p. 105.

30. *Major Barbara*, Act III, *Collected Works*, Vol. XI, p. 340.

31. *Major Barbara*, Act II, *Collected Works*, Vol. XI, pp. 290 f.

32. *Major Barbara*, Act III, *Collected Works*, Vol. XI, pp. 347 f.

33. Ibid., p. 348.

34. Ibid., p. 320.

35. Victor Serge, *Les Hommes dans la prison* (1930), trans. by Richard Greeman as *Men in Prison*, New York, 1969, p. 85.

36. R. F. Rattray, *Bernard Shaw, A Chronicle*, Luton, England, 1951, p. 167, henceforth referred to as *A Chronicle*.

37. Henderson, *Man of the Century*, p. 607.

38. Brit. Mus. Add. MS. 50619 A-D.

39. See also Ruskin, "The Relation of Art to Morals," *Works of John Ruskin*, edited by E. T. Cook and A. D. Wedderburn, 39 vols., London, 1902–12, Vol. XX,

pp. 77 ff. See also Vol. III, p. 92; Vol. V, p. 19; Vol. XXX, p. 173. See also Henry
Ladd, *The Victorian Morality of Art*, New York, 1932, pp. 173 ff.; 339 ff.; G. F.
Carritt, *The Theory of Beauty*, New York, 1914, pp. 47 ff.; J. Buckley, *The Vic-
torian Temper*, pp. 152 ff.

40. Shaw, *Major Critical Essays*, p. 288.
41. *Man and Superman*, Act I, *Collected Works*, Vol. X, p. 23.
42. *The Clarion* (London), 1 June 1906.
43. Ibid.; see also Archer in *The Tribune* (London), 14 July 1906; Henderson,
Man of the Century, p. 606.
44. On the deathbed scene, see Shaw's letter to Barker, 21 August 1906, in Purdom,
Bernard Shaw's Letters to Granville-Barker, p. 69; see also Shaw's letter to
Trebitsch, 5 May 1910, Berg Collection.
45. Henry M. Hyndman, *Further Reminiscences*, London, 1912, p. 13; see also
Pearson, *Bernard Shaw*, p. 103; Arthur Nethercot, *The First Five Lives of Annie
Besant*, London, 1961, p. 216.
46. *The Doctor's Dilemma*, Act IV, *Collected Works*, Vol. XII, p. 167.
47. Ibid., *Collected Works*, Vol. XII, p. 165.
48. Richard Wagner, "An End in Paris," *Prose Works*, trans. by W. Ashton Ellis,
8 vols., London, 1892–99, Vol. VII, p. 66; *Gesammelte Schriften*, Leipzig, 1907,
Vol. I, p. 142. The text is: "I believe in God, Mozart, and Beethoven, and like-
wise in their disciples and apostles. . . . I believe in the Holy Spirit and the truth
of the one indivisible art. . . ."
49. *Mr. Whistler's Ten O'Clock*, Chicago, 1907, pp. 9–11.
50. *Misalliance*, Preface, *Collected Works*, Vol. XIII, p. 100.
51. *The Doctor's Dilemma*, Act III, *Collected Works*, Vol. XII, p. 144.
52. *The Doctor's Dilemma*, Act IV, *Collected Works*, Vol. XII, p. 177.
53. Letter to Granville-Barker, 21 April 1907, in Purdom, *Bernard Shaw's Letters to
Granville-Barker*, p. 82. See also Colbourne, *The Real Bernard Shaw*, p. 165; Rattray, *A Chronicle*, pp. 171 f. See further Desmond MacCarthy, *The Court Theatre: 1904–1907*, London, 1907.
54. *Getting Married*, *Collected Works*, Vol. XII, p. 281.
55. Ibid., p. 343.
56. *The Quintessence of Ibsenism*, "The Technical Novelty in Ibsen's Plays," *Collected Works*, Vol. XIX, p. 145.
57. Quoted by Henderson, "George Bernard Shaw Self-Revealed," in *Fortnightly
Review*, LXXVIII (1926), 434.
58. "Wagner as a Revolutionist," in *The Perfect Wagnerite*, *Collected Works*,
Vol. XIX, p. 200.
59. Henderson, *Man of the Century*, p. 587.
60. *The Shewing-Up of Blanco Posnet*, Preface, *Collected Works*, Vol. XII,
pp. 380 f.
61. Tolstoy, *The Power of Darkness*, Act I: *Vlast tmy*, L. N. Tolstoi, *Sobranie
sochinenii*, 20 vols., Moscow, 1960–64, Vol. XI, pp. 42–43.
62. *Blanco Posnet*, *Collected Works*, Vol. XI, p. 464.
63. Ibid.
64. Letter to Tolstoy, 14 February 1910, cited in Henderson, *Man of the Century*,
p. 589. See also Aylmer Maude, *Life of Tolstoy: Later Years*, London, 1930,
Vol. II, p. 463.
65. *Misalliance*, Preface, "Parents and Children," *Collected Works*, Vol. XIII, p. 4.
66. *Misalliance*, *Collected Works*, Vol. XIII, p. 200.
67. Ibid., p. 201.
68. *Fanny's First Play*, Induction, *Collected Works*, Vol. XIII, p. 269.
69. *Fanny's First Play*, Act III, *Collected Works*, Vol. XIII, p. 314.
70. Ibid.

71. Ibid.
72. Ibsen, *An Enemy of the People*, Act IV: *En Folkenfiende*, edited by Oluf Holck, Oslo, 1962, p. 71.
73. *Fanny's First Play*, Act III, *Collected Works*, Vol. XIII, p. 315.
74. Ibid., p. 323.
75. *Overruled*, Preface, *Collected Works*, Vol. XIV, p. 158.
76. *Our Theatres in the Nineties*, Vol. II, pp. 13–15, *Collected Works*, Vol. XXIV, pp. 14 f.
77. See *New Review*, VIII (1893), 183 ff.; *The Spectator* (London), no. 70 (4 February 1893), 155 f.
78. *Music in London*, Vol. II, p. 94, *Collected Works*, Vol. XXVII, p. 99.
79. W. Archer in *The Theatrical World for 1896*, London, 1897, p. 8.
80. *Emperor and Galilean*, Act III, trans. by W. Archer, *Ibsen's Prose Dramas*, London, 1901, Vol. IV, p. 273.
81. *Emperor and Galilean*, Act V, trans. by W. Archer, *Ibsen's Prose Dramas*, Vol. IV, p. 336.
82. *Androcles and the Lion*, Act II, *Collected Works*, Vol. XIV, p. 138.
83. Ibid., p. 135.
84. Ibid., p. 139.
85. Ibid., p. 146.
86. See J. R. Planché, "Extravaganza and Spectacle," *Temple Bar*, III (1861), pp. 531 ff.
87. See M. Meisel, *Shaw and the Nineteenth Century Theater*, pp. 334 ff.; G. Rowell, *The Victorian Theatre*, London, 1956, p. 70; *The Extravaganzas of J. R. Planché*, Vol. II, p. 66.
88. *Androcles and the Lion*, Preface, *Collected Works*, Vol. XIV, pp. 22 ff.
89. Ibid., p. 24.
90. Quoted in Colbourne, *The Real Bernard Shaw*, p. 171.
91. *Androcles and the Lion*, Epilogue, *Collected Works*, Vol. XIV, pp. 147, 151, 158.
92. Letter to Ellen Terry, 8 September 1897, *Collected Letters*, p. 803.
93. *Pygmalion*, Preface, *Collected Works*, Vol. XIV, p. 202.
94. G. Lanson, *Histoire de la littérature française*, 12th ed., Paris, 1912, pp. 1008 f.
95. See Meisel, *Shaw and the Nineteenth Century Theater*, pp. 169 ff.
96. "How to Write a Play; An Interview with Hayden Church," *Glasgow Evening Times*, 7 February 1939, cited in Henderson, *Man of the Century*, p. 730.
97. *Pygmalion*, Act V, *Collected Works*, Vol. XIV, p. 286.
98. *Pygmalion*, Epilogue, *Collected Works*, Vol. XIV, p. 303.
99. Ibid., pp. 290 f.
100. Ibid.
101. *Pygmalion*, Preface, *Collected Works*, Vol. XIV, p. 199.
102. *Pygmalion*, Act III, *Collected Works*, Vol. XIV, p. 256.
103. Ibid., p. 252.
104. *Buoyant Billions, Farfetched Fables, Shakes versus Shav*, Preface, London, 1950, p. 4
105. Quoted in Ervine, *Bernard Shaw: His Life, Work and Friends*. See further Shaw's letter of 22 February 1913, in *Bernard Shaw and Mrs. Patrick Campbell*, p. 92.
106. Letter to Mrs. Patrick Campbell, 8 November 1912, *Bernard Shaw and Mrs. Patrick Campbell*, p. 54.
107. Letter to Mrs. Patrick Campbell, 9 June 1913, ibid., p. 131.
108. From Mrs. Patrick Campbell, 5 February 1913, ibid., p. 85; see further Shaw's letter of 20 March 1913, ibid., p. 108.
109. To Mrs. Patrick Campbell, 24 May 1913, ibid., p. 128.

110. From Mrs. Patrick Campbell, 10 August 1913, ibid., p. 152.
111. To Mrs. Patrick Campbell, 11 August 1913, ibid., p. 153.
112. To Mrs. Patrick Campbell, 12 August 1913, ibid., p. 154.
113. From Mrs. Patrick Campbell, 13 August 1913, ibid., p. 158. See also her letter of 15 August 1913, ibid., p. 159.
114. From Mrs. Patrick Campbell, 28 June 1939, ibid., p. 384.
115. Letter to Ada Tyrell, 17 April 1940. Quoted in Ervine, *Bernard Shaw: His Life, Work and Friends*, p. 451.
116. In *Fabianism and the Empire*, London, 1905.
117. "Common Sense About the War," in *What I Really Wrote About the War* (1914), *Collected Works*, Vol. XXI, p. 114. See also Shaw's Introduction, ibid., pp. 1–22.
118. "Common Sense About the War," *Collected Works*, Vol. XXI, p. 82.
119. *The New Statesman*, 19 December 1914.
120. "Common Sense About the War," *Collected Works*, Vol. XXI, p. 99.
121. Beatrice Webb, *Diaries, 1912–1924*, edited by Margaret Cole, 2 vols., London and New York, 1952–56, Vol. I, p. 62.
122. *O'Flaherty, V.C.*, *Collected Works*, Vol. XV, p. 227.

HEARTBREAK HOUSE

1. "Armaments and Conscription, A Triple Alliance Against War," in *The Daily Chronicle*, 18 March 1913, reprinted in *What I Really Wrote About the War*, *Collected Works*, Vol. XXI, p. 8.
2. *O'Flaherty, V.C.*, *Collected Works*, Vol. XV, p. 212.
3. *Heartbreak House*, Preface, *Collected Works*, Vol. XV, p. 40.
4. *Pen Portraits and Reviews*, *Collected Works*, Vol. XXX, p. 442.
5. For this, and other indications as to sources, see Meisel, *Shaw and the Nineteenth Century Theater*, pp. 316 f.
6. *Heartbreak House*, Act II, *Collected Works*, Vol. XV, p. 120.
7. Ibid., p. 118.
8. *Heartbreak House*, Act III, *Collected Works*, Vol. XV, p. 139.
9. Ibid., pp. 141 f.
10. *Heartbreak House*, Act II, *Collected Works*, Vol. XV, p. 120.
11. *Heartbreak House*, Act III, *Collected Works*, Vol. XV, p. 145.
12. G. R. Porter, *The Progress of the Nation*, London, 1851, p. 631.
13. Webb, *Diaries, 1912–1924*, entry for 1914, p. 50.
14. See Lawrence Langner, *G. B. S. and the Lunatic*, New York, 1963, pp. 20 ff.
15. *Heartbreak House*, Preface, *Collected Works*, Vol. XV, p. 3.
16. Letter to Trebitsch, 20 July 1919. Berg Collection.
17. Brit. Mus. Add. MS. 50531. Shaw noted that Part I was finished 14 February 1919; Part II is dated March 19, 1918 to April 9, 1918. Part III was finished 16 May 1918. Part IV was begun 21 May 1918 and finished 15 March 1920. Part V was begun 16 March 1920 and finished 27 May 1920.
18. See Langner, *G. B. S. and the Lunatic*, pp. 32 ff.
19. See *Back to Methuselah*, Postscript, The Oxford World's Classics edition, London, 1944.
20. Ibid.
21. *Back to Methuselah*, Preface (1920) *Collected Works*, Vol. XVI, p. xxxi.
22. Purdom, *Bernard Shaw's Letters to Granville-Barker*, pp. 198 f.
23. *Back to Methuselah*, Postscript (1944), p. 270.
24. Ibid.

25. *Back to Methuselah*, Preface, *Collected Works*, Vol. XVI, p. lxxxix.
26. *Saint Joan*, Preface, *Collected Works*, Vol. XVII, p. 17.
27. *Back to Methuselah*, Preface, *Collected Works*, Vol. XVI, p. lxxxvi.
28. Ibid., p. lxxxix.
29. Samuel Butler, *Evolution Old and New*, London, 1879, p. 51.
30. Ibid., pp. 381 f.
31. See Hugo de Vries, *Die Mutationstheorie*, 2 vols., Leipzig, 1901-3, trans. as *The Mutation Theory*, 2 vols., Chicago, 1909-10.
32. *Back to Methuselah*, Part V, *Collected Works*, Vol. XVI, p. 252.
33. See August Weismann, *The Evolutionary Theory*, trans. by J. A. Thomas, London, 1904, chapters on "Life and Death," and "The Duration of Life."
34. *Misalliance*, Preface, *Collected Works*, Vol. XIII, p. 3.
35. *Everybody's Political What's What*, London, 1945, p. 287.
36. "*Sjalamord*" in Strindberg, *Samlade Skrifter*, Vol. XXII, pp. 128 ff.
37. *Back to Methuselah*, Part IV, *Collected Works*, Vol. XVI, p. 142.
38. See also *Misalliance*, Preface, *Collected Works*, Vol. XIII, p. 4.
39. *Back to Methuselah*, Part V, *Collected Works*, Vol. XVI, p. 218.
40. Ibid., p. 257.
41. Ibid., p. 225.
42. Ibid., p. 253.
43. Ibid., p. 255.
44. Ibid., p. 262.
45. Butler, *Evolution Old and New*, p. 56.
46. *Back to Methuselah*, Postscript, Oxford World's Classics, p. 264.
47. *Back to Methuselah*, Part II, *Collected Works*, Vol. XVI, p. 80.
48. Julian Huxley, *Evolution: The Modern Synthesis*, London, 1942, p. 458.
49. Ervine, *Bernard Shaw: His Life, Work and Friends*, p. 496.
50. Jules Quicherat, *Procès de condamnation et de réhabilitation de Jeanne d'Arc*, 5 vols., Paris, 1849; T. Douglas Murray, *Jeanne d'Arc, Maid of Orleans, Deliverer of France*, London, 1902; Pierre Champion, *Procès de condamnation de Jeanne d'Arc*, Introduction, Paris, 1907; Anatole France, *Vie de Jeanne d'Arc*, Paris, 1911.
51. See Langner, *G. B. S. and the Lunatic*, pp. 67-76.
52. For these and other critical notices, see Ervine, *Bernard Shaw: His Life, Work and Friends*, pp. 502 ff.
53. Langner, *G. B. S. and the Lunatic*, p. 60.
54. See also Hans Stoppel, "Shaw and Sainthood," in *English Studies*, XXXVI (April 1955), 49 ff.
55. See Henderson, *Table Talk of George Bernard Shaw*, New York and London, 1925, p. 403; Henderson, "Bernard Shaw Talks about Saint Joan," *Literary Digest International Book Review*, II (March 1924), 286.
56. *Saint Joan*, Preface, *Collected Works*, Vol. XVII, p. 50.
57. See also Shaw, "A Crib for Home Rulers" (1888), reprinted in *The Matter with Ireland*, edited by Dan H. Laurence and D. H. Greene, New York, 1952, p. 23.
58. See Hernando de Acuña, "*Al Rey nuestro Señor*" (1580?), in *The Oxford Book of Spanish Verse*, Oxford, 1942, p. 104. See further *Orlando furioso*, canto XV, stanzas 25 f.
59. G. W. Hegel, *The Philosophy of Fine Art*, trans. by F. B. P. Osmaston, 4 vols., London, 1920, Vol. IV, p. 317. For a good general discussion see W. T. Stace, *The Philosophy of Hegel; A Systematic Exposition*, New York, 1924.
60. *Saint Joan*, Preface, *Collected Works*, Vol. XVII, p. 38.
61. See also Shaw, *Major Critical Essays*, p. 75.
62. *Saint Joan*, Preface, *Collected Works*, Vol. XVII, p. 39. See also ibid., pp. 28, 41.

63. Ibid., p. 42.
64. Ibid., p. 5.
65. Ibid., p. 18; see also ibid., p. 21.
66. Ibid., p. 13.
67. Ibid., p. 50.
68. See also H. C. Lee, *A History of the Inquisition in the Middle Ages*, New York, 1888, Vol. I, pp. 106 ff.
69. *Saint Joan*, Scene VI, *Collected Works*, Vol. XVII, p. 130.
70. Henderson, *Man of the Century*, p. 741.
71. *Saint Joan*, Preface, *Collected Works*, Vol. XVII, p. 130.
72. See also Sylvan Burnet, "Bernard Shaw on Tragedy," in *PMLA*, LXXI (December 1956), 888 ff.
73. *Saint Joan*, Preface, *Collected Works*, Vol. XVII, p. 51.
74. *Saint Joan*, Scene V, *Collected Works*, Vol. XVII, p. 103.
75. *Saint Joan*, Scene VI, *Collected Works*, Vol. XVII, p. 146.
76. *Saint Joan*, Preface, *Collected Works*, Vol. XVII, p. 54 f.
77. Ibid, p. 49.
78. Rattray, *A Chronicle*, p. 230.
79. Yousuf Karsh, *Faces of Destiny*, Chicago and New York, 1946, cited in Rattray, *A Chronicle*, p. 270.

THE CART AND THE TRUMPET

1. *Saturday Review* (London), April 13, 1895; *Our Theatres in the Nineties*, Vol I, *Collected Works*, Vol. XXII, p. 95.
2. Shaw, Preface to *Three Plays by Brieux* (1911), 4th ed., New York, 1912, p. xxiv.
3. Letter of 8 January 1895 in *Life and Letters of Henry Arthur Jones*, by Doris Arthur Jones, London, 1930, p. 140.
4. *Three Plays for Puritans*, Preface, *Collected Works*, Vol. IX, pp. xxiv f.
5. *Androcles and the Lion*, Preface, *Collected Works*, Vol. XIV, p. 24.
6. See Anthony S. Abbott, *Shaw and Christianity*, New York, 1964.
7. See also Ferdinand Baldensperger, *Goethe en France*, Paris, 1904, pp. 143 ff.
8. *Plays Pleasant and Unpleasant*, Vol. II, Preface (1898), *Collected Works*, Vol. VIII, pp. vii ff.; *Immaturity*, Preface (1930), in *Prefaces by Bernard Shaw*, London, 1934, pp. 641 f.; Henderson, *Table Talk of George Bernard Shaw*, p. 111.
9. *Dramatic Opinions and Essays*, 2 vols., New York, 1916, Vol. I, p. 607; *Our Theatres in the Nineties*, 30 March 1895, *Collected Works*, Vol. XXIII, p. 80.
10. See Emanuel Swedenborg, *Heaven and Hell and its Wonders*, New York, 1956; *The Four Doctrines*, New York, 1929; *The Divine Love and Wisdom*, London and New York, 1912, pp. 44 ff.; E. Swift, *Manual of the Doctrines of the New Church*, New York, 1885, *passim*.
11. See Gustave Kahn, *Les Origines du symbolisme*, Paris, 1906; A. Barré, *Le Symbolisme*, Paris, 1911; L. F. Cazamian, *Symbolisme et poésie*, Neuchâtel, 1947; Kenneth Cornell, *The Symbolist Movement*, New Haven, 1951; Anna Balakian, *The Symbolist Movement*, New York, 1967, pp. 12 ff., 72 ff.
12. Richard Wagner, *Quatre poèmes d'opéra, précédés d'une lettre sur la musique*, Paris, 1861. Reprinted as "Zukunftsmusik" in *Gesammelte Schriften und Dichtungen*, 4th ed., Leipzig, 1873, Vol. VII, p. 142.
13. "*Richard Wagner et Tannhäuser à Paris*" (1861), in Baudelaire, *Oeuvres complètes*, Paris (Pléiade), 1956, p. 1050.
14. Stéphane Mallarmé, "*Richard Wagner, Rêverie d'un poète français*" (1885), in Stéphane Mallarmé, *Oeuvres complètes*, Paris (Pléiade), 1956, pp. 541 ff. See also Haskell M. Block, *Mallarmé and the Symbolist Drama*, Detroit, 1963, p. 49.

15. Mallarmé, "Crise de vers," in *Variations sur un sujet, Oeuvres complètes*, p. 367. See also Shaw, *The Perfect Wagnerite, Collected Works*, Vol. XIX, p. 270.

16. Mallarmé, "La Musique et les lettres," *Oeuvres complètes*, p. 649.

17. *The Perfect Wagnerite, Collected Works*, Vol. XIX, p. 277. See also pp. 198 ff.

18. Ibid, p. 280.

19. Ibid., p. 273.

20. See also Edmund Wilson, "The Music of Ideas," in *The Triple Thinkers*, New York, 1938. See also the discussion in Meisel, *Shaw and the Nineteenth Century Theater*, pp. 38 ff.

21. In R. Mander and J. W. Mitchenson, *Theatrical Companion to Bernard Shaw*, London, 1954, p. 6.

22. Jean Paul, "*Über die natürliche Magie der Einbildskraft*" (1796), quoted in Albert Beguin, *L'Âme romantique et le rêve*, 3rd ed., Paris, 1963, p. 189. See also René Wellek, *History of Modern Criticism*, Vol. II, New Haven, 1955, pp. 101 ff., 174 ff.

23. *Buoyant Billions, Farfetched Fables, Shakes versus Shav*, Preface, p. 4.

24. Thomas Mann, *Tristan, Der Tod in Venedig und andere Erzählungen*, Frankfort am Main, 1966; Mann, *Stories of Three Decades*, trans. by H. T. Lowe-Porter, New York, 1936.

25. Sigmund Freud, *Beyond the Pleasure Principle* (1920), in *The Standard Edition of The Complete Psychological Works*, edited by James Strachey, 24 vols., London, 1953–66, Vol. XVIII.

26. *Man and Superman*, Epistle Dedicatory, *Collected Works*, Vol. X, p. xxvi.

27. *Three Plays for Puritans*, Preface, (1900), *Collected Works*, Vol. IX, p. xxxix.

28. Alfred Tennyson, *In Memoriam*, CXXXI. (1850), *Works of Alfred Lord Tennyson* 9 vols., London, 1907–8, Vol. III.

29. Letter to Florence Farr, 28 January 1892, *Collected Letters*, p. 332.

30. To H. A. Jones, 2 December 1894, *Collected Letters*, p. 463.

INDEX